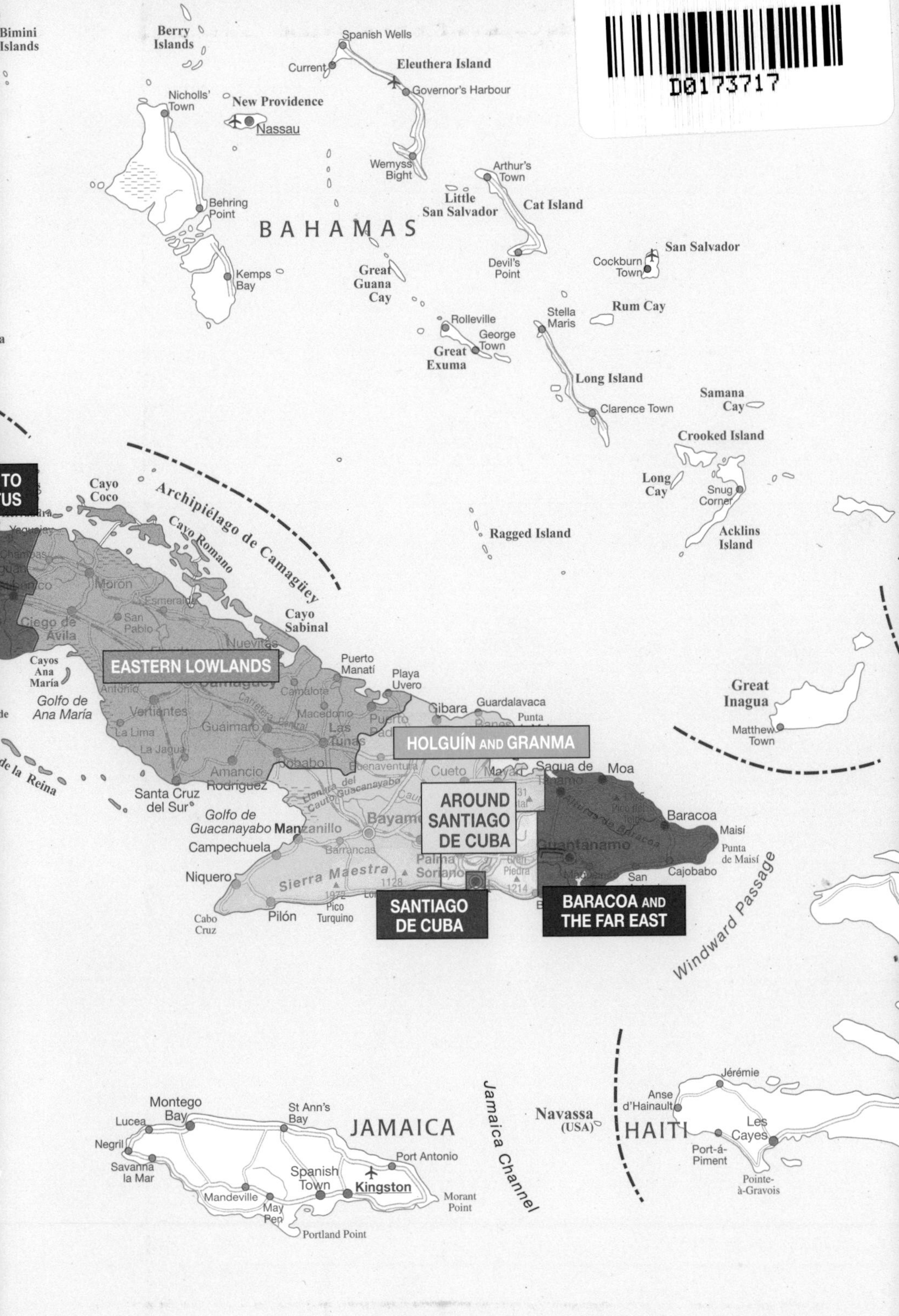

Bimini Islands
Berry Islands
Spanish Wells
Current
Eleuthera Island
Governor's Harbour
Nicholls' Town
New Providence
Nassau
Wemyss Bight
Arthur's Town
Little San Salvador
Cat Island
Behring Point
BAHAMAS
Kemps Bay
Great Guana Cay
Devil's Point
Cockburn Town
San Salvador
Rolleville
George Town
Great Exuma
Stella Maris
Rum Cay
Long Island
Clarence Town
Samana Cay
Crooked Island
Long Cay
Snug Corner
Acklins Island
Ragged Island
TO US
Cayo Coco
Archipiélago de Camagüey
Cayo Romano
Morón
Esmeralda
Ciego de Ávila
San Pablo
Cayo Sabinal
Nuevitas
Cayos Ana María
EASTERN LOWLANDS
Golfo de Ana María
Vertientes
La Lima
Guáimaro
La Jagua
Puerto Manatí
Playa Uvero
Camalote
Macedonio
Las Tunas
Gibara
Guardalavaca
Punta
HOLGUÍN AND GRANMA
Great Inagua
Matthew Town
Amancio Rodríguez
Santa Cruz del Sur
de la Reina
Golfo de Guacanayabo
Manzanillo
Campechuela
Niquero
Cabo Cruz
Pilón
Pico Turquino
Sierra Maestra
Bayamo
Barrancas
Palma Soriano
Cueto
Mayarí
AROUND SANTIAGO DE CUBA
SANTIAGO DE CUBA
Sagua de Tánamo
Moa
Baracoa
Maisí
Punta de Maisí
Guantánamo
Cajobabo
San
BARACOA AND THE FAR EAST
Windward Passage
Jamaica Channel
Montego Bay
Lucea
Negril
Savanna la Mar
St Ann's Bay
JAMAICA
Port Antonio
Spanish Town
Kingston
Mandeville
May Pen
Morant Point
Portland Point
Navassa (USA)
Jérémie
Anse d'Hainault
HAITI
Les Cayes
Port-á-Piment
Pointe-à-Gravois

INSIGHT GUIDES

CUBA

Contents

Travel Tips

Maps

THE BEST OF CUBA: TOP ATTRACTIONS

From wonderful views and heroic sights to colonial architecture and great music venues, here at a glance are Cuba's greatest attractions.

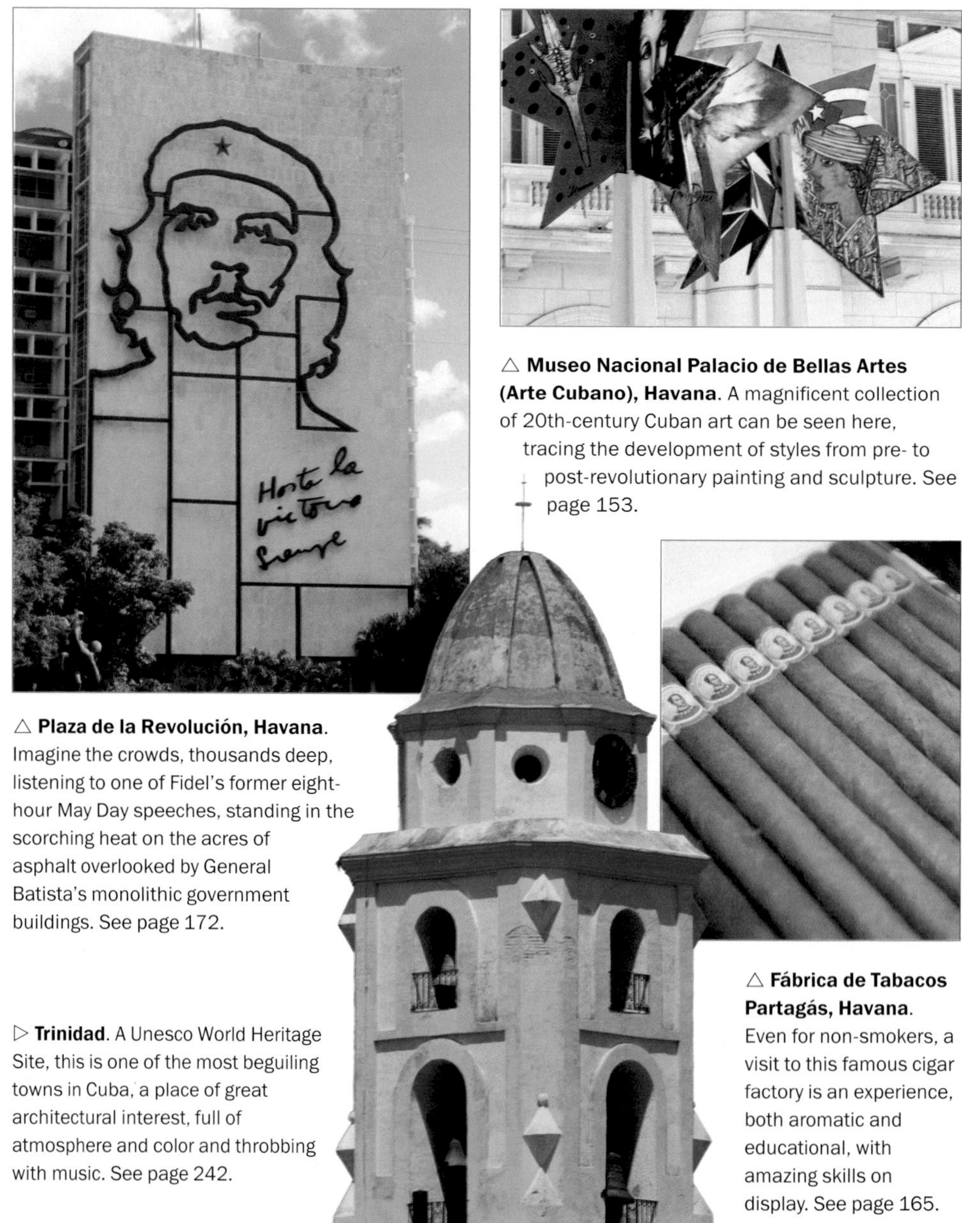

△ **Museo Nacional Palacio de Bellas Artes (Arte Cubano), Havana.** A magnificent collection of 20th-century Cuban art can be seen here, tracing the development of styles from pre- to post-revolutionary painting and sculpture. See page 153.

△ **Plaza de la Revolución, Havana.** Imagine the crowds, thousands deep, listening to one of Fidel's former eight-hour May Day speeches, standing in the scorching heat on the acres of asphalt overlooked by General Batista's monolithic government buildings. See page 172.

△ **Fábrica de Tabacos Partagás, Havana.** Even for non-smokers, a visit to this famous cigar factory is an experience, both aromatic and educational, with amazing skills on display. See page 165.

▷ **Trinidad.** A Unesco World Heritage Site, this is one of the most beguiling towns in Cuba, a place of great architectural interest, full of atmosphere and color and throbbing with music. See page 242.

△ **Valle de Viñales**. When the mists hover over the tobacco fields leaving only the tops of the palm trees and the sheer-sided, limestone *mogotes* on view, this is one of the most beautiful places on earth. See page 195.

△ **Callejón de Hamel, Havana**. Where exuberant art and music mix – this is the place to be on a Sunday afternoon. See page 169.

◁ **Casa de Velázquez, Santiago de Cuba**. Construction of Cuba's oldest house was started in 1516. It is now a fascinating museum. See page 287.

△ **Parque Nacional Desembarco de Granma**. The mangroves, swamps, and razor-sharp grasses in this national park still give an idea of how unwelcoming the landing site was for the *guerrilleros* on their arrival from Mexico. See page 277.

▽ **Cementerio Santa Ifigenia, Santiago**. Most of Cuba's famous sons and daughters, including José Martí, are buried here. There is an eclectic mix of mausoleums and graves. See page 290.

▷ **Monumentu Che Guevara, Santa Clara**. Fans of revolutionary history should make the pilgrimage to this giant monument, with its dramatic statue, the bas-relief of Che's letter to Fidel on leaving Cuba for Bolivia, and the mausoleum where the eternal flame burns for Che and his comrades interred there. See page 228.

THE BEST OF CUBA: EDITOR'S CHOICE

With its varied natural beauty, from mountain top to pristine beach, and a troubled history that has spawned dramatic architecture and monuments, Cuba is fascinating, intriguing, and exciting. Here are the editor's top tips for making the most of it.

The palm-fringed shores of Cayo Levisa.

BEST UNSPOILT BEACHES

Cayo Levisa. On the north coast of Pinar del Río province, Cayo Levisa is a small dive resort reached by a short boat trip. See page 199.
Cayo Sabinal. A wildlife reserve with deserted, pristine white-sand beaches north of Camagüey. See page 260.
María La Gorda. Located in the far west of the island, this lovely beach flanks waters ideal for diving and snorkeling. See page 200.
Cayo Jutías. A small cay off the north coast of Pinar del Río, a lovely stretch of white sand and calm, shallow water. See page 199.
Playa Los Cocos. Some 8km (5 miles) from the beach resort of Playa Santa Lucía, this is a broad sweep of beach with a fishing village at one end and a few beach bars at the other. See page 260.
Playa Maguana. Not far from Baracoa, the trees come down to the sweep of white sand in a curved bay where there is just one hotel and beach bar. See page 307.

Statue of Antonio Maceo, in the Plaza de la Revolución, Santiago.

BEST HEROIC SITES

Monument to Che, Santa Clara. A dramatic statue overlooks the Plaza de la Revolución, while underneath is a museum and a mausoleum where the remains of Che Guevara and some of his fellow fighters are interred. See page 228.
Monument to Antonio Maceo, Santiago. The impressive monument to the great 19th-century independence fighter dominates the Plaza de la Revolución at the entrance to the town. See page 283.
Playa Girón. The site of the Bay of Pigs invasion in 1961, 'The First Imperialist Defeat in Latin America,' is commemorated in the Museo de Girón. See page 221.
Mausoleum of José Martí, Santiago. The Father of the Nation lies in a splendid marble mausoleum, where an armed guard is changed every half hour, accompanied by martial music. See page 290.
Moncada Barracks, Santiago. The unsuccessful attack on Moncada in 1953 launched the revolution. A museum gives details. See page 284.
Parque Nacional Desembarco de Granma, Niquero. On the edge of the Sierra Maestra, this is where the guerrilla war began, in 1956. There is a walkway through the mangroves to the sea. See page 277.

BEST PLACES TO HEAR MUSIC

Casa de Cultura de Habana Vieja. Performances are held in the theater or in the churchyard. See page 340.

Casa Música Habana. Matinées and late-night performances of salsa, son, swing, and rock. See page 340.

La Zorra y el Cuervo, Havana. Famous jazz club on La Rampa. See page 341.

Casa de la Trova, Santiago. One of the most famous *casas* in Cuba. See page 287.

Casa de las Tradiciones, Santiago. An intimate local venue where you will hear authentic traditional music. See page 341.

Casa de la Música, Trinidad. On La Escalinata, there's music and dancing until the early hours. See page 341.

Casa de la Música, Trinidad.

BEST HAVANA PLAZAS

Plaza de Armas. Havana's oldest square is lit at night by antique lamps, and is a center of action at all hours. See page 138.

Plaza de la Catedral. The baroque cathedral and handsome colonial buildings surround the square, where café tables invite you to sit and enjoy a *mojito*. See page 141.

Plaza Vieja. The square has been renovated with great care over recent years and is now one of the most gracious in the city. See page 148.

Plaza de la Revolución. The site of the stark memorial to José Martí and the illuminated mural of Che Guevara. The vast square is not beautiful, but it is impressive. See page 172.

Parque Central. This leafy square, home to the elegant Hotel Inglaterra, is always buzzing with life, especially in the *esquina caliente*. See page 152.

BEST OUTDOOR ACTIVITIES

Walking in the Valle de Viñales. Take walks with local guides through the breathtakingly beautiful valley. See page 195.

El Guafe trail. Birds, butterflies, dry tropical forest, and ancient ceremonial sites can be seen along the path. See page 278.

Hiking in the Sierra Maestra. Great hiking in the national park and up to the highest peak, Pico Turquino, for views of the forest and down to the Caribbean Sea. See page 275.

Exploring the waterfalls of the Sierra de Escambray. Bracing walks and cooling dips amid pristine scenery. See page 233.

Scuba diving on the Isla de Juventud. One of the best of Cuba's scuba-diving sites. See page 309.

Waterfall in the Sierra de Escambray.

Delivering a celebration cake by horse and cart in Santiago.

Old American car, Trinidad.

Trinidad musicians.

THE ISOLATED ISLAND

Cubans find it difficult to buy soap, yet have the best health-care system in Latin America. It is such contradictions that explode prejudices and make the island such a fascinating place to visit.

Musical instruments are everywhere.

It is difficult to be unemotional about Cuba. This Caribbean island thrills the senses, befuddles the mind, and tugs at the heart. It is a magical place, full of romantic images: conga drums pounding late into the night; spicy dark rum; baseball, ballet, and dazzling nightclubs; light-hearted street art; quick conversations spiked with sexual innuendo and wicked humor; people who are warm, expressive, and affectionate; music emanating from every window – all enveloped within the aroma of hand-rolled cigars.

There are also more somber images of Cuba: frustrated youths willing to risk their lives in search of a future elsewhere; an outmoded communist system, exacerbated by the privations engendered by a US trade embargo, that is failing its citizens; political repression; crumbling buildings, empty stores, and overcrowded buses. It is a place of great contrasts: immaculately dressed schoolchildren emerge from tumbledown tenements. Political opponents portray it as a dictatorship, yet the people are infectiously exuberant.

Che Guevara wall sign, Santa Clara.

Cuba's isolation, however, is becoming a thing of the past. The Ministry of Tourism is eager to reinvent the island as a sophisticated vacation destination, to bring in much-needed income: pristine cays with empty swathes of sand are being transformed into modern beach resorts financed by foreign capital. Colonial city mansions are being converted into boutique hotels. Tourists, however, are shielded from the harsh realities of life on the island. It is a rare traveler who experiences the blackouts, the fuel and water shortages, the inadequate food rations, the long lines, leaky roofs, and heavy-handed bureaucracy that are daily hardships for the average Cuban.

For most visitors, Cuba is a taste of the good life, a tropical retreat, and an exotic escape. Even so, the average tourist will not leave Cuba unaffected. Slowly but surely this Caribbean island gets under your skin and touches your soul. Opinions – often contradictory – of the island and its people form quickly. Cuba is an unforgettable experience.

A Baracoa resident relaxing on the doorstep.

THE CUBANS

Multiracial and multicultural, the vivacious Cuban people are universally hospitable and friendly. Most appear to support their government, but may not always feel free to express their opinions frankly in public.

How do you describe the Cuban character? Words like fun-loving, spontaneous, and warm come to mind (not to mention long-suffering). Regardless of their status in society, Cubans tend to be a generous people. This generous nature, closely linked to the gregarious spirit that characterizes the country, is embedded in the Cuban psyche. For one Cuban to label another stingy is to tag him or her with one of the worst character flaws imaginable. The song written by popular songwriter Juan Formell and sung by his band, Los Van Van, captures the idea: 'My hands are always empty, giving when there's nothing to give. Oh, but what can I do? These are the hands that I have!'

Cirilo Villaverde's famous 19th-century novel Cecilia Valdés o La Loma del Ángel explores, brilliantly, the theme of the children of white 'masters' and their black slaves, and the prejudice they faced.

Sharing a joke in Trinidad.

A mestizo people

Barely a trace remains in Cuban culture today of the peoples who were here when Christopher Columbus arrived in 1492. For the most part, Cuba's 11.4 million people are a mixture of European, African, and indigenous ancestry. The government prefers to emphasize national rather than racial identity, so rarely releases statistics on race, and for a while it deleted all questions about race from the official census. But some unofficial sources calculate that 70 percent of the population are of mixed race.

With the onset of slavery in the 16th century, many Spanish colonizers satisfied their sexual appetites with their slaves – a practice that was common throughout the Americas. The criollo children born of these unions suffered as much social prejudice as did the black slaves.

From the late 1840s, Chinese immigrants began to form an important segment of the Cuban population. According to historian Juan Pérez de la Riva (author of *Slavery and Capitalism in Cuba*), about 35,000 Chinese were brought from Canton to the island to work as servants in conditions similar to those endured by African slaves. Eventually, more than 100,000 came to Cuba. Though only vestiges remain today, until the 1970s Havana's Chinese neighborhood was one of the city's most prosperous. The so-called *Barrio Chino* in central Havana has been revived over the past few years, and now has a popular market and foodstands attracting both local people and tourists, although it is but a shadow of its former self (see page 166).

Equality for all

Though once common, terms such as *El Chino* (the Chinese man), *El Negrito* (the black one), and *La Mulata* (the mixed-race woman) are rarely used today – even mentioning racial distinctions is a social taboo (although Chino, as a nickname, does still exist). In the 1950s, skin color was a divisive issue. Black people had very little access to good jobs or professions, and were not allowed to join certain clubs or attend private schools.

With its promise of 'equality for all,' the revolutionary government has gone a long way toward diminishing the effects of racial discrimination. Today, Cubans of all races and ethnic backgrounds are born in the same hospitals, attend the same schools, and are buried in the same cemeteries. But some sociologists argue that, although opportunities for black people advanced quite dramatically after Fidel Castro took power, the country still suffers from institutional racism. There are only a handful of black people in the upper echelons of the government, and only about a quarter of Cuba's Communist Party are black or mulatto; and there's evidence that black people have not benefitted proportionately from employment in the lucrative tourism industry during the recent boom. According to Carlos Moore, a black Cuban exile scholar, the color of power in Cuba has not changed at all.

Shopkeeper and companion in Sancti Spíritus.

> *In leafy Parque Vidal, the main square of Santa Clara, the double sidewalks that once provided separate walkways for black and white people are still visible.*

The Catholic Church

The Catholic Church was officially separated from the Cuban Government with the birth of the republic in 1902. Until the revolution, though, the government considered the Catholic Church its natural ideological ally. As in most Latin American cultures, it served as the foundation of an ordered society. But with the pronouncement of the socialist government in 1961, organized religion was condemned to disappear, and Marxism-Leninism replaced Catholic dogma. The church was not outlawed, but the government viewed it as a dangerous rival and a focus for dissent.

For many years practicing Catholics were punished by limited access to schools and job opportunities. To attend Mass was to 'lapse into the past,' and the 'past' was regarded by revolutionaries as a Bad Thing. But religious observation continued in private, and after the break-up of the eastern bloc, reappeared in public again.

The papal visit

A landmark event occurred in January 1998, when Pope John Paul II visited the island – the only place in Latin America that he had not yet toured. The paradox was not lost on observers: that a Pope who had spent much of his papacy fighting communism should meet a Marxist like Fidel, who had completely relegated the role of the Catholic Church and institutional religion under his regime.

The Pope was keen to advance the cause of religious freedom and human rights in Cuba; whereas Castro hoped to benefit from the international prestige of the event (demonstrating that his regime had nothing to hide), and to exploit the fact that the Pope had publicly opposed the US embargo, so as to isolate the position of the US Government and the Miami exile community.

The Cuban state's position on religion has altered somewhat in recent years. Practicing Catholics are allowed to join the Communist Party, and the state is now officially described as 'secular' rather than 'atheist.' There seems to be far greater tolerance of religious observance than there was before, and while the number of people attending Catholic services is not high, neither is it negligible, especially among elderly people.

Procession of the Miracles, San Lázaro church, El Rincón.

The power of Santería

Although all forms of religious devotion were proscribed for many years, Santería has survived. It is a mixture of Catholicism and traditional West African beliefs brought here by slaves in colonial times. Although it began as a religion of Cuba's black population, Santería followers now come from all walks of life. It is estimated that at least 90 percent of Cubans have participated in some form of Santería ritual, despite the fact that for many years it, too, was discouraged by the state.

As in Catholicism, Santería priests, called the *babalawos*, offer guidance and counsel, but the source of their divine wisdom differs. Instead of consulting a supreme being, *babalawos* use various instruments to interpret the wishes of the *orishas* or gods. Each sign carries many myths and stories that the priest will interpret for his client. A *babalawo* might advise a patient to sprinkle Catholic holy water around their home in order to chase away evil spirits. If the problem is caused by the spiritual presence of a dead loved one, they might instruct the patient to 'steal a mass.' To do this, the patient would attend a Catholic Mass where the souls of the dead are being prayed for, and when the priest mentions the names of the dead who are being honored, they would whisper the name of their loved one. The annoying spirit then floats away and leaves the person in peace. (See page 76 for more on Afro-Cuban religions.)

Santería practitioner dressed all in white.

Women's rights

Women walking alone on the street are often bombarded with overt sexual comments from men. These *piropos* (flirtatious remarks) range from a courteous compliment to a blatant invitation for sex. Many Cuban women, however, accustomed to this from an early age, are capable of giving just as good as they get. *Cubanas* may be victims of *machismo* in some areas of life, but they appear remarkably self-confident.

Many years of official policy designed to achieve the 'equality of women' have undoubtedly improved the lot of women in Cuba, but it has by no means dissolved the island's deep-rooted *machismo* spirit. Far from liberating them socially, the government's goal of incorporating women into the workforce has actually led to their having two jobs: one at the workplace and the other in the home, doing most of the cooking, shopping, cleaning, and child-minding. However, this is not so different from what happens in the US and many European countries.

Raúl Castro's wife, Vilma Espín, who died in June 2007, championed women's rights and lobbied for men to do more in the home and, especially, with raising children. She founded the Federación de Mujeres Cubanas (the

MOTHER'S DAY

The role of mother is revered in Cuba, and Mother's Day, in mid-May, is a major event. Some say it's the only day in the year when the mail is bound to arrive on time, for the importance of Mother's Day cards getting delivered on the day is not taken lightly. Buses are crammed with people carrying flowers and gifts, and everywhere you go you see people carrying large, square cakes, brightly iced in pink or blue, that are handed out of baker's stores by the dozen. Flower sellers, their trucks filled with blooms, do a roaring trade outside cemeteries as people come from far and near to visit the graves of their departed mothers.

Federation of Cuban Women) in 1960, and in 1975 drew up the Family Code, which obliged men to share housework and childcare. While this is obviously difficult to enforce, it was a move in the right direction.

Through education, women are now involved in all aspects of the economy and the community. However, there are still very few women in the higher echelons of government and those with most prominence are family. Celia Sánchez, like Vilma Espín, was linked with the Castro brothers in the Sierra Maestra, and was hugely influential, but she too is now

Female factory workers in Baracoa.

dead. Of the next generation, only Dr Aleida Guevara (daughter of Che) and Mariela Castro Espín (daughter of Raúl and Vilma) are given worldwide political exposure in addition to their jobs in pediatrics and sex education. As in many Western countries, women are a small minority in the Council of Ministers and in the Armed Forces high command where real power lies.

A negative side effect of the revolution has been the increasing divorce rate. According to government statistics, about 5 percent of marriages ended in divorce in 1953. It is now estimated that, among Cubans aged from 25 to 40, a remarkable 60 percent of marriages fail. One reason for this is the lack of independent living space for newlyweds, who are forced to live in cramped apartments with their families. The decline of the influence of the Catholic Church has also been a factor, though another reason for the rise is the fact that the revolutionary government has made it much easier to obtain a divorce: all it takes is a few hours and about half a month's salary. Again, this should be seen in relation to the situation elsewhere: the US has the highest divorce rate in the Western world (44 percent), followed by the UK and Canada. Not as high as in Cuba, but indicative of a growing trend.

Mother and son, Trinidad.

Homophobia and gay rights

Born of two essentially patriarchal cultures, Cubans are largely *machista*, and traditionally homophobic. Although official statistics estimate Cuba's homosexual population to be between 4 and 6 percent, the real figure is likely to be much higher since many gay people maintain public heterosexual relationships in order to avoid harassment. Since the early 1960s, thousands of gay people have fled the island, including a large contingent that left during the Mariel boatlift of 1980 (see page 81).

However, there is more official tolerance of gay people these days. Homosexuality was legalized in 1979, and generally discrimination is less institutionalized today, although police harassment, for example, still exists. The movie *Fresa y Chocolate (Strawberry and Chocolate)*, about a gay intellectual who falls in love with a straight Communist Party militant, brought the gay issue to the forefront in the early 1990s; it played to full houses in Havana and won several international awards.

Groups of gay men and women have begun to form associations and to meet formally to discuss gay rights – a move that even a few years ago would have raised quite a storm. Also, many believe that a great deal depends on where gay people work. Intellectuals and university students are far more tolerant of individual sexual preferences than are blue-collar workers or farmers – but this is the same the whole world over.

Mariela Castro, director of the National Center for Sex Education and an activist for LGBT rights, was instrumental in getting a law passed in 2008 allowing sex change operations. She also campaigns for effective Aids prevention and is an executive member of the World Association for Sexual Health. She has produced a prolific academic output and has had a considerable impact on the acceptance of the human rights of transvestites, homosexuals, and bisexuals in Cuba.

A girl's 15th birthday, her 'quinceañera,' is a milestone, requiring extensive celebrations. Those who can afford it assemble a photo album, with the girl posing in a number of gowns, including a frothy wedding dress.

The generation gap

Members of the older generation, who remember the time before the Revolution, are now enjoying the fruits of their labors. The ones who made the choice to remain in the country after the exodus of the early 1960s are now benefitting from the state health service, seniors' care homes, and pensions. Their income may be meager, but at least they have a roof over their heads.

Their children, now in their 40s, have been brought up on revolutionary dogma. They have learned how to work the system and many families know how to exploit the state to maximum advantage. There may be a bureaucrat, who can get round rules and regulations; a farmer, who can keep them supplied with food; someone who works in tourism to bring in hard currency; an academic who can access the internet; and a relative in Miami who can send funds.

Guantánamo schoolgirls.

The family works together as a unit to maximum advantage.

The younger generation, however, is potentially a pressure cooker waiting to explode. They see the material benefits their contemporaries are enjoying in Miami and around the world and they yearn for the clothes with designer labels, the iPods, the smart phones, and the laptops, none of which is available to them. Teenage rebellion, subversive music, even something as simple as leaving home and living independently, are all impossible dreams. The state controls where they live, their careers, their income, and their entertainment. It is no wonder that some still risk the shark-infested sea to reach the promised land.

Street sweeper, Santa Clara.

Make do and mend

'*No es fácil*' is an expression that is frequently heard, meaning 'Life's not easy.' The daily grind to make ends meet is referred to as '*la lucha*,' the struggle. Trying to make a peso salary worth the equivalent of US$20 last until the end of the month is an uphill struggle even with subsidies that mean housing, health care, and education are all paid for. Tourists marvel at the old American cars still on the road, held together with the apocryphal elastic band, and the unspoilt houses stuffed with antiques, but 'make do and mend' has been essential since the Special Period of economic hardship after the fall of the Soviet Union.

Nothing is thrown away in Cuba. Plastic bags are washed and used over and over again. Men make a living out of refilling disposable cigarette lighters. '*Poncheros*,' puncture repairmen, are constantly in demand. Housewives spend all morning going round the '*agropecuarios*' and black markets until they have secured enough food to feed their families that day.

'*No hay*' (there isn't any) is a phrase frequently heard in shops.

A ponchero at work on a Bayamo street.

Support or discretion?

It is difficult for an outsider to know exactly how Cubans feel about their government and society. If they are critical, they are unlikely to express it openly. On the one hand, people talk with apparent sincerity about the 'triumph of the revolution,' and appear supportive of Castro. On the other hand, there are those who find the system insupportable, and who make their feelings known by leaving – or trying to. Most people would like some of the consumer goods and freedoms that tourists take for granted, but tend to blame shortages and hardships on the *bloqueo*, as they call the US embargo, while they wait, no doubt with mixed feelings, to see what changes are in store.

DECISIVE DATES

Replica of a Taíno sculpture, Bariay Bay.

Pre-Columbian period (6000 BC–AD 1492)

c.6000–3000 BC

First waves of native American settlers, pre-ceramic hunter-gatherer groups, known as the Guanahatabeys, the ancestors of the Ciboneyes.

c.AD 600

Arawak-speaking Taínos reach Cuba, arriving in hollowed-out tree-trunk canoes. They dominate eastern and central Cuba, although Ciboney groups are never entirely displaced. Taínos bring a more settled, agricultural way of life.

c.1490

Native population estimated at more than 100,000.

Spanish settlement (1492–1762)

1492

Columbus sights Cuba.

1508

Sebastián de Ocampo circumnavigates the island.

1509

Diego de Velázquez's first expedition.

1511–15

Velázquez returns to found Baracoa, followed by six other initial settlements *(villas)* around Cuba.

1512

Cacique Hatuey, the great Taíno chief, is burnt at the stake. Indigenous resistance crumbles. Subsequently most of the indigenous people are massacred, die of disease, or become forced laborers under the *encomienda* system.

Christopher Columbus.

1515

Santiago de Cuba becomes the capital.

1519

Havana is moved from the south coast to its present position on the north coast.

1523

The first African slaves are brought to work in the mines and on plantations.

1537

First slave revolt crushed.

1546

French pirates plunder the eastern town of Baracoa.

1555

French forces sack Havana. By order of Felipe II (1527–98) fortresses are built to protect Havana and Santiago.

c.1560

Fewer than 3,000 indigenous people remain.

El Morro fortress, Havana.

Nineteenth-century wood engraving of slaves harvesting sugar cane in Cuba.

1607
Havana named official capital.

1668
English expedition under Henry Morgan sails to Puerto Príncipe (modern Camagüey) and sacks the town.

1682
The Inquisition comes to Cuba, and strikes first in Remedios, which is torched after a Spanish priest discovers 'devils.'

1717
Tobacco trade declared a Crown monopoly.

The British occupation (1762–3)

1762
Havana falls to a massive British invasion force. The port is opened up to international trade, breaking the monopoly of the Spanish Crown.

1763
Havana is returned to Spanish rule as Britain swaps Havana for Florida (the Treaty of Paris).

Sugar boom and slavery (1774–1840)

c.1790s
Sugar replaces tobacco as Cuba's most valuable export. African slaves are imported in huge numbers to work on the plantations.

1795
French Haitian landowners flee the slave revolution and settle in Oriente (Cuba's eastern province).

Early 1800s
The price of sugar and land soars. Beginnings of independence movements in Cuba. Simón Bolívar leads anti-colonial revolts across Latin America.

1837
Latin America's first railroad in operation between Bejucal and Havana.

Two wars of independence (1868–98)

1868
Carlos Manuel de Céspedes liberates his slaves near Manzanillo and issues call to arms against Spanish overlords, sparking the Ten Years' War.

1869
Rebels issue Constitution of Guáimaro.

1871
José Martí, independence fighter, poet, and journalist, is exiled to Spain; he later settles in New York.

1873
Céspedes replaced as rebel leader.

1878
Peace treaty signed. Rebel factions split.

1879–1880
The 'Little War' breaks out.

Independence fighter, José Martí.

1886
Spain abolishes all slavery.

1892
José Martí founds the Cuban Revolutionary Party from exile in the US.

1895
The Second War of Independence, led by Martí, who dies in the first battle at Dos Ríos.

1896
Antonio Maceo, who took over the independence leadership role, is killed in western Cuba. Máximo Gómez returns from exile and continues the struggle. Spanish forces

initiate a 'scorched-earth' policy in the countryside.

1898
Battleship USS *Maine* sunk in Havana's harbor after an explosion, which prompts the US to enter the conflict. Spanish forces defeated at the Battle of San Juan Hill. Spain signs a peace treaty ceding control of Cuba to the US.

Corruption and coups (1901–59)

1901
The Platt Amendment adopted: Guantánamo naval base ceded to the US, which claims the right to intervene in Cuban affairs. Provokes widespread Cuban anger.

1902
Tomás Estrada Palma is inaugurated as president.

1906–9
Marines invade to protect US interests.

1912
Afro-Cuban Black Uprising is savagely repressed.

1924–33
General Machado's presidency is prone to venality and violence. General strike forces him to flee.

Trophy from the Bay of Pigs invasion, Museo de Girón.

1934
Fulgencio Batista stages a coup. Puppet president is installed under army control. Abrogation of Platt Amendment, but Guantánamo left in US control.

1940–4
First Batista presidency follows national vote.

1952
Batista seizes power and cancels elections.

1956
Fidel Castro's guerrilla force sails from Mexico in the Granma. Hideout established in Sierra Maestra.

Cartoon depicting Uncle Sam as Cuba's savior.

1958
Guevara opens second front in Sierra del Escambray. Batista flees.

The revolutionary years (1959–90)

1959
Castro enters Havana. First land reform introduced; literacy and public health campaigns launched.

1960
Nationalization of major companies.

1961
US-backed invasion results in Bay of Pigs fiasco. Castro declares socialist nature of revolution.

The flag of Cuba.

1962
Cuban Missile Crisis brings world to brink of nuclear war. Cuba brought further into Soviet orbit. US economic blockade begins in earnest.

1964
Castro pays first visit to USSR.

1965
Che Guevara resigns posts and leaves for Africa.

1967
Guevara killed in Bolivia.

1976
Right-wing terrorist group

Antonio Maceo.

bombs plane, killing all 73 Cuban athletes on board.

1980
Mariel boatlift: 120,000 leave Cuba – legally – for Miami.

1989
Execution of General Ochoa for alleged drug smuggling and corruption.

The 'Special Period' and recovery (post-1990)

1991
Russian economic aid axed after end of the Soviet Union; food and fuel shortages begin.

1993
Dollar legalized; limited forms of private enterprise allowed. Economic privations continue.

1994
Crisis of the boat people: 35,000 Cubans try to flee to Miami. US tightens immigration controls.

1996
Draconian Helms-Burton legislation passed by US Congress tightens the embargo's stranglehold.

1998
The Pope visits Cuba and criticizes the US embargo.

1999
Five-year-old Elián González survives a rafting accident en route to the US. Despite fierce protests in Miami, Elián is returned to his Cuban father.

2002
Nearly half the sugar mills close; 100,000 workers lose jobs.

2003
75 dissidents sentenced to jail terms of up to 28 years. Worldwide condemnation.

2004
The UN's Human Rights Commission votes to press for human-rights inspections.

2006
Castro hospitalized in July; temporarily hands over power to his brother, Raúl.

2008
Raúl Castro confirmed as president. Fidel remains party leader until 2011.

2009
Raúl Castro removes Fidelistas from Council of Ministers. The US lifts the prohibitions on travel and remittances by Cuban Americans that were imposed in 2004.

2010
The Roman Catholic Church negotiates the release of the remaining 52 of the 75 political prisoners arrested in 2003, most of whom leave for Spain. Cubans are permitted to build and improve their own homes.

2011
Cubans are allowed to buy and sell their own homes.

2012
Hurricane Sandy hits Santiago and the east, causing death and destruction with 124mph (200kph) winds.

2013
Self-employment rises by 445,000. Cubans are allowed to travel abroad and to buy new cars. Castro announces process to end dual currency.

Cuban man holding Cuba's two currencies.

A statue of the Taíno warrior Hatuey.

CONQUISTADORES AND PIRATES

Long before Columbus arrived, Cuba had been populated by groups of indigenous people, who were to be subjugated to the conquistadores. Early colonial history was turbulent, as booms and busts in gold and sugar changed its fortunes.

The first European to glimpse the coast of Cuba was Christopher Columbus, who, on his initial voyage in 1492, pronounced it the most beautiful land 'that eyes had ever set upon.' This beautiful land had, of course, been discovered several thousand years beforehand by peoples Columbus assumed were Indians – a misnomer that has stuck.

The first groups of indigenous people to colonize Cuba were pre-agricultural hunter-gatherers. Quite how and when they first arrived is not known for certain, but it seems that they arrived in different waves of migration from about 6,000 years ago, from the Orinoco delta of modern-day Venezuela, from Central America, and possibly also from Florida and the Mississippi basin.

Historians have attempted to classify these indigenous peoples with different names at different times. Once known as Guanahatabey, they are more commonly referred to as Ciboney, but they all shared a common pre-agricultural, pre-ceramic heritage. Their cultures were characterized by the use of shell implements, and they lived in caves or basic settlements across the island.

Some Taíno finds can be seen in the Museum of Anthropology in Vedado (Havana), and in the little Archeological Museum in Baracoa, close to the spot where a famous Taíno tobacco idol was found.

From about AD 600 onward these hunter-gatherer groups were displaced gradually in some parts of Cuba by waves of new immigrants – the Arawak-speaking Taíno peoples.

A depiction of Columbus's arrival in Cuba.

The Taínos had followed the arc of the Antilles islands in their hollowed-out tree-trunk canoes, arriving from the region of the Orinoco delta. The Taínos brought with them a more settled, agricultural way of life, and they were the dominant group of peoples when Columbus arrived, although some earlier indigenous groups still survived.

The Taínos lived in communities of palm-thatched homes, described by Columbus as looking like large tents, scattered randomly around as if in a camp. For food, they combined fishing and hunting with agriculture – growing staple crops like cassava, peppers, beans, and sweet potatoes, and fruits such as guavas and pineapples.

Their society had a hierarchical structure, at the apex of which were hereditary chiefs *(caciques)* and shamans *(behiques)*. The shamans presided over curative rituals, linked to the worship of a pantheon of gods and ancestor spirits. Taínos believed in an afterlife, and revered idols, called *cemíes*, lovingly carved out of hardwoods, stone, or coral, which they kept in special shrines.

Columbus's very first contacts with the island's native peoples were marked by mutual curiosity and, it seems, a certain respect, even if this wasn't to last for long. Columbus made sure his sailors took nothing from the first dwellings they entered, but no doubt this was partly because he was more interested in gold and pearls than in the fishing nets, spun cotton, silent dogs, and tame wild birds that they encountered.

A Taíno figure, Baracoa.

A Taíno zemi statue.

Columbus noted, 'They very willingly traded everything they had, but they seemed to me a people short of everything.' However, he admired their happiness and generosity. His sailors brought back to Europe tobacco, syphilis, and news of a world ripe for conquest.

Spanish conquest

The Spanish first settled on the island of Hispaniola (present-day Dominican Republic and Haiti), where they enslaved and brutalized the indigenous population. Soon they started to look west, hoping to find gold in Cuba.

However, their reputation preceded them, and some *caciques* were determined to resist. The most famous of these was the great warrior Hatuey, who had witnessed Spanish massacres in Hispaniola and fled to eastern Cuba. When the conquistador Diego Velázquez landed in Baracoa in 1511 at the head of an expedition to settle the island, Hatuey fought back.

But despite a long game of hide-and-seek in the caves and mountains of the east, Hatuey and

SPEAKING WITH THE GODS

The Jeronymite friar, Ramón Pané, recorded Taíno customs in his *Account of the Antiquities of the Indies* in the late 15th century. Of their ceremonies he writes: 'To purge themselves, they take a certain powder, called *cohoba*, snorting it up the nose, which intoxicates them in a way that they don't know what they're doing; and in this way they say many incoherent things, in which they affirm that they are speaking with the idols.' Once thought to be tobacco, *cohoba* is now believed to be the crushed seeds of an acacia-like tree – *Anadenanthera peregrina*, still used today by some Venezuelan indigenous groups, and known as *yopo*.

The island's name derives from a native term for the island, Cubanacán, and not, as some believe, the Spanish for barrel (cuba), after the barrel-shaped hills seen by the first sailors.

his followers were eventually captured and put to the stake in 1512. When offered baptism at his execution, the chieftain asked if there were any Christians in heaven; when told that there were, he proclaimed that he preferred to burn as a pagan.

Bartolomé de las Casas at the execution of an Indian chieftan.

Between 1512 and 1514, Velázquez and his men founded the seven original 'villas' of Cuba – Baracoa, Santiago, Bayamo, Camagüey, Trinidad, Sancti Spíritus, and Havana. The Spanish then set about rounding up the indigenous population for use as forced labor. Resistance continued sporadically for the next couple of decades, but the outlook was bleak.

Champion of the people

Only a few brave Spaniards dared to speak out against what they were seeing. The most famous champion of the native peoples was Bartolomé de las Casas, the so-called 'Protector of the Indians.' As one of the first settlers in Cuba in 1513, he had exploited indigenous slaves in the mines and on his estate, but he turned against this system when a Dominican priest refused him absolution. On becoming a Dominican friar he campaigned passionately for the just treatment of native peoples, but he failed in his goal of abolishing the harsh *encomienda* system, which granted Spanish conquistadores land and the right to use the inhabitants of that land as forced labor.

Although gold made some of the first settlers astonishingly rich, the supply quickly petered out. The conquistadores soon found other, more tantalizing, rewards: Hernán Cortés set off to conquer Aztec Mexico, and soon afterward Francisco Pizarro toppled Inca Peru. Plundered gold and mined silver began streaming into the Spanish coffers, and soon Cuba was reduced to the status of supply post for the more lucrative plundering of South and Central America. While the ports of Panama overflowed with riches, and soldiers shod their horses with silver, the island's seven settlements remained little more than wretched provincial villages.

Cuba's strategic position, however, saved it from oblivion. Treasure from the New World still had to be brought back safely to Spain via the Caribbean Sea, which was becoming infested with foreign pirates. A system of fortresses was established on the orders of Spanish king Felipe II, so that treasure could be conveyed in short hops from port to port.

Havana was moved from the south to its current spot on the north coast, and acquired massive new walls and fortifications that took more than 40 years to build (see page 157). It became the key point in Spain's whole transportation system: fleets from Cartagena in Colombia, San Juan in Puerto Rico, and Panama City converged here for resupplying, while Latin America's first shipyard turned out merchant and warships. At the eastern end of the island, Santiago de Cuba was fortified as a secondary port.

A 16th-century engraving depicting Cortés sailing to Cuba.

First signs of wealth

These military accouterments, however, did not make life in the towns any less squalid. On the contrary, the constant parade of seamen and desperate adventurers did the reverse, turning both Havana and Santiago into warrens of taverns, brothels, and muddy, narrow streets. Even so, some of the wealth rubbed off, and merchants could make modest fortunes loading up the galleons with provisions for the long journey to Spain.

With the proceeds of these sales, Cuba attracted a rudimentary upper class who constructed some magnificent stone buildings – a smattering of which still survive in Old Havana today. Like colonial overlords everywhere, the Spaniards trapped in this remote backwater tried desperately to hang on to their heritage: *caballeros* (gentlemen) would wear finery and frills despite the tropical heat, keep in touch with the latest in the arts in their European homeland, and host lavish dinner dances in the midst of plagues of malaria and yellow fever.

As one traveler to Cuba remarked: 'The palaces of the nobles in Havana, the residence of the governor, the convents, the cathedral, are a reproduction of Burgos or Valladolid, as if by some Aladdin's lamp a Castilian city had been taken up and set down again unaltered on the shore of the Caribbean Sea. And they carried with them their laws, their habits, their institutions and their creed, their religious orders, their bishops and their Inquisition.'

Pirates on the rampage

Despite Spain's best efforts, the uninhabited swamps of Florida and the island maze of the Bahamas became havens for freebooters and buccaneers of every nationality, ready to pounce on any ship passing along Cuba's coast. The more brazen found the cays and islands off Cuba's south coast to be perfect bases for their activities.

The most famous (or infamous) names in the history of piracy all touched on the island's coast, and many became embroiled, over the years, in the shifting patterns of war between Spain and more recent interlopers in the Caribbean, the English, the French, and the Dutch.

Drake and Morgan

It was England's Francis Drake (1540–96), a favorite of Queen Elizabeth I, who started the habit of calling in at Cabo de San Antonio,

Havana's port was heavily fortified.

Cuba's westernmost point, for fresh water and turtle eggs on the way to and from raids on Cartagena and Panama.

The most ruthless and successful buccaneer of all arrived in the following century. This was Henry Morgan, son of a well-to-do Welsh farmer, who was hired by the English Government in 1668 to seek intelligence on Spanish activities in Cuba.

Morgan took this as a license to sail his 750 men the 80km (50 miles) inland to Puerto Príncipe (modern Camagüey) and attack it. The Spanish governor got wind of his plan and had a force drawn up to meet Morgan, but, he reported, 'the pirates were very dextrous.' The Spaniards were defeated and the town forced to surrender. Morgan locked the inhabitants in the churches, and set about sacking the town.

According to chronicles, Morgan's men 'fell to banqueting … and making great cheer after their customary way, without remembering the poor prisoners, whom they permitted to starve in the churches. In the meanwhile they did not cease to torment them daily after an inhuman manner, thereby to make them confess where they had hid their goods and money, though little or nothing was left them. They punished also the women and little children.' Morgan then went on to sack Panama City, and after retiring to London was appointed Governor of Jamaica.

In 1715, the biggest Spanish treasure fleet ever gathered started off from Havana loaded with nearly 7 million 'pieces of eight,' and thousands of bars of silver. This time, it was nature rather than piracy that was to prove the venture's undoing. Though the fleet waited until after the hurricane season, it ran straight into a storm in the Gulf of Florida. Nearly 1,000 of the 2,500 passengers lost their lives, and wreckage littered the entire Florida coast, to be picked off by passing buccaneers.

The tyranny of 'white gold'

Dramatic as these events were, Cuba's real future was being shaped in its first sugar fields. When Columbus first landed in the Americas, sugar was one of the most valuable commodities in Europe, imported for a fortune from the Orient and weighed out by the tablespoon. He quickly realized the Caribbean's potential, and on his second voyage he brought the first sugar-cane roots from the Canary Islands and planted them in what is

THE INQUISITION STRIKES

The Inquisition descended most famously on the town of Remedios in 1682, when the parish priest declared that the village had been invaded by 800,000 devils (more than 1,000 devils per inhabitant – which is quite a lot). After burning the odd, possessed victim, soldiers torched the settlement, ordering the villagers to move to relatively useless land, where the town of Santa Clara was being established. This could be Cuba's first real-estate scam: the property was owned by the priest who had 'discovered' the devils, and who hoped to rent it out at a tidy profit. The villagers, however, defied pressure and rebuilt their town.

today the Dominican Republic. Within a century, the cultivation of sugar cane had spread across the Caribbean islands and to the coast of Brazil.

Cuba started off as a comparatively minor sugar producer – cattle ranching and then tobacco were more important initially – but gradually more and more lush forests of mahogany and ceiba were uprooted to make way for sugar-cane plantations, while boatloads of slaves were transported from Africa to work on them. The first African slaves were brought to Cuba as domestic servants, but before long they were being forced to work in the mines and on sugar or tobacco plantations. With the indigenous population wiped out, the Spanish needed an alternative source of labor and Africans were deemed more robust and resilient. Even Fray Bartolomé de Las Casas (see page 31) had spoken out in favor of the African slave trade, as a way of protecting his beloved 'Indians' from rapacious exploitation. And before long, a second phase of brutalization had begun.

Until the late 18th century, the slave trade was run under license from the Spanish Crown, although a sizable illegal slave-smuggling trade existed too. The trade was initially on a far smaller scale than it was to become in the 19th century, but thousands of peoples from across Africa – from countries like Senegal, Mali, and Sierra Leone; Yoruba-speaking peoples from present-day Nigeria; Bantú peoples from the Congo and Angola; and even from as far away as Mozambique – were hauled across the ocean, all bringing different cultural traditions and languages. With the slaves came African gods, myths, and rituals, which the Christian priests could not eradicate despite their zeal.

Life on the plantations was terribly harsh – thousands died from overwork, disease, and poor nutrition, and beatings were common. There was a severe dearth of women, as slavers preferred importing young men, who were stronger and therefore represented better value. Women were often raped by their overseers, and slave families could be broken up by the selling of their children.

An 18th-century engraving of Havana harbor with chain across the entrance.

Desperate measures

There were uprisings throughout the colonial period, one of the first taking place as early as 1537, when slaves rose up and joined in an assault by French pirates on the city of Havana, and the Spanish lived in constant fear of slave rebellion. Some slaves, termed *cimarrones*, chose to escape, fleeing to the mountains where they sometimes developed small communities (*palenques*), possibly joining too with remnant indigenous communities, but they always lived under the fear of recapture by slave-hunters and their savage dogs.

Just outside Santiago stands a monument to slaves who fled from the harsh conditions of forced labor in the copper mine, El Cobre, in the 18th century. Other slaves, in desperation, even chose to commit mass suicides, many believing that after death they would be resurrected in Africa.

The Last Supper

Just how bizarre Cuban rural society had become by the end of the 18th century can be seen by the events that took place near Santa María del Rosario, a village southeast of Havana. The account comes from historian Manuel Moreno Fraginals (1920–2001), a leading authority on plantation slavery in Cuba, and was captured in the classic Cuban film *La Última Cena (The Last Supper)* made in 1976 by Cuban director Tomás Gutiérrez Alea.

In a fit of religious fervor, the Count de Casa Bayona (whose former home now houses the Colonial Art Museum in Havana) invited a dozen of his slaves to a feast on Maundy Thursday (the day before Good Friday). Acting out the role of Jesus Christ, he washed the feet of each slave personally. When the overseer refused to give the slaves a holiday on Easter Sunday, as had been promised by the count, because the Bible teaches that Sunday should be a day of rest, they rose up in rebellion, burning the plantation to the ground.

Hearing the news, the count arrived with armed horsemen to supress the uprising. Horrified at what he perceived to be the ingratitude of the 12 slaves who had feasted with him, he ordered that they should be hunted down and executed. Their heads were placed on pikes in the cane fields as a warning to their fellow-workers that, whatever the Bible might say, all men were not created equal in Cuba.

African slaves in the sugar fields.

THE CORNISH IN EL COBRE

El Cobre copper mine has a link with the English county of Cornwall, a prominent tin-mining area. The Spanish abandoned the mine in the early 19th century, and a visiting English businessman, finding it still had rich copper deposits, founded the Cobre Mining Company, and imported steam engines and labor from Cornwall. Thousands came in the 1830s, but harsh conditions and mosquito-borne yellow fever resulted in a high death rate, and the number of workers dwindled. By 1870 the enterprise was over: the seam was becoming exhausted, and the destruction caused by the uprising against the Spanish (see page 43) was the final straw.

1901 cartoon satirizing US involvement in Cuba.

THE STRUGGLE AGAINST COLONIALISM

Cuba was one step behind the liberal changes spreading through Latin America in the 19th century. But Spain's 'Ever Faithful Isle' eventually fought for independence from Spain. Inevitably, it then came within the sphere of US influence.

In the early 1800s, every Spanish possession in the New World successfully rose up against colonial rule – except Cuba and Puerto Rico. In Havana, barely a voice was raised in support of the romantic liberation movements being led by heroes such as Simón Bolívar and José de San Martín, much to the embarrassment of modern Cuban historians. On the contrary, Cuba became Spain's military springboard for the many attempts to reconquer her tattered empire, which dragged on for decades and left much of South and Central America in ruins. A short-lived movement for Cuban independence was quelled by Spain in 1823, and relative calm returned.

By 1825 the Spanish had reluctantly given up on the New World and retreated to its two loyal Caribbean possessions – the more valued of which, for the next 40 years, would remain Cuba – referred to in Madrid as 'the Ever Faithful Isle.'

Carlos Manuel de Céspedes.

The Cafetal Museo La Isabelica near Santiago, now under Unesco protection, was the plantation house of a coffee estate belonging to a family of French descent, who had fled from Haiti's slave rebellion.

Predictions of ruin

Cuban Creoles, masters of a slave society, were in fact desperate to avoid independence. They had been kept in a state of constant terror since the bloody slave rebellion in neighboring Haiti in the 1790s: French refugees had landed on the beaches around Santiago, starving, desperate, telling wild tales of race slaughter, laced with lurid images of voodoo and throbbing African drums. Napoleon's army was defeated on the shores of the new black republic, and white Cubans were worried that their island might follow suit. 'There is no country on earth where a revolutionary movement is more dangerous than Cuba,' declared one planter, predicting 'the complete ruin of the Cuban race.'

Even so, greed was stronger than fear. The expansion of the slave population during the later 18th and early 19th centuries was unparalleled, for two main reasons. First, in 1762, the British had captured the heavily fortified city of Havana, after storming the main forts guarding the harbor. This was simply a consequence of a wider war Britain was waging against France and her ally, Spain. They then trained the very guns that were meant to protect the city against its own walls, forcing its capitulation in just two weeks. The Governor of Havana was sent back to Spain in disgrace, but the heroic resistance of the captain commanding El Morro fortress, Don Luís de Velasco, earned him a posthumous ennoblement from his king.

The British divided up the tremendous spoils of the city's public monies and warehouses, and then endured sickness and disease, until Havana was returned to Spain a mere seven months later. Spain regained possession of her beloved colonial city only by handing Florida over to the British. However, an important legacy of the occupation was that the British had allowed Havana to trade freely with other nations, thus breaking the monopoly that Spain had enjoyed since the 16th century, and this liberalization vastly increased the trade in slaves. Once broken, this monopoly could not realistically be reimposed by the returning Spanish. Freed from this economic straitjacket, the Cuban economy boomed, and there were real incentives to increase production of its chief commodity: sugar.

Secondly, the Haitian rebellion destroyed the sugar plantations there, pushing sugar prices sky-high, and many of the refugees who resettled in Cuba brought with them expertise and improved production techniques. Cuba soon became the world's biggest producer of 'white gold.' It was a new era of fabulous wealth and sudden fortunes.

Latin America's first railroad was built in 1837 from the Güines sugar fields to Havana, using the labor of African slaves, Chinese workers, and indentured Irishmen. Thirteen workers perished for every kilometer of track laid.

Slaves' lives were hard and short, and owners began to fear rebellions.

HUMAN LIFE DEVALUED

German naturalist Alexander von Humboldt lived in Cuba at the beginning of the 19th century. He calculated the meridian of Havana and studied the local flora and fauna around Trinidad, where he witnessed life on the sugar plantations. He was appalled by the attitude of Cuban slave owners: 'I have heard discussed with the greatest coolness whether it was better for the proprietor not to overwork his slaves, and consequently have to replace them with less frequency, or whether he should get all he could out of them in a few years, and then have to purchase newly imported Africans.'

Dependence on sugar and slaves

Nothing could stop sugar cane consuming the countryside – citrus fields were replanted, the last forests uprooted, even tobacco plantations were plowed over (growth of the crop being restricted to the narrower fields of the province of Pinar del Río). A steadily increasing supply of slaves was needed for the plantations, especially as workers survived for an average of only seven years. The number of slaves in Cuba stood at 40,000 in 1774, but by 1867 when the last known slave ship landed its cargo, an estimated 600,000 Africans had been imported.

Africans were bought and sold in newspaper classifieds, next to advertisements for horses and farm implements. In a rare gesture of leniency, some planters allowed their slaves to dance at night to drums, praying they were not communicating news of rebellion. Uprisings did occur, and were brutally repressed. By the mid-1820s, blacks outnumbered whites on the island.

A new 'sugarocracy' arose in Cuba: the sugar center of Trinidad sprouted resplendent palaces with names like Hope, Gamble, and Confidence. Their owners could afford to take shopping trips to Europe, bringing back Persian carpets, Italian paintings, and French chandeliers. Sumptuous mansions transformed Havana from a 'large village,' in foreigners' eyes, to Spain's 'jewel of the Caribbean,' a city of elegant iron grilles *(rejas)*, gracious curlicues, and beautiful stained glass. The streets were paved with granite imported from New England, and trade with the United States boomed – the beginning of a relationship that would dominate much of Cuba's modern history.

The wind of change

The 19th century brought with it new ideas of liberation, independence, and emancipation, that swept through empires and their colonies. The slave revolution in Haiti, US independence from Britain, and Latin American countries' independence from Spain, all led to changes in outlook. Cuba was not immune, though modernization came late as a result of entrenched economic interests. A few *criollos* (Cuban-born Spaniards) began to sympathize both with the abolition of slavery and independence from the corrupt and inflexible Spanish administration, but their power was limited.

Their liberal views should be seen in the context of the European (principally British) push to abolish slavery, with some of the more enlightened Cubans recognizing the beginning of the end of enforced labor. In 1811, Spain abolished slavery at home and in all its colonies except Cuba, Puerto Rico, and Santo Domingo. Under British pressure, Spain signed treaties to ban the Atlantic slave trade in 1817 (even receiving £400,000 from Britain for doing so) and 1835, but this was completely ignored in Cuba and the trade continued covertly until the 1860s. In neighboring Jamaica, slaves were emancipated in 1833, but they would have to wait until 1886 in Cuba, a delay that caused more than a few rumblings of discontent among the oppressed, and understandable fear among the landowning, slave-owning class, whose economic interests were at stake.

> *When in 1848 President Polk offered US$100 million to buy Cuba, Spain's foreign minister commented that his country 'would rather see it sunk into the ocean.'*

Lithograph from the Grand Cuban-American Fair, 1896.

Cubans started to seek reforms and greater autonomy from Spain. Politically, they fell into three groups: those who favored annexation to the US; those who favored complete independence from Spain together with the abolition of slavery; and those who wanted to remain part of Spain but with a separate constitution and greater autonomy. There were three attempts at annexation, supported by slave-holding southern states, but all failed because the North and the abolitionist South were vehemently against annexing another slave-holding country.

The push for freedom

By the 1860s, Cuba was producing about a third of the world's sugar and was heavily dependent upon slaves and indentured labor-

A United States version of the Battle of San Juan Hill.

ers from China to do so. Spain was intransigent in refusing to allow political reforms to give the colony more autonomy within the empire and it came to the point when many Cubans were at last ready to end Spanish colonial rule. In 1868, a small-plantation owner, Carlos Manuel de Céspedes, freed the slaves at one of his plantations near Manzanillo, and declared Cuba independent, sparking off the Ten Years' War with Spain. The revolutionaries realized that they would only win against Spain if all Cubans, including free blacks and slaves, presented a united front. Free and runaway slaves swelled the Liberation Army's ranks. Known as *mambís* – a word that meant 'rebel' in the African Congo – they often fought with machetes for lack of guns, and went barefoot and near-naked for want of boots and uniforms.

Antonio Maceo, the 'Bronze Titan,' was a black soldier who rose from the ranks to become major-general and one of the most popular leaders in the struggle. Like a character in a García Márquez novel, he is said to have survived innumerable assassination attempts, fought in 900 battles, been wounded 25 times, and lost his father and nine of his 13 brothers in the war. Many pro-Spanish whites were afraid that he would attempt to become president, and gathered under the slogan: 'Cuba, better Spanish than African!'

Adventurers came from around the world to join the struggle against Spain. One was former American Union army officer Henry Reeve, who was captured and shot by a Spanish firing squad. Left for dead, he survived and became a leading general and anti-slavery voice, remembered as *El Inglesito*, 'the little Englishman.' But the war ground on for a decade, took 200,000 lives, and ended in stalemate. The Moret Law, passed in 1870, freed all children of slaves born after 1868 and any slave lucky enough to live to be over 60, but slavery itself was untouched. The Zanjón Convention, which brought the war to an end, enabled a limited number of Cubans to elect representatives to the Spanish *Cortés* (parliament), but there was no autonomy. The war left the economy crippled, and, with land prices at a level lower than they had been in years, US companies began to invest heavily in Cuban real estate, developing a significant financial interest in the country's future. They bought up many sugar plantations and sugar mills and, as sugar beet started to dominate the European market, Cuba became ever more dependent on the US to buy its main crop.

Finally, in 1880, the *Cortés* approved the law of abolition, although this amounted to little in the way of freedom. The law introduced an eight-year *patronato* (tutelage) for all slaves, whereby they had to continue working for their owners with no pay. It took a royal decree in 1886 to make the *patronato* illegal, and finally abolish slavery in Cuba. It probably had as much to do with the changing working conditions as it did with morality. Free and contract workers, together with more efficient processing techniques, allowed economies of scale.

The fighting starts again

The end of the Ten Years' War solved nothing, and Cuba was like a volcano waiting to erupt. There were other, unsuccessful attempts at rebellion, but the most successful was fostered in the US. In 1895, the carnage began again with the Second War of Independence, this time led by the great Cuban theorist José Martí (see page 42). A lawyer, poet, and journalist, Martí's writings, and his organizational activities among Cubans living in the US in the 1870s and 1880s, had infused the independence movement with ideas of social justice: the goal was not just a free Cuba, but a Cuba without its vast inequalities of wealth and racial divisions. Unfortunately, he was killed in his first battle in 1895. However, the seemingly indestructible Antonio Maceo was still around to keep the flame of revolution burning, until he too was killed in a skirmish with Spanish troops on the border of Havana and Pinar del Río provinces, at the end of 1896. The tragedy left the Cuban cause in the hands of another stalwart veteran of the earlier war, General Máximo Gómez, who had been persuaded by Martí to return from exile to help lead the independence struggle.

Unable to engage the elusive rebels directly, Spanish forces started a scorched-earth policy in the Cuban countryside, executing *guajiros* (farmers), burning farms, and putting the survivors into labor camps. The strategy failed, and by 1898, the Spaniards were exhausted and at the point of withdrawing. But another colonial power had been watching the conflict with increasing interest: the United States of America.

Enter the United States

As long as a century before, North American thinkers had decided that Cuba was crucial to their country's strategic interests. Throughout the 1800s, there were calls for outright

A Spanish depiction of the Battle of San Juan Hill.

AN ENGLISH VIEW

In 1895 the young English officer Winston Churchill took his winter leave in Cuba as war correspondent for the London *Daily Graphic.* He found the jaunt 'awfully jolly,' especially as he was able to celebrate his 21st birthday in a war zone. Churchill had his first experience of being fired upon while having breakfast, but the guerrillas melted into the countryside and he spent most of his visit 'wandering round and round in this endless humid jungle.' Initially sympathizing with the rebels, he began to feel sorry for the Spanish losing their 'Pearl of the Antilles.' 'They felt about Cuba just as we felt about Ireland,' he wrote.

José Martí

From the tiniest Cuban village to cities across Latin America are images of this romantic visionary whose greatness is undisputed.

Born in 1853, Martí began his career as an independence fighter at 15, when he helped start an anti-colonial newspaper, *The Free Fatherland*, in Havana and denounced a fellow student for marching in a Spanish procession. He was charged with treason and sentenced to hard labor in a stone quarry. A frail youth, the experience ruined his eyesight, gave him a hernia and permanent scars on his ankles from the shackles he wore (in later life, he always wore a ring made from these shackles). After six months, Martí was sent into exile in Spain – the beginning of a journey that took him to France, England, Mexico, Guatemala, back secretly to Cuba, to exile again in Spain, escape to France, then to the US and south to Venezuela.

Statue of José Martí, an undisputed hero.

Exile in the United States

In 1881 Martí finally settled with his family in New York City, a center for Cuban exiles, and was initially intoxicated with the United States ('One can breathe freely,' he wrote. 'For here, freedom is the foundation, the shield, the essence of life.')

The enthusiasm was short-lived, however, and Martí soon saw the United States as the greatest threat to Latin American independence. He viewed as crucial the prevention of 'the annexation of the peoples of our America by the turbulent and brutal North which despises them... I have lived within the monster and I know its entrails – and my sling is the sling of David.'

For 15 years in the United States Martí kept up a punishing routine of political organizing, lecturing, purchasing weapons, and writing firebrand speeches, newspaper columns, essays, and exquisite, avant-garde poetry (his *Versos Sencillos* were married to the music of *Guajira Guantanamera* in the 1960s in what became the unofficial Cuban national anthem). He ate little, slept only in snatches, but glowed with nervous energy. Traveling to Florida – always in a heavy black suit and bow tie, his pointed moustache neatly clipped – Martí visited cigar factories to recruit Cuban exiles to his cause. Cuba would not be truly free, he argued, without economic, racial, and sexual equality – thus adding an inspiring social element to the potent rhetoric of nationalism.

A Tragic Conclusion

Martí, though, was not content to remain an intellectual. In 1892, he founded the Cuban Revolutionary Party. Three years later, plans were made to rekindle the independence struggle: a message, hidden in a Havana cigar, was sent to General Antonio Maceo in Cuba.

Martí and Máximo Gómez landed secretly on the southeast coast, in a tiny boat that was nearly dashed to pieces in the middle of a storm. Escaping to the sierra of the Oriente, they were joined by hundreds of supporters. But life as a guerrilla was harsh: Martí's emaciated frame was weighed down by a heavy coat, pack, and rifle, and he often fell on the mountain trails.

On May 19, 1895, near Bayamo, Martí went into his first day of battle carrying a picture of his daughter over his heart. He was shot dead almost immediately as he charged toward the enemy, without ever having drawn his gun. A martyr to the cause, he has been worshiped by Cubans ever since and only Che Guevara is as instantly recognizable and revered. Today, José Martí's words have been appropriated by both sides of the political divide: Fidel Castro views him as the home-grown ideologue of the Revolution, while right-wing Miami Cubans named their anti-Castro broadcast stations Radio Martí and TV Martí.

annexation, and several filibustering expeditions set out from Florida to the Cuban shores, hoping to provoke a popular revolt that would cause Cuba to fall 'like a ripening plum into the lap of the Union' (in the happy phrase of John Quincy Adams). Four US presidents even offered to buy Cuba from the Spanish during the first half of the 19th century, seeing the island as part of the natural orbit of their increasingly powerful and expansionist country. With more than US$100 million invested by 1898, there were many in Washington who worried that radicals would take over an independent Cuba.

American emotions had already been whipped up by the press. Newspaper barons William Randolph Hearst (Orson Welles's model for *Citizen Kane*) and Joseph Pulitzer (who would give his name to America's greatest journalism prize) competed to offer the most lurid and heart-rending tales of the Spanish troops' cruelty: images of Cuban streets awash with blood, bayoneted babies, and deflowered virgins became daily fare for millions from Kansas to New York.

'Remember the Maine!'

The pretext for intervention came on February 15, when the USS *Maine* – a battleship sent to protect US interests – mysteriously blew up in Havana harbor, killing 260 people. Hearst and Pulitzer both claimed that the explosion on the *Maine* was caused by a Spanish mine (it was Hearst who coined the immortal, and very catchy, slogan, 'Remember the Maine, to hell with Spain!'), and though some Cubans today subscribe to the belief that it might have been a deliberate explosion caused by the US itself to precipitate their involvement in the war, the evidence points to an accidental munitions explosion in the hold. Today there is a monument to the *Maine* in Havana on the Malecón.

Within a month, President McKinley had declared war; three months after that, the US Navy had blockaded the Spanish Navy in the harbor of Santiago de Cuba, at the eastern end of the island. A huge American expeditionary force landed north of the city. It was led by an obese veteran of the Indian wars, General William Shafter (1835–1906), and accompanied by a boatload of eager, albeit diarrhea-ridden, journalists.

The 1898 Currier and Ives lithograph Our Victorious Fleets in Cuban Waters.

Although the US Congress passed an amendment stating that they were not claiming sovereignty in Cuba, nationalists quickly had cause to doubt the benefits of US assistance. Shafter and his men took one look at the ragged Cuban Army and refused to allow them into battle, publicly blaming their lack of shoes and poor weapons, but in private appalled that so many of them were black and mulatto (mixed race) – the reporter Stephen Crane called them 'real tropic savages.' Shafter suggested that the Cubans keep up the rear, digging trenches and latrines. Unsurprisingly, the commanding general, Calixto García, refused to cooperate.

The Spanish Army had very little fight left in it, but a showdown of sorts came at the Battle of San Juan Hill, on the outskirts of Santiago. The American Rough Riders were led in a famous charge by Edward Roosevelt, a short-sighted weakling as a child who had taken up *machista* pursuits from tiger hunting to soldiering in compensation. The Spanish were defeated, although the Americans took heavy casualties. Roosevelt's first missive to the US President was sheepish, but the national press hailed it as an extraordinary military achievement. Roosevelt rode the wave of popularity on to the governorship of New York and, in 1901, the presidency. Two days after San Juan, the Spanish Navy made a quixotic sally from Santiago only to suffer a rapid defeat.

It had been a 'splendid little war,' as one US official noted, giving the Americans an instant empire (Puerto Rico, Guam, and the Philippines were snapped up at the same time). General Shafter arranged a victory march through the streets of Santiago, but the Cuban forces were barred from participating.

Afro-Cuban soldiers found that peace did not bring prosperity.

The highjacked revolution

The US set up a military government to administer the country. After 30 years of fighting, Cubans had, in fact, traded one set of colonial masters for another. In 1901, US Congress agreed to withdraw its troops in exchange for guarantees that the country would remain an American protectorate. The so-called Platt Amendment – composed in Washington to be included verbatim in the Cuban Constitution – allowed the United States to intervene in Cuban internal affairs: it forced Cuba to lease them naval bases at Río Hondo and

UP WITH THE USA

Not everything the US did during its military occupation was repressive. Positive aspects included setting up state education, eliminating a famine, improving sanitation, and eradicating yellow fever based on discoveries by Cuban scientist, Carlos J. Finlay. The economy was restored to relative health, and sugar exports were encouraged under an import preference system. Public administration and the judiciary were reformed and an electoral system introduced, leading to the election of a constituent assembly that in 1901 approved a liberal constitution separating Church and State and introducing universal adult male suffrage.

Not all Americans were caught up in the jingoism of the US defeat of Spain in 1898: the vitriolic Mark Twain wrote that the Stars and Stripes should be replaced by a Skull and Crossbones.

Guantánamo Bay, and gave the US the right to veto Cuba's trade or loan pacts with third countries. Understandably, news of the legislation caused rioting around Cuba, but the US military governor made it clear to the constitutional convention in Havana that the *yanquis* would not be leaving on any other terms. Tomás Estrada Palma, Cuba's first president, reluctantly signed the amendment.

Uncle Sam lectures four 'children,' including Cuba in this 19th-century political cartoon.

The independence that wasn't

The Stars and Stripes came down in May, 1902, and Cuba began its stunted, compromised freedom. In the coming years, US Congress sent in the Marines on a regular basis to protect American interests, and even reinstated US military rule entirely from 1906 to 1909. None of the social reforms envisaged by José Martí was enacted; elections were held, but were usually fraudulent, and corruption was rife. At the same time, American investment in Cuba rocketed. United States companies snapped up land at bargain prices, and even set up mini 'colonies' for American immigrants in places such as Isla de la Juventud.

The final tragedy of Cuba's false freedom was the 'Black Uprising' of 1912. Afro-Cubans – many of whom had fought courageously in the Wars of Independence – were disgusted to find that the new republic was happy to leave them in effective serfdom. They formed their own political party, the Partido Independiente de Color, only to have it banned.

Finally, open rebellion spread throughout the country. Cuban forces led by General Monteagudo crushed the uprising with the help of US Marines and, more viciously, local Creoles, who took revenge on the Afro-Cubans in retaliation for a century and a half of fear.

'It is impossible to tell the number of dead,' the general soon reported, 'because it has degenerated into widespread butchery in the hills.' One contemporary writer stated, 'entire families were machine-gunned in their *bohíos* [huts].' An estimated 3,000 Afro-Cubans were massacred in two months. The 'black fear' had been wiped out with blood, and Cuban racism was more brutally ingrained than ever.

THE AGE OF DECADENCE

From the 1920s to the 1950s, Havana was a playground for wealthy Americans seeking guilt-free sex, alcohol, and gambling. The mafia and corrupt Cuban politicians joined forces to preside over this hedonistic era.

At the height of Prohibition in the United States, which lasted from 1920 to 1933, 'personal liberty' became the euphemistic reason for thousands of US tourists to take the short boat ride to Cuba from Florida, to drink and have the sort of fun they wouldn't have at home. Havana became a symbol of decadent pleasure, and the flow of Americans visiting for sun, sex, and alcohol turned into a flood after World War II.

Havana quickly became the prostitution capital of the Western hemisphere. Businessmen could choose their mulatta for the weekend from photos at the airport; the notorious Casa Marina specialized in 13-year-old girls and boys from the provinces (with only a minor surcharge for virgins). Lovely, long-legged mulattas trod the boards of the Tropicana, while the more adventurous visitors headed for live sex acts in seedier surroundings; a regular show-time favorite was Superman, who measured his spectacular erection by lining up 12 silver dollars side by side. Stars like Errol Flynn and Gary Cooper visited every winter in their luxury yachts. George Raft, who specialized as a film-star gangster, was full-time host of the Red Room at the Hotel Capri.

And the whole, rum-soaked party went on to the fabulous rhythms of mamba, rumba, and *son*. Cuba's 12-piece bands, musicians all decked out in white tuxedos, were in demand from Manhattan to the Parisian Left Bank, though the big money in Havana went to American jazz bands and front-liners like Nat King Cole.

Grand hotels, like the Sevilla-Biltmore (now the Mercure Sevilla), sprang up during Havana's heyday.

Strong-man government

Gerardo Machado was elected President in 1924. A populist, he invested in public works projects and tried to diversify the economy, helped by the rise in tourism. However, the Great Depression after the US stock-market crash in 1929 and a sudden fall in sugar prices in the late 1920s left him faced with strikes and demonstrations. Students, the middle classes and labor unions were united in opposition, but all rebellion was met with violence. Troops were regularly called out to break strikes; demonstrators were gunned down; hired thugs, called *porros*, abducted and tortured enemies of the regime, who then 'disappeared.' The US considered intervening again to prevent civil war and its ambassador began negotiations in 1933, but this interference was the last straw for the nationalists, who called a general strike. Machado hopped on a plane to Miami, supposedly carrying five revolvers and as many bags of gold bullion. The new government was equally incapable of restoring peace, facing more strikes, mob attacks, and occupations of factories. In the ensuing chaos, the figure who took control was a young army sergeant, a mulatto of humble social origins called Fulgencio Batista, part of a revolt of non-commissioned officers. In quick succession he took the rank of colonel, then gained full control of the army and became a general. Before long, he emerged as the major player in Cuban politics, managing the government through a string of puppet presidents. The 'Batista Era' had begun.

wage, pensions, social insurance, and an eight-hour day. It was never fully implemented. Batista remained unpopular, however, opposed by students and radical nationalists who felt the full force of political violence. In 1944 he lost the elections to their candidate, Dr Ramón Grau San Martín, of the Partido Revolucionario

During Prohibition, refined Havana nightclubs raged all night and the casinos rivaled those of Las Vegas.

Sloppy Joe's, a famous Havana bar.

In 1934, the US Government, perhaps confident that its interests were secure, repealed the Platt Amendment that guaranteed its power of intervention, although the Americans retained their lease on the naval base at Guantánamo. By 1940, Batista had wearied of running Cuba through others and ran for president himself, winning an apparently fair election.

Batista's government, supported by the armed forces, and US and Cuban business interests, was nationalist, populist, corrupt, and violent. He pacified labor unions by passing social welfare legislation, and by public works, housing construction, and other job creation projects. In 1940 he introduced a new Constitution that included universal suffrage, a minimum

Cubana-Auténtico, who was followed in 1948 by his protégé, Carlos Prío Socarrás. High sugar prices kept them afloat, but neither president did anything to stem rampant corruption nor the grinding poverty in the countryside, social inequalities, unemployment, illiteracy, and minimal health care.

In 1952, Batista staged a coup, suspended constitutional and democratic government, and began a harshly repressive dictatorship.

Havana and the Mob

In a city where fabulous sums could be made from booze, drugs, gambling, and prostitution, it is not surprising that the American Mafia was not far behind. The Mob gained a foothold during the Prohibition years, using Cuba as a base for running rum to the Florida Keys. A far more lucrative opening came in 1938, when Batista invited Meyer Lansky to take over the operation of two crooked casinos and a racetrack. Known as 'the Jewish godfather,' Lansky was the brains behind the US's national crime syndicate, formed by uniting the various warring families in the 1930s.

Lansky soon had the places 'reformed.' The establishments flourished, and more casinos soon followed, with regular kickbacks to Batista brokered by Lansky. What was better, as far as the Mafia was concerned, was that the whole thing was perfectly legal.

In 1953, Batista appointed Meyer Lansky his personal adviser on gambling reform, to clean up Havana. Games were regularized, and the secret police employed to arrest and deport card sharps. The irony was not lost on many people. When he was asked why American gangsters were so welcome in Cuba, the US Ambassador replied: 'It's strange, but it seems to be the only way to get honest casinos.' The Batista dictatorship was the climax of Cuba's age of decadence, a time when corruption reached mythic proportions. The revitalized casino industry was part of a massive push to promote tourism: a new airline opened, visas were waived for visiting Americans, and all new hotels were granted tax-free status. The number of hotel rooms in Havana nearly doubled in six years. Oiling the gears was a Byzantine system of bribes – Meyer Lansky is said to have deposited more than US$3 million in Batista's personal bank account in Switzerland and, according to one observer, they were 'like brothers.'

Meanwhile, the secret police became less secret and more savage in hunting down opposition figures. Corpses of tortured dissidents were strung from lamp posts as a warning to anyone

Federico García Lorca.

Fulgencio Batista.

PARADISE FOUND

The Spanish poet Federico García Lorca came here in 1930 and stayed for three months. 'This island is a paradise,' he rhapsodized in a letter to his parents. 'If I ever get lost, they should look for me either in Andalucía or Cuba.' Already a recognized poet, Lorca was befriended by a string of habanero bohemians and took full advantage of Cuba's pleasures. The atmosphere of sexual liberation apparently made him more overt about his own homosexuality than he had been in his own country: it was in Cuba that he wrote *The Public*, the first Spanish work to feature male lovers, although only two scenes were published in his lifetime.

who dared to speak out against the roulette wheels and poker machines in Havana.

The lure of the tropic

Cuba's combination of unlimited sensual pleasures, lawlessness, and corruption – along with the *frisson* of danger – exerted an almost irresistible fascination for the many writers and artists who passed through Havana.

Ernest Hemingway visited throughout the 1930s for marlin fishing, and then moved to Cuba permanently. Although he regularly drank himself into a stupor and could become aggressive, Hemingway's streak of midwestern puritanism was strong enough for him to remain largely innocent of the seedier side of Havana life.

No such qualms restrained the English writer Graham Greene. During a brief visit in 1957, Greene explored romantic, decadent Cuba and immortalized it in his novel *Our Man in Havana*. Greene found the Cuban capital a place 'where every vice was permissible and every trade possible,' and lapped up 'the brothel life, the roulette in every hotel, the fruit machines spilling out jackpots of silver dollars, the Shanghai Theater where for one dollar twenty-five cents one could see a nude cabaret of extreme obscenity with the bluest of blue films in the intervals.'

Last days of indulgence

For many, the disparity between Cuba's fun-loving image and brutal reality was becoming too great. Many Cubans were disgusted with the levels of corruption into which their country had sunk, and the spectacle of the opulent, Mafia-run casinos alongside Cubans sleeping on the sidewalks and in burned-out cars. Even some foreigners felt moral qualms. As the Cuban-American writer Enrique Fernández-Más put it: 'On the road to pleasure, your driver could turn around at a stop light and show you photos of bodies bloodied with bullets and young faces ripped apart by tortures so savage – vividly described by the *revolucionario* driver – that the daiquirís, the sweet roast pork, the yummy yams, the fine Havanas, the hot sex, nothing tasted good any more.'

High times in a Havana nightclub, 1946.

But not everyone noticed the changing of the winds. In 1957, Lansky opened his own hotel, the Riviera, on the Malecón. It was the largest in Havana. Ginger Rogers performed in the hotel's Copa Room on opening night; Seemingly oblivious to what was going on in Cuban politics, Meyer Lansky stayed put. This time the consummate gambler got it wrong. He gambled everything on Havana – and, as he later put it, 'I crapped out.' After the revolution, the casinos were closed, the Mob's properties nationalized. Havana's age of decadence was at an end.

Fidel Castro addresses the people of Santa Clara, c.1959.

THE REVOLUTION

The 1959 Revolution was one of the 20th century's most distinctive political triumphs for the underdog, but conflict with the US and support from the USSR brought the world to the brink of nuclear war.

As the age of decadence flourished in Havana, the roots of a revolution were beginning to take hold in the countryside. Under Batista's rule, a small elite enjoyed a grand lifestyle, while the majority of the rural population endured appalling poverty. Few had running water, electricity, or access to health care or education. A quarter of all Cubans were unable to read or write, and a quarter of adult males were unemployed. The country was rife with corruption, oppression, and inequality.

You may still see slogans – especially in and around Santiago – declaring 'Es Siempre el 26' (It is always the 26th), a reference to the 26th July Movement and the attack on the Moncada barracks in Santiago.

Fulgencio Batista and his wife in 1959.

The Moncada attack

One year after Batista began his second term in office, a brazen young lawyer named Fidel Castro concluded that an armed uprising was the only way to end the dictator's reign. This was not Castro's first attempt at power. A year earlier he had tried to run for a seat in Congress but, in a Machiavellian move by Batista, the elections were surreptitiously canceled.

Hoping to spark a mass uprising, on July 26, 1953, Castro and 128 of his fellow anti-Batistas mounted an attack on the Moncada army barracks in Santiago. But as the music of Carnival blared in the background, the young revolutionaries were brutally defeated. Despite being a total failure, the coup marked the beginning of the Cuban revolution. Six rebels died in the attack, and 55 more were later killed by the police. Those who escaped, including Castro, took refuge in the Sierra Maestra, but soon afterward were rounded up and jailed. Fortunately for Castro, the arresting officer was sympathetic to the cause, and took him to a local jail rather than the government prison where he would surely have been killed.

History will absolve me

For Batista, having Castro executed in secret would have solved many problems, but Castro's capture had become public knowledge, so any such attempt would have fomented further anti-government sentiment, so he had to put the rebel on trial. Acting as his own lawyer, Castro delivered a five-hour speech that would sink deeply into the minds of the Cuban underclass when eventually smuggled out of jail. He called Batista the worst dictator in Cuban history, and described in detail the sorry living conditions of the majority of the Cuban people. He also called for universal education, agrarian reform, and a total restructuring of the government, then delivered his famous words: 'Condemn me if you will. History will absolve me.'

Castro meets Che

Sentenced to 15 years, Castro was imprisoned on the Isle of Pines (now the Isle of Youth). While there, he read the works of Marx and studied successful peasant uprisings. He also lectured to fellow inmates and plotted the revolution that would bring him to power. After serving less than two years, he was released under a government amnesty on Mother's Day in May 1955 (El Día de La Madre is a major event in Cuba), a decision that Batista would later regret.

Soon after his release, Fidel Castro and his comrades went into exile in Mexico. There, he met a young Argentine doctor, Ernesto 'Che' Guevara, and together they created the 26th of July Movement (M-26), named for the attack at Moncada in 1953. M-26, which had roots in Cuba's 19th-century struggles, was the philosophical foundation that became synonymous with Castro's revolution. Castro traveled to New York and Miami to raise money for the impending revolt, gathered guns and ammunition, and campaigned for support from abroad.

In November 1956, Castro, Che, and 80 other revolutionaries left Mexico and sailed to Cuba. After several days floundering in stormy seas, they landed on December 2 at Playa Las Coloradas, about 160km (100 miles) west of Santiago. The plan had been to arrive in Santiago at the end of November, to assist a potential uprising led by M-26 member Frank País, but the delayed arrival of Castro and his men meant that this uprising was crushed in just a few hours. A few days after they disembarked from their boat they were ambushed by Batista's troops who captured and killed most of the crew.

Among the dozen survivors were Castro, his younger brother Raúl, and Che. Joined by a

Cuban revolutionaries in Havana, 1959: (from left) Raul Castro, Antonio Núñez Jiménez, Che Guevara, Juan Almeida and Ramiro Valdés.

> *The yacht, Granma, on which Fidel's revolutionaries sailed to Cuba, was named by its first (English-speaking) owner for his grandmother. Later, Granma became the name of Cuba's newspaper, and a whole province.*

group of peasants and a few fellow revolutionaries, the ragged band quickly slipped away into the Sierra Maestra where they founded the Rebel Army. One of those who joined them was a wealthy and spirited revolutionary named Vilma Espín, who became Raúl Castro's wife, founded the Federation of Cuban Women, and remained active in politics until her death in June 2007 (see page 20).

Guerrillas in the mountains

Entrenched in the mountains, the Rebel Army saw themselves as warriors of the common people, and set out to spread their revolutionary ideas. During the next few years, they set up an informal government, drew up a manifesto, organized schools and hospitals in rural areas, and established their own radio station, Radio Rebelde, to campaign for a democratic Cuba. Needing the support of the underground movements in Havana, they aligned themselves with the Students' Revolutionary Directorate and the Civic Resistance Movement.

In a clever public-relations coup, the rebels smuggled Herbert Matthews, a reporter for the *New York Times*, into their mountain camp for a clandestine interview with Castro. Swayed by the boisterous bravado of Fidel and his men, Matthews' account praised the Rebel Army and gave the world a romantic first impression of the dashing young revolutionary. Batista insisted that Matthews' story was fabricated, and Castro was actually dead. Days later, the *New York Times* responded with irrefutable evidence: a photograph of Matthews and Castro smoking cigars together in the mountains.

With his name and face now known the world over, public support for Castro in Cuba multiplied. In March 1957, students stormed the Presidential Palace in an attempt to kill Batista, while another group took over a radio station and falsely announced his death. The following year a general strike was called in support of the Rebel Army, and disgruntled naval officers tried to stage a rebellion in the port of Cienfuegos.

Juan Almeida and Celia Sánchez hide from the gunfires of Batista's bomber planes in the Sierra Maestra.

The turning point of the revolution came in July 1958, when a battalion of Batista's forces surrendered to Castro's troops after a 10-day siege. The Rebel Army, which by this time was about 50,000 strong, charged ahead.

Followed by troops, Castro advanced into Santiago, Raúl into northern Oriente, and, in the most decisive move of all, Che Guevara into Santa Clara. By December 1958, the rebels had shattered Batista's army, which retreated in defeat. A terrified Batista fled the country to the Dominican Republic. The following morning,

As Castro delivered a victory speech, a flock of white doves was released into the air and one of the birds landed on his shoulder. This was taken by followers of Santería as an omen that he had been chosen to deliver them from oppression.

people all over the island rejoiced. Ebullient revelers danced in the streets, applauding Batista's downfall. In Havana, throngs of peasants stormed into the casinos, which had been off-limits to them for years. Some vandalized the slot machines, while others brought their pigs in to have a look.

Victorious Cuban soldiers at the Bay of Pigs.

After announcing the triumph of the revolution from the balcony of Santiago's town hall on January 2, 1959, the handsome 32-year-old Castro took off with his guerrillas for a victory drive to Havana. Euphoric crowds cheered as they passed through the countryside. When they arrived in the capital a week later, tens of thousands of supporters welcomed them.

At the Riviera Hotel, workers walked out of their jobs. Meyer Lansky, the boss, found himself in the kitchen cooking dinner for guests as his wife waited tables. For Lansky and his cronies, the good life was over. Words from Castro's speech echoed in his head: 'We are ready not only to deport the gangsters, but to shoot them.' Lansky knew he meant it. He moved his gambling business to the nearby Bahamas, and offered a large bounty for Fidel Castro's head.

A new Cuba

Cubans in New York and Miami celebrated the fall of Batista and made plans to return to the island. The revolution was praised worldwide as a true victory for the Cuban people, and even the US Government was initially optimistic about the changes taking place.

In the spring of 1959, a victorious Castro declared himself the prime minister of Cuba, and Che Guevara was appointed president of the National Bank. Hundreds of Batista supporters were jailed, many of them executed, and by the following year sweeping political changes were taking place across the country.

The new government passed an agrarian reform act which limited private land ownership; under Batista, 70 percent of the land had been owned by a mere 8 percent of the population. Fidel's regime also confiscated foreign-owned industries in an effort to end US control of the island (North Americans owned more than 165 major companies including 90 percent of the public services and 40 percent of the sugar industry).

Farms, plantations, oil refineries, and communications systems were nationalized. The government also outlawed racial discrimination, created a low-income housing program, made free health care and education available to all, and implemented new policies for farming, sports, music, the arts, and defense.

The redistribution of wealth meant instant rewards for the peasant class, but just as quickly, the middle and upper classes were stripped of the privileges they had enjoyed. Already having had their homes confiscated, many feared what might come next, and fled to Miami. Forbidden to take any possessions with them, most left with nothing more than the clothes on their backs. Women sewed their wedding rings into the hems of their dresses to smuggle them out. Once in Miami they established a vocal anti-Castro community of exiles that criticized the new government, and looked forward to the day they could return to their homes.

In 1960, Fidel Castro delivered his first speech to the United Nations and was introduced to Soviet Premier Nikita Khrushchev. While in New York, he also met the radical American Black Power leader Malcolm X.

At about that time, the US began to see Castro as a threat to its national security, and mysterious things started happening. A French ship, *La Coubre*, delivering Belgian armaments, inexplicably exploded in Havana harbor as unidentified low-flying planes flew over the city. The US was the prime suspect.

FIDEL THE SURVIVOR

The Cuban leader estimates that there have been 20 CIA-inspired attempts on his life; one agency director, William Colby, expressed surprise, saying he was aware of only five. Some of them were part of Operation Mongoose, aimed toppling the communist government. The ingenious (if ineffective) ways of attempting to assassinate Castro (apart from simply shooting him), included contaminating his cigars with botulism, giving him a toxic dose of LSD, lacing a chocolate milkshake with cyanide, and smearing his wet suit with tuberculosis spores. Cuban exiles in Miami and the mafia were the CIA's natural partners in crime, but their plots failed.

In response, Castro took an aggressive stance. In January 1961, he expelled 11 US diplomats. Soon after, the two countries severed diplomatic relations, and the US began an economic embargo that brought the import of American goods to a halt. It further isolated the island by persuading all but two Western-hemisphere nations (Canada and Mexico) to cut trade and diplomatic ties with Cuba.

The Bay of Pigs

In April 1961, a CIA-trained brigade of 1,500 mercenaries, mostly Cuban exiles from Miami,

A revolutionary poster (now in Havana's Museum of the Revolution) invites Batista to flee the country.

landed at Playa Girón in the Bahía de Cochinos (Bay of Pigs), hoping to instigate an anti-Castro coup. The invasion was a complete fiasco. The element of surprise was lost because US bombers attacked Cuban airfields days beforehand; the raids failed to destroy the Cuban airforce, leaving the attackers open to assault from the air. The counter-revolutionaries were no match for Cuba's military, led by Castro; and local people, whom it was hoped would be sympathetic to the exiles' cause, were strongly pro-Castro.

Within 72 hours the US brigade was defeated. A few men were killed, the rest taken prisoner. For their release, the US traded $50-million worth of medicines that Cuba had been unable

Che

Decades after his death, 'Che' Guevara is a Marxist hero, an icon by government decree, and model for Cuba's ideal socialist man.

Guevara is known throughout Cuba simply as Che, an affectionate Argentine expression equivalent to 'buddy,' 'pal,' or 'mate.' Each morning, Cuban schoolchildren recite the patriotic slogan: 'Pioneers of communism, we shall be like Che.' Throughout the country, posters of his handsome face hang on thousands of living-room walls and women swoon as if he were a movie star. When the bio-pic *Che* (Steven Sodebergh, 2008) was screened at the Latin America Film Festival in Havana, the actor Benicio del Toro got a standing ovation for his portrayal of their favorite hero.

Che Guevara, iconic revolutionary.

Born in Argentina in 1928, Guevara came from a left-leaning, middle-class family. As a child he developed severe asthma that later brought about his decision to become a doctor. As a medical student he traveled through South America on a motorbike and after graduation in 1953 he took off again to travel through South and Central America, seeking political adventure.

Government Posts

After witnessing the CIA-inspired overthrow of the socialist Árbenz government in Guatemala in 1954, Guevara moved to Mexico, where he met the then exiled Fidel Castro. Soon afterward, he joined the 26th of July Movement and was later to command the decisive guerrilla attack in Santa Clara that led Batista to flee Cuba. He also became Castro's principal ideological counselor and closest friend.

Once the government was established, he supervized the appeals and firing squads of opponents and Batista officials. As Minister for Industry he instituted agrarian reform, and as president of the National Bank of Cuba, he negotiated trade agreements with Eastern-Bloc countries. In 1960 he wrote a book called *Guerrilla Warfare* that became a manual for revolutionary strategies in the Developing World. In it, he advocated the use of guerrilla tactics to defeat imperialism; moral rather than material incentives for work; and working-class solidarity.

Beyond Cuba

During the 1960s, an entire generation of radical youths idolized his purist Marxist beliefs, selfless devotion, and relentless work ethic, and his dramatic image blessed protest movements in Paris, London, Washington, Montreal, Tokyo, Bombay, and Baghdad.

A member of the macho world of brave guerrilla fighters, Guevara was impetuous, daring, and reckless. He was also a brilliant intellectual who spoke French, wrote poetry, and represented Cuba in international chess competitions. In 1965 he resigned from his posts (some say he'd fallen out with Castro over the growing influence of the Soviet Union in Cuban affairs) and, after a brief spell fighting in the Congo, he attempted to foster revolution in the Bolivian highlands. The campaign proved a disaster and Guevara was captured and killed by the cia-backed Bolivian Army in 1967.

Castro declared three days of national mourning, then spent years creating a Guevara cult. After the collapse of the Soviet Union, Castro tried to rekindle some revolutionary passion by implementing a nationwide 'Let's Be Like Che' campaign. Then, in 1997, Che's mortal remains were discovered in Bolivia and returned to Cuba (see page 228).

Che Guevara remains Latin America's most celebrated modern revolutionary. The French philosopher Jean-Paul Sartre described him as 'the most complete human being of our age,' and *Time* magazine listed him as one of the 100 most influential people of the 20th century.

to buy due to the embargo. Castro emerged as the clear victor, while US President Kennedy was humiliated. The invasion was seen by Cubans as a blatant imperialist stunt, and relations between the two countries worsened still further. The incident also garnered support for Castro throughout Latin America, and rendered him fearful of a US military invasion. The United States did little to alleviate those fears, instigating covert activities including plots to assassinate Castro (see page 55).

By the end of 1961, Castro's platform for a freely elected democratic government had changed. Following the Bay of Pigs invasion he had shocked the world by pronouncing Cuba's revolution to be a 'socialist revolution.' Some believe his conversion to Marxism was merely a pragmatic move to gain favor with the Russians, without whom the island did not stand a chance of surviving the US embargo.

Khrushchev welcomes Castro to Moscow.

On the brink of war

In order to support socialist Cuba, the USSR supplied economic aid, as Castro had anticipated, and shipped nuclear missiles to Cuba to defend the island. The threat of nuclear weapons stationed just 140km (90 miles) away was too much for the US Government, and in October 1962, the Soviet Union and the United States came face to face with the reality of nuclear war, over what has gone down in history as the Cuban Missile Crisis.

The US demanded that the Soviets remove the missiles, and threatened to bomb Cuba if they refused. The world watched in horror as the possibility of war came uncomfortably close. The Soviets eventually relented and an uneasy peace was restored.

Despite the fact that an agreement was reached, the US was not happy with the outcome. In 1963, President Kennedy relegated relations with Cuba to fall under the US Trading with the Enemy Act, which tightened the embargo and prohibited all commercial and personal contact between the two nations. The US became the only country in the world to forbid its citizens to travel to Cuba; the political impasse became even more intractable.

Castro was incensed that he had not been consulted during the talks between the two superpowers, but the reality was that he had thrown in his lot with the Soviets and was powerless to prevent them from dictating terms. He had to content himself with an unwritten assurance that the US would not sponsor a further invasion of Cuba, and with the fact that, for the briefest of periods, he'd managed to turn the tables on his enemy in the insecurity stakes.

May Day parade in Havana, 1981.

SOCIALISM OR DEATH

During the 1960s and 1970s, Cuba played a role in world affairs out of all proportion to its size. Since then, progress has been curtailed by crippling domestic problems, taxing even Fidel Castro's ingenuity.

Although resolved diplomatically, the Cuban Missile Crisis (see page 57) provoked even more Cold War hostility from the United States, and pushed Castro firmly into the Soviet camp. In addition, it helped to turn the country into an audacious socialist experiment and a feisty Third World power.

Cuba's Communist Party was restructured in 1965, and the following year, despite Soviet disapproval, Castro was determined to export his revolutionary ideals. In 1966 he claimed that the Andes would become the next Sierra Maestra. But the Soviet Union (which provided money and arms) pressed Castro to pursue a less independent foreign policy. It seems that Che Guevara was determined to carry out a policy of directly fomenting revolution, with or without Soviet support, and left Cuba to fight first in Africa and then Bolivia.

Friends and foes

With the death of Guevara in Bolivia in 1967, Castro realized he had to take a different path to global influence. In 1968 he personally endorsed the Soviet invasion of Czechoslovakia, and cemented the bond with his powerful ally. Castro then directed his energy inward. To lessen Cuba's dependence on the sugar industry, he tried to diversify the economy through industrialization. But thousands of educated Cubans had fled and the country lacked skilled labor. The US embargo limiting the import of industrial equipment was another hindrance, and the industrialization plan failed. Sugar, once again, became the main force of the economy.

Big Brother is watching

In the name of the revolution, the 1960s marked the beginning of decades of political

Fidel Castro speaking in Havana, 1965.

NEIGHBORHOOD WATCH

To help dissuade counter-revolutionary activities, Castro created neighborhood-watch groups known as Committees for the Defense of the Revolution (CDRs). These organized labor and implemented health and education programs, but also served as vigilantes and as the Big Brother of the revolution. Members monitored their neighbors and reported all non-conformist behavior to the government. Still in operation, there are more than 100,000 CDRs on the island, comprising about 75 percent of the population. Membership is voluntary, but belonging to a CDR brings a guarantee of social benefits; not belonging may possibly bring trouble.

repression. Anyone seen as non-supportive of the government was deemed 'socially unacceptable,' and thousands of these 'dissidents' were jailed.

Police sealed off the bohemian neighborhoods of Havana and interrogated artists, writers, and intellectuals. Non-supportive poets were silenced. Education and cultural policies became more severe, labor unions were disbanded, and the media fell under absolute government control. By the late 1960s, an ideological straitjacket had smothered the country.

After poor sugar harvests in 1963–4, Castro called upon the whole nation to meet a target of 10 million tonnes of sugar by 1970. Everyone spent time working in the fields but the goal was never met.

while Cuban students were invited to study in Moscow. Financial aid steadily increased and was measured in billions of dollars. At the time, Cuba was receiving generous shipments of oil priced far below standard OPEC rates, while its

Cuba's literacy campaign created the most literate population in Latin America.

Practicing Catholics, Protestants, Jews, and Santeros were persecuted – any religious affiliation was deemed anti-revolutionary. Prostitutes were sent to vocational schools for rehabilitation, homosexuals were imprisoned in labor camps, and all remnants of bourgeois society were eliminated throughout the island.

Throughout the 1960s, the 'better-dead-than-red' communist-obsessed US continued covert activities against Cuba, including more CIA-backed assassination attempts on Castro. In addition, several of Cuba's trade missions in Europe were bombed by anti-Castro terrorists.

As a result, the Soviet Union beefed up its military and economic support to Cuba. Eastern-bloc technicians were sent to the island sugar crop was bought at inflated prices. About one-half of all Soviet aid to the Developing World poured into Cuba. Boosted by Soviet weapons and fighter planes, Cuba's defense system developed into the most powerful military force in Latin America, much larger than those of Brazil or Mexico.

The heady 1970s

For most Cubans, the 1970s are remembered fondly as the heady days of the revolution. With the utmost confidence, Castro became the international spokesman for Developing World causes, traveling to South America, China, Vietnam, and Africa. In 1974 the Soviet premier Leonid Brezhnev visited Cuba and publicly endorsed his Caribbean comrade. In front of enraptured crowds, the two men predicted that communism would some day triumph throughout the world. The next year, the Organization of American States lifted its sanctions against Cuba and many Latin American nations resumed ties with the country.

Economically, Cuba advanced, and the gains of the revolution were indisputable. Unheard of in most Developing World countries, Cuba's health-care system eliminated infectious diseases, drastically lowered the infant mortality

Cuban soldiers in Angola.

rate, and curtailed population growth. The number of doctors grew from 6,000 to more than 25,000. The government also paved roads throughout the countryside, built low-rent apartment buildings, and eradicated illiteracy. Cubans felt proud.

International involvement

Although Cuba's political system was redesigned to mimic the Soviet model, Castro remained very much his own man. This was especially so when it came to foreign policy. He saw Cuba as part of the non-aligned movement, but nevertheless got heavily involved in Africa. Capitalizing on Cuba's Afro-Cuban heritage, he aligned himself with left-wing revolutionary movements. In 1975 he flexed his military muscles by sending 20,000 soldiers to Angola. Cuban troops fought on the side of the Marxist SWAPO government, following South Africa's decision to assist Angolan UNITA rebels. This conflict continued a tradition of Cuban assistance with what Castro saw as anti-imperialist movements in Africa, which went back to the days of Che Guevara. In 1978 he did the same for Ethiopia.

But Angola was Cuba's greatest triumph – as attested to by Nelson Mandela, who says the defeat of South African troops there helped precipitate the downfall of the apartheid state in his own country.

> *By the late 1980s, Cuba was heavily in debt to the USSR and was forced to cut food rations. In an attempt to rejuvenate the revolutionary spirit, Castro revised the ¡Patria o Muerte! (Fatherland or Death) slogan to ¡Socialismo o Muerte!*

Back on his own side of the world, Castro befriended left-leaning leaders in nearby Jamaica and Grenada and, in 1979, hosted the annual conference of the non-aligned nations. That same year Cuba also supported the Soviet invasion of

Afghanistan, and the socialist revolution in Nicaragua which brought the Sandinistas to power.

In 1976, the Cuban Communist Party finally approved its new Marxist-Leninist constitution. This constitution redrew provincial boundaries, creating 14 provinces and the federal district of Havana. It also created the assemblies of People's Power *(Poder Popular)*, governing bodies of elected officials who delegate power at municipal, provincial, and national levels. The National Assembly elected Fidel Castro president of the Council of State and Raúl Castro first vice president.

Family slogan painted on a wall in Baracoa.

Socialismo o Muerte

At the beginning of the 1980s, Cuba was still a Latin American symbol of independence from US imperialism, but the quality of life in the country was beginning to decline. Productivity dropped off, and health care, education, and social services deteriorated. Castro blamed the country's problems on the 'workers who do not work and the students who do not study,' and then fired numerous government economists.

Many of Cuba's economic problems, however, were caused not by lazy workers or students but by blatant mismanagement. The government had appointed Communist Party members to professional positions for which they were not qualified, destroyed the plantation system, and refused to develop the tourism industry. And a political system designed for the Soviet Union did not translate well to Cuba.

In 1980 public protests escalated to the point that the government permitted anyone who wanted to leave to do so – including, it is said, many criminals who were freed from prison in order for them to leave. That year, 125,000 Cubans fled to the US in the so-called Mariel boatlift (see page 81), adding to the several hundred thousand who had left in the early years of the revolution.

In 1985, the Cubans in Miami set up Radio Martí, an anti-Castro propaganda station aimed directly at Cuba. The station's reports of how great was life in the US stirred up even more discontent, although Castro limited this by jamming its frequency.

Criticisms and scandals

On the international level, Cuba received harsh criticisms for its human-rights violations. A report filed by Amnesty International condemned the country for its abuse of political prisoners, and the beatings, psychological torture, and solitary confinement taking place in Cuba's prisons became a thorny issue.

In 1989, more public disgrace fell on the country. General Arnaldo Ochoa, a much-decorated military figure, and six other military officials, were charged with corruption and drug trafficking. Found guilty of pocketing millions of dollars and allowing Colombian cocaine smugglers to use Cuba as a waystation en route to the US, the officers were put before a firing squad.

The Eastern Bloc crumbles

As the Ochoa scandal shook the country, communist dominoes in Eastern Europe were beginning to tumble. When Mikhail Gorbachev assumed power in Moscow and put forth his *perestroika* economic reforms, many predicted that Soviet money would flow less freely, causing chaos for the Cuban Government. But Castro made it quite clear that he had no interest in multiparty governments or a free-market system. Ever ready with a well-honed phrase, he said: 'For us to adopt *perestroika* would be like living in our home with another man's wife.'

Members of Cuba's Communist Party agreed with their leader. For them, *perestroika*

Fidel Castro and Mikhail Gorbachev during an official visit to Cuba in 1989.

LIVING ON THE LIBRETA

The ration book *(libreta)* was introduced in 1962, initially as a temporary measure in the face of the US embargo, but generations of Cubans have grown up knowing no other system. The principal of providing every Cuban with the basic staples for a balanced diet is no longer affordable and the government wants to reduce subsidies. What is available on the *libreta* has been whittled down and now provides less than a third of the daily calories needed per person. Free lunches have been eliminated from the canteens of state companies and Cubans see the end of the *libreta* in sight. To increase the supply of food to the markets, the government has now started to transfer more land to private farmers. 'The land is there to be tilled,' said Raúl, 'and we must offer producers adequate incentives.'

However, although fruit, vegetables, cereals, and pulses are now available in free farmers' markets *(agropecuarios)*, they are expensive relative to the price paid for goods listed in the *libreta*, and beyond the reach of many. Since potatoes and peas were removed from the *libreta* in 2009, the price has risen from around 1 centavo per lb to 5 and 17 centavos respectively, a huge increase for Cuban families who spend 60–70 percent of their household budget on food, a proportion that is likely to rise.

and Gorbachev's other main goal – *glasnost* (transparency and freedom from censorship) – were dirty words. Untouched by the looming crisis, party members were a privileged class in Cuba. With access to food, cars, gas, travel abroad, and imported goods, they bitterly resisted change.

When the USSR finally fell apart in 1991, the impact on Cuba was devastating. At a stroke, the country lost annual subsidies of US$6 billion in economic aid, $1 billion in military assistance, 10 million tons of oil, and $6 billion worth of imported goods. It also now had to sell its sugar at market value. The scarcity of available oil paralyzed Cuban industry and transportation. Adding to the turmoil, Cuba's sugar harvest was the lowest in 30 years.

The 'Special Period'

Beset by economic crises, but unwilling to adopt either *perestroika* or *glasnost*-style reforms, the government implemented a belt-tightening survival strategy known as the 'Special Period in Time of Peace.' In order to compensate for the loss of Soviet subsidies, Castro told the Cuban people to work harder and be patient. He then demanded sacrifices like none they had ever known before.

Energy consumption was drastically reduced, oxen replaced tractors in the fields, and food rations were slashed to a minimum survival level. Government-produced television programs instructed citizens on how to grow their own vegetables, make their own candles and soap, and turn dried banana skins into sandals. Horse-drawn buggies were put back in service, and inexpensive, low-grade oil was substituted to fire electric plants, causing a pall of dirty smoke over Havana.

In addition, the government imported a million Chinese bicycles and ordered the people to start pedaling. Encouraging Cubans to adopt cycling, Fidel Castro told them: 'Expanding the use of the bicycle is an indicator of cultural advancement.' But for the millions of secretaries, teachers, and factory workers who had to spend hours a day riding to work, it was more like pedaling back in time.

The 'Special Period' – which only officially ended in 2005 – meant that life for the average Cuban citizen was bleak. People watched in dismay as the crowded apartments in which they lived slipped even further into disrepair. Electric wires dangled precariously in the streets, telephones rarely worked, and elevators were often out of order.

Typical Old Havana neighborhood grocery store.

Times get tougher

Hungry, frustrated Cubans soon grew tired of waiting in long lines for pitiful goods. Sugar, coffee, and rum – the backbone of the Cuban economy – became a luxury for most people. And while Cubans had lived with the *libreta* or ration book since the early 1960s (see page 63), fewer and fewer goods seemed to be actually available.

Patients had to get used to bringing their own sheets to hospitals, and surgeons were allotted only one bar of soap a month with which to wash their hands. Herbal remedies replaced drugs, and hemp was used for sutures.

In schools, textbooks were shared among several children, and work in exercise books written in pencil so it could be erased and the books passed on to the next class. Factories sat idle, there were no fertilizers for crops, and harvests rotted in the fields for want of methods of distribution. Newspapers and magazines shut down for lack of paper. Toilet tissue, toothpaste, shampoo, and aspirin became luxury items. Cubans had to buy in what were then dollar shops – but first they had to get access to dollars.

Capitalist tinkerings

Faced with rousing discontent, Castro made some compromises that in the past were non-negotiable. In 1991, he eased travel restrictions abroad, released some political prisoners, permitted more free speech than ever before, and granted autonomy to farmers, who were now permitted to sell a proportion of their surplus produce on the open market, often at cripplingly high prices.

It was a sign of just how serious the crisis had become when, in 1993, Fidel Castro swallowed his pride and legalized the use of the American dollar, to which previously only a few privileged citizens (including high-ranking members of the Communist Party) had had access.

Man selling beans at a farmers' market in Santa Clara.

Queuing at the butcher shop.

THE CESSNAS INCIDENT

In February 1996, Cuban MiGs (Russian-built fighter planes) shot down two unarmed Cessnas piloted by members of the Brothers to the Rescue organization (see page 82), on the lookout for rafters crossing to Miami. The Cessnas had crossed into Cuban airspace in defiance of a warning issued by the Cuban authorities, who viewed these flights as violations of an agreement with the US to clamp down on those encouraging emigration from Cuba. The Cessnas' four Miami Cuban crewmen were killed, and the subsequent outcry in the US helped smooth the passage of the Helms-Burton legislation, which President Clinton had previously opposed.

In the same year Castro permitted people to go into business for themselves by offering licenses in more than 100 categories, including mechanics, fishermen, farmers, taxi drivers, hairdressers, and restaurateurs. The self-employed had to pay a small fortune for a trading license and in income tax, thus putting a sharp brake on both private enterprise and dollar investments from Miami Cubans.

Meanwhile, to make up for the loss of Soviet subsidies and to combat the United States embargo, Cuba began to woo new investors – notably Canada, Mexico, and members of the European Union – in what are commonly known as 'joint ventures.' These countries pumped hundreds of millions of dollars into the economy, above all into tourism, but also in the fields of nickel mining, oil exploration, and the pharmaceutical industry.

Pope John Paul II with Castro during an official visit in 1998.

Sanctions stepped up

During the 1990s, Castro alluded to a reconciliation with the US – something that proved a phantom hope, even in the more relaxed atmosphere of the post-Cold-War era. In 1992, the powerful Cuban-American lobby in the US helped ensure the passing of the so-called Torricelli Act, which sought to tighten sanctions in an effort to bring down the struggling Cuban regime. It prohibited subsidiaries of US companies from trading with Cuba, and linked any repeal of sanctions to Cuba hosting free and fair elections.

Sanctions were ratcheted up again in 1996, when the then US president, Bill Clinton, gave way to pressure from Cuban Americans and approved the Helms-Burton legislation (see box), named after its sponsors in the US Congress. Among other provisions, the Helms-Burton legislation raised the threat of suing any company worldwide that did business with Cuba involving assets on the island that had been confiscated by the Castro regime in the 1960s. Consequently, relations between the US and countries that were investing in Cuba – especially Canada and some members of the European Union – came under strain.

The legislation also helped to polarize the debate on sanctions within the United States – some powerful business and humanitarian interests spoke up against the continuation of sanctions, which they believed had failed in their primary objective of bringing down the Castro regime, and which sections of the business community thought were denying US companies valuable investment opportunities. Some, too, believed that the influential Cuban-American lobby had overreached itself.

The US embargo (called the *bloqueo* in Cuba) also attracted international disapproval. In 1997, 143 countries in the UN General Assembly voted against the embargo, with just three in favor (the US, Uzbekistan, and Israel). The figures for the same resolution in 1992 were 59 in favor, 3 against, and 71 abstentions.

Papal visit

Cuba's regime was also given a shot in the arm by the much-publicized visit of Pope John Paul II in January 1998. Castro agreed to release some 300 political prisoners ahead of the papal visit; the Pope, for his part, criticized Cuba on human-rights issues, but he also spoke out indirectly against US sanctions, calling any such embargo 'deplorable.' This saw the US Government relax the embargo slightly: direct flights between Miami and Havana resumed in July 1998, and more North American politicians and business people began visiting Cuba, though under tight restrictions.

Dollars or death

However, Cuban society was showing the strain. Decriminalizing the dollar had a devastating effect on a society brought up at least to pay lip service to egalitarianism. The island essentially became divided into two classes – those with dollars, and those without. Dollars could be acquired through fair means or foul: on the one hand they might be sent by relatives living abroad, or earned through a thriving business; on the other hand, they could be gained from black-market dealing or prostitution. Many Cubans also converted their hard-earned pesos into dollars at government exchange bureaux known as *cadecas*, but they received a miserable return – with an average monthly salary worth less than US$10.

Counting freshly printed Cuban convertible peso notes.

For those with dollars, life improved beyond measure, hence the booming, clandestine economy. Fear that the dollar sector was getting out of control – that some people were becoming 'too rich' – led to a seesaw economic policy: shop openings were followed by sudden closures, and laws were passed and repealed without notice. Police would appear at the door at 6am to close 'illegal' businesses – the dispossessed businessman only discovering in that morning's edition of *Granma* that some new law had been enacted, making his business illegal. Such tactics, together with high taxation, fines, and overwhelming bureaucratic control, created tremendous insecurity and unease in a population that felt it must earn dollars in order to survive.

Attending a protest in Havana.

CUBA IN THE 21ST CENTURY

Raúl Castro has succeeded his brother, but Fidel remains a strong presence. Early changes appear to be predictable, and most believe Cuba's immediate future will still be controlled from within the state.

As Cuba moved into the 21st century, the Revolution was already four decades old, and in many ways the island seemed to be stuck in a time warp. But change was on the way. The demise of Cuba's great *caudillo*, Fidel Castro, has been predicted for decades, and in July 2006, when he underwent urgent intestinal surgery, he handed over supreme power 'temporarily,' to his younger brother Raúl, the head of the Revolutionary Armed Forces. This marked the effective beginning of the post-Fidel phase, and a further step was taken in February 2008, when Raúl was inaugurated as president by a newly formed National Assembly. Fidel remained head of the Communist Party until 2011, and Raúl promised that his brother would be consulted on matters of national importance. This confirmed that, at least in the near future, things would remain the same.

> *'The commander in chief of the Cuban revolution is unique,' Raúl said, after being unanimously confirmed as president. 'Fidel is Fidel; as we all know, he is irreplaceable.'*

However, Raúl is introducing some changes, with greater economic and personal freedom for Cubans. The state still has great control over its population through organizations like the neighborhood CDRs (see page 59); and the army is firmly wedded to the state, benefiting as it does from a network of companies, most visible of which is the tourism enterprise, Gaviota, as well as ministerial appointments for senior officers.

A food market stall holder, Baracoa.

International deals

In November 2004, in response to tighter US sanctions, Castro banned commercial transactions in dollars, which would have to be exchanged for *pesos convertibles* (CUC). But Cuba's economic future appeared to be picking up – so much so that in 2005, the authorities declared the end of the 'Special Period' that had been in place since the fall of the USSR. However, the world economic slowdown and three hurricanes in 2008 forced the government to demand new sacrifices of its citizens.

The economy has been helped by Cuba's continued tourism growth, along with the shift away from older mainstays. In 2002, the government finally recognized that the sugar industry was no longer sustainable. It closed nearly half the processing plants, and in 2007 the harvest was the leanest in a century. Nowadays, exports like nickel are far more valuable than sugar.

Agreements with China and, above all, Venezuela, have helped Cuba thwart US attempts to isolate it diplomatically and economically. The late President Hugo Chávez of Venezuela, a firm admirer and ally of Fidel, agreed massive oil deals on favorable fixed terms, which alleviated Cuba's energy crisis. In return, Cuba exported some 30,000 doctors and health-care workers to Venezuela. This is the most obvious example of a strategy of 'health diplomacy,' which sees Cuban doctors working in other Latin American countries and also in West Africa, although many Cubans complain that their own health service has suffered as a consequence.

Socialist posters adorn walls and billboards throughout Cuba.

Options for change

For decades, many observers outside Cuba presumed that the regime would collapse after its charismatic leader was removed from power, died, or was incapacitated. This scenario envisaged a flood of dollar-rich Cuban exiles from Miami and New Jersey sweeping into the island on a tide of capitalist counter-revolution, with Cuba turning into a type of Puerto Rico. But the reality seems different; Cuba appears unlikely to undergo either this type of radical transformation or the one that occurred in Europe's former Eastern Bloc countries.

Other options include a move to a more capitalist model, as seen in China, where there is still a totalitarian type of control. This was an economic model that Fidel refused to adopt in the 1990s, but in July 2007, Raúl said that Cuba might have to turn to foreign investment and has acknowledged that 'structural and conceptual changes' are needed.

The major initial change has been a move to transfer land to private individuals, to stimulate agricultural production – an acknowledgment that state-controlled agriculture was inefficient and could not feed the population. Self-employment is being encouraged in a wider range of professions to reduce pressures on the state wage bill. The government has also allowed the legal purchase of a variety of consumer goods – cars, computers, cell phones, and DVD players – which is good for those who can afford them, but a computer costs three times the average annual wage and new cars are an astronomical price. Cubans are also now allowed to buy and sell their homes, although mediators such as real estate agents are illegal.

Domestic challenges

In the meantime, the challenges facing the administration are legion. Wages and state pensions have been increased slightly, but they are still minimal by Western standards. The administration has the difficult task of trying to keep the generation of young Cubans – born well after the Revolution – from wanting to leave the island, while at the same time maintaining social provisions in health and education.

The disparity in incomes between those with access to foreign currency and those without continues to grow. Those with relatives in Miami who send them remittances are the ones who can afford to buy houses and cars, while prosperous casa particular owners now travel abroad and improve and extend their houses. The proposed unification of the peso convertible and the peso cubano may help develop a more egalitarian society by improving the performance of the domestic economy.

However, the chances of violent upheaval in Cuba seem to have receded. The years ahead will bring change and transition, but it seems likely to be largely peaceful, and controlled by internal authorities rather than from abroad.

Cuba's internal political opposition is weak, and although the US seeks to fund opposition groups, many dissidents choose to retain their independence. In 2002, the so-called Varela Project was organized by one prominent dissident, Oswaldo Payá, and called for a number of political and economic reforms. The petition gained 11,000 signatures, but came to naught, and the following year, a crackdown saw 75 opposition figures imprisoned. This led to widespread international condemnation. In 2010, one of those prisoners, Orlando Zapata Tamayo, died after a hunger strike of 80 days. In 2012, Payá himself was killed in a road accident in mysterious circumstances, prompting further outcries in the US and Europe, where the official version of events was widely disbelieved.

The role of the United States

Of course, the position of the United States has a significant role to play in future developments in Cuba. Relations between the two are still stuck in a time warp. There is an ongoing debate in the US about the merits of sanctions, with some groups believing US policy to have been hijacked by the influential Cuban-American lobby. But the United States' official foreign policy is still resolutely anti-Castro. It was hoped that when Obama took office he would remove travel restrictions and allow ordinary Americans to visit Cuba, but this has not happened.

The US refuses to deal with what it considers a 'succession' government rather than a 'transitional' one, and states that it will only end sanctions once Cuba is committed to free and fair multiparty elections, and all political prisoners are released.

Raúl Castro, his brother's heir.

FUTURE LEADER

The Bush administration refused to deal with a Cuban government that contained members of the old guard, but a number of them remained prominent in the Council of State. Most of the younger technocrats groomed by Fidel were removed by Raúl amid rumors that their personal ambitions were counter-revolutionary, and replaced by figures from the military. The Council initially got older rather than younger. But, in 2013, Raúl announced that he would relinquish power when his term of office ends in 2018, promoting 52-year old Miguel Díaz-Canel Bermúdez to First Vice President, effectively nominating his successor.

Fidel Castro

He was a major player on the world stage for five decades, but will he go down in history as a megalomaniac dictator or unique statesman?

Fidel Alejandro Castro Ruz was born in Birán in Oriente in 1926. His father, Ángel Castro y Argiz, was a Galician immigrant who made his money out of sugar and investments. His mother, Lina Ruz

A youthful Castro in New York in 1955.

González, who had been a servant in his father's home, bore Fidel, his two brothers, Ramón and Raúl, and his four sisters, Angelita, Juanita, Enma, and Agustina, all out of wedlock. The couple only married after Ángel's first wife died, when Fidel was 15 years old. With a farm employing 300 people, the Castros were wealthy, but not of the cultured class.

Prone to temper tantrums, the young Castro was a troublesome child, maybe because of his illegitimacy and being raised in foster homes. Sent to a Jesuit boarding school in Santiago de Cuba, he was initially teased about his crude manners, but he proved an able student, both intellectually and in sport.

Later, he attended Belén College in the capital, before going on to obtain a law degree from the University of Havana, where he frequently instigated student protests. It was during this period that he honed his skills in oratory.

After graduation, Castro briefly practiced law, but since he refused to accept money from his impoverished clients, he had to survive on the largesse of his family. In 1948 he traveled to Colombia where he was arrested for inciting anti-imperialist demonstrations.

That same year he married Mirta Díaz-Balart, a wealthy philosophy student with family ties to Batista. The couple honeymooned in Miami and New York, and received US$1,000 from Batista as a wedding gift. In 1949 their son, Fidelito, was born, but five years later they divorced. Mirta remarried and left Cuba, and has never spoken publicly about her ex-husband.

A charismatic leader

In 1959, Castro swept into the limelight with his Christ-like demeanor and outlaw charisma, and seized control of Cuba. As an international statesman and icon of the radical left, he mesmerized cheering crowds in cities all over the world, from Baghdad to Hanoi and Prague. For many years, he was the self-proclaimed leader of the developing world. He saw eight US presidents come and go, and passed from being the world's youngest political leader to being the longest-serving head of state.

Castro set about ruling his island with absolute power, surrounding himself with an entourage of yes-men who would cater to his ego and bathe him in adulation. His national security apparatus, embedded in every crevice of the island, helped maintain total authority. Anyone opposing him was labeled subversive and harassed or jailed. However, unlike most dictators, there is no street named after him, his birthplace is difficult to get to and not promoted. There is no personality cult.

Many have deserted him – his children, Alina and Fidelito, now live abroad, and Alina attacked him in a book published after she fled to the US in the 1990s. Others, the *fidelistas*, revere him as the man who brought them cradle-to-grave health care, free education, and social security benefits. He has had many names, including El Comandante and El Jefe Máximo (The Maximum Leader).

Castro's personal life

If Castro the politician is hard to understand, Castro the man is even more elusive. Although a public figure, he gained a reputation as a very private person and a master of self-concealment. Fiercely intelligent and strictly disciplined, he never admitted defeat. When working, he rarely got a good night's sleep, for to sleep is to be off-guard. Instead of going to bed, he would take short naps at his office.

Though believed to be fluent in English, Castro does not speak it in public. He reads voraciously, but he stopped puffing on his trademark cigars in the 1980s, as part of a public no-smoking campaign. Although the true nature of his abdominal surgery in 2006 has been kept secret, his illness has no doubt curtailed many of his hobbies – gardening, swimming, fishing, and driving his Jeep, although playing chess is something he can probably still do as well as ever.

Castro with his friend and supporter, the late Hugo Chávez, president of Venezuela, in 2006.

Rumors abound, stating that Castro had hundreds of romantic encounters and fathered dozens of children. But following his divorce, he was linked publicly to only one woman, Celia Sánchez. A vivacious upper-middle-class *cubana* and devoted companion during the rebel campaign, Sánchez was the love of his life. A champion of social causes, she was always popular with the Cuban people, and also held substantial power in the government. Celia's death from cancer in 1980 reputedly hit the Cuban leader hard.

Gabriel García Márquez, the Nobel Prize-winning Colombian author, is a long-standing friend of Fidel's – the two men first met in 1959, and the writer was one of the first people outside Castro's inner circle to see him after his illness. He greatly admires Castro, and has said: 'He has the nearly mystical conviction that the greatest achievement of the human being is the proper formation of conscience, and that moral incentives, rather than material ones, are capable of changing the world and moving history forward. I think he has been one of the greatest idealists of our time and this, perhaps, may be his greatest virtue, although it has also been his greatest danger.'

Taking a back seat

Castro is still an icon for some, especially on the Latin American left. At home, Castro named his younger brother Raúl as his successor in 1997, some nine years before illness forced him to take a back seat, and in February 2008 Raúl was inaugurated as president. 'I am not eternal,' Fidel has said. 'Suddenly, one discovers that almost everything is behind and that life has its limits.' However, he is also reported to have said, 'I am a revolutionary and revolutionaries do not retire.' He no longer holds any official government post but acts as elder statesman, meeting with Pope Benedict in 2012, setting the stage for peace negotiations between the Colombian government and rebel fighters, and, in 2013, calling for restraint by the US and North Korea to avoid nuclear war.

Believers clad in white prepare for a Santería ceremony.

BELIEFS AND RELIGIONS

The mixture of African and Hispanic cultures in Cuba is nowhere more apparent than in religion, where African spiritual beliefs blend comfortably with Catholicism.

Spanish Catholic priests working in Cuba were always seen to be politically conservative in colonial times, siding with the white, upper-class elite, first against the native Taínos and later against the imported African slaves. They opposed independence from Spain in the 19th century and opposed the Revolution in the 1950s. Church and State were separated under the new constitution approved in 1901 under the influence of the USA, and the US occupation allowed Protestantism to get a foot in the door, but compared with other Latin American countries religion was not a major part of people's lives. Although there are some magnificent cathedrals and churches in the cities, few villages had a church and most Cubans rarely went to Mass. Fidel Castro was educated by Jesuits, but the Church received no favors from him after the Revolution, and most priests headed for Miami. Practicing Catholics were banned from joining the Communist Party, effectively keeping them out of any position of authority.

A boveda, or spirit altar.

Christmas was abolished in the 1960s because it interfered with the sugar harvest. By the time it was reinstated in 1997 a whole generation had grown up not knowing what it was all about.

Resolving conflict

Eventually, however, Castro mellowed and the regime became more tolerant on issues of race, sex, and religion. He stated that there was no conflict between Marxism and Christianity and was particularly supportive of liberation theologists and their quest for a just society. The Pope condemned the US trade embargo in the late 1970s, prompting Castro to invite him to visit Cuba. During the 1980s, Castro allowed the import of Bibles, permitted the issue of visas to priests and missionaries, and authorized the construction of new churches. In the 1990s a new Cardinal was appointed after a gap of more than 30 years. Communist Party membership was opened to religious believers, congregations rose, and baptisms soared.

In 1996 Castro took off his fatigues, donned a suit and tie, and went to visit Pope John Paul II at the Vatican. The Pope reciprocated in 1998, Cuba being the only Latin American country he had not visited by that time. He criticized free market ideology, which he saw as promoting excessive individualism and undermining the role of society. The two men clearly found common ground on the need for social justice despite disagreeing on such fundamental matters as abortion and contraception.

Huge crowds greeted the Pope at the open-air Masses held all over the country, and there is a bust outside the Basílica del Cobre near Santiago commemorating his visit. At the Pope's request, Castro reinstated Christmas Day as a public holiday, but more major reforms on human rights and political prisoners were ignored.

Slaves were not allowed to practice their native religion and were ostensibly converted to Catholicism, but many Spanish masters chose not to notice that when their slaves observed a saint's day they were really celebrating their own *orishas*. It was because of this that the *lucumí* syncretized, or merged, the Spanish saints with their own *orishas*, many of whom shared similar characteristics. The term Santería was originally used derisively by the Spanish to mock the Africans' seeming over-devotion to the saints but later became a generally recognized term to describe the

A youth carries a basket containing a hen on his head during a santería initiation ceremony.

Santería

From the mid-16th century until the end of the slave trade, hundreds of thousands of Africans were forcibly removed from their cultures and brought to Cuba. Although there were many nations affected, speaking hundreds of different languages, the most numerous were the Yoruba-speaking peoples from Nigeria, Dahomey, and Togo, who were collectively known as *lucumí*. They brought with them their deities, or *orishas*, which together with their legends and customs, such as animal sacrifice, communication with the deities via trance, and sacred drumming, became the basis of the syncretic Regla de Ocha cult, or Santería (the 'Way of the Saints').

THE COLOR OF LOVE

St Valentine's Day is special in Cuba, when women dress up and step out with their boyfriends or husbands and families. Havana's Malecón is thronged with couples late into the night, restaurants and bars have long lines outside, and sellers of fabric roses encased in plastic bubbles and little heart pins do a brisk business. Women frequently wear the color of love – yellow or gold – on this day; Oshún, the goddess of rivers, beauty, and love, is always dressed that way. Outside her flower-filled shrine at the Basílica del Cobre near Santiago flower sellers offer yellow sunflowers in her honor.

religion. Over the years the number of deities has dwindled and now only about two dozen regularly receive tribute at the rites known as *toques de santo*. However, the number of believers is thought to be equal to that of Catholicism and includes prominent Communist Party members. The vast majority of *santeros* consider themselves also to be Catholics, have been baptized, and often require initiates to be baptized too.

Every *orisha* has his or her rules and regulations, including a code of conduct, dress, decoration, and diet that believers must follow, together with specific chants and rhythms to be beaten on the sacred *batá* drums.

Each *toque de santo* begins and ends by calling upon Elegguá, guardian of roads and doors, who stands at the crossroads of the human and the divine and controls our destiny. Nothing should be done without his permission. Elegguá is dressed in red and black, and in the Christian calendar he is equivalent to the Holy Child of Atocha, caring for travelers and pilgrims.

Olofi, or Olorun, (syncretized with both the Father and the Holy Spirit) is the supreme creator of all things, but he is believed to have handed over care of the world to Obatalá (Our Lady of Mercy), who is dressed entirely in white and is the god of peace, truth, wisdom, and justice. His son is Orula, or Ifá, (syncretized with St Francis of Assisi among others), the lord of divination who communicates only with his *babalawo*, or priest; the latter predicts the future by casting eight pieces of coconut or turtle shell, known as the *ékuele*.

The most powerful *orisha* is Changó (syncretized with St Barbara), lord of fire, thunder, war, drums, and virility, and dressed in red. He is the son of Yemayá (Virgin of Regla, the patron saint of Havana Bay), who is mistress of the seas and goddess of motherhood and is dressed in blue and white. Her other son, Oggún (St Peter), is also a war god and patron saint of blacksmiths. Both of them compete for the affections of Yemayá's sister, Oshún (Virgin of Charity, and Cuba's patron saint), the sensual dancing goddess of rivers, beauty, and love. Oyá (St Teresa of Avila) is the goddess of winds and lightning and the queen of

A Santería cabildo (temple) in Palmira.

Anybody dressed all in white is likely to be an Iyawó – someone recently initiated into Santería, and undergoing a year of communion with the orishas. The necklaces are sacred: each one represents one of the orishas.

the cemetery. Babalú Ayé (syncretized with St Lazarus) dresses in purple but is covered in sores and limps on crutches, being the god of leprosy, venereal disease, and a number of skin diseases and problems.

Palo Monte

Regla de Palo Monte, or Regla Conga is a cult that was brought to Cuba by slaves from the Bantu-speaking regions of the Congo basin. Palo Monte is found mostly in the provinces of Havana and Matanzas but is more fragmented than Regla de Ocha, with which it co-exists harmoniously as they are both non-sectarian and non-proselytizing. It is divided into several different sects, the most well known being the *mayomberos*, *kisimberos*, and *briyumberos*.

Ceremonies involving rum and tobacco (and sometimes gunpowder) are used to predict the future, using the forces of nature to perform good or evil magic. Its main supernatural spirit is *nganga*, who lives in an iron container or earthenware pot along with the *mpungus*, or saints. As with the other religious cults, Palo Monte's ceremonies utilize drum rhythms that are exciting and energizing.

A Palo Monte initiation ceremony.

THE SECRET SECT OF ABAKUA

Abakuá, or *ñañiguismo*, is a secret, closed sect, rather than a religion, and has been compared to freemasonry. It is only open to men, has a distinctly macho outlook, and embraces the fraternal aims of mutual assistance, hence the phrase 'Friendship is one thing and the Abakuá another.' Members follow seven secret commandments, have secret signs, and perform arcane ceremonies wearing special vestments. The sect originated among slaves from the Calabar or Cross River region of southeastern Nigeria and southwestern Cameroon and was first noted in the first half of the 19th century, although no one is quite sure when it started. It is found principally in Havana, particularly around Guanabacoa, Regla, and Marianao, but also in Matanzas, Cárdenas, and Cienfuegos.

Ñañigos are also called *diablitos* (little devils), when they dress in the ceremonial outfit – a multicolored checkerboard costume with a tassel-topped conical headpiece – for their Carnival dances. Their rhythmic dance music contributed to the development of the rumba, and it is believed that Ñañigos invented the *guaguancó* type of rumba. They have also been involved in most forms of Cuban popular music, with many commercial recordings made in their secret language, the musicians being aware that their chants could only be interpreted by fellow Ñañigos.

A cigar store Indian outside a store in Little Havana.

DREAMING OF MIAMI

Over the decades thousands of Cubans have fled to Miami as political or economic refugees. Ironically, the remittances they sent back to their families helped keep the Cuban economy afloat during its most difficult period.

In 1959–62, hundreds of thousands of wealthy Cubans left the island in the aftermath of the revolution, either in fear because they had supported the Batista regime, or because of the increasingly evident socialist slant of Castro's policies.

Landless peasants and poor farmers then came from the countryside and took over the vacated mansions. Their children grew up in cities living lives very different from their own, some becoming doctors, professors, and engineers. Yet many Cubans still wished to emigrate to Miami.

In 1980, after a week-long crisis in which thousands of Cubans sought asylum in Havana's foreign embassies (11,000 in the Peruvian embassy alone), Castro announced that anyone who wanted to leave could do so. Around 125,000 promptly did, aided by small craft from Miami, in what became known as the Mariel boatlift.

For the Castro regime, these people were traitors or *gusanos* (worms), and were denounced by the state media as *escoria* (scum). Castro ensured that thousands of criminals were disgorged from Cuban prisons to join the exodus. But the refugees turned out to be mostly respectable, hard-working people: doctors, teachers, academics, and members of Castro's new educated class. In other words, people who owed their status to the revolution they had rejected.

What had gone wrong? Why, after 20 years of a revolution marked by great social changes, of a revolution that was still popular in some sectors, and that was marked by a vehement anti-Americanism, did so many Cubans still yearn for a life in the United States?

Diving from the rocks in front of the Malecón, Havana.

Opportunity stifled

Most of the people who seek to leave Cuba say the revolution has failed because it denies two freedoms: political and, especially for young people, economic. They complain bitterly about the lack of opportunity to 'get on' in the world. Those who have trained to be professionals often can't afford a house and many married couples live with their children in a single room at their parents' house. Doctors earn less in a month than a waiter or a taxi driver can make in tips from tourists in a day.

As one young émigré – an agricultural engineer – said, 'In the United States I will have the chance to live my life. I may fail – there's always a risk. But at least I will have had the chance. Here, if you do not conform, if you are not a revolutionary man, you have no chance to succeed. None at all.'

Home away from home

These emigrants have settled in different Cuban-American communities across the United States, including New Jersey, but most Cubans make the tropical city of Miami their home – near enough to Cuba to keep alive their dreams of a successful return or of counter-revolution.

Escaping the 'Special Period'

The obsession with Miami reached a peak in the early 1990s, when Cuba faced crippling hardships after the fall of the Soviet Union, and people were so desperate to leave that they were willing to risk their lives on a fragile raft. Many had no idea of the difficulties they faced. A distance that seemed small on a map took many days, even weeks, to reach. All too often, empty rafts would wash up on the Florida Keys. The horror stories did not deter those determined to leave, usually sailing with a large painted banner to catch the attention

Would-be Cuban emigrés attempt to cross the Florida Straits in a makeshift boat.

José Martí stayed in Miami in the 19th century, while plotting the overthrow of Spanish colonial rule. Cubans fled there in the 1930s during the brutal dictatorship of Machado. Castro visited exiled Cubans there in 1955 when seeking funds for the overthrow of Batista. After more than a hundred years, Miami has taken on a strong Cuban flavor – the city is essentially Spanish-speaking, largely because of its dominant Cuban community; restaurants and stores sell American-made replicas of Cuban brands, and the scent of strong, sweet 'Cuban' coffee fills the air of Little Havana (the coffee is not from Cuba, of course – federal politics ensures that no goods from the island ever reach the United States).

of the Brothers to the Rescue, an exile organization that launched planes from Miami to search for rafters.

Between 1989 and 1994, more than 10,000 rafters made it to Miami. The Cuban coastguard stopped a further 37,800. Castro claimed that the US precipitated the crisis by refusing to grant sufficient entry visas, and said he would no longer prevent Cubans from leaving, sparking a mass exodus – between August and September 1994, around 2,000 rafters a week set sail. The US authorities feared the consequences of a mass migration like that of the Mariel boatlift, and started to ship those picked up at sea to internment camps at its Guantánamo military base. In the weeks following the start of the 'rafters crisis' during the summer of 1994, people in Havana began to get used to the sight of bodies washing up in the bay – many of them chewed up by sharks. Although about 40,000 Cubans made it to the United States that year, it is estimated that between five and nine thousand died in the attempt.

The crisis led to talks between the United States and Cuba, whereby the Cuban authorities agreed to clamp down on the would-be refugees, rafters picked up at sea would be returned home, and the US would grant 20,000 visas a year by lottery to Cubans seeking to leave the island. This lottery proved popular – each year the numbers applying for US visas doubled until 1999 when the US State Department claimed it had received as many applications as there were families living in Cuba.

Baseball is equally popular in Cuba and the US.

An ongoing exodus

To this day, Cubans still try to make the sea crossing, although not in the numbers seen during previous crises. Some are put off by reports – true or not – of Cubans going to Miami but ending up disillusioned by the rampant consumerism, the widespread waste of resources, the long hours of work needed to maintain the coveted lifestyle, the threat of unemployment, and the difficulties of being confronted with large medical bills and tussles with insurance companies.

New legislation in 2013 relaxed travel restrictions, leading to a 35 per cent increase in Cubans legally traveling abroad. Cubans no longer have to get an exit visa before traveling and can remain abroad for two years before returning to renew their passport. The most popular destinations are the US, Mexico, and Spain, with some Cubans flying overseas more than once a year. Many will probably not return to Cuba and there has been an upsurge in the

CUBAN MULES

Many seats on the flights from Miami and Los Angeles are bought by Cubans with a US visa and a green card. Resident in the US, they supplement their income by traveling back and forth, shopping to order. Spare parts for old cars, computer equipment, and other specialized goods are delivered personally to Cuban customers after 'negotiations' with customs officers. Many things that are unobtainable in Cuban shops are brought in surreptitiously by these 'mules,' who are ostensibly visiting their families. Every so often there is a crackdown and goods are confiscated if a mule is deemed to have come into the country too frequently.

number of Cubans crossing into the US from Mexico, but the majority are using the system to travel as tourists.

The grass is always greener

While those in Cuba dream of life in Miami, the old guard there still dreams of returning to Havana. Veterans of Batista's time and the Bay of Pigs still gather in Miami's Little Havana to plot and scheme over cups of coffee at the Café Versailles. Old men now, they still cling to their dream that the Castros will be overthrown and they will return home. Miami-based terrorist organizations such as Alpha 66 and Omega 7 have carried out several unsuccessful incursions into Cuban territory. Exile leaders admit that the bombs that exploded in Havana's hotels in the summer of 1997, killing an Italian tourist, were organized and paid for in Miami.

These desperate acts, though, are the work of the older generation. Cuban-Americans born in the USA, or those who have arrived since the Mariel boatlift, have a different way of taking on the regime, using their prosperity to fund businesses in Cuba. Most of Cuba's *paladares* (family-run restaurants) started up using Miami money, either as a loan or by direct investment. Many Cubans who left on rafts returned as tourists or entrepreneurs, helping friends and family set up new businesses that have changed the once moribund face of Havana. Now that Cubans are allowed to buy houses, Miami money is helping there too, although surreptitiously, as foreigners are not yet allowed to own property.

Cubans without Miami connections resent this: they see the families of exiles able to live well while they suffer on a monthly ration that barely lasts a week. Havana's shopping malls have been fueled by the spending power of those who receive money from abroad.

Woman embraces a relative at Jose Martí airport in Havana.

Ironically, some argue that remittances sent by the exile community helped prevent economic collapse during the 'Special Period.'

Not all Miami Cubans feel the same about remittances – some people complain that their families back home are too demanding, seeing them as cash cows to be milked at every opportunity. Many are working-class people with mortgages and heavy financial commitments who can find the burden of helping families in Cuba too much for them.

Room for dialog

These days, too, there is more contact between the two communities than there was in the aftermath of the revolution, when political refugees vowed not to return until Castro had been ousted. Subsequent refugee groups like the *marielitos* and the rafters, having left Cuba for economic rather than political reasons, are not at all troubled by the idea of taking vacations in Cuba. The Miami Cuban community no longer has a monolithic approach to the Cuban state. The majority remain anti-regime, but most now back calls for dialog rather than confrontation with the Cuban Government.

The 'Christmas Laws,' passed after the revolution to confiscate émigrés' property, remain in force today. Anyone who emigrates legally still forfeits their possessions and their inheritance rights.

Journeys 'home' increased after the resumption of direct flights from Miami to Havana in 1998, but the policy swung back six years later, when President George W. Bush tightened travel restrictions. Then, US-based Cubans were only allowed to visit 'close family,' and only once every three years, for no longer than two weeks.

The election of Barack Obama and a Democrat administration in the White House in 2009 saw the end of travel restrictions for Cuban-Americans (although not for all Americans) and unrestricted family visits are now allowed. There is a steady flow of visitors on the flights from Florida and Los Angeles. In March 2008, Raúl Castro similarly made some cosmetic changes and allowed Cubans to stay in hotels previously restricted to foreign guests, and to rent cars at state-run agencies. Few Cubans can afford a beach holiday in Cayo Coco, but at least they are now allowed to accompany their Miami relatives if the latter are paying.

Demonstration in Miami in favor of keeping Elián González in the US.

INTERNATIONAL BATTLE

One of the most dramatic immigration cases took place in 1999. Five-year-old Elián González was one of a handful of people who survived when the small craft in which he had been traveling overturned. His mother and nine others drowned. His father (divorced from his mother) called for Elián's return to Cuba, and a fierce international custody battle ensued between relatives in Miami (backed by Cuban-American organizations) and the US Government, backing Elián's father in rare agreement with the Cuban regime. Elián did return home, to the jubilation of thousands of Cubans who had supported government-organized rallies.

CUBA'S TRANSPORTATION SYSTEM

Fascinating, exotic, frustrating, and divisive, depending on your standpoint, the beleaguered transportation system is a visible microcosm of Cuba's economic woes.

In the late 1980s, oil supplies from the Eastern Bloc that had provided the island with 90 percent of its fuel began to dry up as the Cuban-sugar-for-Soviet-oil deal came to an end. Scarcity of fuel meant that outside the main cities motorized transportation virtually vanished, a situation that has changed little today. Roads are all but deserted, oxen pull plows that till the fields, and horses and carts ply the streets of provincial towns in place of buses.

But, most noticeably, bicycles are everywhere – more than 1 million were imported from China in the early 1990s, and in this make-do-and-mend society many of them are still going strong. It's as if the clock has been turned back to a pre-industrial age. Cycling has become part of the fabric of everyday life, with special parking lots for bicycles and tire-repair shops everywhere. Bicycle taxis – bici-taxis – vary in design from town to town, depending on when and where they were imported from China.

The island's current tribulations and its decades of isolation from the Western world have resulted in other memorable forms of transportation. Wonderful old Cadillacs get top billing, but also look for veteran motorcycles with sidecars or bicycles with sidecars carrying the whole family, and on the railroads anything from ancient steam trains to trolley buses that can run along the tracks.

Coco-taxis: these are a fun way to get around Havana and some other cities, as long as you don't have luggage. They use less fuel than conventional taxis and are therefore cheaper.

A motorcycle is a precious commodity, tirelessly maintained despite the chronic shortage of spare parts for models obsolete in the rest of the world.

Coches, or horses and carts, serve as buses and taxis all over the island. An average ride will cost just a few pesos.

Queuing for buses in Havana may look haphazard but everyone knows their place in the line.

THE STRUGGLE TO GET AROUND

Buses (called *guaguas*) are overcrowded and poorly maintained; lines get long at peak times and cancellations are common. Cubans still need to book in advance for a seat on a crowded long-distance Astro bus – tourists have to use Víazul, the dedicated convertible peso service (see page 319).

Hitchhiking *(la botella)* is a way of life for Cubans of all ages, but definitely not for tourists, as anyone who was kind enough to pick you up would risk a fine. This is not any old hitchhiking: state officials, called *amarillos* because they wear yellow jackets, supervise crowds of hitchers at designated places, usually on the edge of towns and cities. Officials wear blue jackets in towns and are known as *azules*. State vehicles are obliged to stop, and *los amarillos* will allocate people to each vehicle on a first-come, first-served basis. Pregnant women and children get priority. Few Cubans own a car unless it is very old or they have access to foreign exchange.

Large pre-1960s trucks provide another form of transport in the provinces.

The ubiquitous bicycle, usually made in China, is the family vehicle throughout Cuba.

Spacious old cars from the 1940s and 1950s are still used as route taxis for Habaneros.

Cuba's coastal areas are idyllic playgrounds for foreign visitors.

TOURISM: SALVATION OR SELLOUT?

Post-revolutionary Cuba viewed the tourist industry with disdain, but nowadays it has no option but to embrace it to prop up the economy.

Revolutionary Cuba, a land of socialist ideals and egalitarian values, once said 'never again' to tourism. Back in the decadent 1950s, Havana, with its sophisticated hotels, clubs, and casinos, catered to the whims of wealthy Americans, and had a worldwide reputation for gambling, drugs, prostitution, pornographic films, and live sex shows. But although the industry was lucrative, much of the infrastructure was foreign-controlled, leaving few in Cuba who actually benefitted from the profits.

There is an old and rather cynical Cuban joke: an adult asks a child the classic question: 'What do you want to be when you grow up?' The child answers: 'A tourist.'

Rejecting excess

Part of Fidel Castro's struggle against Batista stemmed from his revulsion at the excesses of tourism, and the neo-colonialism it represented. Castro denounced tourism as a vulgar example of the dichotomy between the haves and the have-nots. After he took power, he promised Cuba would never again be a playground for the rich and beautiful. Instead it would rely on the sugar industry and other natural resources to fuel its economy.

The new government immediately set about closing casinos and nightclubs, the prostitutes were rounded up and sent to learn useful trades, and the hotels were put to use as vacation retreats for local workers. During the 1960s and 1970s, many of the foreign visitors to Cuba were either journalists or people wanting to express solidarity with the revolution. Others were Eastern Bloc communists on government-paid Cuban vacations.

Tourists find their way around Trinidad.

The government promoted 'social tourism,' whereby sympathetic visitors from around the world were invited to the island to visit model communities, hospitals, schools, and other places where the achievements of socialism were put on display. But between 1963 and 1975, the island received only about 3,000 foreign visitors a year.

However, when the economy began to show signs of strain in the early 1980s, the government had to reconsider its policy toward tourism, and 'health tourism' became the new trend. Foreigners were invited to Cuba for a first-rate face-lift or a coronary bypass at a much lower cost than they could have found at home. But by the mid-1980s, the government realized that this was not going to provide the economic boost and foreign exchange the island needed, and it launched an international campaign to promote pleasure tourism. After the collapse of the Soviet Union, this campaign became much more aggressive.

Tourism is gold

'In the past we feared that tourism would defile us,' Castro told his compatriots, 'but tourism is gold.' So began the push to make tourism the new business frontier of the island – one that saw investors from places like Europe, Mexico, and Canada being offered extremely non-socialist incentives that would allow them to operate in Cuba for at least 10 years without paying taxes on their income.

Progress came quickly. In 1995, tourism became, for the first time, the island's biggest source of hard currency. In 1984, fewer than 200,000 foreign tourists visited Cuba; by 1998 there were more than a million – nowadays, more than 2.8 million visitors come to Cuba each year, bringing in excess of US$2.5 billion into the Cuban economy. It is estimated that if the US were to lift the travel ban for all Americans, more than 1 million would immediately book holidays in Cuba.

A pact with the devil

Having come full circle, the tourism industry has created embarrassing ideological problems for the government. Tourism employs more than 80,000 people, but this represents only about 2 percent of the overall workforce. Tourism jobs are highly sought after because they offer access to tips in foreign currencies or convertible pesos (CUCs). Many teachers, doctors, and engineers leave their professions to work in more lucrative jobs as waiters or bellhops. Tourism has also bred corruption. Cubans wishing to work in a foreign currency/CUC enterprise often have to bribe managers for the privilege of doing so.

The superb colonial architecture, impressive scuba diving, fishing, and fine flora and

A fleet of Transtur tourist buses along the Malecón.

Nicolás Guillén wrote Tengo (I Have) in the 1960s to celebrate the Cuban people's renewed access to the beaches and hotels. After several decades of again being excluded, Cubans are once again enjoying their beaches.

fauna attract a certain number of high-spending tourists, but many more are deterred by the dilapidated infrastructure and the relatively poor standard of service.

Sex tourism

Sex tourism flourishes undercover, despite occasional crackdowns. Everything is available for both genders, straight and gay, and the market is very active. There are many scantily clad girls (called *jineteras* after the Spanish word for jockey) who hang around tourist spots, just as there are buffed-up young men (pingueros) parading their bodies as night falls in Old Havana. Many have come from the provinces and have to pay bribes to avoid being sent back. Their dream is to find a tourist (yuma) who will take them abroad and offer them a comfortable life.

Tourism apartheid

The most distasteful aspect of Cuba's tourism industry was the division it created between local people and tourists. Isolated from the public, many beach resorts were enclaves operating a system of 'tourism apartheid.' Since 2008, Cubans have been permitted to stay at hotels, but only if they can afford to pay in CUCs, which initially eliminated all but the fortunate few. However, domestic tourism is now increasing at much faster rates than foreign tourism. In the summer months, the traditional Cuban holiday period, beach resorts are kept open by the influx of Cuban families. In 2013, some 625,000 Cubans stayed at beach hotels, 100,000 more than in 2012. Surveys show that they were a mixture of self-employed business people, those whose relatives abroad paid for the vacation, athletes, artists, tourism workers, and Cubans returning from missions abroad. Varadero is their most popular destination.

Handicrafts for sale on Varadero beach.

DANGEROUS LIAISONS

More often than not, the sex scene these days revolves around bars and clubs, either through none-too-subtle flirtation that in some places can border on harassment or through young pimps. These days, few *jineteras* are prepared to offer their services for the sake of a dress or a meal – many make more money in a week than a government minister earns in a year. Western men should also know that the age of consent in Cuba is 18 and picking up a young girl is likely to be a blackmail trap. There are also the parallel, though much smaller, types of sex tourism: Western women with young Cuban men, and same sex-liaisons.

Dancers in Havana's Callejón de Hamel.

CUBA'S SIZZLING SOUND

There's nowhere else like it: for 'Cuba,' read 'Rhythm.' Here you will find a depth of musical talent that is, perhaps, unequaled anywhere in the world.

Music and Cuba have been synonymous for considerably more than a century; in no other communist country have music and revolution marched so closely, hand in hand. Even during the final build-up to the 1959 revolution, at the dramatic closure of that legendary era when Havana was a fantasy island playground for American tourists, the bands played on and visitors rushed to the city's casinos, bars, hotels, glitzy nightclubs, and beaches.

Revolution never quashed the music: film footage of Castro's guerrillas moving toward Havana shows Che Guevara with a guitar on his back. All through the 'Special Period,' the state still supported musicians, and the music began to launch a new flush of tourism.

Many people were introduced to Cuban music by the Buena Vista Social Club, liked what they heard, and went on to discover much more about the island's rhythms, its musical history, and changing styles.

Musicians entertain in a Havana café.

The beat goes on

Today, music is the state tourist board's golden egg; millions of visitors flock to Cuba for the same reasons the Americans once did: the rum, sun, sex, music, and dancing (no gambling, however, which is strictly counter-revolutionary). Ironically, they often travel in the same, now patched-up, Oldsmobile taxis to the same still glitzy nightclubs, bars, and hotels built by the Americans and abandoned in 1959. The Hotel Nacional, where Sinatra sang and American high society (and gangsters) partied, is still hugely impressive; the breathtaking Tropicana nightclub still sees dancers in towering headdresses parade across galleries between the palm trees, and singers today perform on the same stage that shook to the voice of the future Queen of Salsa, Celia Cruz, and the delights of Nat King Cole. Hotel Rivera's elegant nightclub is now the Palacio de Salsa (Salsa Palace).

The ruffle-sleeved shirts survive yet the decadence is gone. But most hotels and restaurants provide some kind of live music, and salsa venues in the capital include the prestigious Casa de la Música, and small rooftop bars like the Pico Blanco in Hotel St John's, a must for smoochy boleros. Compay Segundo's old haunt, the beer garden El Tropical, is today a landmark venue for the raunchy Cuban salsa called *timba* (see page 98), and the narrow alley, the Callejón de Hamel, in the Vedado district hosts rumba drumming, dancing, and singing on Sundays.

Music wherever you go

Visitors today are never far from music, with *timba* trombones ricocheting around the narrow streets, scorching jazz drumming rising from basement bars, and sweet guitar melodies in Buena Vista style, drifting from pavement cafés in Old Havana. The 70-year-old song *Guantanamera* is as ubiquitous as images of Che Guevara, and the evocative *Chan Chan* is a reminder of the impact the *Buena Vista Social Club* movie and album has had on the surge of tourism since the late 1990s.

While tourist hotels worldwide offer cheesy stereotyped shows, Cuba's conservatoire-trained musicians treat tourists to music that is often of a spectacularly high standard (although they trot out plenty of *Guantanameras*, as well) and they are often internationally acclaimed, even Grammy-winning artists, such as the Afro-Cuban jazz pianist, Chucho Valdés (founder of the trailblazing band, Irakere), who is a regular at the rooftop Jazz Café, playing with his scat-singing sister, Mayra, or his own small group.

Breaking it down

Many tourists visit Cuba for the salsa dancing, often on special packages, and the chances are that leading salsa bands like Los Van Van (see page 98) will provide music for their classes back home and the live soundtrack to their vacation. To navigate the overwhelming range of music, the local radio stations Taíno (bilingual and for tourists) and Rebelde (mixing news, interviews, and music, in Spanish) are more useful than the solitary newspaper, *Granma*, and Cuban TV presents home-grown bands live and on video.

Cuba is a great place to salsa.

While Havana is the epicenter of Cuban music, it doesn't hold the monopoly on variety or excitement. Santiago, in the eastern state of Oriente, is equally rich in traditional and modern music, and its Carnival (held in late July) beats Havana's hands down.

Santiago is a heavily African city with its own musical identity. The dance music conga sensation, Sur Caribe, is an upbeat salsa-rap big band, influenced by the winning combination of violins and trombones pioneered by Los Van Van but also involving traditional Santiago carnival instruments – the raucous *corneta china* (Chinese cornet) and portable drums made world-famous in the 1930s by Desi Arnaz, and still alive and kicking in conga bands today. Led by Ricardo Leyva, the *orquesta* has a string of albums under its belt and regularly tours abroad. In contrast, Septeto Típico de Tivoli is a neo-traditional *son* band, the *corneta* replacing the conventional trumpet.

Trova

Santiago is a focus for the *trova* song style, supported around Cuba in *casas de la trova*. Santiago's is a celebrated meeting place, where singers, composers, guitarists, and friends met to drink rum, smoke cigars, and be transported by the guitar melodies, vocal harmonies, sensual rhythms, and lyrics inspired by the country life and work, patriotic or revolutionary themes.

Some guitarists once lived a troubadour's life, playing *trova* songs alongside soldiers during the 19th-century Independence War with Spain and during Castro's guerrilla war. The latter spawned a *nueva* (new) *trova* movement linked to Latin America's 1960s revolutions, and key figures Pablo Milanés and Silvio Rodríguez are now superstar elder statesmen who perform internationally. Their songs are almost as familiar as those of their international contemporaries and their successors, including Carlos Varela and Amaury Pérez, have moved closer to rock's singer-songwriter tradition.

One of Havana's celebrated *trova* hang-outs is the Bodeguita del Medio, a small bar in Old Havana where writers, poets, and musicians rehearsed new works and debated revolution. Today, tourists crowd the bar, and crane their necks to read their autographs, most famously that of Hemingway, with whom the bar is most closely associated. *Trova* musicians' repertoires roam through guitar-based styles, and include the ubiquitous *son*, which is at the root of most popular Cuban music, including salsa.

Eliades Ochoa, of Buena Vista Social Club fame rehearsing in Havana.

THE BUENA VISTA SOCIAL CLUB

The 1990s brought an upsurge of interest in traditional Cuban music with the release of the *Buena Vista Social Club* movie and album. Pride of place among the elderly stars 'rediscovered' by American guitarist, composer, and singer Ry Cooder went to Compay Segundo, half of the superb 1950s duo, Los Compadres, who came out of retirement and recorded a Grammy-winning CD in 1998. He was still touring the world in his nineties, but died in 2003. Sadly, most other 1950s greats have since died, too: pianist Rubén González in 2003, and vocalists Ibrahim Ferrer in 2005, and Pío Leyva in 2006. Only Omara Portuondo is still going strong.

Son

Son became universally familiar through the Buena Vista Social Club phenomenon. Its origins lie in Oriente province, against a backdrop of late 19th-century coffee and sugar plantations. By the 1920s, it had reached Havana, and rapidly adapted to an urban style. *Son* is both truly African and truly Cuban, built around call-and-response singing, with rough, often high-pitched lead voices and repetitive guitar riffs working in rhythmic harmonies with the hand percussion. Most crucial are the two hard-wood blocks *(claves)* clacking out the *clave* rhythm, which underlies Cuban popular music. *Clave's* syncopated beat forces dancers into action and musicians into the basic rhythm around which they can improvise.

Polo Montañez, the much-loved guajiro singer.

In 1920s Havana, country migrants initially busked on the streets and in cafés, but their infectious sweetness and catchy rhythms seduced wider audiences, and trios expanded to more sophisticated sextets and septets, boosted by bongos, double bass, and trumpets. In salons and dancehalls the guitars would be replaced by pianos. Don Azpiazu's big-band recording of *El Manicero (The Peanut Vendor)* in 1931 ignited an international rumba craze. Although known as rumba, his popularized son differs from the Afro-Cuban rumba that originated in slave communities and involves drumming, dancing, and chant-singing.

Rumba

Rumba is thought to have emerged among the Congolese dock workers in the late 1800s in the port of Matanzas, following the abolition of slavery. The original drums were boxes taken from the docks, but are now polished, finely tuned instruments, often played in multiple, differently tuned 'nests.' The word 'nest' describes both the music and the parties at which it is played. Master conga drummers have played key roles in the development of original new styles, including the imaginative percussionist Changuito's role in Los Van Van, and that of the late Angá Diaz, who developed a symphonic sound.

Matanzas still has some of the most brilliant *rumberos* in Cuba: Los Muñequitos de Matanzas (The Little Dolls) and Clave y Guaguancó both perform at international festivals and the city's squares. Of the scores of varieties of rumba, three main types are preserved: *guaguancó, yambú*, and Columbia, each with specific drums, rhythms, and dance styles. One of Cuba's most famous singers, the late Lázaro Ros, who died in 2005, could sing in around 800 different African languages, and his rumba group, Olorun, worked with rock groups that blended Afro-Cuban religious music with modern styles. A true rumba is a profound experience that can be shared in street sessions in Matanzas, near the Teatro Sauto, and at Rumba Saturdays in Havana's Vedado district.

Country music: *guajira*

Cuba's country music, *música guajira*, is rooted in Andalusia in southern Spain, descended from the Spanish peasants who came to the island two centuries ago, but blends influences from the African cultures of fellow workers. It was originally a form of after-work escapism for exhausted Spanish farmers and cattle herders, and for African workers in the sugar-cane plantations, tobacco fields, and factories. Like country workers elsewhere, they would pull out a guitar and sing, with family and friends joining in, adding touches of their own.

Its gorgeous melodies are carried on lilting acoustic guitars or *laoud* (a version of the Arabic *oud*) with verses in the poetic song tradition, praising landscapes, detailing everyday lives and loves, and adding improvised gossip.

Many *guajira* singers, including Compay Segundo, were known for harmonizing duets. Compay's Buena Vista companion, Eliades Ochoa, is a quintessential *guajiro* with his cowboy hat, nimble-fingered guitar playing, and high-pitched, soaring voice, but it was the late Polo Montañez's raw countryman's voice that reignited the traditional sound in two great albums, *Guitara Mía* and *Guajiro Natural*. ('Discovered' relatively late in life, Montañez died, far too young, in a car accident in 2002.)

Guajira music still inspires national pride today, and was central to the Buena Vista Social Club's repertoire, and its success.

Music fills the air in Santiago.

Taking country music to town

Musicians who rose beyond the family porch left the land to busk or play in town bars and cafés, and, if lucky, to perform on the radio. Most significant composers and performers ended up in the cities; the early 20th-century composer Guillermo Portabales recorded songs whose sensual lilting melodies, accompanying images of ox-cart drivers and untouched landscapes, have resonated with economic migrants everywhere.

In 1950s Havana, country duo Celina y Reutilio performed romantic, upbeat songs that were heavily African-influenced and delivered in harmonies led by Celina's powerfully expressive voice. Celina González became an ardent defender of the New Cuba through her long-running country-music radio show.

It was the 1930s radio singer, Joseíto Fernández, who launched the classic La *Guajira Guantanamera* onto the world. The song, about a girl from Guantánamo, became popular through a 1935 radio soap opera, but had lyrics based on a poem by independence hero and poet José Martí. It is now heard in every tourist niche in Cuba. *Guajira* music still inspires national pride today.

Danzón to cha-cha-chá

A small but significant French element in the Cuban mix is traceable to the late 18th-century arrival in Oriente (eastern Cuba) of French colonizers' families and slaves escaping the Haitian revolution. They brought the *contredanse*, a variation of the English country dance, played by trios on piano, violin, and flute, and this laid the foundations for the elegant dances called *danzón*. Expanded into orchestras called *charangas*, they gradually incorporated a mild African syncopation, which extended its popularity. The most significant Havana *charanga* was run by flautist Antonio Arcano, and featured the double-bass player Israel 'Cachao' López and his brother, the pianist Orestes. In the late 1930s, they invented a mutant version with a syncopated ending they called mambo, which was declared devil's music for some years. But the 1940s hit records by the brilliantly eccentric Cuban pianist Pérez Prado spread mambo's popularity to the US, and from there, around the world in a sanitized, softened guise by the band leader Xavier Cugat. Mambo was the dance craze in 1950s Manhattan, and laid the trail to salsa.

Member of a local rock band rehearsing in Cienfuegos.

Another offshoot of the *danzón*, the cha-cha-chá, had fewer African qualities than mambo, and was deliberately tailored by its creator Enrique Jorrín (director of Orquesta América) for American tourists and dancers. The first cha-cha-chá, *La Engañadora*, in 1953, ignited a fever that overwhelmed mambo's popularity around the world. The greatest *charangas* remained in Cuba – Orquesta Riverside, and the sensational Orquesta Aragón, still playing today.

Son montuno to timba salsa

As the *danzón* was being modified into the cha-cha-chá, a blind Cuban musician of Congolese descent, Arsenio Rodríguez, updated the *son* by extending the repetitive instrumental section to create *son montuno*. The master *tres* guitarist manipulated the slackly strung, resonating strings to create a searing, unmistakably Cuban sound, which has been extensively imitated by modern groups, including Sierra Maestra.

Throughout the 1940s and 1950s, La Sonora Matancera occupied an important place in the story. Formed in Matanzas in the 1920s, it moved to Havana in the late 1940s, and introduced a fireball singer named Celia Cruz who became everybody's favorite. Cruz's male counterpart was Beny Moré, a sensational dancer, singer, and arranger who spent the 1940s in Mexico City, performing mambos and boleros (made for his searingly expressive high voice) and appearing in Mexican movies. Back in Havana, 'El Bárbaro del Ritmo' (the Barbarian of Rhythm) launched his horn-driven Banda Gigante (Big Band), noted for its up-tempo arrangements of brass, percussion, and

TIMBA SALSA

Salsa comes in many varieties all over Latin America, but in Cuba the dancers' soundtrack is a sizzling mutation called *timba*. The trail to *timba* was laid by young musicians creating music for the post-revolutionary era. Chucho Valdés' Afro-Cuban big band Irakere transformed jazz, and Juan Formell's Los Van Van reinvented dance music through brassy, swinging *songo* rhythms. *Songo* is a feast of conversations between violins and trombones, with jagged rhythms that backed hit songs packed with gossip and catchphrases. Irakere's ex-flautist, José Luís Cortés, founded NG (New Generation) La Banda in the 1980s and crystalized the *timba* sound with brass choruses, funk-bass lines, and risqué slang. NG was a university for *timba* stars including the brilliant Issac Delgado, who took it into America's salsa charts, and heart-throb, Paulito F.G.

The 1990s opened to David Calzado's outrageous Charanga Habanera, whose compellingly edgy songs caused fan hysteria, official panic, and a ban. The acrobatic break-dancing female singers left to found the stunning Azucar Negra. Manolin 'El Medico' de la Salsa and Manolito y su Trabuco continue a more conventional line, but Los Van Van's dreadlocked vocalist, Mayito, remains frontman for the still-dynamic band. Today's stars include the electronic-acoustic orchestra, Chispa y los Complices, which is infecting *timba* fans worldwide.

interlocking piano, whose influence continued into salsa.

The Cuban variety of salsa is called *timba* (see page 98), and was a product of experimentation by the dazzling Los Van Van, and its founder and bass player, Juan Formell, with the original *songo* rhythm created for the band by conga player Changuito, which brought some of the power and drama of rock and funk into Cuban music. Formell's exchanges between violins and trombones were the sensation of the 1980s and 1990s, and Los Van Van remains the premier dance group on the island. Their albums are hugely popular and their songs, full of wry observations and street slang, capture the mood of their audience in any decade.

Timba is the soundtrack to 21st-century Cuba, through its propulsive, edgy rhythms, braying trombone choruses, and driving funk bass lines. Contemporaries of Cortés, including the popular idol Issac Delgado, followed a more traditional singer/band route, but he broke the rules by recording a hit in New York with leading 1980s salsa producer, Ralph Mercado. The popular singer, Adalberto Alvarez, has shifted toward a more pan-Caribbean beat, but remains 100 percent Cuban, while the trombone band Dan Den, founded by the pianist Juan Carlos Alfonso, became popular for its modern, electronic sound. Other key salsa bands include Yumurí y Sus Hermanos and the Vocal Sampling. This six-piece a-capella group reproduces perfectly the sound of an entire salsa band, using only their mouths, cupped hands, and slapped bodies, and are an international phenomenon. The radical Bamboleo introduced shaven heads, break dancing, and sexual routines to the musical scene, but the wildest 1990s bunch, David Calzado's Charanga Habanera, once banned from performing live because of their 'lewdness,' inspired the new wave of rap-based acts that are popular today.

Los Van Van reinvented dance music with swinging songo rhythms.

The jazz thing

From the 19th century onward, the sea links between Havana and New Orleans enabled important musical interchanges: Afro-Cuban rumba became a basic part of New Orleans' jazz musical vocabulary, and African-American jazz came to Havana almost at birth.

Modern Cuban musicians understand both European-style musical theory and Afro-Cuban traditions and those skills have been exploited particularly in the new jazz. Pioneering the move, Cachao López made a series of legendary recordings of *descargas* (jam sessions) in the 1950s with leading soloists from the dance bands, expanding the ad-lib solo slots in popular music to become the entire piece. *Descargas* is still an inspirational best-selling CD, as fresh today as in 1959.

Jazz is central to Cuban music, though many exponents are easier to catch live during foreign tours. Irakere, the 15-piece group founded in 1970 by pianist Chucho Valdés, fused North American jazz idioms, and has operated as a university for young soloists, including *timba* pioneer, José Luís Cortés. Two original members, Paquito D'Rivera and Arturo Sandoval, are now international stars based in the US, and Valdés is an elder in Cuban music, professor at the University of Havana, and a multi-Grammy-winning solo artist who occasionally still rejoins Irakere. His recent reunion concerts and recordings with his father, Bebo Valdés, who has lived outside Cuba since 1960, produced some marvelous, moving musical conversations.

A reggaeton dance competition at a Union of Young Communists beach party.

The electronic invasion

The 1990s international explosion of hip-hop slowly but inevitably penetrated the Cuban scene, via illicit American radio and TV, which, of course, captivated the imagination of Cuban youth. The pioneering Orishas emerged in Cuba as a popular rap duo but transferred to Paris and sprang a future Grammy-winning album, *A lo Cubano* (In the Cuban style), on the market. Its fusion of electronic and 'live' Cuban rhythms, rapped and sung vocals, influenced today's thriving Cuban hip-hop scene.

This scene is officially endorsed by the government, and showcased annually at the Havana Hip-hop Festival, held every August, and for which the state provides the sound system. Early on, Fidel Castro apparently performed alongside rappers Doble Filo at a baseball game, and today, the state supports more than 500 hip-hop artists, many with international reputations.

There is also a thriving underground music scene, not approved by the government. Much

CUBAN HIP-HOP

Lyrics by Cuba's 500-plus approved hip-hoppers focus on social issues, criticism, and humor, and their electronic beats vie with 'live' brass, guitars, and percussion. After the first Havana Hip-hop Festival (1995), Castro legitimized the underground, and encouraged newcomers like Obsesión and Amenaza – who re-formed in Paris as the Grammy-winning Orishas and put Cuba on the rap map. Subsequent compilation albums including *Hora de Abrir los Ojos* (Time to Open Your Eyes) and *Cuban HipHop All-Stars* exposed the scene, and the international DM Ahora! label showcases the rap big band Interactivo, and rap-poet sensation, Telmary.

of it, like reggaeton, is influenced by US trends and also other Latin music, but with a Cuban feel. Young Cubans record it in makeshift studios and distribute it on home-made CDs and memory sticks. A fusion of reggae, rap, Latin, and electronic rhythms, reggaeton has swept the dance floors with its sensual beat and raunchy lyrics, despite the lack of government support.

Cultural interchange with US Latin artists and Latin American performers is increasing and, as Cuban music has become more widely known, so has international music become more influential in Cuba. In addition to the renovating an old theater, Maxim Rock, with state-of-the-art technology for performances. One of the leading metal/Latin/thrash bands is Tendencia, from Pinar del Río, which fuses hard rock with Afro-Cuban rhythms, using the *batá* drum. Led by singer Kiko Mederos, a high-school teacher and director of the town's Casa del Joven Creador, they have toured abroad and have a fan base in Spain.

New generation

Groups like AfroCuba, Cuarto Espacio, and Perspectiva continue the musical explora-

Chucho Valdés and his band, Irakere.

> *Metaleros listen to heavy metal; Repas are salsa and reggaeton fans from Havana's poorer suburbs; Mikis are into techno and crave all the latest electronic gadgets, like iPods, cell phones, and MP3 players.*

Latin styles this also includes rock music, originally the pariah of the revolution for its 'foreign, noisy, and scandalous beats.' It was only in 2007, with the creation of the Agencia Cubana de Rock, that official approval was eventually given, on the basis that 'if you can't beat 'em, join 'em.' Forever fearful of youthful rebellion, the government chose to entertain and control,

tions. Prominent among a new generation that emerged from the Buena Vista Social Club project is pianist Roberto Fonseca, who made his name with the singer Ibrahim Ferrer, and mesmerizes with sparkling, inventive performances that betray his early experience as a drummer. In 2007, his album *Zamazu* was released to international accclaim. Composer and pianist Omar Sosa is another who blends Cuban, African, and European music with jazz, to great effect. This restless search for new music has characterized the story of Cuban music for centuries, and shows no sign of diminishing. Whatever your musical taste, you will find much to please you in Cuba, in clubs and bars, at high-profile festivals, or simply in the city streets.

A performance of Don Quixote by the National Ballet of Cuba.

THE ARTS

Elitist and derivative art of colonial times was replaced in the 20th century by a creative, inclusive, home-grown tradition. Literature, dance, and cinema have all flourished, too, although censorship has inevitably taken its toll.

Cuba has one of the most vibrant artistic histories in the Caribbean, largely owing to its location and cross-cultural history. Forming a maritime crossroads between Europe, Africa, and the Americas, it has long fed off a cultural exchange across the Atlantic Ocean.

Although the island was originally inhabited by various indigenous groups (see page 29), relatively few pre-Columbian artifacts have been discovered in Cuba, especially when compared with the marvels that have been unearthed in Peru or Mexico, for example. However, a few beautiful Taíno pieces have survived, including stone and wooden idols, and wooden ceremonial seats.

With the rapid extermination of the indigenous population, whatever else there may have been of the non-material side of native culture died out too, leaving an almost blank cultural slate. The culture of the Spanish invaders was tempered by the influx of African slaves, French plantation owners escaping from the Haitian revolution in 1790, and Chinese indentured laborers in the second half of the 19th century. America's intercession in Cuba's war against Spain in 1898 added yet another cultural outlook – best exemplified in the grandiose Capitolio building in Havana, which closely resembles the Capitol in Washington, DC.

Art in the 20th century

During the colonial period, the pictorial arts were dull and staid – stiff portraits of wealthy ladies and tepid landscapes tended to decorate aristocratic homes and offices, mimicking the high-society tastes of Europe. In the 20th century, however, things began to change. The rise in nationalism in the political arena was reflected in the arts, with writers and artists getting inspiration from Afro-Cuban images and culture. The generation of painters of 1927–50 is known as La Vanguardia. They were influenced by the modernism of post-Impressionist European artists as well as the vibrant landscapes and people they saw around them in Cuba. From 1900 to the end of the 1950s, Cuban art gained international acclaim and, thanks to the many foreign artists visiting the island, Havana became one of the most celebrated cultural centers in Latin America.

Theatre performance in Havana.

Cuba's most prominent artists from this era include René Portocarrero (1912–85), who created fantastic versions of Havana and beautiful Creole women, and Wifredo Lam (1902–82), who incorporated the mystical dimensions of his Afro-Cuban heritage with erotic and magical symbolism. Lam spent much of his life in Madrid and Paris, and was greatly influenced by Picasso's cubist legacy. Other major artists were Leopoldo Romanach (1862–1951), with his robust country people and gloomy interiors; Fidelio Ponce (1895–1949), who painted young women, children, and saints in faint monochromes; Mariano Rodríguez (1912–90), who famously incorporated roosters into all his vivid, powerful paintings; Amelia Peláez (1897–1968), who evoked the Cuban spirit in her tropical still-lifes; Servando Cabrera (1923–81), who painted robust countrymen and some impressive nudes; and Antonia Eiriz (1929–95), who fascinated the art world with her Goya-esque monsters and ghostly nightmares.

The work of all these artists has been displayed in galleries in Europe and the United States, but the best place to see a wide selection of their works is in the Arte Cubano section of the Museo Nacional Palacio de Bellas Artes in Havana (see page 153).

Post-Revolutionary art

Painting is a field in which Cuban artists have managed to retain a fairly healthy degree of

Cara a Caro (Face to Face) by René Portocarrero.

REVOLUTION AND THE ARTS

Castro introduced an aggressive program of cultural reforms that tried to enhance artistic expression. In 1959, one of the first acts of the new government was the creation of the Instituto Cubano del Arte e Industria Cinematográficos (Cuban Film Institute; ICAIC) and the Consejo Nacional de Cultura (National Cultural Council; CNC). The Escuela Nacional de Arte (National School for Art; ENA), founded in 1962, served as the cradle for new artists and teachers in painting, music, dance, and drama.

State sponsorship opened the door to many artists but compromised their freedom of expression. In 1962 Castro defined his policy toward artists and intellectuals: 'Within the revolution, everything; outside the revolution, nothing.' During the mid-1960s, those with differing opinions about the cultural program, or were noncommittal, were removed. Many liberal artists were condemned to silence, persecuted as 'anti-social elitists,' or exposed as homosexual; others sought asylum. The most unfortunate were sent to prison or to one of Cuba's new labor camps. Directors and writers became more cautious as they were forced to fulfill the artistic and cultural requirements. Socialist ideology began to dominate, and the Education and Cultural Congress increased censorship. Hundreds of actors, writers, and directors lost their jobs in the early 1970s as the totalitarian ring tightened.

freedom of expression, in spite of the difficulties involved. Surviving the sclerosis of socialist realism, the contemporary generation of Cuban artists has developed diverse styles, many with strongly anti-establishment undertones, through their often abstract art.

Afro-Cuban mythology and folklore are more apparent in Cuban art than ever before, as seen in the works of Manuel Mendive (b. 1944), one of Cuba's most famous contemporary artists. An initiate in Santería and Palo Monte, he has cultivated an intricate, primitivist style laden with Afro-Cuban symbolism, and

Painting by Mariano Rodríguez.

Víctor Manuel's (1897–1969) stunning 1924 painting Gitana Tropical (Tropical Gypsy), with its echoes of Cézanne and Gauguin, symbolizes the beginning of modernism in Cuban art.

his work is appreciated worldwide. You can see his paintings in the Arte Cubano section of Havana's Museo Nacional de Bellas Artes. Look out, also, for the work of Flora Fong (b. 1941), of Cuban-Chinese descent, who combines Caribbean colors with a light touch that hints at her ethnicity. She also works with ceramics, stained glass, and textiles.

Artecalle, or street art, developed in the 1980s, whereby young artists displayed their highly expressive work outdoors, away from the official galleries where their paintings could be censored. The streets of Havana became a living exhibition where painters not only displayed their canvases, but also turned the streets into studios in which they created their work. Because of its dissident style, this rejection of official art was finally suppressed. Some exponents were harassed by the police and most of their work was confiscated. Many young artists left Cuba, although some established their

Rural scene by Eduardo Abela.

names abroad without breaking their ties with the government. Many of these artists, who trained in the 1980s and were part of a movement where everything was questioned and deconstructed, are still based in Cuba, while exhibiting regularly around the world.

Carlos Garaicoa (b. 1967) studied thermodynamics before enrolling at the Instituto Superior de Arte in 1989. He uses a multidisciplinary approach including architectural models, drawings, photographs, and videos to portray the failure of modernism as a catalyst for social change.

Tania Bruguera (b. 1968), an installation and performance artist, divides her time between Havana and Chicago, creating, teaching, and exhibiting, while her work is held in collections ranging from the Wifredo Lam Center in Havana to the Museum of Modern Art in New York. Much of her work concerns issues of power and control. Controversially, in 2009 at a gallery in Havana, she told the audience that for one minute they could say whatever they liked into the microphone. Several chose to ask for freedom and democracy – the government denounced it as 'an anti-cultural event of shameless opportunism.'

José Angel Toirac (b. 1966) came to public attention with his 1996 *Tiempos Nuevos* series in which he portrayed Castro in well-known

Ceramic art at Martha Jiménez Pérez' studio in Camagüey.

advertisements, such as Marlboro and Calvin Klein, interpreted to illustrate the way in which Cubans are caught between two rival systems.

Theater

The 19th century was a golden age for Cuban theater, as philanthropists financed the construction of magnificent auditoriums, and going to the theater became an increasingly popular pastime. Notable playwrights emerged, such as Gertrudis Gómez de Avellaneda, José Jacinto Milanés, José María de Heredia, and Joaquín Lorenzo Luaces, whose work is still appreciated today. However, the beginning of the 20th century saw the decline of drama. The government was indifferent, playwrights

Two of Cuba's best playwrights, Eduardo Manet and José Triana, went to live in Paris. Manet's Las Monjas (The Nuns) has been translated into more than 30 languages. Triana's Worlds Apart premiered in Stratford-upon-Avon.

struggled and audiences dropped off. By the middle of the 20th century playwrights were lucky to get their work staged and performances usually lasted for one night only.

In the 1950s ten *salitas*, 'pocket theaters,' were opened in Havana, attracting regular audiences. New playwrights emerged, some of whom became the greats of the 20th century. The most important were Virgilio Piñera (1912–79), Carlos Felipe (1911–75), and Rolando Ferrer (1925–76). There was an eclectic mix of Spanish melodramas, romantic comedies, British and Broadway hits, and European avant-garde, as well as Cuban dramas. The success of the pocket theaters allowed plays to be staged in larger venues and to run for several weeks instead of days, increasing quality and professionalism. The government took an interest and playwrights were paid for their works, and received copyright.

The momentum continued after the revolution. In 1959, 48 Cuban plays were produced, more than the total shown in 1952–8, while in the 1960s almost 400 Cuban plays were premiered. Drama was divided more or less between realistic and experimental. From 1965–70 the theater reflected the artistic and ideological struggles going on in the country;

ART IN CAMAGÜEY

Not all artists gravitate to Havana. Camagüey also has a surprising number, whose studios are usually open to visitors (see www.pprincipe.cult.cu). Nazario Salazar Martínez is known for ceramics, paintings, and graphic design. Orestes Larios Zaak is a painter but you can see other artists at his workshop working on ceramics, ironwork, and paintings. Lorenzo Linares Duque is known for landscapes and paintings of cockerels. Martha Jiménez Pérez is a painter and sculptor, whose work can be seen in the Plaza del Carmen. Ileana Sánchez Hing is a Naïve painter whose recent work includes colorful paintings of gay and lesbian couples.

few theater companies traveled abroad and few foreign companies visited, leaving Cuban theater isolated and xenophobic.

The 1970s were the dark ages. In 1971 the first national Congress of Education and Culture approved repressive measures relating to art and culture, including removing homosexuals from positions of contact with youth. Many actors, directors, designers, and playwrights lost their jobs; a list was made of forbidden plays and authors; theater groups were disbanded and others created, including the Bertolt Brecht Political Theater. Audiences voted with their feet. Subsequently, the 1970s saw the creation of Teatro Nuevo, a grass-roots movement with state support whose best example was the Grupo de Teatro Escambray. Living in a rural community, so as to understand the lives of the people, they worked collectively. Alibio Paz, a member of the group, became a notable playwright, concentrating on contemporary themes and debate in the context of rural traditions and cultural attitudes.

Gradually, although nothing was said officially, a less dogmatic period followed in the 1980s. Some of the previously banned theater workers were allowed back in and playwrights' work was published. It was too late for some, who had either died or fled the country, but some playwrights who suffered in the 1970s, such as Tomás González and Eugenio Hernández Espinosa, were rehabilitated. In the 1990s many of the works of the 1950s and 1960s were rediscovered, while among new authors were Abilio Estévez, Alberto Pedro Torriente, Joel Cano, Ricardo Muñoz, Reinaldo Montero, and Raúl Alfonso. Ideological debate is now tolerated, and many of the issues currently under discussion in society are being aired on the stage. There is a wide range of theater companies, from conventional to experimental, street theater, rural, provincial, political, or works for children, interpreting a wide range of foreign and national plays.

Havana street theater performance by psychiatric hospital patients.

Dance

Although touring companies visited, including the great Romantic ballerina Fanny Elssler in 1842 and Anna Pavlova in 1917, there was no home-grown ballet in Cuba until the Sociedad Pro-Arte Música started ballet evenings in 1931. Its conservatory produced Alicia Alonso, the most influential Cuban dancer and ballet director ever, and the two Alonso brothers, Alberto (dancer and choreographer) and Fernando (dancer, ballet director, and husband of Alicia). Born Alicia Ernestina de la Caridad del Cobre Martínez Hoyo on December 21, 1920, she trained with the School of American Ballet in New York before becoming a professional ballerina. A detached retina forced periods of inactivity, but she continued to dance, working with many of the leading choreographers such as Anthony Tudor. She was known for her classical style and flawless technique, and her interpretation of *Giselle* is a benchmark against which all others are judged.

In 1948 Alicia and her husband returned to Havana to set up her own company, Ballet Alicia Alonso, and two years later came a school. She continued to perform abroad, using her earnings to fund her Cuban enterprises. When Castro was fighting in the Sierra Maestra she sent him a message appealing for support. He did not forget and soon after the revolution he came knocking on her door. He asked what she needed to create a ballet and she requested a ballet school and funding to maintain a company. She got it. Her company was converted into the Ballet Nacional de Cuba and the National Ballet School was created. State funding provides free ballet education to anyone in Cuba selected on the basis of talent. The company has won international acclaim for its repertoire, which includes classical and modern works, many by Cuban choreographers. When not touring abroad, the company performs mainly in Havana's Gran Teatro or Teatro Nacional. Despite no peripheral vision and increasing blindness, Alonso still directs the company, having memorized all the major works.

Members of the British Royal Ballet pay tribute to Alicia Alonso at García Lorca Theatre, Havana.

The world-famous ballet star, Carlos Acosta (b. 1973), owes his training to the National Ballet School and is a protégé of Alicia Alonso. He currently dances with the Royal Ballet in London and in 2009 he helped to organize a visit by the company to Cuba, the first time for more than 30 years that an international dance company had been to the island. Spectacularly popular, thousands watched the classical and avant-garde dances on outdoor screens when tickets sold out. In 2010, Alicia Alonso, aged 89 and blind, took the Ballet Nacional de Cuba to tour the UK in sell-out performances.

The Camagüey Ballet, founded shortly after the Revolution, once had an impressive reputation, but has lost some of its best dancers to the bright lights of the capital. Contemporary dance is also flourishing. Danza Contemporánea de Cuba, under Miguel Iglesias, grew out of Conjunto Nacional de Danza Modernas, begun by Ramiro Guerra in the early post-revolutionary years. Another company, Ballet Rakatan, fuses contemporary and traditional dance styles with flamenco and Afro-Cuban rhythms. The Ballet Folklórico Cutumba, based

Carlos Acosta is acknowledged as one of the greatest dancers ever, on a par with Rudolf Nureyev and Mikhail Baryshnikov. His soaring leaps have earned him the nicknames of 'the flying Cuban' or 'Air Acosta.'

in Santiago de Cuba, performs vibrant ritual dances and chants from the Afro-Cuban cultures, and there are many amateur dance groups across the country that dedicate their efforts to maintaining elements of African culture.

Performance by Danza Contemporánea de Cuba.

Literature

Cuba has produced some outstanding writers, some of whom have an international reputation: Guillermo Cabrera Infante (see page 109); Alejo Carpentier (1904–80), who moved to Paris in 1966 where he served as Cuban Ambassador; poet, playwright, and critic Severo Sarduy (1937–93); and poet and novelist José Lezama Lima (1910–76). All are leading lights of Latin American literature. Backtracking to the 19th century, Cuba's brightest star was poet and revolutionary, José Martí (see page 42).

Before the Revolution, many Cuban writers had gone abroad, and several returned during a period of literary renaissance in the early 1960s, when they received preferential access to housing and a guaranteed income. Writers like the poet Nicolás Guillén were given official patronage by the revolutionary government, and some were even sent overseas as cultural attachés.

However, the international literary scandal known as the Padilla Affair changed all that. In 1968, Herberto Padilla (who died in Alabama in 2000) won an award for his book *Fuero del Juego (Out of the Game)*, a collection of poems that discredited the myths of revolutionary society. Though the award was given by a prestigious international jury, the book was banned in Cuba, and Padilla was arrested. This caused an outcry among intellectuals abroad, including writers like Gabriel García Márquez and Jean-Paul Sartre, who had until then been supportive of Castro's regime.

After this, a large number of writers were marginalized and their books taken out of circulation. The era of limited toleration of literary dissent had ended. Many writers left, including Guillermo Cabrera Infante, winner of the 1997 Cervantes Prize, the most prestigious Spanish-language literature award, who is often described as Cuba's greatest 20th-century author. He lived in London from 1965 until his death 40 years later, and remained highly critical of Castro and his regime.

In 1987, the Cuban leadership re-evaluated the issue of artistic censorship, and in the 1990s, because of the massive exodus of writers and artists, the government took a more lenient attitude toward literary taboos.

In addition to the writers mentioned above, other Cuban writers well worth reading – both those who stayed and those who left – are anthropologist Miguel Barnet (b. 1940), whose best-known work is *Biografía de un Cimarrón (The Autobiography of a Runaway Slave)*, published in 1967; Lydia Cabrera – famous for her studies into Afro-Cuban religions – who died in 1991; Lisandro Otero González (1932–2008), whose most recent work, *Charada*, was published in Havana in 2004; and Reinaldo Arenas, whose openly gay lifestyle led to his imprisonment, and who left for Miami in the Mariel Boatlift. He committed suicide in New York in 1990. His autobiography, *Before Night Falls*, was made into a highly acclaimed movie in 2000. His major work was *Pentagonia*, a series of five novels published over a number of years.

Guillermo Cabrera Infante.

Cuban writers now find it easier to express their ideas without heavy censorship, and many poets and novelists feel they are carrying on where literature left off in the 1960s. Popular authors such as Pedro Juan Gutiérrez and Leonardo Padura Fuentes write about the difficulties of making a living in Havana and are openly critical of the sacrifices demanded by the state.

Nicolás Guillén (1902–89) was a lifelong communist and after the revolution enjoyed the prestige of being Cuba's National Poet.

Cinema

Film is the most favored of the arts. Cuban cinema kicked off with the arrival of Castro and the Cuban Institute of Cinematography (ICAIC). A militant cinema industry set about promoting the advantages of the socialist system. Cuban documentaries were shown in the most remote corners of the island. Inspired by this movement, other Latin American film-makers created political documentaries that became a vehicle for left-wing liberation movements around the world.

In 1986 one of the best film schools in the world was founded in San Antonio de los Baños (see page 184) by Colombian novelist Gabriel García Márquez, Argentine poet and film-maker, Fernando Pirri, and Cuban film-maker, Julio García Espinosa. Thousands of students from Asia, Africa, and Latin America have studied there, and it is relatively free from following the constraints of the official party line.

The leading light among Cuba's film directors was Tomás Gutiérrez Alea (1928–96). His 1969 movie *Memorias del Subdesarrollo (Memories of Underdevelopment)*, about a middle-class Cuban who refuses to leave for Miami in the

FILM FESTIVALS

The New Latin American Film Festival, founded in 1979 and held in Havana every December, may not be as well known in Europe as the festivals in Cannes and Venice, but it attracts film-makers and actors from all over the world. Its prestigious Coral prizes are the Latin American equivalent of the Oscars. The International Low-Budget Film Festival, founded in 2003 by the late film-maker Humberto Solás, is held in Gibara in Holguín province in April every year, showcasing films that have cost less than US$300,000 to make. There are categories for documentaries, short feature films, and experimental video projects.

early 1960s but is unable to fit into revolutionary society, is a modern classic. His 1966 comedy *La Muerte de un Burócrata (Death of a Bureaucrat)* is also well worth seeing; and *Fresa y Chocolate* (1994), co-directed by Juan Carlos Tabío, created a stir inside and outside Cuba.

Although Cuba is full of creative energy, most cultural institutions felt the crunch of economic crisis during the 'Special Period' in the 1990s. The film industry was all but shut down and most new movies were made with foreign money. Book publishing was badly hit, too. Writers, artists, actors, and film-makers struggled to survive. Fortunately, things are picking up again now.

Economic woes also saw a return to a harsher government attitude, and it seemed that the period of relative tolerance had been a false dawn. Movies such as the well-received 1995 comedy *Guantanamera* and Oscar-nominated *Fresa y Chocolate* (both directed by Gutiérrez Alea and Juan Carlos Tabío) were severely criticized by Castro in a speech in 1997, arousing fears among the artistic community – and those who simply enjoyed cinema – of a return to the dark days of total censorship.

The head of ICAIC, Alfredo Guevara (a life-long communist and friend of Castro), gave an emotional press conference defending the movies. But after a flurry of resignations and a meeting between Castro and leading artists, the official position prevailed, and Guevara stated that artistic 'mistakes' had been made, and that the artistic community must be careful not to damage public morale or values.

Poster for the groundbreaking film, Fresa y Chocolate.

A still from the 2005 movie Habana Blues.

Contemporary Cuba in film

Recent movies depicting contemporary Cuba include *Suite Habana* (2003), directed by Fernando Pérez Valdés. A documentary without dialog, chronicling a day in the life of several real people in the city, it has been widely praised. It can be interpreted as critical and subversive or as a tribute to the resilience of people supporting the revolution. *Habana Blues* (2005) is a Spanish-Cuban co-operative effort, directed by Benito Zambrano, a Spaniard who studied at the San Antonio de Baños film school and who has described the movie as his homage to Havana. *El Cuerno de la Abundancia* (*Horn of Plenty*, 2008), directed by Juan Carlos Tabío, is an affectionate comedy based on a true story of a family in a small town who hear they may have inherited a fortune in London. It follows their hopes and dreams, their struggles against bureaucracy, their greed and their fights, until they discover that the inheritance has gone to a branch of the family in Miami.

Fruit stall at the Camagüey farmers' market.

THE ESSENCE OF CUBAN FOOD

The items on Cuban menus may all seem pretty similar, but there is good-quality food to be found, although not always in the obvious places, along with some delicious fresh fruit – not to mention the cocktails.

Most Cuban food is simple. It is the fare of *el campo* (the countryside), which reflects local harvests and earthy suggestions of its Spanish and African roots. It allows, for instance, a dish of Galician inspiration to be served together with African-style accompaniments. Cuban cooking isn't fancy, but Cubans love food.

The Cuban staples

If Cuban creole *(criollo)* cuisine had a national dish, it would, without question, be roast pork *(puerco or cerdo)* served with black beans *(frijoles)*, white rice *(arroz)*, and plantains *(plátanos)*, which is what people eat at New Year celebrations. Rice and beans are traditionally prepared in two forms: kidney beans with rice, known as *moros y cristianos* (Moors and Christians), or black beans with rice *(congrí)*. A delicious soupy stew of black beans *(potaje)* is sometimes served alongside plain white rice.

Food gets into the music. The island's most famous singer, Beny Moré, teased the marranito, the little pig: 'We're going to make you jamón (ham) and chicharrón (pork scratchings').

Black beans – a Cuban creole staple ingredient.

Root vegetables are also popular accompaniments, particularly *yuca* (also called cassava, a starchy tuber), *malanga*, and *boniato*. *Malanga* is not unlike yuca, and *boniato* is a tasty kind of sweet potato.

Chicken *(pollo)* appears on many menus – invariably fried. Fish *(pescado)* is usually *pargo* (snapper) or any plain steak of white fish that is simply called *pescado*.

The ingredients, herbs, and spices most used in traditional Cuban cooking are cumin, oregano, parsley, sour oranges, and *ajo* – garlic. *Sofrito*, a paste of chopped onion, garlic, and green pepper sizzled in oil, is the basis of many dishes. In these days of scarce ingredients, a popular seasoning for vegetables and meat is a tasty mixture of sour orange, garlic, and oil, called *mojo*. You won't often find meat stews on a menu, but look out for the *ajiaco*, a classic infusion of meat and vegetables.

Although you can see piles of seasonal vegetables in markets, you don't often find them in restaurants. Salad often means a heap of grated white cabbage slightly pickled with a vinegar dressing. However, when you do get fresh produce – tomatoes, for example – they can be delicious, full of flavor, and invariably organic.

During the 'Special Period,' the tough years after the collapse of the Soviet Union when there were shortages of absolutely everything, Cuba became the land of 'no hay' – which means, 'there isn't any,' and people had to learn to cook with whatever was available. Lean times forced a new kind of cuisine upon the Cuban people, who became masters of improvisation, stretching and enhancing rice with whatever was available, planning vegetarian meals in a culinary culture obsessed with meat.

Delicious home-cooked food at a paladar.

The opening of farmers' markets *(agropecuarios)* in 1994 made a wider choice of ingredients available. These are markets where farmers sell their surplus produce, after the state has bought its quota, and you will find a wide range of goods on sale, from fresh vegetables to meat, eggs, and honey. The food you eat in *paladares* will have come from an *agropecuario*. Unfortunately these products are relatively expensive and most local people can't afford them.

Some things, such as beef, lobster and shrimp, are primarily for the export and tourist markets and can only be bought in *pesos convertibles* (CUC). If you stay in a *casa particular* (see page 322) and order dinner (in some towns your *casa* may be the best place to eat), your host may ask you if you would like *pollo de mar* (sea chicken), as if the word lobster should not even be mentioned. But if you want it, it will be available.

Fruit

Fruit in Cuba is a delight, and so are the juices made from it. Everything is harvested in season, when it is at its peak: sweet, juicy pineapples, grapefruits that need no sugar, mangos like you've never tasted before, and bananas – the

THE VERSATILE PLANTAIN

Cuban cooking exalts lowly ingredients. Take, for instance, the plantain, *el plátano*. You can fry it ripe *(maduro)* in slices, green *(verde)* in paper-thin chips *(chicharitas)*, or in thicker (green) wedges, to be squashed and fried again for tostones. You can boil chunks, ripe or green, mash them with a fork, drizzle with olive oil, and sprinkle with crunchy fried pork rinds for *fu fú* – a dish of west African origin and something of an acquired taste. You can fill mashed plantains with *picadillo*, minced meat, and melted white cheese to make a *pastel de plátano*. In fact, you can do just about anything except eat them uncooked.

Sugar is the basis of Cuba's fine rum, but also for one of its favorite non-alcoholic drinks, guarapo, which is the cloudy, sweet juice of raw, pressed sugar cane. You will see it being sold from carts in the street.

small, chunky ones are the best. Avocados, too, are at their perfect, creamy best when picked straight from the tree. Unless you buy it in markets you are most likely to come across fruit on the breakfast table of a *casa particular* or the breakfast buffet in a hotel. Despite being plentiful and cheap it is rarely offered as a dessert. Freshly squeezed fruit juices can be found in many bars, in whatever variety is most available – ask for *jugo natural* to get the real thing.

Cakes in Cuba – often thickly iced in bright colors and ultra-sweet.

Sweet treats

The role of dessert on Cuban menus is usually played by ice cream (and it is generally very good, too) or the ubiquitous *flan*, a caramel custard. Cubans do, on the whole, have a sweet tooth – you just need to look in a bakery window at the fluffy pink and baby-blue iced confections to realize that. If you are in Cuba for Mother's Day (the second Sunday in May) you will see special versions of these cakes being handed out of bakers' storefronts to waiting crowds and, everywhere you go, notice people carrying them home, often one in each hand, or balancing them on bicycle handlebars.

In the east of the island, try the *cucurucho* for the ultimate in sweetness. This is grated coconut, sometimes flavored with fruit juice and (mostly) sugar and sold in ingeniously fashioned banana-leaf wrappings.

Cuban rum

The first thing that comes to mind in relation to drinking in Cuba is rum. Along with cigars, this is Cuba's best-known product. Rum, of course, is a sugar-based alcohol, and Cuba has always had plenty of sugar. The best-known and biggest brand is Havana Club. There are various types, but you will most often find Añejo 3 Años, Añejo Reserva, and Añejo 7 Años, of which the latter is the best. There is also a white rum, Añejo Blanco. Although Bacardi rum originated in Cuba (in Santiago) it is no longer made or sold here. The Bacardi family, fiercely opposed to Castro, had their business appropriated and left the island after the Revolution. Bacardi is now made in Puerto Rico.

A good, aged rum (*ron* in Spanish) can be drunk neat, like a brandy or whisky (ask for *ron de siete años*), but white or three-year-old rum is used as the basis of Cuba's famous cocktails: the *mojito* (rum, lime, mint, and soda water), the *daiquirí* (rum, lime juice, sugar, and crushed ice), the *piña colada* (rum with pineapple juice and coconut), and the Cuba Libre. The latter – which means Free Cuba – originated at the end of the 1898 War of Independence and was made with rum and Coca-Cola.

Beer and wine

As well as rum, Cubans are also very fond of beer, which is hardly surprising in this hot climate. Cristal, a light beer made by the Mayabe Brewery, can be found all over the island. The same brewery makes Mayabe, ordinary and extra, which has more flavour. Hatuey beer is made in Havana but is not always easy to find. Bucanero is made in Holguín and found mostly in the east, while Tínimo, made in Camagüey, can be difficult to obtain outside that city.

You can buy wine in some places, certainly in the better hotels and restaurants, but don't expect to find it everywhere. There is small-scale wine production in Pinar del Río province (see page 191), sold under the Soroa label, but most of the available wine comes from Chile or Argentina.

Home-grown coffee

Cuba produces and consumes some excellent coffee, mainly Arabica, the majority of which is grown in the Sierra Maestra region where the mountainous climate is ideal. Ask for a *café con leche* if you want coffee with hot milk – this is normally drunk at breakfast time. A *café cubano* or *cafecito* (little coffee) is small and strong like an espresso, except that it will come ready sweetened unless you ask for it '*sin azúcar*,' although many Cubans, known for liking sweet things, think this is a little bit odd.

Havana Club white rum is usually used for cocktails such as the mojito; the dark version can be drunk neat.

MOJO CRIOLLO

This is the classic sauce for pork, but it is also used to add flavor to vegetables, such as *malanga*.

For four people:

8 garlic cloves, chopped, 1 tsp salt
1 tsp ground oregano (optional)
½ tsp ground cumin (optional)
½ cup sour orange juice
½ cup olive oil

Mash the garlic and salt to form a paste. Blend in the spices. Add the sour orange juice and leave for 30 minutes; stir in the olive oil. Sour orange juice appears in many Cuban recipes but you can substitute sweet orange juice and lime or lemon juice.

Eating out

A good *paladar* or a meal in a *casa particular* will introduce you to Cuban food at its best, far removed from a soulless state restaurant.

State-owned restaurants can be identified by the credit card stickers on the door. A few are good, particularly in Havana, but most are boring, offering poor-quality food and even worse service. They will invariably charge you in CUC$. They do, however, offer some variety in cuisine, with Italian, Spanish, or Chinese the most common. Resort hotels usually have buffet and à la carte restaurants where you can find something you like, although the food often appears recycled or reheated. At the cheaper end of the state sector are fast-food joints, burger bars, or fried chicken places for a greasy snack. Bars and cafés have snacks and light meals for lunch but sandwiches are usually cheese, ham, or cheese and ham, made with stodgy white bread.

In Santiago and other towns in the east of the island, the government has opened a few restaurants that charge in pesos Cubanos. They are designed to appeal to Cubans and offer them affordable dining to improve their social wellbeing, but there is nothing to stop tourists eating there too, at a fraction of the cost of a CUC establishment. There are some teething problems but many are worth trying. Street stands also charge in pesos, selling lunch-time sandwiches and stodgy pizza, but check these carefully if you are concerned about hygiene. Most are best avoided.

Illegal Eateries Legalized

For many years after the 1959 revolution, family-run restaurants were illegal, as was virtually every kind of private enterprise. They operated clandestinely, yet everyone knew where they were; even policemen and party members could be seen eating in them. Then, in 1994, the law was changed and these establishments, called *paladares*, could start doing business more openly. Cuba was suddenly full of *paladares* offering cheap home cooking – usually serving the traditional menu of pork, beans, and rice.

In 1996, the government realized that it had created a highly successful, profitable sector of the economy that was making some people too wealthy. Consequently, *paladares* had to register, meet strict public-health standards, and pay both a license fee and devastatingly high taxes – as much as US$1,000 a month in Havana, regardless of how many meals were served. As a result, many *paladares* went out of business or were driven underground again.

Now, however, the state is encouraging private enterprise and has relaxed some restrictions, particularly on the number of covers and employment of staff from outside the family. There has been another explosion in the number of privately-run restaurants, many of which, with money sent by family in Miami, have invested in equipment and décor and are very good.

International dishes are often on the menu at top hotels and resorts such as Havana's Hotel Nacional.

Home Cooking

The alternative to eating out is to eat in your *casa particular*. This may lack the atmosphere of a good *paladar*, but has the advantage of allowing you to order exactly what you want, when you want it. You can be sure that the food will be bought and cooked fresh that day and any special dietary requirements can be met.

Vegetarians often find that this is by far the best option, and many *casa* owners have become quite skilled at providing meat-free meals. You may need to check, however, that beans are not cooked with the traditional lard, and some vegetarians prefer to travel with their own cooking oil, which they lend to their hosts.

Yargelis Savigne, world champion triple jumper.

SPORT

One irrefutable triumph of the revolution has been in the domain of athletics. Cuban sportsmen and women regularly dominate world-class opposition, and sporting opportunities for all are regarded as a right.

In 1944, the young Fidel Castro was voted athlete of the year at Belén College in Havana, where baseball was his specialty. 'If I hadn't been an athlete, I wouldn't have been a guerrilla,' Castro has said. He was once offered a professional contract to pitch for a US team but, by his own admission, he was not major-league material. Had Castro's arm been better, he might never have taken up arms against Batista, and the world would have been a very different place. Cuba might still be a playground for wealthy Americans, and it is extremely unlikely that there would have been a large sign displayed outside the Cuban national sports training center, proclaiming '*Fidel: Atleta Número Uno*.'

Sport in revolutionary Cuba is seen as an integral part of one's physical and moral education. In the words of Castro himself, 'Sport is an antidote to vice.'

Baseball is a national obsession.

The right of the people

Less than a month after taking power, Castro addressed Cuba's assembled sports organizations and declared: 'It is a shame that sport has been so undervalued. Less than 10 percent of our youth participate in sports. We must promote them at all costs. We must inundate every corner of the island with sports equipment. We should strive to improve our athletes rapidly.'

Another Castro quotation is plastered around sports arenas: 'Sport is the right of the people.' With the creation of the National Institute of Sports, Physical Education and Recreation (INDER) in 1961, Cuba began to fulfill this pledge. Today, nearly half the population has participated in organized sports.

At the base of Cuba's sporting pyramid are its 80,000 elementary school children. Every year students compete in the School Sports Games. Those who excel are eligible to be tested for admission to the Schools for Sports Initiation (EIDE), which trains students ranging in age from 11 to 16. EIDE students attend regular classes, but they are also given advanced coaching and face high-level competition. Those who perform best graduate to one of the Schools of Higher Athletic Performance (ESPA) where students hope to be noticed by a coach from the national ESPA in Havana.

Incentives

It took more than a decade for this system to make an impact on the sports world, but when it did, it did so with a bang. Teófilo Stevenson (1952–2012), a heavyweight boxer from eastern Cuba, won a gold medal at the 1972 Olympics in Munich. Stevenson won another gold at the 1976 Games in Montreal, where another great Cuban athlete, Alberto Juantorena (b. 1950), won gold medals in the 400- and 800-meter races – the first man ever to win both events in one Olympic Games. Stevenson won a third gold medal in Moscow in 1980. They are two illustrations of another Cuban sports philosophy: 'The greatest incentive that can be given to an athlete,' Castro said in 1959, 'is security in their retirement and a proper reward for champions.' Juantorena holds several official posts in Cuban sport and is a member of the IAAF Council.

Brothers training in a makeshift gym at the back of their home.

International events

Overall, Cuba has performed very well at international sporting events for a nation of its size. In the Pan-American Games, Cuba stands second behind the US in the overall medals table. Its greatest success in these games came in 1991, when it played host to the event. Cuba had staked significant prestige on the outcome, managing to stage the games despite the financial strictures caused by the collapse of the Soviet Union and the subsequent loss of Soviet subsidies. The risk paid off, with Cuba becoming only the second nation ever to displace the US at the top of the tree – an obvious reason for national pride.

The nation has likewise punched above its weight at the Olympics, although it has slipped slightly in the table of nations. At the 1992 Olympics in Barcelona, Cuba was the fifth-highest medal winner with 31, surpassing larger countries such as France and Britain. In Atlanta in 1996, they came eighth with 25 medals; in Sydney in 2000 they came ninth in the overall table; in Athens in 2004 they came 11th, winning 27 medals, including nine golds; in Beijing in 2008 they came 12th, winning 24 medals (two gold, 11 silver, 11 bronze); and in London in 2012 they came 16th, with 14 medals (five gold, three silver, six bronze).

Although it has a good record in athletics and some martial arts like judo and taekwondo, the real mainstay in terms of medal-winning is in boxing – one of the island's sporting passions. 'To beat an American is the most important thing,' said one Cuban boxer. 'Knocking out an American is better than knocking out a better boxer. It's transcendent.'

Baseball

Another Cuban passion is baseball, which came to the island at the end of the 19th century, when the North American influence was starting to outweigh that of Spain. The first games were played in around 1865 between Cuban dock workers and US sailors. Spanish authorities associated the game with the cause of Cuban independence – and revenues from baseball games did, indeed, support José Martí's independence movement. As a result, the game was banned in parts of the country in 1895.

Repeated visits from US Marines after independence heightened baseball's popularity, as did the increasing numbers of North American players seeking Caribbean warmth and winter paychecks. Though the sport was originally the realm of Cuba's economic elite, it quickly caught on among all classes of society.

All over Cuba you will see evidence of the game's popularity. Even the smallest community has a baseball field, and in city streets you will see small boys practicing shots – even when they only have a stick, and perhaps a tin can for a ball.

The Cuban national baseball team wait for play in the dugout.

GOLD MEDALIST – YARGELIS SAVIGNE

Born in 1984 in Niceto Pérez, 'Yayi,' as she is known in Cuba, is a prime example of the success of the Cuban sports education system, having attended the Rafael Freyre EIDE Sports School on the outskirts of Guantánamo. With professional coaching, she progressed through National School Games to National Junior Championships until she made the national junior team in 2001. At her international debut she won the 2002 CAC Junior crown for the long jump in Barbados. As a senior, she joined the Cuban team for their 2005 European tour, competing in the triple jump and the long jump. That year was her breakthrough: she won silver in the triple jump at the World Championships in Helsinki and bronze at the World Athletics Final in Monaco.

By 2007 Savigne was a world champion triple jumper, winning gold at the World Championships, Osaka (15.28 meters), the Pan-American Games, Rio de Janeiro, and the World Athletics Final in Stuttgart. In 2008 she took the gold at the World Indoor Championships in Valencia. In 2009 she won gold at the World Championships in Berlin, followed that with silver at the World Indoor Championships in Doha, and came first at the Ibero-American Games in Spain in 2010. Since then her distances have reduced. She is coached by Milán Matos and the Olympic long jump champion Iván Pedroso and is managed by high jump champion, Javier Sotomayor.

Major-league riches

The island dominated baseball when it was a full Olympic sport in 1992–2008, winning three of the five golds awarded. The only blemishes came in 2000 in Sydney, when they were beaten into silver-medal position by the US, and in 2008 in Beijing when they were beaten by South Korea.

Defections, however, have become increasingly common, and some of the island's finest players have abandoned Cuba for multimillion-dollar contracts and the chance to play in prestigious United States major leagues. Dozens of Cuban baseball players have defected since the early 1990s, but not all of them elect to stay in the United States – many go on to a third country to negotiate a lucrative contract which is free of US baseball's rules on exclusive rights.

Cuba does export some of its athletic talent through official channels, and INDER has traditionally taken half the earnings of coaches and athletes who go abroad legally to work and compete. Cuban sports personnel work in some 40 different countries and, in 2002, the authorities came to an agreement with Japan's professional baseball leagues for Olympic stars like slugger Orestes Kindelán and third-baseman Omar 'El Niño' Linares to play there. But when it comes to the United States, that avenue is firmly closed. INDER refuses to sanction players leaving for the US, and the US does not permit the wages of professional players to go back to Cuba. The Cuban government had a change of heart in

In 2013 President Castro announced that Cuban athletes would be allowed to sign contracts with foreign teams and keep up to 80% of their prize money as long as they returned to Cuba for major competitive events. Pay rises were also granted to try and prevent defections.

Training on the beach at Trinidad.

THE PRIZE

The year 2006 saw the inaugural World Baseball Classic – the only international competition in which top stars from the US major leagues tend to compete. Initially, it seemed that Cuba was going to be prevented from competing in the US by the American authorities, as prize money would fall foul of anti-Cuban financial sanctions. But the Cuban team received the all-clear when they offered to donate any prize money to victims of Hurricane Katrina, and went on to surpass their hosts in the tournament. They beat the Dominican Republic in the semi-final, but, eventually lost in the final to Japan.

2013, however, to try and deter defections of athletes when competing or working abroad, both through pay rises and allowing those winning medals to receive bonuses, with special performance incentives and prizes for baseball players.

Two of the greats

Among Cuba's outstanding athletes of the 1990s were the runner, Ana Fidelia Quirot, who triumphed in the 800-meter race at the World Championships in 1997 – having made a remarkable comeback from a severe burns accident – and the phenomenal high jumper, Javier Sotomayor (who enjoys the additional prestige of having been a deputy in Cuba's National Assembly). Sotomayor can rightfully lay claim to the title of greatest high jumper of all time. At the age of 16 he set a new record for that age group by clearing 2.33 meters. He frequently broke the world record (pushing the mark up to 2.45 meters in 1993 – a record that still stands); claimed Olympic gold in 1992 (Cuban boycotts meant he missed the 1984 and 1988 Games); and won World Championship golds in 1995 and 1997.

World champion Javier Sotomayer.

Sporting controversy

However, Sotomayor was stripped of the gold medal he won at the 1999 Pan-American Games in Winnipeg, Canada, when he allegedly tested positive for cocaine. The Cubans reacted angrily, accusing the United States of doctoring the tests in order to tarnish Cuba's sporting reputation. Castro launched a campaign to try and clear Sotomayor's name and Cuba refused to suspend him. After his ban was reduced from two years to one, Sotomayor came back to win a silver medal in high jump in Sydney in 2000.

After more than 20 years in the limelight, and after testing positive for an anabolic steroid (an allegation he strongly denied), Sotomayor retired in October 2001, just before his 34th birthday – a grand old age for a high jumper.

OPEN TO ALL – BIG AND SMALL

In Havana, top budding gymnasts train at the Provincial School for Gymnastics, in an ornate colonial building on the Prado. While they hone world-class routines, elsewhere in the building a group of five-year-olds might be working on cartwheels. Despite the disparity between these extremes, there is an air of accessibility to the elite athletes that meshes nicely with the irony of this formerly exclusive club being put to popular use. It is difficult to imagine a top-level national athlete in any other country training alongside primary-school kids, but, like so many of Cuba's apparent contradictions, it seems to work.

View of Trinidad from the Museo Romántico.

Viñales valley.

Old Havana street leading to Capitolio.

Trinidad backstreet.

INTRODUCTION

A detailed guide to the entire archipelago of Cuba, with principal sites clearly cross-referenced by number to the maps.

A proud fisherman.

Most visitors to Cuba spend at least a few days in Havana, one of the most exciting capital cities in the world, despite being a relatively young one. Havana is where five centuries of Cuban history coalesce with the merging of peoples from Europe, Africa, China, and, of course, the Americas, a city saturated with romance, nostalgia, and intrigue. Although sadly dilapidated in parts, it should not be missed, as there is nowhere else like it in Latin America for architecture and culture. A visit here can easily be combined with one of the many beach resorts that have been developed along the north coast, from the well-established Varadero to the luxury now found on the cays, formerly the lonely preserve of fishermen and birds.

However, the 'real Cuba' lies out in the provinces. With a judicious combination of short domestic flights, organized tours, comfortable long-distance buses, taxi rides, and rental cars, you will be able to penetrate the less-frequently visited hinterland.

A watchful youth.

For a pure taste of rural life, to the west of Havana lies the province of Pinar del Río, the tobacco-growing region that is one of the lushest and most spectacular parts of the island. A journey to the central south coast should include visits to Playa Girón on the Bay of Pigs, the wildlife-filled Zapata peninsula, the port of Cienfuegos, and Cuba's colonial jewel, Trinidad. Inland, Santa Clara provides the last resting place of Che Guevara, a Mecca for students of the revolution. The sandy cays off the north coast offer idyllic beach vacations, while the Isla de la Juventud off the south coast is a major diving center.

The rural heartland is the slowest and least-visited part of Cuba, where cities such as Camagüey and Holguín are interesting stopover points, steeped in history and with beach resorts within easy reach. The east has its own thriving identity and traditions. Santiago, Cuba's second city, is often a few steps ahead of Havana in culture and music. The little colonial town of Baracoa is a delight, and exploring the highways, remote beaches, and craggy mountains of the Oriente remains one of Cuba's great adventures.

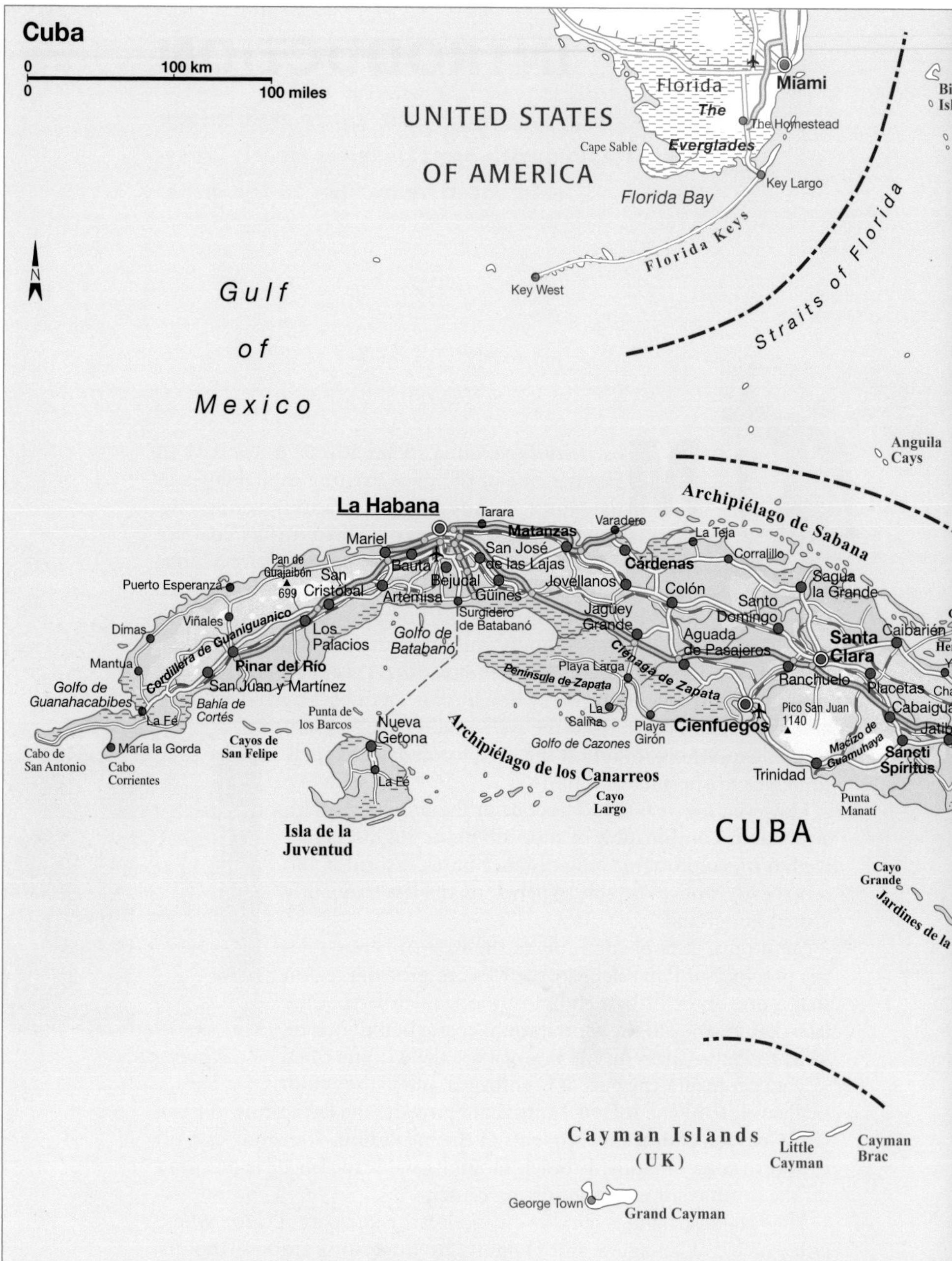
Cuba
0 100 km
0 100 miles
UNITED STATES
OF AMERICA
Florida
The Everglades
Miami
The Homestead
Cape Sable
Key Largo
Florida Bay
Florida Keys
Key West
Straits of Florida
Gulf of Mexico
Anguila Cays
Archipiélago de Sabana
La Habana
Tarara
Matanzas
Varadero
La Teja
Corralillo
Mariel
Bauta
San José de las Lajas
Cárdenas
Pan de Guajaibón 699
San Cristóbal
Bejucal
Güines
Jovellanos
Colón
Sagua la Grande
Puerto Esperanza
Artemisa
Surgidero de Batabanó
Jagüey Grande
Santo Domingo
Viñales
Los Palacios
Golfo de Batabanó
Aguada de Pasajeros
Santa Clara
Caibarién
Dimas
Cordillera de Guaniguanico
Pinar del Río
Ciénaga de Zapata
Playa Larga
Península de Zapata
Ranchuelo
Placetas
Mantua
San Juan y Martínez
Golfo de Guanahacabibes
Bahía de Cortés
La Fé
Punta de los Barcos
Nueva Gerona
La Salina
Playa Girón
Cienfuegos
Pico San Juan 1140
Cabaiguán
Cabo de San Antonio
María la Gorda
Cayos de San Felipe
Golfo de Cazones
Archipiélago de los Canarreos
Macizo de Guamuhaya
Sancti Spíritus
Cabo Corrientes
La Fé
Cayo Largo
Trinidad
Punta Manatí
Isla de la Juventud
CUBA
Cayo Grande
Jardines de la
Cayman Islands (UK)
Little Cayman
Cayman Brac
George Town
Grand Cayman
CARIBBEAN SEA

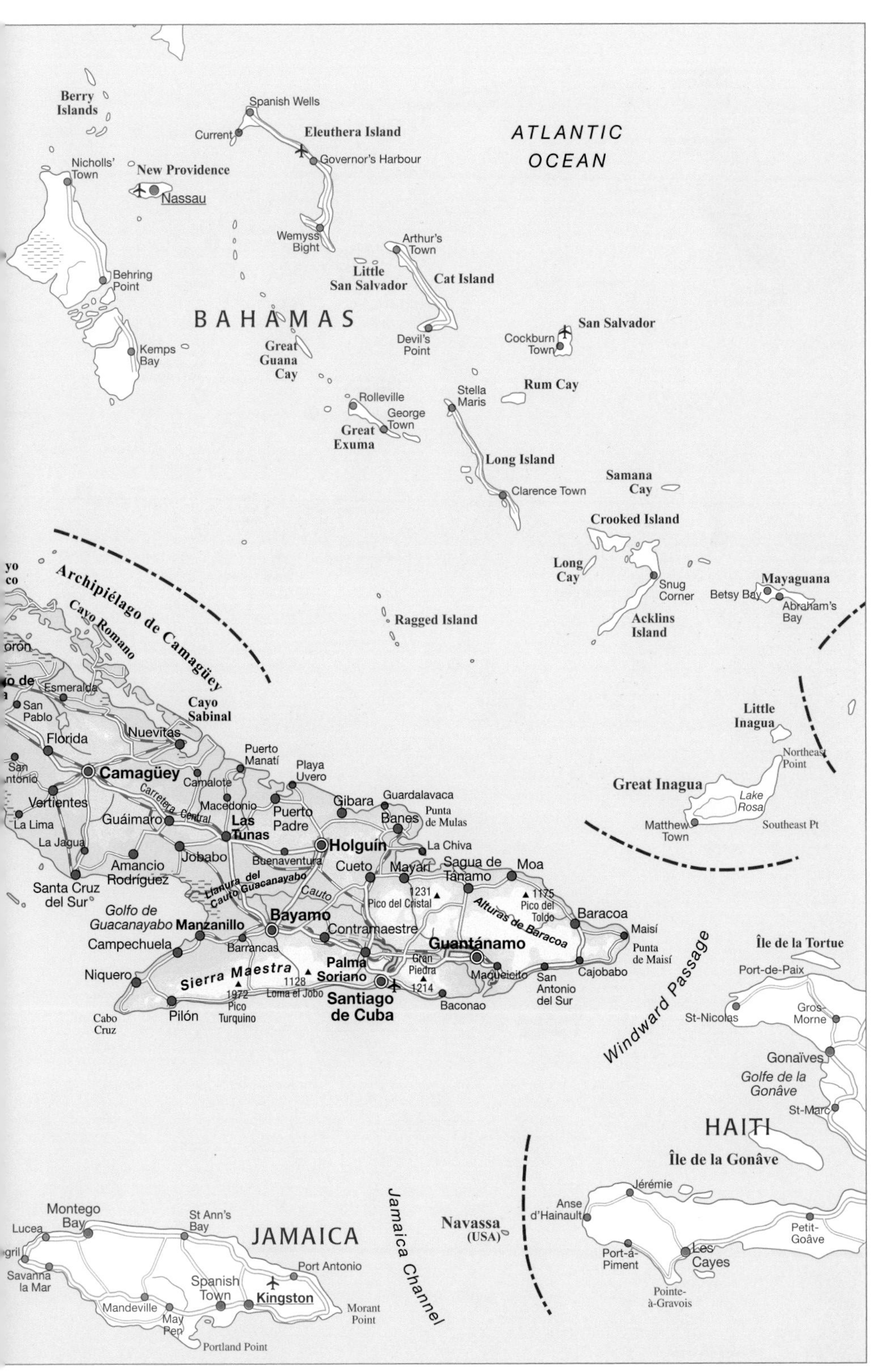
ATLANTIC OCEAN
BAHAMAS
Berry Islands
Spanish Wells
Current
Eleuthera Island
Governor's Harbour
Nicholls' Town
New Providence
Nassau
Wemyss Bight
Arthur's Town
Behring Point
Little San Salvador
Cat Island
Kemps Bay
Great Guana Cay
Devil's Point
San Salvador
Cockburn Town
Rum Cay
Stella Maris
Rolleville
George Town
Great Exuma
Long Island
Clarence Town
Samana Cay
Crooked Island
Long Cay
Snug Corner
Acklins Island
Betsy Bay
Mayaguana
Abraham's Bay
Ragged Island
Little Inagua
Northeast Point
Great Inagua
Lake Rosa
Matthew Town
Southeast Pt
Archipiélago de Camagüey
Cayo Romano
Cayo Sabinal
Esmeralda
San Pablo
Nuevitas
Florida
Camagüey
Vertientes
La Lima
La Jagua
Guáimaro
Carretera Central
Camalote
Macedonio
Puerto Manatí
Playa Uvero
Las Tunas
Puerto Padre
Gibara
Guardalavaca
Banes
Punta de Mulas
Holguín
La Chiva
Jobabo
Buenaventura
Cueto
Mayarí
Sagua de Tánamo
Moa
Amancio Rodríguez
Santa Cruz del Sur
Llanura del Cauto Guacanayabo
Cauto
1231
Pico del Cristal
1175 Pico del Toldo
Alturas de Baracoa
Baracoa
Golfo de Guacanayabo
Manzanillo
Bayamo
Contramaestre
Guantánamo
Maisí
Punta de Maisí
Campechuela
Barrancas
Gran Piedra
Niquero
Sierra Maestra
1128 Loma el Jobo
Palma Soriano
1214
Maqueicito
San Antonio del Sur
Cajobabo
1972 Pico Turquino
Pilón
Santiago de Cuba
Baconao
Cabo Cruz
Windward Passage
Île de la Tortue
Port-de-Paix
St-Nicolas
Gros-Morne
Gonaïves
Golfe de la Gonâve
St-Marc
HAITI
Île de la Gonâve
Jérémie
Anse d'Hainault
Petit-Goâve
Port-à-Piment
Les Cayes
Pointe-à-Gravois
Navassa (USA)
Jamaica Channel
JAMAICA
Montego Bay
Lucea
St Ann's Bay
Port Antonio
Savanna la Mar
Spanish Town
Kingston
Mandeville
May Pen
Morant Point
Portland Point

Miramar, Playa, Siboney
Hotel Riviera
Monumento a Calixto García
Malecón
PARQUE JOSE MARTI (SPORTS GROUND)
Swiss Embassy US Interests' Section
Estrecho de la Florida
Casa de las Américas
Hotel Presidente
(Calzada)
Calle 3
Calle 5
Calle 7
Calle 9
Calle 11
Calle 13
Calle 15
Calle 17
Calle 19
Calle 21
Calle 23
Calle 25
Calle 27
Calle 29
Avenida Washington
Monumento al Maine
Edificio Focsa
Hotel Nacional
Hotel Victoria
Hotel Capri
Avenida O
Avenida N
Avenida M
Avenida L
Avenida K
Avenida J
Avenida I
Avenida H
Linea
Museo de la Danza
Iglesia del Sagrado Corazón de Jesús
Avenida de Los Presidentes (G)
Avenida F
Avenida E
Avenida D
Avenida C
Avenida B
Avenida A
Paseo
COPPELIA Ice Cream Park
Hotel St John
Museo Casa de Abel Santamaría
Humboldt
Hornos
Principe
Vapor
Jovellar
San Lázaro
Hamel
Concordia
Neptuno
San Miguel
San Rafael
San Martín (San José)
Valle
Zanja
Salud
Jesús Peregrino
Pocito
Torreón San Lá
Museo de Artes Decorativas
Hotel Habana Libre
Hotel Vedado
Parque John Lennon
(Rampa)
Universidad de La Habana
Julio Antonio Mella
Calzada de Infanta
Casa de la Amistad
VEDADO
Museo Antropológico Montané
Museo Napoleónico
Mariana Grajales
Estadio Juan Abrahantes
San Francisco
Espada
Hospital
Aramburu
CENTR (CENT
Allende
Castillejo
Soledad
Oquendo
La Tropicana
Castillo del Príncipe
Quinta de los Molinos
Calle 2
Calle 4
Calle 6
Calzada de Zapata
Avenida Salvador Allende (Carlos III)
Casa de Cul de Centro Ha
Enrique Barnet (Estrella)
Lugareño
Bruzón
Desagüe
Benjumeda
Almendares
ESTADIO RAMON FONST
Xifré
Plasencia
Retiro
Árbol Seco
Subirana
Franco
Peñalver
Santo Tomás
Clavel
Santa Marta
CEMENTERIO DE COLÓN
C. Protestantes
Calle 31
Calle 32
Calle 35
Calle 37
Calle 39
Calle 41
Terminal de Omnibuses Astro
Teatro Nacional
Ministerio del Interior
19 de Mayo
Aranguren
Plaza de la Revolución
Paseo
Legado Cultural Hispánico
Monumento José Martí
Julia Borges
Avenida de Colón
Avenida Carlos M. de Céspedes
Territorial
Ave. 20 de Mayo
P. Vidal
(Zaldo)
Arroyo (Avenida Manglar)
San Martín
Palacio de la Revolución
Avenida Rancho Boyeros
Calzada de Ayestaran
Panchito Gómez
Masón
General E. Núñez
M. Abreu
L. Ferrocarril
Amenidad
Pedroso
Bellavista
Panorama
Hidalgo
San Pedro
Estancia
Marino
Lombillo
Ermita
Auditor
San Pablo
CERRO
Estación de Ferrocarriles 19 de Noviembre
Avenida de la Independencia
3ra
2da
Tra
Este
Factor
Tulipán
La Rosa
Ayuntamiento
Clavel
Mariano
Pje. Vista Hermosa
Pedro Pérez
Patria
Estadio Latinoamericano
Universidad
Campos
Estévez
Santa R
Fernandina
Romay
San Joaquín
Cádiz
Zequeira
Borrego
Unión y Ahorro
Connill
José Martí Airport

Havana
El Morro (Castillo de los Tres Santos Reyes Magos del Morro)
Via Monumental
LA HABANA DEL ESTE (EAST HAVANA)
Avenue 1 RA
Tunnel de la Bahía de La Habana
Canal de Entrada
Castillo de San Carlos de la Cabaña
CASABLANCA
Castillo de San Salvador de la Punta
Estudiantes de Medicina
Máximo Gómez
Malecón
Hotel Deauville
PARQUE CESPEDES
Avenida del Puerto
Catedral de La Habana
Plaza de la Catedral
Plaza de Armas
LA HABANA VIEJA (OLD HAVANA)
PARQUE CENTRAL
Barrio Chino (Chinatown)
Capitolio
Nuestra Señora de la Caridad del Cobre
Fábrica de Tabacos Partagás
PARQUE DE LA FRATERNIDAD
Palacio de Aldama
Cruise Terminal Sierra Maestra
Plaza Vieja
Estación Central de Ferrocarriles
Estación La Coubre
Bahía de La Habana
Ensenada de Atarés
Castillo de Atarés
Regla/Guanabacoa
Regla
Avenida Simón Bolívar (Reina)
Máximo Gómez (Monte)
Avenida de España (Vives)
Avenida de Italia (Galiano)
Paseo de Martí (Prado)
Avenida de Bélgica (Monserrate)
Avenida de las Misiones
Desamparado
San Pedro
0 500 m
0 500 yds

Havana's capitol building.

OLD HAVANA

Restored grandeur reveals the might of Spain's most precious colonial city, but Old Havana is more than a living museum. Street life is vibrant and noisy, and just as interesting as the fine architecture.

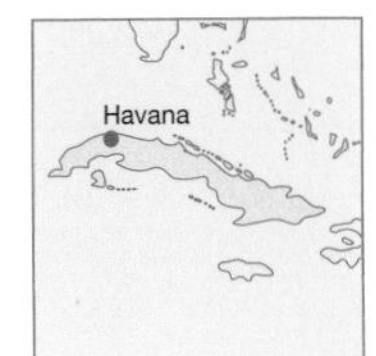

Seen from a distance, Havana looks spectacular. Waves crash over the city's famous seaside promenade, the **Malecón**, where lovers stroll past pastel-colored buildings. Stone fortresses turn golden in the Caribbean light, recalling the days when Havana was the jewel in the Spanish Crown, its harbor full of galleons loaded with South American silver.

The Malecón links two important districts. First, **La Habana Vieja** (Old Havana), a mixture of beautifully renovated squares and buildings, and narrow, noisy streets where Cubans live in cramped conditions. Second, **Vedado**, which was modeled on Miami; most of its tallest buildings are the hotels originally financed by the US Mafia in the 1940s and 1950s. Here, and in the other main western suburb, Miramar, farther afield, the pre-revolutionary mansions of the rich are today occupied either by Cuban families – whose homes crumble splendidly amid lush foliage – or by a number of embassy officials, foreign investors, and Cuban bureaucrats.

Havana is exhilarating, exhausting, with a neurotic, anxious edge to life. It is one of the most fascinating places on earth – a city of great paradox and tremendous presence. As well as Cuba's political and economic center, it is also the focus of Cuba's artistic life, its youth culture, and its aspirations for the future.

La Habana Vieja, Old Havana, is the city's vibrant beating heart. This is where most visitors to Cuba spend the first day or two of their visit, and it's a tremendous place to begin any vacation.

The compact grid of narrow colonial streets, graceful squares, and aristocratic mansions that make up Old Havana was, for some 350 years, the entire city. It was only in the 1860s that the massive city walls were knocked down and *habaneros* began distinguishing the district as 'old.' For

Main Attractions

- Plaza de Armas
- Plaza de la Catedral
- Casa de la Obra Pía
- Plaza Vieja
- Capitolio
- Museo Nacional Palacio de Bellas Artes
- Museo de la Revolución
- El Morro
- Castillo de San Carlos de la Cabaña

Fishing from the Malecón wall.

many years, the area was allowed to languish – which was a blessing in disguise, since it meant Havana escaped the Disneyland-style restoration of some other colonial Caribbean cities. Castro's government prioritized putting money into developing the impoverished countryside, and left the capital untouched.

Colonial havana rescued

In spite of the decay, evident everywhere after such chronic neglect, the 1959 revolution saved Old Havana. During the Batista regime, the area had been scheduled for demolition: cars could not easily pass down the narrow streets, and more land was needed to satisfy the fever for high-rise hotels, casinos, and nightclubs.

Since the old city was placed on the Unesco World Heritage List in 1982, and with the added incentive of turning it into a major tourist attraction, the authorities, under the directorship of the indefatigable Dr Eusebio Leal Spengler, the city historian, have embarked on an ambitious process of restoration. This has rescued sections of the city from decay, and restored many buildings to their former glory, but in other areas, buildings continue to collapse after bad weather. Still, some 150 of Havana's remaining buildings date back to the 16th and 17th centuries, 200 from the 18th, and 460 from the 19th, which makes it the best-preserved colonial city in the Americas.

The restoration of the island's most historical site resulted in demographic changes in what was once one of the liveliest *barrios* (neighborhoods) in the city. People were moved out of the northern part of Old Havana in their thousands, their homes becoming cafés, restaurants, hotels, and museums. Most were rehoused in the less picturesque (but at the time far more comfortable) projects of Alamar that disfigure the city vista east of El Morro. As a result, the well-kept and well-policed streets and squares are now thronged with tourists rather than residents. However, current thinking has become more sensitive to social change, and people are allowed to remain in or return to the renovated buildings.

Vestiges of the life that filled Old Havana can still be seen in the grid of largely unrestored streets between Calle Brasíl (Teniente Rey) and the train station, where hundreds of families inhabit crumbling mansions. Music blares from every window, washing hangs from balconies, boys practice baseball shots, scraggy dogs scavenge for food, and life is lived outdoors to escape the heat of crowded rooms in which air conditioning is not an option.

The heart of the Old City

The **Plaza de Armas** is Havana's oldest square, and the best place to begin any walking tour of the city. In the evening, antique filigree lamps illuminate the space, and on many nights an orchestra plays in the open air. It is the focus for much of the street life of the restored city, and is surrounded

Bookstall in the Plaza de Armas.

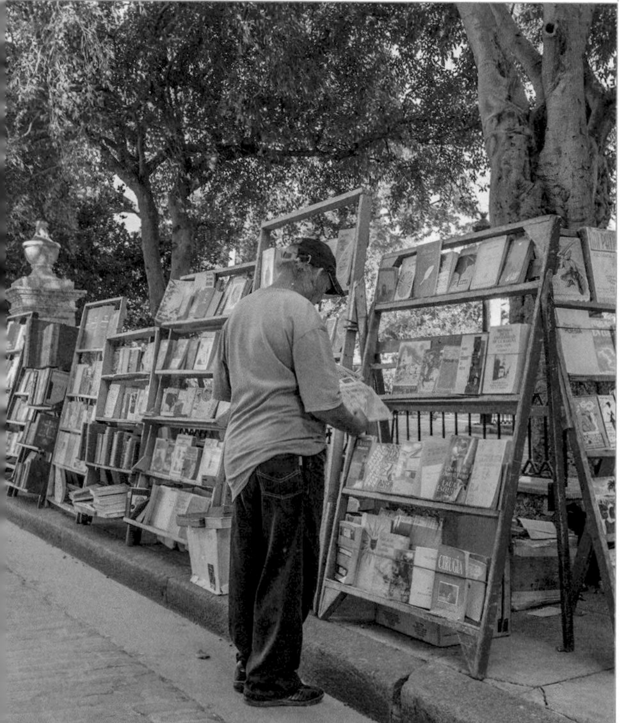

by cafés, bars, and restaurants, such as La Mina (see page 159). In the center of the leafy square is a statue of Carlos Manuel de Céspedes, rebel president and leader of the first War of Independence in the 1860s. A small secondhand book market, which sells revolutionary literature in various languages, is held here (Wed–Sat 10am–6pm); and you will often see costumed troupes of entertainers – stilt-walkers, dancers, and drummers – performing here.

The majestic building on the west side of the plaza, perhaps the finest example of Baroque architecture in Havana, is the **Palacio de los Capitanes Generales** ❶. Completed in 1780, this was home to the Spanish Governor until independence, and of the US Military Governor for the few years thereafter. Cuban presidents lived here until 1917, when they moved to the Capitolio and this became the mayor's office.

Today the palace houses the **Museo de la Ciudad** (City Museum; Tacón 1, between Obispo and O'Reilly; tel: 7-861 5001; daily 9.30am–6pm, last tour 5pm), which has by far the most lavish of Havana's many collections of colonial artifacts. You can visit independently but you get to see more if you take the guided tour. Keep an eye out for the machete of independence fighter General Antonio Maceo, and the dining room with 400 plates hanging on the walls. The King of Spain's Hall was kept constantly ready in case His Majesty ever decided to inspect Havana, though no monarch ever did so. The courtyard garden is delightful, hung with vines and bougainvillea, with a statue of Christopher Columbus at its center.

Nearby, on the south side of the Plaza de Armas, is the **Museo Nacional de Historia Natural** (Obispo 61, between Baratillo and Oficios; tel: 7-863 9361; www.mnhnc.inf.cu; Tue 1pm–5pm, Wed–Sun 10am–5pm), an educational museum with permanent and temporary exhibitions and often full of school children. Among its wide collection of flora and fauna is a beautiful exhibition of Cuban snails.

At the plaza's northeast corner is **El Templete** ❷ (Baratillo 1, between O'Reilly and Narciso López), a Doric-style temple with three large paintings by French artist Jean-Baptiste Vermay inside. One canvas is said to be the first in Cuba to portray black and white people in close company. A column marks the spot where the city was refounded in 1519 as 'La Villa de San Cristóbal de la Habana,' with a Mass being said under the sacred ceiba tree. The original tree was uprooted by a hurricane in 1828 and replacements have been planted several times. The current descendant is still credited with magical powers, partly because ceibas are considered sacred to the Yoruba religion (on which Santería is based). During an annual festival on November 16, *habaneros* celebrate that first Mass: thousands of people fill the square, and often wait many hours to fulfill a ritual – circling the tree three times

El Templete.

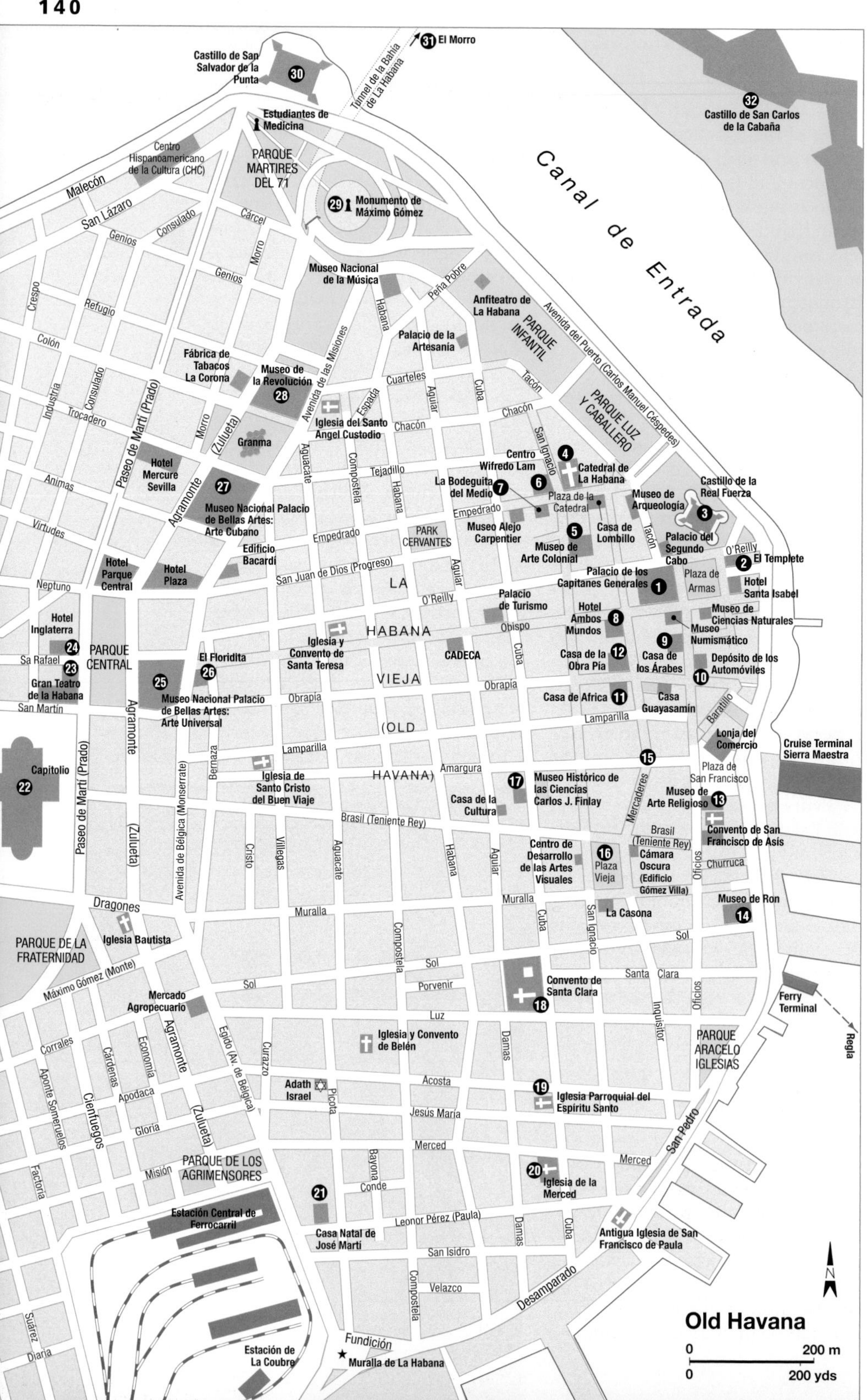

Old Havana
Canal de Entrada
Castillo de San Salvador de la Punta
El Morro
Túnel de la Bahía de La Habana
Castillo de San Carlos de la Cabaña
Estudiantes de Medicina
Centro Hispanoamericano de la Cultura (CHC)
PARQUE MARTIRES DEL 71
Monumento de Máximo Gómez
Museo Nacional de la Música
Anfiteatro de La Habana
PARQUE INFANTIL
Palacio de la Artesanía
Fábrica de Tabacos La Corona
Museo de la Revolución
Granma
PARQUE LUZ Y CABALLERO
Iglesia del Santo Angel Custodio
Centro Wifredo Lam
Catedral de La Habana
Castillo de la Real Fuerza
La Bodeguita del Medio
Plaza de la Catedral
Museo de Arqueología
Hotel Mercure Sevilla
Museo Nacional Palacio de Bellas Artes: Arte Cubano
Museo Alejo Carpentier
Casa de Lombillo
Museo de Arte Colonial
Palacio del Segundo Cabo
El Templete
Edificio Bacardí
PARK CERVANTES
Hotel Parque Central
Hotel Plaza
Palacio de los Capitanes Generales
Plaza de Armas
Hotel Santa Isabel
LA HABANA VIEJA (OLD HAVANA)
Palacio de Turismo
Hotel Ambos Mundos
Museo de Ciencias Naturales
Museo Numismático
Hotel Inglaterra
Iglesia y Convento de Santa Teresa
CADECA
Casa de la Obra Pía
Casa de los Árabes
Depósito de los Automóviles
PARQUE CENTRAL
El Floridita
Gran Teatro de la Habana
Museo Nacional Palacio de Bellas Artes: Arte Universal
Casa de Africa
Casa Guayasamín
Lonja del Comercio
Cruise Terminal Sierra Maestra
Capitolio
Iglesia de Santo Cristo del Buen Viaje
Museo Histórico de las Ciencias Carlos J. Finlay
Casa de la Cultura
Plaza de San Francisco
Museo de Arte Religioso
Convento de San Francisco de Asís
Centro de Desarrollo de las Artes Visuales
Plaza Vieja
Cámara Oscura (Edificio Gómez Villa)
Museo de Ron
La Casona
Iglesia Bautista
PARQUE DE LA FRATERNIDAD
Convento de Santa Clara
Mercado Agropecuario
Ferry Terminal
Regla
Iglesia y Convento de Belén
PARQUE ARACELO IGLESIAS
Adath Israel
Iglesia Parroquial del Espíritu Santo
PARQUE DE LOS AGRIMENSORES
Iglesia de la Merced
Estación Central de Ferrocarril
Casa Natal de José Martí
Antigua Iglesia de San Francisco de Paula
Estación de La Coubre
Muralla de La Habana
Malecón
San Lázaro
Genios
Consulado
Cárcel
Morro
Crespo
Refugio
Colón
Peña Pobre
Habana
Avenida del Puerto (Carlos Manuel Céspedes)
Avenida de las Misiones
Cuarteles
Espada
Aguiar
Cuba
Tacón
Chacón
San Ignacio
Industria
Trocadero
Paseo de Martí (Prado)
(Zulueta)
Animas
Aguacate
Compostela
Tejadillo
Empedrado
Virtudes
Agramonte
San Juan de Dios (Progreso)
O'Reilly
Neptuno
Obispo
Sa Rafael
San Martín
Obrapía
Lamparilla
Baratillo
Amargura
Bernaza
Mercaderes
Avenida de Bélgica (Monserrate)
Brasil (Teniente Rey)
Cristo
Villegas
Oficios
Churruca
Dragones
Muralla
Sol
Máximo Gómez (Monte)
Porvenir
Santa Clara
Luz
Inquisitor
Damas
Corrales
Economía
Cárdenas
Egido (Av. de Bélgica)
Curazzo
Acosta
Aponte Someruelos
Cienfuegos
Apodaca
Picota
Jesús María
Gloria
Merced
San Pedro
Misión
Factoría
Bayona
Conde
Leonor Pérez (Paula)
San Isidro
Velazco
Desamparado
Suárez
Diaria
Fundición
N
0
200 m
200 yds

and placing coins at its roots to bring good luck in the coming year. Visitors to the temple are encouraged to do the same.

Nearby stands the beautiful **Hotel Santa Isabel**, which was originally built in the 18th century as the Palacio del Conde de Santovenia; a ruin for many years, it has now been restored to five-star status (see page 323), and is one of the nicest in the city.

Across the street from El Templete is the **Castillo de la Real Fuerza** ❸ (tel: 7-864 4490; daily 9am–6.30pm), the oldest building in Havana. This powerful fortress, complete with drawbridges, iron cannon, and murky green moat, was built between 1558 and 1577 on the orders of Felipe II after the city was sacked by French pirates in 1555.

Topping its tower is the city's symbol, the bronze figure of **La Giraldilla de la Habana** (a replica, in fact – the original is in the Museo de la Ciudad). Called Iñez de Bobadilla, she was the wife of conquistador Hernando de Soto, who left Cuba to search Florida for the fountain of youth. Instead, he found only miserable death. La Giraldilla spent every afternoon for four years in the tower, watching for his return. From the roof there are good views of the harbor.

The impressive Baroque building on the northwest side of the square is the **Palacio del Segundo Cabo**, which was the headquarters of the Spanish vice-governor in colonial times. It has a beautiful courtyard, but is currently closed for renovation.

Plaza de la Catedral

Two blocks north is the **Plaza de la Catedral**. This beautiful square was once a rather seedy place, known as Plazuela de la Ciénaga (Little Swamp Square). It was the place where the city's rainwater drained, and was once dominated by the 16th-century Zanja Real or 'Royal Ditch' (see page 147). The site of a fish market before construction began in the 18th century, it was the last square to be built in Old Havana.

It is named for the Baroque **Catedral de La Habana** ❹ (Empedrado, corner of San Ignacio; tel: 7-861 7771; Mon–Fri 10am–3pm, Sat 11am–2pm, Sun Mass 9.30am–noon; free, but small charge to go up the tower), which dominates the square and forms part of the most harmonious collection of buildings in the city.

Officially termed the Catedral de la Virgen María de la Concepción Inmaculada, but better known as the church of Havana's patron saint, San Cristóbal, the building was finally finished in 1777, after several setbacks. It was begun as a church by the Jesuits in 1748, but was halted when King Carlos III ordered them out of Cuba in 1767, and gained cathedral status only in 1793. There are bells in both of the towers: the shorter tower has a bell from the Cuban city of Matanzas; the taller one, a bell from Spain. At midnight on New Year's Eve, the cathedral bells ring and crowds gather to rap at the great wooden doors for luck in the new year. The interior holds an altar of

WHERE

On one side of La Mina restaurant is a tiny store, the Casa del Agua, which dispenses glasses of pure water from a natural source, kept cool in old ceramic urns. On the other side (actually in Calle Obispo) is an atmospheric store in the oldest surviving house in Havana, where antiquarian books are displayed in glass-fronted cabinets.

Havana's 18th-century cathedral.

La Giraldilla on the Castillo de la Real Fuerza is a symbol of Havana.

Carrara marble inlaid with gold, silver, and onyx.

For many years the cathedral held the supposed ashes of Columbus, though most people now believe they were those of his son, Diego. Brought from Santo Domingo in 1796, they were returned to Spain after Cuba won independence in 1899.

Colonial homes

On the east side of the square is the **Casa de Lombillo**, built in 1741. The former mansion of a Cuban slave trader, it housed Cuba's first post office, and is now the headquarters of Dr Eusebio Leal Spengler, the city historian. Beside the Casa de Lombillo is the **Casa del Marqués de Arcos**, built in 1742 for Cuba's royal treasurer and now an art gallery.

Directly opposite the cathedral is another beautiful colonial building, the **Palacio de los Condes de Casa Bayona**. Constructed in 1720 for Governor General Chacón, with a lovely central courtyard shaded by a huge palm tree, it houses the **Museo de Arte Colonial** ❺ (San Ignacio 22, corner Empedrado), but is currently closed for renovation.

The mansion contains some impressive *vitrales*, the stained-glass windows and panels that are a Cuban specialty, including the distinctive swing doors known as *mámparas*. Upstairs, there are also superb wooden **Mudéjar** (Arab-inspired) ceilings, known as *alfarjes* (see page 163).

Just off the southwest corner of the square is the **Callejón de Chorro**, a tiny cul-de-sac where a wonderfully restored Art Nouveau building houses the **Taller Experimental de Gráfica** (Experimental Workshop of Graphic Arts). Here you will find good-quality silk screening and printing for sale, and you can often watch local artists at work in the studios.

Next around the square is the **Casa de Baños** (Bathhouse), rebuilt in 1909 over a 19th-century original; the water was fed directly into the baths from the Zanja Real water ditch. A plaque marks the spot. Today, the building houses the Galería Manuel, which sells excellent art, clothes, and Tiffany-style lamps. Next door, taking up most

Marble statue of a sleeping boy at the Museo de Arte Colonial.

RESTORATION

The huge amount of restoration work going on in Old Havana may mean that some of the sights are closed for renovation – a process that may be short-lived or may take several years to complete. Similarly, some of the places under restoration at the time of writing may once again be open. Many of the protective hoardings have become canvases for works of art, with some intriguing murals. The process is a fascinating one, as buildings that were under wraps and encased in scaffolding, billowing building dust, emerge in a pristine state. A splendid book about the restoration program, highly illustrated with photographs showing buildings before and after they were rescued from collapse, can be found in bookstores.

of the west of the square, is **El Patio** restaurant (see page 160). This beautiful colonial building was formerly the **Casa de los Marqueses de Aguas Claras**, the 16th-century former home of Governor General Gonzalo Pérez de Ángulo. Outside, a talented house salsa band plays for those sipping cool *mojitos* on the terrace or at tables and chairs set in the floodlit square. Inside, the palm-filled courtyard is the setting for a formal and somewhat overpriced restaurant, where you may be serenaded with music from the grand piano if there's no competition from the salsa band.

Farther along, next to the cathedral, in the elegant Casa del Obispo Peñalver, is the **Centro Wifredo Lam** ❻ (San Ignacio 22, corner Empedrado; tel: 7-861 3419; Mon–Sat 10am–5pm), a cultural center dedicated to one of Cuba's most famous 20th-century artists (1902–82). It exhibits the works of contemporary artists from Cuba and the rest of the world, and is one of the venues for the Havana Arts Biennial, which has been running since 1984.

Calle Empedrado

Leading off the Plaza de la Catedral to the east along Calle Empedrado, you come to the **Museo de Arqueología** (Tacón 12, between Empedrado and O'Reilly; tel: 7-861 4469; www.ohch.cu; Tue–Sat 9am–5pm, Sun 9.30am–noon), in a mansion once owned in the 18th century by a freed slave, Juana Carvajal, who inherited it from her owner, Lorenza Carvajal. The museum contains both Cuban and Peruvian archeological finds, while outside, on the corner of Tacón, Empedrado, and Oficios, you can see an archeological dig with remnants of the old sea wall and the Boquete fish market.

West of the cathedral, Calle Empedrado's first main sight is the famous bar and restaurant, best known for its Hemingway connections, **La Bodeguita del Medio** ❼, which started life in 1942 as a grocery store. The story is that poets and writers from a nearby print shop used to drop by to check their galleys here, so the owner first offered a few drinks, then lunch. Gradually, more and more tables were set up, until the place became the epicenter of Havana's bohemian life, frequented by talented writers such as Alejo Carpentier and Nicolás Guillén. Cuba's national drink, the *mojito*, was perfected here.

Today, La Bodeguita is still informal and atmospheric, although the only Cuban bohemians here are likely to be working as waiters. Photos and memorabilia from famous diners clutter the walls, which have been tattooed with so many signatures that they are almost black. A sign over the bottles in the front bar was supposedly written and signed by regular customer Ernest Hemingway: '*My Mojito in La Bodeguita, My Daiquirí in El Floridita*.' Not perhaps, his most profound statement, but typically pithy, and a whole lot less banal than some other people's contributions to the great graffiti debate that plasters the bar's walls. According to Tom Miller in *Trading With the Enemy*

WHERE

Even if the subject matter of some of Havana's museums does not particularly appeal to you, they are usually worth visiting for the buildings alone, mostly set around shady, flower-filled courtyards, some cooled by gently splashing fountains.

Restaurant El Patio in the Plaza de la Catedral.

WHERE

On Obispo you will find an Infotur office (between Bernaza and Villegas) and an Infotur kiosk (corner of San Ignacio), as well as the Etecsa office (corner of Habana) with phone kiosks and internet access; and a branch of Cadeca (between Aguiar and Habana) for exchange facilities and ATMs (see page 349).

(see page 357), it was a hoax anyway, made up by Papa's drinking pal Fernando Campoamor to attract customers. If so, it has certainly worked: from morning to closing, the barman can't pour out *mojitos* fast enough. Errol Flynn was another frequent visitor, but nowadays the mix is mainly camera-toting tourists and *jineteros* (hustlers).

Farther along on the same side of the street is the **Fundación Alejo Carpentier** (Empedrado 215, between Cuba and San Ignacio; tel: 7-861 3667; www.fundacioncarpentier.cult.cu; Mon–Fri 8.30am–4.30pm; free), dedicated to the Cuban writer (1904–80). The lovely house, also called the Casa de la Condesa de la Reunión, built in 1870, has a lovely central courtyard and contains many interesting artifacts. Carpentier's widow donated the house and contents (along with the rights to all his royalties), to be used as a museum run by a non-governmental, non-profit organization.

One block south along Calle Cuba is **Calle O'Reilly**, named after a Spaniard with Irish ancestry, Alejandro O'Reilly, who was the first Spanish governor after the island was handed back by the British in 1763. A plaque on the corner of Tacón reads 'Cuba and Ireland: Two island peoples in the same seas of struggle and hope.'

Opulent Calle Obispo

Calle Obispo is one of the best-known and most pleasant streets in Old Havana: it was the first street in the old city to be pedestrianized and restored. It is also one of the busiest, and contains a number of places visitors will find useful, including tourist information offices and exchange facilities. One classic 1920 guidebook to Havana likens Obispo's open-air stores to caves, with windows full of 'diamonds and Panama hats, tortoise shells, Canary Island embroidery and perfumery.' Café windows were stacked with chocolate and almond cakes, wine stores offered Russian liqueurs in miniature glass bears.

Things have changed a lot since the 1920s, but though Havana is still far from being a consumer paradise, many expensive-looking stores have opened, all selling goods for *pesos*

Bustling Calle Obispo.

convertibles (known as CUCs), at prices well out of the reach of all but a handful of Cubans – even those who have access to convertible currency. They stock everything from designer clothes to bed linen and smart sunglasses, although there are still a few, but dwindling, Cuban peso stores with almost nothing for sale. You can also see, and buy, the work of local artists displayed in small upstairs rooms or the spaces they rent at the front of private houses.

The famous pharmacy, **Droguería Johnson** (on the corner of Aguiar), has been restored to its former opulent splendour, with polished mahogany benches and ceramic medicine jars, and is now a pharmacology museum in addition to selling pharmaceuticals in CUCs. **Farmacia Taquechel** (Obispo 155, between Mercaderes and San Ignacio) dates back to 1896 and has also been restored, with floor-to-ceiling mahogany shelves supporting beautiful porcelain jars containing herbal remedies and potions.

Another wonderful old pharmacy, **Sarrá**, on the corner of Compostela and Brasil (also called Teniente Rey), has also been refurbished and returned to its original state, as part of the city restoration program.

Heading back down Obispo toward Plaza de Armas, you pass the **Hotel Ambos Mundos** ❽ (No. 153). For CUC$2 you can visit room 511 where Ernest Hemingway wrote *For Whom the Bell Tolls*. The room is tidily kept, with an antique typewriter (though not Ernest's) and several copies of 1930s US magazines. The rooftop bar is a regular stop on the tour-group trail. The public areas of the hotel have been extensively refurbished and there is a wonderful piano bar in the lobby. Opposite the hotel hangs a bell marking the original site of the University of Havana, founded here in January 1728. This bell originally tolled to signal the beginning of students' classes.

South along Calle Oficios

The next, cobbled section of Obispo leads back to the Plaza de Armas. South out of the plaza on Calle Oficios, is the **Casa de los Árabes** ❾ (Oficios 16, between Obispo and Obrapía; Tue–Sat 9am–5pm, Sun 9am–1pm; free). A surprising number of Cubans are of Middle Eastern origin and this beautiful colonial mansion celebrates Arab culture. On the first floor is a small museum of costumes, tiles, and carpets. Upstairs is a beautiful, tiled fountain, where worshipers wash before attending prayers in the adjoining one-room mosque. A knowledgeable and friendly curator will unlock the upstairs rooms and take you in. His little tour is given free, but a donation is much appreciated. Next door is a restaurant, Al Medina, in which you can eat *tabbouleh* and *hummous* and other eastern dishes in a pretty courtyard (see page 159).

Across the street is the **Depósito de Automóviles** ❿ (Car Museum; Oficios 13, corner Justiz; tel: 7-863 9942; Tue–Sat 9.30am–5pm, Sun 9.30am–1pm) – although just about any street

Lots of artists have studios in Calle Obispo and the surrounding streets.

Stained-glass mediopuntos are one of the loveliest features of Havana architecture.

in Havana could claim this title. Here resides a fabulous collection of venerable roadsters and limos, including vehicles in which revolutionary young bloods like Camilo Cienfuegos and Celia Sánchez would tour around Havana on affairs of state.

On the corner of Oficios and Obrapía is the **Hostal Valencia**, the first colonial home in Old Havana to be converted into a hotel. Its rooms are grouped around a vine-draped courtyard with a pleasant bar and a restaurant. It's a lovely place to stay, but is regularly invaded by sightseers during the day.

Around Obrapía

Turn right into Calle Obrapía and you pass the **Casa de Oswaldo Guayasamín** (Obrapía 111, between Mercaderes and Oficios; tel: 7-861 3843; Tue–Sat 9am–4.45pm, Sun 9am–1pm; free), the house of one of Latin America's foremost 20th-century artists. Though Ecuadorean by nationality, Guayasamín (1919–99) always had a close affinity with Cuba, and belonged to the left-leaning artistic community that found inspiration here. There are a few original paintings in the house, which mainly stages temporary exhibitions. The third of four portraits Guayasamín painted of his friend, Fidel Castro, can be seen in the Fundación La Naturaleza y el Hombre in Miramar (see page 181).

Plaza de San Francisco flower girls.

Farther along Obrapía is the **Casa de Africa** ⓫ (Obrapía 157; tel: 7-861 5798; Tue–Sat 9am–5pm, Sun 9am–1pm; free), with an impressive display of African artifacts, many of them donated by the city's African embassies. The third floor is dedicated to the Afro-Cuban religions of Santería, Abakuá, and Palo Monte (see page 76).

Opposite, at No. 158, is the delightful lemon-yellow **Casa de la Obra Pía** ⓬ (www.ohch.cu; tel: 7-861 3097; temporarily closed for renovation), once the home of the Calvo de la Puerta family. The *obra pía* (pious act) commemorates Martín Calvo de la Puerta's action in providing dowries for five orphan girls every year. The imposing doorway leads into a creeper-strewn courtyard and one of Old Havana's finest colonial mansions. Built in 1665 and enlarged in the 1700s, the building's best rooms are upstairs.

Highlights include the rare *cenefas* – painted floral borders – on the staircase, and the elegant, open-sided dining room. On the roof are the small rooms where the family's slaves were housed. A room on the first floor is dedicated to Alejo Carpentier, housing some of his photographs and personal effects, and his car, a Volkswagen Beetle.

A waterfront square

Walking in the rest of the Old City can be pleasant in any direction. Returning to the Hostal Valencia and walking south along Oficios brings you to another historic square, the **Plaza de San Francisco**. At its center is the Fuente de los Leones (Lion Fountain), built in 1836, and on one side the immense and refurbished business center in a former commodities market, the **Lonja del Comercio**. The main landmark here, however, is the **Convento de San Francisco de Asís** ⓭ (Tue–Sat 9.30am–5pm).

First built in 1608 and rebuilt in 1737, San Francisco has a 40-meter (130ft) bell tower that is one of the tallest on the continent and was once Havana's best lookout for pirates. The building was taken over by the British in 1762–3 and, as it had been used for Protestant services, Catholic *habaneros* would never again worship in it. Since the 1840s, it has been a customs office, a post office, and a warehouse. Its two cloisters house a *Museo de Arte Religioso* (Museum of Religious Art). One of the strangest exhibits is the pickled remains of Teodoro, a Franciscan monk, in jars set into the left side of the church. The beautiful cloisters are perhaps more interesting than the items on display. The Basílica Menor is now a venue for classical recitals, often held in the early evening.

If you continue a short way south along the waterfront you will reach the **Museo del Ron** ⓮ (Avenida del Puerto 262, between Sol and Muralla; tel: 7-861 8051; Mon–Thu 9am–5pm, Fri–Sun 9am–4pm; guided tours), one of the most fascinating museums in the city. The tour takes you through the whole process of rum production and ends with sampling and an opportunity to buy. The highlight for many people is the extensive model railroad running around a model of a sugar refinery. The adjoining Havana Club bar is wood paneled and appealing, and sometimes has live music. There is also an art gallery exhibiting contemporary Cuban artists' work.

Calle Mercaderes

Stretching away from Plaza de San Francisco on all sides are newly restored cobbled roads and freshly painted mansions, many of them now cafés, stores, or art galleries. Walking west along Calle Brasil (Teniente Rey) where you can see excavated parts of the old watercourse, the Zanja Real, you reach the Plaza Vieja, and off to the right runs the traffic-free **Calle**

This historic square takes its name from the adjacent 16th-century Convento de San Francisco de Asís.

ART DECO

While Old Havana is famous for its colonial architecture, there are some remarkable examples of the Art Deco style, worth seeking out during a tour of the old city. On Avenida de las Misiones stands the beautiful Edificio Bacardí, an extravagant confection topped with the statue of a giant bat, which was the Bacardí family emblem. Formerly the headquarters of the Bacardí Rum Company, which was based in Cuba until the family fled the island in the early 1960s, the building, dating from 1929, is a strange mixture of Swedish granite, Cuban limestone, tiles and terracotta, resembling a giant three-dimensional mosaic. You can get a great view of this landmark building from the roof terrace of the Hotel Plaza on the northeast corner of the Parque Central.

Art Deco ornamentation on the Barardí building.

Mercaderes ⓯, one of the prettiest and best-restored streets in the old city.

Mercaderes houses the **Museo de Chocolate** – really a café with displays related to chocolate making and consumption, which serves cups of delicious, thick, pure chocolate. If lining up in temperatures of 35°C (95°F) to drink cups of hot chocolate in an air-conditioned interior seems odd, cold chocolate is also available.

At No. 115, you'll find one of the many elegant stores springing up in Old Havana – the **Tienda El Navegante** (www.habaguanex.ohc.cu), beautifully fitted out in polished wood, which sells maps and navigation charts, both old and new. The **Casa del Tabaco** (Tue–Sat 10am–5pm; free) is a fascinating little museum/shop, well worth a quick visit. Many of the exhibits were donated by the world's most famous ex-smoker, Fidel Castro himself. Notice the cigar box in the shape of the house where Castro was born. You can also buy cigars fresh from a large humidor. Then there is the **Maqueta de la Habana Vieja** – a scale model of the old city – a little garden with a statue of Simón Bolívar, and the **Casa de Simón Bolívar**, funded by the Venezuelan Government, where music is played in a blue-and-white courtyard.

Plaza Vieja

Back now to the **Plaza Vieja** ⓰ (Old Plaza), built in the 1500s to create a space for bullfights and fiestas, and once one of Old Havana's principal squares. A famous fountain with four dolphins once stood here, but it fell victim to 1930s 'modernization.' For decades an underground parking lot ruined any chance the square had of being picturesque, while the surrounding buildings crumbled. But this has all changed and, with the exception of one building, where work is still in progress, the renovations are now complete. The plaza is again one of the most beautiful in Havana, and a place where children are brought to play ball games.

On the northeast corner, on the roof of a yellow-and-white wedding cake of a building, is the **Cámara Oscura** (Calle Brasil, corner of Mercaderes; tel: 7-866 4461; daily 9.30am–5.20pm). An

Bronze statue of El Caballero de Paris.

EL CABALLERO DE PARIS

Outside the Convento de San Francisco is a statue of a man nicknamed El Caballero de Paris (The Gentleman of Paris). There are many stories attached to this figure, but the most commonly accepted is that he was a man who became insane while in prison in the 1920s, falsely accused of theft. (In other versions he was incarcerated simply because he was insane – something that used to happen under General Machado's regime.) On his release he wandered the streets of Havana, wearing a flowing cloak even in the hottest weather, never begging even when destitute, and distributing flowers and feathers to passers-by. He became a much-loved figure in the city, which erected this monument in his memory. You will often see people stroking the statue's prominent beard, which is said to bring good luck. The beard has been rubbed to a shiny gold, as has one of the elegant fingers on his left hand.

There are also a number of explanations given for his unusual name: while it is agreed that he did not come from Paris, theories range from one that his French wife-to-be died in a shipwreck while on her way from France to Cuba, to the more mundane explanation that he had worked in a Havana restaurant called the Paris.

El Caballero died in a psychiatric hospital in 1985, at the age of 86, and is buried within the church.

elevator takes you to the eighth floor, where there are amazing views over the city, and the camera obscura hones in on details of nearby buildings as well as the general vista.

On the **southeastern** corner of the plaza, the amazing Art Nouveau **Hotel Palacio Viena**, built in 1906, was for a long time a *solar* – a residential hotel where many families lived cheek by jowl – but is currently undergoing much-needed restoration, to be reopened by Habaguanex as the Hotel Palacio Cueto.

To the south of the square is the former home of the Conde de Ricla, a Spanish captain general, now an art gallery known as **La Casona** (Muralla 107, corner of San Ignacio; tel: 7-861 8544; www.galeriascubanas.com; Tue–Sat 10am–5.30pm). This fine 18th-century colonial house has various galleries of contemporary art and glasswork, and some rare murals on the stairway. Its trio of *mediopuntos* is among the best examples of stained-glass windows in Havana. The building also houses the **Galería Plaza Vieja**, which specializes in Afro-Cuban works.

On the southwestern corner of the square is a restaurant-bar, the **Cervecería Taberna de la Muralla**, with its own organic microbrewery, very popular after a hot day of sightseeing around the city. On the western side, in the colonial Casa de las Hermanas Cárdenas, is the **Centro de Desarrollo de las Artes Visuales** (San Ignacio 352, between Brasil and Muralla; tel: 7-862 3533; www.cnap.cult.cu; Tue–Sat 10am–5pm), which focuses on contemporary works by Cuban and other Latin American artists.

Just to the northeast of the plaza is the **Museo Histórico de las Ciencias Carlos J. Finlay** ⓱ (Calle Cuba 460, between Amargura and Brasil; tel: 7-863 4824; Mon–Fri 8am–5pm, Sat 8am–3pm), a museum dedicated to the history of science in Cuba. It's named after the doctor who discovered the vector for yellow fever, once a massive killer, but now eradicated. The museum includes an elegant neoclassical lecture theater (where Albert Einstein once gave a lecture) and an atmospheric 19th-century pharmacy.

Architectural detail of one of the city's colonial churches.

The Plaza Vieja has been returned to its former glory.

A trio of churches

Heading south down San Ignacio and turning right on Santa Clara you come to the **Convento de Santa Clara** ⓲ (Cuba 610, between Luz and Sol; tel: 7-861 3335; Mon–Fri 8.30am–5pm), an enormous 18th-century former convent that was renowned as a refuge for dowerless girls. It contains a vast, tree-filled main courtyard, the Clarisa nuns' cells, and lovely cloisters.

There is a small *hostal*, used mainly by educational groups, and still partially under renovation. The convent now houses a conservation institute where all the restoration techniques being utilized in the renovation of Old Havana are honed, including carpentry, the restoration of old tiles, and the making of new ones. All the works in the old town have been undertaken using, wherever possible, the same materials and techniques as used by the original craftsmen.

South of here, on Calle Acosta, is the delightful **Iglesia Parroquial del Espíritu Santo** ⓳ (Mon–Sat 8am–noon, 3–6pm, Sun 9am–noon), one of Havana's oldest churches. Built in the 1670s as a religious retreat for 'free negroes,' this fully renovated gem displays Moorish influence on its facade and the cedar ceiling, and features catacombs with roofs supported by tree trunks. The chapel vault has a mural (sadly almost erased by the passage of time) depicting the Dance of Death.

A little farther down Calle Cuba you will reach the lavish **Iglesia de la Merced** ⓴ (Mon–Sat 8am–noon, 3–5pm, Sun 8am–noon), dating from 1746. This is one of Havana's most famous churches as it is dedicated to Santa Mercedes, who becomes Obatalá in the Santería faith. On September 24, hundreds of worshipers – often wearing white (white is Obatalá's color) or carrying white flowers – congregate here to pay tribute. And at any time of the year, you may see white-clad Santería devotees worshiping here. Note the flower sellers all around, for flowers are a common gift of thanks for requests granted by the saints. The church itself is dark and ornate with wonderful trompe l'œil frescoes and a peaceful, leafy cloister.

View of the Capitolio's impressive dome.

Along the waterside

The atmosphere changes as you hit the busier streets on the fringes of Old Havana. This is not an area that attracts many visitors, but there are a few sights worth seeing if you have time to spare.

By the harbor, where Calle San Ignacio meets the dock road (here called Desamparado), is a pretty little former church, now beautifully renovated, the **Antigua Iglesia de San Francisco de Paula** (Mon–Fri 9am–5pm, Sat 9am–1pm). It has an interesting collection of modern art with a Christian theme and some fine stained glass. A variety of classical concerts take place here on some evenings, and it is also the base for the musical group called Ars Longa.

Farther along the waterfront you come to some interesting remnants of the old city walls, the **Cortina de La Habana**. Slaves worked for 23 years to build these walls, which were 1.5 meters (5ft) thick and more than 10 meters (30ft) tall. The first walls were begun in 1674, but were altered and expanded up until the late 18th century. They ringed the old city until 1863, when they were torn down to allow for expansion.

Nearby stands a stark, dramatic monument to the Belgian ship ***La Coubre***. Carrying armaments for the Cuban Army, it blew up on March 4, 1960, killing 72 sailors and dock workers: was it an accident or – as the Castro government has always maintained – the work of the CIA?

Three blocks north up Avenida de Bélgica (Egido), on Leonor Pérez (confusingly also called Leonor Paula), is the house where Cuba's most revered figure was born. The **Casa Natal de José Martí** ㉑ (Leonor Pérez 314, between Picota and Egido; tel: 7-861 3778; Tue–Sat 9.30am–5pm, Sun 9.30am–1pm) is a small, simple house, painted yellow and blue in typical Havana style. Martí was born here in 1853 and it was his home until he was five years old.

The house contains letters, first editions, manuscripts, photos, even locks of his hair. There is sometimes a line to get in, as the house is a popular place for school visits. It is worth seeing simply because Martí is such an iconic figure (see page 42).

Around the corner stands the Moorish-Victorian **Estación Central de Ferrocarriles** (Central Train Station) – unmissable with its soaring twin towers.

Capitolio and the Gran Teatro

Officially, the sights that follow belong in Central Havana, but they are so closely integrated with Habana Vieja that we have included them in this chapter.

From the station, follow Avenida de Bélgica (Egido) northward. This is a broad, busy street with a number of CUC stores that sell soap, shampoo, and the like to local people who have access to *convertibles*. It follows the line of the old city walls north past a small farmers' market – an *agropecuario*. Turn left along Dragones to the enormous,

SIGHTSEEING IN STYLE

Outside the Capitolio there are always a number of 1950s limousines – Buicks, Chevrolets, Packards, Chryslers. But unlike the many beat-up models you see traveling slowly and noisily around town or stopped with their hoods open while the driver works wonders with a screwdriver, these have shiny bodywork and gleaming hubcaps. They belong to Grancar, a state-owned company that specializes in taking visitors for tours around the city – or as far afield as they want to go. Driving through Havana in one of these limos is a great experience, and not as expensive as you might think, as all rates are strictly controlled. You do, however, usually get a better deal if you ring the company office (tel: 7-648 7338) rather than making an arrangement with a driver on the street.

Iglesia Parroquial del Espíritu Santo.

grandiose **Capitolio** 22 (Paseo de Martí, between San Martín and Dragones; tel: 7-861 0261; closed for renovations until about 2015), which dominates the skyline all around.

Built in 1929–32 by General Machado as the new presidential and governmental palace, it closely resembles the design of the Capitol in Washington DC, continuing the process of Americanization begun in 1902 when the United States effectively took over from Spain as Cuba's colonial master. Before the revolution it was the home of the National Congress, but it now houses the Cuban Academy of Sciences.

The huge bronze doors and marble floor of the domed entrance hall are impressive, as are the broad staircases, but the most magnificent feature is the 17-meter (56 feet) statue of Jupiter, representing the state. Weighing nearly 50 tonnes, it is said to be the third-largest indoor statue in the world and the largest in Latin America.

The 24-carat diamond set in the floor of the entrance hall is point zero, from which all measurements are taken in Cuba. Outside, at the foot of the grand flight of stairs, many old American cars wait to offer visitors a taxi ride, as do horse-drawn carriages and coco-taxis.

Standing next door to the Capitolio is the flamboyant **Gran Teatro de la Habana** 23 (Paseo de Martí 458; tel: 7-861 3077 or 5873), completed in 1837, and housing El Teatro García Lorca, where the Cuban National Ballet performs. It contains several auditoriums – the gold auditorium is grand, if surprisingly small inside, with plush red seats and a bewitching painted ceiling. The Baroque theater building also houses cultural institutions – ballet dancers, opera singers, and theater companies rehearse here, and tours are sometimes offered. There are regular performances by the national ballet and opera companies, usually on weekends, and it's well worth getting a ticket if you can.

Parque Central

The Gran Teatro occupies part of one side of the **Parque Central**, which, with its stately royal palms (many

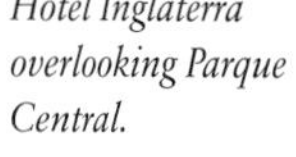

Hotel Inglaterra overlooking Parque Central.

bearing tourist graffiti from the 1940s and 1950s), always seems to be buzzing with activity from early morning until midnight. In the center is a white marble statue of José Martí. The corner of the park nearest the Capitolio is called the Esquina Caliente (Hot Corner) where men gather and debate (hotly), mainly about baseball.

Next door to the Gran Teatro is the splendid, neo-Baroque facade of the **Hotel Inglaterra** ㉔, so named because it was popular with early travelers from England. The sidewalk outside its doorways, nicknamed 'the Louvre Sidewalk,' has been one of the busiest spots in Havana for generations. The covered café here is a great place for people watching, but you will get plenty of hassle from the street.

Initially, in the mid-19th century there was a two-story building here called Café y Salones de Escauriza, subsequently renamed El Louvre. This was a popular place for pro-independence conspirators to speak, and one such occasion in 1869 prompted Spanish soldiers to open fire. Not all Spaniards were so ruthless: an officer protesting the execution of eight Cuban students in 1871 broke his sword against the door, and a plaque commemorates his bold, humanitarian gesture. The building opened as a hotel in 1875, was given a third floor in 1886, and a fourth in 1914, when it became one of the most opulent places to stay in the Americas. The Arab-influenced dining room off the lobby is still impressive.

On the east side of the Parque Central is the *Arte Universal* section of the **Museo Nacional Palacio de Bellas Artes** ㉕ (San Rafael, between Zulueta and Monserrate; tel: 7-861 5777; www.museonacional.cult.cu; Tue–Sat 10am–6pm, Sun 10am–2pm; combined ticket available for this and the *Arte Cubano* section, see page 155). Housed in the old Asturian cultural center on Calle San Rafael, it contains Latin America's largest collection of antiquities, as well as works by Goya, Rubens, Velázquez, Turner, Gainsborough, and Canaletto, many of which were left behind by Batista's family and cronies when they fled after the revolution.

TIP

You have to check your bags in when you go into either the Museo de la Revolución or the Bellas Artes. You are allowed to take a camera with you into the former, but they are forbidden in the latter.

Havana school pupils.

Hemingway's bar

Just southeast of the Palacio de Bellas Artes is **El Floridita** ㉖, made famous as Ernest Hemingway's favorite haunt (it features in his novel *Islands in the Stream*). It was frequented by the Hollywood set who came to Havana in the 1950s – Errol Flynn, Frank Sinatra, Ava Gardner, Gary Cooper, and Marlene Dietrich were all regulars. *Esquire* magazine in 1953 ranked it with the 21 Club in New York, the Ritz in Paris, and Raffles in Singapore as one of the best bars in the world. It is claimed that the *daiquirí* cocktail was perfected here, though it was probably originally invented in Santiago province as an anti-malarial potion for miners. Certainly it was at El Floridita that the drink became famous, and Hemingway even invented his own version, the '*daiquirí* special,' which is still served.

Not much else is the same as in Hemingway's day, when it was an informal, old-fashioned place, with ceiling fans and a three-piece band. Today it has been renovated and polished up into one of the most expensive restaurants in Cuba, with a life-size bronze statue of Hemingway near his favorite seat, on the far left of the original wooden bar. It still serves the best, if overpriced, *daiquirís* in town, but, although friendly, the bar lacks the atmosphere of the Bodeguita del Medio (see page 143), and it is, of course, another blatant tourist trap.

The Prado

Running north from the Parque Central is the **Prado** (officially known as the **Paseo de Martí**), the historic, popular promenade lined with trees and lion statues, that stretches all the way to the Malecón. The Prado officially divides Central Havana from Old Havana, and forms an easy landmark in the transition between the touristy Old Town and the real city of working *habaneros*. This boulevard, with its raised walkway set with colored marble and stone, has seen better days. Construction began in the late 1700s, to build a promenade outside the old city walls, and continued until 1852 (by which time the walls had collapsed),

SEALING DEALS AND TYING KNOTS

The Prado is important territory. The area between Colón and Refugio has become widely known as an unofficial real estate market. Formerly, Cubans were not permitted to sell property – only to exchange it. '*Se permuta*' signs pinned to doors and balconies around the city meant the residents wanted to exchange their house for another. As part of Raúl Castro's economic liberalization program, however, new laws allow Cubans to buy and sell their homes. The job of middleman, or real estate agent, is still illegal, but they can be found touting their wares. No one really knows the value of property in Havana, which was all expropriated after the 1959 Revolution, so people gather on the Prado to make deals. Sometimes the equivalent of thousands of dollars changes hands, in a country where the average wage translates at around US$20 a month.

At Prado No. 306, on the corner of Calle Animas, is the **Palacio de Matrimonios** (Wedding Palace), where on Monday, Wednesday, Friday and Saturday you can see wedding parties in hired tuxedos and frothy white dresses make their grand entrances and exits. Take a look inside, too, at the gilded, chandeliered luxury of this former aristocrat's palace. The non-religious ceremony has a strong socialist feel – the man promises to help his wife with housework and childcare (though few Cuban men ever do).

White weddings are still as popular as ever.

and its buildings were once home to Havana's richest, most aristocratic families. Some of them are extraordinarily beautiful – and extraordinarily dilapidated. Renovation work is proceeding, but slowly, and there is a great deal to do.

The area began to decline in the early 20th century when the mansions of the rich were mostly turned into casinos and nightclubs. The upper levels became notorious brothels, adorned with skimpily dressed girls who would stand on the balconies to lure in custom. Now, however, it is full of ordinary people going about their daily business or simply taking a stroll. Furthermore, some of the old buildings nearby have been turned into schools, and as they have no playgrounds, you will often see the children in their red and white uniforms having sports lessons or just playing on the Prado's raised walkway. Sometimes there are small art markets or open-air concerts; it is a place where spontaneous events happen.

Take a short detour off the Prado to the ornate **Hotel Mercure Sevilla**, which was a notorious Mafia hangout, and featured prominently in Graham Greene's *Our Man in Havana*: secret agent Hawthorne stayed in Room 501. Beautifully restored since the mid-1990s, the Sevilla has a wonderfully Spanish ambiance, with a cool lobby and a delightful blue-tiled patio café, complete with fountain.

Museums of art and revolution

Between Agramonte (Zulueta) and Avenida de las Misiones are two of Havana's most important museums, presenting two very different aspects of Cuba. The first of them, in a modernist building dating from 1954, is the excellent *Arte Cubano* section of the **Museo Nacional Palacio de Bellas Artes** ㉗ (National Museum of Fine Arts; Trocadero, between Zulueta and Monserrate; Tue–Sat 10am–6pm, Sun 10am–2pm; combined ticket available for this and the Arte Universal section, see page 153).

The museum reopened in 2001 after five years of extensive renovation. It contains the largest collection of works by Cuban artists in the country, and the excellent 20th-century section includes pieces by Wifredo Lam, Carlos Enríquez, René Portocarrero, and Eduard Abela, well displayed in a series of interlinked air-conditioned galleries. It is generally considered the best museum in the city.

Directly opposite the Fine Arts Museum is the **Monumento Granma**, which is part of the **Museo de la Revolución** ㉘ (Refugio, between Zulueta and Monserrate, also known as Avenida de las Misiones; tel: 7-862 4091; daily 10am–5pm), housed in the former presidential palace. The 18-meter (56ft) yacht, *Granma*, was used by Fidel, Che, and 80 other guerrillas to cross from Mexico to Cuba in 1956. The boat is painted brilliant white with green trim and set in a huge glass case as one of the revolution's great icons. Around the yacht, in a fenced-off and closely guarded

Geometric sculpture at the Arte Cubano section of the Museo Nacional Palacio de Bellas Artes.

area, are other relics of the revolution: a tractor converted into a tank by rural guerrillas; an old Pontiac with a double floor for smuggling arms and documents; and the bullet-riddled delivery van used for an attack on the Presidential Palace in 1957 in an unsuccessful attempt to assassinate Batista. March 13, the anniversary of the attack, in which 35 rebels and five palace guards were killed, is commemorated each year.

There are also airplanes and a tank that were used to repulse the CIA-backed Bay of Pigs invasion (the invading boats are decorated with a skull and crossbones), and a fragment of the U2 spy plane shot down over Cuba shortly before the Missile Crisis of 1962. The star-shaped monument to the Heroes of the New Fatherland, with an eternal flame, is just like the Kremlin's master model in Moscow. Every day at 3pm a changing of the guard ceremony is held here.

The Presidential Palace was worked in and lived in by all Cuba's presidents from its completion in 1913 until 1957, when Batista built the present Palacio in what is now the Plaza de la Revolución. The delicious white-and-gold interior was created by Tiffany's, of New York.

The memorabilia laid out with quasi-religious reverence in these splendid rooms offers a vivid picture of the revolution, and the earlier struggle for independence. There are blood-stained uniforms from the failed attack on the Moncada Barracks in 1953, as well as the heavy black coat that Fidel wore during his trial, when he made his famous 'History will absolve me...' speech. Information panels about the exhibits do not all have English translations, the exhibits are getting rather worn, and the displays are old-fashioned. Allow several hours to see it all.

Music museum and waterfront castle

Not far from the Presidential Palace, at the bottom of the Avenida de las Misiones, before it meets the Malecón, the **Museo Nacional de la Música** is currently closed for renovation, but its extensive collection of Cuban

A Mariano Rodriguez painting in the Arte Cubano section of the Museo de Bellas Artes.

instruments is temporarily housed at Obrapía 509, between Bernaza and Villegas.

Set proudly and unmissably on an island in the middle of a swirl of traffic and parkland is the **Monumento de Máximo Gómez** 29, honoring one of the great campaigners for Cuban independence, although he actually came from the Dominican Republic.

On the waterfront opposite stands a small 16th-century fortress, the **Castillo de San Salvador de la Punta** 30. Like El Morro, across the water, the fortress was designed by Italian engineer Juan Bautista Antonelli during the reign of the Spanish king Felipe II. On the seafront there are metal floor plans of all the fortresses around the harbor.

Fortresses across the bay

From Old Havana, a tunnel dips beneath the bay to the **Castillo de los Tres Santos Reyes Magos del Morro**, which is usually known simply as **El Morro** 31 (daily 8am–8pm; cost is lower if you simply want to walk round the ramparts). This 16th-century fortress, with 3-meter (10ft) -thick walls constructed from blocks taken from Cuba's coastal reef, took more than 40 years to complete. It still dominates the eastern skyline, especially at night when floodlit. The views from here are superb, whether around the bastion's vertiginous ramparts, back toward the city, or out to sea, from where the main **lighthouse** can be seen 33km (18 nautical miles) away. It is absolutely stunning at sunset.

The castle was once a vital part of the city's defenses. On the lower level, closer to the harbor, is the **Batería de los Doce Apóstoles** (Battery of the 12 Apostles), with each of its 12 cannons bearing one of their names. In colonial times, these guns would be fired to announce the closing of the city gates – a rite now re-enacted in the neighboring fortress of San Carlos de la Cabaña (see page 158).

A great chain used to run between El Morro and the Castillo de la Punta in Old Havana. The chain closed the bay to pirate ships in the days when Sir Francis Drake sailed these seas.

Watching the world go by in one the many streets that have not been renovated.

Museo de la Revolución.

WHERE

To reach the fortresses take a taxi (around CUC$5), any bus that runs through the tunnel, or the HabanaBusTour from the Parque Central (CUC$5), which allows you to hop on and off all day; the Playas del Este route includes La Cabaña. From El Morro to Castillo de San Carlos it's about a 20-minute walk. Travel agencies also run tours.

The pirate Henry Morgan was told by former English prisoners in Havana that he would need at least 1,800 men to take the city – he did not even try. Bizarrely, there are still several pieces of modern artillery directed out from El Morro toward the Straits of Florida, in symbolic defiance against a *yanqui*-inspired invasion.

There are three **museums** at El Morro castle, focusing on navigation, the history of the castle, and on pirates. You will also find one of Havana's most atmospheric restaurants, Los Doce Apóstoles, just outside the wall (see page 159).

Castillo de San Carlos

The **Fortaleza de San Carlos de la Cabaña** ㉜ (daily 9am–10pm) was built from 1764–74, after the departure of British invaders. It, too, has two interesting **museums**. One of them documents the fortress in colonial days, when many independence fighters were shot here. A good number of Batista's followers met the same fate after the revolution in 1959, when Che Guevara used the fortress as his headquarters (the focus of the second museum).

In the first year of the revolution, those found guilty of such crimes as murder and torturing prisoners under the Batista regime were executed here. Bullet holes from the firing squads pepper the walls by the front gate.

At 9pm every evening, the atmospheric ceremony of the **firing of the cannon** (called *El Cañonazo*) is conducted in period military dress, in commemoration of the obsolete practice of closing the city gates. Although nowadays they only fire blanks, the noise is authentic, and the ceremony is fun, especially as local people often outnumber tourists.

Much of the fortress is in a fairly dangerous condition – there are a lot of sheer drops from the high walls, which are neither roped off nor signposted, so take care when exploring and keep a close eye on children. You will find an excellent restaurant, La Divina Pastora, at the foot of the fortress on the waterside (see page 159), as well as several upscale tourist shops selling arts, crafts, and clothes.

El Morro fortress, built to defend the city.

RESTAURANTS, PALADARES, BARS, AND CAFÉS

PRICE CATEGORIES

Price categories are for a three-course meal for one with a beer, or mojito. Wine puts the price up:
$ = under $25
$$ = $25–35
$$$ = over $35

Restaurants

Al Medina
Casa de Los Arabes, Calle Oficios 12, between Obrapía and Obispo
Tel: 7-867 1041. Open daily noon–11pm. **$$**
Tasty Arabic dishes, falafel, hummus, and couscous in the courtyard of a lovely old colonial mansion attached to the Casa del Arabe. Good for vegetarians.

A Prado y Neptuno
Prado, corner Neptuno
Tel: 7-860 9636. Open daily noon–midnight. **$$$**
Modern restaurant opposite the Hotel Parque Central on one corner and Hotel Telégrafo on the other. A good place for a pizza and cold beer, where you can watch the baseball on TV. The food is better than the service.

La Barca
Avenida del Puerto 16, corner Obispo
Tel: 7-866 8807. Open daily noon–midnight. **$$$**
Opposite the old yacht club overlooking the seafront road and the water, a pleasant open-air restaurant with good Spanish dishes, seafood, and steaks. Part of the Habaguanex chain and efficiently run.

La Bodeguita del Medio
Calle Empedrado 207, off Plaza de la Catedral
Tel: 7-867 1374. Open daily noon–midnight. **$$$**
Bohemian atmosphere with creole cooking in this old Hemingway haunt, but the quality of the food and service suffers due to the constant flow of tourists. Walls downstairs are decorated with the autographs of celebrities who have eaten here over the years, but the roof terrace is a more congenial place to sit. Reservations advised.

Bar Cabaña
Calle Cuba 12, corner of Peña Pobre (by the seafront)
Tel: 7-860 5670. Open daily 10am–midnight. **$$**
Good *criolla* and international food served in an unpretentious setting.

El Castillo de Farnés
Avenida de Bélgica (Monserrate) 361, corner of Obrapía
tel: 7-867 1030. Restaurant open daily noon–midnight; bar daily 24 hours. **$–$$**
Pictures of Fidel and Raúl adorn the bar – this is supposed to have been one of their favorite haunts and they came here with Che at 4.45am on January 9, 1959 after Castro's victory speech on arrival in Havana. Spanish food. The chickpeas *(garbanzos)* with ham are a specialty and are worth trying. Good for people watching, or sit inside in the cool restaurant at the back.

La Divina Pastora
Fortaleza de La Cabaña
Tel: 7-860 8341. Open noon–11pm. **$$$**
At the foot of the Cabaña fortress, La Divina Pastora offers a stunning view of the Havana skyline, particularly at sunset. A good place for a meal or a drink before the 9pm *cañonazo* (see page 158). The food is average and the service slow but the setting is worth it.

Los Doce Apóstoles
Castillo del Morro
Tel: 7-863 8295. Open daily noon–11pm; bar 11pm–2am. **$$**
Next to the El Morro Fortress and named for its battery, this restaurant serves fish and pork dishes with all the trimmings, though the setting is arguably better than the food.

La Dominica
Calle O'Reilly, corner of Mercaderes.
Tel: 7-860 2918. Open daily noon–midnight. **$$**
You can sit inside or out at this lovely courtyard restaurant. Good pizzas from a wood-fired oven, pasta, and other Italian-influenced dishes. Good band.

El Floridita
Calle Obispo 557, corner Monserrate
Tel: 7-867 1300/1301. Open daily noon–1am. **$$$**
Havana's most fabled dining spot, and Hemingway's favorite for his *daiquirís* (the best in town, but not cheap), is elegant but dark and overpriced. You pay for the name (and the waiters' red jackets) as well as for the food. Main courses include grilled lobster, shrimp flambéed in rum, turtle steaks, and other exotica. If you just want to check it out, you could simply opt for a *daiquirí* at the bar.

Hanoi
Calle Brasil (Teniente Rey) 507, corner of Bernaza
Tel: 7-867 1029. Open daily noon–midnight. **$**
Despite the name, the food is *criolla*. Lots of pork, shrimp, and rice; good-value set three-course meals or *combinados*. Cheap cocktails, live music, and a relaxed atmosphere.

La Lluvia de Oro
Calle Obispo 316, corner of Habana
Tel: 7-862 9870. Open daily 8am–early hours. **$**
This is a good place for a snack and a drink in the heart of the main shopping street, with excellent live (and sometimes loud) music in the afternoons and evening. Popular bar.

Café el Mercurio
Calle Oficios, corner of Plaza de San Francisco
Tel: 7-860 6118. Open daily 9am–midnight. **$$**
Good spot for breakfasts and for light meals throughout the day – salads, omelets, etc. Not so good for evening meals, and service can be erratic.

La Mina
Plaza de Armas
Tel: 7-862 0216. Bar/restaurant open daily noon–midnight, café from 10am. **$$$**
Cuban *criolla* cooking, or sandwiches and pasta, are served in a restaurant with a beautiful courtyard where peacocks stroll and a broad terrace right on the Plaza de Armas. Very popular with tourists. Plenty of musicians, artists wanting to draw you, and people in traditional dress wanting to be photographed with you – for money, of course.

Los Nardos (Sociedad Juventud Asturiana)
Paseo de Martí (Prado) 563, between Teniente Rey and Dragones
Tel: 7-863 2985. Open daily noon–midnight. **$**
This is a quirky and popular place, with a busy, buzzing atmosphere. No reservations taken, so you have to wait in a well-regulated line outside till a table is free. Decorated with soccer memorabilia, with trophies from the 1930s. Good wine list. Huge portions of pork, lamb, Uruguayan beef, chicken, fish, shrimp, and lobster with all the trimmings. The service is efficient and friendly. You don't have to stand in line if you go to the restaurants upstairs: El Trofeo, which serves Cuban and international food, or El Asturianito,

serving Cuban and Italian food, with good pizzas.

Café del Oriente
Calle Oficios 112, Plaza de San Francisco
Tel: 7-860 6686. Open daily noon–midnight. **$$$**
This is an extremely elegant and formal restaurant, with a jazz trio and a full international menu, the sort of place where smoked salmon and filet mignon are served by very attentive waiters.

El Patio
San Ignacio 54, Plaza de la Catedral
Tel: 7-867 8504. Open daily noon–midnight. **$$$**
Go for the fabulous location, in an old colonial palace, rather than the food. You can eat either on the ground floor, surrounded by palms and serenaded from the grand piano, or upstairs in the Parillada del Marqués. Reserve a table overlooking the plaza. International menu.

The Roof Garden
Hotel Sevilla, Calle Trocadero 55
Tel: 7-860 8560. Open daily 7–10.30pm. **$$$**
The food is good but the views are the reason many people come here for dinner, with panoramic vistas of Old Havana on three sides. Wonderful, elegant, candlelit ambiance, really special when they throw open the huge windows to let in the evening breeze off the sea.

Café Taberna
Calle Mercaderes 531, corner of Brasil (Teniente Rey)
Tel: 7-861 1637. Open daily 11am–midnight. **$$**
This was the first coffee house opened when the British took Havana in 1762, and was named after its owner Juan Batista de Taberna. Now it's the place to go for a lobster or shrimp dinner and a show by the remaining members of the Buena Vista Social Club with dancing. Hugely popular. You can just have a drink at the bar and enjoy the music if you don't want to eat there.

El Templete
Avenida del Puerto 12–14, corner Narciso López
Tel: 7-866 8807. Open daily noon–midnight. **$$$**
Next to La Barca and under same management, this place is slightly more elegant, upscale, and expensive. You can eat inside or in the open air overlooking the waterfront. The food is very good, prepared by a Spanish chef, and you can choose from a variety of meats, fish, or lobster.

La Torre de Marfil
Calle Mercaderes 121, between Obispo and Obrapía
Tel: 7-867 1038. Open daily noon–midnight. **$–$$**
Chinese/Cuban food, in pleasant surroundings with lanterns and Chinese decorations. They pride themselves on serving the best piña colada in Havana, with or without rum, which you can add yourself.

Vuelta Abajo
Hotel Conde de Villanueva, Calle Mercaderes 202, between Lamparilla and Amargura
Tel: 7-862 9293. Open daily noon–11pm. **$$$**
Named after a tobacco region in Pinar del Río, this cool, stone-arched restaurant specializes in old *criolla* favorites, such as *pescado trapiche* – fish with ginger, and *fonguito* – steamed, seasoned plantain.

Paladares

El Chanchullero
Teniente Rey 457, between Bernaza and El Cristo, Plaza del Cristo
Tel: 7-861 0915; www.el-chanchullero.com. Open daily 1pm–midnight **$**
Great atmosphere, lively crowd and music. This hole in the wall bar serves excellent drinks and tasty tapas or meals. The owner Yosvany has opened another restaurant in Alamar (5th G, 16204 between 162 and 162D in Zone 6), which is less touristy.

Doña Blanquita
Paseo de Martí (Prado) 158, first floor, between Colón and Refugio
Tel: 7-867 4958. Open daily noon–midnight. **$**

El Patio.

One of Havana's oldest *paladares*, but not necessarily the best. The food can be variable. However, it's pink, kitsch, and great fun, with plastic flowers and candles on the tables. Try for a table on the sweet little balcony overlooking the Prado.

Doña Eutimia
Callejón del Chorro, Plaza de la Catedral
Tel: 7-861 1332. Open daily noon–10.30pm. **$**
This historic *paladare* is a good place to try traditional Cuban food such as malanga fritters or tostones and the ropa vieja is highly rated, while lobster and other seafood is excellent value. Pleasant decor in a traditional setting tucked away just off the Plaza. Reservations usually required.

Ivan Justo
Aguacate 9, corner Chacón
Tel: 7-863 9697. Open daily noon–11pm. **$$**
Difficult to find, no sign, up a narrow staircase on the corner, but reservations recommended. You can eat inside or on the roof terrace, which is pleasant on a warm night. Imaginative food from this experienced chef, with specialties such as suckling pig and paella. Large portions.

La Julia
Calle O'Reilly 506, between Bernaza and Villegas
Tel: 7-862 7438. Open daily noon–11pm. **$**
One of the real old-style *paladares*, this is the kind of place where you feel as if you are a guest in someone's home, although the dining room opens out onto the street. Stick to the excellent *comida criolla*, featuring some of the best *frijoles* (fried beans) you will find, together with good prices and good service from a friendly family. Avoid the lobster.

Los Mercaderes
Mercaderes 207, between Lamparilla and Amargura
Tel: 7-861 2437. Open daily noon–10.30pm. **$**
There are three elegant dining rooms in this traditional colonial house with high ceilings and lofty doorways, beautifully kept by owner Yamil. Cuban food is the specialty and seafood is plentiful and imaginatively prepared. There is a good, if limited, wine list and excellent *mojitos*, while service is attentive.

La Moneda Cubana
Empedrado 152, between Mercaderes and San Ignacio
Tel: 7-861 5304; www.lamonedacubana.com. Open daily noon–late. **$**
Dine inside with views along Mercaderes or Empedrado or up on the rooftop with a fabulous view to La Cabaña and from where you can hear the 9pm cañonazo. Well-prepared and tasty Cuban dishes, attentive service, pleasant decor, good value for money.

Bars and Cafés

Hotel Ambos Mundos
Calle Obispo 153
Take the ornate elevator to the rooftop bar for a drink with a wonderful view. The ground-floor piano bar is pleasant, too, in a hushed and intimate kind of way.

Bosque Bologna
Calle Obispo 424
A cheerful place on this busy street, with green-painted trellises, and live music day and night.

Café el Escorial
Mercaderes 317, corner Muralla
A European-style coffee house serves coffee grown in the Sierra de Escambray and roasted and ground in-house. Enjoy sandwiches and a variety of cakes at one of the tables outside on the corner of Plaza Vieja.

Bar El Louvre, Hotel Inglaterra
Parque Central
The terrace bar is a great place for people watching. Among other things there are good fresh fruit juices, homemade lemonade, and what some say are the best ham and cheese sandwiches in Havana (and there's internet access in the lobby). There is always a group of musicians playing, and as often as not it's *Guantanamera*.

Bar Monserrate
Avenida de Bélgica (Monserrate) 401, corner of Obrapía
Good, reasonably priced cocktails in a bar with a laid-back, local atmosphere, next door to the far more swish and expensive El Floridita.

Café O'Reilly
Calle O'Reilly 203, between Cuba and San Ignacio
An atmospheric little bar with a spiral staircase leading to a small upper room where you can sit on the tiny balcony and drink one of the best cups of coffee in Havana. Good fruit juices, too. Tapas and other snacks are available. On the adjacent corner the bar has an open-air barbecue area with a few tables.

Café Paris
Calle San Ignacio 202, corner of Obispo. Open daily 9am–1am.
Live music and a vibrant atmosphere, with good drinks but only average food. Always busy and popular; get a table near the street so you can enjoy people watching as well as the band.

PRICE CATEGORIES

Price categories are for a three-course meal for one with a beer, or mojito. Wine puts the price up:
$ = under $25
$$ = $25–35
$$$ = over $35

El Floridita.

CUBA'S COLONIAL ARCHITECTURE

Colonial architecture in Havana may not be as decorative as that found in other Spanish colonies such as Peru, but it has a simple, solid elegance.

Old Havana is, without doubt, the finest showcase of colonial architecture in Cuba, but its features are seen all over the island. Other cities particularly worth visiting for their architecture are Camagüey, Gibara, Remedios, Santiago, and, especially, Trinidad.

The strongest influence on Cuban colonial architecture came, of course, from Spain, in particular from Andalusia, where the so-called Mudéjar style – a fusion of Christian and Arabic architectural traditions that developed in medieval Spain – predominated at the time of the colonization of Cuba. Many of the early buildings in Havana were built by Mudéjar craftsmen, who came by ship from Seville and Cádiz and adapted the styles they knew to suit the conditions in the Caribbean: primarily the hot climate and the relative paucity of materials. The talent of these craftsmen lay above all in carpentry. Woods such as mahogany and cedar were abundant in Cuba at that time, and were used to construct ceilings, doors, columns, and railings, as well as furniture.

The other predominant style is Baroque, which reached Havana in the late 18th century, and was primarily used in the building and decoration of churches. This more flamboyant, sophisticated architecture proved to be a perfect medium for expressing the new-found confidence of a nation enjoying its first real economic boom – though the wealth was concentrated in the hands of a few. While undoubtedly grander than anything that had gone before, fusion with the existing Mudéjar styles kept Cuban Baroque relatively simple.

The high-timbered ceilings of the Parador de los Tres Reyes restaurant in Camagüey are typical of 19th-century colonial architecture.

The louvered and stained-glass windows of the Museo de Arte Colonial offer a magnificent view of the unequal twin towers of Havana's cathedral.

Restrained Baroque: the swirls on the facade of Havana's cathedral are typical of Cuban Baroque. Because the local limestone was hard to work with, the style was less elaborate than that found in Europe, and some believe that to be a good thing, more in keeping with the Caribbean surroundings.

Many families use antique furniture and retain pre-Revolutionary fittings for lack of modern alternatives.

HOW TO BE COOL IN CUBA

The most striking features of Cuban colonial design are solutions to the problem of how to keep cool – namely, by creating the maximum amount of shade and ventilation.
Courtyards: many houses were laid out around a courtyard, with arcades enabling residents to move from room to room in the shade.
Doors: these were very tall and had small windows or *postigos* that could be opened to provide light and ventilation without having to disturb the residents' privacy by opening the whole door.
Ceilings: vaulted ceilings *(alfarjes)* were not easy to build but were higher than flat ones and kept rooms cooler.
***Mamparas:* these swing doors, with decorative glass panels and fancy woodwork, were popular in the 1800s and allowed air to circulate between rooms.**

Much of Old Havana has now been restored to its former glory by the Cuban tourism company, Habaguanex.

The Palacio de Ferrer in Cienfuegos is an ornate late 19th-century mansion with sea views over the harbor from its tower.

An 18th-century engraving of Havana's Plaza Vieja, notable for its grand houses and fine arches.

Night-time view over Centro Habana.

CENTRO HABANA AND VEDADO

Centro Habana is a run-down but colorful place with crumbling tenements and crowded markets, while Vedado's broad streets are quieter, more elegant, and the centerpiece is the stark, impressive Plaza de la Revolución.

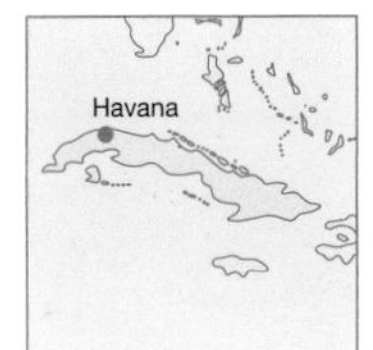

Bounded by the giant avenues of the Malecón to the north, Prado to the east, and Calzada de Infanta to the west, **Centro Habana** is a dilapidated, overcrowded district seething with life and noise. It dates mostly from the 19th century, when Havana, having burst out from its city walls, began to spread across the swampy lands and rocky pastures to its west. The restoration program has spread to Centro, notably to the Malecón, Monte, Cayo Hueso, and parts of Chinatown, but most of this district is as it has been for decades – tumbledown, narrow streets lined with tall, crumbling mansions divided between a dozen families into *ciudadelas* (little cities).

But look beyond the crumbling facades and you will see that many of these houses are true palaces, even if their glory has faded: pizzerias lit by priceless chandeliers; a narrow passageway lined with lofty marble columns; a pink marble bathroom with gold fittings, but nevertheless waterless and sometimes shared by 30 families. The street theater of everyday Havana lights up each corner and offers visitors a different kind of experience – of life as it really is lived in the city.

Cigar factories

The famously strong Partagás cigars (see page 202) have been rolled since 1845 at the **Fábrica de Tabacos Partagás** ❶ (Partagás Cigar Factory; Industria 520, between Dragones and Barcelona; tel: 7-862 4604; Mon–Fri 9am–1.30pm; regular 40-minute tours every 30 mins; tickets must be bought in hotel lobbies; no photos; store open daily 9am–5pm) just behind the Capitolio, but while renovation of the site is in progress, the factory is temporarily at San Carlos 812, between Sitios and Peñalver in Centro Habana. Real cigar smokers should resist the temptation to buy from the *jineteros*

Main Attractions
- Fábrica de Tabacos Partagás
- Malecón
- Hotel Nacional
- Callejón Hamel
- Coppelia Ice Cream Park
- Plaza de la Revolución
- Cementerio de Colón

The Partagás Cigar Factory.

Old trains on display in front of Parque de la Fraternidad.

(hustlers) gathered outside. Despite the stories they tell, most of their cigars are fakes and definitely not worth the high asking price. The equally famous **H. Upmann** cigar factory at Amistad 407 also offers guided tours. Some of the best Montecristos are rolled here.

Flanking the southern side of the Capitolio is the **Parque de la Fraternidad**, a busy, pleasant park with the Friendship Tree at its heart. This ceiba tree was planted in the soil of 17 nations by the delegates of the 1928 Pan-American conference to cement friendship between the countries of the Americas. On the west side is this area's main bus terminal, and you will see long lines for the buses.

The Queen's Avenue

The hectic **Avenida de la Reina** effectively forms the southern boundary to Centro Habana for most tourists. Somewhat confusingly, this street is also known as Avenida Simón Bolívar, and becomes Avenida Salvador Allende as it heads out toward Vedado. Two sites are worth noting among the multitude of stores and apartment blocks along its length. First, a magnificent Gothic church with lovely stained-glass windows, the **Iglesia del Sagrado Corazón de Jesús**; and a short way farther on, the splendid **Casa de Cultura de Centro Habana** (Avenida Salvador Allende 720, between Soledad and Castillejo; tel: 7-878 4727), which is always alive with musicians, dancers, and other aspiring artistes, who rent magnificent, decaying practice rooms for a pittance.

Running southwest from the east end of Reina is Calle Máximo Gómez, better known as **Monte**. This area has been crumbling away for decades but is now in the process of renovation. The imposing 19th-century mansions were once the summer homes of the city's colonial aristocracy, as it was cooler here than in the rest of the city during Havana's steamy summers.

The street begins to the south of the Parque de la Fraternidad, at the busy farmers' market of **Cuatro Caminos** – the largest market in the city, with separate sections for fruit and vegetables, meat, flowers, and prepared foods. There is a *guarapera* selling freshly pressed sugar-cane juice for around a Cuban peso a glass. This entire area is good for peso street food, such as peanut *turrón* (nougat) candy bars, reasonably cheesy pizza, *refrescos*, and *granizados* (shaved ices flavored with syrup), for those with stronger stomachs. The area has some good *paladar* restaurants, too. Opposite the market, there's an interesting herbalist with strong links to Santería, selling medicinal herbs alongside votive jars, candles, and bead necklaces dedicated to the *orishas* or gods of the religion.

Waitress at a Chinatown restaurant.

Chinatown

Easily reached by heading west along Dragones from the Capitolio is the **Barrio Chino** ❷ – Havana's once huge but now tiny Chinatown, centered on calles Cuchillo and San Nicolás. The first Chinese arrived in Cuba in the mid-19th century to build the country's railroads, but the community lost much of its homogeneity after the revolution, and has to a large extent been integrated into wider Cuban society. Still, many people in the area have distinctly Asiatic features and, confusingly, almost everyone is known by the nickname 'Chino.'

This area used to be notorious as the center of Havana's red-light district. Times have changed, and the infamous **Shanghai Theater** – described in Graham Greene's *Our Man in Havana*, and which once specialized in live sex acts and pornographic movies – has now re-opened as a nightclub specializing in karaoke. Castro and Hemingway were both regulars of the once-renowned Restaurante Pacífico, at the end of Calle Cuchillo on San Nicolás, but these days the food is not distinctively Chinese. Hemingway's son Gregory described a 1950s visit to the Pacífico with a five-piece Chinese orchestra on the second floor, a whorehouse on the third floor and, on the fourth floor, an opium den. On Calle Cuchillo, a small, not especially Chinese market is a hive of activity and does sell a few unusual things – fresh lychees and goose eggs for example – but watch out for pickpockets. There are also several places specializing in Chinese medicine.

The neo-Romanesque Santería church, **Nuestra Señora de la Caridad del Cobre** ❸ (calles Manrique and Salud) is to be found at the edge of Chinatown. This glorious frescoed and golden church – its dark interior lighted by candles and full of incense, flowers, and choral music – is undergoing lengthy restoration, so you won't yet be able to appreciate its beauty. Just inside the door is a shrine to the eight saints who are the most powerful *orishas* of the Santería faith.

The Malecón

The area of Centro Havana that most tourists visit is to the north. Emerging from the Castillo de la Punta at the end of the Prado, the 5km (3-mile) **Malecón** seafront stretch is Havana's main artery, running straight through to Vedado. Hitchhikers, runners, young couples, families,

WHERE

Take Avenida de Italia, also known as Galiano, down from Chinatown to the Malecón. This noisy commercial street, lined with crumbling tenements, has lots of *agropecuarios* (produce markets) and CUC stores. It is also home to the Casa de la Música. Set on the first floor of a huge apartment block, it looks unprepossessing but is known for its great music.

Havana street scene.

wheeler-dealers, prostitutes, elderly women walking the dog – such is the cross section of city life you will see here. Salsa bands rehearse in the buildings above, while children splash in the crashing (and heavily polluted) surf, or play makeshift games of baseball, fearless of the traffic as they run out to collect their balls, and musicians sit on the sea wall and play, hoping for a few pesos from tourists who show an interest. On weekend nights the Malecón turns into one huge party, when hundreds gather to dance and drink rum.

The first ornate building you see is the **Centro de Cultura Hispano-Americano**, with its second-floor balcony supported by caryatids (classical, draped female figures). Known as the Casa de las Cariátides, it has been extensively renovated and now stages temporary art and photographic exhibitions.

Many houses along the seafront here, having suffered from decades of neglect, are now undergoing desperately needed renovation, with many individual buildings having been sponsored by different Spanish provinces. Consequently, you find severely dilapidated, overcrowded buildings standing next to smartly painted new ones.

There are plans to completely rebuild the dangerously pitted seafront walkway. The spectacle of the sea roaring up against the Malecón is a part of the Havana scene, but the 'big seas' (during storms, giant breakers can reach up to 10 meters/30ft) do tremendous damage to roads, paths, and buildings. In winter, the road is often closed to traffic, and on some occasions the sea wall is severely breached, flooding Centro Havana.

For the time being, at least, you can still enjoy the dramatic spectacle from September to April – the biggest and best waves are to be seen in Vedado, by the Hotel Riviera and the statue of Calixto García, where the Malecón meets Presidentes. In contrast, when the tide is low and the sea calmer, you can see the remains of 19th-century stone baths carved from the limestone at the Old Havana end of the Malecón. The area, known as

Waves batter the Malecón.

the **Elysian Fields**, was a fashionable place to see and be seen. There were once separate bathing areas for men and women, and for blacks.

The Hotel Deauville at Malecón and Avenida de Italia (Galiano) is one of Centro Habana's only tourist hotels – a pretty grim-looking building, although the interior has been refurbished. Halfway along the promenade is the **Monumento a Antonio Maceo** ❹, a huge bronze statue of the 19th-century revolutionary hero. There is a code to the city's equestrian statues of heroes: when the horse is rearing up, with both hoofs in the air, the subject died in battle; if only one hoof is raised, the man died of wounds sustained in battle; if the horse has all four hoofs firmly on the ground, the hero in question died peacefully in his bed. Maceo's horse is rearing since he died fighting the Spanish in 1896. Close by is the 18th-century watchtower, the Torreón de San Lázaro.

The large tower block behind the statue, reached by sinuous drive, was built before the Revolution as a bank, but it is now Cuba's flagship hospital, the Hospital Nacional Hermanos Ameijeiras.

A couple of blocks inland is **Callejón de Hamel** ❺ – take San Lazaro behind the hospital, then turn left on Calle Hospital (see page 169).

Vedado

West of Centro Habana, the Malecón courses through to the green and leafy suburbs of Vedado. The district was loosely modeled on Miami: the streets are identified by numbers (running east to west) or letters (running north to south); and some Art Deco buildings vaguely recall the shabbier corners of South Beach in the 1970s, before its restoration. With palm trees lining many streets, it is a pleasant place to stroll or to stay, particularly if you want to take advantage of the nightlife on your doorstep.

The suburb is heralded by the twin towers of the **Hotel Nacional** ❻, Havana's most splendid hotel, perched on a rocky outcrop overlooking the Malecón. Modeled in the 1920s on the Breakers Hotel in

TIP

There is a television station in Vedado's hotel zone, from which Fidel Castro traditionally made his speeches. When he was due to arrive the streets were blocked off and residents were not allowed out on their balconies.

Restoring a vintage car on the Callejón de Hamel.

CALLEJÓN DE HAMEL

Anyone who takes an interest in Afro-Cuban religions and the powerful, percussion-driven music and dance that accompanies their ceremonies, should check out the Callejón de Hamel in the district of Cayo Hueso – a tiny backstreet off San Lázaro and Lucena in northwestern Centro Habana. The area has been dedicated to Palo Monte and Santería, with shrines to various *orishas* and tiny stores selling art and artifacts. The walls and houses have been plastered with enormous, boldly colored murals, pieces of sculpture, old typewriters, and bathtubs turned into seats. The project was initiated in 1990 by artist Salvador González. A nattily dressed man with the air of a showman, he is fired by his religious heritage, and there is considerable local pride in his achievement, especially considering the scarcity of available resources.

It's interesting to see at any time, but Sunday is the best day to go (noon–3pm), when an Afro-Cuban band strikes up with *batá* drums and fierce dancing for the mixed crowd of tourists and local people. The atmosphere is good, but it gets very crowded, so take care of your valuables, or better still, leave them behind in your hotel. You are welcome to take photos, but expect to make a contribution. Women sit at the gated entrance offering good-luck charms and fortune telling for an 'offering,' and the bands' CDs are for sale.

Palm Beach, Florida, it has serene gardens with conveniently placed chairs and tables, good views of the sea and a long, shaded veranda with comfy wicker chairs where you can escape the hubbub of the city for a while. The café bar has walls lined with pictures of those who stayed here in its glory days – movie stars such as Errol Flynn, Frank Sinatra, Ava Gardner, and Clark Gable, plus more recent celebrity visitors, such as Naomi Campbell.

The Malecón rolls on past the **Monumento al Maine** ❼, dedicated to the 260 US sailors who were killed when their ship blew up in Havana in 1898 (see page 43). A plaque on the monument declares, 'Victims Sacrificed by Imperialist Voracity in its Eagerness to Seize the Island of Cuba.' The US eagle that once topped the two graceful columns was felled by an angry mob with a crane in 1960.

The **US Interests' Section of the Swiss Embassy** – a faceless mass of concrete and tinted glass – lies a little father west. Throngs of over-dressed Cubans, hoping to join the '*Señores Imperialistas*' with an entry visa, gather in a little park on Calzada and K as they wait to be interviewed by the US consulate.

Protests against US policies are also held here and monuments come and go in line with events. These have included tit for tat measures: an electronic billboard scrolling out illuminated propaganda was blocked by 138 black flags, each with a white star, symbolising those who had died as the result of violent acts against Cuba since 1959.

A couple of blocks south, on calles 13 and L, is a building right out of Gotham City, designed by the firm of architects (Shreve, Lamb, and Harmon) who built the Empire State Building in New York. The families of many famous revolutionaries lived here. Next door, by the park, is the Hospital Camilo Cienfuegos, specializing in eye diseases. Another Vedado landmark is the blunt, curved **Edificio Focsa** ❽: although reminiscent of Stalinist architecture, it was actually built in the capitalist 1950s, and the Russians liked it so much that they copied the design for 10 buildings in Moscow.

La Rampa

The Hotel Nacional overlooks the junction of the Malecón and Calle 23 – known as **La Rampa**. This famous commercial artery houses many of the city's airline offices, the International Press Center, a few nightclubs, an excellent jazz club, and a whole host of fairly cheap but good snack bars.

One block away, off Calzada de Infanta, is the **Casa Museo de Abel Santamaría** ❾ (Calle 25 164, between O and P; Mon–Fri 10am–4pm; free), home of the joint leader (with Fidel) of the 26th of July Movement in the 1950s, tortured to death after the failed Moncada attack of 1953. Castro attended many meetings here. The building's main entrance is on Calle 25 next to Pain de Paris, but there is another on O and there are two elevators, helping conspirators make a

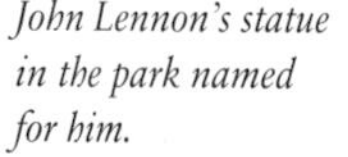

John Lennon's statue in the park named for him.

quick getaway if necessary. Today, the apartment on the sixth floor contains Santamaría memorabilia.

To the west is the **Hotel Habana Libre** ⑩, a tall building emblazoned with a bold blue-and-white ceramic mural. Inaugurated three months before the fall of the Batista dictatorship as the Havana Hilton, Fidel and his embryonic government took over an entire floor for several months in 1959. The first-floor café was the scene of a famous poison attempt on Castro, who used to spend late nights here chatting to kitchen staff – the cyanide capsule intended for his chocolate milkshake broke in the freezer. The café disappeared in a refurbishment that replaced the atmospheric 1950s interior with a bland, modern design.

Opposite the Habana Libre is the famous **Coppelia Ice Cream Park** ⑪, built by the revolutionary government to replace the notoriously elitist Vedado ice-cream parlors (where poorer and darker-skinned clients need not even have bothered lining up). The domed building, occupying a whole block, was designed by Mario Girona in 1966, based on an idea by Celia Sánchez, friend and companion of Fidel Castro and heroine of the Sierra Maestra campaign. It was in the park that the opening scenes of the 1994 film *Fresa y Chocolate* were filmed – the title refers to the two most common flavors, sometimes the only ones available – strawberry and chocolate.

Tourists are entitled to wait for two hours or more with everyone else if they wish to buy ice creams and pay in *moneda nacional*, but it is quicker (and more expensive) to pay in CUCs at one of the stands on the fringes of the park. The ice cream is less rich and creamy and more icy than it used to be – because of the cost.

Around the university

Two blocks southeast of here, the **Universidad de La Habana** ⑫ is a lovely group of classical buildings in golden stone placed around a cool and leafy garden, reached by climbing an impressive flight of steps at the head of San Lázaro. Anyone can stroll around the campus, and it is a good place to meet

Statue of Alma Mater in front of Havana's university.

THE POSADA DEBÂCLE

In 1976 former CIA agent Luís Posada Carriles was jailed in Venezuela for his part in bombing a Cuban airliner, en route from Caracas to Havana, killing all 73 people aboard, but he escaped nine years later. Posada also admitted being involved in the bombing of the Copacabana Hotel in Havana in 1997, in which an Italian tourist was killed, but later retracted his confession. In 2005 he was charged with illegal entry to the US. To the anger of both Cuban and Venezuelan authorities, which wanted him extradited, the charges were dropped in 2007, even though the us Justice Department described him as dangerous and 'an admitted mastermind of terrorist bombs and attacks.' In 2011 he was acquitted of 11 charges of perjury, obstructing the course of justice and immigration fraud.

The Hotel Nacional.

young Cubans, who love to practice their English. In the Faculty of Biology lies the **Museo Antropológico Montané** (Felipe Poey Building, Plaza Ignacio Agramonte; Mon–Fri 9am–noon, 1–4pm), with an excellent collection of pre-Columbian artifacts including the famous wooden Taíno Tobacco Idol, dating from around the 12th century, found in Maisí, at the far eastern tip of Cuba.

Opposite the university is a stark **monument to Julio Antonio Mella**, containing the ashes of the student who founded the Cuban Communist Party and was assassinated in Mexico in 1929. On January 28 – José Martí's birthday – a tremendous torchlit march starts from the monument.

Around the corner, the **Museo Napoleónico** ⓭ (San Miguel, 1159, corner of Ronda; tel: 7-879 1460; Tue–Sat 9.30am–5pm, Sun 9.30am–noon) is housed in a delightful mansion with a small garden. Much of this unexpected collection of Napoleonic art and memorabilia was brought by Julio Lobo, a 19th-century politician and sugar baron, from his travels in Europe. It includes Napoleon's death mask (made by one of his doctors who later moved to Santiago de Cuba, where he performed the first cataract operation), pistols from the Battle of Borodino, and a fine library.

Where Calzada de Infanta meets Avenida Salvador Allende (also called Carlos III) you'll find the **Quinta de los Molinos** ⓮ (closed to the public), reached via a tree-shaded drive. This was the site of 18th-century snuff mills built alongside the Zanja Real watercourse to Old Havana (see page 147), and parts of the 16th-century aqueduct have been incorporated into the water garden and grotto. Now quiet and neglected, the gardens were popular in colonial times, when the rich owners of summer palaces nearby could inspect slaves before they went to market. They are now home to La Madriguera, a center for young artists and a music venue known for rap, reggaeton, and rumba.

Revolution Square

South of here is the **Plaza de la Revolución** ⓯, the governmental heart

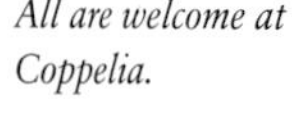

All are welcome at Coppelia.

of modern Havana. It is an extraordinary place – a vast, bleak square, big enough to hold the masses that came to hear Fidel's famous eight-hour May Day speeches, but normally empty of anyone except camera-toting tourists and the taxis that brought them. The exception to this is October 9, the anniversary of Che's death, when schoolchildren come here to lay flowers.

The whole region has been given over to eastern European-style monolithic architecture, where bureaucrats labor behind concrete walls. Yet the Revolution is not to blame: most of the buildings, including the Martí monument, went up during Batista's time, when the dictator expressed his taste for intimidating, uninspired design, as seen in the gray former Justice Ministry, finished in 1958, that now houses the Central Committee of the Communist Party.

At the center is the mighty **Monumento José Martí** ⓰ (tel: 7-859 2347; Mon–Sat 9am–5pm), which houses an informative museum, including the original design plans for the plaza and Martí monument. Ascend the monument (extra charge) for an impressive 360-degree view of the city: Habana Vieja looks a very long way away. Behind the monument is the monolithic Palacio de la Revolución, where senior ministers, including Fidel Castro, have their offices. Visitors are not permitted to photograph the palace, or loiter behind the monument.

The Ministerio del Interior is Cuba's most sinister and secretive organization (although vast, it has just one number listed in the phone book, which no one ever answers), yet it is housed in Cuba's most photographed building. The outside wall has a giant mural of Che Guevara executed in black metal, and best viewed at night when clever lighting gives the face an eerily three-dimensional look. The plaza is also the location of the Television and Radio Information and Communications Building, the Biblioteca Nacional, and the Teatro Nacional de Cuba (tel: 7-879 3558) – a stark building containing three theaters, the lively Café Cantante, a piano bar, a discotheque in the basement, and a

Musicians on the Malecón.

FACT

There is a philatelic museum – the Museo Postal José Luis Guerra Aguiar (Avenida Independencia, between 19 de Mayo and Arangurén; open Mon–Thu 8am–5.30pm, Fri 8am–4.30pm) – to the northeast of the square, with exhibitions of stamps from all over the world.

large sculpture garden where works by Cuban artists are displayed. On the east side of the plaza is the terminus for Astro, the long-distance bus company used by Cubans.

Avenida de los Presidentes

From the Plaza de la Revolución make your way (on foot or by taxi, depending on stamina) along the broad Avenida G, also called the **Avenida de Los Presidentes**, which crosses La Rampa, and is lined with lush, formal gardens and the former homes of the rich, most now government buildings. En route, you pass a monument to the murdered Chilean president Salvador Allende, and a gigantic marble tribute to past Cuban presidents. Once a favored hangout for disaffected youths, it has now been cleaned up. Where Avenida G meets the Malecón stands a monument to Calixto García.

A couple of blocks west, at Calle 17, between Avenidas D and E, is the **Museo de Artes Decorativas** ⓱ (tel: 7-830 8037; Tue–Sat 10am–5pm). It has a wonderful collection of European and oriental decorative arts, especially porcelain, which is displayed in a series of furnished rooms ranging from a rococo salon and Regency dining room to a gorgeous Art Deco bathroom. Many of the treasures in this museum belonged to María Luisa, Condesa de Revilla de Camargo, a member of the wealthy Gómez Mena family. She lived here from the 1930s until she fled after the revolution, leaving her collections of fine art hidden in the basement.

Where Avenida G crosses Línea, you find the delightful **Museo Nacional de la Danza** (Línea 365, corner G; tel: 7-831 2198, www.balletcuba.cult.cu; Tue–Sat 10am–6pm, Sun 9am–1pm), where guided tours are available of the personal collection of Alicia Alonso, and other memorabilia from the Ballet Nacional de Cuba.

Next door to the Hotel Presidente is the elegant cultural center, the **Casa de Las Américas** ⓲ (Calle 3 52, corner l; tel: 7-838 2706; www.casadelasamericas.org; Mon–Fri 8am–5pm). Housed in a landmark Art Deco building, it contains archives, a fine collection of Latin American art in the Sala Latinoamericana, and contemporary Cuban art in the Sala Contemporánea, and hosts workshops, lectures, and other cultural events. There is also a good book and music shop. Next door, the Galería Haydée Santamaría also exhibits the work of Latin American artists, including paintings, sculptures, engravings, and photography.

At the intersection of Avenida de los Presidentes and the Malecón, beside the Calixto García monument, the José Martí sports ground, built in 1961, is a fine example of the use of concrete in the 1960s, painted in bright colors to relieve the effect on the eye. From here, the Malecón heads west. There is an artisans' market, the Feria del Malecón, on the corner of Avenida D, and just beyond rises the Hotel Riviera, built by mob boss Meyer Lansky as a last attempt to re-create Las Vegas in the Caribbean. Lansky had a suite on

The mural of Che Guevara in Revolution Square.

the 20th floor, which can be booked by hotel guests. The interior of the Riviera is still pleasantly evocative of the 1950s, but the hotel has been both dwarfed and outclassed by the Hotel Meliá Cohiba next door, which was Cuba's first five-star hotel (see page 324).

Paseo

If you turn inland again by the Riviera, parallel with Avenida de los Presidentes is Paseo, another of the major thoroughfares of Vedado, which runs from the Malecón to the Plaza de la Revolución. The main point of interest along this street is the **Casa de la Amistad** (Paseo 406, between calles 17 and 19; tel: 7-830 3114), in a beautiful coral-pink 1920s mansion. This is the head office for the Cuban Institute for Friendship among the Peoples and also houses the Amistur travel agency, which specializes in social tourism. However, of more interest to the visitor may be the restaurant and bar and the music on offer; there is usually something going on here.

A few blocks away, on Calle 8, between 15 and 17, is the **Parque John Lennon** ⓳, a nicely landscaped park occupying one block, where the centerpiece is a realistic bronze statue of John Lennon, lounging nonchalantly on a park bench and inscribed with the line '*Dirás que soy un soñado, pero no soy el único*' (You may say that I'm a dreamer, but I'm not the only one). The statue was unveiled by Castro himself in December 2000. It's a favorite hangout spot for young people and there are occasional concerts.

City of the dead

You could turn right (west) on Paseo or get a taxi from Plaza de la Revolución – there are usually several there – to the **Cementerio de Colón** ⓴ (Columbus Cemetery; entrance on Calzada de Zapata; tel: 7-830 4517; daily 8am–5pm; guided tour), with its arched entrance gate, one of the largest necropolises in the world. Work began in the 1860s, when *habaneros* ran out of catacombs. A competition for its design was won by a Spaniard, Calixto de Loira y Cardosa. Although the Latin motto reads 'Pale Death enters both hovels and the palaces of kings,' Calixto ensured the dead could be separated by social status. He died before it was completed and became one of the first to be buried here. Wealthy *habaneros* competed to create the most impressive tombs, and the result is a morbid atmosphere that would have appealed to Edgar Allan Poe: a stone forest of Grecian temples and columns, crucified Christs, and angels of mercy. The mausoleums are an eclectic mix of Gothic and neoclassical styles, and stone dogs lie at their masters' feet.

Cubans make pilgrimages to the tomb of Amelia Goyre de la Hoz, La Milagrosa (The Miraculous One), who died in childbirth. She was buried in 1901 with her child at her feet, but when exhumed the child was supposedly found in her arms. Nobody seems clear about *why* she was exhumed, but she is an object of devotion.

Casa de las Américas.

Leaping from the rocks in front of the Malecón.

RESTAURANTS, PALADARES, BARS, AND CAFÉS

PRICE CATEGORIES

Price categories are for a three-course meal for one with a beer, or mojito. Wine puts the price up:
$ = under $25
$$ = $25–35
$$$ = over $35

Restaurants

1830
Malecón 1252 and 22, Vedado
Tel: 7-838 3090. Open daily L & D. **$$$**
Located just before you go under the tunnel to Miramar at the mouth of the Río Almendares in the Torreón de la Chorrera castle by the sea, this romantic restaurant is known for its cabaret shows and salsa dancing on Wednesday and Sunday nights. There is a bar, live music, and a pleasant garden on the waterfront where you can dance.

Casona de 17
Calle 17 60, between M and N, Vedado
Tel: 7-838 3136. Open noon–midnight. **$$–$$$**
Serves reasonably priced Cuban dishes, and more international food in the elegant surroundings of an old villa, opposite the Focsa Building. Two air-conditioned indoor restaurants and an Argentine-style barbecue-grill on the patio.

Polinesio
Hotel Habana Libre, Calle 23, Vedado
Tel: 7-838 4011. Open daily noon–midnight. **$$–$$$**
Attached to the Hotel Habana Libre but with access from the street, so it feels a bit less like a hotel restaurant. The food is also different, as they serve a variety of Chinese and Indonesian dishes. Once a Trader Vic's, and still with the same decor, it has been in operation for decades and is highly regarded.

Sociedad Asturiana Castropol
Malecón 107, between Genios and Crespo, Centro
Tel: 7-861 4864. Open daily noon–midnight. **$$**
Two very good restaurants in one location. Downstairs is a grill, where the food is cooked over coals and you eat in a beautiful central patio. Upstairs offers a more varied menu of meat or seafood with an excellent wine list served in an elegant air-conditioned dining room or on the balcony overlooking the Malecón and the sea. Music and a show start after 10pm Thursday to Sunday nights, going on late, with a cover charge.

Unión Francesa de Cuba
Corner of 17 and 6, overlooking Plaza John Lennon, Vedado
Tel: 7-832 4493. Open daily L & D. **$–$$**
International food is served in the main dining room and Cuban food on the roof terrace. A pleasant spot for a quiet lunch or relaxed dinner, surrounded by a nice garden, there is an extensive menu but for the best deal go for one of the set menus – a simple three-course meal including a drink for CUC$10–15. Their home made ice cream is good, fruit-flavored, and served in the fruit from which it is made.

Enjoy a mojito before your meal.

Paladares

Los Amigos
Calle M, between 19 and 21, Vedado
Tel: 7-830 0880. Open daily noon–midnight. **$**
Popular with Habaneros as well as tourists, this *paladar* offers good classic Cuban food that's a good value, unpretentious, and tasty. The interior design is nothing special, but the service is good and the food comes quite quickly.

Le Chansonnier
J 257, between 15 and Línea, Vedado
Tel: 7-832 1576; www.lechansonnierhabana.com. Open daily L & D. **$$**
A very elegant restaurant in a handsome Vedado mansion, with tall windows and doors and high ceilings hung with chandeliers, all tastefully decorated. The food and multilingual service are among the best in Havana.

Decameron
Línea 753, between Paseo and 2, Vedado
Tel: 7-832 2444; Email: restaurantedecameron@gmail.com. Open daily L & D. **$$**
It doesn't look like a restaurant from the outside, but ring the bell and enter this small *paladar* to find two antique-filled rooms, one of which is lined with clocks. Very good Cuban food at reasonable prices, but note that they

add a 10 percent service charge.

El Gringo Viejo
Calle 21 454, between E and F, Vedado
Tel: 7-831 1946. Open daily noon–11pm. **$**
'The Old Gringo' is popular for its efficient service as well as the menu, which features seafood as well as the usual offerings. The decor is wall-to-wall movie memorabilia.

La Guarida
Calle Concordia 418, between Gervasio and Escobar, Centro
Tel: 7-866 9047; www.laguarida.com. Open daily L & D. **$$–$$$**
You must book well in advance as this *paladar, which* featured in the famous Cuban film *Fresa y Chocolate* – or, rather, the film featured the crumbling tenement building, and the *paladar* followed two years later. It is always full of tourists, and if a tour party is in service suffers. The decor is kitsch and eclectic, the food is varied and excellent, and portions are 'nouveau' without being small. The prices are high, as the restaurant trades on its movie connections, but it is well worth a visit.

Café Laurent
M 257, between 19 and 21, Vedado
Tel: 7-831 2090; http://cafelaurentcuba.com. Open daily L & D. **$$–$$$**
A very upscale *paladar*, that's modern and elegant, with efficient service and a high standard of fusion cuisine – the closest you'll come to fine dining. Located in the penthouse, you emerge from the elevator into a dining room with wonderful views over Havana from the huge windows and the terrace.

Mediterráneo Havana
Calle 13 406, between F and G, Vedado
Tel: 7-832 4894; http://medhavana.com. Open daily L & D. **$$**
Eat inside or on the upstairs terrace overlooking the street. If you are craving something other than beans and rice and want some good pasta, pizza, risotto, a decent tiramisu, or even just some variety in the seafood, this is the place to come. There is also a good bar; try the strawberry *daiquirí*. Very good value and friendly service.

Las Mercedes
Calle 18 204, between 15 and 17, Vedado
Tel: 7-831 5706. Open daily noon–midnight. **$$**
Smart, with good-quality furniture and table linens. The room is decorated with fairy lights, and Jorge Pérez and his family provide a friendly atmosphere and like to get to know their customers. Some visitors eat here every night of their stay in Havana, appreciating the home cooking.

El Monguito
Calle L, between 23 and 25, Vedado
Tel: 7-831 2165. Open daily noon–midnight. **$**
Opposite the Havana Libre hotel, this small restaurant in the family living room serves traditional, tasty *criolla* food: pork, chicken, and fish with *congrís*, fried plantain and salad. Plastic tables and chairs are decorated with plastic flowers – the outdoors brought indoors.

San Cristóbal
San Rafael 469. Centro
Tel: 7-860 1705. Open daily L & D. **$$**
This is a beautiful restaurant in a lovely old building, whether you sit in the dining room or on the covered patio area. It's famed for the warm, multilingual hospitality as much as for the food, and is justifiably popular, so reservations are essential. The platter of starters is magnificent, and rum and cigars follow an excellent meal.

La Tasquita
Jovellar 160, between Espada and San Francisco, Centro
Tel: 7-873 4916. Open daily noon–2am. **$**
Very good food at excellent prices make this a place that's well worth seeking out. Meat dishes such as pork, chicken, or fish come with all the trimmings: rice and beans, sweet potato, and good salads. Its modern interior, with clean and minimalist furnishings, contrasts with most antique-filled places. Unusually, this is a non-smoking *paladar*.

Bars and Cafés

Bar-Café Centro de Prensa
Calle 23, corner of Calle O, Vedado
A pleasant place for a drink, where you can feel as if you are joining the intellectual café society. It closes at 7pm, though.

Hotel Nacional
Calle O and 21, Vedado
An excellent *mojito* or *daiquirí* on the hotel's broad, landscaped terrace overlooking the sea is one of the delights of Havana, especially when the sun is going down.

Café Neruda
Malecón, 353–7, between Galiano and Aguila
A great, modern, open-air bar with a glass front, located in the shell of a ruined building on the seafront. Run by Habaguanex, it has flair and style while prices of drinks, meals, and snacks are moderate. It is a very popular place to stop while strolling along the Malecón and there are usually lines of young couples waiting outside on weekend nights.

Opus Bar
Calzada, corner of Calle D, Vedado
Above the Teatro Roldán, this is a tranquil, comfortable bar.

Doorman at the Hotel Nacional.

An old Chevrolet at Marina Hemingway.

AROUND HAVANA

The area around Havana contains an eclectic mix of things to see – from classy Miramar in the west to the Parque Lenin, a delightful botanical garden, a couple of Hemingway sites, and an eastern beach.

Visitors to Havana generally concentrate on La Habana Vieja, Centro, and Vedado, but there are other areas not far away that are well worth visiting if you have time.

Continuing westward from Vedado, where the previous chapter left off, you will soon come to the suburb of Miramar, which is divided from Vedado by the Río Almendares. You can cross into Miramar by tunnel, close to the bay, or farther inland by the road bridge, an extension of La Rampa (Calle 23).

Miramar

Miramar ❶ is a suburb of broad, tree-lined avenues, once the home of Havana's wealthiest residents, and still pretty smart compared with much of the city, although many of the buildings have seen better days. It is also an area that seems to have no center, perhaps because it was modeled on Las Vegas, rather than on colonial Spanish cities. High-rise hotels, luxury apartments to rent to foreigners, and business centers have sprung up all over the area.

Quinta Avenida (Fifth Avenue) is a broad promenade, planted with vividly flowering trees and bushes, where most of the foreign companies who have chosen to defy the US ban and invest in Cuba have their offices. Signs are everywhere: Benetton, Castrol, Bayer, Philips. It is also the home of the city's foreign embassies, housed in beautiful buildings set in lush gardens.

Quinta Avenida is home to one of the city's quirkiest museums – the **Museo del Ministerio del Interior** (Avenida 5, corner Calle 14; tel: 7-203 4432; Tue–Fri 9am–5pm, Sat 9am–4pm), which catalogs the history of the police force as well as the CIA's numerous attempts to destabilize the Cuban state and to assassinate Castro.

A little farther along, between calles 24 and 26, there is a pretty little park, shaded by enormous, ancient banyan

Main Attractions
- Miramar
- Tropicana
- Marina Hemingway
- Parque Lenin
- El Rincón
- Finca Vigía
- Santa María del Mar

A weathered facade in Miramar.

trees. Heading from here toward the sea you will come to the **Maqueta de la Habana** (Calle 28 113, between 1st and 3rd Avenues; tel: 7-202 7322; Tue–Sat 9.30am–5pm). This vast scale model of the city took 10 years to construct, and is the largest of its kind after a model of New York. Every street, every house, every vacant lot, every tree is faithfully represented, made out of cigar boxes; different colors show from which periods the districts date.

Back on Quinta, farther west at No. 6502, between 62 and 66, the giant **Russian Embassy** towers over Miramar. This huge, ugly complex of offices and apartments once housed the various delegations of the Soviet Union. Now the independent former Soviet states have moved out and have their own embassies, leaving the greatly reduced Russian mission somewhat lost and lonely, but hard to overlook.

Close by, on the seafront, is the **Acuario Nacional** (National Aquarium; 3rd Avenue, between calles 60 and 62; tel: 7-202 5872; www.acuarionacional.cu; Tue–Sun 10am–6pm), which has an endangered-species breeding program, and treats injured animals before returning them to the wild. Unfortunately, it also stages three dolphin and sea-lion shows throughout

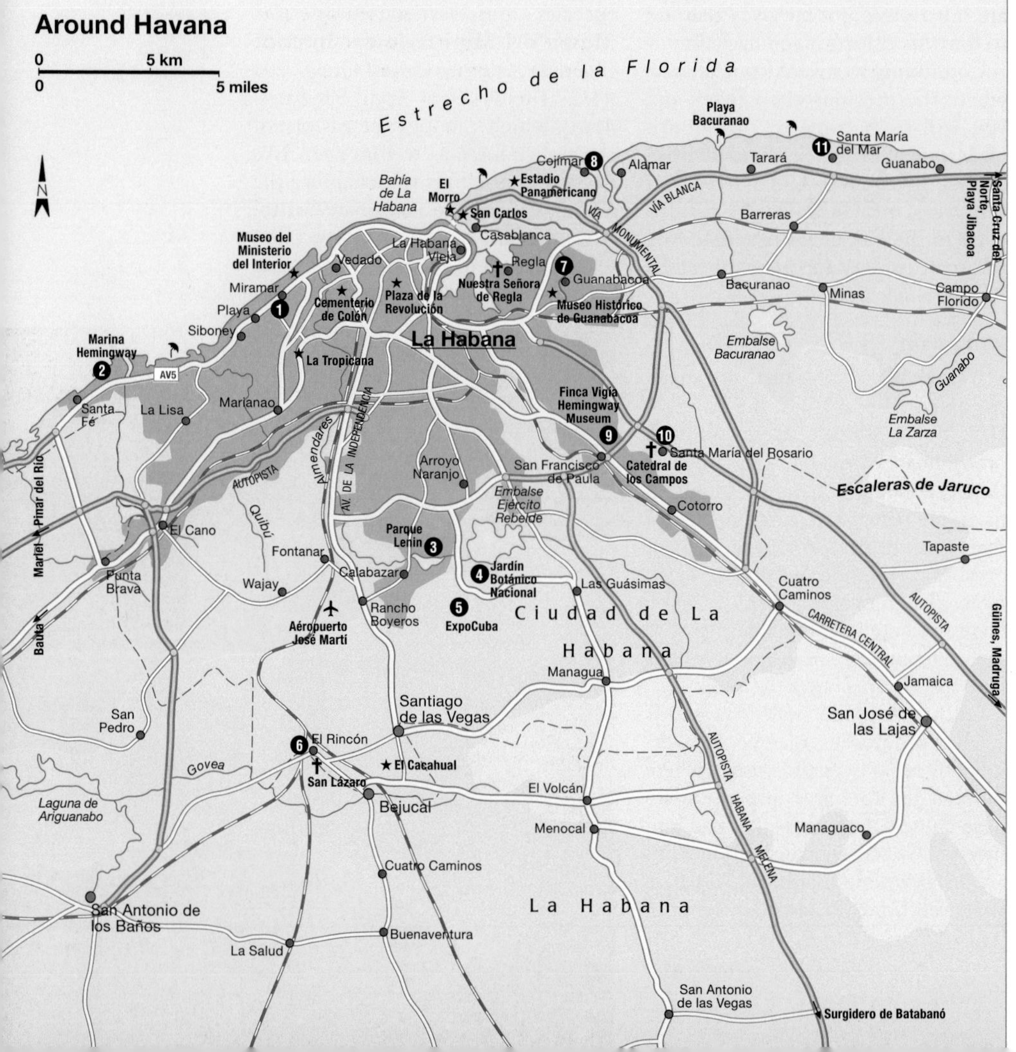

the day (small extra charge) and is a great favorite with local families, especially on weekends, when it gets quite crowded. Note that Cuba is in the habit of capturing wild dolphins, removing them from their natural habitat and families so they can be confined and trained for human entertainment, a practice condemned by conservation groups worldwide. Opposite is a little complex of bars and restaurants.

Just inland from the Russian Embassy, on the western end of Avenida 7, is the **Fundación La Naturaleza y el Hombre Antonio Nuñez Jiménez** (Avenida 5B, between calles 66 and 70; www.fanj.org; Mon–Fri 9am–4pm; advance booking essential). This fascinating place displays the canoe in which naturalist Antonio Núñez Jiménez and his team traveled from the source of the Amazon to the sea in 1987. There is a wealth of objects gathered from the indigenous people they met, including lots of erotic ceramic figures. The foundation also has an excellent photographic collection, and Oswaldo Guayasamin's portrait of Fidel Castro.

Retracing your steps eastward, another attraction is the **Teatro Karl Marx** (Primera Avenida, corner Calle 10; tel: 7-209 1991), which is good for concerts and movie premieres.

Southern and western suburbs

South of Miramar, in Marianao, is the **Tropicana** nightclub (see page 182), while to the west extend endless green suburbs, such as **Cubanacán** and **Siboney**, where many government offices are located, and a lot of party functionaries live. Cubanacán is also the location of the Instituto Superior de Arte, and a large conference center.

At the farthest outskirts of Havana, in what was once a fishing village called Santa Fé, is the marine resort called **Marina Hemingway** ❷. There are hotels and villas for rent, several expensive restaurants and duty-free stores, and a popular center for sport fishing, sailing, and scuba diving (see page 345). From the marina, the coastal road carries on west toward the province of Pinar del Río. It passes a few small resorts, such as **Playa Baracoa**,

The stark Russian Embassy building.

Maqueta de la Habana.

A Night at the Tropicana

Cuba's unique brand of escapism is showcased here in breathtaking glamor, a colorful spectacle where cabaret meets carnival.

The roulette tables may be gone, but little else has changed in the Tropicana – which has been Havana's most famous cabaret spot since it opened in 1931, and the only place of its kind that has operated more or less continuously from the days when the Mafia and their hedonist friends lavished money on nightlife in Havana, through the austere years of the revolution. Internationally famous as one of the best shows in the world, the Tropicana (Calle 72 4504, between Avenida 43 and 45, Marianao, western Havana; tel: 7-267 0110; www.cabaret-tropicana.com) has all the glitz and glamor of a casino show, without the casino. It has been called the Moulin Rouge with Cuban music and rhythm.

Stage beneath the stars

Doors open from 8.30pm for drinks or dinner and shows start at 10pm nightly except Monday, weather permitting, lasting 1 hour and 45 minutes. Billed as an open-air paradise '*bajo las estrellas*' (under the stars), it is often forced to cancel shows in the rainy season. The place is lit up like a Christmas tree: blue neon signs announce the entrance, and a huge fountain with statues of frolicking naked women is bathed in blue and red. A small band warms up the crowd at the entrance, to add to the carnival atmosphere.

The setting is breathtaking. Tables fan out like sunbeams around the semicircular stage, with enough room to seat 1,400 and stand many more; tropical trees enclose the amphitheater in a sheltering cocoon; among the foliage, large neon lights spell out the names of legends who performed here in pre-revolutionary times, such as Carmen Miranda and Nat King Cole. On a good night, the warm tropical air is seductive and the stars are visible through the treetops. This being Cuba, there may also be the odd cat running around the audience's legs, bringing the tone back down to earth.

Tropicana's extravaganza has changed little over the decades.

A tropical extravaganza

With the triumphant blare of a 20-piece band, the show begins. Women in silver lamé coats and top hats float across the stage on trapezes. Dancers leap past in a blur of feathers, glitter, and long legs. A bizarre pageant may be thrown in. Then, as if to mock the power shortages elsewhere, dancers appear with giant, blazing candelabras sprouting bizarrely from their heads.

It's the sort of extravaganza preserved elsewhere in the world only in casinos, although many of the costumes have echoes of carnival processions in Rio de Janeiro or Trinidad. Cubans love their vast, hectic, titillating shows, but few can afford a night at the Tropicana; lesser versions can be seen around the island – the best, also called the Tropicana, in Santiago de Cuba.

One reason the Tropicana has survived is that it brings in tourist revenue: entrance fees are 75, 85, or 95 CUCs depending on the seat and the age of the quarter-bottle of rum (with mixer and cigar – the smoke can be overpowering) included. The most expensive seats are closest to the stage; you get a better view from the mid-range ones, which are slightly raised. Transportation, snacks, or dinner (the food and service are heavily criticized) can be arranged at extra cost. The Tropicana is a prime haunt for Cuba's most gorgeous *jineteras* (prostitutes) who hunt out single men, and introduce themselves as 'dancing students' who just happen to be catching the show. The discotheque attached to the club goes on, very loudly, till 2am.

and **El Salado**, pleasant, sleepy places with wooden houses along the seafront and small rocky beaches, before it reaches Mariel (see page 190).

Parque Lenin to El Rincon

Directly south of Havana on the airport road (officially called Rancho Boyeros, but Avenida Independencia on most street signs) is **Parque Lenin** ❸ (park daily, attractions Wed–Sun 9am–5pm; park free, but charges for some amenities and attractions), a vast stretch of gently rolling parkland with tall trees and bamboo stands. After years of stagnation in the 'Special Period,' the park is slowly gaining a new lease on life. Some rides and shows, and the 19th-century miniature steam railroad, have reopened and there are new cafés serving Cubans in pesos and foreigners in CUCs, although often only on Sundays. Among the attractions is an artificial lake with rowboats, a monument and museum dedicated to the park's creator, Celia Sánchez; and a giant, well-tended stone head of Lenin – one of the last such monuments in the world.

South of the park is the largest botanical garden in Latin America, the **Jardín Botánico Nacional** ❹ (Wed–Sun 9am–4pm, Mon–Tue by arrangement through your hotel). Looking after the vast areas of pasture and woodland is quite a struggle, and some areas are sorely neglected. The beautiful Japanese Garden is well maintained, however, and there are attractive greenhouses with large collections of tropical, desert, and temperate flora (there are poinsettias the size of Christmas trees), as well as an extensive herb garden, which supplies medicinal plants to many of Havana's *yerberos* (herbalists). The entrance fee includes the services of a knowledgeable guide. The garden has a herbal tearoom, a botanical bookstore, a plant store, and one of Cuba' very few vegetarian restaurants (see page 187).

Across the road **ExpoCuba** ❺ (Wed–Sun 10am–5pm) is a sprawling area of pavilions celebrating Cuba's achievements in science, health, education, and the arts.

About 8km (5 miles) down Avenida de la Independencia from the Parque Lenin turning is the small town of **Santiago de las Vegas**, a sleepy place that wakes up just once a year for the **Procession of the Miracles.** On the eve of December 17, the day of San Lázaro – patron saint of the sick, and also worshiped by followers of Santería (see page 77) – people come from all over Cuba to the little church of **San Lázaro at El Rincón** ❻, just south of town, to pray for help or forgiveness. Thousands of people – a mixture of penitents and those who come just to join in – process slowly through the town to the church, where the pilgrimage culminates with a Mass held at midnight. The scenes inside the church are often emotional, with people shouting '¡Viva Lázaro!' '¡Viva Cristo!' Spirits run so high that the security forces always turn out in force in case of trouble.

Insignia for the members-only Club Náutico la Habana located at Marina Hemingway.

The eastern suburbs

The suburbs east of Havana offer a slice of life you won't see in the city,

Trying out a vintage kart on display at Marina Hemingway.

FACT

En route to Regla or Casablanca on the ferry, you may see passengers dropping paper into the sea – this means they are hoping to rid themselves of their problems in a Santería ceremony.

but if you only have a short time in Cuba you will have plenty to do in Old Havana and Vedado, and if you have longer you will almost certainly be visiting some of the better-known towns on the island. These small towns, although they get a mention, will not be high on most visitors' lists.

The ramshackle little town of **Casablanca** can best be reached from Old Havana by ferry *(lancha)*, which will pick you up at the foot of calles Luz and Santa Clara and take you to the other side of the harbor. An alternative is to walk about 15 minutes from the fortress of La Cabaña. Casablanca is famous for the statue that dominates the bay, the figure of Christ, carved from Italian marble, and very similar to the more famous one in Rio de Janeiro. Sometimes known as **El Cristo de Casablanca**, it was carved by Cuban sculptor Jilma Madra, and inaugurated in December 1958, shortly before the fall of Batista. In the early years of the revolution the statue was struck by lightning and the head fell off. The government had the figure repaired – to the consternation of some communists who felt it a 'waste of the people's money' to repair a religious monument. The other noticeable structure here is the domed, white **Observatorio Nacional** (no public access). You can continue on from Casablanca east to Matanzas via the electric Hershey train, built when the Hershey family operated the sugar refinery at Santa Cruz del Norte (see page 187).

If you want to visit **Regla**, the best way to get there is also by ferry from the foot of calles Luz and Santa Clara in Old Havana, but it is not the same ferry that goes to Casablanca. Regla is ringed by heavy industry, but the old town is still quite pleasant, and its main forms of transportation are trucks and horse-drawn carts. The main reason people come here is to visit the early 19th-century **Iglesia de Nuestra Señora de Regla**, (daily 7.30am–5.30pm). This church is dedicated to the black Virgen de Regla, the patron saint of Cuba's sailors. Her counterpart in Santería is Yemayá, goddess of the sea. You will see worshipers making offerings here,

Classic American car in Guanabacoa.

SMALL TOWN WITH BIG CONNECTIONS

If you have your own transportation, and time to spare, you might like to make a brief trip to the southwest of Havana (some 37km/22 miles along the Autopista del Mediodía), to San Antonio de los Baños, which may be the most filmed small town in the developing world. Just 8km (5 miles) away is the Escuela Internacional del Cine (International Film School), whose students, drawn from 50 countries in Latin America, Asia, and Africa, often use San Antonio and its residents in their graduating projects. Gabriel García Márquez is one of the three founders and a benefactor of the school, which he has often visited to teach classes in screenwriting. Other notables who have worked with the school include Robert Redford and Francis Ford Coppola.

San Antonio is known, too, for its annual International Humor Festival (in April), and has a small Museo del Humor, which exhibits satirical cartoons. It is also the birthplace of both the composer-singer Silvio Rodríguez (in 1946), whose political lyrics have made him a national icon; and of the late Eduardo Abela (1889–1965), whose cartoon character, El Bobo (The Fool), which appeared in a daily newspaper in the 1930s, created biting social criticism. El Bobo is now the town symbol, standing at its entrance. There is a gallery named after the artist, but it exhibits the work of local artists and does not contain his works.

many dressed in blue, or wearing blue-and-crystal beads – the colors of Yemayá. Her day is September 8, when there is a procession in her honor. The church also has an altar to Santa Bárbara, twinned in Santería with Changó, god of war and *machismo*. Offerings here are in red, the color of Changó. His feast day is celebrated on December 4. The **Museo Municipal de Regla** (Calle Martí 158, between Facciolo and La Piedra; tel: 7-797 6989; Tue–Sat 9am–5pm, Sun 9am–1pm) has information and displays of Yoruba culture and the links with Santería.

Guanabacoa

Santería is strong in **Guanabacoa** ❼ as well, a town renowned in Cuba for its connections with Afro-Cuban religions. Though the outskirts are grim and faceless, the town has an agreeable **plaza** and several interesting churches (in the process of restoration).

The **Museo Histórico de Guanabacoa** (Calle Martí 108, between Versalles and San Antonio; tel: 7-897 9117; Tue–Sat 10am–5pm, Sun 9am–1pm) is best known for its exhibitions on Afro-Cuban cults. There is also a lot about local resistance to the British invasion of 1762. Less heroically, Guanabacoa was a nexus for the slave trade. Wander along **Calle Amargura** (Bitterness Street), where slaves were dragged en route to their executions. A festival celebrating Cuba's African roots is held in Guanabacoa the last week of November every year.

Guanabacoa also has an interesting Jewish cemetery, started at the beginning of the 20th century, containing graves of victims of the Machado dictatorship and a memorial to those who died in the Holocaust.

Driving to Guanabacoa, you take a turning off the Central Highway, 5km (3 miles) east of Havana. By public transportation, you could take bus Ruta 3 from Parque de la Fraternidad or the ferry to Regla and then another bus from there to Guanabacoa. There are also guided excursions that include the town on a trip to nearby Cojímar.

Cojímar to Santa María del Rosario

The former fishing village of **Cojímar** ❽, 16km (10 miles) from Old Havana, is popular for its Hemingway connection, but now it is a concrete mess. The seafront took a battering in the 2008 hurricanes and the wharf where Hemingway kept his boat, the *Pilar*, was smashed. Hemingway used the village as the setting for *The Old Man and the Sea* and celebrated his Nobel Prize here in 1954. There is a bust of the author made from boat propellers donated by local fishermen and housed in a gazebo by the cube-shaped Spanish fortress, now occupied by the military.

Just off the highway before Cojímar is the **Villa Pan Americana**, a complex of sports amenities, apartments, and a hotel built for the 1991 regional games. The volunteers who took on

The late Gregorio Fuentes, pictured here in Cojímar, was Hemingway's fishing guide for nearly 30 years.

Fire-breathing dancer in Guanabacoa.

the huge task of building the complex now live in the athletes' apartments, though some are still used by athletes competing at the nearby stadium (Estadio Panamericano).

Across an inlet to the east of Cojímar lies **Alamar**, a suburb built by volunteers, known as micro-brigades, after the revolution. Originally planned for 40,000 people, it now has closer to 100,000, mostly in a depressing array of five-storey walk-up apartment blocks. Despite – or because of – the grim surroundings, a strong musical culture has sprung up in Alamar. Many young bands rehearse in this dingy neighborhood, which stages an annual international rap festival, held in August at the **Casa de la Cultura de Alamar**.

Southeast on the *autopista* (Via Monumental) is the suburb of **San Francisco de Paula**, 12km (8 miles) from the city center, with the Hemingway Museum at **Finca Vigía** ❾ (tel: 7-891 0809; http://fincafoundation.org; Wed–Mon 10am–4pm, closed when it rains). Journalist Martha Gellhorn, soon to be Hemingway's third wife, was not content to live in a room at the Hotel Ambos Mundos. She found a house called Finca Vigía – a former cattle farm on the site of a Spanish fort. The couple bought it in 1940 for US$18,500, and, although Gellhorn later divorced him, Hemingway stayed on at the *finca* for most of his life. The house lies at the end of a long, leafy driveway and is surrounded by lush gardens. The views over Havana are splendid. The mansion looks much as he left it, but was meticulously renovated by a joint US-Cuban project to restore the house and preserve the author's papers. Among the relics are 9,000 books, Hemingway's original Royal typewriter, and innumerable bullfighting posters and animal heads – mementoes from Spain and Africa. Visitors can only look in through the open doors and windows, but you get an excellent view of the large, airy rooms and their contents. Close to the main house is a four-story tower, from which the estate gets its name – *vigía* means 'lookout.' The pool where Ava Gardner swam naked and Gary Cooper once lolled, tanning his famous torso, is still there and his boat is in the gardens.

Finca Vigía has been beautifully renovated in recent years.

Santa María del Rosario ❿ nearby is a lovely place with tall trees, colonial houses, and pleasant inhabitants. The main attraction is the 18th-century **Catedral de los Campos**, best visited on Sunday afternoon (Mass is at 2.30pm) – the only time you can be fairly sure of seeing the Baroque paintings and statues. Across the shady plaza is the restored **Casa del Conde de Bayona**, home of the Count of Bayona, a sugar baron notorious for executing a group of rebellious slaves. The execution site is marked on the **Loma de la Cruz** (Hill of the Cross), up a steep street from the plaza. The plain wooden cross was erected as a warning to other slaves, and two flanking crosses were added in 1959 to represent the thieves crucified with Christ.

Map on page 180

Playas del Este

Beyond Alamar stretch a series of beach resorts known collectively as the **Playas del Este** (Eastern Beaches). This is where *habaneros* come to enjoy the sea and sand. The closest beach is **Playa Bacuranao,** on a small horseshoe-shaped inlet. A favorite with Cuban families, it is packed in July and August.

After this is Tarará, where there is a marina and a famous hospital where victims of the Chernobyl nuclear explosion are treated. Then comes a 16km (10-mile) stretch of open sea, sand dunes, and coconut palms. The sand starts at **El Mégano** and continues to **Santa María del Mar** ⓫, which has a good beach and is the nicest section of this coast, with a number of seafront hotels. Farther on is **Guanabo**, an old seaside town with a lively beach and a number of wooden bungalows built in the 1920s and 1930s, which are very popular with Cubans. Much of this stretch of coast can be seen by taking a ride on the hop-on, hop-off HabanaBusTour.

Farther east lies **Santa Cruz del Norte**, site of Cuba's largest rum distillery (home of Havana Club). Inland is the decommissioned **Central Camilo Cienfuegos** sugar mill, founded by the Hershey Chocolate Company during the sugar boom in 1917.

The coast road continues past attractive **Playa Jibacoa**, a good spot for family vacations with some good walking opportunities, and then reaches the **Litoral Norte** (North Coast), where beach resorts sit amid coastal vegetation. While much of the route along the Vía Blanca is attractive, there are also parts spoiled by heavy industry and smelly oil wells right by the sea.

Golden sands and coconut palms typify the Playas del Este.

RESTAURANTS AND PALADARES

PRICE CATEGORIES

Price categories are for a three-course meal for one with a beer, or mojito. Wine puts the price up:
$ = under $25
$$ = $25–35
$$$ = over $35

Restaurants

El Aljibe
Avenida 7, between calles 24 and 26, Miramar
Tel: 7-204 1583. Open daily noon–midnight. **$**
Open-air dining; the very popular specialty is *pollo al aljibe*, chicken with rice, beans, potatoes, and salad – a delicious recipe on an otherwise unprepossessing menu. First opened in 1947, it closed in 1961, but was reopened in 1993 by the state with the original owner bringing his famous dish back to life.

El Eco-Restaurant El Bambú
Jardín Botánico, Carretera El Rocío, Km 3.5, Boyeros
Tel: 7-643 7278. Open daily (for foreign tourists) L only. **$**
Eat all you want for a set price from a huge array of vegetarian dishes, ranging from soups, salads, and rice dishes to puddings and fresh fruit juices. Most products are grown on the premises, and cooked with solar power.

La Fontana Grill, Bar & Lounge
Avenida 3ra 305, corner Calle 46, Miramar
Tel: 7-202 8337; www.lafontanahavana.info. Open daily noon–11.30pm, bar open until 6am. **$$$**
Excellent grilled or roasted meats, a range of seafood, and lots of variety on the Cuban menu, plus impeccable service, attracts Cubans and foreigners alike, and its popularity means that reservations are advisable, particularly at night. The location is beautiful, with seating in the open air by the fish pond or indoors by an aquarium, and it's a good choice for a special night – with wine, it can cost around CUC$100 for two.

El Tocororo
Calle 18 302 and Avenida 3ra, Miramar
Tel: 7-204 2209, 202 4530. Open daily noon–midnight. **$$$**
Housed in an attractive Miramar villa, with a striking array of Art Nouveau lampshades. The *criolla* food is good and tasty. Book ahead as it is often used by tour groups.

Paladars

La Cocina de Lilliam
Calle 48 1311, between avenidas 13 and 15, Miramar
Tel: 7-209 6514; www.lacocinadelilliam.com. Open Tue–Sat noon–3pm, 7–11pm. **$$**
Lovely setting with tables set in a pretty garden. Very good and tasty Cuban and Spanish-influenced dishes, which are popular so reservations are recommended. At this paladar they bake their own bread and make ice cream with unusual flavors.

La Esperanza
Calle 16 105, between Avenidas 1 and 3, Miramar
Tel: 7-202 4361; www.paladarlaesperanza.com. Open Mon–Sat 7pm–11.30pm. **$$**
Small and intimate, with the atmosphere of a 1950s salon, this is a top-of-the-range paladar and reservations are essential. Excellent cocktails prepare you for a delectable meal, and Hubert is an attentive host.

Tending the crops at a Viñales tobacco plantation.

VIÑALES AND THE WEST

Cuba's westernmost province is one of its most beautiful, a lush and lovely landscape where tobacco, bananas, and pineapples are grown, where fields are tilled by ox-drawn plows, and white sandy beaches are never far away.

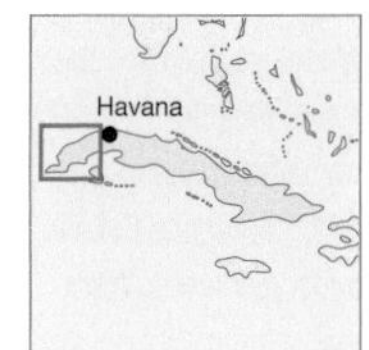

Main Attractions
- Las Terrazas
- Soroa Orchideario
- Parque Nacional de la Güira
- Pinar del Río
- Viñales
- Cayo Levisa
- Punta María La Gorda

Jutting out to the west of Havana, the province of Pinar del Río looks and feels quite different from the rest of Cuba. This is the country's tobacco heartland. Physically, it is dominated by a string of rounded limestone mountains called *mogotes*, around Viñales; in their shadows are lush green tobacco fields – *vegas*. Southwest of the *mogotes* lies the area known as Vuelta Abajo that produces the world's finest tobacco leaves, the dream of cigar connoisseurs from Paris to New York.

The atmosphere in Pinar is several degrees more gentle and relaxed than the rest of Cuba – a fact that the great Cuban intellectual Fernando Ortíz has argued is a legacy of the centuries-old tobacco tradition. While eastern Cuba is devoted to sugar cane – a crop whose harvesting is back-breaking work in the fierce Caribbean sun – the cultivation of tobacco is refined, intimate, and even elegant. Pinar's plantations are minuscule compared to the endless cane fields of the east, and only require a fraction of the numbers of workers. Everything is done by hand, from the picking of the leaf to the rolling of the cigars. In some *vegas*, linen nets protect the plants from the sun while harvesters remove their hats, so as not to bruise the fragile, valuable leaves.

Pinar del Río has historically been one of the least-developed provinces of Cuba. For centuries, the central government looked first toward the east (after Havana, that is), and even vacationing *habaneros* avoided Pinar in favor of the beaches of Varadero and attractions of Santiago. One of the revolution's aims was to bring Pinar more up to par with the rest of the country, but rural life is still somewhat reminiscent of the 19th century. Bullock carts are often the main form of transportation and regularly block traffic on highways. The use of oxen and mules for transportation is not exclusive to

The white sands of Cayo Levisa.

WHERE

Just before Artemisa, a large town south of Mariel, you will find the fascinating but unmarked ruins of the 19th-century La Bellona sugar plantation. Walls and columns are spread over a large area, the most identifiable structures being the main house and the slave quarters, which have a tall iron gate and the remains of a watchtower at one end.

this region, but Pinar's reliance on them is greater than elsewhere, partly because oxen are used for plowing the tobacco fields – their hooves do far less damage to the soil than tractors. Thatched *casas de tabaco*, with steeply pitched roofs for drying the leaves, still dot the landscape, although some have been replaced by similar sheds roofed with sheets of corrugated iron. You will see traditional palm-thatched cottages – *bohíos*. At a time of severe building shortages, the government began constructing new *bohíos*, using traditional, abundant, natural materials. The villages are small and dreamy, each with a crumbling colonial church, palm-fringed plaza, and the inevitable bust of José Martí.

Head west, *compañero*

In its efforts to bring Pinar closer into the national fold, the Castro government pushed through an impressive six-lane *autopista* (highway) from Havana. Today it is little used; except for a few trucks and army vehicles, your rental car or tour bus is likely to be the only moving thing. Clustered in the shade under bridges are droves of hitchhikers going to buy food in the provinces or visit relatives – be generous with your space since many of them may have been waiting for hours. In the summer, when students are on holiday, the problem is worse, but always exercise caution. Frequently, people stepping out into traffic to hitch a lift have been hit by vehicles.

Following the highway, the provincial capital of Pinar del Río, 178km (110 miles) from Havana, can be reached in only three hours. Slower, but more appealing, is the old Carretera Central, a two-lane road that winds through smaller towns and is thick with cyclists. The third and most picturesque option is the rough-and-ready Carretera Norte, which follows the coast. Note that it is considerably easier to get out of Havana and join any of these three routes by first following the coastal road to **Mariel ❶**. During the summer of 1994, *balseros* (rafters) embarked on the hazardous crossing toward the US from all along this coast, in a great refugee crisis that strained political relations between the two countries. Mariel was also the scene of a great exodus in 1980, when more than 120,000 Cubans were allowed to leave, picked up in boats from Miami. This busy port is very industrial, with a cement works and a special development zone (similar to a free trade zone, with legislation and labor laws favoring investors). In 2014 the presidents of Cuba and Brazil opened the first phase of a huge container terminal – the most modern port in Latin America.

Beyond Mariel, the scene grows more rural. The coast road passes glorious blue seas edged with scrubby beaches, and inland the landscape is agreeably pastoral. Many roads are unmarked, but local people will give directions. If heading inland, the road from Mariel soon joins the highway or links up with the Carretera Central at Guanajay. Although all Cuban

The verdant and fertile Viñales valley.

autopistas are now pretty well provided with fuel and rest stops, drivers should remember to fill up with gas before heading to the remoter parts of the province.

The verdant sierra

Traveling through the interior, the highways enter the steep hills of the **Sierra del Rosario**. The first detour, just before the provincial boundary, is the biosphere reserve and eco-resort of **Las Terrazas** (there's a small charge, payable at checkpoints). In 1967 the government built a colony here, on 5,000 hectares (12,300 acres) of land, in an attempt to assist the rural community after indiscriminate logging had all but denuded the countryside. The terraces were created to help prevent further soil erosion. Now run as a tourist complex on principles of sustainable development, the little colony flourishes, its forested terraces tumbling down to a long artificial lake that is lit at night and has a small café suspended over the water on a pier. A recent addition to the area's tourist attractions is a zip line, called a canopy tour, across the lake into the trees. The community is the base for several artists who sell crafts and paintings from their workshops. There is also a **museum** of pre-Columbian artifacts. The Hotel Moka (see page 326) here is a beautiful modern hotel built in traditional Cuban style.

At the **Eco-Center** (Centro de Investigaciones Ecológicas) you can hire guides who specialize in the forest's flora and birdlife and will lead you on forest trails. The San Juan River Trail ends at the fabulous **Baños de San Juan** where you can bathe in a deep mountain pool fed by a waterfall. You can also rent bicycles.

Just across the provincial border, 8km (5 miles) from the main highway, is **Soroa** ❷ – less a village than a crossroads in the dripping forest (much of the sierra has been declared a Unesco Biosphere Reserve). Soroa is best known for its **Orchideario** (Orchid Garden; tel: 48-522 558; guided tours daily 8.30am–11.40am, 1.40–4pm), maintained behind large gates: on its extensive, pleasant grounds are some 700 types of orchid, more than 200 of

DRINK

The area around Soroa and San Cristóbal is the only region in Cuba where grapes – introduced from Spain – are grown for wine production. The industry is still in its infancy, but some of the wines are worth trying.

Braving the waterfall at Soroa.

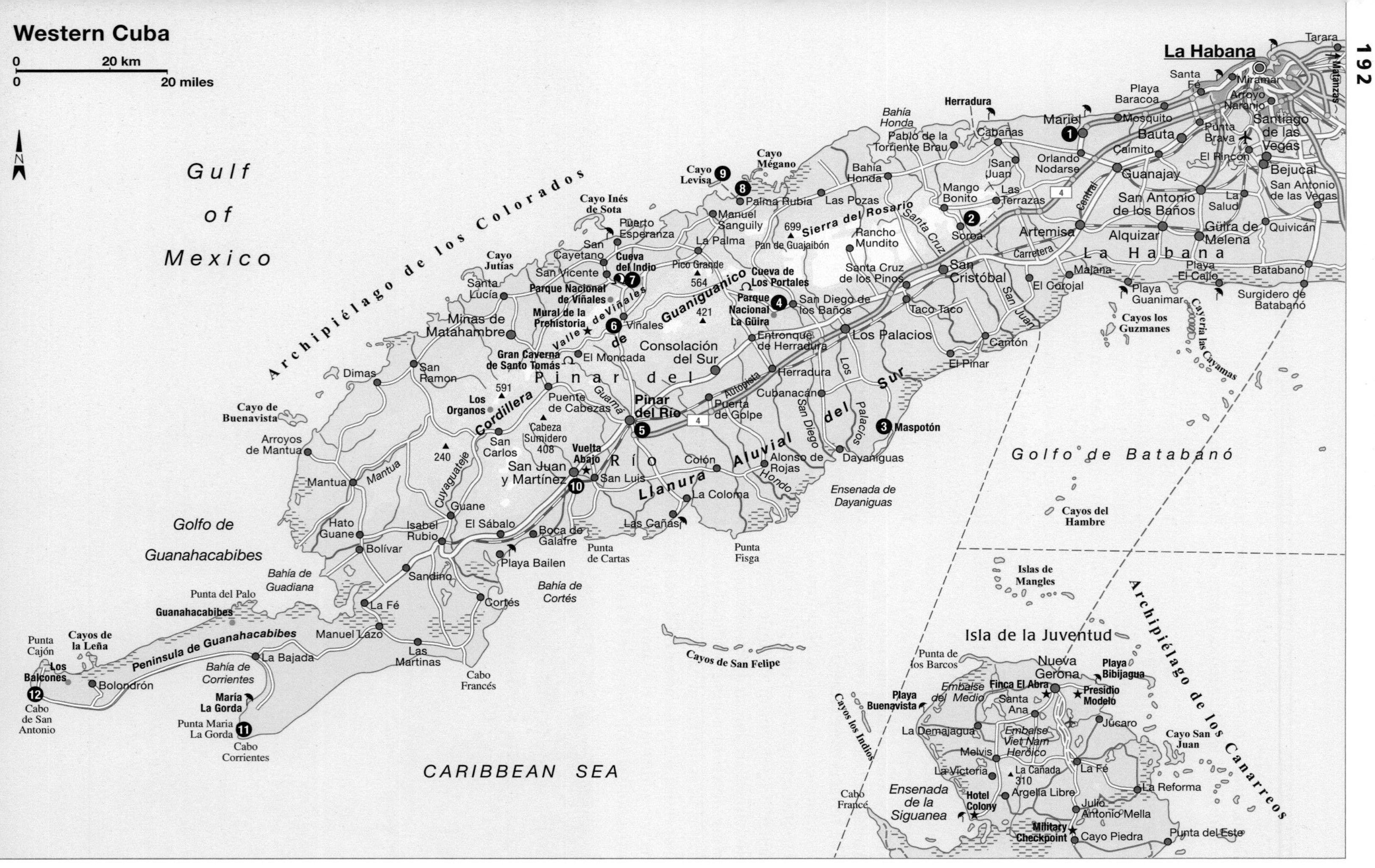
Western Cuba
0 20 km
0 20 miles
N
Gulf of Mexico
Archipiélago de los Colorados
Golfo de Guanahacabibes
Golfo de Batabanó
Archipiélago de los Canarreos
CARIBBEAN SEA
La Habana
Matanzas
Tarará
Miramar
Arroyo Naranjo
Santiago de las Vegas
Bejucal
San Antonio de las Vegas
Quivicán
Batabanó
Surgidero de Batabanó
Santa Fé
Punta Brava
El Rincón
La Salud
Güira de Melena
Playa El Cajío
Playa Baracoa
Mosquito
Bauta
Caimito
Guanajay
San Antonio de los Baños
Alquízar
La Habana
Mariel
Orlando Nodarse
Artemisa
Majana
El Corojal
Cayería las Cayamas
Playa Guanimar
Cayos los Guzmanes
Cabañas
San Juan
Las Terrazas
Herradura
Mango Bonito
Soroa
San Cristóbal
Cantón
El Pinar
Bahía Honda
Pablo de la Torriente Brau
Santa Cruz
Taco Taco
Rancho Mundito
Santa Cruz de los Pinos
Los Palacios
Maspotón
Dayaniguas
Ensenada de Dayaniguas
Las Pozas
Sierra del Rosario
San Diego de los Baños
Cayo Mégano
Palma Rubia
Pan de Guajaibón
Cueva de Los Portales
Parque Nacional La Güira
Entronque de Herradura
Herradura
Cubanacán
San Diego
Alonso de Rojas
Hondo
Manuel Sanguily
La Palma
Cayo Levisa
Pico Grande
Guaniguanico
Consolación del Sur
Puerta de Golpe
Autopista
Colón
La Coloma
Punta Fisga
Las Cañas
Llanura Aluvial del Sur
Pinar del Río
Puerto Esperanza
Cueva del Indio
Viñales
Valle de Viñales
Cayo Inés de Sota
San Cayetano
San Vicente
Parque Nacional de Viñales
Mural de la Prehistoria
El Moncada
Guamá
Puente de Cabezas
Vuelta Abajo
San Luis
San Juan y Martínez
Punta de Cartas
Boca de Galafre
Bahía de Cortés
Playa Bailen
Cayo Jutías
Santa Lucía
Minas de Matahambre
Gran Caverna de Santo Tomás
Los Organos
Cordillera
Cabeza Sumidero
San Carlos
El Sábalo
Cortés
Cabo Francés
Cuyaguateje
Guane
Isabel Rubio
Sandino
Las Martinas
San Ramon
Dimas
Mantua
Hato Guane
Bolívar
La Fé
Manuel Lazo
Arroyos de Mantua
Cayo de Buenavista
Bahía de Guadiana
La Bajada
Bahía de Corrientes
María La Gorda
Cabo Corrientes
Punta María La Gorda
Punta del Palo
Guanahacabibes
Peninsula de Guanahacabibes
Bolondrón
Cayos de la Leña
Los Balcones
Punta Cajón
Cabo de San Antonio
Cayos del Hambre
Islas de Mangles
Cayos de San Felipe
Isla de la Juventud
Nueva Gerona
Playa Bibijagua
Presidio Modelo
Finca El Abra
Santa Ana
Júcaro
La Fé
Julio Antonio Mella
Cayo Piedra
Military Checkpoint
Argelia Libre
La Cañada
Embalse Viet Nam Heróico
Embalse del Medio
Punta de los Barcos
Playa Buenavista
La Demajagua
Melvis
La Victoria
Hotel Colony
Ensenada de la Siguanea
Cayos los Indios
Cabo Francés
Cayo San Juan
La Reforma
Punta del Este

them indigenous, and most of them in flower between December and March. You can also go hiking, birding, or horseback riding from here.

Signposts by the road also direct hikers to a *mirador* (lookout) – a 20-minute walk – and a **waterfall**, as well as the **Villa Soroa-Castillo en las Nubes** complex (see page 326). This is a good place for a break from the road, with a pleasant dining room (although the food is only average) and views across the sierra to the plains from a sunny, silent terrace. Soroa is now very much a part of the tourist trail but this is still a pleasant place to sit and watch the river and listen to the cicadas – an amazing rattling sound that rolls through the forest like a Mexican wave. Visitors can stay at the Villa Soroa in cabins set in a lush landscape or in one of the *casas particulares* along the road.

West of Soroa, the Carretera Central passes the provincial town of **San Cristóbal**, whose red-tiled roofs and colorful buildings are falling to pieces. As in all such outposts, motor vehicles are few and far between. Slightly to the southwest, on the railroad track, is **Los Palacios**, and a rough dirt road that heads to the remote and barely populated southern coastline. In the swampy land here is **Maspotón** ❸, where a Club de Caza (hunting club) operates small bungalows. Pigeon and wild duck are common in the winter months, and trout fishing is good year-round.

Che's redoubt

Back on the Carretera Central, the route passes the **Presa La Juventud** (Lake of Youth), and there's a detour north to the village of **San Diego de los Baños**. This pretty little town, by the side of a gorge cut by the fast-flowing Los Palacios River, was once famous for its spa. The healing waters were discovered by a freed slave, whose skin was covered in lesions until he bathed in a local spring. Public thermal baths were inaugurated in 1951 but they have been closed since the passage of Hurricane Ike in 2008. Glowing in the gloom of the bathhouse is a milky radioactive pool that is said to stimulate the hypothalamus

POLO MONTAÑEZ

Born Fernando Borrego in San Cristóbal in 1955, Polo Montañez became popular both within and outside Cuba for his *guajiro* (country) music. His first and best-known album was *El Guajiro Natural* (The Authentic Countryman). Polo joined his father's band when he was 10 years old, and never stopped playing or singing, even when he had to take on a variety of manual jobs to earn a living. He rarely left Pinar del Río, and never strayed from his roots. His music was undeniably Cuban, yet it was unlike any other, for he developed his own distinctive style. There was widespread mourning when Polo died following a car accident on his way home from Havana in November 2002. The lively Cultural Center in Viñales, not far from his home town, has been renamed the Polo Montañez Center in his honor.

A tranquil lake in the Viñales valley.

Guayabita del Pinar is a liqueur specific to the region.

area of the brain and rejuvenate the nervous system.

The tropical forests of the **Parque Nacional La Güira** ❹ can be reached by road, or by crossing the suspension bridge across the river by the spa. This was part of an aristocratic estate in colonial times and still contains a mansion and sculpted garden. The surrounding forest, dotted with lakes, plays host to a rich birdlife and is home to the native Cuban deer.

The neighboring **Cueva de Los Portales** was the HQ for the Western Army under Che Guevara during the 1962 Missile Crisis, and was declared a National Monument in 1987. You can visit free of charge, although if there is a guide there he will appreciate a tip. A path leads into a tunnel, parallel with the Río Caiguanabo, and off to one side is the chamber from where Guevara led his operation. Stalagmites and stalactites are interspersed with evidence of his occupation, but this is not a museum as such. The camping complex here has a dozen comfortable cabins set among lawns and pines joined by rope walkways. It was designed by Celia Sánchez and is a pleasant, inexpensive place to stay, although it is primarily for Cubans and foreigners can only stay there if there is space.

Provincial capital

The one exception to the prevailing laid-back atmosphere of the province is the hectic regional capital, **Pinar del Río** ❺. A settlement has existed here since the 1570s, but development really began only after 1774 – comparatively late in the Spanish colonial period. Pinar lacks the clear grid pattern that makes many other Cuban towns so straightforward to explore. The streets are unusually narrow and confusing, and packed with cyclists. Be warned, too, that for a relatively small place, the town contains a significant concentration of *jineteros* (street hustlers).

The main street, José Martí, has a number of impressive, if decrepit, buildings: the **Palacio Guasch**, dating from 1909, stands out for its fairytale Moorish design mixed with other architectural styles. It is in a somewhat

View of the mogotes across the fertile Viñales valley.

sorry state, but houses the **Museo de Ciencias Naturales Tranquilino Sandalio de Noda** (Natural History Museum; Martí Este 202, corner Avenida Pinares; tel: 48-753 087; Tue–Sat 9am–6pm, Sun 9am–1pm), crammed with stuffed animals and with a curious collection of concrete dinosaurs in the courtyard.

A short walk east is the **Museo Provincial de História** (Calle Martí 58; Tue–Sat 9am–5pm, Sun 9am–1pm), housed in a colonial mansion and with a collection of local memorabilia ranging from 18th-century furniture to the pistols, radios, and rifles of local revolutionary heroes. Next door, the fully restored, neoclassical **Teatro Jacinto Milanés,** dating from 1838, is one of the prettiest theaters in the country.

More interesting for visitors are two factories in Pinar. Near Plaza de la Independencia, at the eastern end of Martí, is the tiny **Fábrica de Tabaco Francisco Donatién** (Maceo 157, corner Tarafa; tel: 48-723 424; Mon–Fri 9am–noon, 1–4pm, Sat 9am–noon; no photos allowed), where a constant stream of tourists watches workers rolling a variety of cigars, and where there is also a small shop opposite, the Casa del Habano. South on Isabel Rubio is the **Fábrica de Bebidas Casa Garay** (Isabel Rubio 189, between Ceferino Fernández and Frank País; Mon–Fri 9am–noon, 1–4pm, Sat 9am–noon; guided tours), which produces a liqueur called Guayabita del Pinar, distilled from sugar cane and the small *guayabita* fruit, a tiny, wild guava that grows around Pinar. Tours take you past the vats of liqueur and end up in the gift shop, where the concoction can be tasted and, of course, bought.

The Viñales Valley

The touristic core of the province lies north of Pinar in the **Sierra de los Órganos**, a region protected as the Parque Nacional de Viñales and dominated by the bizarre flat-topped mountains that protrude sheer from the fields on the valley floor. These *mogotes* are fists of hard limestone that were left behind when the softer rock around them eroded over millions of

EAT

Nearly all the *casas particulares* in Viñales cook excellent food for their guests at very reasonable prices – and some of them mix a mean *mojito*, as well.

An ornate but crumbling building houses the Museo de Ciencias Naturales.

The Guajiro

Looking like a cowboy who's lost his steers, the *guajiro* is usually seen welded to his horse, shaded by his broad-brimmed hat.

The Cuban peasant farmer – the romanticized version of the *campesino*, or rural worker – is country-born and bred, devoted to the land, fiercely independent, and firmly set in his ways. Both by tradition and preference, he lives in a *bohío*. These rustic cottages, their roofs thatched with palm leaves, can still be seen, with rocking chairs tipped up on the front porch, a horse tethered at the door, a television aerial atop the roof, chickens scratching in the yard, and a few pigs rooting outside.

Independent spirit

The stereotypical *guajiro* is taciturn and mistrustful of outsiders, especially people from the city and farming bureaucrats – the ones who set quotas and prices for whatever they've told him to plant. Recently, more and more *guajiros* – persuaded by the state – have joined with others to form larger cooperatives, but he still guides his ox-pulled plow through the fields, dressed like his predecessors in old boots, baggy pants, long-sleeved shirt, and broad-brimmed straw hat; breaking his dawn-to-dusk day with a midday meal then relaxing with a cigar and a shot of rum.

A guarijo at work in Holguín.

The first *guajiros* were the tobacco farmers of western Cuba, sons of Spaniards who revolted against the Spanish tobacco monopoly in 1717. Although plantations based on slavery soon dominated Cuban agriculture, they always co-existed with small farms owned and worked by free men. No matter what the crop or where they grew it, these farmers had little in common with the plantation owners, who operated on a totally different scale, with a large workforce of slaves. They also had little in common with freed slaves.

Though unsophisticated, the *guajiro* has unwittingly made his contribution to Cuban fashion with the *guayabera*, a white cotton shirt donned for a down-home *guateque*, or party. In the 1800s, Cubans rebelling against Spain adopted it for dress parade; early 20thcentury Havana bohemians brought the look into their clubs; and it remains the favorite dress shirt of many Cubans.

Cultural heritage

Typically, the *guajiro* enlivens the *guateque* with a dance called a *zapateo* that expresses his exuberant energy, a toe-and-heel jig that keeps couples hopping around between shots of *aguardiente* (raw rum) and hunks of roast pork.

Despite lacking formal education, the *guajiro* brought poetry to the Cuban countryside in the form of the *décima*, which originated in 16th-century Spain. It consists of 10 octosyllabic rhymed lines, improvised and usually sung in counterpoint, accompanied by three main instruments – a guitar, a *tres* (similar to a mandolin), and a lute – with *claves* (wooden sticks) and a dried gourd for percussion. The songs usually describe the *guajiro*'s life of joy and pain, trust and deception, success and failure, but are sometimes witty polemics on a current topic.

Typical of rural Cuba is the *guajira* ballad, first sung by roving troubadours, and much later commercialized for radio. The most famous one that groups of musicians play in every square and bar in Cuba where tourists congregate, is Joseíto Fernández's *La Guantanamera*, in praise of a girl from Guantánamo, using verse written by independence hero José Martí: 'I am a sincere man from the land where the palms grow... Guantanamera, *guajira*, Guantanamera...'

years. In the Jurassic period the *mogotes* were the pillars of vast caves that subsequently collapsed; today, covered in luxuriant foliage, they have the air of overgrown ruins.

From Pinar, a narrow road with splendid views winds 27km (17 miles) up into the sierra until it reaches **Viñales** ❻. The long rows of single-story houses and the porches on which people sit in rocking chairs, are colorfully painted. Local residents have discovered the benefits of tourism: Viñales has more rooms to let than any small Cuban town except Trinidad; there were said to be nearly 300 at the latest count. There are a couple of lively music venues (see page 201) and a general air of friendliness. Viñales has been badly hit by hurricanes in recent years and the loss of the avenue of trees down the main street in 2008 changed the leafy aspect of the town.

At the east end of the main street (Salvador Cisneros), almost opposite the Cupet gas station, is the pretty little **Jardín Botánico** (daylight hours; donation appreciated), first planted in the 1930s and maintained by the same family ever since. A wide selection of flowers and fruits is cultivated, as well as some oddities, like a tree decorated with beer cans, and another with plastic dolls' heads. They will show you around and tell you the name of everything, before offering you slices of seasonal fruits on their shady porch.

There's a little Museo Municipal at the western end of the street (No. 115) in the house of local War of Independence heroine, Adela Acuye (1861–1914). It gamely stays open until 10pm, but seems to receive few visitors.

A good way to get to know the area is to take the little tourist bus that runs from the main square (8.30am–6pm, CUC$5). The tour lasts about an hour and takes in all the main sights and hotels; you can get off where you like, and continue on a later bus.

There are two hotels worth visiting even if you aren't staying there. The **Hotel Los Jazmines** (see page 326) has the most attractive position and its views across the valley are exceptional.

FACT

Some 4km (2½ miles) from Viñales is a small community called Los Acuáticos, founded in 1943 by a santero, Antoñica Izquierdo. The residents venerate water, and bathe three times a day in the clean water here, which they believe keeps them healthy, and they refuse outside medical care.

INSIDER KNOWLEDGE

The Parque Nacional de Viñales has a Visitors' Center, in a bright yellow building just past the Hotel Los Jazmines, 3km (2 miles) from Viñales. It offers a limited amount of information on the area's agriculture and geology, as well as guided walking tours (available in English) into the valley, stopping to visit a tobacco-drying house. It is convenient if you are staying in the Hotel Los Jazmines, but if you are in a casa particular, the owner will probably be able to arrange similar walks more cheaply (although you are less likely to get an English-speaking guide). In Viñales, everyone knows someone who can oblige. If you want horseback trekking, for example, a guide and horse will be produced and a price quoted; and if you want to buy cigars, you'll be spoiled for choice.

A Viñales tobacco plantation worker

The **Hotel La Ermita** (see page 326) is closer to Viñales – a 20-minute walk, above the town to the east. It has more distant views of the valley, but at dusk the scenery is stunning: the sun turns brilliant orange as it slides behind the mountains while a thin mist gathers in the valleys, isolating the distant strings of palm trees in a haunting tropical soup.

Agricultural heartland

It is a short drive (or a pleasant walk) from Viñales into the shaded valleys between the *mogotes*, whose rich, red soil is perfect for tobacco growing. Along the isolated tracks, *guajiros* (farmers) cycle past wearing straw hats and puffing huge cigars, or trot past on horseback. In the fields, simple wooden or iron plows are pulled by placid oxen *(bueyes)* rather than tractors, and these animals are often used to pull carts as well. You will see the steep-roofed *secaderos*, sheds in which tobacco is dried, and the small homesteads where farming families live. Most of the farmers here grow a mixture of tobacco, maize, bananas, and pineapples, all on a small scale, and most keep a pig and some chickens, as well as the working *bueyes* and horses.

The **Mural de la Prehistoria**, an enormous, garish painting that covers the flank of the Dos Hermanas Mogote, about 4km (2 miles) west of Viñales, was commissioned by Castro in the 1960s to portray the emergence of Socialist Man from the primal wilderness. One of Diego de Rivera's students, Leovigildo González, took on the commission, directing dozens of local painters. It is regularly touched up by artists who dangle precariously from the cliff top on rope swings.

A collection of caves

The *mogotes* are riddled with underground rivers and limestone caves. Heading north of Viñales, the road passes the **Cueva de San Miguel**, a small cave through which you walk to reach **El Palenque de los Cimarrones**, a bar, restaurant, and museum (noon–4pm). A couple of miles farther on, in manicured grounds amid towering rocks, is the **Cueva del Indio** ❼ (Indian Cave; daily 10am–5.30pm;

The tranquil beach at Cayo Jutías.

regular tours last 25 minutes) – so named because the indigenous Guanahatabey people used it as a cemetery and refuge during the Spanish Conquest. You climb steps to the cave then follow a contorted limestone tunnel down to an underground lake, on which you can take a boat trip (part of the guided tour).

There is a pleasant hotel, El Rancho San Vicente, with a restaurant and a bar set beside a deep natural pool, with shacks outside selling touristy goods. You can visit the spa with its sulphurous water and have a mud bath, massage, physiotherapy, or acupuncture (usually closed in the low season). There's also the Cueva del Indio restaurant, open for lunch only, where you buy tickets to visit the cave.

Seventeen kilometers (10½ miles) southwest of Viñales, in the village of El Moncada, is the **Gran Caverna Santo Tomás** (daily 9am–5pm; 90-minute guided tour), said to be Cuba's largest cave system. Visitors are provided with headlamps (like miners' lamps) but the lack of other artificial light makes it unsuitable for the claustrophobic.

Cayos Jutias and Levisa

A well-signposted road leads westward and then north from El Mondaca, passing mangrove swamps on the last part of the journey, to **Cayo Jutías**, a tranquil little sandy beach reached via a long causeway. (There's a gas station at Santa Lucía, just before you get to the causeway.) You pay CUC$5 to gain access. A *ranchón* (thatch-roofed restaurant and bar) is open for lunch and drinks until 6pm right by the shore. There are thatched umbrellas for shade on the beach and a kiosk where you can rent snorkeling equipment or sunbeds. Snorkeling is best right out on the reef beyond the sea grass. Take insect repellent, as flying insects can be a nuisance.

The road north of Viñales runs 25 km (15 miles) through spectacular countryside directly to the coast, ending up at **Puerto Esperanza** a small, soporific fishing outpost, where benches are laid out beneath palm trees by the mangrove-lined coast. Just past the Cuevo del Indio, on this road, is a more oft-traveled route: a turn-off east leads through La Palma to **Palma Rubia** ❽, from where it is a 25-minute boat trip to **Cayo Levisa** ❾: get there by 9.45am at the latest to catch the 10am sailing, or there isn't another departure until 6pm. Return ferries are at 9am and 5pm. This small island has the best beaches in Pinar del Río province, with sparkling white sands. There is a comfortable, unpretentious resort where, thanks to the fishing industry, lobster is the specialty. This is a place to chill out, though there is some good diving – the nearby reef has abundant black coral and other rarities.

The coastal route heading back to Havana via **Las Pozas** and **Bahía Honda** is often rough, potholed, and narrow, so should be approached with caution. The Sierra del Rosario, Soroa, and Las Terrazas can also be accessed

Stalactites in the Cueva del Indio.

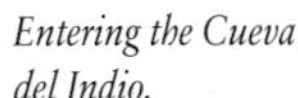

Entering the Cueva del Indio.

Cayo Jutías lighthouse.

from just east of Bahía Honda. This is a return to more traditional sugar-growing areas, and in winter harvest time the road can be jammed with trucks. The views of the Caribbean are pleasant, but the beaches are not the best, and much of the coastline is taken up by mangroves rather than sand. The best of them is probably **Playa Herradura**, some 8km (5 miles) off the main road, to the north of Cabañas.

The Vuelta Abajo to Cabo de San Antonio

Heading west from Pinar del Río, the route passes the town of **San Juan y Martínez** ❿. Between here and **San Luis** is the district of **Vuelta Abajo**, generally regarded as the place where the finest tobacco leaves in the world are grown. Despite its tiny size, the most famous – and therefore the most photographed – field of all is the **Hoyo de Monterrey**.

Increasing numbers of travelers venture west beyond this point. Although the roads are in reasonable condition, invasions of land crabs can cause havoc with your car tires at breeding times (March and April). The Carretera Central leaves the hills for more monotonous terrain. You pass the planned city of **Sandino** – named after the Nicaraguan revolutionary hero, and partially populated by Cubans forcibly transferred from the Escambray mountains during the 1960s for supporting the counter-revolution – and end up at the fishing outpost of **La Fé**.

You can continue west from La Fé to **La Bajada**, where the road branches south to **Punta María La Gorda** ⓫ (Fat Maria's Point), named for an obviously well-fed Venezuelan girl abandoned here after being kidnapped by pirates. The beach is lovely, but most people come for the diving. There are some sheltered offshore reefs of black coral, some good wrecks to explore, a wide range of marine life, and great visibility. The **International Diving Center** offers a range of dive packages including accommodations and food.

La Bajada marks the beginning of the **Península de Guanahacabibes Biosphere Reserve** and the site of the Guanahacabibes' last stand against the Spanish. At the information center you can arrange an entry permit and guided walks. The area has an excellent reputation for birdlife, including several rare endemic species. The roadway along the **Bahía de Corrientes** sparkles with fine, white-sand beaches, and dolphins may sometimes be seen in the blue seas of the bay. Beyond this, the Gulf of Mexico stretches into the distance. Cuba's most westerly point, **Cabo de San Antonio** ⓬, is 52km (32 miles) on a good road from La Bajada. There is a small new hotel and marina, near the Roncali lighthouse, built in 1849. Diving and fishing are offered in addition to refueling and provisioning for visiting yachts. There are a few caves to explore and some pretty beaches, but otherwise the region is very isolated.

Snorkelling at Punta María La Gorda.

RESTAURANTS AND BARS

PRICE CATEGORIES

Price categories are for a three-course meal for one with a beer, or mojito. Wine puts the price up:
$ = under $25
$$ = $25–35
$$$ = over $35

Restaurants

Las Terrazas

La Fonda de Mercedes
Building 9, Apt 2, Las Terrazas,
Tel: 48-578 647. Open daily 9am–9pm. **$**
Just below the Hotel Moka, this is a very popular but small *paladar*, so it's best to make evening reservations. Traditional recipes are served on the patio of this apartment.

El Romero
Las Terrazas
Tel: 48-578 555. Open daily 9am–10pm. **$**
This vegetarian restaurant is in the 'eco-community' between Pinar del Río and Viñales. All ingredients are home-grown and organic, and dishes are quite innovative, too.

Pinar del Río

El Mesón
José Martí Este, opposite Palacio Guasch
Tel: 48-822 867. Open noon–10pm. **$**
This *paladar* serves a typically Cuban menu with lots of pork, but it is probably the best in town and popular with local residents.

Rumayor
Carretera Viñales, Km 1.5
Tel: 48-763 051. Open Fri–Wed noon–10pm. **$–$$**
Restaurant and amphitheater surrounded by garden and trees. The house specialty is smoked chicken (*pollo ahumado*). Known for its Tropicana-style cabaret Fri–Sun, starting at 11pm, followed by a disco until about 3am.

Viñales

Fernando's
Carretera a La Ermita Km 1.
Tel: 48-696 628 Open daily L & D. **$**
Near Hotel La Ermita and if you are staying there, this *paladar* has better food and is worth the walk. Lovely setting, live music at night, attentive service and fresh, local food.

Finca Agroecológica El Paraíso
Carretera al Cementerio Km 1.5.
Tel: 48-695 187. Open daily L & D. **$**
Large and plentiful servings of organic vegetables are perfect for vegetarians, although tasty meat dishes also served. The family is friendly and the service is helpful.

Restaurant Jurásico, Mural de la Prehistoria
Carretera Pinar del Río–Viñales
Tel: 48-796 260. Open daily noon–7pm. **$$**
The mural may be a bit odd but the food is great. Charcoal-grilled pork with all the trimmings is the specialty.

El Olivo
Salvador Cisneros.
Open daily L & D. **$**
This Mediterranean paladar is a welcome change from rice and beans. Good fish, pasta, paella, and even cheese. The service is slow but the food is tasty.

Palenque de los Cimarrones
Carretera Puerto Esperanza, Km 36.
Tel: 48-796 290. Open daily 11am–4pm. **$$**
Reached through the Cueva de San Miguel. Grilled chicken and game are the specialties. You get an Afro-Cuban show with your lunch, and on Friday and Saturday nights there is a cabaret followed by a disco.

Bars

Viñales

Casa Polo
Calle Salvador Cisneros, beside church in the plaza
Named after the singer Polo Montañez (see page 193), this place is open all day, serving drinks and snacks, with taped music. Live music, often very good, starts around 10pm, followed by a disco, till about 2am.

Patio del Decimista
Calle Salvador Cisneros, 102
A lively spot, where you can sit at tables, inside or out, with a rum or a beer. Live music every night from 9pm or 10pm.

El Viñalero
Calle Salvador Cisneros, 105
Renovated in 2009, this is a very local, friendly spot for a beer or rum – and if there's no music you can sit on the terrace and hear the music from the Decimista opposite.

Pouring glasses of fresh sugarcane juice.

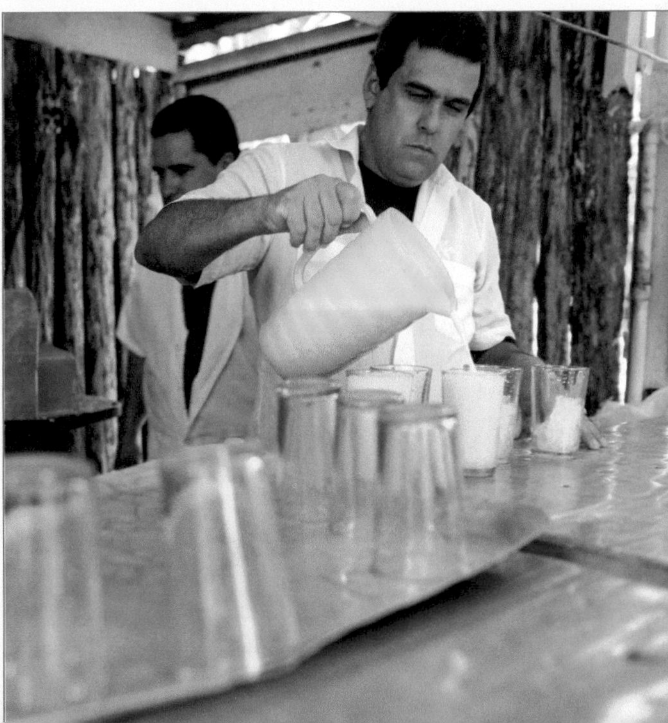

SECRETS OF THE CUBAN CIGAR

Thanks to the ideal climate and soil, plus centuries of expertise in cultivating the tobacco crop, Cuba produces the world's finest smokes.

The big fat Cuban cigar holds almost as important a role in the national identity as rum and salsa. Tobacco is grown on smallholdings in parts of eastern, central, and western Cuba, but the most highly prized comes from the *vegas* (plantations) around the town of San Juan y Martínez and San Luís in the western province of Pinar del Río, in an area called the Vuelta Abajo.

It is this region's leaves – the most important of which are grown under cheesecloth to protect them from direct sunlight – that end up in Havana's cigar factories, to be made into world-famous brands such as Cohiba, Montecristo, and Romeo y Julieta. Around 100 million cigars are exported each year, and the industry is one of the island's chief hard-currency earners.

In order to stamp out the black market in counterfeit cigars, official cigar boxes now bear a holographic seal. A box of Cohibas bought on the street may look much like the real thing, with the packaging and cigar bands pilfered from a factory, but the tobacco is likely to be inferior. It's best to buy from an official shop (the best are in tobacco factories), where prices are much higher but still only a fraction of what you would pay abroad.

If you get the chance to inspect the contents of a box before you buy, check that the cigars are of a similar color (the darker the color, the stronger the flavour), and that if you squeeze them they readily spring back into shape and don't crackle.

The finished product – sealed boxes of genuine Montecristo cigars.

Harvesting of tobacco is done by hand from January through March, with two or three leaves picked from each plant every five days, starting from the bottom.

The harvested leaves are sewn together in pairs and hung on a pole to dry for about 50 days before being stacked for fermentation.

Five types of leaves are used to make a cigar: 'fillers,' ligero, seco, and volado, mixed together in the middle to determine the flavor, wrapped in the 'binder,' capote, which is then enveloped in the soft, silky 'wrapper,' capa.

CUBAN CIGAR FACTORIES

Cigars for domestic consumption are made in small-scale factories across the country, while those for export are produced in Havana's large, famous factories such as Partagás and La Corona.

The highlight of a factory visit is seeing a room full of *torcedores* (cigar rollers) dexterously blending together the filler, binder, and wrapper leaves. The best rollers can produce as many as 150 cigars a day. All rollers are allowed to smoke as many cigars as they want on the job. To help pass the time and prevent boredom, a lector takes the podium to read from a newspaper or book.

Visitors are often allowed to watch other parts of the cigar-making process, such as the sorting of leaves into their various strengths, and the color grading, banding, and boxing of the final product. Before cigars can leave the factory, *catadores* (tasters) smoke random samples from selected batches to ensure their quality.

t was the women who traditionally sorted tobacco leaves by lacing them across their thighs, giving rise to the myth that igars are rolled on the thighs of dusky maidens.

lejandro Robaina (1919–010) was the only grower) have a brand of cigar amed in his honor after a fetime of producing the ery best leaves for wrapping igars on his privately owned 0-acre (16-hectare) farm in inar del Río.

Every brand of cigar has its own emblem and many of the old labels have become collectors' items.

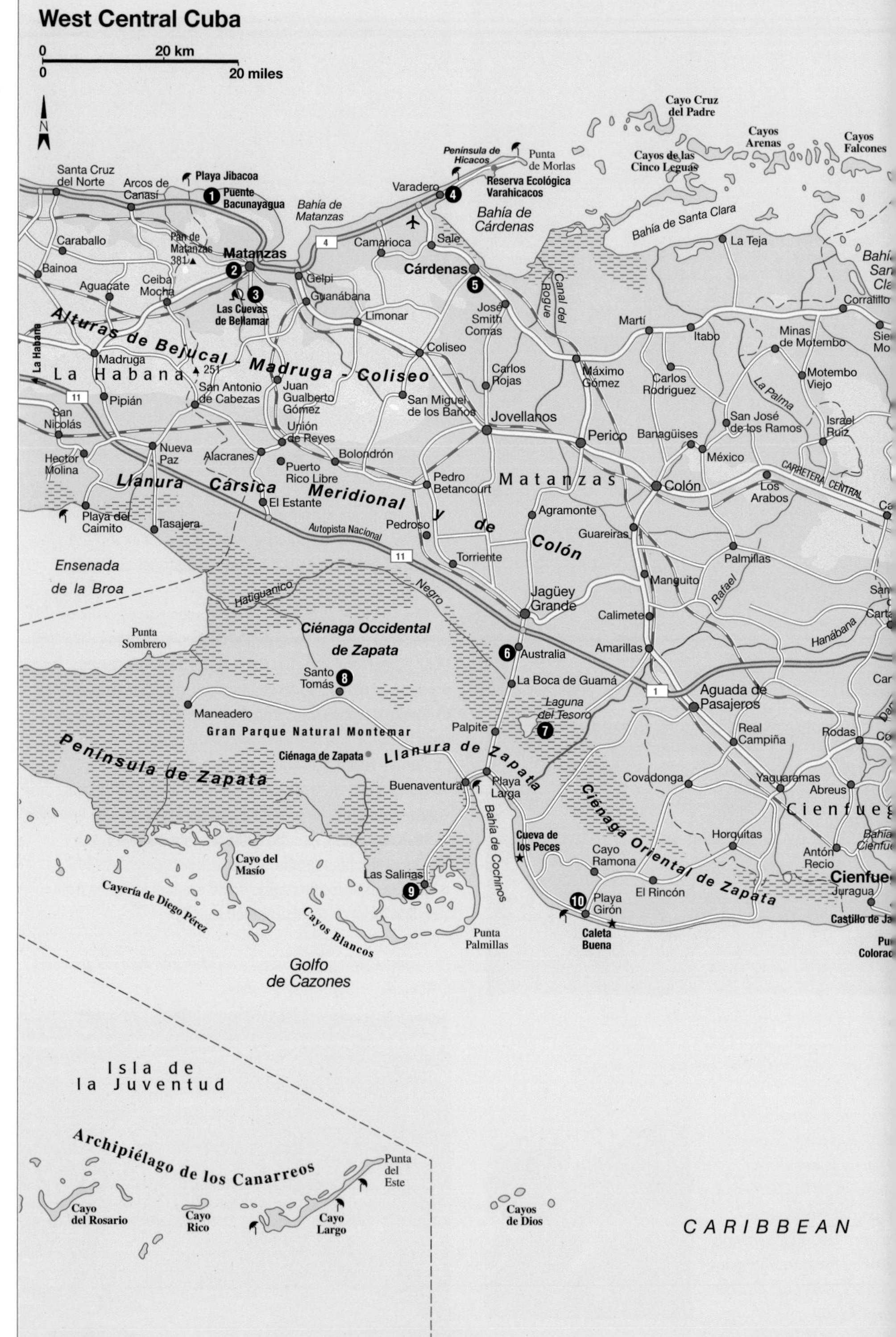
West Central Cuba
0 20 km
0 20 miles
Playa Jibacoa
Puente Bacunayagua
Matanzas
Las Cuevas de Bellamar
Varadero
Península de Hicacos
Reserva Ecológica Varahicacos
Cárdenas
Bahía de Matanzas
Bahía de Cárdenas
Bahía de Santa Clara
Cayo Cruz del Padre
Cayos de las Cinco Leguas
Alturas de Bejucal - Madruga - Coliseo
La Habana
Llanura Cársica Meridional y de Colón
Matanzas
Jovellanos
Colón
Perico
Jagüey Grande
Australia
La Boca de Guamá
Laguna del Tesoro
Ciénaga Occidental de Zapata
Santo Tomás
Gran Parque Natural Montemar
Península de Zapata
Llanura de Zapata
Playa Larga
Bahía de Cochinos
Cueva de los Peces
Ciénaga Oriental de Zapata
Playa Girón
Caleta Buena
Las Salinas
Ensenada de la Broa
Golfo de Cazones
Cayos Blancos
Cayería de Diego Pérez
Aguada de Pasajeros
Cienfuegos
Isla de la Juventud
Archipiélago de los Canarreos
Cayo del Rosario
Cayo Rico
Cayo Largo
Punta del Este
Cayos de Dios
CARIBBEAN

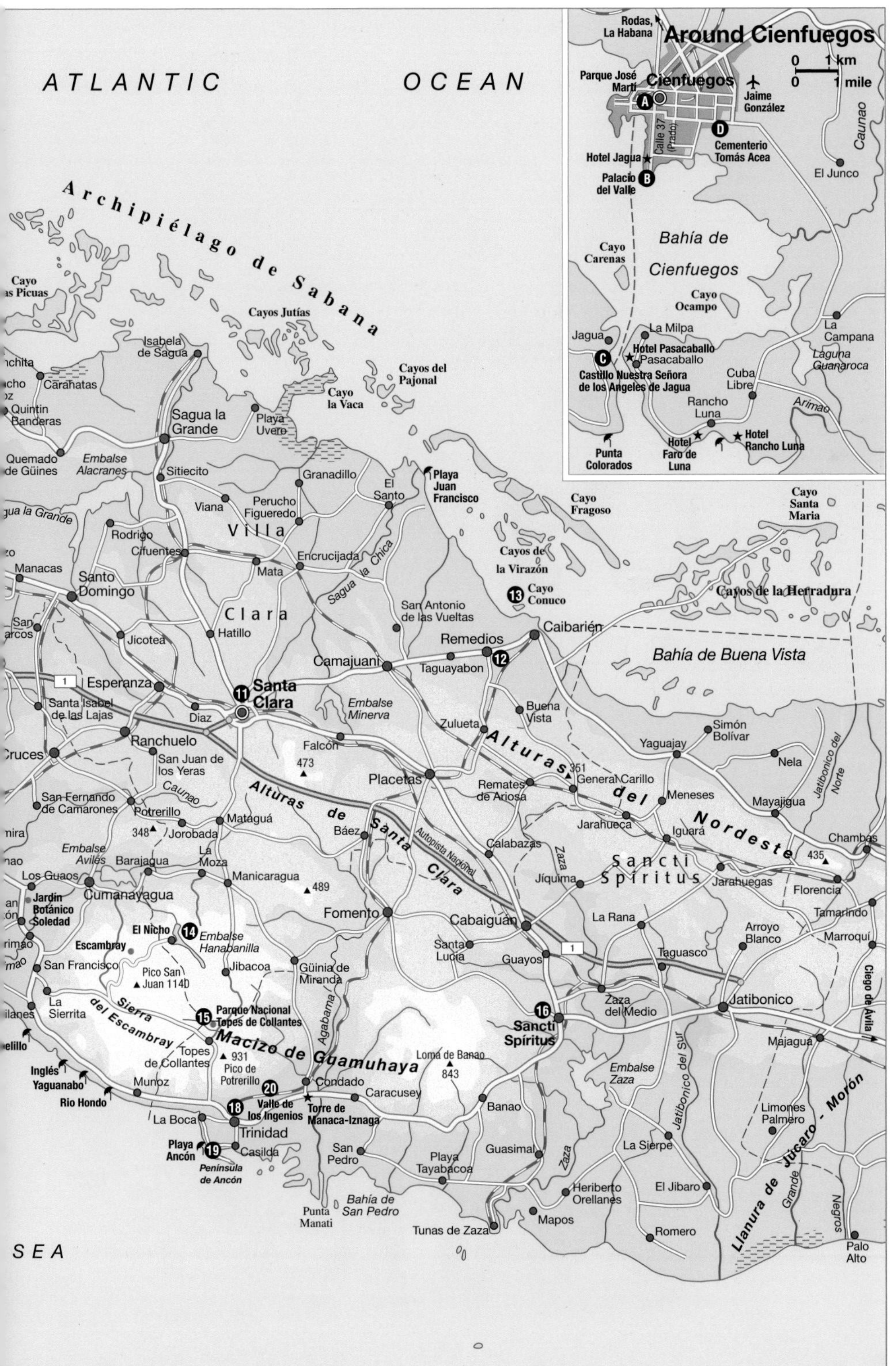

ATLANTIC OCEAN
Archipiélago de Sabana
Around Cienfuegos
Cienfuegos
Bahía de Cienfuegos
Bahía de Buena Vista
Villa Clara
Sancti Spíritus
Alturas de Santa Clara
Alturas del Nordeste
Macizo de Guamuhaya
Sierra del Escambray
Llanura de Júcaro - Morón
Santa Clara
Sagua la Grande
Remedios
Caibarién
Placetas
Cabaiguán
Fomento
Cumanayagua
Trinidad
Sancti Spíritus
Jatibonico
Parque Nacional Topes de Collantes
Valle de los Ingenios
Torre de Manaca-Iznaga
Playa Ancón
Península de Ancón
Cayos de la Herradura
Cayo Santa María
Bahía de San Pedro
SEA

Handicraft barrow, Varadero.

 Maps on pages 204, 208

VARADERO AND MATANZAS

Cuba's prime resort for package tourism, Varadero is a world apart from the rest of the island, including the area's own peaceful hinterland and the nearby cities of Matanzas and Cárdenas.

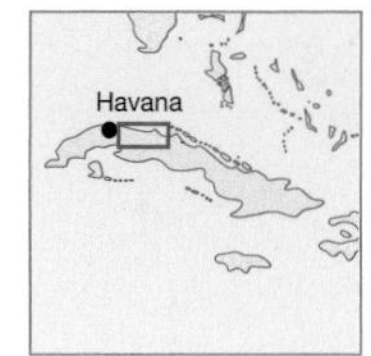

Main Attractions

- Puente Bacunayagua
- Matanzas
- Teatro Sauto
- Cuevas de Bellamar
- Varadero
- Xanadú
- Cárdenas

The province of **Matanzas** is the second largest in Cuba, yet most visitors will never go there unless they are staying in the glitzy beach resort of Varadero. This finger of land has become a tourist enclave, where tens of thousands of hotel rooms attract foreigners in search of sun, sea, and sand. Many visitors never step outside Varadero except, perhaps, for a day trip to Havana, which means that the rest of the province ticks over at a leisurely pace. In the rural areas and villages, bicycles and horses are the typical mode of transportation, and oxen are more reliable in the fields than worn-out old tractors. Rusting, mothballed sugar factories bear witness to the collapse of the industry that once supported the nation's economy; tourism is now the engine of growth.

The province couldn't have a grander point of entry than the **Puente Bacunayagua** ❶. This impressive bridge, the highest in the country, spans the 112-meter (370ft) -deep gorge of the Bacunayagua River, dividing the provinces of Havana and Matanzas. The Yumurí Valley meanders away to the distant mountains beyond. Turkey vultures wind lazy circles above the near-silent gorge. Cicadas sing. Few vehicles pass. There is a small restaurant and café here – an obligatory pit stop for bus parties, and deservedly so: the view is impressive.

Puente Bacunayagua.

Matanzas

About 20km (12 miles) east is the provincial capital of **Matanzas** ❷, founded more than 300 years ago. The highway passes right by the city's supertanker port, capable of receiving 150,000-tonne oil tankers and linked by pipeline to the Cienfuegos Oil Refinery, 187km (116 miles) to the south.

Matanzas Bay was first navigated by Sebastián de Ocampo in 1509, but the city itself wasn't established until October 1693, when Severino de Balmaseda, the provisional governor of Cuba, traveled from Havana to Matanzas with a team of surveyors to parcel out lots to new settlers from the Canary Islands. The city's name means 'slaughter,' and was originally thought to refer to a massacre of a local indigenous tribe, but recent study suggests it had more to do with the killing of herds of pigs kept nearby to resupply ships.

Local farmers started out growing tobacco, but by the end of the 18th century they had converted to sugar. Sugar and the slave trade made the city immensely rich, and during the 19th century the local aristocracy became major patrons of the arts. Matanzas developed a rich café society and many poets and artists made their home here. During the 1895–8 War of Independence, it was the center of a battle between Spanish general Arsenio Martínez Campos and two of Cuba's most important national heroes, Máximo Gómez and Antonio Maceo. On January 1, 1899, in **Plaza de la Vigía**, in the center of town, the Spanish Army handed over control of the town – not to the Cubans, but to General J.P. Sanger of the US Army.

The square still has a reminder of that conflict: the **Statue of the Unknown Soldier**, erected in 1919 on the spot where Matanzas was founded. Here, too, is the neoclassical **Teatro Sauto** Ⓐ, which has glorious ceilings and wonderful acoustics. Unusually, it also has a floor that can be raised to convert it into a ballroom. It was built in 1862–3 by Daniel Dallaglio after he won a competition. It is open for visitors (tel: 45-242 721; daily 9am–5pm) and for performances of theater, opera, and dance, usually on weekends. In the past such international stars as Sarah Bernhardt (1844–1923), Andrés Segovia (1893–1987), and, more recently, the renowned Spanish dancer and choreographer Antonio Gades have performed here to audiences of 650 people, seated in wrought-iron seats.

Adjacent to the square is the **Museo Histórico Provincial** in the **Palacio del Junco** Ⓑ (Milanés, between Magdalena and Ayllón; tel: 45-243 464; Tue–Fri 10am–6pm, Sat 1–7pm, Sun 9am–noon), which holds hundreds

The Museo Farmacéutico in Matanzas has a vast and fascinating array of items.

of documents and artifacts relating to the history of Matanzas. Slavery in the sugar plantations is given unusually detailed treatment here. The house itself was built in 1840 by a wealthy sugar plantation owner.

To the south of the theater toward the river you find the **Parque de los Bomberos** (Firemen's Park), with an elegant neoclassical fire station and a perfectly preserved vintage fire truck. On the same side of the street as the nearby **Galería de Arte Provincial** (daily 9am–5pm) is **Ediciones Vigía**, which produces limited editions of marvelous handmade books: you can tour the workshops (Mon–Fri 9am–4pm). The street crosses the Río San Juan at the rotating **Puente Calixto García**, a bridge built in 1849. A couple of blocks west of Plaza de la Vigía on Calle 282 stands the neoclassical **Catedral de San Carlos Borromeo** **C**, currently undergoing restoration.

The Pharmacy museum

Perhaps the most important attraction in Matanzas overlooks the main square, **Parque La Libertad**: it is the **Museo Farmaceútico** **D** (Calle 83/ Milanés 4951, between Santa Teresa and Ayuntamiento, tel: 45-223 197; Mon–Fri 10am–6pm, Sun 8am–noon), housed in the three-story dispensary of two 19th-century doctors, Juan Fermín Figueroa and Ernesto Triolet. Considering the shortage of common medications in present-day Cuba, this may be one of the best-stocked pharmacies in Matanzas. Among the most important pieces here are porcelain medicine flasks, hundreds of pharmacy books, and a dispensary table that won a bronze medal at the 1900 International Exposition in Paris. Displayed in an adjacent laboratory are ancient utensils, a wood-burning brick oven, and an *alambique*, or still, in which water, alcohol, and essential oils were distilled for medicinal purposes.

Don't leave town without visiting the **Ermita de Monserrate** sanctuary, currently under renovation on a hill, at the northern end of Calle 306 (Domingo Mujica), which offers a panoramic view of the city and the Yumurí Valley beyond.

Bellamar Caves

There are many interesting caves in the region. The most important are **Las Cuevas de Bellamar** **3** (Mon–Sat 9am–8.30pm, Sun 9am–5pm; 45-minute tours at half past the hour in the morning, and 15 minutes past in the afternoon), 5km (3 miles) southeast of Matanzas. After a slave working an open lime pit in 1861 discovered the cavern, 1,000 tonnes of rock had to be broken and extracted to clear the entrance; the work revealed one of the Caribbean's largest and most beautiful underground formations. According to a US traveler, Samuel Hazard, writing in 1897, anyone who hadn't visited the Bellamar Caves hadn't really seen Cuba. This is a slight exaggeration, but the caves are impressive. The Salón Gótico (Gothic Hall), 80 meters (265ft) long and 25 meters (80ft) wide, contains stalagmites with

Las Cuevas de Bellamar.

The Mantanzas-Varadero hop-on-hop-off double-decker tour buses make it easy to travel between the area's main sights.

names such as La Mano de la Mujer (The Woman's Hand) and La Capilla de los Doce Apóstoles (The Chapel of the Twelve Apostles). The Lago de las Dalias (Lake of Dahlias), a rocky area covered with water, is famous for thousands of tiny calcite crystals covering its roof, walls, and floor. Tours run from Varadero, but if you are coming from Matanzas, and don't have a car, take a taxi, or the No. 12 bus from Parque Libertad, which runs every two hours.

The **Vía Blanca** highway powers 32km (20 miles) eastward from the caves to Cuba's most famous international beach resort, passing towering onshore oil rigs that fly the Cuban and Canadian flags, representing one of the island's joint ventures. At night, the sky is lit up by the eerie orange glow of gas flares.

Varadero

The resort of **Varadero** ❹ is flashy in a Cuban kind of way. Nowhere else on Cuban soil can you find such a high concentration of oceanfront restaurants, nightclubs, and luxury hotels. Varadero is the ideal place to vacation if you don't want to meet too many Cubans. They are allowed here, but few can afford the rates at the foreign-run hotels unless a relative from Miami is treating them. Take a leisurely stroll along its palm-fringed, white-sand beach, considered one of the finest in the Caribbean, and you're likely to encounter lots of Spaniards, Italians, Canadians, and Germans – but few local people. This is Varadero's biggest problem: because there are few Cubans, there is very little atmosphere. But if you are looking for a straightforward beach vacation, relatively free of *jineteros*, in a good modern hotel with cable TV; with air conditioning that works; a pool and a jacuzzi; a golf course left over from the 1950s; and restaurants serving pizzas and hamburgers, then this is the place for you. The seas are warm and crystal blue but, really, you could be anywhere in the Caribbean. This is one of the few places in Cuba where women can sunbathe topless. Despite the very open sexuality of Cuba, topless bathing is, perhaps surprisingly,

Xanadú is now a boutique hotel.

VISITING VARADERO

If you are staying in Havana and want to check out Varadero there are four buses a day (see page 319). Taxi drivers hang around the Víazul office trying to tempt you to go with them instead – and if there are more than two of you it is usually a viable option. You can also go by tour bus, which most Havana hotels will arrange. If driving, the divided highway is good (it's 144km/90 miles from central Havana). A small toll (currently CUC$2) is payable on entry to Varadero at a toll gate that doubles as a checkpoint to ensure Cubans have an official reason to enter the resort. Any bus will drop you off at Matanzas en route, but a more interesting option is the Hershey electric train from Casablanca station. There are four or five trains a day, journey time from 2.5 to 4 hours.

illegal, although it is tolerated in resorts like Varadero.

Many package-deal tourists fly directly to Varadero and never leave, so almost the only Cubans they will encounter are on the hotel staff. Foreign hotel firms pay the Cuban Government, on average, the equivalent of US$400 a month for each employee. The government pockets that money and pays workers in Cuban pesos. Hotel jobs in Varadero are much sought-after, however, due to the access to tips and the better food they provide. Staffers at the hotels usually share the tips so that kitchen workers benefit as much as the front-of-house team.

The early years

Varadero has been something of a private preserve for much of its history. Local tribes once lived here, but the earliest historical mention of it dates from 1587, when the merchant Don Pedro Camacho began mining salt, both for local use and for Spanish fleets that dropped anchor in Havana.

Throughout the 1600s and early 1700s, pirates preyed on the few inhabitants of the 18km (13-mile) **Península de Hicacos**, along which Varadero is located. In 1726, José Antonio Gómez bought the peninsula and used it to produce salt and rear livestock. Thirty-six years later, the Varadero Hacienda – consisting of 1,140 hectares (2,800 acres) of land from Paso Malo to Hicacos Point – was sold to an aristocrat called Bernardo Carrillo de Albornos, whose heirs were still in possession of the land in the mid-19th century.

Varadero's tourist history started in the 1870s, when families from nearby Cárdenas began visiting. In that decade, they built the first palm-thatched frame houses on the northern coast, while the southern coast remained the preserve of fishermen. The beach's fame grew, however, luring visitors from Havana, who in those days arrived by ox cart. The year 1915 marked the inauguration of the Hotel Varadero – the fledgling town's first resort. Three years later, the Cuban Congress passed a law authorizing annual rowing regattas at Varadero Beach, which soon became a highlight of the local social calendar.

Xanadu

Then in 1926, the chemicals magnate Alfred Irénée Du Pont (who had made his fortune manufacturing dynamite during World War I) scored a real-estate coup with the purchase of 512 hectares (1,265 acres) of prime Varadero property for as little as four centavos per sq meter (11 sq ft). The lavish vacation home he built, **Xanadú**, is still standing today – one of the few tourist attractions in Varadero worth visiting. Located right on the beach, the mansion was finished in 1930 at a cost of US$338,000 – an astronomical sum back then. These days, it is a boutique hotel (very popular with golfers) with an expensive restaurant.

Even if you don't eat there, you can see the first floor and visit the bar on the top floor for a sunset drink and

Playing in the sand on Varadero beach.

a fine view. The mahogany ceilings and banisters are all original, as are the Italian marble floors and the 1932 organ, one of the largest privately built organs in Latin America. Don't overlook Samuel Taylor Coleridge's poem *(In Xanadu did Kubla Khan a stately pleasure-dome decree...)*, reproduced in full on the wall; or the beautiful terrace with a sweeping view of the Atlantic. There is an adjacent golf course, but the small, flat area does not make for a very satisfying game.

Foreign investment

Du Pont, who continued to buy up oceanfront property through the 1930s and 1940s, was not the only land speculator in Varadero. Others invested here, often with the complicity of corrupt Cuban officials or those with Mafia connections. The **Casa de Al**, which evokes those years, is now a restaurant housed in a mansion once owned by Chicago gangster Al Capone.

In 1950, the Hotel Internacional was constructed for US$3 million. That sparked a development boom that continued right up until the 1959 revolution. Dozens of mansions arose from one end of Varadero to the other, along with golf courses, gambling casinos, and hotels with links to the so-called 'Jewish godfather' Meyer Lansky and other notorious figures of organized crime.

Cárdenas cathedral.

It all came to a screeching halt in 1959. A state-approved tourist pamphlet says that two months after Batista's overthrow, the Cuban Government passed Law 270 'proclaiming the people's full right to enjoy all beaches.' Even so, for many years the only kind of tourists Castro's regime welcomed was solidarity brigades from the Soviet Union and other sympathetic countries. It was only with the end of aid from the USSR that Cuba began to court large-scale tourism from capitalist countries.

It was in Varadero that the first joint venture between the Cuban Government and foreign capitalists was inaugurated in 1990 – the US$26-million, 607-room Hotel Sol Palmeras. Since then the same firm, Spain's Grupo Sol Meliá, has built more hotels. As part of its ambitious development program for the area, the Ministry of Tourism has allowed development right to the end of the peninsula (which looks like a giant building site). Even the old 'Campamiento Internacional,' where Cuba's youthful pioneers once stayed alongside young foreigners from solidarity brigades, has been bought for development. There are investors here from across Europe, Latin America, the Caribbean, and even China – a Chinese restaurant has recently opened. Problems with cash flow and water supplies sometimes hinder progress.

Parks and natural sites

Aside from Xanadú, Varadero offers very few sites of historical interest. Visitors with time to spare might like to check out the **Parque de Diversiones** (Amusement Park) at Avenida Tercera, between calles 29 and 30. There is a tiny **tobacco factory** on Avenida Primera and Calle 27, and the equally diminutive **Museo Municipal de Varadero** (Tue–Sat 10am–6pm) on Avenida Playa and Calle 57, which has interesting exhibits of local flora and fauna, and some oddities, such as a two-headed shark. Varadero's municipal park, the **Parque Retiro Josone**, located between calles 54 and 59, has a pleasant flamingo lake where you can rent boats.

Halfway along the peninsula, past the main hotel stretch, the tiny, 2 sq km (0.7 sq-mile) **Reserva Ecológica Varahicacos** (daily 9am–4.30pm) gives some idea of what the peninsula was like before tourism. The Patriarca Playa trail (charge) takes you 300 meters/yds to see El Patriarca (The Patriarch) – a giant endemic cactus. At more than 500 years old, it is thought to be the longest-lived plant in Cuba, and is perhaps the only living thing in the country to have been around in the pre-Columbian age. The aboriginal paintings in the limestone **Cueva de Ambrosio** are interesting. This small cave, discovered in 1961, contains 50 well-preserved prehistoric drawings.

Cárdenas

Rent a car in Varadero and head into northern Matanzas province. The distance is minuscule but the difference in lifestyles is astonishing. Only 15km (9 miles) south of Varadero, across Cárdenas Bay, lies **Cárdenas** 5 (pop. 104,000), a city founded in 1828. In 1850, Cuba's national flag was raised for the first time here. A plaque commemorating this can be seen on the wall of the Hotel Dominica on Avenida Céspedes. On May 11, 1898, after Spain had been defeated in the Spanish–American War, Cárdenas was shelled by US Navy ships commanded by Admiral William T. Sampson. As in many provincial Cuban towns, traffic in Cárdenas consists of horse-drawn carts rather than cars, which sit in backyards, immobilized by the lack (or the cost) of gasoline.

Cárdenas became the center of world media attention in 2000 as the home town of Elián González, the 'tug of love' boy (see page 85). The

Jellyfish warning on the Varadero shore.

Varadero at sunset.

streets of this small dusty town were once filled with his image, but now that he has grown up it is almost as if the huge media circus never happened, except that the town now has the **Museo de la Batalla de Ideas** (Calle 12 and Plaza Echeverría; Tue–Sat 9am–5pm, Sun 9am–1pm). Housed in a well-restored 19th-century building, and inaugurated by Castro in July 2001, the six-room museum documents in lively detail the tireless campaign for the repatriation of 'Eliancito,' as the little boy was known. Exhibits on display include a striking modern sculpture of José Martí holding a child in his arms.

Cárdenas is also home to the eclectic **Museo Municipal de Oscar María de Rojas** (Plaza Echeverría between Avenidas 4 and 6 Este; Tue–Sat 9am–5pm, Sun 8am–noon), named for a local revolutionary hero. This natural history museum has several exhibition halls devoted to Cuban coins, weapons, shells, butterflies, minerals, pre-Columbian objects, and documents from the various revolutions and wars of independence. At the end of Calle Céspedes is a small **fortress** (**La Fuerte Roja**), now a café and a popular meeting place for local people.

Local transportation, Cárdenas

On Avenida 4 Este is the **Casa Natal de José Antonio Echeverría** (Tue–Sat 9am–5pm, Sun 8am–noon), the birthplace of the student killed in 1957 while leading the attack on Batista's Presidential Palace. The house itself is beautiful, and there is a monument to the student in the park outside, which is also named after him.

The city has a fine cathedral, the **Catedral de la Inmaculada Concepción** (often closed, except for Sunday Mass), on Parque Colón, with a statue of Columbus dating from 1858, said to be the first erected in Latin America. There is a mausoleum in the **Plaza de la Independencia**, containing the remains of 238 patriots who fell fighting Spanish colonialism in the late 19th century.

Matanzas Province

The province of Matanzas has seen its glory days fade as an exporter of sugar. About 10km (6 miles) south of Cárdenas, off the road to Santa Clara, is the former sugar mill Central Azucarero José Smith Comás, decommissioned and now a museum. It is interesting to see the production process but the star of the show is an 1888 steam engine, still used to transport tourists.

Southeast of Matanzas the potholed Carretera Central offers a route toward Santa Clara, an alternative to the main *autopista*, passing by or through some pretty colonial settlements including **Jovellanos**, an old slave town with a strong Afro-Cuban tradition, which was named after an 18th-century Spanish philosopher and statesman; and on to **Colón**. This is another colonial settlement with a busy main street and sleepy squares, with some impressive, if crumbling, neoclassical architecture.

You then cross into Santa Clara province. Independent travelers may like to know that Jovellanos and Colón both have a Cupet gas station.

RESTAURANTS AND BARS

PRICE CATEGORIES

Price categories are for a three-course meal for one with a beer, or mojito. Wine puts the price up:
$ = under $25
$$ = $25–35
$$$ = over $35

Restaurants

Matanzas

Frenesí BBQ
Calle 1, corner Calle 212 on Playa Allende
Tel: 58-213 234; www.frenesibbq.com/en.
Open Mon, Wed, Fri–Sun 10am–10pm. **$**
Attractive position on the waterfront overlooking the Bay of Matanzas, with shaded tables on the terrace of an unremarkable house. The three-course set lunch is a bargain and delicious, but the grill menu is extensive.

Restaurante Romántico San Severino
Santa Teresa 7903, between Contreras and Milanés, in front of Parque de la Libertad
Tel: 45-281 573; www.frenesibbq.com/en.
Open daily L & D. **$**
A new restaurant in a delightful old building with traditional tiled floors, high ceilings and antique furniture in the salon. The food is adventurous and high quality, prettily presented with friendly service.

Varadero

Resort hotels in Varadero specialize in buffets with lots of fresh fruit, and outdoor grills, where you can get lunch without leaving the beach. The specialty restaurants in the big hotels serve decent food and are open to all. Relaxation of restrictions has led to many *paladares* being opened, some of which serve much better food than the hotels, with a friendlier atmosphere.

Casa de Al
Villa Punta Blanca, Carretera Las Américas
Tel: 45-616 8050. Open daily noon–midnight. **$$**
Formerly Al Capone's house, now a quiet place for a drink or meal in a lovely location by the sea. All the dishes are themed with gangster names such as Mafia Soup or Godfather Salad. Sit indoors or outside on the terrace.

La Gruta
Parque Josone
Tel: 45-667 224. Open daily 3.30pm–10.30pm. **$$**
Part of the restaurant is in a cave, and reservations are essential if you want a table inside, as it is small and popular. Essentially Cuban food, but most people choose the lobster and/or shrimp with rice and trimmings, all nicely cooked and tasty. The wine is expensive, but the food is good value.

Mesón del Quijote
Avenida las Américas, next to El Castillito water tower
Tel: 45-667 796. Open daily noon–midnight. **$$**
A jolly, intimate restaurant with a Spanish theme. Well-cooked paella and grilled lobster feature, but the steak is also good. Reasonable prices, although lobster always adds to the bill.

Paladar Nonna Tina
Calle 35 5, between Avenida 1 and Playa
Tel: 45-612 450. Open daily noon–11pm. **$**
An Italian chef guarantees authentic Italian pasta, pizza, focaccia, and other delicacies from her mother country. This unprepossessing *paladar* is worlds away from the resort hotels, but it is always busy.

Salsa Suarez
Calle 31 103, between Avenida 1 and 3
Tel: 45-614 194. Open daily L & D. **$$**
International recipes and Cuban specialties like *ropa vieja* (with a twist) feature on a menu that changes every two weeks. The chef uses interesting flavours from Mexican, Italian, and other Mediterranean cuisines with some imported ingredients, including foie gras and cured ham. Service is very good too.

La Vaca Rosada
Calle 21 102
Tel: 45-612 307. Open daily 6pm–11.45pm. **$$**
The Pink Cow is very popular for its cocktails, pizzas, seafood, and much more. Great atmosphere, and lovely dining on the rooftop terrace, if it isn't too windy. Friendly service and a very professional *paladar*.

Varadero 60
Calle 60, corner Avenida 3
Tel: 45-613 986. Open daily L & D. **$$–$$$**
A bit more expensive than some *paladares* but still reasonable. Chicken, pork, and beef dishes are well prepared and attractively presented on huge plates, but the star of the show is the tower of lobster served with grilled pineapple. Desserts are also good and the staffers are attentive and multilingual.

Waco's Club
Avenida 3, between Calles 58 and 59, close to Parque Josone
Tel: 45-612 126. Open daily noon–10.30pm **$$**
A former Olympic rower has turned his home into a *paladar*, now a great place to come for lobster, shrimp, and other tasty meals. Friendly and multi-lingual waiters provide excellent service.

Xanadú
Mansión Xanadú, Carretera Las Américas, Km 8.5
Tel: 45-668 482; www.varaderogolfclub.com.
Open daily noon–10.30pm. **$$$**
A stylish place for lunch or dinner, with good French food. Check out the cool bar on the third floor.

Bars

Varadero

Resort hotels have a wide variety of bars, indoors or on the beach, with or without live music. One independent bar worth visiting is at Mansión Xanadú (see page 211). Any bartender will have a long list of cocktails that are fun to try.

Hotel buffet, Varadero.

Reddish Egret in a coastal lagoon on the Zapata Peninsula.

THE ZAPATA PENINSULA

The best known of Cuba's wildlife havens, the Zapata peninsula is a refuge for many bird and animal species. Nearby Playa Girón earned its place in history during the Bay of Pigs invasion.

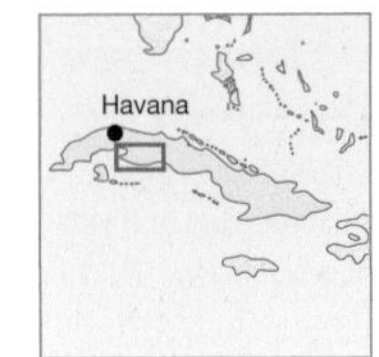

The half of Matanzas province that lies to the south of the *autopista* from Havana is mainly low, marshy terrain that is primarily a destination for visitors interested in the rich Cuban wildlife to be found here, or those who want to visit the Bay of Pigs for historical reasons. It is not a place where people come to admire the towns or cities. The main town for the area is **Jagüey Grande** and the Entronque de Jagüey is the intersection of the *autopista* with the access road to the peninsula. This is the heart of the world's largest citrus operation – a 40,000-hectare (103,000-acre) grove of orange and grapefruit trees. Mangos are also grown on an industrial scale, mostly for processing into juice, pulp, and preserves.

Just south of the *autopista* is the town of **Australia** ❻, dominated by its decommissioned sugar mill *(central)*. The mill was Fidel Castro's headquarters during the battle at the Bay of Pigs, and part of it is now a municipal museum, the **Museo Memorial Comandancia de las FAR** (tel: 45-912 504; Tue–Sat 8am–noon, 1–5pm, Sun 8am–noon). The next long, straight stretch of road leads to the turn-off for the Zapata peninsula, with monuments to the fallen of the Bay of Pigs all along the roadside.

Close by is the **Finca Fiesta Campesina**, a tourist venture with a little zoo, shops, coffee bars, and a small cabin-style hotel, the **Bohío de Don Pedro**, tucked round the back of the property (see page 221). It is an obligatory stop on the Zapata tour, and has surprisingly appealing gardens where you can sip fresh-fruit *batidos* (milkshakes) in the bar, watch a man extract sugar-cane juice *(guarapo)* for you to try, and inspect the coffee growing on the hillside. There is even an original kind of lottery where you are asked to bet on which hole a guinea pig will run into on its release.

Main Attractions
- Criadero de Cocodrilos
- Laguna del Tesoro
- Santo Tomás
- Las Salinas
- Playa Girón
- Museo de Girón

Rocky coastline in the Bay of Pigs.

TIP

Víazul runs daily buses from Havana to Trinidad via Entronque de Jagüey, Playa Girón, and Cienfuegos. The bus from Varadero to Trinidad stops at Jagüey Grande but goes on to Santa Clara. Drop-off is easy, but return buses are often full. There are usually taxis at the gas station, but the peninsula is best explored with a rental car.

The Centro de Información La Finquita (tel: 45-913 224; open daily 8am–8pm), next to the café, can arrange a taxi to Playa Larga or Playa Girón.

The Montemar Biosphere Reserve

The **Península de Zapata**, 156km (97 miles) southeast of Havana, was named for its similarity in shape to a shoe (*zapato* in Spanish). An enormous swamp, it has been a refuge, first for indigenous Taíno people, later for buccaneers and charcoal makers. The entire region is now a Unesco Biosphere Reserve, the **Gran Parque Natural Montemar**.

Most of the Zapata peninsula is barely above sea level and is flooded every year during the rainy season (June through October). About 30 percent is slightly higher, supporting a wide strip of forest some 16km (10 miles) from the southern coastline. Other elevated patches of terrain are scattered throughout the swamp, and clumps of trees grow on these patches like tiny islands. The western, triangular part of the Zapata peninsula is entirely unpopulated.

The whole area is described on maps as the Ciénaga de Zapata, divided into east and west, with the Llanura de Zapata in between (*ciénaga* means swamp, *llanura* means plain).

Many narrow, linear canals are visible from the air, connecting lagoons with the surrounding shallow seas. These were all excavated by hand by the desperately poor charcoal makers a century or more ago, to facilitate lumber transportation. There are many hidden sinkholes, so always stick to designated trails when walking. (And remember to carry plenty of bottled water, as the swamps are very hot.) Much of the swamp area is covered with a thick mat of peat, which acts as a gigantic mattress during the dry season. The underlying hard sediment of limestone frequently shows through, and, below ground, it is eroded into a network of caverns.

The Zapata's forests were once abundant in cabinet-quality hardwoods like ebony, mastic, and mahogany. Regrettably, these virgin forests have been thoroughly exploited over

Playa Larga.

the centuries, and even the tallest trees today are only secondary growth. More recent logging has produced unsightly corridors through the forest. Moreover, feral pigs and the introduced white-tailed deer have devastated the plant life of the undergrowth and altered the balance of the forest species. As a result, species that you might expect to grace the forests – like orchids, ferns, bromeliads, and vines – are rarities.

Crocodile farm

Crocodiles are rare in Zapata. Two species exist – the American crocodile, and the rarer Cuban crocodile. On the road to Playa Larga, just before you reach La Boca de Guamá, is the **Criadero de Cocodrilos** (Crocodile Farm; tel: 45-913 224; daily 9am–6pm, shows 9am–4.30pm) where several species can be seen.

From **La Boca de Guamá** boats carry passengers through a canal to the **Laguna del Tesoro** ❼ (Treasure Lagoon; speedboats every 30 minutes from 9am–6pm; slower ferries run about four times a day). The lake got its name because, it was said, indigenous Taíno people of the area threw all their valuables into it rather than surrender them to the Spanish. There's a romanticized mock Taíno village at Guamá populated by life-size statues of Taínos by the sculptor, Rita Longa, as well as an interesting hotel complex. Some artifacts have been found here, but no gold.

Snail kites *(Rostrhamus sociabilis)* are abundant here. They are raptors that feed, unsurprisingly, on snails, which they extract from the shells, using their long curved beaks. One indigenous name for them was *kiewe balielie* (lord of the snails). You will also find the endemic *manjuarí* (garfish or pike) – its teeth, snout, and body are a crude parallel to those of a crocodile, and its lineage goes back some 70 million years.

Birdlife of the peninsula

Birds are the main attraction in the peninsula, with a total count of 190 species. Most of Cuba's endemic species can be found here: the bee hummingbird, Cuban parakeet, Gundlach's hawk, blue-headed quail dove, Cuban tody, Cuban trogon, two species of blackbird, two types of woodpecker, and a couple of very small owls. Some species, such as the Zapata wren and rail (close to extinction), are unique to the swamp, while others can be found in few other places – the Zapata sparrow, for instance, is only found here, in Cayo Coco, and the desert area of Baitiquirá, near Guantánamo.

Playa Larga, at the head of the Bahía de Cochinos (Bay of Pigs), is where you find the headquarters of the national park (tel: 45-987 249, email: pnacionalcz@enet.cu; daily 8am–4.30pm) and where you can organize trips with accredited guides (mandatory). You need your own transportation though, or else a taxi. The hotel at Playa Larga is often booked by tour groups, but there are also a few *casas particulares*, some of which, like the hotel, are on the beach.

One of the best places for ornithologists lies north of the village of **Santo**

THE BAY OF PIGS

Not far from the palm trees and tourist bungalows of Playa Girón is a defiant billboard depicting a raised rifle and the words: 'Playa Girón – La Primera Derrota del Imperialismo en América Latina' (The First Imperialist Defeat in Latin America). The battle began shortly after midnight on April 17, 1961, when the 2506th assault brigade – a cia-trained force of some 1,500 mercenaries and Cuban exiles – landed to force the overthrow of Fidel. However, El Jefe Máximo was ready for them with Soviet-built T-34 tanks and a few T-33 fighter jets, and, after two days of intense air and land battles, the 2506th surrendered. Of the invading force, 107 were killed and 1,189 were taken prisoner. Most were later released back to the US in return for a US$53-million consignment of medicines and food. Castro, who led the people's militia in the battle, lost 161 men and women (five of these were civilians). The Museo de Girón was built at the landing site to commemorate the events. Outside, you can inspect a couple of tanks used in the defense. Inside are two rooms full of documents, photos, and weapons and an array of artifacts, among them a 12.7mm anti-aircraft battery used against US planes, and a map showing the mercenaries' route from Puerto Cabezas, Nicaragua. The invasion was preceded by an unsuccessful bombing raid on the Cuban Air Force, which put Castro on full alert. You can see a video compilation of footage from the era.

A tank at the Museo de Girón that was used to repel the US invasion.

Tomás ❽, west of Playa Larga. Many migrant birds show up here from October through April, after having flown all the way from the United States or Canada. The majority are warblers (more than 30 different species), but there are also herons, terns, and several birds of prey.

At **Las Salinas** ❾, 25km (15 miles) southwest of Playa Larga, the scenery is spectacular: flamingos swoop across the milky, saltwater lagoons, and crocodiles meander out across the dirt roads. The area is virtually uninhabited – there are just a dozen or so families who work in the reserve or fish for a living. Fly-fishing is becoming popular but only six anglers are allowed into the reserve at any one time, and must be accompanied by a guide who will navigate through the channels and flats. You can wade or fish for several different species from the flat-bottomed skiffs. From **Playa Larga** (one of the landing sites in the notorious 1961 invasion (see box), the road skirts the edge of the Bahía de Cochinos as it runs south toward Playa Girón. Some wide canals can be found slightly inland beyond **Los Hondones** (about 10km/6 miles from Playa Larga) where water birds abound. They include coots, gallinules, ducks, whistling ducks, herons, ospreys, jacanas, migratory buntings, and peregrine falcons.

Speedboats make regular trips from the Boca de Guamá to the Laguna del Tesoro.

Fish Cave

Farther along this stretch of road, look for the many monuments to the Cuban dead of the Bay of Pigs invasion, and stop off at some of the beautiful sinkholes *(cenotes)* surrounded by forest, which are connected to the nearby sea by underwater tunnels. These flooded caverns in the limestone are full of tropical fish in all colors of the rainbow. The water is crystal clear even deep down, and surprisingly cold. You can snorkel or scuba dive in most of these *cenotes*, which is like swimming in an aquarium.

Sadly, one of the largest and loveliest, the **Cueva de los Peces** (Fish Cave; daily 9am–4pm), has been spoiled by over-development. It is well signposted, and there are restaurants, a bar, and loungers on which you can sit by the lagoon and admire the scenery. You can rent snorkeling gear, and even though loud music ruins the ambiance, the swimming and the fish are still lovely. There is an abundance of lizards too, some tame enough to feed on scraps under the tables.

Playa Girón

The village of **Playa Girón** ⑩ holds an important place in Cold War history: this was the site of the United States' disastrous 1961 Bay of Pigs invasion (see page 219), about which you can learn in the commemorative **Museo de Girón** (tel: 45-984 122; daily 8am–5pm). The village is low and spread out, with an unattractive hotel, a collection of single-story concrete houses, and horses tethered everywhere.

At the junction there are two incongruous blocks of apartments, and here the road turns inland to Cienfuegos across a fertile plain where vegetables are grown on an industrial scale. An alternative track continues along the coast, approaching Cienfuegos from the south, but it is very rough and should only be attempted if you have a four-wheel-drive vehicle.

The western side of Playa Girón is a sanctuary for local fauna. You need authorization to go through the gate and follow the old solid-fill causeway that has slowly killed all vegetation. Flocks of rosy flamingos and spoonbills can be seen, feeding in the shallow salty lagoons, alongside other waders such as white ibises, black-necked stilts, sandpipers, and plovers.

At Playa Girón itself, you can bathe and snorkel off the beach or at several spots along the shore (designated with signs) where the seas are shallow. Farther out to sea, where the Caribbean shelf sinks vertically to hundreds of meters, scuba divers will be able to see rare black corals, spiny oysters, and ocean fish species such as amberjack and little tunny.

A little farther along the bay to the south is another excellent place to dive, the lovely cove of **Caleta Buena** (the charge includes buffet lunch, see below), which is also blessed with spectacular sponges and red coral.

RESTAURANTS

PRICE CATEGORIES

Price categories are for a three-course meal for one with a beer, or mojito. Wine puts the price up:
$ = under $25
$$ = $25–35
$$$ = over $35

Restaurants are few and far between in this region, and by far the best food can be found in *casas particulares*, where the hosts usually serve good *comida criolla* as well as fresh fish and seafood.

Boca de Guamá
Tel: 45-913 224. Open daily 9am–6pm. **$–$$**
The tourist center at the crocodile farm has shops and a restaurant, which is a regular lunch stop for tour parties, so it can be crowded if your visit coincides with one of them. The food is pretty mediocre, with the standard set meal of chicken, fish, or pork, but you can also try crocodile meat if you are feeling adventurous. It tastes rather like a tough mixture of all three when fried.

Bohío de Don Pedro
Finca Fiesta Campesina, South of Entronque de Jagüey
Tel: 45-912 825. Open daily 7am–9.30pm. **$**
The Bohío is not the place to head for if you are looking for a gourmet meal, but it is a reliably good pit stop on the way down to the Zapata peninsula. There is a bar, a few shops, bathroom facilities, and a pleasant garden with animals to look at while you have a drink or something to eat.

Caleta Buena
Open daily 10am–5pm for drinks; lunch 12.30–3pm. **$**
You pay CUC$15 for a day package, which includes drinks and lunch as well as swimming in the pretty cove where the snorkeling is lovely, which makes it quite a good deal. Diving is also available for an extra (but not exorbitant) charge.

Hostal Enrique
Caletón, Playa Larga.
Tel: 45-987 425. Open daily L & D. **$**
A casa particular cum paladar, serving excellent food and drinks, popular with some tour parties as well as people staying in the area. Seafood is a specialty and the desserts are delicious.

Punta Perdiz
Open daily 9am–4.30pm. **$**
This is a reasonable café serving drinks, snacks, and lunch (the usual food is on offer). It's the location that is the attraction: set between Cueva de los Peces and Playa Girón, where you can go snorkeling, there is a dive center, and boat trips are available.

BIRD BONANZA

Birders will be delighted with the rich variety of birds in Cuba. Some are easy to find, but you need an expert guide if you want to discover the island's more secretive inhabitants.

The Bee Hummingbird (Mellisuga helenae) is the world's smallest bird at 5–6cm (2–2.4 inches).

Cuba has a wide range of habitats: from beaches to coastal mangrove swamps, broad plains to rugged mountains, cactus semi-desert to remaining indigenous forests of cedar and ebony. Like many other large islands in the world, Cuba contains a rich collection of rare birds found nowhere else on earth, of which 21 are endemic species. A total of 357 species of birds has been recorded on the island, more than half of which use it as a winter resting spot as they migrate from North to South America.

In western Cuba an easily accessible site for birding is the Sierra del Rosario. In the semi-deciduous tropical forest you can find the endemic Cuban Solitaire, as well as the Cuban Tody and the Cuban Trogon.

The Zapata peninsula is one of the best regions, particularly around Santo Tomás and the salt flats of Las Salinas, or the Laguna del Tesoro. The mixed habitat of mangrove swamp, thick scrub, forest, and saltpans attracts a wide range of birds, including most of the endemic species.

In the province of Camagüey, a good place to go is the Hacienda La Belén, in the Sierra de Najasa, a forest reserve and home to the Giant Kingbird as well as the endangered Cuban Parakeet, the Cuban Pygmy Owl, and the Cuban Vireo.

Despite the proliferation of tourist amenities, Cayo Coco and the other north-coast cays near Morón are good places to see endemic sub-species, although the main attractions here are the water birds.

The east is no less rewarding, with the mountains of the Sierra Maestra, the Cuchillas del Toa, and the surrounding coast offering a variety of birds at different altitudes and habitats, including tanagers, orioles, todies, hummingbirds, and woodpeckers.

The forest-dwelling Cuban Trogon (Priotelus temnurus), known as the tocororo, bears all the colors of the Cuban flag and is the national bird.

The endemic Cuban Green Woodpecker (Xiphidiopicus percussus) is known locally as the carpintero, or carpenter bird.

The swamps, mangroves, and wetlands of Cuba provide food and shelter for many migrating species as well as endemics.

TOURS AND GUIDES

Regulations stipulate that you must have a guide to enter a national park in Cuba, and these are, of course, the best places to see birds. This will be organized for you, along with your accommodations and meals, if you book a place on a birding tour with a foreign agency. Alternately, you can do day trips with a Cuban agency such as Ecotur (www.ecoturcuba.tur.cu), which has offices around the country and can take you off the beaten track to see birds in Pinar del Río, Cienfuegos, Villa Clara, or Morón. If you are traveling independently, however, you can usually arrange a specialty guide when you need one by going to the local offices of the national parks. You will have to arrange your own transportation but the guide can take you to all the best places and make sure you see the species you want to see. On the Zapata peninsula, go to the headquarters of the Parque Nacional Ciénaga de Zapata in Playa Larga (tel: 45-987 249, email: pnacionalcz@enet.cu), where trips cost CUC$10 per person and some guides speak English.

The male Red-legged Honeycreeper (Cyanerpes cyaneus) is a brilliant violet blue with a turquoise crown, black wings and tail, showing a flash of yellow under his wings in flight.

The Cuban Pygmy Owl (Glaucidium siju) is found in a variety of forest habitats. It has a pair of 'false eyes' on its neck.

The Cuban Tody (Todus multicolor) is a tiny, colorful bird which nests in short tunnels dug out of clay or tree cavities, usually found near rivers and in woodlands.

Manaca-Iznaga estate, Valle de los Ingenios.

SANTA CLARA TO SANCTI SPÍRITUS

In addition to hectares of sugar cane, Cuba's heartland has some lovely towns, such as buzzing Santa Clara, with its Che Guevara monument, and the little-visited gem of Remedios, plus stunning landscapes in the Escambray Mountains.

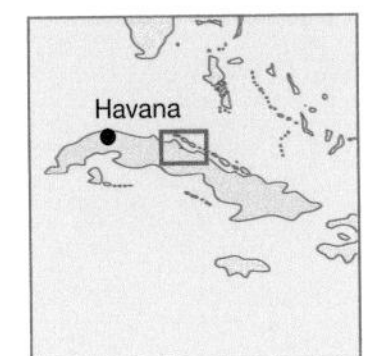

Main Attractions
- Santa Clara
- Tren Blindado
- Monumento Che Guevara
- Remedios
- Embalse Hanabanilla
- Topes de Collantes
- Sancti Spíritus

East of Varadero begins a fertile green belt of land: Cuba's agricultural backbone. Formerly a monoculture with sugar cane as far as the eye can see, nowadays orchards, rice fields, vegetable farms, and enormous cattle ranches eat up the terrain and feed much of the island's population. Buses, trucks, tractors, carts, cars, bicycles, and animals all share the road, presenting a slow but picturesque parade of life in the countryside. The Ocho Vías Autopista, projected as an eight-lane highway all the way to the eastern tip of the island, is completed only as far as the other side of Sancti Spíritus. Along the way are a handful of CUC-only service stations. These offer gas, oil and air, rest rooms (of varying quality), drinks and food (proper meals in some cases), and usually one or two stores.

With a population of 800,000, **Villa Clara** province runs the gamut of rural backdrops. There are sleepy fishing villages, pretty coves, and offshore cays to the north; colonial towns and sugar-cane plantations in the center; the rolling hills of the Alturas de Santa Clara to the east; and the majestic Escambray Mountains to the south.

Santa Clara's old town

Santa Clara ⓫ (pop. 210,000), the provincial capital, lies 276km (171 miles) east of Havana on the Autopista Nacional, and is well worth visiting. A university town with a large student population, it is busy and lively, day and night. There is always something going on and the music scene in particular is very active.

Santa Clara was founded in 1689 by 17 families from Remedios who, it is alleged, had been persuaded that legions of demons were afflicting their settlement (see page 33). Whatever the truth of the matter, land was parceled out and these families became the local oligarchy, building

Stopping for a chat in Santa Clara.

TIP

The views from the rooftop bar of the Hotel Santa Clara, overlooking Parque Vidal, are the best in town.

up the settlement and their fortunes by growing tobacco and sugar, rearing cattle, and working the Malezas copper mines, as well as trading with both ends of the island. In the 19th century, prosperity increased with the arrival of the railroad in 1873, and in 1895, when the island was divided into six provinces, Santa Clara became the capital city of the large province of Las Villas.

In December 1958, Che Guevara's derailment of an armored troop train on its way to Santiago de Cuba, and his seizure of the city, was the decisive victory in the struggle against Batista: this seminal moment is commemorated at sites across the town, most importantly, in Che's monument and mausoleum (see page 228). It is this that brings most visitors to Santa Clara, but this pretty little city has far more to offer for those with time to spare.

Around Parque Vidal

Santa Clara's main square is the delightful, leafy **Parque Vidal** Ⓐ, with a graceful central gazebo used for concerts. A monument marks the spot where Independence hero Leoncio Vidal was killed in 1896, and benches line the promenades that cross and encircle the park – in earlier days, a fence separated the inner promenade for whites from the outer area for blacks. Colonnaded buildings from the late 19th and early 20th centuries line the square; they include the **Casa de la Trova,** and the ugly **Hotel Santa Clara Libre** Ⓑ, distinguished by a facade still riddled with shrapnel from the 1958 campaign.

On the plaza's north side is the **Museo de Artes Decorativas** Ⓒ (Parque between Lorda and Luis Estévez; tel: 42-205 368; Wed–Mon but check hours as they vary), in one of the city's loveliest colonial buildings. Rooms are sumptuously furnished with colonial pieces in many different styles, but dating mainly from the 19th century.

On the nearby corner is the lovely **Teatro La Caridad** Ⓓ (tel: 42-208 548), built in the 1880s, financed by the philanthropist Marta Abreu de Estevez to bring culture to the poor people of Santa Clara. The theater, now a respected national monument, was renovated in 2009.

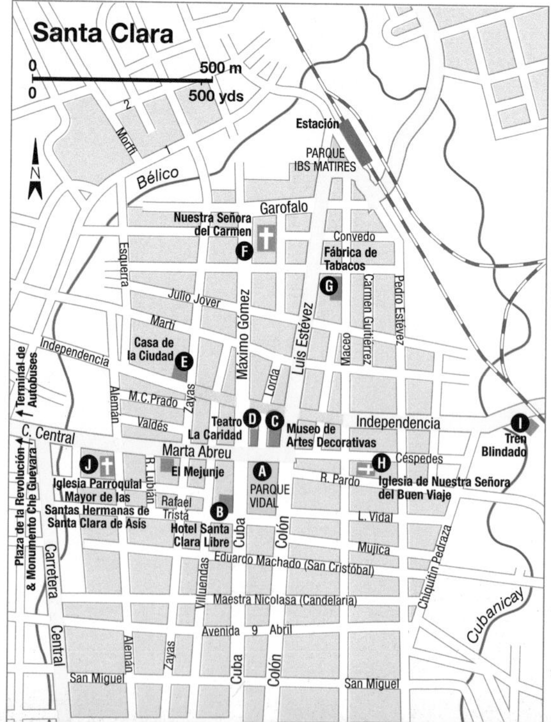

The armored troop train derailed by Che Guevara in 1958.

Marta's parents had earlier used their fabulous wealth gained from sugar and slavery to establish the city's first free clinic and primary school, in 1878. The school, a block behind the theater, was used successively as a convent, a trade school, and the incipient Ministry of Education in the early 1960s, but is now the Restaurante Colonial 1878.

Santa Clara's six-block-long **boulevard**, running along Calle Independencia one street to the north of the plaza, is an enticing, brick-paved mall with iron grilles, colonial lamps, and benches at each crossing. At the western end is the **Casa de la Ciudad** **E**, an attractive old mansion with a motley array of exhibits, where concerts are sometimes held; and the **Fondo de Bienes Culturales**, where local arts and crafts are sold.

Farther north, up Calle Máximo Gómez, you reach an attractive church, **Nuestra Señora del Carmen** **F** (Parque El Carmen; tel: 42-205 217), built on the very hill where Santa Clara's founding families held their first Mass. Leaving the church, go left along Calle Berenguer for a couple of blocks before turning right to the **Fábrica de Tabacos** **G** (Maceo between Julio Jover and Berenguer; tel: 42-202 211; Mon–Fri 9–11am, 1–3pm; buy your ticket in advance from an agency or from the shop on the opposite corner) on Calle Maceo, where there is a very good tour. Going down Maceo and turning left on Calle R. Pardo you will find the appealing **Iglesia de Nuestra Señora del Buen Viaje** **H** (Pedro Estevez, corner Buen Viaje; tel: 42-206 332), which is well worth visiting for its hybrid of architectural styles.

Armored Train and Che's resting place

Taking a short walk east along Calle Independencia from Parque Vidal and across the river brings you to the **Tren Blindado** **I** (Armored Train) and museum (tel: 42-202 758; Mon–Sat 8am–5pm). This train, loaded with 408 government soldiers and munitions, was sent from Havana to stop the Rebel Army's advance, but was derailed at a critical moment

Stunning monument to Che Guevara.

during the battle for Santa Clara, when it was attacked by 23 rebels with guns and Molotov cocktails on December 29, 1958. To prevent the men and munitions getting through, Che himself ripped up the lines with a bulldozer, derailing the train, and subsequently winning the battle. Both the bulldozer and three of the train's five carriages have been preserved in situ.

Two blocks west of Parque Vidal, on Calle Marta Abreu, a sign above a brick facade announces **El Mejunje**. Artists, intellectuals, and bohemians of all ages meet here to sip beer and *infusiones* (herbal teas), to listen to a poetry recital or a musical group, to dance, or just to sit and chat. The cultural potion is just right for laid-back Santa Clara, and there's no place quite like it anywhere else in Cuba.

A couple of blocks farther along Calle Marta Abreu is the early 20th-century cathedral. This is the grandly named **Iglesia Parroquial Mayor de las Santas Hermanas de Santa Clara de Asís** ❶. Going west from the church, Calle Marta Abreu joins the Carretera Central, which continues west to the circunvalación (beltway/ring road). Just south of the junction of the two roads is the **Plaza de la Revolución Ernesto Guevara,** the usual place for revolutionary gatherings. It is dominated by one of Cuba's finest revolutionary statues, the **Monumento Che Guevara:** a giant figure of Che, shown with his arm in a sling – he broke it when he fell from a building during the battle for Santa Clara in 1958. The bronze statue bears the legend 'Hasta La Victoria Siempre' (Ever Onward to Victory), a refrain that **appears** on many a billboard around **Cuba.**

Beneath Che's statue is the **Mausoleo** (Tue–Sun 9am–5pm; no cameras; free), where the remains of Che and 29 of his co-revolutionaries were interred in 1997, after being recovered from Bolivia. The mausoleum, with its low ceiling and construction almost entirely of stone, has the look and feel of a cave. By Che's resting place, a lamp casts a light in the shape of a five-pointed star, and an eternal flame (originally lit by Fidel) burns.

THE TOWN OF COMANDANTE CHE

On December 28, 1958, Che Guevara's rebel troops attacked Santa Clara. Two days later, with the aid of townspeople (who braved air raids and snipers to help build barricades and mix Molotov cocktails), the rebels emerged victorious. They cut Batista's communications with the east of the island by derailing a train carrying government troops on their way to fight Fidel Castro and his Revolutionary army. The dictator saw the writing on the wall, as the rebels got ever closer to Havana, causing him to flee Cuba on New Year's Eve. Many older Santa Clara residents remember the battle well and will recount fascinating details of the events. To this day, the town remains Guevara's city: his wife, Aleida, is a native of the town; the names of institutions and numerous monuments attest to the affection in which he is held.

The monument complex named after him, in the vast Plaza de la Revolución, was inaugurated on December 28, 1988, and every year on that date a concert is held, with Cuban and Latin American singers. The huge bronze statue of Che carrying a machine gun stands above a bas-relief scene of his battles and an inscription of the letter Che wrote to Fidel when he left Cuba to continue the struggle in Latin America. It was designed by José Delarra (1938–2003), an avid admirer of the Argentine rebel, who created a further 14 sculptures depicting scenes of the exploits of Che and his guerrilleros in the province of Villa Clara.

When the handless mortal remains of this rebel icon were discovered after a lengthy search in Bolivia in 1997, they were brought to Cuba for burial. His flag-draped coffin lay in state in Santa Clara – the scene of his greatest triumph – for three days, and lines of those wishing to pay their final respects stretched back more than 3km (2 miles). In the town's Plaza de la Revolución Ernesto Guevara, on October 8, 1997, Fidel Castro made a speech as the coffin, and those of six companions from his Bolivian campaign (including one Bolivian and a Peruvian), were laid to rest in the specially constructed mausoleum beneath the monument to Che. It is now a highly revered site, visited by individual Cubans and groups of school children, as well as tourists.

Few visitors fail to be moved by the aura of reverence.

There is also an interesting museum, the **Museo Histórico de la Revolución** (tel: 42-205 985; Tue–Sun 9am–5pm; free), featuring revolutionary memorabilia, some primitive broadcasting equipment used at Radio Rebelde, set up by Che at La Mesa mountain station, and some great photographs. There is also sometimes a video about Che and his role in the revolution.

Remedios

Some 48km (30 miles) to the north-east of Santa Clara (heading toward the north coast) is **Remedios ⓬**, a sleepy, engaging little colonial town and the oldest settlement in the province of Villa Clara. Founded by Vasco Porcallo de Figueroa in 1513–15 as probably the third of eight *villas*, it was moved in 1544 and in 1578 and never achieved the status of the other *villas*. A fire in 1692 meant that all the colonial buildings were built after that date. There has been very little recent urban development here, something the town has in common with Trinidad. While it may not be as picturesque as Trinidad, Remedios scores top marks for its tranquility and lack of tourists.

Remedios did not enjoy an auspicious start, being ravaged during repeated raids by French, English, and Portuguese pirates. If that were not enough, it was subsequently occupied, according to one of the town's priests, by 'infernal legions of demons,' and a number of families decamped to found the settlement of Santa Clara. Commercial incentives may have also had something to do with the migration. However, many of the inhabitants ignored their cleric's warnings and stayed put.

Plaza Martí

Plaza Martí, the town's pleasantly spacious central square, has a charming bandstand and is the only town in Cuba to possess two churches on its main plaza. The most stunning edifice in Remedios is the restored **Iglesia Parroquia Mayor de San Juan Bautista de Remedios** (Mon–Fri 9am–noon, 2–5pm, or during Mass at other times, or seek out the church warden at the rear), bordering the east side of Plaza Martí. The old church, built in 1692 on the foundations of an earlier one, was severely damaged by a 1939 earthquake, but a millionaire penitent underwrote a 10-year renovation, discovering gold painted altars and carved beams under layers of encrusted paint and false ceilings.

The church is a religious treasure: parts of the elaborate cedar-wood altar are carved in Arab style and encrusted with 24-carat gold, seen in its full glory when the lights are turned on. The decoration continues along the edge of the mahogany ceiling – which is a breathtaking example of a Mudéjar-style vaulted ceiling (*alfarje*), and was discovered only during the restoration work in the 1940s. The ceiling is particularly rare for its floral decoration. Also overlooking

Plaza Martí, Remedios.

Bici-taxi in Santa Clara.

the square is the attractive but rundown church of the **Virgen del Buen Viaje** (currently closed awaiting restoration), though its interior seems very plain after a visit to the Parroquial Mayor.

On the north side of Plaza Martí is the splendid **Museo de la Música Alejandro García Caturla** (Mon–Sat 9am–noon, 1–5pm, Sun 9am–1pm), originally the home of Alejandro García Caturla, a lawyer who devoted his life to music and became one of Cuba's most famous avant-garde composers. Caturla broke with the conventions of his class in every way. He married a black woman and, after her death, married her sister. His worst crime, though, was his incorruptibility: in 1940, at the age of 34, he was murdered by a policeman he was about to sentence for beating up a prostitute; there are suspicions that there may have been underlying political motives. The museum exhibits Caturla's personal effects, scores, musical instruments, and recordings of some of his compositions. There are also art exhibitions, and information on other musicians and bands from the area.

Street festivals

Remedios is famous for its strange and passionate street festivals, known as *parrandas*, which evolved from the percussion street bands, known as *repiques*, that advance through the streets to arouse people for the predawn Mass held to honor San Juan de los Remedios on December 24. In the 19th century, this religious celebration developed into a street fair, with costumes, parades, music, and food.

The fascinating **Museo de Arte Popular las Parrandas** (Tue–Sat 9am–noon, 1–6pm, Sun 9am–1pm), two blocks off the plaza at Máximo Gómez 71, displays the instruments heard during the celebrations. Neighboring districts (Carmen, identified by a sparrowhawk and a globe, and San Salvador, whose symbol is a rooster) spend the week between Christmas Eve and New Year's Eve competing for the best *carroza* (parade float). For months beforehand, artists and engineers secretly plan and build a so-called

Plaza Martí, Remedios.

trabajo de plaza, a great tower of light that represents their neighborhood; it can reach up to 28 meters (90ft).

The *parrandas* start when darkness falls, with the unveiling of these incredible confections, and continue until dawn, with musicians playing traditional polkas. Paraders carry handmade lanterns and banners, there are tableaus on dazzling floats, and fireworks as thrilling as they are menacing. Nearby Placetas and Zulueta maintain similar traditions. Enjoy the tranquility of Remedios while you can: its days as a sleepy backwater may be numbered, as it has become a picturesque and popular tourist stop on the road to Camagüey Cays.

The northern islands

Ten kilometers (6 miles) northeast of Remedios is the rather run-down fishing port of **Caibarién**, where boats dot the harbor. The wharves and warehouses along the waterfront recall the town's one-time importance as a shipping port. Caibarién has some rather mediocre beaches, on a promontory jutting out into the sea, and there is also a nautical base on the bay northeast of the port, where local people practice sailing, windsurfing, and kayaking to compete in national and international competitions.

From Caibarién, you can drive to **Cayo Conuco** ⓭. This 145-hectare (363-acre) cay is a former cholera quarantine post, now a biosphere reserve, and a trail leads uphill to one of the most delightful campgrounds in Cuba. *Cabañas* (cabins) nestle in the woods, and campers can swim, fish, ride horses, cook outdoors, and enjoy nature. They share the cay with numerous species of animals, including iguanas and jutías (a type of rodent), as well as 172 species of plants. Remember to take insect repellent with you.

On the coast east of Caibarién, a causeway (*pedraplén*) runs out 45km (28 miles) to **Cayo Santa María** and the smaller cays closer to shore. All these cays, called the **Cayos de la Herradura**, are, or soon will be, developed for tourism. Cayo Santa María is an increasingly popular resort. There are already at least a half-dozen luxury hotels distributed among the cays, all but one of them offering all-inclusive holidays, and there are plans to construct many more.

The Escambray Mountains

South of Santa Clara, the scenery of the province folds from pastoral farmland into the Escambray Mountains. At **Manicaragua,** the road splits, giving you the option to head straight on to Trinidad or west to the Embalse Hanabanilla and on to Cienfuegos.

The **Embalse Hanabanilla** ⓮ is an enormous reservoir at the top of an 8km (5-mile) climb from a turning after the village of La Moza. Perfectly located in a gorgeous location by the lakeside, with hills all around, is the Hotel Hanabanilla. You may decide simply to enjoy the views and cool off in the swimming pool, but if you wish you can also fish for large-mouth bass, hike through the woods, visit

Musicians perform on the bandstand in Remedios.

The elaborate altar in the Parroquial Mayor.

TIP

Topes de Collantes offers visitors an opportunity to see the national bird, the vividly colored tocororo, otherwise known as the trogon.

nearby waterfalls, or take a boat across the lake – a trip that is highly recommended for the glimpse it provides of mountain life.

Farmers who work small plots along the shore have their own animals, keep bees, and grow most of their food – fruit, vegetables, and coffee. Bags of beans and jars of honey and royal jelly are sometimes for sale. Coffee is a 'state crop' and, legally, only the state can buy or sell the beans, but farmers often ignore the law.

From here you could continue west on winding roads toward Cienfuegos, but our route, for the moment, goes east through the Sierra del Escambray, Cuba's second most famous mountain range (after the Sierra Maestra in the Oriente), with its highest peak, the Pico San Juan, topping 1,140 meters (3,700ft).

1Even at the height of summer, when temperatures in Trinidad or Santa Clara reach 40ºC (100ºF), you may still need a sweater here. Some of the heaviest rainfall in Cuba feeds the Escambray's lush jungle, where trees are laden with bromeliads and delicate waterfalls greet you at every turn; look out for the giant umbrella-like ferns, a prehistoric species. This is also an important coffee-growing region. On the lower slopes, jungle gives way to pastures and royal palms.

The Escambray provided a perfect hideout for counter-revolutionaries in the 1960s. The number of anti-Castro guerrillas, who ranged from hardened CIA-trained fighters to local farmers adversely affected by Castro's land reforms, had reached an estimated 3,000 by 1962, when the revolutionary government instigated a campaign to defeat the *bandidos* (bandits). Counter-insurgency units combed the area, driving the bands into more and more difficult terrain until they had no option but to surrender or fight. Even so, the last groups were not killed until 1966. (There is a museum about this struggle in Trinidad; see page 246.)

Topes de Collantes

If, instead of turning off, you continue south from Manicaragua, the road twists and turns through spectacular

Cayo Santa María.

scenery, with every bend offering new views of tropical vegetation, interspersed with plantation forests of eucalyptus and pine. Parrots (*cotorras*) and other bird species abound, though casual observers are more likely to hear than see them.

Eventually you come to the undulating, wooded **Parque Nacional Topes de Collantes** ⓯, 770 meters (2,528ft) above sea level. A wide variety of trees and exotic plants flourish here: as well as pines and eucalyptus, there are cedar and mahogany, among others, and orchids enjoy the damp climate.

The unattractive Kurhotel here was originally built in the 1930s as a tuberculosis sanitarium, and later developed for wider health tourism use; it still offers good hydrotherapy facilities. Tourists stay either at the Kurhotel or at the Hotel Los Helechos (both Gaviota hotels, www.gaviota-grupo.com), which offer air-conditioned rooms, saunas, mineral baths, massages, and herbal therapies.

For most visitors, the appeal of Topes lies in the walks, through beautiful scenery, and the exotic **waterfalls** nearby – especially **Salto Vega Grande** and the sweeping, uniquely shaped **Salto Caburní,** a 75-meter (250ft) fall. This hike involves a fairly testing 6km (4-mile) round trip; bring plenty of drinking water, sunscreen, and swimming gear. You have to pay to enter the National Park, and guides are compulsory. If you come here independently, arrange one through the information office at the park entrance (tel: 42-540 231). Many visitors come to Topes on a day trip from Trinidad (see page 242); if you are one of them, you will find the round trip by taxi costs about CUC$25–35. Cubatur or Cubanacán in Trinidad will also arrange excursions, and their Jeep or truck safaris are rewarding six-hour trips with lunch, hiking, and swimming.

From Topes the road continues dramatically downhill to Trinidad (22km/13 miles), with some stunning views of the coastline. If you are driving, be sure to stay in low gear: brake pads can wear out quickly on a hot day (for Trinidad, see page 241).

Parque Nacional Topes de Collantes.

The Yayabo Bridge.

Sancti Spíritus

The Carretera Central and the Autopista Nacional east from Santa Clara cut through the central plains to reach the city of **Sancti Spíritus** ⓰ (pop. 87,400) – capital of the province of the same name. Although the city in no way rivals the splendor of Trinidad, on the province's south coast, it is one of Cuba's seven original *villas* founded by the conquistador Diego Velázquez in 1514 and has a very pleasant atmosphere. The people are friendly, and there is little in the way of *jinetero* (hustler) hassle, since the town is off the main tourist routes. Avoid the ugly, industrial new town and head for the neoclassical **Parque Serafín Sánchez** and the center of the old city located to its south.

Serafín Sánchez was an independence hero who died in battle in 1896, having fought in three wars. His birthplace is now open as the **Casa Natal de Serafín Sánchez Valdivia** (Céspedes Norte 112, between Sobral and San Cristóbal; tel: 41-327 791; Tue–Sat 8am–5pm), to the north of the square on Céspedes Norte.

Sancti Spíritus had an unfortunate early history: it had to be relocated from its original site after the area's native inhabitants – a plague of stinging ants – decided to fight off the invaders; and then the new city was twice burned and destroyed by pirates. Therefore, none of this city's historic buildings is as old as those in Trinidad, though it does still have some delights.

Chief among them, on the **Plaza Honorato del Castillo** (also called the Plaza de Jesús), is an enchanting church, one of the oldest in Cuba, the **Iglesia Parroquial Mayor del Espíritu Santo** (Tue–Sat 9–11am, 2–5pm; free). Originally constructed of wood in 1522, it was rebuilt in stone in the 17th century after being destroyed by pirates. The tower was added in the 18th century and the cupola not until the 19th. With its rich, burnished-yellow exterior and peaceful location, this well-preserved church is one sight in the city that should not be missed.

Just to the south is the **Museo de Arte Colonial** (Calle Plácido Sur 74, between Guairo and Pancho Jiménez;

El Nicho, one of the picturesque waterfalls near Topes de Collantes.

A HEALTHIER CITY

The young Winston Churchill was a visitor to Sancti Spíritus in 1895, when working as a newspaper correspondent for the London Daily Graphic. Riding with the Spanish army, he became involved in a skirmish with Cuban independence fighters at Arroyo Blanco, to the east of the city. He narrowly escaped being shot, and later recalled the experience in his memoirs: 'There is nothing more exhilarating than to be shot at without result.' Arriving in the city, he was distinctly unimpressed, dismissing it as 'a very second-rate and most unhealthy place.' Perhaps he had drunk from the River Yayabo, for years the city's only source of water. There is still a tradition of drinking the river water, filtered of course, and served in a porrón – a small earthenware jug.

tel: 41-325 455; Tue–Sat 9am–5pm, Sun 8am–noon), housed in an attractive colonial mansion, and well worth visiting for its decor and furnishings alone. Built in the 18th century by the Iznaga family, the wealthy local sugar barons, the palace is notable for having 100 doors.

The church, the nearby colonial houses of cobbled Calle El Llano, and the **Puente Yayabo,** the sturdy bridge across the Río Yayabo, built by the Spanish in 1815, have all been declared national monuments. Puente Yayabo is the only colonial arched stone bridge left in Cuba. By the river at the attractive villa, **Quinta Santa Elena**, is the **Museo de la Guayabera** (Padre Quintero, between Llano and Manolico Díaz) charting the history of this iconic Cuban shirt and exhibiting some worn by famous people. You can even have a shirt made for you at its store, La Alforza.

Embalse Zaza

Cuba's largest man-made lake, the **Embalse Zaza,** just to the southeast of the city, is known for the size and number of its large-mouth bass and trout, while the surrounding woods harbor both mourning doves and white-winged doves, which attract seasonal hunters. There is a hotel here – the Hotel Zaza – that will organize excursions for visitors; and an international fishing competition is held here in September. The reservoir area is also extremely popular with birders, as the mangrove-choked marshes of the River Zaza provide a habitat for large numbers of water birds.

Sancti Spíritus old town.

RESTAURANTS

PRICE CATEGORIES

Price categories are for a three-course meal for one with a beer, or *mojito*. Wine puts the price up:
$ = under $25
$$ = $25–35
$$$ = over $35

Caibarién

Saramar
Calle 14 1502, between 15 and 17
Open daily 11am–11pm. **$**
A pleasant paladar offering the best food in the area and accepting payment in either CUCs or *moneda nacional*. Offers excellent value.

Remedios

El Pirámide
Andrés del Río 9
Open daily L & D. **$**
Run by a former employee of one of the resorts on the cays, this is an excellent paladar in a cosy upstairs dining room, with an extensive menu and delicious seafood. Service is friendly and attentive.

Santa Clara

El Alba
Rolando Pardo (Buen Viaje) 26, between Maceo and Parque
Tel: 42-203 935.
Open daily noon–3pm, 6–10pm.
$
Simple but plentiful Cuban food, popular with locals as well as tourists because you can pay in pesos cubanos, so it's frequently crowded. The walls are painted with cartoons.

NaturArte
Calle Nueva, corner Carretera a Sub-Planta
Tel: 42-298 354.
Open daily 10am–11pm.
$
Away from the town centre, but worth the trip – food is cooked on the grill (parrillada) and served under shady trees and among leafy plants. This is a cultural project and there is an art gallery and handicrafts exhibition, while pheasants and parrots patrol the garden.

Sancti Spíritus

Mesón de la Plaza
Máximo Gómez 34
Tel: 41-328 546. Open daily 10am–10pm. **$–$$**
An agreeable place furnished with heavy wooden tables and chairs, popular at lunch time with tour parties, but quieter in the evening. There is usually live music. The house specialty is *ropa vieja* (old clothes) – strips of beef stewed with peppers and tomatoes, served with rice.

Picturesque street in Trinidad.

CIENFUEGOS AND TRINIDAD

Two historic but very different cities and a splendid stretch of coastline, with one of Cuba's favorite beaches, offer a cultural interlude after the sugar fields and mountains of the interior.

Cienfuegos province is dominated by green rolling countryside, peppered by small sleepy towns and *bohíos* – palm-thatched cottages. Palm-fringed fields run down to the Alturas de Santa Clara in the east and the distant blue Escambray Mountains in the south. The 1959 revolution brought change to what was once primarily an agricultural region, and it has, around the city of Cienfuegos at least, become highly industrialized.

Cienfuegos

The road to Cienfuegos city from the *autopista* runs through the small town of Rodas: a pleasant but sleepy place, best known for its Ciego Montero spring, the origin of most of Cuba's fine mineral water. **Cienfuegos** ⓱ is known as the 'Pearl of the South.' It's a lovely city with most of its colonial buildings now fully restored.

Europeans first sighted the area in 1494 during Christopher Columbus's second voyage, but no settlement was established until 1819 when Louis de Clouet, a Frenchman who had emigrated to New Orleans, founded the colony of Fernandina de Jagua. It was renamed Cienfuegos the following year in honor of Cuba's Spanish governor general, who invited further settlers from Louisiana. With a little imagination you can appreciate the attempt by its French founders to give the city a certain Parisian feel, with its parks, tree-lined boulevards, and colonnades. In 1869, a group of Cuban nationalists led by Juan Díaz de Villegas rebelled against the Spanish Government, and in October 1895, Major-General José Rodríguez organized the Cienfuegos Brigade, which later played a key role in the battle of Mal Tiempo during Cuba's second War of Independence.

Following the 1959 revolution, Cienfuegos received massive investment from the Soviet Union, which

Main Attractions

- Cienfuegos
- Jardín Botánico Soledad
- Iglesia Parroquial de la Santísima Trinidad
- Museo Romántico, Trinidad
- Convento de San Francisco de Asís, Trinidad
- Playa Ancón
- Valle de los Ingenios
- Torre de Manaca-Iznaga

Catedral Purísima Concepción.

turned the region into a major industrial center. At its height, the province of Cienfuegos had 12 sugar mills that could grind 39,000 tonnes of raw *caña* (sugar cane) daily, but many of them have now closed. Its port – the only deep-water terminal on Cuba's south coast, and home to a sizable fishing and shrimping fleet – handles around 30 percent of the country's sugar exports. Here you will also find the largest cement plants and oil refineries in Cuba.

The historic center

The historical center of the city is the **Pueblo Nuevo** district, which is quite a pleasant shopping center – although only for those who can use convertible pesos. However, there are more CUC stores in Cienfuegos than there are in other cities, and the residents do seem to enjoy a higher standard of living. Most of the city's best buildings are around **Parque José Martí** Ⓐ, the square where the first settlement was founded on April 22, 1819, under the shade of a *majagua* tree. A bandstand now marks the place where the tree once stood. There is a series of statues to the city's illustrious citizens, including one to José Martí, guarded by lions, as well as a triumphal arch, inscribed with the date 20 Mayo, 1902 – commemorating the birth of the Cuban Republic.

The Catedral Purísima Concepción, dating from 1870, dominates the square and has an impressive, but shabby, interior, complete with marble floors. Nearby, on the north side, is the neoclassical **Teatro Tomás Terry** (officially known as the Teatro de Cienfuegos; Avenida 56, 2701, between Calles 27 and 29; tel: 43-551 772; daily 9am–5pm), inaugurated in 1890. It was named after a rich sugar baron who arrived in Cuba as a poor Venezuelan émigré, and made a dubious fortune by buying up weak and sick slaves, nursing them back to health, and then reselling them at a profit. The ornate interior of the theater is made almost entirely of precious Cuban hardwoods with classical reliefs and nymphs providing some of the decoration. National and local

Trinidad has a history of producing good-quality pottery and linens.

performances are staged here, ranging from National Ballet productions to local comedy acts.

On the opposite side of the square, the **Museo Histórico Provincial** (tel: 43-519 722; Tue–Sat 10am–6pm, Sun 9am–1pm) focuses on the city's role in the War of Independence, and is housed in a magnificent building that used to be the Casino Español, a cultural and political institution. The marble staircase is huge and grand and the rooms contain art and furniture as well as historical exhibits. On the west side of the plaza, the **Casa de Cultura Benjamín Duarte**, which occupies the former Palacio de Ferrer, the home of a rich sugar baron, is closed for renovation. It's a fine building, with a wide marble staircase and attractive wall tiles. There is a tower on the corner that was used to view shipping in the harbor, but is also great for looking out over the town.

Next door, the Unión de Escritores y Artistas de Cuba – the Writers' and Artists' Union (UNEAC) – has a pretty, flower-filled garden with wrought-iron furniture. There's a small movie theater and an art gallery here, and live bands perform on weekends.

The streets around the Plaza José Martí hum with activity: particularly traffic-free **Boulevard San Fernando**, where food and souvenir vendors, flower sellers, boot blacks, and other entrepreneurs ply their trades. Northwest of the Plaza, on a small peninsula called Cayo Loco, is the interesting **Museo Histórico Naval Nacional** (Naval Museum; tel: 43-516 617; Tue–Sat 9am–6pm, Sun 9am–1pm). There is a good deal of military history here, but many exhibits relate to the fishing industry, and there are some archeological and natural history items too.

The main street, however, is the broad Calle 37, usually called the **Paseo del Prado** – a more fitting name for the longest boulevard in Cuba. It is bordered by some beautiful but unpretentious colonial buildings, most of which are still private residences. South of Avenida 46, just before it hits the waterfront, the street is known as the Malecón. Always busy, and filled with traffic and gossiping crowds, it is the hub of the city's nightlife. The

Colonial bell tower, Cienguegos.

street is lined with statues, busts, and plaques commemorating Cienfuegos's most notable past citizens, as well as yet more impressive colonial houses.

Palacio del Valle

One of Cienfuegos's best-known landmarks is at the very end of the Prado. At the south end of the Malecón you reach Punta Gorda, where gracious French-style mansions and plantation houses can be found. You can't miss the vast, unattractive Hotel Jagua, formerly a notorious casino hotel run by Batista's brother. However, the main attraction is the adjacent **Palacio del Valle** ❸. This kitsch mansion, done up in Moorish Revival style with a few other styles mixed in for good measure, was commissioned by businessman Acisclo del Valle. He brought in an Italian architect, and craftsmen from Morocco and France, and materials were imported from Spain, Italy, and the USA. The building was finished in 1917. After the 1959 revolution, the del Valle family fled Cuba, and for many years the palace served as a government hotel school. Then, in 1990, the Hotel Jagua, situated across from the Palacio, converted it into an expensive Italian restaurant.

Watching the sunset over Cienfuegos Bay from the third-floor balcony of the Palacio is unforgettable (they charge you CUC$2 to go onto the terrace during the day but not at night). The cocktails are expensive compared to other places, but it's worth it for the view.

Another attraction on the waterfront overlooking the bay in Punta Gorda is the Club Cienfuegos (Calle 37, between 10 and 12; tel: 43-512 891), formerly the Cienfuegos Yacht Club and still a hive of activity, with a sailing center, tennis courts, restaurants, and other social amenities. The eclectic building, with twin-domed towers linked by a balcony, is painted a brilliant white.

Around Cienfuegos

The best way to visit the **Castillo Nuestra Señora de los Angeles de Jagua** ❸ (daily 9am–4pm; guides available) on the southern side of the beautiful Bahía de Cienfuegos is to take a ferry (*lancha*) from a terminal

Climb to the top of Palacio del Valle for fabulous views.

BENY MORÉ

A bronze statue on the Prado at the junction with the Boulevard (Avenida 54) in Cienfuegos honors the musician Beny Moré, who was born in nearby Santa Isabel de las Lajas in 1919. He got his breakthrough when he won a radio competition in the early 1940s, and went on to record with the Trio Matamoros. Beny was equally at home with Afro-Cuban music as with mamba or the country music known as *guajira*. When many other stars left Cuba after the revolution, he remained, yet he was already famous in Mexico and much of Latin America, and could have had a good career outside his homeland. He is particularly loved in Cienfuegos because, at the height of his fame in the 1950s, he chose to record with the little-known Cienfuegos-based Orquesta Aragón and helped them reach a wider audience.

just south of the Parque Martí (Avenida 46, between calles 23 and 25). It departs at 8am, 1pm, and 3pm, and returns at 6.30am, 10am, and 3pm; the journey takes about 45 minutes, and costs just CUC$1. The colonial fortress was built in 1733–45 by Joseph Tantete of France to defend the area against pirate attacks, and you enter across a drawbridge over a dry moat.

If you have a car or want to hire a taxi, take the road that follows the eastern side of the bay. After about 2km (1 mile) you pass the **Cementerio Tomás Acea** Ⓓ an impressive neoclassical cemetery overlooking the bay. Guides are available here if you want a tour of the graves and monuments. You will eventually end up at the ugly, Soviet-built Hotel Pasacaballo – strangely, although it is built directly across the bay from the Castillo de Jagua, all the rooms face the other way.

About 6km (4 miles) east of Pasacaballo, just where the road veers inland, is the Hotel Rancho Luna, a no-frills resort popular with Cubans on weekends. Non-residents can use the Rancho Luna facilities (including the only good beach close to Cienfuegos) for around CUC$5. Scuba diving and snorkeling are also available here.

The road to Trinidad

En route to Trinidad, between the villages of San Antón and Los Guaos and about 23km (15 miles) east of Cienfuegos, you will come to the **Jardín Botánico Soledad** (at Pepito Tey; tel: 43-545 115; daily 8am–5pm). Now a national monument, the vast garden is well worth a visit. Established in 1899 by Edwin Atkins, the American owner of the Soledad sugar plantation (now called Pepito Tey), it is home to some 2,400 species, including 285 types of palm tree.

The original aim was to produce more resistant strains of sugar cane, and from 1919 Harvard University was involved in scientific research into different types, but Atkins gradually became more interested in planting exotic species. The gardens have been in state hands since 1961 and scientists have developed sections devoted to medicinal plants, fruit trees, orchids, and palm trees.

The tower on the Casa de Cultura in Cienfuegos.

NUCLEAR CITY

The views from the Castillo de Jagua (see page 240) are impressive, but they encompass not only the delights of the coastline and the inland sea of the Bay of Cienfuegos. You also get a view of the eyesore which is the Hotel Pasacaballo and, in the distance, one of Cienfuegos's most curious and eerie sites: the concrete dome of the Soviet-designed Juragua Nuclear Power Plant, known as Ciudad Nuclear, or 'Nuclear City.' Construction of two 440-MW reactors began in 1983 to avoid dependence on oil imports and improve electricity supplies, but were only 60 percent complete when the USSR collapsed. Attempts were made to renegotiate the contract on commercial terms, but Cuba was unable to meet the proposed payments and construction was halted in 1992.

A stately avenue in the Jardín Botánico Soledad.

Trinidad's cathedral, officially known as the Parroquial Mayor.

From Cienfuegos, you can also reach Embalse Hanabanilla (see page 231) and Santa Clara (see page 225) by taking the scenic road via Cumanayagua to Manicaragua, across the foothills of the **Sierra del Escambray**.

The main road between Cienfuegos and Trinidad proceeds south, across a delightful hummocky landscape, until it reaches the sea. **At La Sierrita**, 32km (20 miles) east of Cienfuegos, you can head inland into the Escambray for one of the most dramatic routes through the mountains to Topes de Collantes, which will take you close to **Pico San Juan** (1,140 meters/3,740ft), the highest mountain in the Sierra del Escambray. The road surface is poor in places, and the inclines are steep and require concentration, but the views are magnificent. (The more usual route to Topes de Collantes runs north from Trinidad, and is one of the most popular trips from the colonial town.) Agencies in Cienfuegos offer tours to El Nicho, on the edge of Embalse Hanabanilla in Cienfuegos province, where there are waterfalls up to 35 meters (105ft) high. It is a beautiful setting surrounded by forest and mountains, and the tour usually includes bathing in pools, hiking, cave visits, and a lunch stop.

Back on the coast road, you pass several small, empty beaches, the first of which is Playa Inglés, about 48km (30 miles) from Cienfuegos. The second is Playa Yaguanabo, 5km (3 miles) farther east, where Villa Yaguanabo offers basic accommodations and meals.

Colonial sugar capital

Located in Sancti Spíritus province, 82km (50 miles) southeast of **Cienfuegos, is Trinidad** ⓲, Cuba's third-oldest settlement and one of the island's jewels. Its red-tiled roofs, pastel-colored buildings, cobblestone streets, laid-back atmosphere, and historic museums make it the main place outside Havana that most visitors include on their itinerary.

Trinidad was founded in January 1514 by Spanish explorer **Diego Velázquez**, at a spot just inland from the Caribbean Sea near the mouth of the Río Arimao. From the outset, Velázquez and his men enslaved the

View across rooftops to Convento de San Francisco de Asís.

local indigenous Taíno inhabitants, but they soon began to die from imported diseases and overwork, and the colonists started to replace them with slaves shipped in from Africa.

Throughout much of the 17th century, pirate raids were frequent in this area. They destroyed the provincial capital of Sancti Spíritus, but spared Trinidad itself and the town became a thriving center for smugglers and the slave trade – the source of much of its wealth.

During the boom years of the sugar industry, in the late 18th century, the area around Trinidad became known as the Valle de los Ingenios (Valley of the Sugar Mills), and fabulous plantation houses began to dot the countryside. When Cuba officially abolished slavery in 1886, the practice continued in more subtle forms for several years, even after the 1895–98 War of Independence. Throughout most of the 20th century, Trinidad remained economically tied to the sugar industry, though tourism is now the main source of revenue for the town.

A protected gem

In 1988, Unesco declared Trinidad and the Valle de los Ingenios a World Heritage Site, but the town had already been recognized as a National Monument back in the Batista years. There are no garish signs or political slogans in the town itself, as these are against the law.

It well deserves the praise heaped on it: painted mahogany balustrades run along the shady colonnades, massive ancient wooden doors open to reveal cool green courtyards beyond, motorized transportation is light, and life in the city moves sleepily along. At night, the town is dark, lit only by low lights or the eerie glow of television screens as the inhabitants settle down to watch an evening soap opera or movie – although the sound of music and laughter emanating from one of the bars or from the Casa de la Trova indicates that not everybody stays at home at night.

Trinidad is divided into the old and the new towns. The Plaza Mayor, where the rich built their mansions, is the centre of **Old Trinidad**. Parque Céspedes is the focal point of the newer town, which is built on a grid system. The sloping streets all have a central gutter to allow rainwater to flow away easily.

The only way to explore Trinidad is on foot. Many of the streets in the old town are closed to traffic and in other parts of the town they are generally narrow and difficult to negotiate by car unless you know them well. Following a simple walking tour takes three to four hours – museum and lunch stops included – although you may enjoy the town so much that you make it last a few days. Sightseeing is best done in the morning, while it's still fairly cool and the streets are less crowded, or in the early evening, when the buildings are bathed in a delicious, pinkish light.

The heart of the city

Any tour of the town will start in the splendid yet intimate **Plaza Mayor**,

Negotiating the streets of Trinidad by bike.

SHOP

Next door to the Museo Romántico is an artex store, selling jewelry, arts and crafts, and other souvenirs. The ARTex chain is represented throughout Cuba; their products are usually good and their prices fair.

one of Cuba's most photographed sights. All the museums and sites of interest are clustered around the square, with its magnificent palm trees, white wrought-iron benches, and small statues, including two bronze greyhounds. The huge, cream-colored cathedral standing at the top of the square is the **Iglesia Parroquial de la Santísima Trinidad** Ⓐ (tel: 41-993 668; daily 10.30am–1pm for visitors, Mass daily 8pm and Sun 9am for worshipers only). Begun in 1817, it is the largest church in Cuba. It is also the only church in Cuba with hand-carved Gothic altars and five aisles instead of three. It is known for its acoustics and it is worth catching a performance by the church choir, Piedras Vivas, singing religious music with a Cuban twist.

If you walk around the plaza in a clockwise direction from the church, you come to the former house of the Sánchez family, now the **Museo de Arquitectura Colonial** Ⓑ (Desengaño 83; tel: 41-993 208; Sat–Thu 9am–5pm), which tells the history of Trinidad's development, with maps and models showing how colonial craftsmen worked. If you are interested in architecture, ask here about two-hour walking tours of the city (they also arrange visits to the Valle de los Ingenios).

Like many buildings in Trinidad, this house, dating from 1735, was painted yellow rather than white, because white was considered too harsh on people's eyes in the strong tropical sun. When the house was restored in the 1980s, sections of yellow were left as a reminder of its original color. The museum includes an exhibition of hand-carved doors and windows, gas-lit chandeliers, and a stockade built to hold 12 slaves at a time.

On the south side of the square, the attractive balconied building contains the **Galería de Arte Universal** (Real 48; tel: 41-994 432; Fri–Wed 9am–5pm) on a site where the conquistador Hernán Cortés is said to have lived before departing for Mexico to conquer the Aztecs. Downstairs the gallery exhibits art. Upstairs there is a shop selling arts and crafts.

If you turn left here, down Simón Bolívar, you pass several impressive colonial mansions, before reaching the **Palacio Cantero** ⓒ, one of the city's most exquisite mansions, housing the city's **Museo Municipal de Historia** (Simón Bolívar 423; tel: 41-994 460; Sat–Thu 9am–5pm), with some fine pieces of colonial furniture and interesting exhibits on the slave trade. There's a Roman-style bathhouse, and a fountain that once spouted eau de Cologne for women and gin for men. However, the finest feature is the square tower, which provides an exceptional view of the whole town.

Within a few paces of the museum are the **Casa del Regidor** (formerly the mayor's residence), and **Callejón de Pena**, a street full of private merchants' houses, and a good place to find excellent arts and crafts, particularly lace and woodwork. If you want to buy, be sure to bargain – it is expected.

Back on the west side of the square, another beautiful mansion houses the **Museo de Arqueología Guamuhaya** ⓓ (Simón Bolívar 457, corner Villena; tel: 41-993 420; Sat–Thu 9am–5pm). There are interesting items relating to the pre-Columbian past with developments being traced to post-Conquest times.

Elegance and romance

A strong contender for Trinidad's best museum is the bold yellow building with arches located on the same side of the square as the church: the **Museo Romántico** ⓔ (Hernández 52; tel: 41-994 363; Tue–Sun 9am–5pm), housed in a sumptuous mansion. The ground floor was built in 1740 and it remained single-story for 70 years until the second floor was added at the beginning of the 19th century. In 1830–60, the Romantic period, it belonged to Nicolás de la Cruz Brunet Muñoz, the Conde de Brunet, who lived in the mansion with his 12 children and a number of slaves. He made his money from sugar and cattle, owning 70 slaves at the time of his death.

In 1974, the house was turned into a museum, and its rooms were filled with period pieces collected from numerous mansions throughout the city. Here, for example, you can see a

FACT

When the original tree in the Plazuela Real del Jigüe reached the end of its life, a cutting was taken and replanted, a custom that has continued through the centuries. The present tree was planted in 1929.

A guide at the Museo Romántico.

priceless 18th-century Austrian writing desk, covered with painted-enamel mythological scenes; a marble bathtub; and a wooden 'throne' from 1808 used as a toilet. In the kitchen there is a limestone water filter and a set of beautiful, custom-made porcelain plates and dishes from the 1820s. The upstairs balcony has fine views over the square.

From religion to revolution

Leaving the museum, walk down Calle Echerrí (also called Cristo) to the intersection with Calle Piro Guinart. Here is the **Archivo de la Ciudad** (City Archives), recognizable by the colorful coat of arms on the facade. Directly in front is the tallest and most famous landmark in Trinidad: the **Convento de San Francisco de Asís** Ⓕ, parts of which date from 1731. The building was enlarged and embellished in 1809 by a Spanish priest, Father Valencia, but, after the construction of the nearby Parroquial Mayor in 1892, the convent ceased to function, and the building was turned into a barracks for the Spanish army.

Then, in 1984, in a perverse twist of history, the former convent was turned into the **Museo Nacional de Lucha Contra Bandidos** (Museum of the Struggle Against Counter-Revolutionaries; Calle Echerrí; tel: 41-994 121; Tue–Sun 9am–5pm), which concentrates on the campaign to weed out anti-Castro guerrillas in the Escambray Mountains during the 1960s. Inside there is a boat in which Cuban exiles came from Florida to destroy the oil tanks at the nearby port of Casilda, and a Russian truck that was used in the search for counter-revolutionaries in the mountains.

The real beauty of this building, however, has nothing to do with politics. Climb the 119 granite and wooden stairs to the top of the bell tower. Once you've caught your breath, enjoy the view: from here, all of Trinidad is clearly visible, as are the blue waters of the Caribbean and the distant, hazy peaks of the Sierra Escambray. It is well worth the climb.

Plazuela Real del Jigüe

Walking to the end of Fernando Echerrí (Cristo), you reach the area

Santería doll dressed in white lace at Templo de Yemaya.

called El Fortuno. In the 18th century this area was home to several foreign pirates who were welcomed by the Trinidadians (*trinitarios* in Spanish), many of whom grew rich from smuggling and trading with the disreputable people they were supposed to fear. The house at Ciro Redondo No. 261 was reputedly built for a French pirate, Carlos Merlin, in 1754.

At the foot of Redondo, turn left into Calle Martínez Villena, heading toward **La Canchánchara**, a bar with live entertainment, and its own house cocktail, the *canchánchara*, made with rum, lime, honey, and sparkling water. The bar is quiet during the day, but comes into its own at night, and is popular with locals as well as tourists.

On the parallel Calle Vicente Suyama (also known as Calle Encarnación) is a makeshift gallery at No. 39 run by professor of art, Carlos Mata: it's typical of several private galleries that cater specifically to foreign tourists, and which have sprouted up around Trinidad since early 1994, when the government began tolerating certain limited forms of private enterprise.

One block along from La Canchánchara to your right is the spot where, in the early 16th century, the so-called 'Protector of the Indians,' Bartolomé de las Casas (see page 31), in the presence of Diego Velázquez, conducted the first Christmas Mass in Trinidad under a stately old *jigüe* tree: this is the **Plazuela Real del Jigüe**, complete with one of Trinidad's best little restaurants.

The next stop, heading up Vicente Suyama 59, is an authentic **Santería house** ❻, with Cuban revolutionary posters and an altar complete with a black Madonna. There's also a rock shaped like an egg, inside a pot full of seawater; the whole contraption is covered with fine lace. If you would like to go in, ask for Israel, the Santería priest, who will explain everything. He is very pleasant and knowledgeable and gives an interesting little tour (a donation is appreciated).

East of Plaza Mayor

To the right of the Iglesia Parroquial Mayor, an ancient flight of cobbled steps marks the end of Calle Rosario.

Playa Ancón is the main tourist resort on the peninsula.

At No. 3 is a house built in 1732 for Fernández de Lara, Trinidad's chief inquisitor, who was responsible for upholding Christianity. Halfway up the steps is an open-air bar, La Escalinata, great for a sunset cocktail, where you can relax with a *mojito* and listen to live bands.

At the top of the steps you will find the **Casa de la Música** **H**, a really lively spot that has live music, including salsa concerts, and impromptu dancing until the early hours. The Casa also has displays of old instruments, and you can buy a variety of Cuban music on CDs and tapes. There is a second entrance on Calle J.M. Márquez.

At the foot of the steps to your left along Fernando Echerrí is the Palenque de los Congos Reales, a bar open day and night where you can often catch an Afro-Cuban dance show or live music while enjoying a drink in the shady courtyard.

Slightly farther east is a triangular-shaped plaza – the **Plazuela de Sagarte**, where some of the oldest houses in Trinidad are to be found. One of these is now the **Casa de la Trova** **I** (daily 9am–1am; free during the day), built in 1717 and decorated with murals. It is popular with tourists and local people who come to enjoy the live music by day and night, and there is always a warm and friendly atmosphere.

One block down the hill and to your right, you come to **Calle Francisco Javier Zerquera** (**Rosario**) again. On the corner at No. 406 is a light-blue house that once belonged to one of Trinidad's sugar barons. Today it is the **Casa de la Cultura Trinitaria** **J** (tel: 41-994 308; daily 7am–11pm) where there is an art gallery and classrooms, dances are held, and concerts and plays are performed. Back up the hill, notice the 18th-century walls made from rocks, bricks, bones, and bottles of all sizes and shapes, and held together with clay, straw, and plaster. The yellow house at No. 79 is the **Casa de los Curas**, the residence for centuries of the parochial church's priests.

Santa Ana and Parque Central

There are two other areas worth visiting outside the heart of the Old Town.

The lush and lovely Valle de los Ingenios.

A 10-minute walk from the Plaza Mayor, the **Plaza Santa Ana** Ⓚ has a beautiful ruined church of the same name. Also on the plaza is the former Royal Prison (Carcel Real), and there is also a restaurant, a gallery displaying local art, and a store. You may also notice a rare statue of Bartolomé de Las Casas, the Dominican friar who fought for indigenous rights in the 16th century.

To the southeast, the **Parque Central** (which is also known as **Parque Céspedes**) Ⓛ has no stunning architecture but is a busy spot, with a church, a movie theater, and the telephone office, while in the center there are pergolas of shady vines and trailing plants. In November, the square is the focus for a week of cultural events and music.

Peninsula de Ancón

Some 12km (8 miles) south of Trinidad lies a spectacular stretch of beach, accessible either by way of **Casilda** or the more scenic route via the small fishing village of **La Boca**, where Trinidad's river disgorges its waters into the sea. The beach here is popular with local people, who can't usually be found at the main tourist resort of Playa Ancón, farther out along the peninsula. Unlike those in the tourist resorts, the beach here is not cleaned daily, but it is quite acceptable, and the area is lively, with *casas particulares* and places to eat.

Playa Ancón ⓳ is an excellent long sandy stretch with warm, clear blue waters. Behind the beach, however, there are lakes and swamps, so take precautions against mosquitoes and the sandflies that appear in the evening. Bathers tend to gather on the sections in front of the Hotel Ancón and the nearby Hotel Costa Sur, where they can be within easy reach of bars and restaurants. You can use the hotel's loungers for a small fee (currently CUC$2), and straw sunshades are available if you can't find a spot under the seagrape trees.

If you don't have a car, the beach can be reached by an irregular and somewhat unreliable bus service, or by taxi (*taxistas* tout for business on the corner of Antonio Maceo and Simón Bolívar). Find other people to fill the cab and make it a more economical journey. There is a public parking lot next to the Hotel Ancón, where taxis and coco-taxis wait to take people back to Trinidad. It is also a great cycle ride, with the road following the twinkling waters of the Caribbean.

The bicycle ride is best done fairly early in the morning or in the late afternoon to avoid the sun at its most powerful. Your hotel, or the owner of your *casa particular*, will probably be able to set you up with a bicycle for around CUC$3 a day. The quality of the bikes varies and they rarely have gears. For a tip (CUC$1) someone will watch your bicycle for you while you are on the beach.

There is a marina at Ancón, opposite Hotel Ancón (tel: 41-996 205), from where you can make excursions by boat or arrange scuba diving. Most excursions are booked through the

Cuba's Caribbean coast offers ample opportunities for snorkelling.

TIP

According to the census of 1795 there were 2,676 slaves in Trinidad. That year, the area's 82 sugar mills produced 680 tonnes of sugar, 1,000 barrels of *aguardiente*, and 700 urns of molasses.

local tour operators, but set off from here. Catamarans go to either Cayo Blanco or Cayo Macho, two offshore cays, which make a nice day trip with snorkeling, lunch, and an open bar.

Valle de los Ingenios

As you leave Trinidad on Route 12, heading northeast toward Sancti Spíritus, or to join up with the Carretera Central going east, the road passes through the spectacular **Valle de los Ingenios** ⓴ (Valley of the Sugar Mills). Like Trinidad, this lush valley is a Unesco World Heritage Site. When it was Cuba's most important sugar-producing region, there were 43 working sugar mills in the valley, but there was a serious downturn in the valley's economy in the mid-19th century. It collapsed completely in 1880 when world sugar prices slumped.

In the rest of Cuba, the more efficient *central* sugar mill was becoming the norm, and the valley's *ingenios* simply could not compete. Many of the magnificent plantation houses and mansions dating from those days are now in ruins, but some still stand, most notably the exceptionally beautiful farm belonging to the Iznaga family, which has been restored.

The quaint little **Tren Turístico**, an old steam train, goes from Trinidad station, south of the town, to Manaca-Iznaga (daily in high season, 9.30am–2pm; CUC$10).

The Tren Turístico goes from Trinidad station to Manaca-Iznaga.

Torre de Manaca-Iznaga

You cannot miss the farm, as it is splendidly indicated by the **Torre de Manaca-Iznaga**, 15km (10 miles) by road from Trinidad (daily 9am–4 or 5pm), which rears proudly out of the green cane fields. Legend has it that the tower was built after a bet between two brothers, in which one had to build a tower higher than the depth that the other could dig a well. In fact, the tower was designed originally as a watchtower to keep an eye on the slaves working in the fields, and has a bell that summoned them to work. Birds of prey circle on the thermals, and a refreshing wind cools you as you climb up above the valley floor.

Down below, local women sell beautiful handmade lace and *guayaberas*, the traditional white cotton men's shirts. The immaculate hacienda (daily 9am–5pm) is an excellent place for a drink of *guarapo*, the freshly pressed sugar-cane juice that is milled by Cuba's only original *trapiche* (sugar press) remaining *in situ*. There are also demonstrations of sugar-cane pressing, in which you can participate, and enjoy the fruits of your labor afterward with a dash of rum. Trips to the *torre* can be arranged through tour operators in Trinidad.

If you are bound for Santa Clara, you should take the road running north from the **Manaca-Iznaga tower to Güinia de Miranda**. This is a little-used and potholed but beautiful route. An alternative route, the road to Sancti Spíritus, curves and dips across a lovely landscape, passing the heights of the Alturas de Banao, and is the main route for buses heading to the east, en route to Santiago de Cuba.

RESTAURANTS AND PALADARES

PRICE CATEGORIES

Price categories are for a three-course meal for one with a beer, or mojito. Wine puts the price up:
$ = under $25
$$ = $25–35
$$$ = over $35

Cienfuegos

Aché
Avenida 38, between 41 and 43
Tel: 43-526 173. Open Mon–Sat noon–10.30pm. **$**
A long-established, professional paladar, which opened in 1996, serves generous cocktails and you can accompany your meal with Spanish or Chilean wine. The house specialty is shrimp, but it is all good, with friendly service.

Casa Prado
Calle 37 4626, between 46 and 48
Open daily L & D. **$–$$**
Good food and large portions, including lovely fresh fish and seafood. Attentive service. Good for couples, families or large parties.

Finca del Mar
Calle 35, between 18 and 20
Tel: 43-526 598. Open noon–midnight. **$$**
Somewhere a bit different for Cuba, with tapas-style dishes and unusual menu items such as ceviche, octopus, or stuffed peppers. Service can be slow if they are busy, but it is a pleasant way to spend an afternoon overlooking the sea with a glass of wine and some seafood. Great cocktails too.

Palacio del Valle
Calle 37, Punta Gorda
Tel: 43-551 226. Open daily L & D. **$$–$$$**
Seafood, including lobster and shrimp, is the specialty in this extravagant, early 20th-century Spanish-Moorish palace, but the food and service do not match up to the decor.

El Tranvía
Calle 37 4002, between 40 and 42
Tel: 43-524 920. Open daily L & D. **$–$$**
A good place for a fun experience. A themed *paladar* with a reconstructed tramcar on the roof terrace and staff all dressed as guards. Live music and good drinks contribute to the friendly atmosphere and make the food seem better than average.

La Verja
Avenida 54, 3306
Tel: 43-516 311. Open daily 11am–3pm, 6pm–midnight. **$$**
The best place to eat in the town center, for its shabby elegance and stained-glass *mámparas* more than the food.

Trinidad

There are now dozens of paladares in Trinidad, although not all of them can be recommended. New restaurants are opening so ask in your *casa* for the latest recommendations.

El Cubita
Maceo 471, between Zerquera and Bolivar
Tel: 52-711 479. Open daily 11am–11pm. **$$**
Attractively decorated, this spacious restaurant, with live music and English-speaking staff, is a reliable option. Good food with a varied menu and tasty drinks from the bar, called Bar Santander after the pottery family in town.

Estela
Simón Bolívar 557
Tel: 41-994 329. Open Mon–Fri 6.30–9.30pm. **$$**
A family-run *paladar* and one of the most popular places to eat in town, so get there early. Tables in the garden, enclosed by a high wall. Food is fresh and tasty with lots of choice and plentiful portions, including heaps of avocado from the tree in the garden in season. Lamb is the house specialty. Friendly hosts, good service.

Guitarra Mía
Jesús Menéndez (Alameda) 19, between Lino Pérez and Camilo Cienfuegos
Tel: 52-703 174. Open daily D. **$$**
Hand-decorated guitars adorn the walls and the music theme is carried through to the food presentation, with guitar-shaped vegetables and musical symbols drawn on the plates. A cosy, intimate *paladar*, serving good food with pleasant service and, of course, live music.

Museo 1514 (Quince Quatorce)
Bolívar 515, between JM Márquez and Hernández Echerri
Tel: 41-994 255. Open daily D. **$$**
The food is generally good here, but most people come for the location, a wonderful old house stuffed with antiques and heirlooms and the tables all dressed with old china. The atmosphere is lifted by live music and professional dancers. The staffers are multilingual and service is good.

San José
Maceo 382, between Joseph Smith and Colón
Tel: 41-994 702; http://restaurantbarsanjose.com. Open daily L & D. **$–$$**
Very good bar and restaurant in colonial style with lovely old tiled floor and wooden tables and chairs. A range of Cuban dishes features on the menu, but there's also pizza, pasta, sandwiches, and ice cream; something for all the family.

Sol Ananda
Real 45, between Bolívar and Piro Guinart
Tel: 41-998 281. Open daily L & D. **$$**
Architect-owned, this delightful, renovated colonial house on the corner of the Plaza Mayor is a feast for the eyes, with chandeliers and antiques, including beds. The food is good and the multilingual service is excellent, managed by the owner's brother.

Interior of Palacio del Valle.

Patio of a Camagüey restaurant.

EASTERN LOWLANDS

This region's economic mainstay is agriculture, although tourism is growing steadily, and though it lacks obvious attractions, the colonial city of Camagüey is worth visiting and there are fine beaches along the north coast.

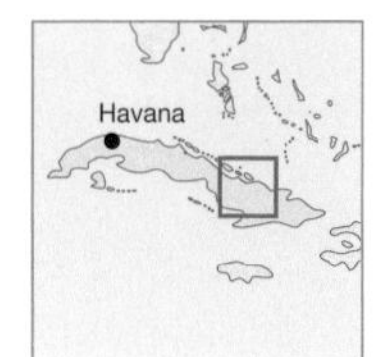

Main Attractions
- Ciego de Ávila
- Los Jardines de la Reina
- Morón
- Cayo Coco
- Camagüey
- Cayo Sabinal
- Hacienda La Belén

The Carretera Central highway continues east from Sancti Spíritus through **Ciego de Ávila province**. With its fertile soils and abundant water, this is Cuba's fruit bowl, producing citrus, bananas, and pineapples, in the most productive plantations on the island. To the north are the Jardines del Rey, of which Cayo Coco, Cayo Guillermo, and Cayo Paredón Grande now make up the third most important tourist development in the country. To the south are the Jardines de la Reina, popular for diving and fishing, while other watery attractions include the two largest natural lakes in Cuba, Laguna de la Leche and Laguna La Redonda, much loved by fishermen, hunters, and birders.

Ciego de Avila

The provincial capital, also called **Ciego de Ávila ❶**, gets its name from a 16th-century rancher named Jácome de Ávila, who cleared the original dense forest here to make a clearing, or *ciego.* He set aside part of his estate as a resting place for travelers on the east–west route, and this quickly became a settlement. Often called the 'Pineapple Town' by other Cubans, its nickname is well deserved. Here, a single variety of pineapple, the sweet and juicy *Española Roja*, is grown in vast quantities that still fall short of demand.

The town, also known as the 'city of portals,' after the large number of neoclassical columns and pillars adorning the houses, is built on a strict grid system around **Parque Martí**, with the usual bust of the hero. There are few buildings of note apart from the **Museo de Artes Decorativas** (tel: 33-201 661; Mon–Fri 9am–5pm, Sat 2–9pm, Sun 8am–noon) and, just south of the square, the neoclassical **Teatro Principal** (Agüero and Honorato del Castillo; tel: 33-222 086), built in the 1920s by a rich socialite, Angela

Setting sail from Cayo Coco beach.

Cycling is a popular mode of transportation in Morón.

Hernández Vida de Jiménez, who battled to create a cultural mecca in her home town. The theater has wonderful acoustics and is still used.

During the first War of Independence in the 1860s, the Spanish colonial government built a 67km (42-mile) defensive string of 43 forts – called **La Trocha** – across the island from Júcaro to Morón, so as to cut the rebellious east off from the rest of the island. At the junction of calles Marcial Gómez and Joaquín de Agüero is the spot where the city was founded, and a 19th-century Mapa Mural shows the first 25 blocks of the town, including the Spanish command headquarters and some of the forts along the military line.

Jardines de la Reina

South of Ciego de Ávila, **Júcaro ❷** is a pleasant, if scrappy, fishing village on the coast, and the point of embarkation for the pristine and enchanting island chain of **Los Jardines de la Reina** (The Queen's Gardens). Visits, which must be organized well in advance, are expensive week-long diving or fishing packages, with accommodations on a floating hotel, the *Tortuga*, moored near Cayo Anclitas, or on live-aboard boats. For more information, contact Avalon (http://cubanfishingcenters.com/, http://cubandivingcenters.com/) or Roxtons (www.roxtons.com), the only operators who currently have authority to run fishing and diving expeditions here. The 200km (125-mile) archipelago has been designated a marine national park.

Morón – the rooster city

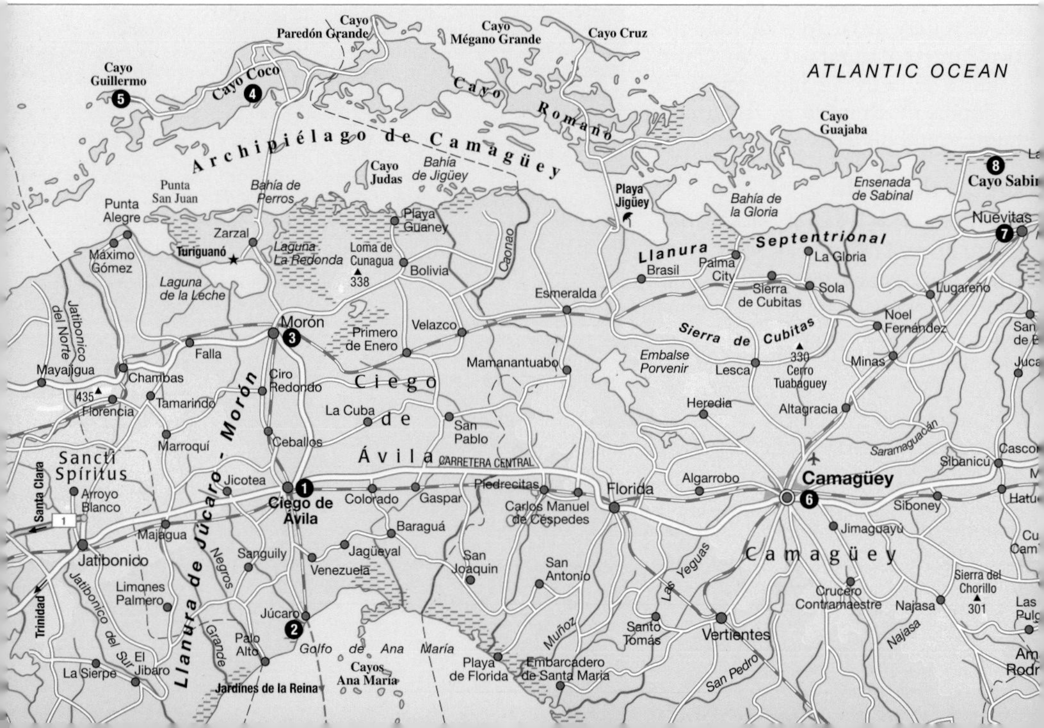

Morón ❸, a real country town where people get around on foot, on bicycles, or in horse-drawn carts, lies to the north of the province and is visited mostly by people wanting easy access to the northern cays but with cheaper accommodations. Nicknamed Ciudad del Gallo (Rooster City), the town's symbol is a crowing rooster, representing the people's triumph over arrogant officialdom. In the 1950s, local citizenry raised money to have the rooster sculpted in bronze as a public monument. Dictator Fulgencio Batista got in on the act and decided to unveil the statue in what would be known as Batista Park. Outraged residents saved their rooster from humiliation by boycotting the inauguration, but the bird was subsequently kidnapped and destroyed by misguided guerrillas.

In the calmer 1980s, Morón's rooster was born anew and placed in the **Parque del Gallo** (Rooster Park), at the entrance to Hotel Morón. The monument was sculpted by Rita Longa and is a replica of the rooster at Morón de la Frontera in Spain. In the adjacent tower an amplified recording of jubilant crowing is electronically set to activate twice a day at 6am and 6pm.

The 1924 eclectic, neo-colonial, two-story train station is a national monument. You can ride on a steam train through sugar-cane fields to the Patria o Muerte sugar museum at the Central Patria. The **Museo de Arqueología e Historia Caonabo** (Calle Martí 374; Mon–Tue 8am–4pm, Wed–Sat 8am–9pm) was built originally as a bank in 1919, but after a spell as the offices of the telephone company it became the municipal museum, showcasing archeology and local history.

North of Morón are popular places for fishing, hunting, and boating: **Laguna La Redonda**, where catfish abound, and **Laguna de la Leche**, milky-white from sodium carbonate deposits that attract flamingos. This is Cuba's largest natural reservoir; its size and central location made it strategically important during the 1895 War of Independence: Cuban *mambí* fighters crossed it on numerous occasions to deliver munitions from Camagüey to Villa Clara, thus evading La Trocha. An Aquatic Carnival is held here, usually in July but sometimes in August or September.

The northern islands

Cayo Coco ❹ covers an area of 595 sq km (230 sq miles) with 22km (13 miles) of white sand and crystal-clear water. There are nine beaches of varying sizes on the northern coast, several of which are now dominated by large, all-inclusive resorts only meters from the shore. A 27km (17-mile) causeway that shoots straight through a mirror of water links the cay to the mainland.

Cayo Coco is named after the white ibis, known locally as a *coco*, one of the island's more striking inhabitants,

TIP

Morón is the last stop on Víazul's Circuíto Norte (Northern Circuit) bus route, which starts in Trinidad and runs via Cienfuegos, Santa Clara, Remedios, Caibarién, Mayajigua, and Chambas. A minibus is used if there aren't many passengers, and service may be canceled in low season. From Morón there is easy access to lovely beaches at Cayo Coco and Cayo Guillermo.

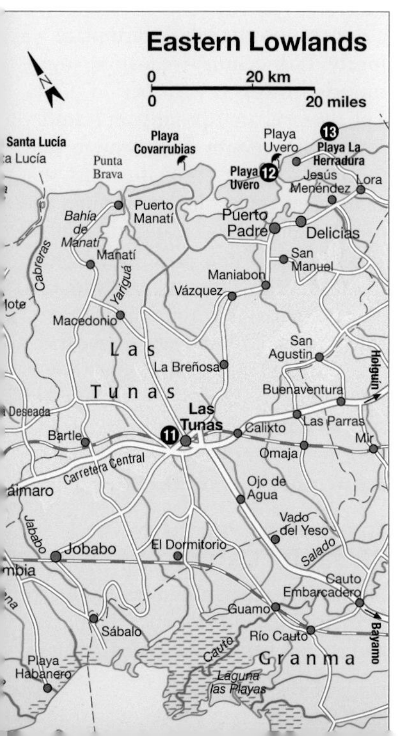

Cayo Coco.

TIP

Unlike most Cuban cities, Camagüey is not constructed on a grid pattern, and it has no central square. A useful reference point is the wide Avenida República, which runs north–south through the center. The city sights are spread out, so taking a bici-taxi (contact Andariegos, tel: 32-295 484), with shade for passengers, is a good option. Guides are available.

along with the rosy flamingo. The area is a protected zone, as much of the wildlife, including 156 bird species, is endangered. Many Cuban ecologists are concerned about the long-term effects of development, especially the way the causeway has obstructed the free flow of currents. The expansion of hotels is also having an impact on wildlife – hotels routinely spray against mosquitoes, for example.

The causeway continues west to **Cayo Guillermo** ❺ – also rapidly developing for 'sea and sand' tourism and as a base for scuba diving and fishing – and east to **Cayo Romano** and **Cayo Paredón Grande**, far less developed, with empty white sand beaches.

Camagüey

The province of Camagüey, the largest in Cuba, has its fair share of sugar-cane fields, rice paddies, and citrus groves, but far more important are its cattle pastures, supporting both dairy and beef cattle. *Vaqueros* (cowboys), wearing broad-brimmed hats and dangling machetes, can be seen herding stock from astride their horses, lassos flying. Rodeos are a popular entertainment.

Camagüey ❻, the capital of the province, is Cuba's third-largest city (pop. 325,000). It was one of Diego Velázquez's seven original settlements, founded as the Villa of Santa María del Puerto Príncipe in 1514. It was twice moved, razed by Henry Morgan's crew in 1668 then rebuilt soon after, with a street plan that seems designed to help ambush future invaders.

Camagüey is a place of beauty, culture, and tradition. The old town is a delight: narrow, twisting streets wind from the river, lined by rows of small, rainbow-colored, stuccoed houses, with lush courtyards set back from the street that can be glimpsed through ancient wooden doors. But don't come expecting to find another Trinidad: Camagüey is quite different.

The city's most famous son, Ignacio Agramonte (1841–73), was the fighting general of Camagüey's rebel forces during the first War of Independence (he died in action in 1873). The **Museo Casa Natal de Ignacio Agramonte** Ⓐ (Avenida Agramonte 459, Plaza de los Trabajadores; tel: 32-297 116; Tue–Sat 9am–7pm, Sun 8.30–11.30am) is a museum in the hero's birthplace – a lovely 18th-century mansion, sumptuously furnished with period pieces. The *tinajones* are a prominent feature – round, wide-mouthed earthenware jugs, modeled on the big-bellied jars that came from Spain filled with wines and oils. Local potters created the Cuban versions to solve a pressing problem: Camagüey had almost no water sources, and rainfall, while abundant, was seasonal. You still see *tinajones* in the shady courtyard of many Camagüeyan households, and water sellers still ply the streets. Ranging in size from large to enormous, some of the *tinajones* still in use were made more than a century ago.

Around Agramonte and Plaza del Carmen

North of here sits the splendid **Teatro Principal** Ⓑ, which draws the biggest audiences when the Ballet de Camagüey

Produce for sale in the Agromercado.

or the local symphony orchestra performs. Calle Padre Valencia brings you back to the attractive 18th-century church, **Nuestra Señora de La Merced** **C** (opening hours vary), across from Agramonte's birthplace on the **Plaza de los Trabajadores.** Considered one of the most splendid churches in the country when it was first built in 1747 and now a National Monument, La Merced has benefitted from (on-going) restoration: the 20th-century decorated ceiling is particularly striking. The ghoulish may go down the steps beside the altar to see the catacombs.

Avenida Agramonte leads you to another important church, also dating from the 1700s: **Nuestra Señora de la Soledad** **D**. Its red brick exterior looks unpromising, but inside you are greeted by glorious decoration on the arches and pillars, topped by a splendid vaulted ceiling. Before continuing south to the heart of the city, you can make a diversion north along Avenida República (which becomes Avenida de los Mártires beyond the train station) to the **Museo Provincial Ignacio Agramonte** **E** (Avenida de los Mártires 2; tel: 32-282 425; Tue–Thu and Sat 10am–6pm, Fri noon–8pm, Sun 10am–2pm), with an eclectic collection ranging from stuffed animals to archeological finds. It is best known, though, for its fine-art collection. A cavalry barracks in the mid-19th century, the building was converted into a hotel in the first half of the 20th century but became a museum in 1955.

Continuing on the route south, you reach **Parque Ignacio Agramonte** **F**, the nearest thing Camagüey has to a main square. The dramatic mounted figure of Agramonte is the centerpiece. On the south side, the 19th-century **Catedral** **G** is worth a peek. Its wooden ceiling is its best feature. If you ask, you may be allowed to climb spiral steps to the bell tower for a wonderful view (donation appreciated).

Another recently restored church is **Nuestra Señora del Carmen** **H**, which lies several blocks west of the square along Calle Martí, on the beautifully restored **Plaza del Carmen.** The old hospital alongside the church is now the offices of the Historiador de la Ciudad, where all the restoration works

Statue of local hero, Ignacio Agramonte.

Camagüey's Gran Hotel and the city beyond.

HONORING FAMOUS SONS

Camagüey has spawned a number of eminent men, several of whom have achieved international fame. Ignacio Agramonte is the great warrior who battled for five years against the colonial Spanish but never lived to see independence (the inhabitants of Camagüey are called *agromonteros* in his honor). **Casa Natal de Nicolás Guillén** (Hermanos Agüero 58, between Príncipe and Cisneros, tel: 32-293 706) is the birthplace (in 1902) of a more recently famous Camagüeyan, the world-renowned writer Nicolás Guillén Batista (see page 110). The house is now an art and cultural studies school, rather than a museum, and though you are free to wander around, there is not much to see other than a small bronze portrait of the poet at the front of the house, and photos and poems on the walls inside. Carlos J. Finlay's birthplace (Cristo 5, between Lugareño and Callejón del Templador; tel: 32-296 745) is also open to the public. He was born in 1833 to a family of mixed French and Scottish origins and later pursued his scientific studies in Paris and Philadelphia. His discovery in 1881 that the Aedes mosquito was the vector for yellow fever affected the world's health. By controlling the mosquito population, the spread of both yellow fever and malaria were checked, a factor of particular importance in the construction of the Panama Canal. Finlay became the chief health officer in Cuba at the beginning of the 20th century and died in Havana in 1915.

are planned. The plaza is dotted with *tinajones* as well as sculptures by Martha Jiménez Pérez of gossiping women, a courting couple, and a man reading a newspaper. The real-life versions can often be seen alongside the statues. There are restaurants here where you can sit and have a drink, or take a break on one of the benches and watch the world go by. While in this area, walk a few blocks south to the **Iglesia de Santo Cristo del Buen Viaje** ❶. The interest here lies mainly in the adjacent **cemetery**, one of the finest in the country, much frequented by local people who like to stroll around, as well as visiting family graves. Running eastward, back toward the center, Calle Cristo has road-side flower-sellers, and a couple of local bars.

San Juan de Dios to Parque Marti

Rivaling the Plaza del Carmen for the honor of being the loveliest place in Camagüey is the restored, 18th-century **Plaza San Juan de Dios** ❶, south of Parque Agramonte. Now a national monument, the square is peaceful and surrounded by brightly colored houses with elegant wooden *rejas* (grilles), and tall doors and windows. The plaza is dominated by the **Iglesia San Juan de Dios**, a small, intimate church with a fine mahogany ceiling and altar. Next door, the old hospital, the first ever built in town, was where the body of Agramonte was brought before his interment in the cemetery. It is believed that he may have been tended by Fray José Olallo Valdés (1820–89), who worked tirelessly to help victims of the cholera epidemic in 1835 and those wounded in the Wars of Independence. He was the last remaining brother of the San Juan de Dios order in Cuba, following religious persecution by the Spanish authorities, and was beatified in 2008 in the first-ever such ceremony in Cuba. Now the hospital is the local heritage office, Centro Provincial de Patrimonio Cultural. Two of the finest buildings on the plaza are restaurants – La Campana de Toledo and the Parador de los Tres Reyes – popular with day-trippers.

The **Agromercado** Ⓚ (farmers' market), on the banks of the river, is a great

Artist's studio, Camagüey.

place to appreciate the *agramonteros*' renowned love of good food. In addition to stands selling fresh produce are simple kitchens serving hot meals. It's a lively spot, shaded by palms and tropical foliage, and with vendors noisily hawking their produce: piles of glossy mangos, tomatoes, and peppers, strings of garlic, and heaps of *mamey*. On the eastern bank of the Hatibonico River, Parque Casino Campestre was used in colonial times for cattle shows, fairs, dances, and other social activities.

Backtracking up Calle San Pablo and turning right on Calle Martí you come to the Plaza de la Juventud, to give it the official name, but local people know it as **Parque Martí** L. This quiet square is dominated by the Sagrado Corazón de Jesús, an imposing neo-Gothic church built in 1920. Its stained glass windows were damaged during the Revolution and restoration started only in 2001. It was completed in 2013, with a new roof and other works, and the whole square has also been given a facelift.

Camagüey province

The city of Camagüey is a cultural oasis in an otherwise arid province, where cows seem to outnumber people. Second in size is **Nuevitas** 7, the Atlantic seaport on the Bahía de Nuevitas. Despite its run-down appearance,

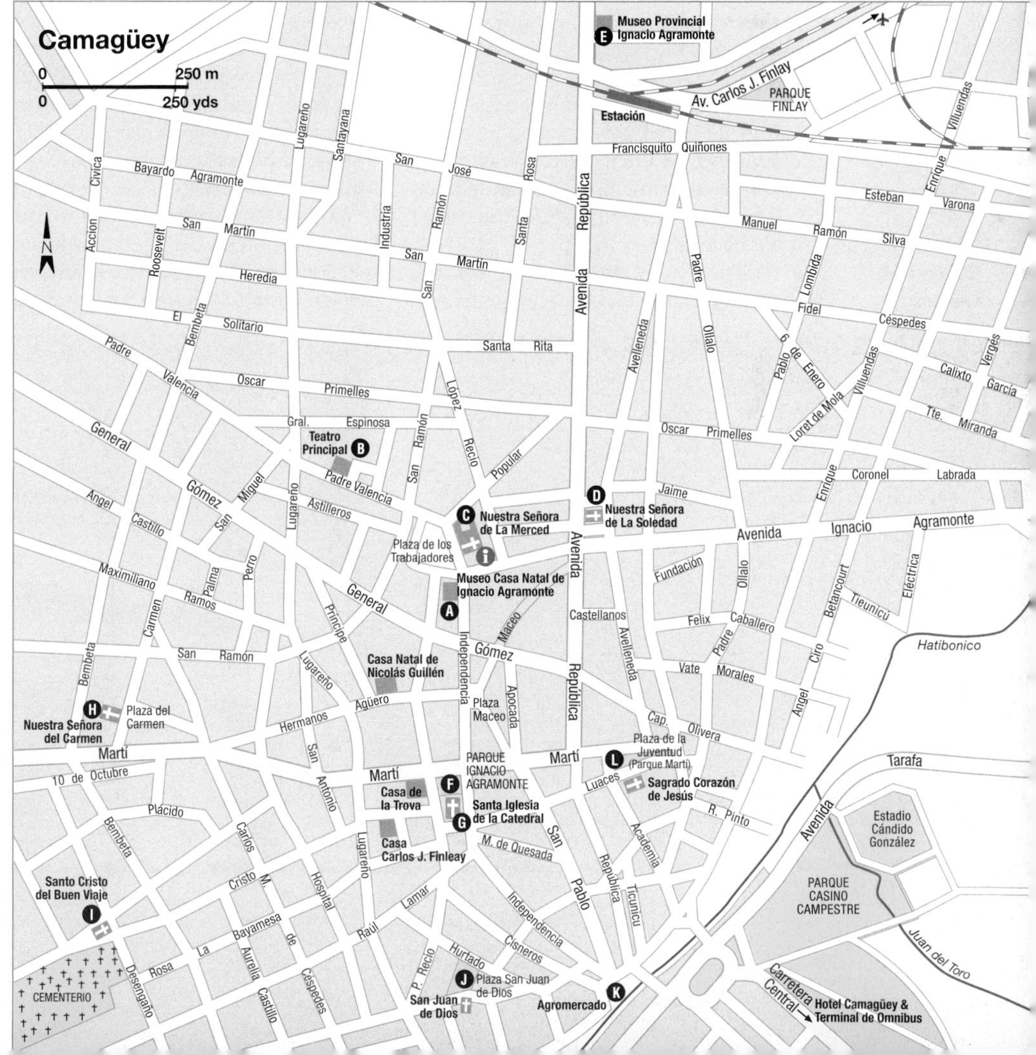

The Spanish name for the prickly pear cactus is tuna, and it is after this plant that the province is named.

Nuevitas is an important trading center for the rural heartland, close to the causeway to the beautiful **Cayo Sabinal** ❽, a cay to the northwest with more than 30km (20 miles) of empty beaches. At Playa Los Pinos, there are basic accommodations and a restaurant. The cay is a nature reserve protecting flocks of flamingos and many endangered birds.

Boat trips are organized from nearby **Playa Santa Lucía** ❾, to the east, to Cayo Sabinal, but the most common route is by road from Camagüey – a journey of 105km (65 miles) through cattle country. At Santa Lucía, the 20km (12 miles) of dazzling white sands are still relatively quiet. There are half a dozen hotels of varying quality strung out along the main road, but not a great deal else. If you don't have your own transportation you can get a bus from Camagüey to Playa Santa Lucía (at 5am or 2pm) for a few pesos Cubanos, or arrange to join one of the shuttle buses taking package tourists from the airport to the resort.

The area is well known for the quality of the diving. Scuba devotees recommend the area for the sheer variety of marine life at underwater sites with 33 known shipwrecks just off the coast. The Shark's Friends International Diving Center offers a variety of boat dives including shark feeding at a site in the channel between Cayo Sabinal and Playa Los Cocos, which is exciting to watch. **La Boca**, a tiny fishing village on **Playa Los Cocos**, 8km (5 miles) west of the main resort, is one of the loveliest spots in Cuba, with a glorious crescent of sand that knocks spots off the strip at Santa Lucía and a couple of seafood restaurants. Behind is a lagoon where flamingos gather.

Guáimaro and Las Tunas

Traveling eastward from Camagüey along the Carretera Central, the only town before you cross into Las Tunas province is **Guáimaro** ❿, whose main claim to fame is that it was the site of the assembly that drew up Cuba's first constitution in 1869.

South of Guáimaro, near the town of **Najasa**, the Sierra Guaicanama-Najasa is the site of the little-visited reserve of **Hacienda La Belén**. The birdlife

The Plaza San Juan de Dios is a national monument.

is especially rich, with many species of parrot; you can also go horseback riding or hiking, and there is a small hotel with a swimming pool. Contact Ecotur, www.ecoturcuba.tur.cu, for details.

There is not much to detain you in Las Tunas province and most people drive straight through without stopping. The provincial capital, also called **Las Tunas** ⓫, was burned down in both wars of independence, and has no colonial landmarks. The main square, Parque Vincent García, is not unpleasant but is spoiled by traffic.

Located close by on Calle Lucas Ortiz is the **Museo Memorial Mártires de Barbados** (tel: 31-347 213; Mon–Sat 10am–5pm). It is set in a two-story wooden house, the former home of fencing champion Carlos Leyva González, who was killed with 72 others when a Cuban plane was sabotaged by terrorists in 1976 (see page 171). En route from Caracas to Havana, the plane made a stopover in Barbados, when the bomber got off, leaving a bomb on board. The museum contains documents, photos, and sports implements belonging to all the victims, but especially to Carlos and to Leonardo McKenzie Grant, who was also born in the town.

The region's most famous son is El Cucalambé, the pseudonym of poet Juan Cristóbal Nápoles Fajardo, whose 19th-century *décimas* (10-line rhyming topical songs) are honored at the annual Cucalambeana Fair, attracting poets and singers from all over Cuba. The town has a traditional dish, a *caldosa* (stew) of meat and vegetables, which is served in tasty form at Quique Marina, a family-style restaurant on the Carretera Central on the western outskirts. Look for terracotta ceramics dotted about the town – Las Tunas is famous for them.

On the north coast, near the town of Jesús Menéndez, are two completely unspoiled beaches, **Playa Uvero** ⓬ and **Playa La Herradura** ⓭. On **Playa Covarrubias**, there is a single all-inclusive hotel. There is nowhere else to stay.

RESTAURANTS AND PALADARES

PRICE CATEGORIES

Price categories are for a three-course meal for one with a beer, or mojito. Wine puts the price up:
$ = under $25
$$ = $25–35
$$$ = over $35

Camagüey

1800
Plaza San Juan de Dios, 113
Tel: 32-283 619; www.restaurante1800.com. Open daily 9am–1am. **$$**
A very upscale *paladar* in the heart of the colonial zone. There is usually a buffet for appetizers and desserts, and a menu for main course options. Good, professional service, plus music and dance entertainment.

Café Ciudad
José Martí corner Cisneros, Parque Ignacio Agramonte
Open daily until 11pm. **$$**
Serves a variety of coffees, some of the best to be found in Cuba, as well as snacks and ice cream. A good place to stop and observe life around the Parque.

Campana de Toledo
Plaza San Juan de Dios, 18
Tel: 32-286 812. Open daily L & D. **$$**
Spanish-style dishes in a colonial mansion with an attractive patio; tables overlook the square or the courtyard. Busy at lunch with tour parties. Next door, Parador de los Tres Reyes (same phone) offers similar fare for a similar clientele.

Papito Rizo
Carretera del Aqueducto, corner Circunvalación, on outskirts of town
Tel: 32-283 348. Open daily 11am–11pm or later. **$**
The best *paladar* in town, according to local people, serving good Cuban food. Friendly staffers speak English and Italian. You'll need a taxi to get there though.

Ciego de Avila

Fonda La Estrella
Honorato del Castillo
Tel: 33-266 186. Open daily noon–midnight. **$**
The best restaurant in town, decorated like an old Spanish inn, with local artifacts on the walls. Cuban food includes *ropa vieja*.

Solaris
Honorato del Castillo
Tel: 33-222 156. Open Tue–Sun noon–3pm, 6–10pm. **$**
On the top floor of a 12-story building with a panoramic view. Enjoy cocktails and *comida criolla* while a pianist plays requests.

Morón

La Atarraya
Laguna de la Leche
Tel: 33-505 351. Open Tue–Sun noon–5pm. **$$**
Built over the lake with a lovely view, La Atarraya serves mostly seafood and fish dishes.

Liberluz
Libertad 148, between Padre Cano and Luz Caballero
Tel: 33-505 054. Open daily noon–3pm, 7–10pm. **$**
A *paladar* and *casa particular*, serving up plentiful meals of *criollo* food. Open-air seating under a canopy of bougainvillea is accompanied by live music and friendly service.

DREAM DIVING

Whether you're a first-time scuba diver or a pro, Cuba offers some of the most exciting diving in the Caribbean, along myriad reefs and cays still relatively untouched by mass tourism.

Cuba's dive sites extend all round the island and no matter where you're staying there's bound to be a dive operator within fairly easy reach. They offer a variety of reefs, walls, tunnels, and wrecks, from old Spanish galleons to modern fishing vessels deliberately sunk as dive sites. Marine wildlife is varied and plentiful and much of it is protected, including turtles and the elusive manatee.

María la Gorda, in the far west, has some of the best diving, in a sheltered bay where it is calm even when the rest of the island has bad weather. Spectacular sponges and colorful coral offer shelter to grunts, grouper, barracuda, and even whale sharks. Visibility here and off the west coast of Isla de la Juventud is usually reliably good. Hotel Colony, on the Isla, is the most famous dive resort in Cuba, with 56 dive sites within reach of a dive boat. Some 40 varieties of coral can be found here, home to myriad fish of many colors, and you swim through tunnels, trenches, and pristine underwater gardens. Farther east in the Jardines de la Reina there is even a live-aboard boat hotel for divers and anglers.

Along the north coast the cays and reefs of the archipelago Jardines del Rey attract moray eels, angel fish, snappers, jacks, lobster, and rays. Marinas offering scuba diving can be found at Varadero, Cayo Las Brujas, Cayo Coco, Playa Santa Lucía, and Guardalavaca. Sometimes they suffer from rough seas if there is a weather front approaching from the eastern seaboard of the US, but generally the water is warm and inviting.

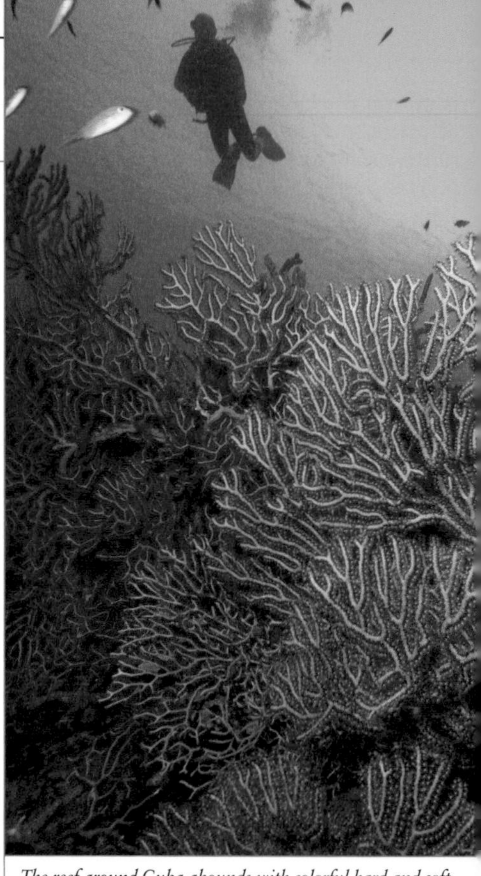

The reef around Cuba abounds with colorful hard and soft corals often seen to best advantage on a night dive.

There are 33 shipwrecks off the coast of Camagüey, including the Virgen de Altagracia near Santa Lucía.

The Goldentail Moray Eel (Gymnothorax miliaris) can be found popping its head out of holes along the reef or among wrecks, its golden tail rarely visible.

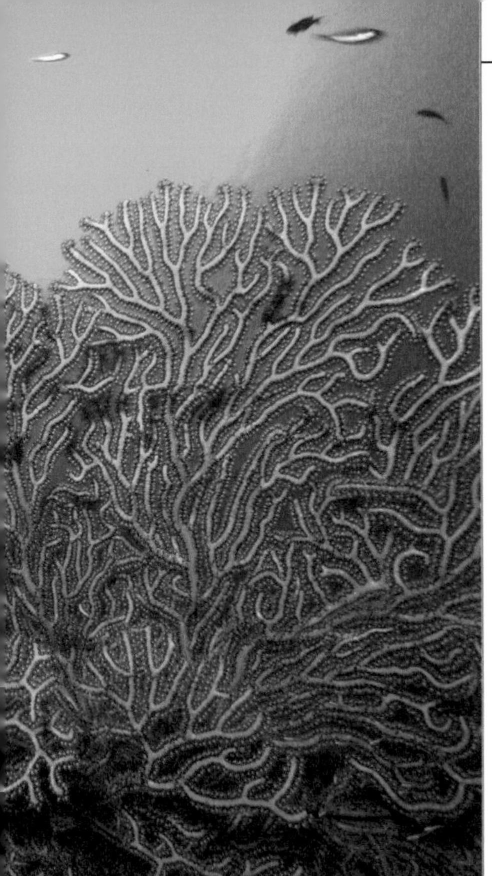

The Atlantic goliath grouper fish (Epinephelus itajara) is found off the eastern coast of Cuba. This impressive fish can grow to 1.8 metres (6ft) and usually swallows its prey whole.

The Brain coral (Diploria Strigosa) is a colony of tiny polyps which secrete the coral skeleton and can live to be 900 years old and grows very slowly, eventually reaching approximately 2 meters (6ft).

Feeding time at Playa Santa Lucía is an exhilarating sight – those brave enough can watch massive bull sharks devour fish hand-fed to them by local dive masters.

SHARKS AND WRECKS

Playa Santa Lucía, north of Camagüey, has some excellent dive sites, with 33 shipwrecks discovered so far. However, it is more famous for its sharks than its wrecks. Staff at the local dive shop, now called Shark's Friends, started to feed a few sharks in the early 1980s but word got around underwater and now some 20 massive bull sharks measuring up to 3 meters (10ft) turn up at feeding time. They congregate and are fed in a channel between Playa Los Cocos and Cayo El Sabinal, close to the wreck of a Spanish merchant ship at a depth of 25–30 meters (80–95ft). The current has to be right and there is only a 45-minute slot, but it is thrilling to watch the dive masters hand-feed them, and the sharks swim up to the dive group, strategically placed a few meters away. No armor is worn but spear guns are kept at the ready, just in case. Watch your air consumption – you may run out if it is too exciting.

The Yellow Tube Sponge (Aplysina fistularis) is a filter-feeder, consuming plankton and detritus, in turn being eaten by reef fish as well as the hawksbill sea turtle.

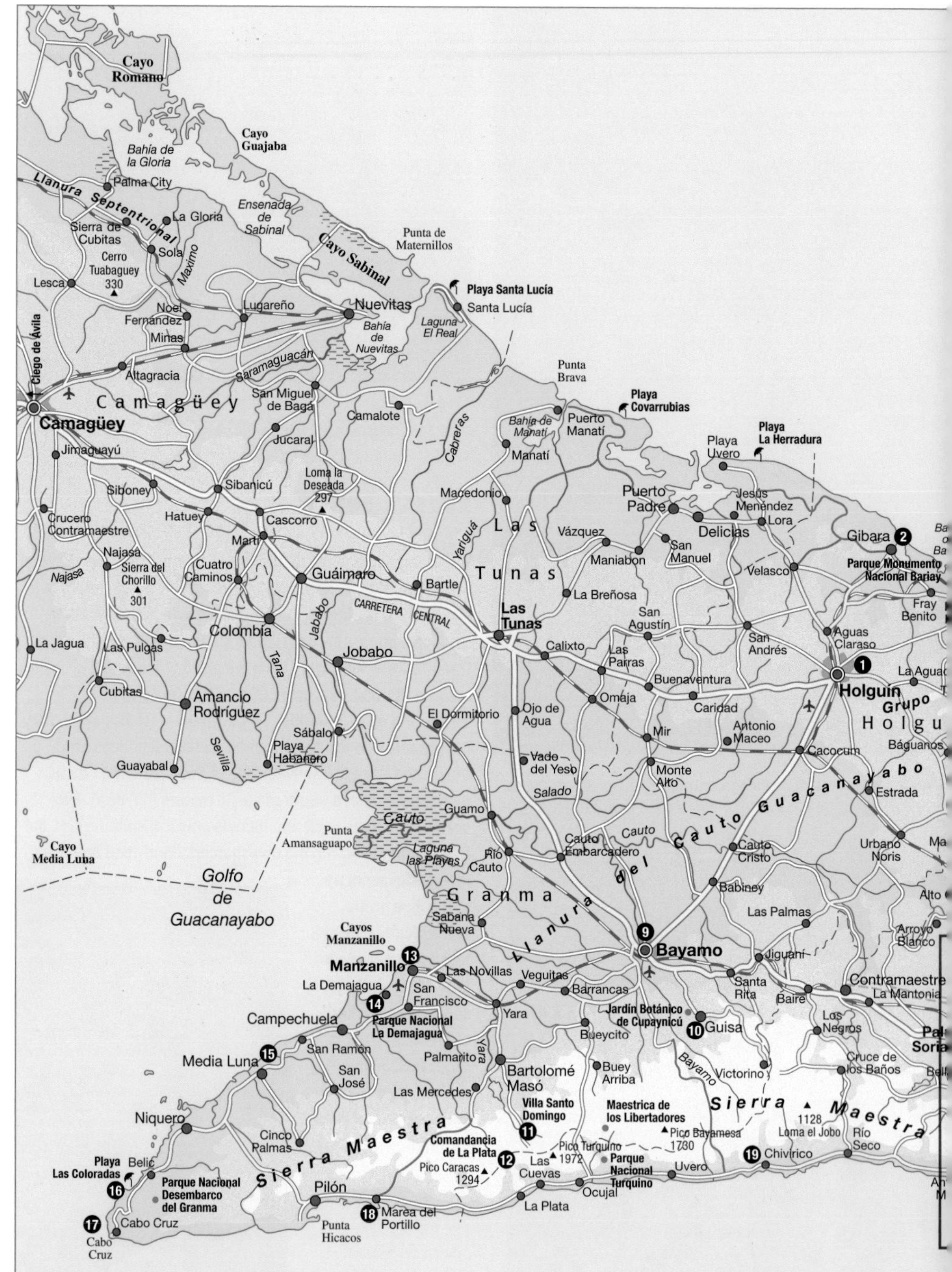
Cayo Romano
Cayo Guajaba
Bahía de la Gloria
Palma City
Llanura Septentrional
Ensenada de Sabinal
Cayo Sabinal
Punta de Maternillos
La Gloria
Sierra de Cubitas
Sola
Maximo
Cerro Tuabaguey 330
Lesca
Playa Santa Lucía
Santa Lucía
Noel Fernández
Lugareño
Nuevitas
Bahía de Nuevitas
Laguna El Real
Minas
Ciego de Ávila
Altagracia
Saramaguacán
Punta Brava
Camagüey
San Miguel de Bagá
Camalote
Playa Covarrubias
Jucaral
Cabreras
Bahía de Manatí
Puerto Manatí
Playa La Herradura
Jimaguayú
Manatí
Playa Uvero
Loma la Deseada 297
Siboney
Sibanicú
Macedonio
Puerto Padre
Jesús Menéndez
Crucero Contramaestre
Hatuey
Cascorro
Las Tunas
Delicias
Lora
Vázquez
Gibara
Martí
Yariguá
San Manuel
Najasa
Sierra del Chorillo 301
Cuatro Caminos
Guáimaro
Bartle
Maniabón
Velasco
Parque Monumento Nacional Bariay
La Breñosa
Fray Benito
CARRETERA CENTRAL
Jabobo
Colombia
San Agustín
Aguas Claraso
La Jagua
Las Pulgas
Tana
Jobabo
Calixto
Las Parras
San Andrés
Holguín
Grupo Holguín
Buenaventura
Cubitas
Amancio Rodríguez
El Dormitorio
Ojo de Agua
Omaja
Caridad
Antonio Maceo
Sábalo
Mir
Báguanos
Sevilla
Playa Habanero
Vado del Yeso
Cacocum
Guayabal
Monte Alto
Salado
Estrada
Llanura del Cauto Guacanayabo
Guamo
Cauto
Punta Amansaguapo
Cayo Media Luna
Laguna las Playas
Río Cauto
Cauto Embarcadero
Cauto Cristo
Urbano Noris
Golfo de Guacanayabo
Babiney
Granma
Las Palmas
Alto
Cayos Manzanillo
Sabana Nueva
Arroyo Blanco
Bayamo
Jiguaní
Manzanillo
Las Novillas
Veguitas
Santa Rita
Contramaestre
La Mantonia
La Demajagua
San Francisco
Barrancas
Baire
Yara
Jardín Botánico de Cupaynicú
Campechuela
Parque Nacional La Demajagua
Guisa
Los Negros
Bueycito
San Ramón
Palmarito
Media Luna
Buey Arriba
Victorino
San José
Bartolomé Masó
Cruce de los Baños
Las Mercedes
Villa Santo Domingo
Maestrica de los Libertadores
Sierra Maestra
Niquero
1128 Loma el Jobo
Río Seco
Pico Bayamesa 1730
Cinco Palmas
Comandancia de La Plata
Pico Turquino 1972
Playa Las Coloradas
Belic
Pico Caracas 1294
Las Cuevas
Parque Nacional Turquino
Uvero
Chivirico
Parque Nacional Desembarco del Granma
Pilón
Ocujal
La Plata
Marea del Portillo
Cabo Cruz
Punta Hicacos
CARIBBEAN SEA

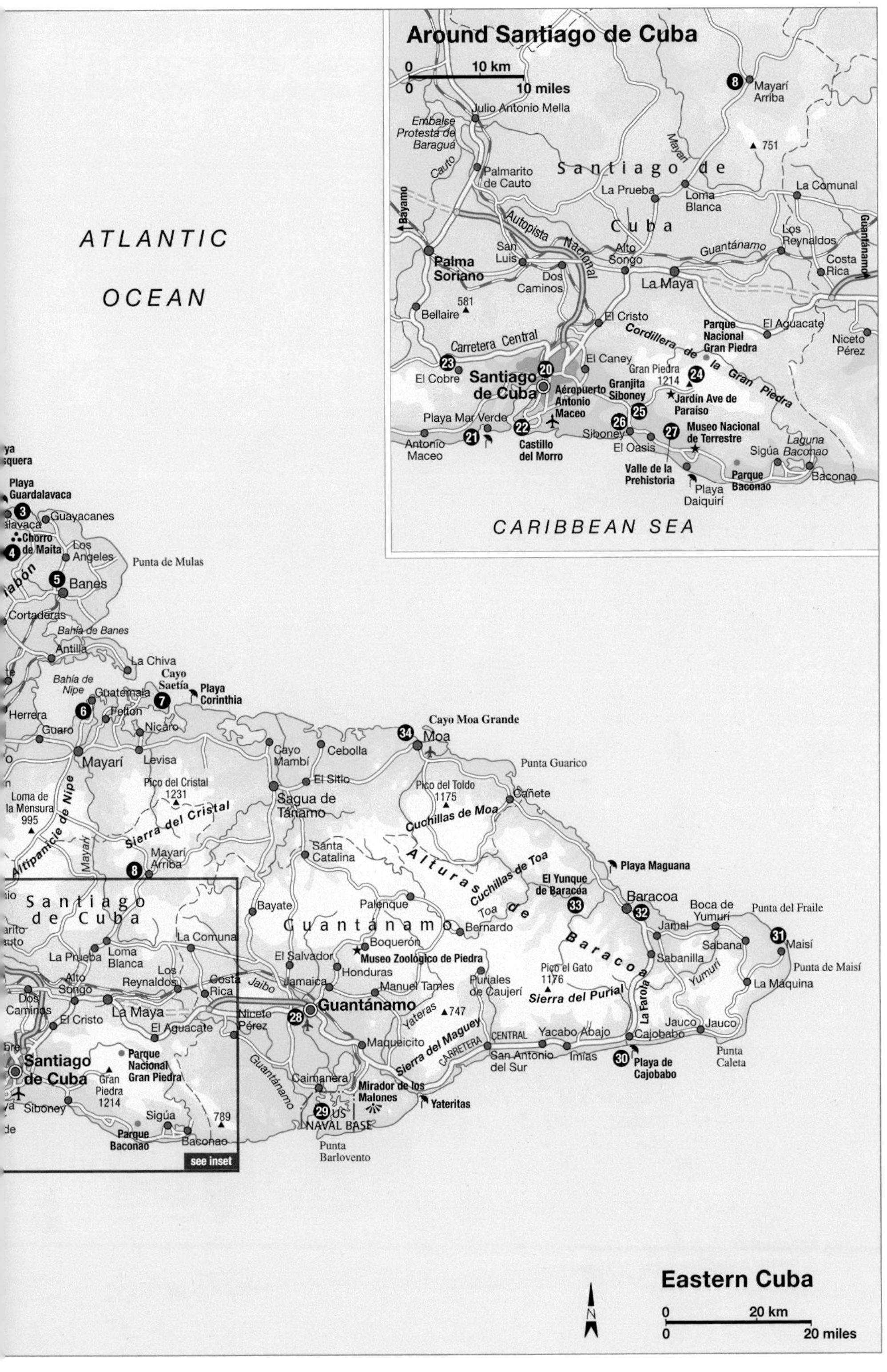

Around Santiago de Cuba
Eastern Cuba
ATLANTIC OCEAN
CARIBBEAN SEA
Santiago de Cuba
Guantánamo
Palma Soriano
Baracoa
Moa
Sagua de Tánamo
Mayarí
Banes
Cayo Moa Grande
Sierra del Cristal
Cuchillas de Moa
Cuchillas de Toa
Alturas de Baracoa
Sierra del Purial
Sierra del Maguey
Cordillera de la Gran Piedra
Parque Nacional Gran Piedra
Parque Baconao
US NAVAL BASE
see inset

Playa Guardalavaca.

HOLGUIN AND GRANMA

From the island's top archeological site to the ragged mountains of the Sierra Maestra, including the Pico Turquino, Cuba's highest peak, this region has much to offer, yet attracts surprisingly few tourists.

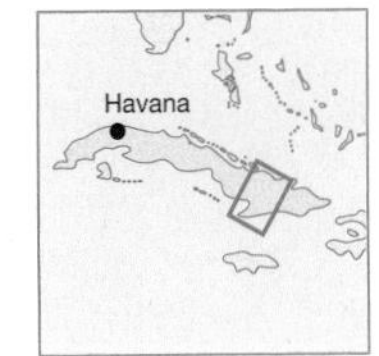

Often called the 'Granary of Cuba' because of its agricultural wealth, the province of Holguín has some 1.3 million people living within its borders, making it second in population only to Havana province. Its capital city, also called **Holguín ❶**, is the fourth-largest city in Cuba, with a population of 300,000. Along with its agricultural importance, it is a relatively active industrial center, having grown rapidly in recent decades, and has two universities, two large hospitals, and a brewery.

Familiarly known as the 'city of the parks,' Holguín is built on the traditional grid system. Five parks lie within the parallel lines of the two main streets, running roughly southeast to northwest: Maceo and Manduley (also called Libertad). The three middle plazas are linked by a pedestrian boulevard along Manduley where you can find cultural venues, restaurants, and cafés, most of which charge in *moneda nacional*.

Parque Calixto García is an expansive square built around the monument to the city's most famous independence fighter, General Calixto García Iñiguez. His birthplace, a block away, is now a museum (Calle Miró 147; tel: 24-425 610; Tue–Sat 9am–4.30pm, Sun 10am–6pm). Families and friends come in the cool of the evening for a stroll or to sit on benches and watch the children playing while music wafts out from the bars and clubs. Fronting the square are a striking Art Deco theater, the local Casa de la Trova, an ARTex bar, ice-cream parlors, the modern provincial library, bookstores, and art galleries. For nightlife, in addition to the Casa de la Trova, there is also the Casa de la Música, a disco on the third floor of the Pico Cristal building, and the Beny Moré center on the corner of Luz Caballero and Maceo.

Main Attractions
- Holguín: Museo Provincial de Historia
- Gibara
- Playa Guardalavaca
- Chorro de Maita
- Bayamo
- Pico Turquino
- Manzanillo
- Parque Nacional Desembarco de Granma

View from the Mirador de Mayabe, near Holguín.

You may find a rodeo taking place in Holguín, where you see this sign.

Holguín's attractions

Most noteworthy is the building known as **La Periquera** (Parrot Cage) – so named ever since Spanish soldiers, in their blue, yellow, and green uniforms, took refuge behind the barred windows during a *mambí* attack in 1868. The building houses the Museo Provincial de Historia (Mon–Fri 9am–5pm, Sat 9am–1pm), where the prized possession is the *Hacha de Holguín* (Holguín Axe), a pre-Columbian figure carved in polished rock; found in 1860, it has become the symbol of the province. There are also displays on slavery, and all kinds of historical memorabilia.

A half-block south of the square, on Calle Maceo, is the **Museo de Ciencias Naturales Carlos de la Torre** (Calle Maceo 129; Sun–Thu 9am–5pm, Sat 1–5pm), with a fine collection of polymitas, the brightly banded snails indigenous to eastern Cuba. There are also lots of taxidermied animals, including a pair of ivory-billed woodpeckers, now almost certainly extinct.

Around the corner, **Parque Peralta,** also known as the Parque de los Flores because people sell flowers here for the cemetery, is the site of the **Catedral de San Isidoro** (1720). Its rough brick arcades harbor carvings of birds and figures, the work of a local artist; other treasures include the original baptismal font.

Tune in to local radio.

The **Plaza de la Maqueta** is a recently restored square one block from Maceo between Mártires and Máximo Gómez, and is well worth a visit. The old market in the center has now become the Lírico theater, and there are shops selling music, instruments, artists' materials, cigars, and handicrafts, along with some art galleries. The small Don José Hotel, on the east side, has a handicrafts shop downstairs. Artwork is everywhere, from statues to carved lamp posts.

Three blocks north of Parque Calixto García, leafy **Plaza Carlos Manuel de Céspedes** is the most picturesque square in Holguín, with a ruined church, the Iglesia San José, in the middle. The main post office and a couple of banks are here.

La Loma de la Cruz (The Hill of the Cross), to the north, is Holguín's most visible landmark and is a place of pilgrimage. It's not far to walk, but when you get there you must tackle the 468 steps leading up to the top. On May 3, 1790, a group led by a Franciscan priest erected a cross on the hill (unfortunately blown down by Hurricane Georges in 1998); later the Spanish built a lookout tower for strategic reasons. The construction of the stone steps was begun in 1929, but not finished until May 3, 1950. The *Romerías de la Cruz de Mayo* is celebrated every May 3 with a procession up the hill.

Gibara, a colonial gem

The farther north you go, the better Holguín province gets. **Gibara** ❷, on the coast, 36km (22 miles) north of the capital, exudes maritime charm and colonial grace. On the road from Holguín you pass through some fabulous scenery with strange, humpbacked hills. An old iron bridge over the

Río Cacoyoquín leads into the town along a seaside drive with a **statue of Christopher Columbus** and a small ruined garrison at the end.

With terracotta roofs, flowering patios, a weather-beaten church, cobblestoned streets, and fishing boats, Gibara is endlessly photogenic, although the town is still recovering from the battering it received from Hurricane Ike in 2008. The **Teatro Colonial** (1889) is a little masterpiece, but the pièce de résistance is the **Museo de Artes Decorativas** (Independencia 19, between Luz Caballero and J Peralta; Tue–Sun 9am–noon, 1–5pm, Thu–Sun also 8–10pm), on the second floor of a magnificent 19th-century mansion. Besides gorgeous *mediopuntos* (Cuba's characteristic, fan-shaped stained-glass windows) and *mamparas* (decorative saloon-style doors), there is a fine collection of furniture and many Art Nouveau pieces. You can climb up to the roof terrace for a view of the town. Also worth visiting is the **Museo de Historia Natural Joaquín Fernández de la Vara** (Maceo 12, between Martí and Luz; tel: 24-844 222; Tue–Sat 9am–noon, 1–5pm, Sun 9am–noon), where there is an excellent collection of butterflies and moths.

In April every year Gibara hosts the Festival Internacional del Cine Pobre (www.cinepobre.com), a celebration of movies made for less than US$300,000. The festival was founded in 2003 by the Cuban film maker Humberto Solás (1941–2008), who championed movies made despite the lack of a financial backer or official approval. He had a prolific output himself, even being nominated for an Oscar, and some of his films were shot in Gibara.

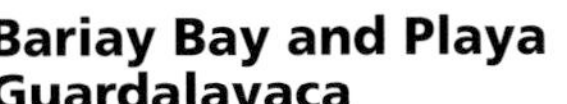

Bariay Bay and Playa Guardalavaca

There used to be a long-standing debate between Gibara and Baracoa about the exact place where the Europeans first landed in Cuba. Nowadays historians agree that the first landfall was made in **Bariay Bay**, east of Gibara. The peninsula has been declared a national monument, **Parque Monumento Nacional Bariay** (daily 9am–5pm). A **monument**,

Gold idol in the Museo Indocubano.

View over the rooftops of Gibara.

Indigenous skeleton from Chorro de Maíta.

designed to symbolize the meeting of European and American aboriginal civilizations, was erected in 1992 to commemorate the 500th anniversary of Columbus's setting foot in America. It sits on the tip of Cayo Bariay, within sight of what is almost certainly the flat-topped mountain he mentioned in his logbook. By road, it is 7km (4 miles) north of Fray Benito, but boat trips are also arranged from Guardalavaca.

Farther east lies northeastern Cuba's main resort area, where the sea is a diaphanous blue and the beaches creamy white, fringed by tropical foliage. Guardalavaca can be reached by bus from Holguín (CUC$5 one way): make a reservation at the Transtur Buró in the Pico Cristal cafetería on Parque Calixto García and catch the bus outside La Begonia café. They frequently offer mid-week or weekend deals with accommodations.

The oldest part of the resort is **Playa Guardalavaca** ❸, which has a village atmosphere with a cluster of hotels, restaurants, and water sports amenities along a pleasant beach, as well as workers' apartments and a commercial center. West of here you reach the powdery white-sand beach at **Playa Esmeralda**. This horseshoe-shaped bay has been taken over by the all-inclusive hotels of the Sol Meliá chain.

At the **Bahía de Naranjo** there is a marina and an aquarium (daily 9am–9pm; charge), with the usual, overpriced dolphin show labeled 'educational.' On the eastern shore of the bay there is a marked nature trail, Sendero Ecológico Las Guanas, with a cave and a lookout.

Playa Yuraguanal and Playa Pesquero, to the west, are dominated by enormous all-inclusive resorts, each with up to 1,000 rooms. They are isolated and there is nothing to do in the immediate vicinity of the hotels, but excursions to Gibara, Holguín, and other towns are within easy reach and the myriad bays are beautiful.

Chorro de Maita to Castro's birthplace

Just south of Guardalavaca, the hilly road passes **Museo Aborígen**

Playa Esmeralda.

Chorro de Maita ❹ (tel: 24-430 201; Tue–Sun 9am–5pm, Mon 9am–1pm), the largest pre-Columbian burial ground known to exist in the Antilles. Archeological excavations have revealed 108 skeletons of the indigenous Taíno people who inhabited the area from *circa* AD 1000 to the end of the 16th century. A section of the graveyard has been excavated to show how the skeletons were buried. Two of the children wear European jewelry, and the presence of a Spaniard indicates that there must have been cross-cultural relationships in the early years.

Over the road is a reconstructed Taíno village, the **Aldea Taíno** (tel: 24-430 422; daily 9am–5pm) – the most authentic of the country's reconstructed indigenous settlements.

Some of the finds from Chorro de Maíta are on display in the tiny but interesting **Museo Indocubano Bani** (Gen Marrero 305, corner José Martí; tel: 24-802 487; Tue–Sat 9am–5pm, Sun 8am–noon, 2–5pm, Fri–Sun also 7–9pm) in nearby **Banes** ❺. The utensils and jewelry are made of delicately carved and shaped shells, rocks, bones, ceramic, wood, and metal. The minuscule gold idol of a woman wearing a headdress and offering a bowl is, arguably, a joint Amerindian-Spanish effort, and is one of the few gold pieces to have been found.

South of Banes, a former United Fruit Company town, the road runs around **Bahía de Nipe**. There is a turn-off to Cueto, and from there a road goes to **Birán**, Castro's birthplace. It has been reconstructed since the revolution; thatched *bohíos* have gone, replaced by rows of identical concrete houses. The old Castro residence still stands in this tiny community. A long avenue of royal palms sweeps up to the front of the elegant pink and yellow wooden house with lacy balconies, which is open to the public as the **Sitio Histórico de Birán** (tel: 24-286 102; Tue–Sat 9am–noon, 2–4pm, Sun 9am–noon; phone ahead – if it rains it is closed). There are lots of family photographs on display, as well as domestic items and an ancient Ford automobile, which belonged to Castro's father.

Guatemala and the central highlands

Back toward Bahía de Nipe, **Mayarí** is an industrial town with little to interest travelers, but **Guatemala** ❻, an old slave town right by the bay, is a gem. There are plenty of gingerbread cottages, built with palm timber and driftwood, each delightfully individual, each a work of art: some have carved wooden gargoyles, others elaborately worked gables; the gardens are lush and colorful. A former exclusive 'whites only' country club is now a bar, selling shots of rough *aguardiente* spirit for around a peso.

At the mouth of the Bahía de Nipe is the 42 sq km (16 sq-mile) island of **Cayo Saetía** ❼, once the exclusive resort of top Communist Party officials; Raúl Castro used to be a regular visitor. The island is home to deer and

Riding through Gibara by buggy and horse.

wild boar, and a variety of imported animals, including ostriches, zebras, and antelope. Although this is a protected reserve, hunting is still allowed under strictly regulatd conditions. It's a delightful spot, with lush vegetation running down to the pristine white sands and just one hotel, the Villa Cayo Saetía (see 334).

The impressive **Sierra del Cristal** mountain range, reaching 1,231 meters (4,000ft) at Pico del Cristal, rolls through Holguín and Guantánamo provinces. The best place to get close to nature is the pleasant hotel at **Pinares de Mayarí**, established in 1988 to study the mountain ecology of the region (see page 335).

Cuba's great hero of the first *mambí* independence struggle, Carlos Manuel de Céspedes, established his revolutionary government at **Mayarí Arriba** ❽ in 1868. The area is covered with coffee plantations established by French planters who fled here in the early 19th century after the slave rebellions in Haiti. From here, a twisting road descends to Cuba's second city, **Santiago de Cuba** (see page 281).

Granma province

Granma province was carved out of the old *Oriente* or Eastern Territory historically controlled by Santiago de Cuba. The peculiar name comes from the cabin cruiser Fidel, Raúl, Che, and their comrades used to sneak into the country from Mexico in 1956 before they took up arms in the mountains. The stunning scenery of the Sierra Maestra is one of the area's main attractions, but so too are the numerous sites linked with the 1950s guerrilla campaign, and with the 19th-century struggle for independence.

Bayamo

Bayamo ❾ (pop. 150,000), the second of Cuba's seven original *villas,* was founded in 1513 by Diego Velázquez. It was located far enough inland to be safe from pirate attacks, and set on the navigable Río Bayamo. This flowed into the **Río Cauto**, the longest river in Cuba and the major transportation route for the eastern end of the island when coastal trade was faster than overland trails. It

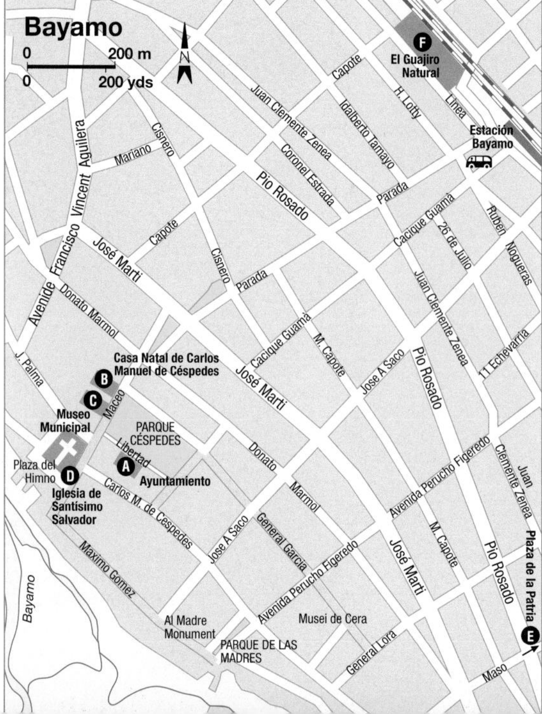

Carlos Manuel Céspedes, who declared rebellion against the Spanish.

wasn't until 1902 that eastern and western Cuba were linked by rail through the center of the island, and the Carretera Central roughly paralleling it was only finished in 1932.

Bayamo is famous for its role in the Cuban independence struggle, being the first city taken by the rebels. In the main square, **Parque Céspedes,** is the **Ayuntamiento** Ⓐ (town hall) where Carlos Manuel de Céspedes, the rebel president, signed the document abolishing slavery in the liberated zones. Across the plaza is the **Casa Natal de Carlos Manuel de Céspedes** Ⓑ (Maceo 57, between Donato Mármol and José Joaquín Palma; tel: 23-423 864; Tue–Sat 9am–5pm, Sun 9am–noon), where he was born in 1819. Built of marble, it emerged unscathed from the independence wars and was for years the local post office.

The museum recounts Céspedes's life, from his days as a law student to the rebel presidency, with documents, photos, period furnishings, and family memorabilia. Next door, at Maceo 55, is the **Museo Municipal** Ⓒ (tel: 23-424 125; Tue–Sat 8am–2pm, Sun 9am–1pm), which has rooms exhibiting natural history, architectural history, and the War of Independence.

Plaza del Himno and the Boulevard

A block from the central square, the **Iglesia de Santísimo Salvador** Ⓓ was the church where *bayamese* patriot Perucho Figueredo first performed a stirring march for the independence fighters that later became Cuba's national anthem. The square outside the church is now called the Plaza del Himno. The church was burned down when Spanish troops re-took Bayamo, and residents decided to torch their own city and flee to the hills. They did, however, save the wooden altar to the Virgen de Dolores, and the stone font at which Céspedes and Figueredo were baptized, which can be seen in the rebuilt church.

A descendant of the Father of the Homeland, Onorio Céspedes, is Bayamo's historian and director of **La Casa de la Nacionalidad Cubana** (House of Cuban Nationality; Plaza del Himno 36, between Antonio Maceo and Padre Batista; tel: 23-424 833).

Running south from Parque Céspedes is the main shopping street, General García, most of which has now been converted into a pleasant pedestrian-only boulevard, sometimes called Paseo Bayamez. Quirky lamps and benches along its length give it artistic interest. Here you can find shops, banks, the telephone and Internet office, post office, pharmacies, cafés, restaurants, and a few small museums, including a waxworks, an aquarium, an archeological museum, and a *maqueta,* or scale model, of the town.

Turn west off the boulevard along Calle Masó and head downhill to the river and a large park. Here a busy market sells meat, seasonal fruit, and vegetables. Open-air concerts are sometimes held here, too, and there

Iglesia de San Salvador and the Plaza del Himno.

is an amusement park and a pleasant swimming spot in the river.

The Plaza de la Patria E is a huge open space with historical monuments and statues, created in 1982 by the architect Miguel Delarrá. To its north is the railroad, to the west is Avenida Amado Estévez, and to the east are the buildings of Reparto Jesús Menéndez. Political rallies, sporting events, concerts, and Carnival (at the beginning of August) are held here. At the base of the administrative building you can see the largest *vitral* in the Americas. There are several open-air cafés and La Taberna, selling local and national beers in *pesos cubanos*.

What was formerly known as Plaza Luis Ramírez López, on Calle Línea between Milanés and William Soler, has been redeveloped as a recreational center called El Guajiro NaturalF. A restaurant, bar, café, and literary center are open daily from 10am until midnight, while from Thursday to Sunday there is an open-air cabaret with live music, and a show with dancers from 8pm until about 3am.

An ornate bandstand in Manzanillo.

Guisa

Guisa ❿ is a pretty village in the foothills of the Sierra Maestra, 14km (8 miles) southeast of Bayamo off the road to Santiago. On a hill overlooking the little town is the Mirador de Guisa, with a restaurant and bar, very popular on weekends as an out-of-town excursion because of the lovely views up into the mountains with a reservoir sparkling in the distance. Calixto García used this hill to take up his position before a battle in 1897 in the War of Independence, and it was used again during the revolution some 60 years later.

Just before you get to Guisa, turn right off the road to the **Jardín Botánico de Cupaynicú** (guides available). Of the 13 botanical gardens in Cuba, this is the third largest, after Havana and Cienfuegos, but it contains some of the oldest trees, at more than 300 years old. A little more than half of the 104 hectares (257 acres) have been left as a protected reserve containing native forest, with the rest divided into fascinating and beautiful collections of medicinal plants and

PEAK FITNESS

To hike up to the Comandancia de la Plata from Villa Santo Domingo costs CUC$20 and to Pico Turquino costs CUC$53 for a two-day hike, both with mandatory guide. Add transportation up to Alto de Naranjo parking lot and back, CUC$5, and CUC$5 to take photos. The overnight stop for Pico Turquino is at Camping Joaquín and, as numbers are limited, this should be organized well in advance. It can be done in one day if your guide is willing. There is also access from the Caribbean side of the Sierra Maestra at Las Cuevas (between Ocujal and La Plata on the coast road). Day trips are offered by Ecotur, in Santiago, for CUC$101, which involve a Jeep pick-up at 5am, a two-hour drive to Las Cuevas, a four-hour hike up, a lunch stop and a four-hour hike down, getting back to Santiago around 7pm. It is tough, so take plenty of water and sunscreen.

It is possible to go up Pico Turquino from Santo Domingo and down the other side to Las Cuevas (or vice versa, 2–3 days), or hike to Pico Turquino one day and Comandancia de la Plata the next, spending the night on the mountain. Go to the national park HQ in Santo Domingo (no phone) soon after 7.30am to ensure there will be a guide available. Even so, you may have to come back another day as numbers are limited, routes may be closed, or the weather may be against you. There is no national park office on the Las Cuevas side and no guides wait there.

edible plants and another of palms. A guided tour is well worthwhile and birders will find it a rewarding visit. There is no public transportation to speak of, so you will need to hire a taxi or rent a car or bicycle.

Into the Sierra Maestra

To experience fully the rugged beauty of the southeastern mountains, the best base is the **Villa Santo Domingo** ⓫, south of the road linking Bayamo and Manzanillo on the coast. The mountain road veers off at **Yara**, passing through the small town of **Bartolomé Masó** and heading steeply up into the heart of the sierra.

During the guerrilla war, Santo Domingo was a rebel camp with a mess hall and workshops. Today, these have been adapted for feeding and entertaining campers. Cabins are partially hidden in the forest by the Yara River. The **Turquino Parque Nacional** offices are at Santo Domingo; come here to arrange a guide (mandatory) for any of the hikes up the mountains. Tours set off at 9am and you should be there some time in advance. Take water and snacks and sunblock, of course. From here a 3km (2-mile) road goes up the steepest (40-degree gradient) incline in Cuba, finishing at Alto de Naranjo (950 meters/3,116ft), a parking lot for the vehicles ferrying walkers. The trail to the right goes to the Comandancia de la Plata, while the trail to the left heads up Pico Turquino.

Castro's old rebel headquarters in the mountains are at **La Comandancia de La Plata** ⓬. The trail is 3km (2 miles) up and down hill; parts of it are steep and if it has been raining it can be slippery and muddy. Halfway there you come to the house of the Medina family, who were the first in the area to help the revolutionaries. Their little family farm looks much the same today, with pigs and chickens roaming around and coffee beans drying on the ground.

At the command station there is a small museum, Castro's bedroom and kitchen, the old hospital and Radio Rebelde hut, all small wooden buildings spread out over the hillside. Quiet, beautiful, and very atmospheric,

A Holguín province farmer in his field.

CÉSPEDES AND CUBAN REBELLION

On the morning of October 10, 1868, Bayamo-born Carlos Manuel de Céspedes rang the great bell at his sugar plantation, La Demajagua, located to the south of Manzanillo. With that stroke he emancipated his slaves and, in the resonant *Grito de Yara* (Cry of Yara), he declared open rebellion against Cuba's colonial rulers, thus beginning the first War of Independence against Spain. As with the US Civil War a few years earlier, emancipation was not the main reason for the war, but it was always an important subsidiary, and became an increasingly necessary weapon. Other landowners were soon to begin freeing their slaves and arming them for battle.

Céspedes's bold action was the climax of 15 years of conspiracy during which he and his friends used Masonic lodges and chess tournaments in Bayamo and Manzanillo as a cover for anti-colonialist plots. He led the rebel forces as president of the Republic in Arms until October 1873, when factional infighting forced him from power. By now almost blind, he accepted his removal with great dignity, and retired to San Lorenzo in the Sierra Maestra to teach letters and chess. He had just finished a chess game one afternoon in March 1874 when Spanish troops raided the town and ordered him to surrender. He refused and was shot down.

you get a good idea of how tough life must have been. Birding is good here and you can see the national bird, the Cuban trogon. After being banned for 50 years, photography is now allowed, for a charge.

Hikes up Cuba's highest mountain, **Pico Turquino** (1,972 meters/6,470ft), are exciting and beautiful (see box). Between outcroppings of mineral and sedimentary rocks, deep-green conifers stand alongside precious cedar, mahogany, and trumpetwood trees. The slopes are dotted with delicate wild orchids and graceful ferns. Although it can be cold and windy, the temperature rarely drops to freezing and there is never any snow. You can't see anything from the summit of Turquino, but the views from just before you reach it are magnificent.

Manzanillo

On the Gulf of Guacanayabo, 48km (30 miles) west of Bayamo, the fine harbour at **Manzanillo** ⓭ made it the main fishing center and principal shipping terminal for the sugar brought in by truck or rail from the little mill towns farther south. However, during the difficult times of the 'Special Period,' the port was closed and 3,000 men lost their jobs. Imports of food and building materials have restarted, but large cargo ships can no longer come in, as the harbor has silted up. Fishing is still an important activity, though.

Like Bayamo, Manzanillo is steeped in rebellion, early on as a smuggling port, then during the Wars of Independence. Cuba's first communist cell was organized in Manzanillo in the 1920s, and the only communist mayor, Paquito Rosales, was democratically elected there in the 1940s. In the same decade, Jesús Menéndez, the incorruptible leader of the sugar workers' union, was assassinated on Manzanillo train station platform.

During the 1950s, Celia Sánchez organized an underground campaign here in support of the 26th of July Movement. The **Celia Sánchez Memorial**, with its colorful tiled murals of sunflowers and doves, is seven blocks southwest of the main

The 19th-century lighthouse at Cabo Cruz.

square along Calle Martí, which is partly a pedestrian-only boulevard.

On the large **Parque Céspedes**, several colonial buildings show a marked Arab influence – particularly the delightful, brightly colored *glorieta* or bandstand in the center of the square. You still see people playing the *órgano oriental*, a type of hand-operated organ brought from France in the 19th century. The **Museo Histórico Municipal** (José Martí 226) is on the park, with colonial history in one section and displays on the 20th-century political struggle in the other. Walk past the little colonial church, Iglesia de la Purísima Concepción, and up Maceo toward the sea. At Villuendas, one block away, you come to the theater, reopened after a closure of 30 years, and opposite is the small Hotel Venus, also restored, to be used by visiting artistes.

On the seafront drive, Avenida 1 de Mayo, you find the little Parque Masó, El Golfo seafood restaurant, and for nighttime entertainment, the cabaret Costa Azul (tel: 23-573 158; show 9pm–1am). From here the Malecón stretches west along the coast, past a statue of singer Beny Moré, a few fish restaurants and road-side stands, and out to the Proyecto Recreativo, a large open public space where there are nightclubs, cabarets, and open-air nightlife. A bit farther on, on a hill overlooking the city, is the multicolored, concrete Hotel Guacanayabo, busy and noisy during the Cuban holiday season but unaccustomed to foreign tourism.

Liberty bell

Parque Nacional La Demajagua ⓮ (Mon–Sat 8am–5pm, Sun 8am–1pm), on the coast just 10km (6 miles) south of Manzanillo, is where Céspedes rang the bell to call for independence and the abolition of slavery in 1868 (see page 275). The plantation is now a park, with the great bell firmly anchored in a stone wall by some old machinery, and a tiny museum. It is a pleasant place to stop on the way along the coast, with pretty views over the sea and cays offshore.

Past La Demajagua, the road follows the coast 50km (30 miles) through cane fields to **Media Luna** ⓯, the little town where Celia Sánchez was born in 1920. Her father was the local doctor and a follower of José Martí. The family home, a green and white traditional wooden house, is now a museum, the **Casa Natal de Celia Sánchez Manduley** (Avenida Principal 111; Tue–Sat 9am–5pm, Sun 9am–1pm). Celia Sánchez became a prominent underground organizer and was the first of the underground movement to make contact with Fidel after the landing of the *Granma*. Eventually, she joined the rebel forces and was a part of the revolutionary leadership up to her death in 1980.

Parque Nacional Desembarco de Granma

The road continues another 23km (14 miles) along the coast to Niquero, a busy town full of horses and carts and *bici-taxis*, with a functioning sugar mill

TIP

The Campismo Popular at Playa Las Coloradas is chiefly for Cuban vacationers, but foreigners are welcome and there are amenities for motorhomes. Reserve through Campismo Popular in Bayamo, or through Cubamar (www.cubamarviajes.cu) in Havana.

Granma coastline.

and a pleasant hotel with a sea view, as well as some interesting French-style plantation houses.

At Playa Las Coloradas ⓰, 17km (10 miles) south of Niquero, there is a pleasant beach and a Campismo Popular site with basic cabins. A little farther is the entrance to the **Parque Nacional Desembarco del Granma.** A visitor center has been built with a replica of the yacht *Granma*, close to the *bohío* of Angel Pérez Rosabal, the first person to help the 82 guerrillas when they landed on December 2, 1956. From the visitor center, where you have to get a guide, you follow a concrete boardwalk to the landing site, crossing the mangrove and saw-grass swamps that Fidel, Raúl, Che, and their band waded through, heavily laden with guns and ammunition while wearing heavy fatigues (see page 52). The rebels were quickly surrounded by Batista's troops, and were nearly annihilated at the tiny village of Alegría de Pío. At one time the revolutionary force was reduced to only 12 men. An annual reconstruction of the event is staged each December by hundreds of young people, making the journey from Mexico before heading off into the Sierra Maestra.

A few kilometers farther, on the left side of the gravel road is the **Sendero Ecológico El Guafe** (charge includes guide), a 2km (1-mile) circular trail through the dry tropical forest. There is plenty of wildlife in the forest and birding is very rewarding. The tallest cactus in Cuba, called El *Viejo Testigo* (The Old Witness), was battered by the 2008 hurricanes but still stands. The guide will also show you evidence of habitation – burial sites and ceremonial areas – by the Ciboney, who once lived in the caves along this coast. Their diet consisted of fish, small animals, and native plants; they collected shells and stones to make tools and weapons, and crushed rocks into colored powder for painting. Clearly visible on the walls of several caverns are black and red (sometimes blue and brown) drawings.

At the end of the road, still within the national park, is **Cabo Cruz** ⓱, with a 19th-century lighthouse and fishing village, marking what is effectively Cuba's most southerly point. There is a restaurant, but if it isn't open when you arrive, a roadside stand by the sea wall sells freshly fried fillets of *minuto pescado* served in a bun, for a few *pesos cubanos*. The marine terrace along this part of the coast is replete with caverns: fissures in the rocky surface expose drops of up to 70 meters (240ft) with vertical walls that open into enormous underwater chambers. Fascinating coralline formations and one of Cuba's largest collections of the coveted queen conch hug the rocky shore. The dry surface of the terrace reveals sturdy cacti poking through the rocks. Lizards scuttle underfoot, while cormorants, egrets, and gulls wheel overhead.

Cuban rock iguanas inhabit the southern coastal region.

The dramatic south coast

Between Media Luna and Niquero a road turning takes you along the

Río Sevilla through sugar-cane plains and the foothills of the Sierra Maestra before coming to the beautifully sited harbor town of **Pilón**. Along the way, just before you get to Ojo de Agua, look for signs and plaques marking the places where three groups of Castro's men crossed the road in underground water conduits on their journey from *Granma* to the Sierra Maestra, aiming to meet up at Cinco Palmas.

From Pilón the road hugs the coast, sandwiched between mountains and the Caribbean, all the way to Santiago de Cuba, with some of Cuba's most dramatic scenery along the way. There are occasional rock falls, and stones get washed up from the beach, so drive carefully, and always watch out for cows, goats, and other animals. Take plenty of fuel, water, and food for the journey. **Marea del Portillo** ⓲, once a small fishing village, has been developed as a medium-sized resort, very popular with Canadians in winter. Diving is possible off the reef, with shipwrecks and coral caves to explore, and guests can take trips into the local mountain villages.

La Plata (not to be confused with the Comandancia de La Plata inland) is the site of the rebels' first attack on Batista's army on May 28, 1957. A museum (Mon–Sat 8am–6pm, Sun 8am–noon) in the village focuses on this battle and other aspects of the guerrilla campaign. Nearby, Las Cuevas has a pleasant beach, and is the trailhead for the climb up to Pico Turquino from the coast (see page 276). The road continues through Ocujal and Uvero to the fishing village of **Chivirico** ⓳, famous for its bat-filled caves, **Las Cuevas de los Murciélagos**, and its **international scuba center**, based at the Hotel Brisas Sierra Mar Los Galeones, before eventually reaching Santiago.

RESTAURANTS AND PALADARES

PRICE CATEGORIES

Price categories are for a three-course meal for one with a beer, or mojito. Wine puts the price up:
$** = under **$25
$$** = **$25–35
$$$** = over **$35

Bayamo

El Polinesio
Parada, between Pío Rosado and Cisneros
Tel: 23-423 860. Open daily L & D. **$–$$**
A *paladar* with live music on the terrace at night. Cuban and international food of better quality than at state restaurants, however, you have to pay in CUCs.

San Salvador de Bayamo
Maceo 107, between Donato Mármol and Martí
Open daily noon–midnight. **$–$$**
Very central, beside the Casa de la Trova, in a large, colonial house with high ceilings and tall doorways, decorated with local historic items and more modern paintings. There is an extensive menu of local dishes and most items are usually available, nicely prepared, and well cooked.

Guardalavaca

El Ancla
Playa Guardalavaca
Tel: 24-430 381. Open daily 9am–10.30pm. **$$**
Perched on a rocky promontory above the sea, a lovely location to dine on seafood and a pleasant change from all the hotel buffets.

Holguín

1720
Frexes 190, corner Miró
Tel: 24-468 150. Open daily L & D. **$–$$**
An elegant restaurant in a colonial building. The quality of the food doesn't match up, but it is OK and the service is attentive. Standard chicken and pork dishes, also lamb, beef, and lobster. There is a pleasant bar in the same building, and live entertainment. On weekends there is an open-air disco on the roof.

1910
Mártires 143, between Aricochea and Cables
Tel: 24-423 994. Open Wed–Mon noon–11.30pm. **$**
In a colonial house, pleasantly decorated and recently extended to provide more dining space. The food is nicely presented and good quality with a wide ranging menu and the service is good.

Delicias Cubanas
Dositeo 76, between Garayalde and Agramonte
Tel: 24-464 397. Open daily L & D. **$**
Portions of tasty food are generous and come with lots of side dishes, so come here hungry. Excellent service and very good food.

Taberna Pancho
Avenida Jorge Dimitrov
Tel: 24-481 868. Open daily 12.15–4pm, 6.15–10pm. **$**
Right by Hotel Pernik and close to Plaza de la Revolución. With rustic wooden tables and chairs, wooden barrels, and traditional music, this is a quiet, pleasant place for a burger and a beer or a full meal.

Plaza de la Revolución, Santiago.

SANTIAGO DE CUBA

Cuba's second city has a heroic revolutionary past, beautiful squares, and a vibrant musical tradition that includes the country's most vigorous carnival.

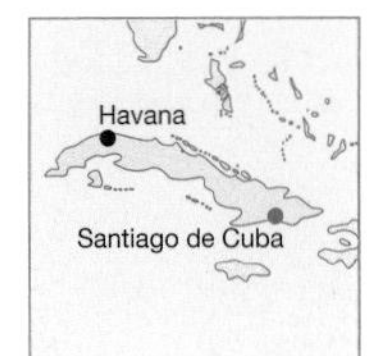

Main Attractions
- Antiguo Cuartel Moncada
- Plaza de Dolores
- Museo Provincial Emilio Bacardí
- Parque Céspedes
- Catedral de N.S. de Asunción
- Casa de Velázquez
- Casa de la Trova
- Cementerio Santa Ifigenia

Nestled alongside a sweeping bay at the foothills of the Sierra Maestra mountains, surrounded by slopes covered with sugar cane, coffee, fruit, and vegetables, **Santiago de Cuba** ⓴ is Cuba's most exotic and ethnically diverse city. Multicultural, it is where many Haitians, both of white French ancestry, and of black African descent, settled after fleeing the slave uprisings in their country at the end of the 18th century, bringing with them the cachet of their Afro-French culture to blend with that of Afro-Hispanic Cuba. Isolated and remote, it is Cuba's second-largest city with a population of 475,000.

The city was badly hit by Hurricane Sandy in 2012, when it lost nearly all its trees, completely changing the formerly leafy aspect of its squares and plazas, although it is slowly recovering. Some areas are traffic-free, but generally the streets are congested and full of fumes in the heat. There is some beautiful colonial architecture – you'll see plenty of graceful hanging balconies, gingerbread latticework, and wrought-iron gates throughout the city, but Santiago suffered greatly from the privations of the 'Special Period' even before it was hit by the hurricane. There is a lot of poverty here and visitors have to put up with harassment from hustlers and beggars. For the same reason, there is more need for care against crime, especially when walking through town alone at night. On the other hand, most of Santiago's residents are extraordinarily friendly and helpful.

Santiago is renowned for producing much of Cuba's most important music, and this rich musical tradition, mingled with the remnants of French customs, gives the city a sensual, somewhat sleazy, New Orleans-like atmosphere. Wandering around can be confusing at times because some of the city's streets have two or three

View over the bay.

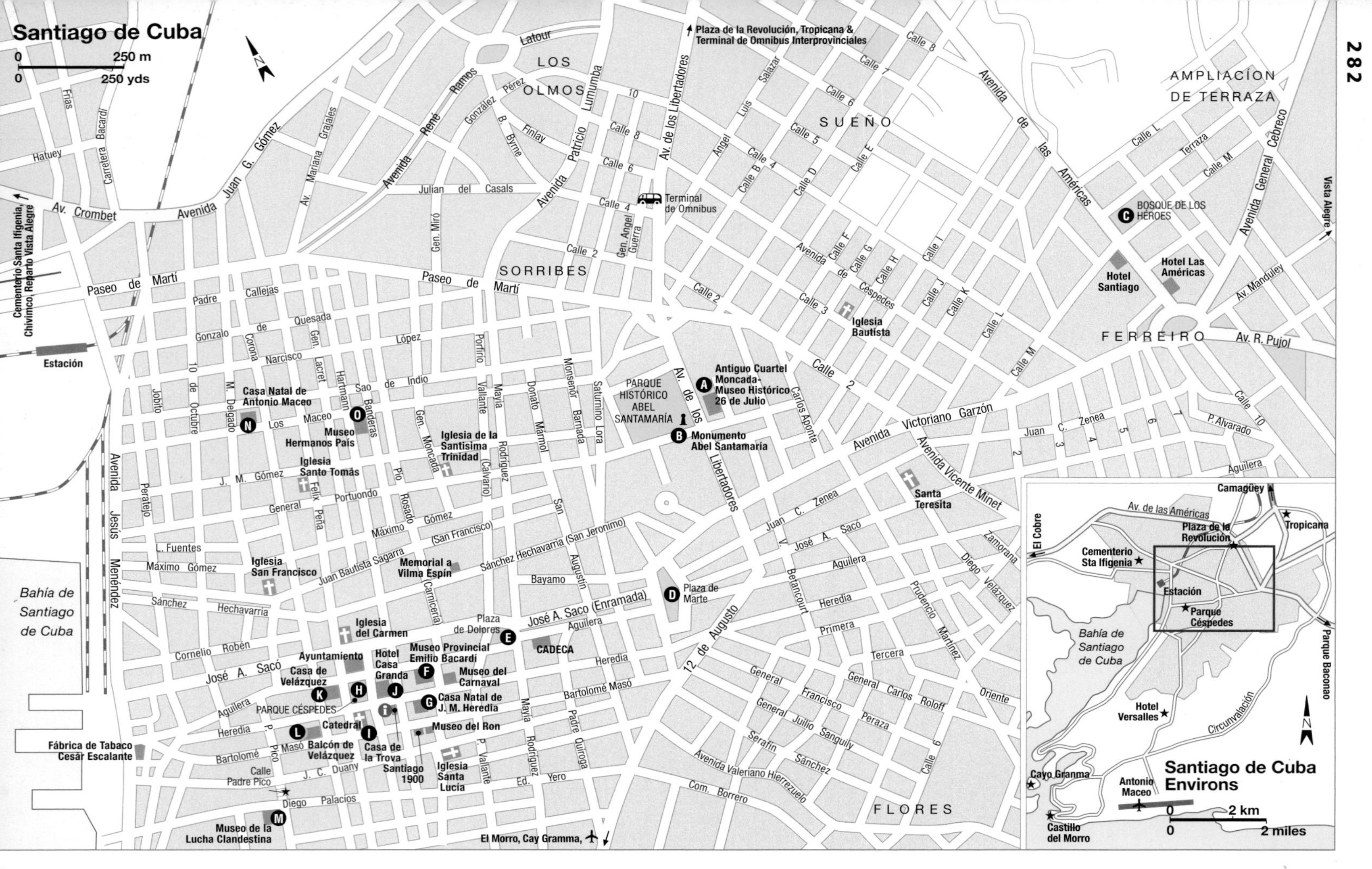
Santiago de Cuba
0 250 m
0 250 yds
LOS OLMOS
SUEÑO
AMPLIACÍON DE TERRAZA
Plaza de la Revolución, Tropicana & Terminal de Omnibus Interprovinciales
Vista Alegre
Cementerio Santa Ifigenia, Chivimco, Reparto Vista Alegre
Av. Crombet
Avenida Juan G. Gómez
Av. Mariana Grajales
Avenida René Ramos
Avenida Patricio Lumumba
Av. de los Libertadores
Avenida de las Américas
Avenida General Cebreco
Av. Manduley
Terminal de Omnibus
BOSQUE DE LOS HÉROES
Hotel Santiago
Hotel Las Américas
FERREIRO
Av. R. Pujol
SORRIBES
Paseo de Martí
Estación
Iglesia Bautista
Avenida de Céspedes
Antiguo Cuartel Moncada-Museo Histórico 26 de Julio
PARQUE HISTÓRICO ABEL SANTAMARÍA
Monumento Abel Santamaría
Av. de los Libertadores
Avenida Victoriano Garzón
Avenida Vicente Minet
Santa Teresita
Casa Natal de Antonio Maceo
Museo Hermanos País
Iglesia de la Santísima Trinidad
Iglesia Santo Tomás
Avenida Jesús Menéndez
Iglesia San Francisco
Memorial a Vilma Espín
Plaza de Marte
Bahía de Santiago de Cuba
Iglesia del Carmen
Plaza de Dolores
José A. Saco (Enramada)
CADECA
12 de Augusto
Museo Provincial Emilio Bacardí
Ayuntamiento
Hotel Casa Granda
Museo del Carnaval
Casa de Velázquez
Casa Natal de J. M. Heredia
PARQUE CÉSPEDES
Catedral
Museo del Ron
Fábrica de Tabaco César Escalante
Balcón de Velázquez
Casa de la Trova
Santiago 1900
Iglesia Santa Lucía
Avenida Valeriano Hierrezuelo
Museo de la Lucha Clandestina
El Morro, Cay Gramma,
FLORES
Camagüey
Av. de las Américas
Tropicana
Plaza de la Revolución
El Cobre
Cementerio Sta Ifigenia
Estación
Parque Céspedes
Parque Baconao
Bahía de Santiago de Cuba
Hotel Versalles
Circunvalación
Cayo Granma
Antonio Maceo
Castillo del Morro
Santiago de Cuba Environs
0 2 km
0 2 miles

 Maps on pages 264, 282

names, but Santiago is still ideal for walking if you can manage the hills of the old city and it deserves several days' exploration.

Founded by the Spaniards in 1514, Santiago was Cuba's capital from 1524 until 1549. Because of its deep, natural harbor and Caribbean coastline, it also served as the center of the island's prosperous slave trade in the 1700s and 1800s. In 1898, Spain's surrender to the United States took place in Santiago, but then the city gradually slipped into second-class status after the government based itself in Havana.

Today, Santiago is the island's only official 'Hero City,' revered for being a bastion of Cuban nationalism and the cradle of the revolution. It was here, on July 26, 1953, that the revolution began with the failed assault, by Castro and his rebels, on the Moncada Garrison, then the second-largest military post in Cuba. It was also here that Castro accepted the surrender of Batista's army in 1959. The town's motto is 'Rebelde Ayer, Hospitalaria Hoy, Heroico Siempre' (Rebellious Yesterday, Hospitable Today, Heroic for Ever).

Monuments to the revolution

The first thing you see when you enter Santiago is the stark **Plaza de la Revolución**, dominated by a vast, equestrian statue: the **Monumento Maceo**. Beneath the monument is a museum containing holograms of revolutionary items connected with the great fighter, one of the major figures in Cuba's 19th-century struggle for independence. The plaza stands at the junction with the Avenida de los Libertadores, a broad street lined with flowering trees and busts of the Moncada rebels.

Some distance down Avenida de los Libertadores you come to the Parque Histórico Abel Santamaría. On the other side of the road is the **Antiguo Cuartel Moncada** Ⓐ, now half elementary school, half museum, the **Museo Histórico 26 de Julio** (Moncada Barracks; entrance on Avenida Moncada; tel: 22-620 157; Tue–Sat 9am–8pm, Sun 9am–1pm), dedicated to the Moncada assault and the 1959 revolution. Batista had the bullet holes filled in, but these have

Santiago back street.

Carnival time, Santiago de Cuba.

TIP

Santiago seems to have more than its fair share of wonderful old cars, many now used as taxis – big old Buicks, Packards, Chevys, Chryslers, Studebakers, Hudsons, Edsels, and Fords. Be respectful – you may find yourself in a 1940s Oldsmobile. If the driver holds the door open for you, it could be gallantry – or ensuring you don't slam it so it falls off.

now been reconstructed for effect. Inside are revolutionary memorabilia: guns, grenades, documents, photographs, Castro's khaki uniforms, and Che Guevara's muddy boots. The museum is visually strong, and there are multilingual guides. Surprisingly, the museum is hardly signposted; you enter by taking a turning left off Avenida de los Libertadores.

Opposite, in a park of the same name, is the impressive **Monumento Abel Santamaría** Ⓑ, a tribute to Fidel's second-in-command in the 1953 attack on Moncada. It was Santamaría's job to create diversionary fire at the nearby hospital – a task he performed too well, in fact: unaware that the main assault had failed, he and his men continued firing until the hospital was surrounded. Despite pretending to be patients, the unfortunate rebels were caught and tortured, and most were executed.

Batista's men gouged out Santamaría's eyes and presented them to his sister, Haydée, a fellow revolutionary, to make her talk, but she realized that he could not have revealed the movement's plans and kept silent herself. Eye hospitals in Cuba now bear Abel Santamaría's name, as does a national medal given to young people who show extraordinary achievement in their studies or work. The park itself is a shady, well-used spot, where plants struggle to survive, boys play baseball, and groups of elderly people take exercise classes.

Ferreiro and the colonial center

Walking south from here, you reach Avenida Victoriano Garzón. If you go left up the avenue you come to the intersection with Avenida de las Américas, locally known as Ferreiro after the family that owned most of the land here before the revolution. This is one of the city's most modern and most wealthy areas, with the landmark red, white, and blue **Hotel Santiago**. Nearby is a buzzing farmers' market, and, next to the **Hotel de las Américas**, a small, rather neglected park, the **Bosque de los Héroes** Ⓒ, which has monuments dedicated to Che Guevara and his comrades who fell in

Statue of Antonio Maceo in the Plaza de la Revolución.

Bolivia. It was the first monument to Che in Latin America. Just east of here, flanking Avenida Manduley, is the attractive **Vista Alegre** district. There are several museums and cultural centers for those interested in Afro-Cuban culture and religion, including the Centro Cultural Africano Fernando Ortiz (Avenida Manduley, 106), the Casa del Caribe (Calle 13, corner Calle 8), and the Museo de la Religión (Calle 13 206, corner Calle 10).

To reach the old heart of town, however, turn right and look for **Hotel Rex**, on the left just before you reach **Plaza de Marte** **D**. Now a basic peso hotel, the Rex is only notable as the place where Fidel Castro and his fellow guerrillas ate the last meal before the Moncada Barracks attack in July 1953. From Plaza de Marte, a noisy square where taxis gather, and goat-pulled carts take children for rides on weekends, head down the busy, commercial Calle Aguilera to **Plaza de Dolores** **E**, a pleasant open space with lots of benches under the trees, as well as the tables of numerous restaurants. It is known as *Bulevar*, and is more a widening of Calle Aguilera than a formal square. The Cafetería la Isabelica here is a local institution, open 24 hours, but watch out for *jineteros*. Also on the plaza is the Complejo Don Antonio, which is a state-run complex of places to eat, including Chinese, Cuban, international, and Italian food. In a former church, the Sala Dolores is known for its recitals of choral and orchestral music.

Santiago's museums

Continuing down Calle Aguilera, you come to the **Museo Provincial Emilio Bacardí** **F** (entrance on Pío Rosado; tel: 22-628 402; www.cnpc.cult.cu; Mon noon–9pm, Tue–Sat 9am–9pm, Sun 9am–1pm; guided tour in English), Santiago's most interesting museum. It was founded in 1899 by Emilio Bacardí Moreau, a Cuban writer and the first mayor of Santiago, although he is more famous for his Caney Rum distillery, which was moved to Puerto Rico after the revolution to produce the re-named and globally popular Bacardi Rum.

The museum contains some first-rate Cuban art (including works

Vintage car on a Santiago backstreet.

TIP

Housed beneath the huge, tiled terrace of the cathedral are a number of small, tourist-oriented stores and a branch of ETECSA (daily 8.30am–7.30pm) where you can make phone calls, buy phone cards, and use the Internet. There's another branch on Calle Tamayo Fleites (same hours).

by the talented José Joaquín Tejada Revilla), some colonial European paintings and memorabilia from Cuba's wars of independence, historic documents, flags, maps, and weapons. There is also an archeology section with indigenous artifacts, an Egyptian mummy – bought by Emilio Bacardí, a keen collector, on a visit to Egypt in 1912 – several skeletons from Paracas in Peru, and a shrunken head.

From here it is a short walk to one of old Santiago's most important and most vibrant streets, **Calle Heredia**, which has a couple of museums worth a quick visit. The most interesting is the small **Museo del Carnaval** (Heredia, corner Carnicería; tel: 22-626 955, Tue–Sun 9am–6pm), where there are some great costumes and *cabezudos* (big-headed carnival figures) and faded photographs depicting carnival's history. In the courtyard you can watch Afro-Cuban music and dance sessions daily (except Saturday) at 4pm – but be prepared to be pulled into the action.

Nearly opposite, the **Casa Natal de José María Heredia** G (Tue–Sun 9am–6pm) is the birthplace of José María Heredia, one of the first Cuban poets to champion national independence. It's a peaceful, attractive house with original furnishings, and occasional poetry workshops are held in the courtyard.

The central square

In the very center of the city is **Parque Céspedes** H, a colonial square with a bust of Carlos Manuel de Céspedes in the middle, where you will find young and old, rich and poor, gathering to exchange news or simply watch the world go by. It is also a place where you are likely to get a lot of requests for money or soap from the persistent *jineteros* (hustlers) of both sexes who congregate here. Many of the city's most venerable buildings are on the square, several of which were repaired and renovated 2013–14, partly to mark the 55th anniversary of the Revolution.

Dominating the park is the **Catedral de Nuestra Señora de la Asunción** I (Tue–Sat 8am–noon, 5–7.30pm, Sun 8–11am, 5–6.30pm; free), a vast basilica rebuilt four times since the first one was completed in 1524, because of earthquakes or pirate

Parque Céspedes.

attacks. The current building dates from 1818, with further restoration and decoration added in the 20th century. There is a good, painted wooden altar, and hand-carved choir stalls, and, it is said, the remains of conquistador Diego Velázquez, though these have never been located.

Directly opposite the cathedral is a splendid neo-colonial white building with blue shutters. This is the **Ayuntamiento** (town hall), from the balcony of which Castro announced the triumph of the revolution on January 2, 1959.

Also on the square is the elegant **Hotel Casa Granda** ❶. The interior, restored in the mid-1990s, has an air of faded grandeur and having a drink on the roof terrace at sunset is delightful. The hotel was once a high-society spot where the Cuban elite gathered on the rooftop terrace to sip rum, dance, and smoke cigars. Anyone who was anyone could be seen here, and famous patrons included many famous movie stars, singers, and sports champions, including baseball legend Babe Ruth. However, during the 1950s it was a sinister place that teemed with US spies and Cuban rebels. One of the hotel's former guests was the author Graham Greene, who came here to interview Castro (the interview never took place) and used the setting for a scene in his book *Our Man in Havana*, when his protagonist, Wormold, stayed here.

Cuba's oldest house

In the northwest corner of Parque Céspedes, distinguished by its black-slatted balconies, is the newly-renovated **Casa de Velázquez** Ⓚ which houses the **Museo de Ambiente Histórico Cubano** (tel: 22-652 652; Sat–Thu 9am–5pm, Fri 2–5pm; multilingual guided tour, camera fee). A solid-stone structure with Moorish-style screened balconies, glorious cedar ceilings *(alfarjes)*, floor-to-ceiling shutters, and two lovely courtyards, the house was built between 1516 and 1530 and is said to be the oldest home in Cuba. In the 16th century, Governor Diego Velázquez used the first floor as his office and the upper floor as his residence. Among its collection are European tapestries, crystal, paintings,

Antique bust at the Museo de Ambiente Histórico Cubano.

Man carrying bird cages, Santiago.

MUSIC ON CALLE HEREDIA

Calle Heredia is a good venue for the arts and you may well witness here some of the finest musicians in Cuba. The local office of the Unión de Escritores y Artistas de Cuba (UNEAC; Cuban Writers' and Artists' Union) stages poetry readings, arts shows, lectures, and literary discussions. Another venue is the unprepossessing ARTex shop, which sells various crafts and souvenirs, and hosts good bands in the relaxed atmosphere of the pretty courtyard at the back.

The most famous venue is the renowned **Casa de la Trova**. Musicians consider it an honor to be asked to play here – treading as they do in the footsteps of a string of Cuban greats – and so it attracts some very accomplished artists. All week long, local musicians perform acts that range from somber Spanish guitar classics to vibrant Afro-Cuban drumming; from solo acts to 12-piece bands; trained professionals to talented amateurs. Upstairs there is a dance floor and lounge used at night, known as the Salón de Grandes Personas. Tables and chairs are set on the wooden balcony running the length of the room above the street. Daytime concerts are held downstairs for a minimal charge. Tour agencies offer evening packages that include transportation, drinks, and a CD, but it is cheaper to come independently. Note that you are not allowed to record the music.

Cuban Health Care

One of the major successes of the revolution was the development of an exemplary health service, now being exported around the world.

The flood of middle-class, educated professionals leaving Cuba after the revolution took with it more than half the 6,000 doctors previously working on the island. Health care was already fragmented and failing the poor so it became one of the key areas for attention, along with the literacy campaign. Private health care was abolished and a state-run, national system was introduced. Huge efforts were made to eradicate infectious diseases, improve maternity care, and reduce mortality rates, while large numbers of young people were recruited to train as doctors and other health professionals.

The next stage, in the 1970s, developed the idea of community health care. Polyclinics were built around the country to provide specialist services not previously available outside big cities. Then, in the 1980s, the Family Doctor program was introduced to provide care on a micro level; each doctor in charge of 120 families, a ratio rarely seen in the developed world and only beaten by Israel.

Better health care has improved life expectancy.

Winning the War on Disease

The success of initial policies enabled the government to embark on preventative care, led by a massive immunization and screening program; 95 percent of the population has been vaccinated against 12 diseases, some of which have been eradicated. Everyone has been tested for HIV and most people are tested annually. Ante-natal screening has prevented any babies being born HIV-positive since 1998. Other indicators also highlight the enormous success in improving the health of the nation: UN statistics show infant mortality fell from 70 deaths per 1,000 live births in 1955–60 to only 5 deaths in 2005–10 (UK down from 24 to 5, US from 26 to 6), while life expectancy rose in the same period from 61 to 77 years for men and from 64 to 81 years for women. This has been achieved with one of the lowest rates of spending per person on health care in the world.

The investment in training has, however, left Cuba with a surplus of doctors. Some of them have left the profession to work in the tourist industry, where they can earn more money as waiters or guides. Others work abroad and have become a valuable tool in the state's foreign policy initiatives. In the 1990s 600 Cuban doctors were seconded to the South African health service for three years to make up a shortfall when their own doctors emigrated. Thousands of doctors operate in Caracas shanty towns in return for a cheap supply of oil. Thousands more work in Brazil under a three-year deal to send health workers to impoverished areas. Although they earn only a fraction of what Brazil pays Cuba for their services, they can save enough to buy a house or car on their return home.

Cuban Medics to the Rescue

Whenever there is a natural disaster or emergency, Cuban doctors and paramedics from the Henry Reeve Medical Brigade are usually first on the scene – they set up field hospitals in Haiti after the 2010 earthquake long before the US emergency services arrived, and have been deployed after earthquakes in Pakistan and China, the tsunami in Indonesia, and major flooding in Guatemala and Bolivia.

Thousands of foreign students from developing countries have trained in Cuba, returning home after years of subsidized education as fully-fledged doctors fluent in Spanish and skilled in salsa.

ceramics, and antiques. *Peñas* (musical performances) are sometimes held here, and you may hear musicians practicing in the courtyards.

Just behind the square, to the southwest, is the **Balcón de Velázquez** Ⓛ (CUC$1 to take photos), an open paved area on the site of the first Spanish fort in the city, which has very good views of the harbor.

Bartolome Maso and Padre Pico

Bartolomé Masó (also called San Basilio) is a cobblestone street lined with antique gas lamps, running parallel to Heredia. Look for the **Restaurante Santiago 1900**, in a grand colonial home that once belonged to Emilio Bacardí. With a series of balconies set around a courtyard with a central fountain, and furnished with 19th-century antiques and crystal chandeliers, it retains some of its original elegance. It's a better spot for a drink than a meal, however (see page 291). The **Museo del Ron** (San Basilio 358, corner Carnicería; tel: 22-623 737; Mon–Sat 9am–5pm) explains the history of rum in Santiago and has an atmospheric little bar for a post-tour rum tasting. The street leads down to Avenida Jesús Menéndez and Parque Alameda, flanking the harbor.

Off to the left, before you reach the harbor, is one of the prettiest streets in the city, **Padre Pico**, which climbs up steps to the top of a steep hill southwest of Parque Céspedes, in the **Tivolí district**. The streets here are lined with houses that were once home to prosperous French refugees fleeing the slave rebellion in Haiti.

At the corner of Padre Pico and Diego Palacios (Santa Rita) is the **Museo de la Lucha Clandestina** Ⓜ (Museum of the Underground Struggle; tel: 22-624 689; Tue–Sat 9am–5pm, Sun 9am–noon; free), a lovely mustard-yellow colonial mansion with fine views of the city, reached via a slope fringed with bougainvillea. It is dedicated to the heroes of the 26th of July Movement and highlights the help that local people gave to the revolutionaries. In 1956 guerrillas fire-bombed the Batista police headquarters here, but it has since been beautifully restored.

Farther south, on Calle Jesús Rabí, is the Casa de las Tradiciones, in a large colonial house with a central courtyard, a great place to come at night for authentic *trova*, and a lot more local than the Casa de la Trova.

Laundry drying in the breeze on a Santiago rooftop.

Changing of the guard at the impressive José Martí mausoleum, Cementerio Santa Ifigenia.

Cementerio Santa Ilfigenia.

The broad, dusty promenade by the seafront is not particularly scenic, but you may want to venture down here to visit the cigar factory, the **Fábrica de Tabaco Cesár Escalante** (Mon–Fri 9–11am, 1–5pm).

Santa Ifigenia

Some distance northwest (taxi recommended) is the **Cementerio Santa Ifigenia** (Avenida Crombet, Reparto Juan G. Gómez; tel: 22-632 723, daily 8am–5.30pm; charge includes a guide). Once segregated by race and social class, the cemetery has both massive mausoleums and unpretentious graves. Carlos Manuel de Céspedes, Emilio Bacardí, and Cuba's first president, Tomás Estrada Palma, are among the famous figures buried here.

The tomb to receive most visitors, though, is that of the patriot José Martí, whose marble vault has the figures of six women carved around the outside bearing the symbols of Cuba's provinces. Buried within the mausoleum is earth from each of the Latin American countries inspired by Martí to assist in the independence struggle; the countries' names are inscribed on wall plaques. The national flag is draped over Martí's sarcophagus, which is so positioned as to catch the sun throughout the day. Accompanied by martial music, a uniformed armed guard is changed every half hour. The remains of 38 of the Moncada rebels are also buried here, in a special wall just inside the cemetery entrance.

Local musician.

Along Calle General Banderas

You could ask your cab driver to return to the center via the **Casa Natal de Antonio Maceo** **N** (Los Maceo 207 between Corona and M Delgado; tel: 22-623 750; Mon–Sat 9am–5pm; free), a modest house where the great man, nicknamed the Bronze Titan, was born. It exhibits photos, personal possessions, and Maceo's battle flag.

From here, you can walk along Calle General Banderas where there is a museum dedicated to two of Santiago's revolutionary heroes, the **Museo Hermanos País** **O** (General Banderas 226, corner Los Maceo; tel: 22-652 710; Mon–Sat 9am–5pm). Frank País was a poet, teacher, and army rebel who led the 26th of July Movement in Oriente. His younger brother, Josué, was also active in the movement. Both were gunned down in the street in separate incidents in 1957, and their boyhood home is a national shrine.

On your way back to the center stop at the memorial to Vilma Espín (1930–2007) (Sánchez Hechavarría, also known as San Jerónimo, between Calvario and Carnicería), opened in April 2010 on the 80th anniversary of her birth, in the house that was the headquarters of the 26th of July Movement. Each exhibition room charts a different period of her life: her childhood in Santiago; her time as a student; as part of the clandestine movement; as a revolutionary fighting in the Sierra Maestra; as a mother and wife to Raúl Castro; and then her important work with the Federation of Cuban Women (FMC).

RESTAURANTS, PALADARES AND BARS

PRICE CATEGORIES

Price categories are for a three-course meal for one with a beer, or mojito. Wine puts the price up:
$ = under $25
$$ = $25–35
$$$ = over $35

Restaurants

Santiago has long been a great place for bars and nightspots, but not so good for restaurants. However, things are now changing with the opening on Avenida Victoriano Garzón of several new restaurants, cafeterias, and food stands, all of which charge in *moneda nacional*.

El Barracón
Avenida Victoriano Garzón, between Martí and Primera. Tel: 22-643 242. Open daily 11am–11pm. **$–$$**
Decorated with a slavery theme; life-size images of slaves at the door to welcome you; the walls are stone, the crockery earthenware, the furniture rustic and wooden. The food is good *comida criolla* with specialties such as lamb or smoked pork, but items are often not available and the service is slow.

El Baturro
Aguilera, corner San Félix
Open daily noon–11pm. **$**
A popular place serving cheap Cuban food.

El Palenquito
Avenida del Río 28, between Calle 6 and Carretera del Caney, Reparto Pastorita, a cab ride east of the center
Tel: 22-645 220, www.facebook.com/ElPalenquito. Open daily noon-midnight **$**
This lovely open-air restaurant under a thatched roof is in a lawned garden that gives it a rural aspect. Much of the meat or seafood is cooked to order on the grill, but there are plenty of other tasty menu items. Service is good, and so are the drinks, including the coffee.

Casa Granda
Hotel Casa Granda, Parque Céspedes
Tel: 22-686 600. Open daily L & D. **$$**
An elegant venue in Santiago's most atmospheric hotel. Eat in the dining room, on the broad terrace, or in the rooftop bar/restaurant. International food and pleasant, if slow, service.

Compay Gallo
San Germán 503, between Carnicería and Moncada
Tel: 22-657 227, www.facebook.com/RestauranteCompayGallo. Open daily L & D. **$**
Modern Cuban cuisine here is artistically designed and delectable. Seafood and meat dishes are all worth trying, the service is attentive, and you may need a reservation for this popular *paladar*.

España
Avenida Victoriano Garzón, corner Cañedo
Open Mon noon–5pm, Tue–Fri noon–4pm, 6pm–midnight, Sat–Sun noon–2am. **$**
One of the new restaurants operating in *moneda nacional*. The outside is blue with tiles reminiscent of public baths, but inside is quite smart with waiters in neat uniforms. Items on the menu are often not available, but it is so cheap you can forgive them.

Santiago 1900
Calle Masó (San Basilio) 354, between Pío Rosado and Hartmann
Tel: 22-623 507. Open daily L & D. **$**
In a beautiful mansion that was the Bacardí family home. There's a great courtyard with a fountain, an upstairs patio, and a dim though elegant dining room. There is often live music, too. Unfortunately the food isn't very good and, like many places, they tend to run out of things. Drinks have to be paid for in CUC$, but ask for the menu in *moneda nacional* for a cheap meal.

Bars

Santiago bars and clubs are pretty much interchangeable, so some of these venues are also mentioned in the Nightlife section (see page 341).

Café de Ajedréz
Plaza Céspedes
A good local bar (small and easy to miss), with great coffee all day and music at night.

Bello Bar
Hotel Meliá Santiago, Avenida de las Américas
A quiet bar on the hotel's 15th floor, with wonderful panoramic views.

Casa de la Trova
Calle Heredia, 208
There's music here, afternoon and evening, and drinks are not expensive.

Patio de ARTex
Calle Heredia, 304
Rum, beer, coffee, and snacks in the patio behind the artex shop; two daily sessions of live music.

Enjoying a drink at the Patio de ARTex.

The Basílica del Cobre.

AROUND SANTIAGO

Several interesting trips can be made from Santiago de Cuba, including one to the spectacular Morro Fortress, to El Cobre, the island's most holy Catholic shrine, an historic coffee plantation, and some great beaches.

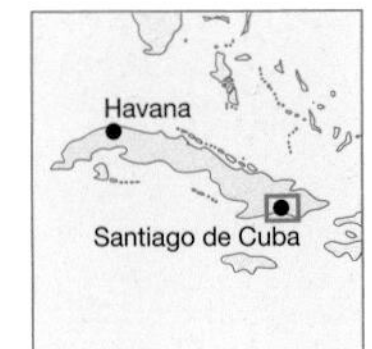

Main Attractions
Castillo del Morro
Cayo Granma
Basílica del Cobre
Gran Piedra
Cafetal Museo La Isabelica
Granjita Siboney
Valle de la Prehistoria

Within easy striking distance of Santiago are several sights that shouldn't be missed. A rental car provides the most convenient way of exploring these, but if you don't want the risk of getting lost they are also accessible either with tour agencies or by hiring a taxi for an individual trip or for the day – make sure you strike a deal and agree an itinerary before you set off.

Most sights are located east of Santiago. West of the city you'll find a scattering of pleasant beaches, such as **Playa Mar Verde** ㉑, not to mention the stunning drive along the coast into Granma province.

The Morro fortress

To the south of the city, perched above Santiago Bay, is the Spanish fortress of **Castillo del Morro** ㉒, now a World Heritage Site, housing the Museo de la Piratería (tel: 22-691 569; daily 8am–8pm). A taxi from Parque Céspedes will cost CUC$15–25 for the round trip, with waiting time. Construction on this stunning fortress began in 1638, to a design by a specialist Italian architect, Juan Bautista Antonelli, son of the man who built El Morro in Havana.

It was destroyed in 1662 by English forces commanded by Sir Christopher Myngs, an expedition in which the pirate Henry Morgan took part, and rebuilt between 1690 and 1710. It has an elaborate labyrinth of drawbridges, moats, passageways, staircases, and barracks, all executed with marvelously precise angles and a geometric beauty – many people think it is more impressive than Havana's fort. Its dark, dank inner cells, complete with built-in iron shackles, once housed African slaves in transit, and a small chapel still contains a wooden cross carved by a 16th-century Spanish artist. Look for the contraption that was used to haul mighty stone balls up from the store to the cannon above. The views across the bay and along the

Castillo del Morro.

coast are splendid. You can have an excellent lunch here (see page 297) or just buy snacks or drinks (and souvenirs, of course) from the stands outside.

The ferry boat to **Cayo Granma** – a small island community just inside the mouth of the Bay of Santiago – departs from the Ciudadmar pier 1.6km (1 mile) along the coast from the small beach at the foot of El Morro (you will see it signposted as you drive up to the fort on the Carretera del Morro). Ferries (CUC$2) depart roughly every hour throughout the day and follow a roundabout route linking the island with several little communities on the bay shores. Ferries also depart from Punta Gorda on the bay, about a CUC$6 taxi ride from the center. The island was formerly called Cayo Smith, for the wealthy English slave trader who once owned it, but the name was changed after the revolution.

Cayo Granma today has about 750 residents, some of whom still fish and build boats for a living, although most commute by ferry to factory and office jobs in Santiago. Since there are no cars or hotels on the island, it has a tranquil, old-time atmosphere. It has a beautiful beach, a small park where local people gather for games of dominoes, a school, a few stores, and a good seafood restaurant (see page 297). Many residents offer rooms, and the island makes a pleasant, relaxing place to spend a night.

The floating Virgin's shrine

Of all the monuments in the Santiago region, the most famous is the shrine to the Virgen de la Caridad del Cobre, 19km (12 miles) northwest of the city. The **Basílica del Cobre** ㉓ (daily 7am–6pm; free) is named for the first open copper mine in the Americas, which supplied the ore for Havana's artillery works, the largest in the New World, around 1600.

Although the mine was producing copper until a few years ago, the place has long been identified with an object that some people believe is far more precious, which three young men found floating in the Bay of Nipe off Cuba's northern coast, in 1608. This is a 30cm (1ft) -tall wooden statue of a mestizo (mixed-race) Virgin carrying the infant Christ on her left arm, and

View of El Cobre.

holding a gold cross in her right hand. At her feet was the inscription, *Yo soy la Virgen de la Caridad* (I am the Virgin of Charity). Legend has it that she had been floating for almost 100 years, since an indigenous chieftain – who had been presented with the statue by the conquistador Alonso de Ojeda in 1510 – had set her adrift to protect her from the evil intentions of other less Christian native *caciques* (chiefs).

Through the years, the Virgin has been invoked to protect freedom, perform miracles, offer consolation, and heal the bitterness of battle. In 1916, at the petition of veterans of the War of Independence, the Pope declared her the patron saint of Cuba. The Virgin's sanctuary was inaugurated on her saint's day, September 8, in 1927, and thousands of worshipers flock to the church every September 8, for the Virgin is also worshiped as Ochún, the magnetic and sensual Santería goddess of love and rivers. Pope John Paul II visited the basilica during a trip to Cuba in 1998, and there is a bust of him outside the main door.

On the hilly drive from Santiago you will pass flower sellers offering yellow blooms that people buy as gifts for the Virgin/Ochún. The cream-colored church, surrounded by bougainvillea, looks stunning against the wooded slopes behind. Inside, above the altar is an air-conditioned niche that holds the diminutive figure of the Virgin, dressed in a gold-encrusted satin gown and crown.

The Virgin is displayed to worshipers during Mass, then the figure is rotated so that it can be seen only by climbing stairs above the Shrine of Miracles, where grateful believers leave braces, crutches, flags, armbands, coins, medals, locks of hair, and other *ex-voto* offerings. There is even a piece of the Berlin Wall, and the athletics shirt of the famous Cuban 800-meter Olympic gold medalist, Ana Quirot. It is said that the mother of Fidel and Raúl Castro laid an offering here for the safety of her boys when they went off to fight in the Sierra Maestra. Well, that worked.

El Cobre attracts hordes of persistent touts and beggars. Be careful if you are carrying valuables, and be firm in refusing to buy statues of the Virgin (unless, of course, you really want one).

From the basilica you can see the **Monumento al Cimarron**, a sculpture commemorating a revolt by African slaves forced to work in the copper mines. A steep hike to the statue will be rewarded with stunning views. In one of the abandoned mines a lake has formed; the high but fluctuating mineral content means that the water – which has proved effective for some skin conditions – can be green one day and blue the next.

Gran Piedra

The highway east of Santiago, which follows the Caribbean coastline, is a marvelous road that slips between the sea and a rocky cactus desert with the blue-green mountains beyond. An 80,000-hectare (200,000-acre) area, the **Parque Baconao**, has been recognized as a biosphere reserve by Unesco.

FACT

Ernest Hemingway donated his Nobel Prize to the Virgen de la Caridad, but unfortunately it was stolen from the Shrine of Miracles. It was soon recovered but is now safely stored away.

The Virgen de la Caridad is an object of veneration.

FACT

The Villa Daiquirí has another historical connection, too: it was on Daiquirí Beach that Teddy Roosevelt and his Rough Riders came ashore during the Spanish–American War of 1898.

Thirteen kilometers (8 miles) into the mountains is a well-marked turn-off to **Gran Piedra** ㉔, taking you from dry and dusty desert into cloud-capped mountains shrouded in rainforest, up a long access road (under-powered or overloaded cars may struggle to make it). Each twist and turn in the road reveals a new vista across the mountains. At 1,214 meters (4,300ft) above sea level, you come to the Gran Piedra (Great Rock), with fabulous views across the mountains and out to sea, where even the lights of Jamaica can be seen on a clear night. It's ideal for climbing. Most people come for the day, but you can stay at the Villa Gran Piedra, an 'eco-lodge' with comfortable rustic cabins along the mountain ridge, and unbeatable views. There is a CUC$1 charge to climb the steps to the Gran Piedra.

Close to Gran Piedra, the **Jardín Ave de Paraíso** (Bird of Paradise Garden; daily 8am–5pm) should not be missed. First laid out in 1860 in the grounds of a coffee plantation, it was subsequently used to provide flowers for hotels, celebrations, and formal presentations. The gardens are beautifully landscaped, covering 45 hectares (111 acres) and the flowers are breathtaking, especially the brilliant *ave de paraíso* for which the garden is named.

In a lovely spot 2km (1 mile) or so along a dirt road east of La Gran Piedra, the **Cafetal Museo La Isabelica** (daily 9am–5pm) is one of the area's few relics of the plantation era. This 19th-century estate, now a Unesco World Heritage Site, gives an insight into what life on a coffee plantation was like. The house originally belonged to a family of French descent, refugees from Haiti's slave rebellion (1789–1804). It is said that the plantation was named for the owner's mistress, an enslaved woman whom he later married.

Back on the main highway is **Granjita Siboney** ㉕ (Tue–Sun 9am–5pm), the farmhouse where Fidel Castro and other rebels planned the 1953 attack on the Moncada Barracks in Santiago (see page 283). It has been converted into a museum, displaying the usual collection of bloodstained clothing and the check from the Santiago

Brontosaurus grazing, Valle de la Prehistoria.

ANTIQUE AUTOS

Before the revolution American cars were freely imported into Cuba, and some of the most flashy models were brought in by Hollywood movie stars and Mafia hoods. Since the US trade embargo in 1961 there have been no new imports and the American cars you see on the roads now date from the 1940s and 1950s, and are held together with a lot of ingenuity and tender care. In the late 1980s, the government began selling some of the old cars to foreign investors, offering Cuban owners new Ladas instead, but many fine examples of old Buicks, Chevys, Studebakers, and others ended up in the Museo Nacional de Transporte Terrestre (see page 297), and in the Depósito de los Automóviles in Havana (see page 145). Many of them are also used as taxis to ferry tourists around.

restaurant where the *compañeros* had their last supper before the failed assault. The weapons were hidden in a well in the garden. The road along the coast is peppered with monuments to those who died at Moncada.

Santiago's coast

The coast east of Santiago was devastated by Hurricane Sandy in 2012, which wreaked havoc and destroyed hundreds of properties on its route to the USA. Boulders and rocks were dragged up from the seabed and thrown inland, and beaches were completely rearranged, many losing their sand. In the village of **Siboney** 26 178 houses were recorded as completely flattened. **Playa Bucanero**, which was popular with package tourists from Canada and Germany, was badly hit and the Club Bucanero Hotel was destroyed.

One unmissable site for anyone interested in Cuban kitsch is the **Valle de la Prehistoria** 27 (daily 8am–5pm), some 24km (16 miles) east of Santiago. This dinosaur theme park was created in 1983, with a collection of life-sized models. There is also a good little museum, the **Museo de Ciencias Naturales**, packed with interesting facts on local flora and fauna.

The **Museo Nacional de Transporte Terrestre** (daily 8am–5pm), up a left-hand turn a little farther east, is also worth visiting for its collection of vintage cars – including the Cadillac that belonged to renowned Cuban singer, Beny Moré – and the display of more than 2,000 miniature cars.

At **Playa Daiquirí** on the coast south of here the daiquirí was invented, as an anti-malarial tonic for miners, even if it was 'perfected' in Havana's El Floridita bar. Unfortunately, Playa Daiquirí is reserved for the military.

The best place to aim for is **Playa Cazonal**, with an all-inclusive hotel, though the shallow water makes for limited swimming. Just beyond lies **Laguna Baconao**, a lagoon surrounded by hills. There's a restaurant, a couple of boats, and a small crocodile enclosure.

The paved road ends by the lake. Beyond lies a restricted military zone – do not go any farther.

RESTAURANTS

PRICE CATEGORIES

Price categories are for a three-course meal for one with a beer, or mojito. Wine puts the price up:
$ = under $25
$$ = $25–35
$$$ = over $35

Casa de Pedro El Cojo
Carretera de Baconao, Km 32, Sigua
Tel: 22-356 210. Open daily, all day. **$**
Just outside Sigua, directly south of La Gran Piedra, this is a pleasant, simple restaurant *(ranchón)* that serves fish (mostly) with the usual accompaniments. Compay Segundo entertained friends here in his latter years, and there is an Eliades Ochoa song of the same name on a *Best of Buena Vista* album.

El Cayo
Cayo Granma, Bahía de Santiago
Tel: 22-690 109. Open daily noon–7pm. **$**
This pretty little blue-and-white building, by the water, houses Cayo Granma's only restaurant. You can eat good *criolla* food here – mainly fish – in pleasant surroundings. Booking for lunch is advisable.

La Jaiba Azul
Baconao
Open Tue–Sun 9am–6pm. **$–$$**
Near the black sand beach, this is a convenient spot for lunch on a day trip out of the city. It specializes in seafood, including lobster. Prices are in *pesos Cubanos*, making it very good value.

El Morro
Carretera del Morro, Km 9
Tel: 22-691 576. Open daily noon–4pm. **$$**
This place serves good *criolla* cooking, with a varied menu that includes spicy shrimps and lobster. It's right next to Castillo del Morro with great views of the coastline. Booking is advisable.

Los Robalos
Baconao
Open Tue–Sun 9am–6pm. **$–$$**
Over the bridge from La Jaiba Azul, giving you a second option, this place specializes in crab dishes.

La Rueda
Calle Montenegro s/n, Siboney
Tel: 22-639 325 399 325. Open daily 9am–9pm. **$**
The food is pleasant and the service friendly, but the main reason this little place is well known is as the birthplace of Buena Vista musician, Compay Segundo. It also goes by the name of Museo/Sitio de Compay Segundo and is decorated with his personal possessions.

Hotel Villa Gran Piedra
Gran Piedra
Tel: 22-686 147, 651-205. Open daily D only. **$**
The restaurant in this 'eco-lodge' is also open to non-residents and serves traditional Cuban food.

Baracoan street musician.

BARACOA AND THE FAR EAST

The US military base of Guantánamo is synonymous with the 'war against terror,' but it is the lush mountain landscape, the pristine beaches, and the laid-back town of Baracoa that draw visitors to the east.

Main Attractions
La Farola
Baracoa
Río Yumurí
El Yunque
Playa Maguana

The main reason most visitors venture east of Santiago de Cuba is to visit Baracoa, the most popular destination in the region, which has been opened up to tourism. If you want to go straight from Santiago to Baracoa, there is a daily Víazul bus. The 4.5-hour journey down the road called La Farola is delightful; views are splendid and bends are tortuous, so it's preferable to have somebody else doing the driving.

However, there are a few other places of interest in the surrounding area for those who have rented a car and want to explore at leisure.

Guantánamo

To get to **Guantánamo** ㉘ you take the Autopista Nacional from Santiago, then, after about 15km (9 miles), go east on the Carretera Central. The road then becomes motorway again about 20km (12 miles) before Guantánamo.

There's no immediately obvious reason to make the trek from Santiago to Guantánamo, but it is a pleasant, well-kept provincial town. It was founded in 1819 and lies between the Jaibo, Bano, and Guaso rivers just north of where they flow into the Bay of Guantánamo. During the 19th century the town received a large influx of immigrants from Haiti and Jamaica, many of them French, fleeing the slave revolt. As a result, some of the architecture has a French Caribbean feel, with pretty wooden balconies and wrought ironwork, although there is a predominance of the neoclassical style of the late 19th- and early 20th-century Spanish Cuba. There is also a rather unfortunate late 20th-century 12-story apartment tower.

City life revolves around **Plaza Martí**, a pleasant leafy square shaded by laburnum trees (glorious in March), and with an attractive golden-colored church, the 19th-century **Iglesia Parroquial Santa Catalina de**

Guantánamo street mural.

TIP

There is a small museum near the Plaza de la Revolución, north of Guantánamo city center, which contains the space capsule in which the first Cuban went up into space.

Ricci. It's worth at spending least an hour exploring the streets around the main square. There are some attractive old houses on the parallel calles Pedro Agustín Pérez and Calixto García, north of Parque Martí, while Los Maceo, one block east, is buzzing with shoppers. Seek out the unusual **market**, a neoclassical structure occupying an entire block.

Musical heritage

The town's French heritage has had a lasting impact on its musical traditions and rhythms. Go to the **Tumba Francesa** (Serafín Sánchez 715, between Jesús del Sol and Narciso López; Tue 9.30am–1pm, Thu 9.30am–noon, Sat 9.30am–2pm) to see the colorful folk dance and music that originated in Haiti, created by freed slaves in the 1890s to preserve the traditions that had grown up on the coffee plantations in the area. The dancers re-create the movements of their ancestors to the beat of the Premier drums and the Catá (a wooden percussion instrument), both of which came from the Dahomeyan region of Africa. There is a shop selling Haitian-style handicrafts and other souvenirs.

Everyone visiting Cuba will hear the haunting *Guajira Guantanamera* song, based on the words of a poem by José Martí. The *guajiro* is not only a peasant farmer (see page 196), but also a rural style of *son*. This developed in the mountains around Guantánamo and became known as *son changüí*. It has a very complex rhythm and much improvisation on the bongos, but it has been kept alive in the **Casa de la Trova** (Pedro Agustín Pérez, corner Crombet; Tue–Sun 9am–noon, 2–6pm, 7pm–midnight) and in the **Casa del Changüí** (Serafín Sánchez 710, between Jesús del Sol and Narciso López; tel: 21-324 178; Tue–Fri 7am–11pm, Sat–Sun 10am–2am). Here you can find the *changüí* bands playing their bongos and marimbulas (African thumb bass).

Caimanera and the base

The only reason most people come here is for a view of the controversial US naval base, one of the last vestiges of the Cold War, and the place now

Plaza Martí.

best known as the site of the infamous Camp Delta, where men suspected of terrorist involvement have been detained in conditions that have aroused widespread disquiet.

Guantánamo itself offers no views of the base, which actually extends to the south of the city. If you want a glimpse of it, there are two options open to you. The first and most difficult option is to pass through two Cuban military checkpoints, to **Caimanera**. The necessary papers can be obtained from the Ministry of the Interior (MININT) office on Calle José Martí in Guantánamo, but independent travelers will find it difficult and very time-consuming to get hold of a pass. Visitors staying at the Hotel Caimanera on a pre-booked itinerary through a tour agent get a pass included in their booking. The hotel is the closest you will get and has a three-story observation tower overlooking the **US Naval Base** 29. Look up: on all sides of town are the omnipresent tunnels where residents are to go in case of an emergency.

Los Malones

For the average visitor, the best view they will get of the US base is through binoculars from the **Mirador de los Malones**, off the Baracoa road about 24km (15 miles) east of Guantánamo. You can arrange a visit by booking a tour at one of Santiago's central travel agencies, ideally a couple of days in advance, or at a *buró de turismo* in the hotel in Guantánamo. The area is controlled by the military and tours are sold by Gaviota, the military's tour agency. A guide will accompany you into the Cuban military zone that surrounds the base and then along a bumpy dirt track to the lookout point. You will be shown a model of the base, and given a few vital statistics before climbing the stairs, where a telescope allows you to pick out vehicles and people moving around, and spot the US and Cuban flags flying by the perimeter fences.

The Stone Zoo

You could make a detour into the mountains northeast of Guantánamo, toward Palenque, where the village of **Boquerón** is home to the **Museo Zoológico de Piedra** (Stone Zoo; Carretera a Yateras, Km 18; Mon–Sat 9am–6pm), the handiwork of Ángel Iñigo, a coffee farmer who has carved more than 100 animals out of the limestone. Some large sculptures are carved *in situ* from outcrops or large boulders, others from smaller rocks, and all stand amid a beautiful garden. Almost all were carved from pictures in books: Ángel has never seen most of the animals he has so faithfully sculpted. The zoo is now run, and the more recent figures carved, by Ángel's eldest son, Angelito. From here, access is prohibited, and you must retrace your steps to Guantánamo and the Baracoa road.

Along the coast

The road east out of Guantánamo passes pleasant little farming communities and beaches at **Yacabo Abajo** and **Imías**. At **Playa de Cajobabo** 30,

Playa de Cajobabo.

Road to Guantánamo.

US Guantánamo

This little piece of the island of Cuba is in fact US-occupied territory with one of the worst human rights records in the world.

The naval base sits in the southeast corner of Cuba, an enclave of US military might, occupying 116 sq km (45 sq miles) of Cuban territory. For decades, it has been one of Uncle Sam's most-favored ports, known to sailors as Gitmo. Founded in 1898 after 600 US Marines landed here to fight in the Spanish–American War, the base was formally established in 1901 by the Platt Amendment. Until 1959 it was a good-time assignment where sailors overindulged in cheap rum and accommodating women. Saloons and brothels dotted the streets of nearby Guantánamo city.

Following Castro's takeover, brothels and bars were closed, commerce between Americans and Cubans forbidden, and security on the base tightened considerably. Many Cubans still worked there, but had to get a bus then walk through the gate after vehicular traffic was prohibited.

Since 1960, Castro has not cashed any of the annual US$4,085 rent checks issued by the US Treasury, as to do so would acknowledge the legitimacy of the base. Guantánamo, according to Castro, is 'a dagger plunged into the heart of Cuban soil,' but it remains in US hands until the two countries agree to end the arrangement, or the US decides to abandon the base. The Platt Amendment was repealed in 1934 and theoretically the US lease on Guantánamo expires in 2033.

Detainee attending a 'life skills' class.

Surrounded by barbed wire, Gitmo is an isolated installation guarded by 500 Marines. About 8,000 people live here, including civilians and military families. It contains housing, a school, health spa, a movie theater, a shopping center, and a McDonald's. Children watch Saturday-morning cartoons picked up by satellite from US television networks, and military planes fly in with supplies. Servicemen and women stationed on the base conduct defense exercises, maintain warships, and monitor Cuban airspace. Rifles slung over their shoulders, they patrol the perimeter, which is mined with explosives. Though neither the US nor Cuba will confirm the figure, it is estimated that about 100 Cubans a year enter the base illegally by swimming through the shark-infested waters or jumping the fence. Dozens of these have died in the attempt. In the early 1990s, the camp held Haitian refugees who fled their country after a coup, and in 1994 it became a temporary refugee center for thousands of Cuban rafters who had been picked up at sea by the US Coast Guard.

The controversy continues

As Cuba poses little military threat to the US, the base had little strategic value except as a thorn in Castro's side, until 2002, when it became the site of the now-notorious Camp Delta, the subject of international controversy, which holds people suspected of belonging to al-Qaeda or the Taliban. There were in fact three camps, one of which has been closed. There was controversy over the insistence of the Bush administration that detainees, despite being held as 'enemy combatants,' should be denied the protection of the Geneva Convention. Terrible stories emerged concerning torture and human rights abuses of the prisoners, who were held indefinitely without trial. The election of President Barack Obama in 2008 brought hopes of change. In January 2009 he suspended the proceedings of the Guantánamo military commission for 120 days and promised that the facility would be shut down within a year. Many prisoners were released or transferred, but 162 remained in December 2013, of which 29 were on hunger strike, 19 of whom were being force fed.

next along the coast, José Martí and Máximo Gómez came ashore to begin the fight against the Spanish in 1895. However, it is not a particularly interesting beach destination. From here, the road divides, turning north to Baracoa, and east to **Punta de Maisí**.

Few people take the road to Maisí. It is in poor repair, and requires a good four-wheel-drive vehicle and a skilled driver, not to mention a strong nerve, as it bends higher and higher up the stone mountain terraces. It passes through dry, scrubby desert land with dramatic mountain scenery rising to the north. The vast limestone terraces are full of caves with stalactites and stalagmites. Below the coffee-growing town of La Máquina, the village of **Maisí** ㉛ sits on a wide coastal plain of dry shrubby vegetation and cacti. There is a lighthouse on Cuba's most easterly point, only 80km (50 miles) from Haiti, but this is a military zone and you will be denied access.

Instead, take the route heading north (inland) from Cajobabo to Baracoa – along the hair-raising but well-maintained road over the mountains. Known as **La Farola** (The Beacon), it twists through some fearsomely acute bends. The crash barriers are disconcertingly broken in places and warning notices appear regularly – 'Caution: 72 Accidents on this Bend So Far.' The risk is compensated for by the wonderful scenery: magnificent mountain vistas, wild jungle, coconut groves, and coffee and cocoa plantations. You will be approached by vendors of wonderful fruit and snacks, such as *cucburuchos*, grated, flavored coconut neatly encased in palm leaves, but if they offer you anything made of polymita snail shells, say no, as they are endangered and protected by international law.

Cuba's first town

Some believe Columbus landed first at **Baracoa** ㉜ in October 1492, but there is little evidence for this. The explorer was looking for the Orient, but no matter: he found the *oriente* (east) of Cuba. 'A thousand tongues would not suffice to describe the things of novelty and beauty I saw,' he recalled. The town nestles beneath El Yunque, a flat, anvil-shaped mountain that was described by Columbus in his log.

Baracoa certainly was Cuba's first town, founded by Diego Velázquez in 1512, and was also the first capital of Cuba and the starting point for the Spanish conquest of the rest of the island. Three years later, Santiago, and then Havana, took over the role of capital. Baracoa remained isolated up until La Farola was built in 1962; prior to that, access was possible only by sea.

The streets, impossibly picturesque in the late afternoon light, are absolute heaven for photographers, with their neat lines of single-story, pastel-colored houses with red-tiled roofs and lush vegetation. This laid-back air is a result primarily of Baracoa's isolation, with Havana 1,070km (670 miles) away. While Baracoa is still well off the main tourist trail, the town's combination of friendly people, attractive scenery, and distinctive cuisine

Baracoa Bay.

A residential street in Baracoa.

make it a great place to spend some time. There are several small hotels and dozens of *casas particulares*, but no large resorts.

The best place to get an overview of the town, the bay, and the unnervingly short runway of Baracoa's tiny airport on the far side is from the gardens of the Hotel El Castillo (see page 336), up a long flight of steps or a steepish slope on a clifftop. The building was originally a castle, built in 1770 to keep out the British; it later became a prison, and more recently a hotel.

Life in Baracoa revolves around leafy **Parque Independencia**, also known as Parque Central, where legend has it that the indigenous chief Hatuey was burned alive by Spanish conquistadors (see page 30): the supposed spot where he died is marked by a bust, directly opposite the entrance to the **Catedral de Nuestra Señora de la Asunción** (Tue–Sat 8am–noon, 2–4pm, Sat 7–9pm, Sun 8am–noon; free), although his death is more likely to have occurred in Yara, near Manzanillo. The church was built in 1805, replacing the original, destroyed by pirates in 1652, and was refurbished in 2011. What is believed to be Columbus's Cruz de la Parra (see box) is kept inside. There are several peso food stands and cafés around the parque, particularly at lunchtime.

The town's two main streets, Maceo and Martí, are where everything happens. Check out the small but lively **Casa de la Trova** (Antonio Maceo 149; Tue–Sun from 9pm), which really gets going at about 10pm, and is a popular gathering place. Dancers are always welcome if you want to join in. In neighboring **Plaza Martí**, each Saturday is 'La Fiesta' – a lively affair with loud street music and plenty of rum, roast pork, and snacks for sale. Farther along Maceo (No. 124) is the **Casa de la Cultura**, where there are exhibitions of modern art by local artists, and regular live music, including a nightly show of Afro-Cuban music using traditional instruments and costumes.

Along The Malecón

Baracoa was particularly badly hit by the hurricanes of 2008, but work is now being done to cheer up the

Parque Independencia,. Baracoa.

Malecón, Baracoa's seafront boulevard. Gaviota has opened a few cafeterías, all called Costa Norte, has opened the new Hostal Río Miel (see page 337), and has renovated the iconic La Rusa hotel (you can't miss it, it's bright yellow). La Rusa was a Russian woman who abandoned the Soviet Union in the 1950s, came to Cuba, and ended up supporting the rebels. Fidel and Che both stayed here, and guests fight over the rooms where they are said to have slept.

At the eastern end of the Malecón is the small but well-preserved **Fuerte Matachín** (1802), which houses a small **Museo Municipal** (tel: 21-642 122; daily 8am–noon, 2–6pm). Outside the fort is a chunky statue of Columbus and a large wooden cross. The museum contains a mixture of displays on the indigenous Taíno, local history, and a few Baracoan characters.

At the western end of the Malecón, close to the bus station, is **La Punta** fortress, now a restaurant (see page 307), with a statue of a defiant-looking Hatuey outside. From here there is a great view of the bay, on the far side of which is a good hotel, the Porto Santo, and a small airport (four flights a week to Havana).

If you climb a flight of steps on the inland side of Antonio Maceo toward a neighborhood called Reparto Paraíso, you pass the outdoor El Ranchón disco, then walk along pretty, rural tracks lined with little houses in lush gardens, with children playing, goats roaming, and chickens pecking in the dust.

The **Museo Arqueológico** (Mon–Fri 8am–5pm, Sat 8am–noon) is tucked away up a narrow path, in the Cueva del Paraíso. It contains objects found in and around Baracoa, including a skeleton of a Taíno chief called Guamá, who fought the Spanish for 10 years. The story is that he was murdered by a single blow to the head, dealt by a man – possibly his brother – whose wife he had stolen. There is also a replica of the Taíno Tobacco Idol, found nearby in 1903, and said to be the most important in the Americas. The original is in Havana's Museo Antropológico Montané (see page 172). The cave is part of the Majayara

Bass saxophonist rehearsing in Baracoa.

A REGIONAL CUISINE

Baracoan food typically uses spices, coconut, and chocolate. Food is cooked in coconut oil and *lechita* (coconut milk), giving the whole town a heavenly smell when cooking starts. Local dishes include *bacón* (a plantain tortilla filled with spicy pork), and *tetí* – small red fish caught in the river estuaries between August and December; they have a gelatinous protective wrapping, which dissolves upon reaching fresh water, and are tasty raw or in omelets. Tamales are mashed plantains wrapped in a banana leaf, instead of the maize used elsewhere. Rice is colored yellow with annato seeds, while 'Indian bananas' are boiled in their pink skins and dressed with garlic and lime juice. The Casa del Chocolate at Antonio Maceo, 121, famously serves hot chocolate with salt as well as sugar.

Banana vendor in a Baracoan food market.

terrace, and there are stalagmites, stalactites, and petroglyphs. Yara and Majana are the two other terraces in this geological area, in between which there are many caves, full of petroglyphs, once used by the Taínos. The museum runs archeological tours of the area.

Excursions from Baracoa

Legend says that those who sleep in Baracoa's **Bahía de Miel** (Bay of Honey) or bathe in the waters of the Río de Miel, will never want to leave. Disappointingly, the city beach, at the eastern end of town, is gritty and gray, and the sea rather muddy. Going east from Baracoa through the small settlement of Jamal, there are some beautiful (and gentle) walks through countryside where the crops are a mixture of bananas, coffee, cocoa, and avocados, where pigs snuffle in the undergrowth and chickens roam. At **Río Yumurí**, 30km (20 miles) east of Baracoa, a boatman is usually available to take visitors on a short trip. The green river is delightful, flowing between high cliffs, and you may see and hear Cuba's national bird, the trogon (also known as the *tocororo*).

Baracoa's horizon is dominated by **El Yunque** ㉝ (The Anvil), looming at 560 meters/1,800ft, to the west of the town. Archeologists have found shells and skeletons left by the Taíno people who, during the conquest, took advantage of the mountain's cliffs and natural lookout points, as did anti-Spanish rebels during the 19th century.

The slopes are cloaked in virgin rainforest, part of which is protected by the rarely visited **Cuchillas de Toa** mountain reserve. This is one of the wildest regions in Cuba, with excellent potential for hiking and some wonderful flora, such as wild orchids. You can climb El Yunque in a couple of hours; bring plenty of water and good footwear, as the path can get muddy and slippery. A guide is compulsory. The path runs from Campismo El Yunque, near the base of the mountain, but you can also rent horses and hire guides for the trip at Finca Duaba, just outside Baracoa, along the Moa road.

A CROSS DEBATE

In Baracoa almost every resident can, and will, tell you the story of the Cruz de la Parra (Cross of the Vine), fashioned from hardwood, which Columbus reputedly brought from Spain and planted here. It vanished and was later found amid the backyard blackberry bushes of a colonizer's house in 1510. This historic cross has survived pirates, fires, vandals, and other hazards, although relic-hunters have chipped away at the edges and it is now about half the size it used to be. Standing 1 meter (3ft) tall, it is now kept safe in the cathedral, with its edges encased in metal.

That, at least, is the story. But did Columbus really bring the cross? The church maintains that he did. So does Alejandro Hartmann, director of the local history museum, the Museo Municipal (in the Fuerte Matachín) in Baracoa. But a host of scholars disagree. Everybody has a conflicting notion – and everyone can back it up with data. In 1989, carbon-dating tests appeared to indicate that Baracoa's wooden cross was planted in Cuban soil in the late 15th century, which supports one strand of the Columbus theory, making it chronologically possible, but it is made from the native seagrape tree *(Cocoloba diversifolia)*, which could not have been brought from Spain. So the mystery deepens, but the cross is still revered.

Nuestra Señora de la Asunción, Baracoa.

The Finca, which, like all the tourist amenities here, is part of the Gaviota chain, has a restaurant that serves Cuban food, and organizes demonstrations showing how local crops, such as cocoa and bananas, are cultivated. At **Playa Duaba**, near the mouth of the Duaba River you can swim in either fresh or saltwater.

The best beach, and one of the finest in Cuba, is **Playa Maguana**, 22km (14 miles) from town, where there's a good hotel, the Villa Maguana (see page 337). A coral reef ensures that the 3km (2 miles) of sugar-white sand is lapped only by gentle waters.

Tour operators, Cubatur (Maceo 149; tel: 21-645 306), Ecotur (Coronel Cardoza 24; tel: 21-643 665), and Havanatur (Martí 202; tel: 21-645 358) in Baracoa can organize excursions to the area led by knowledgeable local guides, who can incorporate interesting additions, such as visits to cocoa farms. Here, you can learn how the cocoa pods are harvested and transformed into a variety of delicious products including chocolate, which you can taste and buy.

The road northwest from Baracoa takes you into Holguín province, along a dramatic route that skirts the mountains and the sea. It is rough going in the early stages, with many potholes, so allow three hours for the drive to **Moa** 34. Unless you are a metallurgist, you won't want to spend much time in Moa. This is mining country, with possibly the world's largest reserves of nickel and cobalt. Nickel production is an important industry, but one that results in belching chimneys and polluted seas and rivers washing up against blackened hills.

FACT

Close to the mouth of Río Yumurí is the Tunel de los Alemanes (German Tunnel). This impressive natural rock formation, through which the road runs, is so-called because, in pre-revolutionary times, a German family lived close by, and charged drivers of motor- and horse-drawn vehicles for passing through.

RESTAURANTS, PALADARES AND BARS

PRICE CATEGORIES

Price categories are for a three-course meal for one with a beer, or mojito. Wine puts the price up:
$ = under $25
$$ = $25–35
$$$ = over $35

Baracoa

There are now some 28 *paladares* in Baracoa that, together with the state restaurants and casas *particulares*, mean you'll never go hungry.

El Buen Sabor
Calixto García 134, between Ciro Frías and Céspedes.
Tel: 21-641 400. Open daily noon–11pm. **$**
Eat on the terrace or indoors. Delicious local dishes and coconut sauce with the fish that is among the best in town. Pleasant, friendly service.

La Colonial
Calle Martí, 123
Tel: 21-645 391. Open daily D only. **$**
A reliable *paladar*. Two small dining rooms and interior patio lively with caged birds. Menu varies, depending on availability.

El Poeta
Calle Antonio Maceo, between Ciro Frías and Céspedes
Open daily L & D. **$**
Good local food including spicy soups and fish cooked in coconut-milk sauce. Be prepared for poetry recitals by the owner and drinking games with rum and sugar cane juice as a finale to dinner.

Porto Santo
Carretera del Aeropuerto
Tel: 21-645 105. Open daily L & D. **$$**
Hotel restaurant with international menu and barbecue, just outside Baracoa.

La Punta
Malecón s/n
Tel: 21-645 224. Open daily L & D. **$$–$**
A pleasant open-air restaurant with a good reputation, within the walls of one of the three forts. Full meals or snacks.

Villa Maguana
Playa Maguana, Carretera a Moa, Km 22.5.
Tel: 21-641 204. Open daily 7am–9.45pm. **$$–$**
A pleasant beach bar and *parrillada* for snacks, meals, and drinks.

Guantánamo

La Cubanita
Calle Martí, 864
Open daily L & D. **$**
A great little *paladar* serving well-cooked *comida criolla*, charged in *moneda nacional* and very cheap.

Taberna Las Ruinas
Calixto García
Open daily 10am–1am.
The shell of a ruined building is the backdrop for this restaurant. It offers an extensive menu for lunch and dinner, and the bar is open late with live music.

Vegetariano
Pedro A Pérez
Open daily noon–2.30pm, 5–11pm. **$**
One of the very few vegetarian restaurants in Cuba.

Bars

Baracoa

Casa de la Cultura
Maceo, 124
Music most nights.

Casa de la Trova
Maceo, 149
Lively at night with traditional *son*.

El Patio de artex
Maceo, 120
Pleasant courtyard bar; live music and other events.

Playa Sirena, Cayo Largo.

SOUTHERN ISLANDS

Most important are the Isle of Youth, with good diving, caves with indigenous paintings, and the prison where Fidel Castro was once incarcerated, and Cayo Largo, with its sugar-white beaches.

Main Attractions
- Isla de la Juventud
- Nueva Gerona
- Museo de la Lucha Clandestina
- Presidio Modelo
- Punta del Este
- Cayo Largo
- Cayo Rosario

Located off the main island's south coast, each of the islands of the Archipiélago de los Canarreos has its own distinct personality. Isla de la Juventud (Isle of Youth) is quiet and rural, with a colorful history as a pirate refuge, home for US settlers, and prison camp for revolutionaries; Cayo Largo has a string of hotels and little else; other cays, like Cayo Rosario, are just virgin specks of sand wallowing in the blue Caribbean.

Isla de la Juventud

Isla de la Juventud, the largest by far of Cuba's subsidiary islands with an area of 3,020 sq km (1,180 sq miles) and a population of around 87,000, can be reached either by plane from Havana or by the ferry that departs from the port of Surgidero de Batabanó. The latter is a time-consuming option, and one that is usually only undertaken by travelers with time to spare. Accommodations for visitors are in Nueva Gerona, the capital, and the Hotel Colony on the southwest coast, a dive resort with a marina. Over the centuries, the island has seen immigrants from Spain, England, Scotland, China, Japan, Jamaica, the Caymans, and the USA, and it has had a similarly varied history in terms of the names it has been given.

Indigenous peoples called it Camarcó or Siguanea, but Christopher Columbus renamed it La Evangelista when he landed here in 1494, on his second voyage to the New World. By the 17th century it was known as Isla del Tesoro (Treasure Island) because of the pirate treasure allegedly buried here (thus inspiring the name, at least, of Robert Louis Stevenson's classic adventure tale, published in 1883). By this time, the Spaniards, who finally got around to colonizing the island in the 1840s, had renamed

The infamous Presidio Modelo, Isla de la Juventud.

TIP

Bus and ferry tickets from Havana via Batabanó must be booked in advance from Empresa Viamar (Astro bus terminal, Havana; tel: 7-870 1841); take your passport. Book your return passage before getting to the island. Take food and drink for the journey with you. There is a 20kg (44lb) weight limit and X-ray checks for luggage. It is easier and cheaper to fly.

it Colonia Reina Amalia. Later names include: the Isla de los Deportados, when it became a dumping ground for criminals and rebels deported from the mainland; La Siberia de Cuba, in recognition of the isolated prison where Castro and others spent several years in the 1950s; Isla de las Cotorras (Isle of Parrots), as the habitat of the brightly colored birds that are still the trademark of the island's bottled water; and, until 1971, Isla de Pinos (Isle of Pines). Finally, it acquired its present name in the 1970s, a symbol of the influx of young people to the island.

In 1971, Cuba began taking students from countries in the Developing World and educating them for free on the island, thus hoping to spread solidarity for the Cuban Revolution across the under-developed world. At its height, the program included 60 boarding schools with 150,000 students. However, the flow of foreign students dwindled, due to economic difficulties in Cuba and political changes in their own countries. The last foreign students completed their studies in 1996, although the schools still remain.

Nueva Gerona

The point of arrival on the island is invariably **Nueva Gerona ❶**, which looks a little like a small village in the USA's West at the turn of the 20th century: the older houses are wooden, with spacious, columned verandas, shuttered windows, and carved doors with brass knockers. The similarity is no accident, since many of the town's first pioneers came from the United States in the early 1900s, lured by unscrupulous US land dealers.

It was these midwesterners who planted the island's first citrus groves, which now cover some 25,000 hectares (62,000 acres). Along the riverside road is a wooden bungalow built by a Swedish-American family whose last surviving member lived there for 60 years before finally returning to the US. Her parents, like hundreds of other Americans, believed the island would soon become another state in the Union by vote of the US Congress.

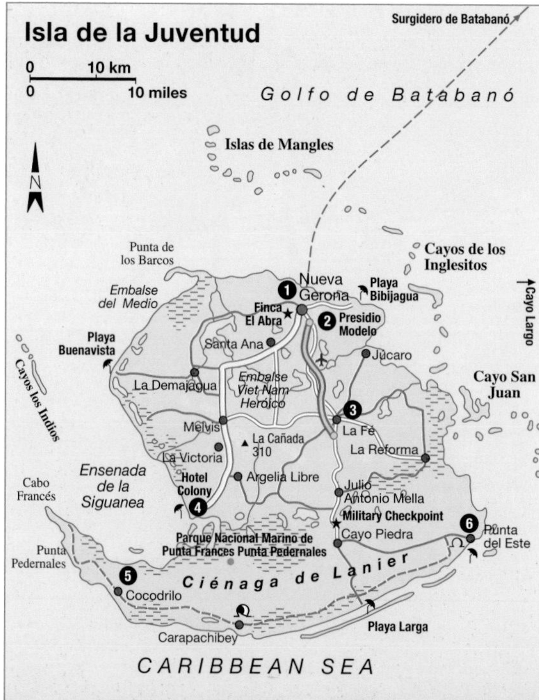

Playing dominoes on a street in La Fé.

They built houses and planted orchards in places they named McKinley, Columbia, Westport, and San Francisco Heights. They spoke English, worshiped a Protestant God, and when they died they were buried in the **Cementerio Americano**, which is maintained today as a historical site. The starkly simple headstones – most dating from between 1905 and 1925 – contrast sharply with the more flamboyant mausoleums, statues, and vaults that decorate the **Cementerio Católico** in town.

Cayman and Jamaican islanders added their Caribbean English to that of the Americans in those early years, while a sizeable group of Japanese settled as farmers. This mix, together with Spanish merchants, Chinese storekeepers, and Cuban landowners, provided a lively diversity in island life.

Today, downtown Nueva Gerona consists of an eight-block grid, so everything is within easy walking distance, including stores and eateries (mostly just snack places). There are also a few nightspots – bars or the Casa de la Cultura – where you can hear live music and join in the dancing.

Main street and Parque Central

Calle 39, also known as Calle Martí, is the main street, a pedestrian boulevard with pretty pink tiles where every building is painted and many house restaurants, shops, bars, and nightlife. The street runs along one side of **Parque Central** (also called Parque Julio Antonio Mella or Guerrillero Heróico). The square is located between calles 37 and 39, running north to south, and between calles 28 and 30 running east to west. Elderly residents sit and watch the world go by during the day but it gets livelier at night.

In the square stands the island's oldest church, **Nuestra Señora de los Dolores**, a typical Latin American colonial-style church, which was built in 1929 to replace an older one that blew away in a hurricane. One of the oldest buildings here, dating from 1853, is the former Casa de Gobierno, now the **Museo Provincial** (Calle 30; tel: 46-323 791; Mon–Fri 9am–10pm, Sun 9am–1pm), which houses exhibits of local interest.

At Calle 39, between calles 24 and 26, is Ecotur (tel: 46-327 101), the main agency that runs highly recommended tours of the island, including the caves at Punta del Este. They are very helpful, and can arrange for a guide and the necessary special permits. Cubanacán (tel: 46-326 369) can also arrange tours.

The **Academia de Ciencias y Planetario** (Calle 41, corner 46; Tue–Thu 8am–7pm, Fri 2–10pm, Sat 1–5pm, Sun 9am–1pm) covers natural history and archeology, and is worth visiting for the replica of the Punta del Este cave paintings if you don't have the time to see the real thing.

On the corner of calles 24 and 45 is the local **Museo de la Lucha Clandestina** (Tue–Sat 9am–5pm, Sun

Nuestra Señora de los Dolores in Nueva Gerona.

8am–noon), devoted mainly to the underground campaign in the run-up to the revolution. *El Pinero*, the ferryboat that carried Fidel Castro and his fellow revolutionaries back to the mainland after their release from prison, is now just a rotted hull on the riverbank between calles 26 and 28. You may be surprised to see a nearby statue of a cow: it is dedicated to **Ubre Blanca** (White Udder), a local cow who broke world milk-production records.

The model prison and La Fé

If you travel a few kilometers east of town in Reparto Chacón, on the road to Playa Bibijagua, you can't miss the **Presidio Modelo** ❷ (Model Prison). It was built between 1926 and 1932 using the plans from a prison in Joliet, Illinois, to house Cuba's hardest cases – most famously Fidel Castro and other revolutionaries after the failed attack on the Moncada Barracks in 1953. As political prisoners, Castro and his *compañeros* fared a good deal better than the common inmates. They were housed in the hospital wing, where they studied and imposed their own group discipline without much interference from the prison officials.

The prison was closed in 1967. An impressive **museum** (tel: 46-325 112; Tue–Sat 9am–4.30pm, Sun 9am–1pm), which includes Fidel Castro's (rather comfortable) old cell, recounts the prison's grim past.

Cuba's 19th-century revolutionary hero, José Martí, also spent time imprisoned on the island in 1870, when he was awaiting deportation to Spain for expressing anti-colonial ideas. For a few months between his grueling prison labors and his exile, Martí stayed at the **Finca El Abra** (Tue–Sat 9am–4.30pm, Sun 9am–1pm), a country estate where the Sardá family nurtured him back to relative health. The farm is located 3km (2 miles) west of town just off the road to the Hotel Colony, near marble quarries – the source of material for the floors, facades, and carved objects seen all over the island.

La Fé ❸, southeast of the island capital, used to be the market town for the surrounding farmlands, and is far

The Presidio Modelo is now a museum.

more attractive than Nueva Gerona, with green parks and tree-lined streets. There is a radio station, public library, post office, and telephone company, while ruins just off the square are all that remains of an old hotel. In the early 20th century, La Fé was a well-known spa resort: the medicinal springs are located nearby, close to the deteriorating hotel and baths.

Not far from the town center is **La Cotorra** spring, in a perfect little park enclosed by an iron fence with a ceramic parrot *(cotorra)* at the gate. This is the spring that supplies the island's bottled water. Inevitably, there are some brilliantly colored parrots that screech at visitors from their cage perches.

Pirates' Coast

From La Fé and Nueva Gerona, roads lead west to the **Hotel Colony** ❹ on **Ensenada de la Siguanea** (Siguanea Sound), completed at the end of 1958, just in time for the rebels to take it over. The bay here is picturesque but too shallow for good swimming – the pool is the best place for that.

Across the bay, though, is **Cabo Francés**, with the spectacular scuba sites of the **Costa de los Piratas**. At more than 50 marked sites, divers can see coral of every shape, size, and color, giant sponges, tropical fish, and crustaceans, underwater caves, tunnels, and rock formations. The site is of particular interest as it contains the sunken remains of a great sea battle between the pirate ships of Thomas Baskerville and the Spanish fleet in the 16th century. And near Punta Francés are three Spanish galleons lying together.

The scuba center at the Hotel El Colony (see page 337) provides full-day diving trips, moving from site to site, with lunch aboard. There is an international marina here, too, as well as plenty of opportunities for deep-sea fishing trips.

The south coast of the island, from **Punta Pedernales** in the west to **Punta del Este** in the east, is breathtaking. However, the entire area inland of Cocodrilo and nearby **Caleta Grande** is a military zone and off limits unless you pre-arrange a visit with Ecotur in Nueva Gerona.

Horse and cart, Isla de Pinos.

This beautiful area is practically uninhabited except for the little town of **Cocodrilo** ❺, settled by English-speaking Cayman islanders at the beginning of the 20th century. Their descendants speak a lilting Caribbean English, though this is beginning to die out as younger generations gradually adopt Spanish. There are numerous magnificent white sand beaches, as yet untouched by tourism and development, but accessible on day trips.

The coast here is backed by thick forests of pine and hardwoods, and the region is separated from the north by the mosquito-ridden **Ciénaga de Lanier** (Lanier Swamp). This geographical isolation once made the area a plunderer's paradise, especially for loggers who felled trees and shipped lumber to all the ports of Cuba and the Caribbean. Reforestation has fortunately been a priority since the early 1960s.

An hour's drive southwest of Nueva Gerona is a **crocodile farm** (daily 9am–5pm) that breeds native crocodiles for release into the wild when they are four or five years old. The caretakers will give you a tour of the hatchery and breeding pens. The Isle of Youth and the Zapata peninsula are the only places in the world where the endangered Cuban crocodile can be found.

Cave paintings of Punta del Este

Punta del Este ❻, in the southeast corner of the island 60km (37 miles) from Nueva Gerona, is beautiful. Except for the ferocious mosquitoes, it is altogether magnificent. It is so far mercifully free of intrusive tourist development, and likely to remain so as long as restrictions on entering the zone remain in place.

Just inland from a sparkling, pristine beach is a series of mysterious **caves** where the indigenous Ciboney inhabitants painted pictographs 3,000 years ago. The caves are one of the most important archeological finds in the Caribbean, first discovered by a shipwrecked French sailor in 1910 and then explored by the Cuban anthropologist Fernando Ortíz in 1922.

Wading through the crystal clear waters of Cayo Largo.

CORAL REEF

From the top of the headland above Punta del Este, a long coral reef is visible about 3.5km (2 miles) offshore. Blue waves crash against the coralline wall in a spray of foam that rolls onto the inner lagoon. The calm, nearly transparent water affords a marvelous view of the sea bed – a clean, sandy plain rippling in undulating zigzag crests that look like tiny dunes. At some points, a fine seagrass carpets the seabed, revealing queen conch shells, with their shiny pink mouths; large king helmets shaded from dark brown to a lustrous cream; and conical top shells. Starfish adorn the sandy bottom, on which white coral appears in a thicket of gorgonians, with delicate hands and multiple fingers swaying in the water. Snorkelers can explore as far as this, and the experience is wonderful, but full diving gear (and some experience) is needed if you want to swim through the coralline wall into the extraordinary reef garden beyond. It is formed of the most varied green, white, yellow, violet, and pink corals imaginable, all surrounded by an almost transparent liquid mass.

These corals can be found only where the sea is less than 100 meters (330ft) deep and where the temperature never drops below 19°C (68°F), so this is a perfect environment for them. At a deeper level, squirrelfish, hogfish, barracudas, and sharks may also be spotted.

The main cave is considered the Ciboneys' Sistine Chapel. It is a single spacious chamber with a fairly low ceiling containing seven natural vaults and more than 235 drawings of circles, arrows, triangles, and serpentine lines. The whole is a great red and black mural that is believed to represent a lunar calendar, including human figures and animals in the world the Ciboney knew and imagined.

Largo, Iguana and Rosario cays

East of the Isle of Youth, myriad tiny cays lie scattered in a wide arc. Most are uninhabited and inaccessible from the mainland. All have delicious beaches of white powdery sand and magnificent diving amongst the coral and the shipwrecks: the Nueva España treasure fleet that went down in 1563 on the reefs somewhere between Cayo Rosario and Cayo Largo provides just a fraction of the more than 200 known wrecks in this area. So far, all but one of these dream islands are undeveloped and only accessible by boat. Plans are afoot to develop Cayo Rico, just west of Cayo Largo, but nothing has happened there yet.

The only cay currently geared to tourism is **Cayo Largo**, which has 27km (17 miles) of white beaches, but is no more than 3km (2 miles) wide at any point. The cay is accessible by plane from Havana or Varadero, and day trips are organized by tour agencies in Havana (see page 351).

In 1985, before Cuba plunged into schemes to attract international tourism, the slogan for this pristine island was 'Thus it all began.' Then came the building boom, the package tours, and the airport disco reception with watery rum cocktails. Even the boat trip to swim and have lunch at lovely **Playa Sirena** has been over-commercialized. An indication of its international tourist status is that Cayo Largo now accepts euros.

Still, Cayo Largo remains popular with travelers looking for sun, sea, and sand, and not much else – anyone interested in Cuba or Cuban people would be better off going elsewhere.

There is, however, an escape: from Cayo Largo, you can take day trips to nearby islets that have no tourist installations at all. But you cannot travel between Cayo Largo and Isla de la Juventud by boat or plane, so you won't be able to 'island hop' and visit both places on the same trip.

Other accessible places include **Cayo Iguana**, inhabited by hordes of these friendly reptiles (which can also be seen on the main island). **Cayo Rosario**, west of Cayo Largo and almost as large, is a crescent-shaped beach, backed by high sand dunes. It is enclosed by a sandbar that forms a natural lagoon of clear blue water over fine pearly sand, with minuscule pink shells piled in the ridges of the seabed. The calm water is lovely for swimming. The cay also has a freshwater river. For the time being at least, the only inhabitants are the large iguanas and other, more elusive, wild animals and birds that exist in this sensitive environment. Long may it last.

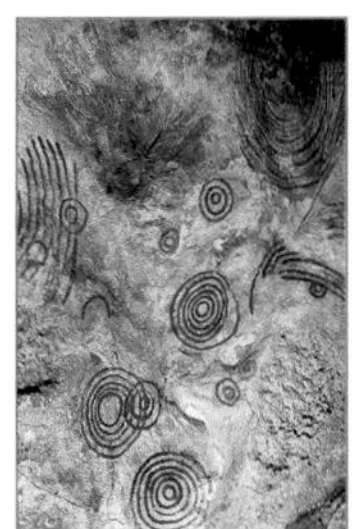

Ancient Ciboney pictographs.

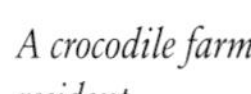

A crocodile farm resident.

Vintage car in a Santiago back street.

INSIGHT GUIDES TRAVEL TIPS
CUBA

Transportation

Accommodations

Activities

A – Z

Language

Further Reading

TRANSPORTATION

GETTING THERE AND GETTING AROUND

GETTING THERE

By air

The availability of flights to Cuba and the airlines in service are subject to change and vary according to season, so always check. There are international airports at Havana, Varadero, Holguín, Santiago de Cuba, Ciego de Avila, Cayo Coco, Cayo Largo, Santa Clara, Las Tunas, Manzanillo, and Camagüey. *Cubana de Aviación*, the national airline, flies scheduled and charter routes between Cuba and other cities in the Americas and Europe, serving primarily Havana, but also Holguín, Santa Clara, Camagüey, and Santiago de Cuba. Most flights are positively no-frills, but Cubana flights provide the cheapest, quickest, and easiest route into Cuba.

From Europe

Cubana (www.cubana.cu or www.cubajet.com) flies from: London (Gatwick), Paris, Moscow, Madrid, and Rome. Flights from London (twice weekly) usually make a stop in Holguín.

Air France (www.airfrance.com) has scheduled flights to Havana from Paris; there are good connections from other European cities.

Iberia (www.iberia.com) operates scheduled flights from Madrid with connections from London and other European cities.

KLM (www.klm.com) flies from Amsterdam with connections from UK and mainland European cities.

Virgin (www.virgin-atlantic.com) operates direct flights from Gatwick to Havana, with a flight time of about 9 hours. These are more expensive than those with a stop in Europe.

There are various charter flights from Gatwick, Luton, Stansted, Manchester, and other regional airports in the UK to Havana, Varadero, and Holguín. Dutch charter airline **Martinair** (www.martinair.com) flies from Amsterdam to Havana, Varadero, and Holguín, usually booked through package-tour operators.

From Latin America and the Caribbean

Cubana flies to and from: Buenos Aires, São Paulo, Santiago de Chile, Santo Domingo, Mexico City, Cancún, Guatemala City, Caracas, San José, Bogotá, and Lima.

Many Latin American and Caribbean airlines also serve Cuba, with scheduled and charter flights available. **Mexicana** (www.mexicana.com) flies between Mexico City and Havana, and there are also frequent flights from Cancún and Mérida in Yucatán. There are regular connections between Havana and various Central American cities with local airlines (www.grupotaca.com); **AeroGaviota** flies from Kingston, Jamaica to Havana via Santiago, and from Montego Bay to Havana via Holguín.

From Canada

Cuba is accessible by air from Montreal and Toronto. **Cubana** runs scheduled flights from Montreal and Toronto, while **Air Canada** (www.aircanada.ca) flies from Toronto to Havana, Varadero, Santa Clara, Holguín, Cayo Coco, and Ciego de Avila. Direct flight time from Montreal to Havana is 4 hours; 3 hours 45 minutes from Toronto. There are also charter flights from Ottawa.

Tourist cards

Remember to keep your stamped tourist card in a safe place as you will need to surrender it when you leave the country. Visitors may also be required to produce their tourist card, along with their passport, when changing traveler's checks, booking into a casa particular or a hotel, if traveling independently. Photocopies of passports are not acceptable – it has to be the real thing.

From the US

Travel restrictions remain in force and US citizens are not allowed to fly to Cuba. However, since 2009, Cuban Americans have been allowed to visit relatives in Cuba regularly and there are direct flights from Los Angeles and Miami to Havana or Cienfuegos (Cuba Travel Services, www.ctcharters.com). Those with their visas (such as accredited journalists, academics, or business travelers) can buy air tickets from **Marazul**, tel: 800-223 5334 or visit: www.marazul.com. There is often a long waiting list on these flights, and US currency restrictions apply.

Americans keen to visit Cuba sometimes travel via Canada, Cancún, Jamaica, or Nassau, although the latter is not recommended as there is a US customs office there that monitors flights arriving from Cuba.

Cuban officials do not stamp travelers' passports; they simply stamp their tourist cards. Visitors from the US are welcome as long as they steer clear of 'subversive' activities.

Airline offices

In Havana, international and domestic airline offices, and some tour operators, are mostly located on La Rampa, a stretch of Calle 23 between Calle M and the Malecón, in Vedado.

On departure

If you do not have a transfer to Havana airport as part of your deal, you should take a taxi. Buses do not go close enough to the airport. Allow at least 45 minutes for the trip from Old Havana to the airport. Be at the airport at least 2 hours before an international flight; security and customs checks can be lengthy.

Airport departure tax for international flights is CUC$25, which must be paid after you have checked in, in cash, in pesos convertibles. You can exchange foreign currency into CUCs at the airport, but this can be time-consuming and best not left until the last minute.

By sea

There are more than 20 marinas and nautical centers for people traveling on chartered (or private) yachts. There is no ferry service. A few cruise lines stop in Cuba, docking in Havana, Cienfuegos, or Santiago de Cuba. The US forbids any vessel from calling at a US port if it has previously stopped in Cuba.

Public transportation

Fuel shortages have prompted drastic cuts in inter-urban and inter-provincial public bus services. Many Cuban cities rely on horse-drawn carts that use the same urban routes that buses once followed. You will also see open-backed trucks, sometimes with a tarpaulin 'roof,' carrying passengers in many towns.

In Havana, thousands of Chinese-made bicycles have been introduced, but there are many more non-cyclists who wait two hours or more for a bus every day. In some places, it is mandatory for Cuban state-owned cars and trucks to pick up hitchhikers; but the farther you go into the countryside the fewer vehicles you see. Tourists are not obliged to pick up hitchhikers but it is rather churlish not to. What is more, local people often make good company and can be very helpful in giving directions on Cuba's poorly signposted roads.

GETTING AROUND

Cuba is a long, thin island, about the length of England, and distances between towns can be greater than expected. All transportation radiates from the Havana hub. There are road and rail links between Havana and Pinar del Río in the west and Havana and Santiago de Cuba in the east, and many towns are also connected with Havana by air. Both Havana and Santiago de Cuba are ports. Their old, historic centers are by the water, with newer suburbs sprawling in an arc around them, making departure by road from the centre to the airport or autopista time-consuming.

From Havana Airport

José Martí International Airport, tel: 7-649 5666 for international flight information; 7-266 4133 for domestic flights. Most international flights operate from Terminal 3, where there is a 24-hour tourist information desk (tel: 7-642 6101, but phones are rarely answered), numerous car-rental desks, bars, restaurants, and an exchange desk. Some charter flights use Terminal 2.

Taxis are always available: the fare is around CUC$25 to the old city, although you may be charged as little as CUC$15 on the return. (The airport is about 18km/11 miles from central Havana.) Drivers gather at the terminal and hustle for your custom. It is illegal for **unlicensed cabs** to drive tourists to or from the airport, and the police keep an eagle eye out for offenders.

By air

Flying is the most convenient way to travel for anyone with limited time and a desire to see various corners of the island. Most services originate from Havana. The national airline, **Cubana** (www.cubana.cu), has regular scheduled flights to 13 Cuban cities from the capital. New destinations are being added all the time, so check with your tour operator or with the airline. The addresses of Cubana offices are:

Havana: Calle 23 64, corner of Infanta, Vedado, tel: 7-838 1039, 834 4446, and at the airport, Terminal 3, tel: 7-649 0410.
Baracoa: Calle Martí 181, tel: 21-645 374.
Bayamo: Calle Marti 58, between Parada and Rojas, tel: 23-423 916.
Camagüey: Calle República 400, corner of Correa, tel: 32-291 338, 292 156.
Ciego de Avila: Calle Chicho Valdes (Carretera Central) 83, between Maceo and Honorato Castillo, tel: 33-201 117.
Holguín: Edificio Pico de Cristal, Calle Libertad, corner of Martí, 2nd Floor, Policentro, tel: 24-468 148 and at the airport, tel: 24-468 114.
Santiago de Cuba: Calle Enramada (Saco) 673, corner of San Pedro (Gen Lacret), tel: 22-651 570/8.
Varadero: Avenida 1era, corner of Calle 55, tel: 45-611 823.

Aerocaribbean and **Aerogaviota** operate flights to Cayo Largo, Cayo Coco, Cayo Santa María, and other popular destinations.

Aerocaribbean: Calle 23 64, corner of Calle P, Vedado, Havana, tel: 7-879 7524, 870 4965.

Aerogaviota: (www.aerogaviota.com, tel: 7-203 0686, 203 0668) operates from a separate, small airport near Havana at Baracoa Beach, Carretera Panamericana Km 15.5, Caimito, Artemisa, tel: 7-209 8002 for airport information.

For most visitors, especially those who do not speak Spanish, it is better to purchase tickets for domestic flights from a hotel reception desk or a recognised travel agency (see page 351). They do not charge commission for making the airline booking.

By bus

City buses, known as **guaguas**, are crowded and uncomfortable, but they are cheap and traveling on them does help immerse you in local life (hold tight to your valuables). They are motorized in Havana and Santiago de Cuba, but in many cities they are horse-drawn and foreigners are not encouraged to use them. A hop-on, hop-off bus service for tourists is in operation in Havana, called the HabanaBusTour, CUC$5 per day, with two routes, one from the Plaza de Armas to Vedado and the other out to Playas del Este via the Castillo del Morro. A similar service runs from Varadero to Matanzas; from Guamá along the coast; Jardines del Rey; Holguín to Guardalavaca and around Viñales.

Long-distance buses are a good, and relatively inexpensive, way of getting around the island.

Víazul is a CUC-only bus service offering fast, comfortable, air-conditioned vehicles, with toilets and plenty of luggage capacity, which operate between the major centers.

From Havana to Santiago there are four buses a day, but the best one is the **express**, the overnight service that leaves Havana at 6pm, as it takes slightly more than 13 hours, and stops only once, in Camagüey. The other services take 14–16 hours (although that is still faster than the train). The cost, currently CUC$51 one way, is the same whether you take the express or not. There are four Víazul buses a day from Havana to Varadero (3 hours), two a day to Viñales (3.5 hours), and three a day to Trinidad (just under 6 hours), one of which starts in Viñales, as well as many other destinations, including a direct service from Varadero to Trinidad, and from Santiago to Baracoa. Be sure to wear something warm, as the air conditioning is fierce.

The Víazul station is by the city zoo on Avenida 26 and Zoológico, Nuevo Vedado, tel: 7-881 1413, www.viazul.com.

Provincial offices are at:
Camagüey: Carretera Central s/n, corner Perú, tel: 32-270 396
Santiago: Avenida Libertadores 457, tel: 22-628 484
Trinidad: entrance on Gustavo Izquierdo on the corner with Piro Guinart; tel: 41-994 448
Varadero: Calle 36 and Autopista Varadero, tel: 45-614 886
Viñales: Salvador Cisneros 63, tel: 8-793 195

At busy times of year, and on popular routes, reserve your ticket in advance, at bus terminals, at the desk at Havana airport, through a **Cubatur** office (in most towns) or, in Havana, through the **Infotur** office at Calle Obispo 524. Online reservations are 8 percent more expensive.

You pay a deposit and receive a voucher, which you exchange for a ticket at the bus station. You still have to turn up about 45 minutes in advance, but it's safer than lining up for a ticket without a reservation.

Some destinations such as Cienfuegos, Trinidad, Pinar del Río, and Viñales can also be reached by transfer service from Havana hotels with Transtur, which charges the same price as Víazul. However, Transtur picks up passengers with reservations from hotels (not casas particulares) in the city, so you can save yourself the taxi fare out to the bus station. You book your seat through hotel reservation desks. Departures are usually early in the morning, but vary according to demand.

There are also long-distance bus services run by **Astro** (Terminal de Omnibus Nacional, Avenida de la Independencia and 19 de Mayo, near the Plaza de la Revolución, tel: 7-870 3397), but these are reserved for Cubans only.

Tour buses

Hotels can book reasonably priced excursions to a wide range of destinations on modern, comfortable, air-conditioned buses. Tourist agencies will also book tours, contact: Cubanacán, Cubatur, and Havanatur (see page 351).

By train

The Cuban railroad was the first in Latin America, but it may be the last in efficiency and comfort today. Trains are crowded and services have been reduced – almost all are now locals that stop at every station. All are achingly slow and prone to breakdown. Little or no food or water is to be had, so take provisions with you, and a flashlight and toilet paper.

Iconic Cuban vehicle.

Puncture repairs

The nearest filling station may be able to help if you have a flat tire. Otherwise, ask around for the local *ponchera*. Since self-employment was legalized, many Cubans have set up puncture-repair workshops. Most of these deal mainly with bicycle tires, but many can handle car inner tubes.

Seats on Cuban trains are always booked well in advance with long waiting lists, but there are always seats reserved for those paying in CUCs. For peace of mind, you should book your ticket a day in advance, and arrive at least an hour before departure to check in, and before 7pm if taking a night train: unassigned seats will be re-allocated to those on the waiting list if you have not confirmed that you are traveling.

In Havana buy your tickets in advance at Ladis (Ferrocuba) office on Arsenal and Aponte, open daily 8am–8pm, tel: 7-860 3161. You must pay in cash, in CUCs, and bring your passport. Trains leave from the Estación Central de Ferrocarril, on Egido (Avenida de Bélgica) corner Arsenal, tel: 7-861 1920.

At many provincial Ferrocuba offices (in the stations) staffers are not accustomed to dealing with foreigners and take the same unhelpful (or downright rude) attitude they inflict on fellow Cubans. They are also unlikely to speak English. Persist if you are told that there are no seats: it is unlikely that this is the case.

From Havana the train to Santiago de Cuba (CUC$30) leaves every other day, theoretically at 3.15pm, taking at least 15 hours, usually many more. In summer an extra train, the *especial*, is also laid on.

Fly/drive

There are several fly/drive options from airports in Havana, Varadero, Camagüey, Holguín, and Santiago. It is convenient because negotiations have been done in advance and your car is waiting when you arrive.

Driving

Renting a car gives the greatest degree of independence, and allows you to reach corners of the island that otherwise would be hard to get to. Highways and secondary roads

Horse-drawn carriages are a common sight in provincial towns.

are fairly well maintained, except for the potholes. Otherwise, driving is safe and Cubans are helpful with directions – though often vague when it comes to distances. There are very few road signs so a good map is essential; or be prepared to pick up hitchhikers who can direct you. Do not drive after dark; Cubans often drive with headlights on full beam and animals may wander onto the road. Away from cities, traffic congestion isn't a problem: you may travel miles without seeing another vehicle – even stretches of the autopista can be empty. In towns, traffic usually moves at the speed of bicycles and horses.

Car rental

Current rental charges range between CUC$45 and CUC$100 per day, depending on the vehicle, plus a deposit of CUC$200–300. The fee and deposit must be paid in advance (cash, non-US credit card, or travelers' checks). Unlimited mileage is included, but insurance and fuel are extra. The tank should be full when you start (check that it is – it's a common scam for staff to underfill it) and you must return the car empty – there are no refunds.

Super Collision Damage Waiver is compulsory. The cost depends on the make and size of the car, but is around CUC$20 for a compact car.

Check the car carefully for damage and scratches. Draw attention to anything you find, and insist that any damages are noted on the paperwork. Car-rental agents have all kinds of ruses for not returning the full deposit. Be sure to take out the maximum insurance cover possible; it is well worth the extra cost, in case of even minor scrapes or mishaps.

If you are involved in an accident or have something stolen from the car, report this to the police and be sure to get the right paperwork (*denuncia*) or you will not be able to claim insurance in Cuba or at home. The business at the police station will be time-consuming and may take many hours.

Cars can be rented through the desks of the major hotels in the cities and beach resorts. The main rental companies are Rex (www.rexcarrental.com), Cubacar, Havanautos, and Transtur (all on www.transtur.cu), and Vía Rent-a-Car (www.gaviota-grupo.com). They are all state-owned and there is little competition. They also rent cars with drivers. Other websites to try include www.havanacarhire.com and www.carrentalcuba.com.

Gas (petrol)

Buying gas used to be a nightmare. It still is for most ordinary Cubans who have no access to CUCs. Tourists and anyone else with convertible currency, however, can now make use of the **Cupet** gas stations, which you will find in all the main towns and, increasingly, in smaller provincial towns all over the island. Cupet stations normally offer minimal mechanical backup, as well as snack bars. Most are open 24 hours.

Private cars and taxis

You may prefer to let someone else do the driving. One way Cubans are making CUCs now is by driving visitors around (though the many crackdowns have hit unlicensed drivers hard). Some charge a flat rate for a half or whole day of sightseeing or for a particular excursion, for example from Havana to Varadero or Havana to Viñales and back. The price should be less than the cost of an organized tour with a state agency if two or more of you are traveling together. Always agree a price before you set off.

It is possible to organize a car and driver for a week – as long as you pay for all their food and lodging.

It will not always be apparent, but some private taxis are licensed and some are not – depending on whether the driver pays the hefty license fee-cum-tax imposed by the government. As you walk around the streets of Havana and other towns and cities you will constantly be asked if you want a taxi – most of these will be private operators, legal or illegal.

There is only one state taxi company: Cubataxi, tel: 7-855 5555 in Havana, although the cars vary. You can call them or pick them up from designated ranks (usually outside hotels, and major museums). They are usually cheap, friendly, reliable, and metered (starting at CUC$1, then up to CUC$1 per kilometer, depending on the car). In 2014, the government announced the privatization of Cubataxi, leasing the cars to their drivers, who will become self-employed. The old Russian Ladas will be replaced by ex-rental cars. **GranCar** tel: 7-881 0992, operates a taxi service in the shiny old vintage cars that all visitors appear to love, at CUC$25–30 per hour.

Coco-taxis

These are the little round, yellow, two-seater motorbike taxis that are fine (and fun) for short distances. They charge a minimum of CUC$3, and CUC$5–10 per hour.

Bici-taxis

These little rickshaw-type vehicles, drawn by bicycles, can be fun and are inexpensive – but agree a fare before you start, usually CUC$1–2 in town centers.

Horse carriages

In provincial towns horse-drawn wagons (called *coches*) provide an inexpensive bus service, and are widely used by local people. In tourist areas, such as Havana or Varadero, more luxurious carriages are available for sightseeing tours.

Cycling

Cycling is the way many Cubans get around, and you will have no trouble finding someone to mend a flat tire (see page 320). There are cycle lanes on many roads outside towns. Bring a strong lock, and be careful where you park, or you may find yourself going home without your bicycle. Don't cycle in the middle of the day when the sun is at its height, nor after dark as roads are poorly lit and you may hit a cow.

ACCOMMODATIONS

HOTELS AND CASAS PARTICULARES

LOOKING FOR A HOTEL

Foreign tour operators and hotel chains pay about half the listed price for groups of 15 or more, giving them space for the attractive packages of which the vast majority of tourists take advantage. Price categories given here reflect the rack rate an independent traveler will pay for a room. Low-season prices can be considerably lower than those provided here.

Tourist hotels are run by a variety of enterprises, and it is possible to ascertain the standard of the hotel from the name of the enterprise that manages it. For example, hotels run by Islazul tend to be two-star or three-star, while those run by Gran Caribe or Cubanacán are often four-star, although the star rating does not equate with what you would expect in a hotel abroad. Any hotel may occasionally lack hot water or air conditioning. In Old Havana there are many delightful boutique hotels in renovated mansions run by Habaguanex (www.habaguanexhotels.com). They come in a variety of sizes, ages, and prices, but the newer the renovation, the better they are; the first to be done up are now in need of repairs and refurbishment. In the resorts, there are joint-venture hotels run by foreign companies, such as Meliá (www.melia.com), from Spain, which runs 26 hotels around the island.

Commissions and Scams

The owners of casas particulares can book rooms for you in other towns, passing you along a network of contacts. This is a reliable service but you will pay an extra CUC$5 per night more than you would pay if you booked independently. Any taxi driver or tout taking you to a casa will receive a CUC$5 commission, too. If you have made a reservation by phone your host will probably meet you at the bus terminal. Don't be taken in by touts trying to divert you to other houses in order to get a commission.

CAMPSITES

Campsites operated by Campismo Popular are in every province. Campers sleep in huts (*cabañas*) not tents. Group showers and latrines prevail. Most sites are designed for Cuban tourists, and open only in July and August but a few are used for international tourism and open all year round. They have better amenities, such as flush toilets and hot water. International sites include Campismo Los Cocos, near Havana, and Villa Santo Domingo in the Sierra Maestra, in Granma province.

Reservations can be made with Cubatur on arrival (see page 352) or, better, booked from abroad through a specialty tour operator.

PRIVATE ROOMS (CASAS PARTICULARES)

Staying in a private house can be the most rewarding way of experiencing Cuba. Not only do you get to know the people more intimately than in a hotel, but there is usually a better standard of service, cleanliness and comfort than in the equivalent or higher value of hotel room. The food served is fresher and often cooked better, and special diets can be accommodated on request. Personal safety is excellent and theft is extremely rare. Your hosts' livelihood can be wiped out if guests complain to the authorities. Renting rooms in private houses has been legal since 1996, but they must be registered with the authorities and are subject to strict regulations. There are illegal, unregistered *casas particulares*, but these can be unsafe.

Casas particulares should display a blue sign, shaped rather like an anchor, on or above the front door.

It is illegal to let unless you register with the government and pay hefty taxes – but people do.

Cuban hosts must fill out a form with visitors' details, and present it to the police. You can now put a legally registered casa on your tourist card as your official place of residence.

There are thousands of *casas particulares* in Havana and provincial towns, especially Santiago, Trinidad, Viñales, and Baracoa. One useful website is www.casaparticularcuba.org, but the best way to find a *casa* is by recommendation from a fellow traveler.

Cuban Addresses

A few points on understanding addresses. An address written as Calle Martí 65, esq. Céspedes means it is at 65 Martí Street on the corner of (or intersection with) Céspedes Street. Similarly, Calle Martí 65, entre 9 y 11 means it is at 65 Martí Street between streets 9 and 11. You will also see Avenida 1ra or Avenida 5ta, which mean 1st Avenue or 5th Avenue. Piso 1º or Primer Piso means first floor. We use the anglicized form in our listings, but you will encounter the Spanish form in written material.

OLD HAVANA

Beltran de Santa Cruz
Calle San Ignacio, 411, between Muralla and Sol
Tel: 7-860 8330
www.habaguanexhotels.com
A lovely 18th-century former mansion, with beamed ceilings, stained glass, and blue-painted balconies. Eleven air-conditioned rooms overlook the courtyard and service is friendly and helpful. Only breakfast is available but there are a lot of restaurants in the area. **$–$$**

Hotel el Comendador
Calle Obrapía, corner of Baratillo
Tel: 7-867 1037
www.habaguanexhotels.com
Small, attractively restored 18th-century house in the heart of Old Havana with harbor views, sister hotel to the Valencia. Quiet, with 14 attractive rooms (with hairdryers) and a tapas bar on the ground floor. **$–$$**

Hostal Conde de Villanueva
Calle Mercaderes, 202, between Lamparilla and Amargura
Tel: 7-862 9293
www.habaguanexhotels.com
In the heart of Old Havana this is a specialist cigar-smokers' hotel (there's a giant model cigar in the lobby and rooms are named after tobacco plantations, but there are three non-smokers' rooms as well). Small and atmospheric, with a beautiful colonial patio, but the peacocks can be noisy through the night. It has its own cigar bar and Cuban restaurant. **$–$$**

Hotel Florida
Calle Obispo 252, corner of Calle Cuba
Tel: 7-862 4127
www.habaguanexhotels.com
Bang in the heart of Old Havana, this 19th-century building surrounds a lovely courtyard with marble floors and pillars. There is an elegant restaurant and a piano bar. Rooms have high ceilings, air conditioning, minibar, 24-hour room service, safe, and satellite TV, but can be noisy if there is a party in the courtyard. **$–$$**

Hostal Los Frailes
Calle Teniente Rey 8, between Oficios and Mercaderes
Tel: 7-862 9383
www.habaguanexhotels.com
A small, attractive colonial building converted to a hotel in the center of Old Havana, with the gimmick of having its bellboys dress up in monks' habits. It has 22 comfortable rooms overlooking the courtyard with air conditioning and private bathrooms but no windows. Four suites with balconies look out on to the street and do have windows. **$–$$**

Iberostar Parque Central
Calle Neptuno, between Zulueta and Prado (Paseo de Martí)
Tel: 7-860 6627
www.iberostar.com
A business hotel of international standard with efficient air conditioning, excellent bathrooms, good service, and a business centre. There is even Wi-fi in the lobby. It has a rooftop pool, a Jacuzzi with great views, a gym, and numerous bars, cafés, and restaurants. The food is good in the extremely formal ground-floor restaurant. **$$–$$$**

Hotel Inglaterra
Parque Central (Prado 416), between San Rafael and San Miguel
Tel: 7-860 8595/6/7
www.hotelinglaterra-cuba.com
Built in 1875, this historic hotel with a cool gold and white lobby, has entertained a long list of celebrities and is a national monument. It has a lovely 24-hour café-bar, with live music from the grand piano or a (rather deafening) mariachi band. The restaurant next door is beautiful, gently lit by chandeliers and stained glass, but the food doesn't live up to the decor. The small rooftop bar holds a salsa cabaret every night except Tuesday. The interior rooms tend to be rather stuffy but quiet, while those with balconies looking out over the Parque Central or the Gran Teatro, next door, are light but noisy. **$$**

Mercure Sevilla Havane
Trocadero 55, corner of Prado
Tel: 7-860 8560
www.mercure.com
The Sevilla opened in 1908 and was hugely popular with the American Mafia in the 1930s. Now operated by the French hotel chain, it has a wonderfully Spanish ambiance, with a cool, tiled lobby and delightful blue-tiled patio café complete with fountain. The ninth-floor restaurant, in what used to be the ballroom, has huge windows thrown open to catch the breeze and spectacular nighttime views – and the food is good. Rooms are simple but adequate. **$$–$$$**

Hotel Santa Isabel
Calle Baratillo 9, between Obispo and Narciso López, Plaza de Armas
Tel: 7-860 8201
www.hotelsantaisabel.com
A beautiful, renovated colonial palace, in the heart of Old Havana – a vision in turquoise and stone with a lovely courtyard. Popular with package tours. The best rooms are on the third floor with balconies overlooking the Plaza, while the café is also good for people watching. Excellent restaurant. One of the nicest hotels in the city but in need of a spruce up to warrant the price. **$$–$$$**

Hotel Saratoga
Prado 603, corner of Dragones
Tel: 7-868 1000
www.habaguanexhotels.com
A renovated neoclassical building opposite the Capitolio, with modern amenities, including Wi-fi in communal areas. Large, comfortable rooms and service are of a high standard. There's a rooftop pool and terrace with a great view over the Capitolio and along the Malecón to Vedado and a good tapas restaurant. **$$–$$$**

Hostal del Tejadillo
Calle Tejadillo 12, corner of San Ignacio
Tel: 7-863 7283
www.habaguanexhotels.com
There are 32 rooms set around two plant-filled courtyards, but only eight have windows letting in daylight and the others are poorly ventilated. There's a restaurant and lively bar, plus babysitting and laundry. Rooms, with lofty ceilings, all have minibars, safes, telephones, and cable TV. **$–$$**

Telégrafo
Prado 408, corner Neptuno
Tel: 7-861 1010
www.habaguanexhotels.com
This hotel first opened in 1860, but moved to this location in 1888 with only one floor. It closed for rebuilding and expansion in the 1990s and reopened in its present, modernized form in 2001. Very smart and efficient, the decor mingles the old with the new, with a state-of-the-art restaurant set amid the bare brick arches of the original building. Beds are comfortable and bathrooms are well equipped. **$–$$**

Hostal Valencia
Calle Oficios 53, corner of Obrapía
Tel: 7-867 1037
www.habanaguanexhotels.com
Just 10 rooms around a glorious vine-draped courtyard in a beautifully restored colonial mansion linked

PRICE CATEGORIES

Price categories indicate the cost of a double room in high season:
$ = under $80
$$ = $80–150
$$$ = $150–250

to El Comendador. Rather noisy in the morning when the water truck arrives, but the rooms are spacious and delightful, with original colonial features. Staffers are very friendly. Usually booked well in advance. **$–$$**

Casas Particulares

Most *casas particulares* in Havana charge about CUC$25–35 per room per night. Breakfast is usually extra (typically CUC$3–5 per person) and is usually large and very good – fresh fruit, fruit juice, coffee, and eggs any way you want them.

Casa Colonial 1715
Lamparilla 324, between Aguacate and Compostela
Tel: 7-864 4914
Roberto and Zoraida are hospitable and informative. They offer two rooms in their colorful colonial house with its high ceilings, tiled floors and stained glass. Each room has a double and single bed, air conditioning and private bathroom. If they are fully booked, Roberto's brother, William and Carmen run another good casa across the road.

Casa Colonial Maritza
Luz 115, between San Ignacio and Inquisidor
Tel: 7-862 3303
Two double rooms on the ground floor and one upstairs on the terrace, in a beautiful colonial house near the harbor, with an internal patio.

Casa Humberto
Compostela, 661, between Luz and Sol
Tel: 7-860 3264
Two large air-conditioned rooms with private bathrooms, and breakfast served on a shady plant-filled terrace outside your door. One tiny double room on the roof, where there's a huge terrace, with hammocks, for all guests' use. Run by a pleasant young couple, Humberto and Miladys.

Casa Maura
Refugio 104, between Morro and Prado
Tel: 7-864 3923
www.casamaura104.com
A very friendly and helpful household in a convenient location. Two rooms in a more modern apartment, each with private bathroom, air conditioning and fan. Maura serves excellent meals and can arrange tours and other activities.

Casa Yamelis
Jesús María 58, between Cuba and San Ignacio
Tel: 7-867 5065
Email: llanesrenta@yahoo.es
A recently renovated apartment in the southern part of the old city near Espíritu Santo and La Merced churches. Only one room, which sleeps three in double and single bed, well equipped with balcony, air conditioning and fan, refrigerator, and safe box.

Federico Llanes
Cárcel 156, between San Lázaro and Prado, 3rd floor
Tel: 7-861 7817
E-mail: fllanes@gmail.com
Good size rooms with tiled floors and air conditioning, new bathroom fittings, a good supply of hot water, and nice touches you don't always find, such as a wall safe, CD player, phone, and desk, as well as plenty of hanging space for clothes. English spoken.

Fefita y Luís
Prado 20, 5th floor, apt B, between San Lázaro and Cárcel
Tel: 7-867 6433
Two rooms. It's centrally located, and the owners, the food, the views of Old Havana and the harbor, and the comfortable beds are all wonderful.

Rafaela y Pepe – Los Balcones
San Ignacio 454, between Sol and Santa Clara
Tel: 7-867 5551
Three comfortable air-conditioned rooms, with balconies, share two bathrooms in this friendly house full of antiques, plants, and bric-a-brac. The elderly couple keep a clean home and offer a good breakfast.

CENTRO HABANA AND VEDADO

Hotel Habana Riviera
Paseo and Malecón, Vedado
Tel: 7-836 4051
www.hotelhavanariviera.com
Built by Mafia boss Meyer Lansky in 1957, it is rather overshadowed by the Meliá Cohiba next door. It has an excellent swimming pool (not always open), complete with original diving platform, and rooms with sea views, although they smell of mould. The lobby retains a 1950s appearance and atmosphere, and there's the lively Copa Room cabaret. **$$–$$$**

Hotel Nacional, Havana.

Hotel Meliá Cohiba
Paseo and Primera, Vedado
Tel: 7-833 3636
www.melia.com
Cuba's first five-star hotel, opened in 1995, on the seafront. It's not pretty, in architectural terms, but it is of an international standard with good service, and most of its 460 rooms have sea views. Filled to bursting with restaurants, cafés, bars, nightclubs, and shops, as well as a gym, a business center and, of course, a swimming pool. Some rooms are equipped for visitors with disabilities. **$$$**

Hotel Nacional
Calle 0 and 21, Vedado
Tel: 7-836 3564/5/6/7
www.hotelnacionaldecuba.com
Once Havana's top hotel, and still pretty classy, although the grandeur is rather faded and there is better food elsewhere. The rich and famous of the city's golden age in the 1940s and 1950s used to stay here – you can see their pictures in the corridors

and the Bar of Fame and take an historical tour on weekdays at 10am and 3pm, and Saturday at 10am. The neoclassical building is undeniably elegant. There are beautiful tropical gardens, tennis courts, and two pools, which can be used by non-guests (CUC$15, but you get CUC$15-worth of food and drink included). There are lovely views along the Malecón, and the Cabaret Parisien is the next best thing to the Tropicana, and cheaper too. **$$–$$$**

Hotel Roc Presidente
Calzada 110, and Avenida de los Presidentes, Vedado
Tel: 7-838 1801
www.roc-hotels.com
Built in the 1920s and one of the first high-rise buildings, the stylish hotel has an impressive marble-floored lobby, filled with antiques. About half the 158 rooms have sea views; some rooms are spacious, others rather small. Totally renovated in 2000, some areas need another makeover and you are recommended to eat elsewhere, but overall it has charm and the service is good. **$$–$$$**

Hotel Terral
Malecón, corner Lealtad, Central Havana
www.habaguanexhotels.com
A new hotel right on the Malecón, the modern rooms have big windows and a great view of the sea, although there is traffic noise. **$$–$$$**

Hotel TRYP Habana Libre
Calle L, between 23 and 25, Vedado
Tel: 7-834 6100
www.melia.com
A time capsule of 1950s design for decades, the Habana Libre is now just another high-rise modern hotel in need of refurbishment. Rooms are spacious and mostly comfortable. The higher you go, the more expensive because of the views, but renovation seems to have started from the top so rooms on the 17th floor are good. The hotel has a pool, several decent bars (including the rooftop Bar Turquino) and restaurants, a bank, and a range of shops. **$$$**

Casas Particulares

Armando Gutiérrez
Calle 21 62, Apt 7, between M and N Vedado
Tel: 7-832 1876
Comfortable and spacious air-conditioned rooms in an apartment on the fourth floor (there is an elevator) with private bath, a terrace with great views, and friendly owners who speak English, Italian, German, and French.

Jorge Coalla Potts
I 456, Apt 11, between 21 and 23, Vedado
Tel: 7-832 9032
www.havanaroomrental.com
Long-established casa with experienced and helpful hosts. Convenient location close to nightlife and good amenities. The bed even has an orthopaedic mattress.

Marta Vitorte
G 301, Apt 14, 14th floor, between 13 and 15, Vedado
Tel: 7-832 6475
www.casamartainhavana.com
Impeccable casa with wonderful views to the sea and over the city, four rooms with air conditioning and private bathrooms, substantial breakfast. This is one of the more expensive casas, Marta is a retired diplomat and speaks English. She also has a refurbished two-bedroom apartment for rent if you want to be self-contained.

Melba and Alberto
Galiano 115, Apt 81, between Animas and Trocadero, Centro
Tel: 7-863 5178; 5-264 8262 (cell/mob)
Email: barracuda1752@yahoo.es
The entrance off the street is not obvious and rather unwelcoming, but once you go up in the elevator to the eighth floor you are in a comfortable home with great views over Havana from the balconies. There are two rooms, one with its own balcony. You can use the kitchenette, which is useful for snacks, but Melba serves tasty, filling meals.

AROUND HAVANA

Miramar

Hotel Comodoro
Calle 84 and 3ra, Playa
Tel: 7-204 5551
www.hotelescubanacan.com
A resort complex that caters for all-inclusive vacations as well as business travelers, with rooms and bungalows – the latter are better, airy and pleasant with kitchens. Excellent swimming pool, and small private beach. The HabanaBusTour stops outside. **$–$$**

Hotel Meliá Habana
Avenida 3ra, between 76 and 80, Miramar
Tel: 7-204 8500
www.melia.com
This is a large modern hotel of international standard (409 rooms, including a number of suites) offering smooth service and all-round excellence. There are rooms with ocean views, five restaurants, three swimming pools, private beach, and a business center (Wi-fi throughout the hotel). Free bus shuttle to Old Havana. **$$$**

Casas Particulares

Casa Estudio Alicia
Calle 36 122, between Avenida 1 and 3, Miramar
Tel: 7-209 1365
One block from a beach and in walking distance of restaurants and bars, this *casa* offers the option of a self-contained studio apartment with kitchen upstairs or a bedroom in the family home downstairs. Transportation and guided tours can be arranged as well as laundry service and breakfast on request. English spoken.

Playas del Este

There are numerous concrete block hotels here,but none is outstanding.

Hotel Club Atlántico
Avenida de las Terrazas, corner of Calle 11, Santa María del Mar
Tel: 7-797 1085/6/7
www.gran-caribe.com
Bright and airy 1950s hotel on the beach with 92 air-conditioned rooms on three floors with no elevator. There is a pool and excellent beach. The all-inclusive buffet meals are no great culinary experience, but there are paladares in the area.
Free shuttle to Havana twice daily. **$–$$**

Casas Particulares

Iriana Suárez and Rosa Machado
Avenida 1ra 50017, between 500 and 504, Guanabo
Tel: 7-796 3959
Delightful seafront setting with a lawn running down to a seawall, and sun loungers on a balcony affording a wonderful view. Light and bright, the room has independent access, and a living area with a kitchenette. Minimum stay of seven nights in January and February. There are other *casas particulares* in this area,

PRICE CATEGORIES

Price categories indicate the cost of a double room in high season:
$ = under $80
$$ = $80–150
$$$ = $150–250

several also on the waterfront or a short walk away. Prices rise the closer you get to the sea.

Casa Julia Fuentes
Calle 474 9B02, between 9B and 11, Guanabo
Tel: 7-796 3633
Email: Julia.fuentes@informed.sld.cu
Two comfortable and clean rooms with independent access, with fridge. Barbeque area in the garden and views over Guanabo to the sea. Julia is helpful and informative and can arrange bike rentals. Good food and paladares close by.

VIÑALES AND THE WEST

Cabo San Antonio

Villa Cabo de San Antonio
Playa Las Tumbas
Tel: 48-778 131 ext 204
www.gaviota-grupo.com
Simple lodging in a small hotel on an isolated beach 4km/2.5 miles from a marina, where you can arrange fishing or scuba diving. Extremely quiet and peaceful although mosquitoes can be a problem at times. Car and bicycle rentals. If arriving by boat, bring cash. This is too remote for banking facilities. **$–$$**

Cayo Levisa

Hotel Cayo Levisa
Tel: 48-756 501
www.hotelcayolevisa-cuba.com
A resort and diving center – the only facility on the cay – with rustic, but air-conditioned cabins with porches, clustered beside the beach. Water sports are available, and there is a bar, a good 'international' and seafood restaurant; massage services. **$$–$$$**

Las Terrazas

Hotel Moka
Complejo Turístico Las Terrazas, Autopista Habana–Pinar del Río, Km 51 (take this turn, then it's 8km/5 miles farther)
Tel: 48-578 600
www.hotelmoka-lasterrazas.com
A beautiful hotel in Spanish-Cuban style in a purpose-built eco-complex. Forest trees pierce its split levels and patios. There are light, airy rooms in the main hotel, little cabins by the lake, and a few simple rooms in wooden huts in Baños de San Juan, 3km (2 miles) from the main hotel. Swim in the waterfall-fed pool, rent a bicycle, swing down a zip line across the lake into the trees, or spend time in the nearby artists' colony. **$**

María La Gorda

María La Gorda
Tel: 48-778 131
www.gaviota-grupo.com
A small-scale resort that's popular with divers, located in the far western region of Cuba. It's a peaceful and isolated place, set amid semi-deciduous woodland. Some rooms are in cabins directly on the beach, the newer ones are behind in the trees, but guests using these sometimes suffer from mosquitoes. Diving and meals can be included in packages; there is nothing else available here so you have to eat either in the restaurant, at the buffet, or have sandwiches in the bar. **$–$$**

Pinar del Río City

Islazul Vueltabajo
Calle José Martí 103, corner Rafael Morales
Tel: 48-759 381
www.islazul.cu
A town-center hotel with 39 small, dark, air-conditioned rooms in a pastel-pink colonial mansion. Ask for a room away from the street, which is noisy. The food is nothing special and overpriced and there may be some hassling in the bar with people trying to sell cigars. Services include car rental, currency exchange, a tourism bureau, and excursions. **$**

Soroa

Villa Soroa
Carretera de Soroa, Km 8, northwest of Candelaria
Tel: 48-523 534
www.hotelescubanacan.com
Rooms and villas (*casitas*) with good amenities in stunning landscaped gardens, plus a large pool. Some rooms have maintenance issues, but generally the hotel is in good condition and the staffers are friendly. Food is buffet style; get there early for the evening meal before the tour parties come in. Hiking round the local sights is organized. If you want to visit and swim but don't want to stay, it's only an hour's drive from Havana, and makes a pleasant daytime excursion (there are lockers for storing clothes). **$**

Viñales

Hotel La Ermita
Carretera la Ermita, Viñales, Km 2
Tel: 48-796 250
www.hotelescubanacan.com
Just above the town of Viñales, nicely located at the edge of the valley. La Ermita is a modern hotel of Spanish colonial design with 62 shabby rooms ranged around a good-sized swimming pool. Balcony rooms are the nicest, but there are great views from almost all rooms, especially lovely at dawn and sunset. Food is average. Non-guests can use the pool for a small charge, and it can get noisy. **$**

Hotel Los Jazmines
Carretera Viñales, Km 25
Tel: 48-796 210
www.hotelescubanacan.com
Los Jazmines is a handsome, colonial-style hotel in a magnificent setting at the top of a hill above the town, with the Viñales valley unfolding beneath. There are vine-draped gardens, a large, deep swimming pool, periodic poolside cabaret, a children's playground, and recreation hall. There are 62 rooms in the main building and 16 cabin-style rooms in an annex – most with balconies, and offering gorgeous views. However, furnishings are tired and stained, maintenance in the rooms is variable and food is poor-to-average. Horseback riding and other excursions are available. **$**

Casas Particulares

Pinar del Río

Villa Colonial José Antonio Mena
Gerardo Medina 67, between Adela Azcuy and Isidro de Armas
Tel: 48-753 173
Aficionados of colonial architecture will appreciate this house, with its columns, stained glass, high ceilings, and decorative work. The bedrooms have a refrigerator and fan, while outside in the courtyard garden there is a Jacuzzi in a gazebo.

Soroa

Hospedaje Estudio de Arte
Km 8.5 on the road past Villa Soroa
Tel: 48-598 116
This *casa particular* is attached to an art studio and paintings are all around the house. The room is spacious and the food is excellent, typical *comida criolla*.

Casa Los Sauces
1 km from autopista on the road to Villa Soroa
Tel: 5-228 9372

Hotel la Ermita, Viñales.

Rooms each have double and single bed; it is a comfortable house with friendly hosts. Ana Lidia works at the Orchidarium, is very knowledgeable about plants and has a beautiful garden.

Viñales

There are more than 280 *casas particulares* in this little town. Most of them offer excellent food. If you get one on the south side of the main street, Calle Salvador Cisneros (left side, coming from Pinar del Río), you get great views of the *mogotes*.

Casa El Cafetal
Calle Adela Azcuy Norte Final, s/n
Tel: 5-223 9175 (cell/mob)
A pretty house set in lush gardens producing fruit and coffee. Señora Marta Martínez is an agreeable hostess, her son is a climbing instructor, and her daughter is a chef. English is spoken.

Ridel y Claribel
Calle Salvador Cisneros, Pasaje B, 203C
Tel: 48-695 127
Two bedrooms on first floor, one with two double beds, the other with a double and a single bed. The rooftop terrace is a lovely place to relax after a busy day. A very friendly family, with some English spoken; helpful in arranging tours; Claribel cooks delicious meals.

Casa Villa Jorge and Ana Luisa
Calle Final de Policlínico 2C
Tel: 48-695 524
Three rooms in an immaculate house with lovely countryside views and even a small swimming pool in the backyard. Very friendly and helpful family, excursions and transportation arranged, delicious food.

Villa Los Reyes
Calle Rafael Trejo 134 and Salvador Cisneros 206C
Tel: 48-695 225
www.villalosreyes.net
Joan and her son run a house with large, comfortable rooms, with air conditioning, refrigerator stocked with beer and water, and tasty meals if required (vegetarian on request). Some English spoken, and Joan offers walking tours and other excursions.

VARADERO AND MATANZAS

Matanzas

Hotel E Velasco
Calle Contreras between Santa Teresa and Ayuntamiento
Tel: 45-253 880
www.hotelescubanacan.com
Built in 1902 on the Plaza Libertad, this glorious neoclassical boutique hotel was reopened in 2011 after a full renovation, including a spectacular lobby bar. Of the 17 rooms, only the suites have windows overlooking the square. The staffers are friendly and the service and food are both good . **$**

Varadero

There are now hotels running the length of the peninsula and Varadero provides some 18,000 rooms in total, most of them in all-inclusive beach resorts run by international companies. There are, however, a few small hotels in the older part of the resort that don't offer the same amenities, but the beach is just as good and you can walk to restaurants and bars.

Hotel Acuazul
Avenida 1ra and Calle 13
Tel: 45-667 132
www.islazul.cu
Located a couple of blocks from the beach. All-inclusive or bed and breakfast available. Basic, but friendly. It has a small pool, bar, and disco and you can use the amenities of the Villa Sotavento and Aparthotel Islazul Varazul. **$**

Los Delfines
Avenida de la Playa with Calle 39
Tel: 45-667 720
www.islazul.cu
Small Islazul hotel, right on the beach in downtown Varadero. Friendly and pleasant but tired and in need of renovation. Food is poor but there are plenty of paladares close by. **$$–$**

Hotel Dos Mares
Corner of Calle 53 and Avenida 1ra
Tel: 45-612 702
www.islazul.cu
A pleasant older building, in Spanish Mudéjar-style, in a great downtown location one block from the beach. The Dos Mares has just 34 well-worn rooms of varying sizes, with two suites for families with children. The food is awful so eat elsewhere, but the staffers are friendly and it is very cheap. **$**

Mansión Xanadú
Avenida Las Américas, Km 8.5
Tel: 45-668 482
www.varaderogolfclub.com
The swish mansion built in 1930 for industrialist Irenée Du Pont, who made the peninsula effectively his own private resort when he bought up most of it in 1926. The property was nationalized after the revolution, but retains most of its original fittings. Great for golf fans, as you get free green fees on the course it overlooks; and you have use of the swimming pool at the neighboring Meliá Las Américas. There's an excellent bar upstairs, with a fine view of the peninsula. Restaurant serves international cuisine (about CUC$30–50 a head including wine). Only six

PRICE CATEGORIES

Price categories indicate the cost of a double room in high season:
$ = under $80
$$ = $80–150
$$$ = $150–250

rooms, so book at least a month in advance. **$$$**

Meliá Las Américas
Autopista del Sur
Tel: 45-667 600
www.melia.com
Next to the Du Pont mansion (Mansión Xanadú), the Plaza América shopping mall, and the golf course – golf is included but you pay for cart rental – this hotel has a fabulous lobby with artworks, palms, and colored glass, and a pleasant sun deck and a good stretch of beach. All-inclusive rooms, suites, and bungalows of varying standards. No children under 18. **$$$**

Meliá Varadero
Carretera de Las Morlas
Tel: 45-667 013
www.melia.com
Next to the shopping mall and convention center, this is another hotel in the Spanish-run Meliá chain, with a spectacular seven-story spiraling atrium with parrots and trailing vines, and even glass elevators. There are 483 rooms and seven suites, all with balconies, most with sea views. Children are welcome here. The food is good. **$$$**

Mercure Cuatro Palmas
Avenida 1era, between 60 and 64
Tel: 45-667 040
www.mercure.com
The complex consists of a hotel on the beach side of Avenida Primera, and villas across the road. The villas provide less expensive accommodations. Both are designed with Spanish-type arcades and galleries beside the Centro Comercial Caiman, and convenient for shopping and restaurants. Helpful staff and a good atmosphere. **$$**

Paradisus Varadero Resort and Spa
Punta Francés
Tel: 45-668 700
www.melia.com
The most luxurious, ultra all-inclusive, five-star resort on the peninsula, with a spacious layout. It's relatively secluded, as is surrounded by the Reserva Ecológica. There are 510 suites in bungalows, with sea or garden views. All the amenities you would expect, with a huge pool, diving, children's club, and a range of entertainment. **$$$**

ROC Arenas Doradas
Autopista Varadero, Km 17
Tel: 45-668 150
www.roc-hotels.com
Two-story chalets, providing 316 rooms, set in 8 hectares (20 acres) of tropical gardens by the beach and backed by the Marina Chapelin. Good value all-inclusive. **$$**

ROC Barlovento
Avenida 1ra, between calles 9 and 12
Tel: 45-667 140
www.hotelesc.com
On the seaside promenade in downtown Varadero, the all-inclusive Barlovento has 272 attractive rooms in two three-story buildings and six houses. Adults only, no children under 16. Convenient for downtown restaurants, cafés, and shops if you want a change from hotel food. **$$**

Sol Palmeras
Autopista del Sur, Km 8
Tel: 45-667 009
www.melia.com
Part of the Las Américas complex, this all-inclusive hotel was Varadero's first joint venture with Spanish investors, dating from 1990. There is a busy, family atmosphere and the lobby has a touch of the jungle, complete with tropical birds; there's a thatched bar on an island in the swimming pool. Rooms, suites, and bungalows are laid out in a horseshoe shape. **$$$**

Villa Tortuga
Calle 7, between Avenida Kawama and Playa
Tel: 45-614 747
www.gran-caribe.com
A pleasant complex of scattered villas, with 292 all-inclusive rooms, close to the beach. Tennis court, nighttime entertainment, and cars for rent. Friendly staff. Good value for money. **$**

Casas Particulares

Matanzas

Hostal Alma
Calle 83 29008, between 290 and 292
Tel: 45-242 449
Email: hostalalma@gmail.com
Two rooms (one double, one triple), both with private bathrooms, refrigerator, and drinks in an attractive colonial house with beautiful stained glass, a large terrace, and a good view from the roof. Friendly host. Breakfast and evening meal are available.

Hostal Azul
Calle 83 29012, between 290 and 292
Tel: 5-273 7903 (cell/mob)
Email: hostalazul.cu@gmail.com
Beautiful mansion, dating from the 1870s, which still retains its original tiles and other architectural features. Two large rooms with big private bathrooms available. English and Italian spoken; very experienced and hospitable owners.

Varadero

Beny's House
Calle 55 124, between Avenidas 1 and 2
Tel: 45-611 700
www.benyhouse.com
A comfortable house, just a short walk from the beach, with a pleasant garden and patio for relaxing. A well kept casa with English-speaking family. Good quality and tasty meals.

Casa Mary y Angel
Calle 43, between Avenidas 1 and 2
Tel: 45-612 383
Email: marisabelcarrillo@yahoo.com
Good location very close to good stretch of beach as well as restaurants and bars. This casa has three bedrooms, all with good bathrooms, and is comfortable and spacious, with plenty of outdoor seating for relaxing in the evening. Excellent fresh home-cooked meals.

ZAPATA PENINSULA

Boca de Guamá

Horizontes Villa Guamá
Laguna de Tesoro, reached by boat from La Boca de Guamá
Tel: 45-915 551
www.hotelescubanacan.com
Mosquitoes are a big problem here and the disco is very noisy, but slap on the insect repellent, cover your arms and legs, and when the last tourist leaves at dusk this becomes a place of peace and loveliness. It is a replica of a pre-Columbian village, with thatched-roof *bohíos* built on wooden bridges over a lake to lodge guests. Cabins have modern amenities, and there is a pool. You can watch flocks of wild parrots descend to feed on the nectar of the bottlebrush trees and the dawn birding tour is recommended. The Villa Guamá was Fidel Castro's idea (in the early 1960s) and he used to be a regular visitor. He always used to sleep in cabin No. 33, so there's usually competition for that room. **$**

Jagüey Grande

Finca Don Pedro
Autopista Nacional Km 142
Tel: 45-912 825
www.hotelescubanacan.com
One km (0.5 mile) south of the Jagüey Grande highway intersection, on the road to Australia and Playa Larga, this small, rustic complex has 10 large log cabins with palm-thatched roofs, own

bathrooms, TV, fan, and refrigerator, and there's a small family-run restaurant. (Just down the road, the state-run Finca Fiesta Campesina serves good *criolla* food.) Mosquitoes can be a problem in summer, so bring repellent and cover your arms and legs at night. **$**

Playa Larga

Horizontes Playa Larga
Tel: 45-987 212
www.hotelescubanacan.com
Renovated in 2009, this hotel offers one- or two-bedroomed cabins with sitting rooms, by a small beach on the eastern edge of the village. It is cheap and cheerful, popular with local people during the summer and tour groups at any time of year – particularly those interested in birding and fly fishing – as it is well placed for exploring the Zapata Peninsula. **$**

Playa Girón

Hotel Playa Girón
Tel: 45-987 241
www.hotelescubanacan.com
A basic beach resort with 282 rooms in rather ugly concrete cabins. There are two pools, scuba diving and snorkeling, and equipment for rent. Bicycles and mopeds can also be rented, and guides can be arranged for visits to the local area. All in all, it is quite a pleasant place to stay if you're not too concerned about the architecture and get a cabin away from the disco (open until 4am). The food is poor, so seek out one of the local *paladares* instead. **$**

Casas Particulares

Playa Larga
Roberto Mesa Pujol
Caletón
Tel: 45-987 307
Email: casamesa@gmail.com
The garden of this house runs down to the beach, where there are palm trees and a volleyball net. There are three rooms for rent, with air conditioning, private bathrooms, and car parking space. There are several other beachfront houses in Caletón also offering a superb location.

Playa Girón
Hostal Luis
Carretera a Cienfuegos, on the corner of Carretera a Playa Larga
Tel: 45-984 258
This house on the main road is modern and well cared for. Luis García Padrón has four rooms for rent and provides secure parking for cars. Friendly and helpful hosts offer excellent food, and English is spoken.

SANTA CLARA TO SANCTI SPÍRITUS

Cayo Santa María

Iberostar Ensenachos
Cayo Ensenachos
Tel: 42-350 300
www.iberostar.com
An upscale and elegant resort spread over two lovely beaches in three sections: 270 rooms in the Park section for families; 190 rooms in the Spa section for adults only; and 46 luxury villas. Rooms are spacious with balconies and concierge service. Board walk to beautiful Mégano beach. **$$$**

Meliá Cayo Santa María
Cayo Santa María
Tel: 42-350 200
www.melia.com
This five-star, adults-only, all-inclusive resort has 360 rooms in bungalows set in 12 hectares (30 acres) of grounds by a gorgeous white beach, but not many have a sea view. A choice of restaurants includes buffet and à la carte, and there are all the usual Meliá resort amenities and services, with a range of water sports. **$$$**

Meliá Las Dunas
Cayo Santa María
Tel: 42-350 100
www.melia.com
A massive, all-inclusive resort, with 925 rooms in two-story buildings in manicured grounds so extensive that golf buggies are required to get around. It's in two parts: adults only and a family section. You can eat in a different restaurant every night of the week and there is a good range of activities and sports. **$$$**

Royalton Cayo Santa María
Cayo Santa María
Tel: 42-350 600
www.royaltonresorts.com
A luxury, adults-only resort on a superb white sand beach. Service is impeccable and the amenities are excellent. Plenty of activities are on offer, but generally, this is a quiet and peaceful place to relax. **$$$**

Sol Cayo Santa María
Cayo Santa María
Tel: 42-351 500
www.melia.com
A family resort, with 298 rooms in one- and two-story buildings set in pretty tropical gardens, some with ocean views. There is a choice of restaurants and bars, three pools, kids' club, and tennis courts, beside the pristine white beach where there are plenty of water sports on offer. **$$–$$$**

Villa Las Brujas
Cayo Las Brujas
Tel: 42-350 199
www.gaviota-grupo.com
A world apart from the mega-resorts in the area, this small hotel was the first on the cays and has only 24 cabins, reached by an elevated boardwalk above the rocks overlooking the beach. A place to come for peace and quiet, unpretentious and excellent value above a beautiful sweep of white sand. The restaurant has indoor or outdoor seating and offers a buffet breakfast, snacks, and à la carte meals. **$$**

Embalse Hanabanilla

Hanabanilla Hotel
Southwest of Manicaragua
Tel: 42-208 461
www.islazul.cu
An unappealing concrete Soviet creation, but with a breathtaking setting on Lake Hanabanilla, at the end of an 8km (5-mile) hill, in the Escambray Mountains south of Santa Clara. The lake is stocked with large-mouth bass and the hotel has its own dock and boats. There are 125 comfortable, air-conditioned rooms, a disco, well-stocked games room, 24-hour bar, and a lovely big pool (under renovation). Both rooms and public areas can be noisy, especially on weekends. The restaurant specializes in lake-caught fish and will gladly cook and serve your catch. It's a good base for hiking, boating, and horseback riding, and there are waterfalls and caves to explore. **$**

Remedios

Hotel E Mascotte
Máximo Gómez 114 (Parque Martí)
Tel: 42-395 144
www.hotelescubanacan.com
A wonderful 18th-century mansion beautifully renovated in 2009 and

PRICE CATEGORIES

Price categories indicate the cost of a double room in high season:
$ = under $80
$$ = $80–150
$$$ = $150–250

part of the Encanto chain. Some of the 10 rooms have French windows opening onto balconies with wrought-iron railings. The food is good and the place oozes nostalgia. It's the only hotel in Remedios. **$–$$**

Santa Clara

Hotel Santa Clara Libre
Parque Vidal 6
Tel: 42-207 548
www.islazul.cu
Basic accommodations: the 159 rooms in the dilapidated 10-story hotel have showers and radios, but don't all have air conditioning. It's not an attractive building, but is conveniently sited on the main square (it's not always easy to park nearby). A better standard of accommodations can be found at *casas particulares* in town. There are good views from the top-floor restaurant (which serves a decent breakfast), and the rooftop bar. The hotel was home to Che Guevara and many of his men after the battle of Santa Clara; its facade is still pock-marked by shells fired during the 1958 battle. **$**

Villa Los Caneyes
Circunvalación and Eucalyptos
Tel: 42-218 140
www.hotelescubanacan.com
On the main *autopista* 1.6km (1 mile) west of the Che Guevara monument, this motel was designed to resemble an Amerindian settlement. The conical thatched-roof huts contain 95 comfortable, spacious rooms, with hot water, TV, refrigerators, and air conditioning. The garden setting is delightful and there are a lot of animals around, although many are caged, as in a zoo. The pool provides the focus, overlooked by a bar, disco, and a restaurant. Those who wish to hunt can make use of the Los Caneyes hunting lodge, and there's bass fishing in Alacranes dam, Cuba's second-largest reservoir. Frequently used by tour groups for overnight stays. Day passes are available for those staying elsewhere. There are taxis into town, and car rental can be organized. Excellent value. **$**

Sancti Spíritus

Hotel E Del Rijo
Calle Honorato del Castillo 12, corner Máximo Gómez
Tel: 41-328 588
www.islazul.cu
A 16-room hotel in a well-restored mansion, built in 1827, that belonged to a renowned local doctor, for whom it is named. Renovation works included stained-glass windows with shutters and wrought-iron fretwork. Comfortable rooms, meals in a pretty courtyard with plants and a fountain, and a central location make it an ideal choice. **$**

Hotel E Plaza
Parque Serafín Sánchez
Tel: 41-327 102
www.islazul.cu
Lovely colonial architecture with a distinctive blue facade and a central garden courtyard. There are 25 large and airy rooms with high ceilings, air conditioning, and satellite TV. Some have balconies overlooking the plaza, which can make them noisy at night on weekends. There's also a restaurant and a 24-hour snack bar. **$**

Casas Particulares

Remedios

La Casona Cueto
Alejandro del Río 72, between Enrique Malaré and Máximo Gómez
Tel: 42-395 350
A gem of an 18th-century house with many of original features, and stuffed with antiques in the huge living room. There is a lovely interior patio with fountain. Owner Jenny Cueto offers two large rooms with modern bathrooms, plus car parking and a roof terrace, and household pets include dogs, doves, and turtles.

Hostal Villa Colonial
Calle Antonio Maceo 43, between General Carrillo and Fé del Valle
Tel: 42-396 274
An attractive colonial house decorated with beautiful tiles and furnished with antiques, run by Frank and Arelys, who are most hospitable. There is a small patio where you can enjoy a *mojito*, two rooms for guests, and a dining room.

Sancti Spíritus

Hostal Las Américas
Carretera Central 157 Sur, between Cuba and Cuartel
Tel: 41-322 984
Email: hostallasamericas@yahoo.es
Modern house in a large and productive garden. Two big rooms with stocked refrigerator, TV, DVD, MP3 player, hair dryer, and safe deposit box. Meals, snacks, and cocktails are available and special requirements accommodated. English and Italian spoken.

Hostal Santa Elena
Calle Santa Elena (Calle del Gas) 42, between Carretera Central and Onza
Tel: 41-329 218
Email: saraelito07@yahoo.es
Quite a distance from the town centre – 25 minutes' walk, or get a bicitaxi – but it's worth the journey. This immaculately clean and well-presented house offers three guest rooms, and Sara and Elio and their staff are welcoming and helpful. German and some English spoken.

Santa Clara

Casa Mercy
Calle San Cristóbal 4, between Cuba and Colón
Tel: 42-216 941; 5-283 6076 (cell/mob)
Email: casamercy@gmail.com
Excellent modernized house in city center, run by friendly, experienced hosts – Omelio, Mercedes, and family – who can manage several languages between them. The guest rooms and bathrooms are separate from the family quarters, upstairs and overlooking the street. Roof terrace, laundry, good cooking, any diet catered for, good cocktails, and rum tasting too.

Hostal Florida Center
Calle Candelaria 56, between Colón and Maceo
Tel: 42-208 161
Traditional 19th-century colonial house around an interior patio garden crammed with plants, orchids galore, as well as dogs, cats, and birds. It was the winner, in 2008, of the architectural conservation award. The guest rooms open on to the patio and have a lot of antique fixtures and fittings for decoration, while mattresses are up to modern standards. Host Angel Rodríguez also runs a *paladar* on the patio and speaks some English, French, and Italian.

CIENFUEGOS AND TRINIDAD

Cienfuegos

Hotel E Casa Verde
Calle 37, between calles 0 and 2
Punta Gorda
Tel: 43-551 003
www.gran-caribe.com
The newest of the boutique hotels in the Encanto chain, this pretty green house at the far end of the peninsula dates from the early 20th century and has been totally renovated with eight well-equipped rooms and huge bathrooms. There is a restaurant and bar, but meals are often taken at Hotel Jagua across the road. **$**

Hotel Jagua, Cienfuegos.

Hotel E Palacio Azul
Calle 37 1202, between calles 12 and 14, Punta Gorda
Tel: 43-551 020
www.gran-caribe.com
Only seven rooms, in a beautiful, pale-blue neoclassical mansion built in the 1920s, converted into a hotel in 2003. Three rooms have balconies, with great views, and all have air conditioning, TV, and a minibar. There's also a small dining room for breakfast and snacks. You get a great view over the harbor from the little turret on the roof and you can use the pool and other amenities at La Unión. **$**

Hotel Jagua
Calle 37 1, between calles 0 and 2, Punta Gorda
Tel: 43-551 003
www.gran-caribe.com
Located 3km (2 miles) south of the heart of the city, this was once a notorious casino hotel run by Batista's brother. Externally, it's monolithic and ugly, but the 145 large rooms have air conditioning, TV, good bathrooms and a great view, although you can't rely on power or water. There's a large pool, but no beach, and a CUC$5 cabaret show every night except Wednesday. **$$**

Hotel La Unión
Calle 31, corner of 54
Tel: 43-551 020
www.gran-caribe.com
By far the most attractive option in town, this huge mansion has interior patios, a pretty pool, and comfortable rooms and suites with antique furnishings. Sauna, Jacuzzi, internet, car rental, bars, and the 1869 restaurant. **$$**

Guajimico

Villa Guajimico
Carretera a Trinidad, Km 45, Cumanayagua
Tel: 43-540 947
www.cubamarviajes.cu
On the coast between Cienfuegos and Trinidad, this hotel specializes in scuba diving. It has 51 small but attractive cabins, with air conditioning, in an attractive rural and remote location overlooking the mouth of Río La Jutía. Take a flashlight and insect repellent. There are 14 dive sites, 10–15 minutes from shore and scuba diving trips run twice a day. Dive gear (and kayaks) available for rent . **$**

Playa Ancón

Brisas Trinidad del Mar
Península Ancón
Tel: 41-996 500
www.hotelescubanacan.com
The most colorful of the Playa Ancón establishments, this mid-range all-inclusive hotel has 240 rooms in two- and three-story blocks around a pool – and its own bell tower. Popular with package-tour groups, it offers dance classes and beach volleyball. A children's program makes it ideal for families. Good water sports, including scuba lessons, tennis and a gym. Bland food, disinterested service. **$$**

Hotel Club Amigo Ancón
Carretera María Aguilar
Tel: 41-996 120
www.hotelescubanacan.com
The three-star Ancón is a rather unattractive five-story block, albeit with a great location, right on the beach. Rooms are small and in need of a face-lift, but are air-conditioned and have bath and radio. There are several bars, a swimming pool, and bicycles for rent. **$$**

Trinidad

Iberostar Grand Hotel Trinidad
Calle José Martí 262 and Lino Pérez (Parque Céspedes)
Tel: 41-996 070
www.iberostar.com
A hotel in a gorgeous renovated colonial building with a green-and-white facade. The 36 standard rooms and four suites are elegant and comfortable, but there's no pool or external patio. No children under 15. **$$–$$$**

La Ronda
José Martí, between Lino Pérez and Colón
Tel: 41-998 538
Renovated in 2012, this traditional colonial building has rooms on two floors around a central patio and a rooftop bar that is lovely for sunset watching at Happy Hour. Friendly staff and good service, including amusing towel art on the bed. **$**

Casas Particulares

Cienfuegos

Bella Perla Marina
Calle 39 5818, corner Avenida 60
Tel: 43-518 991
Email: bellaperlamarina@yahoo.es
A period piece, built in the 1950s, with furniture and fittings from that era. Two rooms and a new suite are available, with private bathrooms, and there's a nice family atmosphere. Hosts are welcoming and knowledgeable about the region, and English and Italian are spoken. Rooftop terrace, lovely garden, extensive views, and good food.

Los Delfines
Calle 35, 4E, between Litoral and 0, Punta Gorda
Tel: 43-520 458
www.casalosdelfines.blogspot.co.uk
At the tip of Punta Gorda, this comfortable and welcoming casa has two rooms. The one on the top floor has access to a delightful terrace, where you can eat your meals with wonderful views over the harbor.

Trinidad

There are hundreds of *casas particulares* in Trinidad, some excellent, some less so, but most

PRICE CATEGORIES

Price categories indicate the cost of a double room in high season:
$ = under $80
$$ = $80–150
$$$ = $150–250

perfectly acceptable. If arriving by bus, you will find people outside the terminal offering rooms. It is better to make advance reservations and always reconfirm by phone a couple of days in advance as at busy times the whole town can be full.

Casa Colonial Muñoz
Calle José Martí 401, between Fidel Claro and Santiago Escobar
Tel: 41-993 673
www.casa.trinidadphoto.com
A lovely, breezy colonial house in the center of Trinidad, with huge shuttered windows in the living room, tiled floors, and family heirlooms. Three large guest rooms, one of which is a duplex, have en-suite bathrooms, refrigerator, air conditioning, and safe box; there is parking, a patio, and roof terrace. Julio (a photographer) and Rosa speak English and keep dogs and horses. Photography workshops, horseback riding, and other excursions are available. Book in advance.

Dr Rogelio Inchauspi Bastida
Calle Simón Bolívar 312, between Maceo and Martí
Tel: 41-994 107
Two rooms and bathrooms with fan and a good supply of hot water. The roof terrace is a delight, with a 360° view. Friendly service and excellent food. Book in advance.

Casa Font
Gustavo Izquierdo 105, between Simón Bolívar y Piro Guinart
Tel: 5-821 9553
www.hostalcasafont.com
One of Trinidad's most stylish casas, with crystal chandeliers in the main reception room, antiques, and stained-glass *mamparas* (swing doors). Three rooms with air conditioning and private baths. Helpful family; good food; English spoken. Reserve in advance.

Hospedaje Yolanda
Piro Guinart 227, between Izquierdo and Maceo
Tel: 41-996 381
Email: yoliaye@gmail.com
Four nice rooms with air conditioning and private baths in huge, busy house. The room on the top floor has views of the coast. The bus station is across the road.

Casa Meyer
Gustavo Izquierdo 111, between Simón Bolívar y Piro Guinart
Tel: 41-993 444
www.hostalcasameyer.com
Another historic house stuffed with antique furniture, chandeliers, and family heirlooms, with the advantage of a lovely courtyard garden at the back where you can relax. Alejandro and his mother, Mercedes, speak English, French, and some German, and provide good food and helpful advice

Hostal Sandra y Víctor
Maceo 613, between Piro Guinart and Pablo Pichs
Tel: 41-996 444
www.hostalsandra.com
Two rooms with private bathrooms and air conditioning, dining room, balcony, and nice back garden patio for relaxing. Pleasant, well-maintained house, and Sandra and Víctor offer good, filling meals with plenty of variety.

EASTERN LOWLANDS

Camagüey

Hotel Colón
Avenida República 472, between San José and San Martín
Tel: 32-283 346
www.islazul.cu
A small, elegant, if slightly jaded, 1920s hotel in downtown Camagüey, with a lovely columned lobby, old wood-topped bar, and a stained-glass window picturing Christopher Columbus landing in Cuba. On arrival you are greeted with a towel and welcome cocktail – a nice touch. Rooms are small, simple, and can be noisy, but have TV and air conditioning. Food is poor; drinks are cheap. **$**

Gran Hotel
Calle Maceo 67, between Agramonte and Gómez
Tel: 32-292 094
www.islazul.cu
The best of the hotels in town, established in 1939 in an 18th-century mansion, right in the heart of Camagüey. Rooms surround a central patio with a fountain. There is a pool where synchronized swimming is offered as evening entertainment. The bar and restaurant (food nothing special) on the fifth floor offers the best views in town (aside from the cathedral bell tower). There is also a 24-hour café on the ground floor. **$**

Cayo Coco

Emperador Laguna Villas & Resort
Avenida de los Hoteles
Tel: 33-301 470
A massive all-inclusive resort complex, partly on a lagoon, a few minutes' walk from the extensive beach. Rooms and suites are in blocks or there are villas on stilts over the lagoon. A lot of sporting amenities, restaurants, and bars. **$$$**

Memories Flamenco Beach Resort
Tel: 33-304 100
www.memoriesresorts.com
An all-suite, all-inclusive resort for all the family on a gorgeous beach, although there are rocks at the water's edge. With 624 rooms, this is a large complex offering a lot of activities for families and couples. Memories also has Caribe Beach on Cayo Coco (formerly Blue Bay), which is not as modern.. **$$$**

Tryp Cayo Coco
Tel: 33-301 300
www.melia.com
Modeled as a simulated colonial township, this 508-room complex is just 100 meters/yds in from a glorious white-sand beach. At the center is the airy town hall, with a colonnaded portico, tiled floors, and a central patio where reception is located. Accommodations are in two- or three-story buildings with terracotta tile roofs, each named for the flower planted in front: azucenas (madonna lilies); *mariposas* (butterfly jasmine); *claveles* (pinks); and so on. Gourmet, à la carte, buffet, barbecue, and other specialties are served in eight pleasantly designed restaurants. There are amenities for all the usual water sports, and catamaran trips to outlying islands are offered. Also on Cayo Coco are the Hotel Meliá Cayo Coco and the Sol Cayo Coco in the same Spanish chain, with good amenities and plenty of entertainment. **$$$**

Cayo Guillermo

Allegro Club Cayo Guillermo
Tel: 33-301 712
www.occidentalhotelscuba.com
An attractive, colourful 212-room hotel (formerly Villa Cojímar) at the eastern end of the island, consisting of bungalows set among lawns and gardens. There's a lovely beach and excellent diving, and kite surfing is particularly good here. The food is not up to the standard of some of the other resorts, but neither is the price. **$$**

Iberostar Daiquirí
Tel: 33-301 650
www.iberostar.com

Large, 4-star, all-inclusive resort with rooms in blocks around the pool. Some have been refurbished, but others are a bit dated. Family friendly, with children's club and other activities. Pleasant strip of beach with thatched umbrellas and palm trees for shade. **$$$**

Meliá Cayo Guillermo
Tel: 33-301 680
www.solmeliacuba.com
All-inclusive hotel, with very good service and attention to detail. The 301 rooms in a low-rise, 5-star hotel on the beach, are decorated in blue with a nautical theme. Thatched umbrellas give shade on the beach and a long pier stretches out into the sea. Good for honeymooners or families. **$$$**

Sol Cayo Guillermo
Tel: 33-301 760
www.solmeliacuba.com
An all-inclusive hotel with rooms and bungalows, the nicest of which are close to the beach. Service is attentive and the food is varied. Good for families; there are plenty of activities and entertainment. **$$$**

Ciego de Ávila

Hotel Ciego de Ávila
Carretera de Ceballo, Km 2.5
Tel: 33-228 013
www.islazul.cu
The usual Soviet-designed 5-story monolith, with 143 air-conditioned rooms and a pool (not always filled), located 3km (2 miles) north of the center. It's popular with tour groups, and very, very cheap. **$**

Hotel Santiago-Habana
Calle Honorato Castillo, between Joaquín Agüero and Chicho Valdés
Tel: 33-225 703
www.islazul.cu
Renovated in 2009, this hotel is in the center of town. It comprises 76 air-conditioned rooms with private bathrooms; those at the front have balconies. **$**

Morón

Hotel Morón
Avenida de Tarafa
Tel: 33-502 230
www.islazul.cu
This is a concrete hotel on the outskirts of town. The 144 rooms (not all currently in operation) have all the usual amenities, with air conditioning and private bathrooms. Suites have their own balconies. The hotel has a restaurant, bars, pool, and tourism bureau. It is very noisy on weekends when there is loud music all day and a pool disco all night. **$**

Najasa

Hacienda La Belén
Five km (3 miles) from Najasa, 54km (34 miles) southeast of Camagüey
Tel: 32-864 349
www.ecoturcuba.tur.cu
One of the nicest rural hotels in Cuba, operated by Ecotur, with only 10 rooms and a pool. Breakfast is included and other meals are available, as are horseback riding, hiking, and birding. Book in advance. **$**

Santa Lucía

Club Amigo Mayanabo
Tel: 32-336 184
www.hotelescubanacan.com
All-inclusive three-star hotel set 100 meters/yds from the beach, with 213 simple but clean rooms and 12 suites in two blocks between pool and beach. Water sports include diving, snorkeling, kayaking, and windsurfing, there are courts for basketball, volleyball, and tennis, and dance classes are available. **$$**

Gran Club Santa Lucía
Tel: 32-365 145
www.hotelescubanacan.com
All-inclusive villa complex, with 108 rooms on a broad stretch of the beach and 144 garden rooms. A lot of activities for all ages, including a disco, games room, bicycle rental and good entertainment for kids. **$$**

Casas Particulares

Camagüey City

Casa Caridad
Oscar Primelles 310, between Bartolomé Masó and Padro Olallo
Tel: 32-291 554
A colonial house with small but very clean rooms, and everything works. The high point of the casa is the lovely garden patio, where you can sit and relax, with vines and trailing plants over a high wall. Very professional host is expert at arranging things. There is also a garage with safe parking.

Casa Miriam
Calle Joaquín de Agüero 525, between 25 de Julio and Perucho Figueredo, Reparto La Vigía
Tel: 32-282 120
Email: miriamhouse29@yahoo.com
Well-maintained accommodations in a modern house north of the center, with two large guest rooms, each with excellent bathroom, good beds, and plenty of storage space. Large roof terrace with pot plants, dogs, and cats. Miriam speaks English, is full of information, and cooks a wonderful breakfast and wholesome three-course meals.

Los Vitrales
Calle Avellaneda 3, between Gómez and Martí
Tel: 32-295 866
Email: requejobarreto@gmail.com
Three rooms in a colonial house with a friendly, English-speaking host – and an extra room in his sister's house upstairs means that groups of eight can be accommodated. New bathrooms, new beds, and many original features, including a colonial-era kitchen (there is a more modern one too) where they serve good traditional meals. There's a pleasant patio bedecked with of flowering plants.

Morón

Morón is convenient for the cays and accommodations here are cheaper than those on the beach. If you just want a day or two of sun, sea, and sand, it is worth staying here and hiring a driver to take you to the best places away from the all-inclusive resorts.

Hostal Alicia
Libertad 90, between Martí and Castillo
Tel: 33-505 194
Email: katiavaz@enet.cu
A clean and comfortable house, run by very helpful owners who can arrange transportation and connections for you. Delicious meals and huge breakfasts to set you up for the day. Very friendly and hospitable.

Maité Valor Morales
Calle Luz Caballero 40-b, between Libertad and Agramonte
Tel: 33-504 181
Email: maite68@enet.cu
This is an upscale and professional household, with English and Italian spoken and a lot of advice and information offered. There are three rooms available: one is very spacious and has two big beds and a kitchenette. The other is smaller and its bathroom is not en suite. The garage has been converted into a dining room where tour parties can be served and huge dinners are offered, but that still leaves plenty of parking space.

PRICE CATEGORIES

Price categories indicate the cost of a double room in high season:
$ = under $80
$$ = $80–150
$$$ = $150–250

HOLGUÍN AND GRANMA

Bayamo

Hotel Royalton
Calle Maceo 53, between Donato Mármol and José Joaquín Palma
Tel: 23-422 290
www.islazul.cu
A small traditional-style hotel on the main square that was totally renovated and reopened in 2010. Rooms are simple but smart, and all have air conditioning and private baths with good showers and hot water. Restaurant and bar downstairs and another rooftop bar and terrace for good views and sunbathing; à la carte breakfast is included in the room rate. Staffers are friendly and service is good. **$**

Villa Santo Domingo
Carretera La Plata, Km 16, Santo Domingo
Tel: 23-565 568
www.islazul.cu
A small hotel in the mountains by the entrance to the National Park, a base for trips into the Sierra Maestra and a fabulous location by a river. There are rooms in rustic single-story cabins or in newer, smarter, two-story wooden houses. The food is awful, but there is a *paladar* down the road that is a good alternative. **$**

Cayo Saetía

Villa Cayo Saetía
Tel: 24-516 900
www.gaviota-grupo.com
A secluded 12-room bungalow hotel, in a nature reserve on an island, was once a hunting ground for the wealthy. The animals, such as antelope and zebra, now roam freely, while enormous iguana stroll in the garden and jutía scuttle in the bush. The cottages, reception, and a restaurant are inland. There is another bar and restaurant on a pristine beach, which is used by catamaran day trips from Guardalavaca. If arriving by car you need your passport and there is a charge to enter. Snorkeling, jeep safaris, and horseback riding. **$$**

Chivirico

Brisas Sierra Mar
Carretera Chivirico Km 60, Playa Sevilla, west of Santiago de Cuba, 12km (8 miles) east of Chivirico
Tel: 22-329 110 and 326 160
www.hotelescubanacan.com
At the foot of the Sierra Maestra, more than an hour's drive from Santiago airport, this older all-inclusive resort is popular with Canadians. Extensive damage by Hurricane Sandy in 2012 has mostly been repaired and the beach has sand again. A variety of restaurants serve decent food or there's a *paladar* across the road; fitness center, shopping mall, freshwater pool, art gallery, games room, disco, and cabaret; Spanish, dancing, and history lessons. Plenty of water sports, tennis, and volleyball, plus good hiking, biking, and birding tours. **$$**

Gibara

Ordoño
Peralta, between Donato Mármol and Independencia
Tel: 24-844 448
www.hotelescubanacan.com
A local landmark and architectural gem, recently restored as a boutique hotel, offering 27 rooms and suites in this picturesque fishing town. The rooftop bar is a great place for sunset watching. The rooms are still in good condition and the food is good, making this a worthwhile place to stay. **$**

Guardalavaca/Playa Esmeralda/Playa Pesquero

Blau Costa Verde Beach Resort
Tel: 24-433 510
www.blau-hotels.com
One of many new all-inclusive hotels in this area, this one is in two sections, and is more luxurious. Blocks of rooms are built around a pool complex a short walk from a pretty arc of sand where there are thatched umbrellas for shade. **$$$**

Brisas Guardalavaca
Tel: 24-430 218
www.brisasguardalavaca.com
All-inclusive, 230 rooms in the hotel and 200 in villas. The hotel part is popular with honeymooners, the villas with families. The hotel section is more lively, but ask for rooms away from the disco. Amenities include a water sports center, pool, disco, tennis courts, bikes for rent, and several restaurants and bars. **$$–$$$**

Club Amigo Atlántico Guardalavaca
Tel: 24-430 180
www.clubamigo.gvc.tur.cu
This amalgamation of older accommodations consists of a moderately priced hotel on the beach, a 1970s hotel set around a pool, and a clutch of newer villas a short walk from the beach. Nothing fancy but good value for money. **$$**

Paradisus Río de Oro Resort & Spa
Tel: 24-430 090
www.melia.com
One of Cuba's most luxurious resorts, this is the best hotel in the area, with a Royal Service section for extra luxury. It's all-inclusive, five star, tasteful, and expensive. There's a spa for pampering and good restaurants, including a Japanese one, although the menu doesn't change often enough for longer stay visitors. **$$$**

Playa Costa Verde
Tel: 24-433 520
www.gaviota-grupo.com
A large, all-inclusive resort, with low blocks of spacious rooms on extensive grounds. Cigar lounge and piano bar, and a number of play areas and pool for small children. Good standard of food, maintenance, cleanliness, and service. Nice beach, but water shoes recommended. **$$$**

Playa Pesquero
Tel: 24-433 530
www.gaviota-grupo.com
A vast all-inclusive resort with 1,000 rooms in blocks surrounding the pool area. Every amenity you could want, a range of entertainment, and a variety of food and good drinks. Staffers are attentive and efficient. **$$$**

Riu Playa Turquesa
Playa Yuraguanal
Tel: 24-433 540
www.riu.com
Pleasant and attractive all-inclusive resort set back from the beach with rooms in several blocks. Be prepared for a lot of walking, with hills and stairs to negotiate, if you are in one of the far-flung blocks, although golf carts are available. A good selection of sports, activities, and entertainment, including a multi-level pool complex with waterfalls.

Sol Río de Luna y Mares
Playa Esmeralda
Tel: 24-430 060
www.melia.com
A 445-room hotel in gardens, with excellent water sports amenities, and several good restaurants. Livelier than the Paradisus next door, but less luxurious. The beach is a lovely horseshoe shape and the water is great for snorkeling around the rocks at the edge. The beach bar doubles as a disco at night. **$$$**

Holguín City

Mirador de Mayabe
Loma de Mayabe

Tel: 24-422 160
www.islazul.cu
In an isolated but scenic spot 10km (6 miles) southeast of Holguín, this is an attractive villa with cabins among trees and a magnificent view over the valley from the pool area. Unfortunately it is very run down and food is poor, although it is very lively and noisy on weekends when Cuban families come for a stayover and to drink and eat around the pool. **$**

Marea del Portillo

Club Amigo Marea del Portillo/ Farallón del Caribe
Carretera Granma Km 12.5
Tel: 23-597 103; 5-970 813 (cell/mob)
www.hotelescubanacan.com
Two all-inclusive hotels, with golf buggy shuttle between the two and shared amenities. The Marea del Portillo section is on the beach, but rather run-down; the rooms and food at Farallón del Caribe are better. A range of excursions is available, including boat trips, horseback riding, and hiking; good scuba diving. Cars and mopeds for rent. Plenty of evening entertainment. Some food items and wine often run out, so bring any supplies you particularly need. **$$**

Mayarí

Villa Pinares de Mayarí
32km (20 miles) south of Mayarí
Tel: 24-503 308
www.gaviota-grupo.com
At 600 meters (2,000ft) above sea level, between Holguín and Moa, this peaceful complex comprises 28 log cabins in a woodland setting. It has a pleasant bar-restaurant, pool, and mountain bike rental, and will book excursions to the Mensura National Park, which is excellent for hiking and birding. There are some lovely waterfalls in the area, notably Capiro, which you can reach on foot or horseback, and Guayabo, the highest in Cuba, which is best visited on your way up to or down from the hotel. Mostly used by tour groups and often closed if no party is expected. **$**

Casas Particulares

Bayamo

Arturo y Esmeralda
Calle Zenea 56, between Wiliam Soler and Capote
Tel: 23-424 051
casabayamo@gmail.com
A modernized house with new bathrooms, air conditioning, roof terrace (with a self-contained room), laundry service, and plenty of good, wholesome food. Friendly and helpful family. The owners currently have four guest rooms and are expanding next door to add four more as funds permit.

Olga Celeiro Rizo
Calle Parada 16, between Martí and Mármol, above Cubana office
Tel: 23-423 859
Apartment with two bedrooms with private bathrooms. There's a balcony off the living room, from where you can take in life on the square below. Friendly hosts offer good meals, including breakfast, and can help arrange excursions.

Gibara

Hostal Las Brisas
Peralta (Malecón) 61, between Juan Mora and Mariano Grajales
Tel: 24-845 134
Excellent location on the waterfront with a terrace for sunset watching. Good rooms and bathrooms, very good food, helpful staff. Short walk to other restaurants and bars.

Holguín

Don Santiago
Calle Narciso López 258, Apt 3, 2nd floor, between Coliseo and Segunda
Tel: 24-426 146
Email: visionatres@yahoo.es
Don't be put off by the exterior of this Soviet-built apartment block; inside is another world. One room in cosy apartment in walking distance of center, good bed, reading lights. Santiago and Consuelo are friendly and knowledgeable, and can make alternative reservations if the room is occupied.

Isabel Sera Galves
Calle Narciso López 142, between Aguilera and Frexes
Tel: 24-422 529
A large colonial house in town center; two rooms and excellent food offered. There's a lovely garden with fruit trees and flowers, cats, and a dog, where you can sit and relax.

Villa Liba
Calle Maceo 46, corner 18
Tel: 24-423 823
Air-conditioned rooms with private baths; reading lights, plenty of storage space; a modern villa in a quiet residential area in walking distance of center. Helpful owner, Jorge, and his wife, Mariela, who is a masseuse and expert in natural medicine, provide vegetarian food on request.

Manzanillo

Adrián y Tonia
Mártires de Viet-Nam 49, between Caridad and San Silvestre
Tel: 23-573 028
A welcoming place on Celia Sánchez memorial staircase. Hosts are helpful and the room is well appointed and comfortable. There is also a suite on the roof with its own entrance, which has a bedroom, living room, kitchenette and bathroom, all well equipped and comfortable. A great roof terrace has a shaded dining table and a higher *mirador* for views of the bay. Garage.

SANTIAGO DE CUBA

Las Américas
Avenida de las Américas and General Cebreco
Tel: 22-642 011 and 687 225/6
www.islazul.cu
Opposite high-rise Santiago de Cuba, in walking distance of the city center, Las Américas has 70 decent rooms. Its restaurant is quite good with a great breakfast and there is usually a pleasant, buzzing atmosphere; the cabaret is very popular and so is the pool. **$**

Balcón del Caribe
Carretera del Morro, Km 7
Tel: 22691 011
www.islazul.cu
A nice, quiet spot by the sea next to the Morro Castle. The hotel, with 72 rooms and 24 *cabañas*, is largely unmodernized but has a pleasant atmosphere, and there's a little cabaret. It is handy for the airport, but it's also under the flight path. **$**

Hotel Casa Granda
Heredia 201, between San Pedro and San Félix, Parque Céspedes
Tel: 22-686 600 and 653 021
www.gran-caribe.com
Overlooking the main square, this landmark hotel built in 1914 is

PRICE CATEGORIES

Price categories indicate the cost of a double room in high season:
$ = under $80
$$ = $80–150
$$$ = $150–250

Santiago's nicest. The interior is splendidly grand, but some rooms are in need of renovation. There is a broad terrace bar overlooking the square. The fifth-floor bar offers fine views over downtown Santiago, and is great at sunset. **$$**

Hotel E San Basilio
Calle Masó 403, between Calvario and Carnicería
Tel: 22-651 702
www.hotelescubanacan.com
Santiago's only 'boutique' hotel, this pretty, pastel-green place is very close to Parque Céspedes. It takes its name from the old name of the street (one that many people still use). There are just eight rooms with air conditioning and TV. Only breakfast is served. Being in the city center it can be noisy. **$$**

Hotel Meliá Santiago de Cuba
Avenida de las Américas, between Avenida 4 and Calle M
Tel: 22-687 070
www.melia.com
Spectacular red, white, and blue modern building with glass-fronted escalators, its 15 stories can be seen all over town. With 270 spacious rooms, 34 suites, and a conference room, it's popular with business guests. Four restaurants, three pools, and a lavish cabaret/nightclub. Good view from rooftop bar. **$$**

Hotel Versalles
Alturas de Versalles, Carretera del Morro, Km 1
Tel: 22-691 016
www.hotelescubanacan.com
On a hillside just outside the city, a pink and white stuccoed gingerbread house of a hotel in lush gardens. There are 61 rooms and one suite, all with garden views from their balconies. There's air conditioning, satellite TV, a restaurant (prices vary from night to night), two cafés, two bars, a large pool (closes at 5pm) and a separate children's pool, a nightclub on weekends, and sporting amenities. Rather inconvenient for the town unless you're a good walker; a metered cab costs CUC$3-4. **$**

Casas Particulares

Casa Dulce
Calle Bartolomé Masó (San Basilio) 552, corner Clarín
Tel: 22-625 479
Email: gdcastillo20@yahoo.es
One lovely room in an apartment on a corner block; huge windows let in light and air. There's a great view over the city and the harbor from the roof terrace, where there is a table for meals and sun loungers for relaxing. Central, convenient, friendly and helpful hostess; English spoken; good food served.

Casa Jesús Pérez Castro
Padre Pico 54, Apt 3, between San Gerónimo (Sánchez Echavarría) and Jaguey (Cornelio Robert)
Tel: 22-658 693; 5-246 5967 (cell/mob)
Despite the unprepossessing exterior, the apartment is clean and comfortable. The spacious, air-conditioned rooms are plainly but comfortably furnished. It is a five-minute walk to the city center, but is away from the noise at night. Jesús is an attentive and professional host who speaks English and can arrange tours and transfers. Meals are fresh and tasty.

Casa Leonardo and Rosa
Clarín (Padre Quiroga) 9, between Aguilera (Marina) and Heredia
Tel: 22-623 574
Leonardo works for the city's conservation office and keeps this late 19th-century house pristine, with lovely stucco on the façade. Inside there are tiled floors, high ceilings and lofty doors and windows. He also restores classic cars. There is a nice garden at the back, with a small fountain and fishpond, and a roof terrace. The rooms are air-conditioned and good and the food is plentiful and tasty.

Casa Nivia Meléndez
General Portuondo (Trinidad) 510, between Hartman (San Félix) and General Banderas (San Bartolomé)
Tel: 22-622 893
Hosts David and Beatriz are English-speaking biologists and are helpful and informative. They can arrange excellent tours around the city and outlying areas with a guide and/or driver. The house is nice and well cared for with a courtyard garden; very homey. Beatriz cooks excellent food with a number of vegetarian delights, while David prepares a great lobster.

AROUND SANTIAGO DE CUBA

Gran Piedra

Hotel Islazul Gran Piedra
Carretera de la Gran Piedra, Km 14.5
Tel: 22-686 147
www.islazul.cu
An 'eco-lodge' with comfortable and spacious rustic cabins and bungalows set along the edge of the mountain ridge (*gran piedra* means large rock). The views are absolutely wonderful when the weather is fine and it is always pleasantly cool. The staffers are friendly and helpful. There is also a café, a restaurant, and a souvenir shop on the road beneath the rock. **$**

Sierra Maestra

Hotel El Saltón
Carretera a Filé, Contramaestre
Tel: 22-566 326
www.hotelescubanacan.com
Northwest of El Cobre, deep in the Sierra Maestra, this place is very rural and extremely beautiful. There are 22 rooms in wooden cabins set by a mountain lake fed by waterfalls. The waterfall that gives the hotel its name is 34 meters/yds high, and you can stand under it for an invigorating shower, or bathe in its pool. The hotel was originally an anti-stress center, and still offers a sauna and massage services. You can take Jeep trips from Santiago to Saltón for the day or weekend, with hiking into the mountains included. **$**

THE FAR EAST

Baracoa

Hotel El Castillo
Calixto García s/n, Loma el Paraíso
Tel: 21-645 106
www.grupo-gaviota.com
High on a cliff, with the best views of the town and El Yunque mountain, this was one of Baracoa's three castles, built in 1770 to keep the British out. It later became a prison. Some of the rooms are in dire need of renovation; the newer ones are good, although you still may not get hot water. The hotel has a gorgeous pool with a barbecue bar and lovely gardens, and serves a good breakfast. . Reached by a steep flight of steps or a curving drive.

Inexpensive, and great value. **$**

Hostal La Habanera
Maceo 68, corner of Frank País
Tel: 21-645 273
www.grupo-gaviota.com
This 10-room hotel with an ocher-facade is in the center of town on a pedestrian street. It has been well renovated, there's cable TV and air conditioning in the rooms, and the beds are comfortable. There's a lovely balcony at the front where you can relax and watch the world go by. Can be noisy at night if the Casa de Cultura next door has loud music – but it's very atmospheric. **$**

Hostal Río Miel
Malecón, corner Ciro Frías
Tel: 21-641 207
www.grupo-gaviota.com
This 12-room hostel on the seafront is the newest offering from Gaviota, having opened in late-2013 with simple accommodations. Located beside La Rusa, it is the better option while everything is new and works. **$**

Hotel La Rusa
Máximo Gómez 161
Tel: 21-643 011
www.grupo-gaviota.com
An aristocratic Russian, who fled the revolution in her own country and lived to see another on her adopted island, founded this simple 12-room hostelry on the waterfront. The low-rise yellow-painted La Rusa is in an enviable location and has attracted many famous guests, including Che. Simple accommodations are good enough for a night or two. High seas can make this a dramatic location. **$**

Villa Maguana
Carretera a Moa, Km 22.5
Tel: 21-641 204
www.grupo-gaviota.com
In a beautiful location on a spectacular and secluded white-sand beach, 20km (12 miles) north of Baracoa, this is one of the very few small and intimate beach hotels in Cuba. There is a restaurant and a beach bar. It has 16 3-star rooms in four blocks and tranquility in abundance. **$**

Casas Particulares

Andrés Cruzata Rigores
Calle Wilder Galano Reyes 23 Alto, between Abel Díaz Delgado and Ramón López Peña
Tel: 21-642 697; 5-246 5755 (cell/mob)
Email: cruzata.bacoa2012@yahoo.es
Air-conditioned rooms are in an upstairs apartment with TV, good bathrooms, a terrace with seating, and a lovely view over the town and the sea. Helpful family can organize things for you and offer services such as laundry. English and French spoken.

Casa Colonial Lucy
Calle Céspedes 29, between Rubert López and Maceo
Tel. 21-643 548
A pretty colonial house with a lovely view over the town and the sea from the roof terrace. Two good air-conditioned rooms with lofty ceilings and refrigerator. Lucy is most helpful in arranging excursions and provides good food. English and Italian spoken.

Daniel Salomón Paján
Calle Céspedes 28, between Rubert López and Maceo
Tel. 21-641 443; 5-291 7403 (cell/mob)
Email: fifi@toa.gtm.sld.cu
Daniel works at the museum and is extremely knowledgeable about the area. He and his family are very helpful and friendly and speak some English. They rent out one room with air conditioning and a large bathroom.

SOUTHERN ISLANDS

Cayo Largo

All the hotels are all-inclusive and flank the beach on the south side of the island. Sol Meliá (www.melia.com) has the two best, while Gran Caribe (www.cayolargodelsur.cu) runs the rest. The price of packages bought in Havana or abroad varies widely, so shop around.

Hotel Playa Blanca
Tel: 45-248 080
www.gran-caribe.cu
Probably the best resort and very popular, with rooms in three-story main hotel or two-story blocks along the white sand beach. All are well appointed, spacious, and comfortable; service is friendly and efficient. Plenty of activities, sports, and entertainment, and food is very good by Cuban standards. Jeep or scooter rental available.
$$–$$$

Sol Pelícano
Playa Lindamar
Tel: 45-248 333
www.melia.com
Good, three-star family hotel on a superb beach. Buffet restaurant, beach bar, and snack and pizza bars. Saltwater pool with children's section. A little tram picks up from the hotel for trips to other beaches.
$$–$$$

Isla de la Juventud

Hotel El Colony
Carretera de Siguanea, Km 46
Tel: 46-398 181
www.gran-caribe.cu
On Southwest coast, 42km (26 miles) from Nueva Gerona, 77 air-conditioned rooms, some in cabins with good amenities. Miles from anywhere and surrounded by swamp and mangrove, people come for some of the best diving in Cuba and the beach is pleasant (bring insect repellent and snacks). Food is poor. Marinas Puerto Sol offers packages covering the hotel, the scuba center, and the marina, which provides deep-sea fishing trips. **$$**

Hotel Rancho El Tesoro
Carretera La Fé, Km 3, on the way to the airport, less than 3km (2 miles) south of Nueva Gerona
Tel: 46-323 035
www.gran-caribe.cu
With 54 very basic air-conditioned rooms, set around a courtyard with a fountain and vines hanging from wooden beams, this hotel has a pool and restaurant. **$**

Villa Isla de la Juventud
Autopista Gerona–La Fé, Km 1.5
Tel: 46-323 290
www.gran-caribe.cu
A modern single-story building houses 20 basic rooms. There's a decent pool and views, and a salsa band plays afternoons and evenings. **$**

Casas Particulares

Isla de la Juventud

Elda Cepero Herrera
Calle 43 2004, Nueva Gerona
Tel: 46-322 774
Separate apartment behind the house with a living room and kitchen.

Odalis Peña Fernández
Calle 10 3710, between 37 and 39, Nueva Gerona
Tel: 46-321 166
Friendly, with good home cooking; Odalis can suggest unusual excursions or find transportation.

PRICE CATEGORIES

Price categories indicate the cost of a double room in high season:
$ = under $80
$$ = $80–150
$$$ = $150–250

ACTIVITIES

FESTIVALS, THE ARTS, NIGHTLIFE, SHOPPING, AND SPECTATOR SPORTS

THE ARTS

Museums

Many of the colonial mansions and public buildings clustered around the historic centers of Cuba's older cities are now museums. Whatever their theme, they are often worth seeing for the beauty of the buildings themselves.

The main museums in tourist centers charge an admission fee of CUC$1–3, but the cost is higher in some of Havana's top attractions, such as both branches of the Museo Nacional Palacio de Bellas Artes (a combined ticket is available), and the Museo de la Revolución. You may also be charged extra for taking photos or videos.

Exhibits are generally labeled in Spanish, though shortened notes are sometimes given in English. The most popular museums usually have at least one guide who speaks English and sometimes French.

Opening hours are notoriously erratic, and buildings can be closed for renovation. Many museums close on Monday, and some open only for the afternoon on Sunday – current opening times of the major museums are given in the main text.

Music

Cubans are crazy about music. It blares from every window and accompanies every activity. Rumba, *son*, and its derivative salsa, *trova* ballads, and *nueva trova* political songs, jazz, country, and classical can be heard and seen on TV, along with modern, US-influenced rap, hip-hop and reggaeton. There is always some group performing live, whether in hotels or in local nightspots.

***Son*, bolero**, and **salsa** are everywhere and live bands playing and singing traditional music can be found in the Casa de la Trova and/or the Casa de la Cultura in any town.

Most of the bars and *tabernas* of Old Havana and tourist centers such as Trinidad feature live bands (see Nightlife, page 339).

Jazz has deep roots and Cuban musicians are creative interpreters. Havana jazz venues are all in Vedado. The genre is at its most exciting when the best Cuban and international jazz musicians gather in the capital for the Havana International Jazz Festival in December (see Festivals, page 339).

The national opera company is based at the Gran Teatro, off the Parque Central. Performances are posted on notices outside, or call the theater, tel: 7-861 3077.

With fantastic acoustics, the church of San Francisco de Asís in Plaza San Francisco is a great venue for classical music. Tickets are available from the venue and recitals are usually at 5pm or 6pm. The main venue for concerts in Havana, however, is the Teatro Amadeo Roldán, in Vedado, tel: 7-832 1168, the base for the Orquesta Sinfónica Nacional and where visiting symphony orchestras play. The Sala Hubert de Blanck, in Vedado, tel: 7-833 5962, specializes in classical concerts and stages contemporary dance. You can also find something going on at the Teatro Nacional de Cuba, on Paseo and Calle 39 (Plaza de la Revolución), tel: 7-879 3558.

Dance

Cubans dance from the moment they can walk and, to Westerners, it seems they all have an innate rhythm, impeccable footwork, and the endless energy expected of a pro. Perhaps that is why Cuba's professional groups are so good, and have become internationally recognized.

Art in Havana

Havana has the lion's share of art treasures – in particular at the Arte Cubano section of the **Museo Nacional Palacio de Bellas Artes** (see page 153), which has the most representative collection of 20th-century Cuban art. The **Casa de las Américas** at Avenida 3era 52, and Calle G, Vedado, www.casa.cult.cu, has an interesting collection of Cuban and Latin-American art, and the **Galería Habana**, Linea 460, between calles E and F, Vedado, www.galerihabana.com, has lively and well-displayed contemporary Cuban works. **Galería UNEAC**, Calle 17, corner of Calle H, Vedado, www.uneac.org.cu, has exhibits by contemporary Cuban artists (in official favor). Calle Obispo in Old Havana is home to a number of commercial galleries/sale rooms for contemporary art. Others are dotted all around the old town.

Afro-Cuban Dance

Now internationally renowned, Clave y Guaguancó was founded to keep Afro-Cuban dance, drumming, and music alive, concentrating mainly on rumba, *son*, and *danzón*. They play Yambú, Guaguancó, Columbias, and carnival music as well as African music from the Yoruba, Arará, Abakuá, Congo, or Bantú. They sometimes perform in Callejón de Hamel (Centro Habana) on

Sunday noon–3pm, and give open-air performances alternate Wednesdays from 5pm, at the Hurón Azul, UNEAC, Calles 17 and H, Vedado.

The Conjunto Folklórico Nacional de Cuba (Calle 4 103, between Calzada and 5ta, Vedado, tel: 7-830 3939, 830 3060, 831 3467) hosts rumba performances on the patio outside the Gran Palenque Bar, Calle 4, between Calzada and 5, every Saturday. Box office opens at 2pm on Saturday before the 3pm performance; there is often a line, so be there early. You can also book a course of dance lessons here (same numbers as above, or go in person).

Tango

Tango is not indigenous to Cuba, but can be found here. The best place for classes and excellent performances is Casa del Tango Edmundo Daubar, Neptuno 309, between Aguila and Italia, tel: 7-863 0097. It's a cross between a music venue and a museum with tango memorabilia dating from the 1940s.

Ballet

The **National Ballet of Cuba**, directed since its creation in 1961 by Alicia Alonso, is world-famous for its fluid grace and technique. The company is often on tour, but when at home it performs at the **Gran Teatro**, Paseo de Martí 458, corner San Rafael (Parque Central), tel: 7-861 3077/8; or the **Teatro Nacional de Cuba**, Paseo and Calle 39 (Plaza de la Revolución), tel: 7-879 3558. The company's ballet school is based at the Gran Teatro, and during the day you can see the young students rehearsing (also see Festivals below).

The Museo Nacional de la Danza covers all aspects of the history of dance with special emphasis on ballet. It is at Línea 365 and G, Vedado, tel: 7-831 2198, housed in an elegant building that is worth a visit in itself (see page 174).

Modern Dance

Cuba's impressive **Contemporary Dance Company** (Danza Contemporánea de Cuba) performs avant-garde and other forms of modern dance. Its base is the **Teatro Nacional de Cuba,** Paseo and Calle 39 (Plaza de la Revolución), but performances can also be seen at the Sala Hubert de Blanck or the Teatro Mella, Línea 657, between A and B, tel: 7-833 5651.

Cinema

Movies are often put on only on weekends or on selected evenings – other than in the main movie theaters in Havana, such as those in Vedado, including the Yara, opposite the Habana Libre, and the Charles Chaplin, farther along Calle 23. These same movie theaters tend to show the pick of the screenings during the annual International Festival of **New Latin American Cinema,** www.habanafilmfestival.com, during the first two weeks of December, drawing stars, directors, critics, and movie buffs from around the world. The Teatro Karl Marx is the venue for some high-profile screenings. In April there is also a film festival, held in Gibara, for low-budget movies, the **Festival Internacional de Cine Pobre de Humberto Solás**, named for the late Cuban director (1941–2008).

Theater

Teatro Bertolt Brecht, Línea and Calle 13. Renovated and now capable of staging a wide range of shows, from musical comedy to political satire, dance, and music.

Teatro El Sótano, Calle K between calles 25 and 27, tel: 7-832 0630, is home to the Rita Montaner company and a place to find contemporary drama and fringe theater events.

Teatro Guiñol, calles M and 19, Vedado, tel: 7-832 6262, stages contemporary youth theatre and drama classes.

Teatro Nacional de Cuba, Paseo and Calle 39 (Plaza de la Revolución), tel: 7-879 3558. Three auditoria, where experimental and children's theater is staged, as well as ballet performances and concerts.

Festivals

All Cuban provinces celebrate a **Culture Week** *(Semana Cultural)* once a year, with music, dance, arts and crafts, and local food.

Havana International Jazz Festival in December, running since 1978, is organized by Chucho Valdés. The festival is based in the Teatro Nacional de Cuba but venues include the Teatro Amadeo Roldán and Teatro Karl Marx, where major performances take place, and there are impromptu performances along the Malecón. Other festivals include the **Havana Contemporary Music Festival** held at UNEAC and Havana theaters in October, and the International **Electrical Acoustic Music Festival** in March. Outside Havana are the **International Son Festival** (October) and the **International Trova Festival** (March) in Santiago, and the **Cuculambeana Festival** of folk music in Las Tunas (June).

The **International Ballet Festival** in October, running since 1986, draws companies from Cuba and abroad. Most performances are in the Gran Teatro or the Teatro Nacional but there are various other venues. **Cubadanza** is a contemporary festival held twice a year (January and August), organized by the Danza Contemporánea de Cuba, with workshops and classes as well as performances.

The **Havana Theater Festival** is held in October with performances of contemporary international and Cuban drama in various theaters or in the open air in plazas, as well as workshops and seminars.

Another highlight of Cuba's events calendar is **Carnival.** Havana now holds its carnival in August – dates have changed over the years. The venue is the Malecón, where flamboyant parades are held throughout the day and night. Santiago de Cuba holds a lively carnival in late July. Again, it is not the traditional pre-Lent celebration, but one that grew out of traditional summer festivals. Varadero has a less spirited festival, with tourist participation, in January and February.

At all these events, popular bands often play for free, and there are midways (fairgrounds) and other attractions. For most Cubans the food fairs, at which basic staples like rice and bananas are sold from the back of trucks at very low prices, are the main attraction.

The *comparsas* (street dances) of Cuba's carnivals are as colorful and symbolic as the floats. In Havana and Santiago, neighborhood groups have rehearsals at least once a week during the year, and even if you miss the carnival, you may be lucky enough to come across a practice session.

A less well-known festival**, Las Parrandas**, takes place in certain towns and villages of Villa Clara province in the week between Christmas and New Year – most famously at Remedios. For a description of this wild and colorful event, see page 230.

NIGHTLIFE

Every hotel in Cuba has one or more bars and many have programmed entertainment, often focused around the pool. Most large hotels have their own disco and cabaret. If you want to be more adventurous, ask around for the best local *peña*, disco, or cabaret, where you will be able to drink rum and dance alongside local people. Local discos are obviously at their liveliest on weekends, but don't get going until 11pm or even later.

The beach resort of Varadero has abundant discos and nighttime shows and cabarets, but the best and most varied nightlife is in Havana.

1830
Malecón, 1252, right by the Miramar tunnel Tel: 7-838 3090
Expensive restaurant open from noon; outdoor dancing to live music at 10pm; cabaret shows and live bands. (See page 176)

Atelier
Calle 17, corner of Calle 6, Vedado
Tel: 7-830 6808
Basement club with small dance floor, open daily 10pm–4am; shows start at 11.30pm, followed by a disco where styles include salsa and rap.

Cabaret Parisién
Hotel Nacional, calles 21 and O
Tel: 7-873 3564
Cheaper than the Tropicana, this show in the Nacional lasts longer and is equally good. Open 9pm–2.30am; show starts at 10pm; reservations required.

Café Cantante Mi Habana
Teatro Nacional, Paseo and Calle 39 (Plaza de la Revolución)
Tel: 7-878 4275
The program varies: sometimes disco, live music of all kinds (usually on weekends), or stand-up (in rapid Spanish). It's a small, lively basement venue and quickly fills up. Open daily 5pm–3am; afternoon and evening performances.

Café de Paris
Calle San Ignacio 202, corner of Obispo
Live and lively music every night (see page 161).

Café Taberna 'Amigos del Benny'
Calle Mercaderes 531 and Brasil (Teniente Rey)
Tel: 7-861 1637
Restaurant and bar (see page 160), with live music from 8pm;good-quality *son* and mambo.

Casa de la Cultura de La Habana Vieja
Calle Aguiar 509, between Amargura and Brasil (Teniente Rey)
Tel: 7-863 4860
Starting around 8pm, nightly performances held either in the lovely theater or outdoors in the churchyard. Large crowds, mostly local people; the atmosphere is enchanting.

Casa de la Música Galiano
Avenida de Italia (Galiano) 255, between Neptuno and Concordia, Centro Habana
Tel: 7-862 4165
Salsa, *songo*, and rock bands; matinee slots from 4pm for up-and-coming bands and prime evening slots from around 11pm for the big guns, when you can pay CUC$20 or more for a ticket (but usually it's far less). Also a music shop and restaurant.

Copa Room
Avenida 5 and Calle 110, Miramar
Tel: 7-834 4228
Cabaret Mon, Wed, Thu 8.30pm–midnight, followed by recorded music; a show followed by a salsa band Fri–Sun 8.30pm-3am.

La Cecilia
Habana Riviera Hotel, Paseo corner Malecón, VedadoTel: 7-204 1562
Music and dancing to a salsa orchestra in the open air. Thu–Sun 10pm–3am.

Pico Blanco
Hotel St John's, Calle O 206, between 23 and 25, Vedado
Tel: 7-833 3740
Live bolero till 1am followed by a disco; also known as the home of '*filín*', or 'feeling'. Fantastic views over Vedado. Open every night 9am–3am.

El Delirio Habanero
Teatro Nacional, Paseo and Calle 39 (Plaza de la Revolución)
Tel: 7-878 4275
Piano bar and salsa. Cooler and quieter than the Café Cantante Mi Habana downstairs. Great views over the Plaza de La Revolución. Open Tue–Sun 6pm till late.

Jazz Café
Galerías del Paseo, Paseo, corner of Avenida 1era, Vedado
Tel: 7-838 3556
Famous jazz club, frequented by Chuchó Valdés, with live music (two sets, 8pm and 11pm). New groups and lots of improvisation. Good food.

El Gato Tuerto
Calle O 14, between 17 and 19, Vedado
Tel: 7-838 2696
A club near the Hotel Nacional. Major artists, *son*, *trova*, boleros, and *filín*. Open daily till 3am.

Club Habana
Avenida 5, between 188 and 192, Reparto Flores, Miramar
Tel: 7-204 5700
Social and sailing club with café-bar, piano bar, and live music and dancing. Fri and Sat karaoke 10.30pm–1am.

Hurón Azul (UNEAC)
Calle 17 351, between Avenida de los Presidentes and H, Vedado
Tel: 7-832 4571
Headquarters of the Cuban Union of Artists and Writers, and mainly a Cuban hangout. Boleros on Saturday night, Trova sin Traba and Peña del Ambia alternate on Wednesday (5–8pm), and there's *son* on Sunday (5–8pm).

Club Imágenes
Calzada 602, corner of C, Vedado
Tel: 7-833 3606
Live bolero, *son*, and traditional music, plus soft piano sounds. Matinées Mon–Fri 3.30–8pm, daily 9.30pm till about 3am.

Club Karachi
Calle K, between calles 15 and 17, Vedado
Tel: 7-832 3485
Mostly Cuban clientele. Recorded and live music; a show at midnight. Open Tue–Sat till 3am and Sun afternoon.

Opus Bar
Calzada and Calle D, Vedado
Tel: 7-832 4521
Housed in the elegant and old School of Music. Live music, cocktails, and snacks. Open 3pm–3am.

El Polvorín
Avenida Monumental, La Cabaña
Tel: 7-860 9990, 863 8295
By the Twelve Apostles restaurant at the foot of El Morro, this is a funky disco bar and reggaeton venue with an excellent outdoor terrace. You can sip *cuba libres* among the big guns that face out over the bay. Popular with hip young Cubans and tourists. Open daily 9pm–3am.

La Red
Calle 19 151, corner of Calle L, Vedado
Tel: 7-832 5415
A mainly Cuban club serving mostly Western music, sometimes reggae, also excellent Cuban rap. Open from 10pm but doesn't get going until midnight, especially on weekends.

Salón Rosado Benny Moré, La Tropical
Avenida 41 and 46, Miramar
Tel: 7-206 1282
The best live salsa venue in Cuba. A big, no-frills outdoor arena. The best (and lesser-known) artists play here Sat–Sun 11pm–2am. Cabaret Wed from 8pm, *peña* Thu, recorded music Fri, dance matinee Sun 3–7pm.

Tikoa
Calle 23 177, between calles N and O, Vedado
Tel: 7-830 9973
Salsa rules on weekends in this lively disco favored by Cubans but Mon–Thu there is usually a singer. Open daily 10pm–2am.

Tropicana
Calle 72 4504, between 43 and 45, Marianao
Tel: 7-267 1717

One of Cuba's many trova hang-outs.

This is the most elaborate and impressive of Cuba's cabarets (see page 182). Any hotel tourism bureau will book seats for you, but the show is expensive: CUC$70–90, depending on your seat and the age of your rum. Open air – it is canceled if it rains. Open till 2am.

El Turquino
Hotel Habana Libre, calles 23 and L, Vedado
Tel: 7-834 6100
Disco on the 25th floor, with occasional live salsa from top groups. The roof opens and you can dance in the open air. Open daily 10.30pm–3am, cabaret 11pm and 1am.

La Zorra y el Cuervo
Calle 23, between N and O, Vedado
Tel: 7-833 2402
Famous jazz club in a La Rampa basement (look for UK-style red phone box at entrance). Live music from 11pm. Open daily 10pm–2am.

Nightlife Outside Havana

Just about every Cuban town has a **Casa de la Trova** (traditional Cuban-style music hall), and/or a Casa de la Música. Cultural events and concerts take place in a Casa de la Cultura and there is usually a Patio de ARTex, a bar/café with an open-air space where you can hear contemporary regional music and comedy.

What's On

Havana's nightlife scene is constantly changing. It is well worth asking in music stores, and at your hotel or casa particular, for venues. The weekly magazine *Cartelera* (free in most hotels, www.cartelera.com) has a reliable 'what's on' section. *Guía La Habana* (also free) is a monthly publication that may also be useful. EGREM (Empresa de Grabaciones y Ediciones Musicales, or Enterprise of Recordings and Musical Editions; http://promociones.egrem.co.cu) publishes a list of what's on at Casas de la Música and other venues around the country.

Santiago

Casa de la Trova
Calle Heredia 208, between San Pedro and San Félix
Tel: 22-623 943
One of the best-known *casas* in Cuba. Famous musicians play here and you can hear *trova*, *son*, and boleros. There is always something going on, and most of it is excellent. Open Tue–Sun, afternoon and evening.

Casa de las Tradiciones
Rabí 154, between José de Diego and García
Tel: 22-653 892
Smaller and more intimate than the Casa de la Trova, this is very much a local venue. Open 3–11.30pm, with live *trova*, *son*, and boleros from 8pm.

Patio de ARTex
Calle Heredia 304, between Carnicería and Calvario
Tel: 22-654 814
In the patio behind the ARTex store, there is often excellent music, with late-afternoon and evening sets. Dance, or just have a drink and enjoy the music.

Tropicana Santiago
Autopista Nacional, Km 1.5
Tel: 22-642 579
Santiago puts its stamp on this glitzy show, with local touches to distinguish it from its Havana namesake. Open 8pm–3am, with disco after the show; tickets cost around CUC$30, but packages are available that include transportation and drinks.

Trinidad

Casa de la Música
On the steps by the Plaza Mayor
Tel: 41-996 622
Music and dancing till the early hours. There's a restaurant, show, piano bar, and music shop, very popular with local people and tourists.

Casa de la Trova
Calle Echerrri 29
Can be great or average, but when it's good, it's very good. Live music day and night, popular with Cubans and tourists of all ages.

Palenque de los Congos Reales
Calle Echerri, corner Menéndez
Tel: 41-994 512
Son and salsa nightly on a small patio; has a lively following. During the day there are often live bands and an Afro-Cuban show.

Las Ruínas de Brunet
Calle Maceo, between Colón and Zerquera
Touristy Afro-Caribbean dance show in a ruined colonial courtyard at 9pm. Daytime activities include *trova*, dance, and percussion classes.

Cienfuegos

Disco El Beny
Avenida 54, between 29 and 31
Tel: 43-451 105
This is the best place in town for dancing. The bar is 1950s style, there is a show every night at 11pm, and the disco stays open until 5am; popular with Cubans and tourists, there is a great atmosphere and very few *jineteras*.

Holguín

UNEAC
Calle Libertad, between Luz Caballero and Martí
A very elegant, restored colonial building, hosting all the major cultural events in the city. There is also a good Casa de la Trova and Casa de la Música in town for a range of music and dance options.

Baracoa

Casa de la Trova
Calle Maceo 149, between Ciro Frías and Pelayo Cuervo
Tiny, traditional place with great entertainment and plenty of locals. Tourists welcome and women are never short of a partner. Open Tue–Sun from 9pm.

El Ranchón
Loma Paraíso, above Calle Calixto García
Tel: 21-643 268
Open-air disco on the hill with a lovely view, popular with the young after other places close; live and recorded music, gets going after midnight.

Santa Clara

Club Mejunje
Marta Abreu 107, between Alemán and Juan Bruno Zayas

Tel: 42-282-572
There is always something going on here, an open-air venue in a ruin with trees and graffiti-covered walls where composers, artistes, and audience mingle for a drink and chat over good music. A different theme every night, from 1950s music, *trova*, and Afro-Cuban folkloric music to a gay disco with transvestite show.

Bayamo

Cabaret Bayamo
Opposite Hotel Sierra Maestra
Tel: 23-421 698
There is a restaurant where you can have a meal before the 9pm show, everything in pesos Cubanos, so very cheap.
Los Beatles
Calle Juan Clemente Zenea, corner Saco
You can't miss the statues of John, Paul, George, and Ringo at the door, looking as though they are waiting to go in. Live and taped music, mostly golden oldies, popular for dancing.

SHOPPING

What to Buy

Nobody goes to Cuba for the shopping. In fact, one of the most striking things for most visitors is the lack of consumer goods – along with the lack of advertising. However, two of the things that Cuba is most famous for – Cigars and rum – are easy to find and make the best gifts. Most countries have import limits on both, which travelers should check beforehand: the standard limit is 50 cigars and two liters of rum. Both items can be purchased in the big hotels or tourist stores, or directly from the cigar factories and rum distilleries that offer tours.

Some recommended places to buy cigars are listed below, and rum can be bought just about everywhere. Habana Club is the best: the cheapest variety is the three-year-old white rum; the most expensive (and this only means about CUC$12) is the *añejo siete años*; in between come the *añejo cinco años* and the *añejo reserva* – these three are all dark rums of different ages. Cuban coffee is well worth purchasing, too; Cubita, Turquina, and Hola are the best brands. Try the Casa del Café on Calle Baratillo, between Obispo and Jústiz.

If you love chocolate, go to the **Museo del Chocolate** on Calle Mercaderes in Havana (really just a café and store) where excellent pure chocolate can be purchased.

If you fall under the spell of Cuban music, as most people do, you will want to splash out on a few **CDs**. Many hotels have a reasonable selection, but keep an eye open for ARTex stores, which have a better-than-average choice (see page 343). Many of the groups that serenade you in Old Havana and elsewhere have their own CDs for sale. The recording quality is not the best, and the music may not sound quite as good once you get it home, but they can make good, nostalgic mementoes.

Handicrafts tend to be of mixed quality in the state-run stores, but the legalization of private enterprise has meant that many Cubans have started painting pictures and making jewelry, embroidery, ceramics, leather goods, and musical instruments.

Foreign interest in Santería and other Afro-Cuban religions has also spawned the proliferation of souvenirs related to these cults, from the colorful necklaces associated with Santería to sculpted figures of the gods (*orishas*).

Second-hand **books** and fascinating **newspapers** and **magazines** from the pre- and early revolutionary era are worth looking out for, too. Across Cuba you will find people selling books in the street or from the front of their houses. The biggest collection is to be found in the market in the Plaza de Armas in Old Havana (Wed–Sat 9am–6pm).

Many **peso bookstores** are depressingly empty of new titles, but books of obvious interest to tourists are being published for sale in CUC stores. The range of titles is improving, but stock is often dominated by illustrated books about Cuba, expensive reprints of Cuban revolutionary volumes (the speeches of Che Guevara or the works of José Martí, etc.), and a limited number of novels in Spanish by 'safe' authors (García Márquez is a favorite).

Export Procedures

Visitors who wish to buy Cuban art should note that they need an export permit. State-run stores and galleries will issue this automatically. You also need a permit if you buy a work from a street market or artist – no matter how inexpensive. Sometimes, the artist will issue a permit, but otherwise you must go to the **Registro Nacional de Bienes Culturales** (National Registry of Cultural Goods) at Calle 17 1009, between calles 10 and 12, Vedado, and allow a minimum of three or four days for processing. Permits cost around CUC$20 and are good for up to five artworks. It is important to get a permit, otherwise your purchases will be confiscated at the airport. This is also true for antiques and antiquarian books, more than 50 years old.

You can take up to 20 loose cigars and up to 50 cigars in their original, sealed packaging, with the official hologram, out of the country without an official receipt. For more than 50 cigars, keep both copies of your official receipt from an authorized state store (one will be retained by customs on your departure) and keep the cigars in their sealed boxes. Anything else will be confiscated. Always keep cigars in your hand luggage when you leave the country.

Buying Cigars

Cigars can be bought on any visit to a factory, such as the **Fábrica de Tabaco Partagás** just behind the Capitolio in Havana (see page 165). Outside Havana, there's the shop opposite the **Fábrica de Tabaco Francisco Donatién** in Pinar del Río; numerous opportunities on *vegas* (tobacco plantations) in and around Viñales; and the **Fábrica de Tabaco César Escalante** in Santiago, and many other places. Hotel cigar stores all have large humidors and usually well-informed staff, and their cigars are often cheaper than in factory stores. If you have left it until the last minute, you can buy cigars at the airport, but the selection is smaller. Some recommended stores are listed below:
In **Old Havana,** the **Casa del Habano,** attached to Hostal Conde de Villanueva, Calle Mercaderes 202, between Lamparilla and Amargura, is an excellent cigar store. **Casa del Ron y el Tabaco**, Monserrate corner of Obispo, sells both rum and cigars. **Tabacos Habana** in the Manzana de Gómez, Zulueta and Neptuno, is open every day 9am–5.30pm. **Habanos** in the Hostal Valencia, Oficios 53, between Lamparilla and Obrapía, is open daily 10am–9pm, and **Palacio de la Artesanía,** Cuba 84, between Cuarteles and Chacón, has a cigar store.
In **Centro**, there's **Romeo y Julieta,** Calle Belascoaín 852, between Peñalver and Desagüe; and **El Palacio del Tabaco**, Reál Fábrica de Tabacos La Corona, Calle Agramonte (Zulueta) 106, between Refugio and Colón, sells fine Corona cigars from the factory.
In Vedado, **Hotel Nacional de Cuba** and **Hotel Meliá Cohiba** both have stores.

In **Miramar, La Escogida,** a fine cigar store, is housed in the Hotel **Comodoro**, on Avenida 3ra, corner of 84; and **Casa del Habano**, Avenida 5ta 1407, corner of 16, is a small but good cigar store.

Don't be tempted to buy cigars from hustlers on the street: most of them are fakes made from cheap tobacco or even banana leaves, whatever the labels say.

General Shopping

The shopping scene in Havana was transformed in the 1990s. The main commercial streets of the pre-revolutionary era are now gradually coming to life, with new and more upscale stores opening all the time. Habana Vieja tends to have smart, expensive stores, geared specifically to tourists, in the renovated streets.

Old Havana

Habana 1791, Calle Mercaderes 156, between Obrapía and Lamparilla, sells its own brands of colognes in gorgeous old-world bottles of heavy glass and sealing wax, beautifully packaged in pure linen bags. One interesting fragrance for men is a woody cologne made from tobacco. They mix bespoke fragrances at prices well below what you would pay in Europe or the US. **La Casa del Perfume**, Calle Brasil (Teniente Rey) between Oficios and Mercaderes, also sells perfumes and colognes and will mix personalized fragrances.

One interesting development is the reopening of once famous department stores such as **Harris Brothers** at Avenida de Bélgica 305, between O'Reilly and Progreso (open daily 9am–9pm), for clothes, food, and more. The **Palacio de la Artesanía**, Cuba 64, tel: 7-866 8072, sells clothing, perfume, music, and souvenirs and is open Mon–Sat 10am–7pm, Sun 10am–1pm. There are several boutiques, aimed at upscale consumers, all open Mon–Sat 10am–6pm, Sun 10am–1pm, including Plaza Vieja, on the corner of Mercaderes and Brasil (Teniente Rey); Paul and Shark, Muralla between Mercaderes and San Ignacio on Plaza Vieja; La Bella Cubana, Oficios, corner Lamparilla, near Plaza San Francisco; and Vía Uno, also on Oficios, corner Lamparilla.

Other interesting places are the **Betania market**, on Amargura, corner San Ignacio (open Mon–Sat 10am–7pm), where you can buy expensive organic products; and the small specialty cultural market at the Casa de los Arabes, Oficios, between Obispo and Obrapía.

Where to Buy Crafts, Books, and Music in Havana

Arts and Crafts

One of the best places for crafts in Cuba is the **Feria de Artesanía,** in Almacenes San José, on San Pedro (Avenida del Puerto), just beyond the ferry for Regla. You will find jewelry, leather goods, carved wooden items, and more. You are expected to haggle. There are smaller, cheaper versions of this market on Calle Simón Bolívar, just off Parque de la Fraternidad (near the Capitolio); opposite the Pabellón Cuba on La Rampa in Vedado, and the Feria del Malecón on the Malecón and corner of Calle D, a few blocks east of the Hotel Riviera.

The **Palacio de la Artesanía**, an attractive colonial building on Calle Cuba 64, Old Havana, has a good selection of crafts, CDs, and other items that make good souvenirs and mementoes.

In Centro, arts and crafts can be found at **ArteHabana,** on San Rafael 110 corner Industria, open Mon–Sat 10am–6pm, with a café open until 7pm, while another option worth checking out is Fin de Siglo, on the pedestrian part of San Rafael, open Mon–Sat 10am–5pm. **Sala Contemporánea** – a gallery selling Cuban arts and crafts – is at Calle 3 and G, Vedado (open Mon–Fri 10am–5pm).

Books

Stands sell second-hand and antiquarian books, including many with revolutionary and political themes, at a market on the Plaza de Armas (Wed–Sat). Prices are fairly high, but there is a good choice. If you are looking for something specific, it's always worth asking around; even if a vendor does not have the book to hand, they may well be able to track down a copy for you if you can wait a day or two.

The bookstores worth checking out include the following:

La Librería Anticuaria El Navío, Calle Obispo, 119, between Oficios and Mercaderes, is one of many very fine, decidedly upscale stores that are springing up all over the restored old town. Selling expensive rare books, first editions, and old postcards, the prices are steep, but it's great for a browse. If you buy, remember that export procedures apply to books more than 50 years old.

La Moderna Poesía, Obispo, 527, corner Bernaza, just off Parque Central. This was the most famous peso bookstore in Havana, but became a dollar, now a CUC, store.

Music

Cassettes and CDs are available all over town. Most hotels have a good selection, as do ARTex stores throughout Cuba. In Old Havana, the music store in the **Palacio de la Artesanía** at Calle Cuba 64 in Old Havana is good. The **Museo Nacional de la Música,** on Avenida de las Misiones, currently closed for renovation, has a store with knowledgeable staff selling an excellent selection of CDs. **Tienda Longina**, Obispo 360 between Habana and Compostela, sells musical instruments as well as CDs and musical souvenirs. The **Centro Wifredo Lam**, San Ignacio 22, corner Empedrado, is another good place for CDs and souvenirs. In Centro, head for the **Casa de la Música**, on Galiano and Neptuno, or **ArteHabana**. In Vedado, one of the best places is the **ARTex** store, La Habana Sí, on Calle 23 and L (opposite the Habana Libre); in Miramar, try the **Casa de la Música** de Miramar, Calle 35, corner of 20.

Centro Habana

The main shopping streets of Centro Habana are **San Rafael, Neptuno**, and **San Miguel**, where you will see many familiar names over the storefronts. **La Época** department store, Avenida de Italia (Galiano) and Neptuno, is good for children's and women's fashion. **La Vajilla**, on Avenida de Italia (Galiano) and Zanja, is a state-run antiques store (prices in pesos). You have to root about a bit, but there's often a gem or two to be found (open Mon–Sat 10am–5pm).

Plaza de Carlos III, on Avenida Salvador Allende, between Arbol Seco and Retiro, is one of the biggest malls in Havana, with restaurants, cafés, banks, and other services.

Vedado

Calle 23, particularly **La Rampa** – the section that runs from the Hotel Habana Libre down to the Malecón – was once the hub of Havana's life, and is inlaid with colored panels by famous Cuban artists.

The **International Press Center,** on the corner of La Rampa and Calle O, hosts exhibitions by Cuban artists, and has a store where you can buy newspapers, magazines, and books (particularly political titles), and a photo center.

On the Malecón and Prado (across from the Hotel Meliá Cohiba) is a glass-fronted shopping mall, **Galería Paseo**, where the first-floor supermarket sells Cuban cheeses, unusual cuts of meat, and breads that are often hard to find.

Pan de Paris, is a French-owned patisserie selling the best bread in Cuba, using imported French flour. They can be found at: Línea, between Paseo and A, Vedado; 106 and 51, Marianao; Vento and 100, Boyeros; and at the entrance to Tarará, Playas del Este. There is also a nice bakeshop called Sylvaín, selling cakes, pastries, and sweets (pay in CUCs), at Línea and 8 (next to Cine Línea).

The **Galerías Amazonas**, Calle 12, between 23 and 25, Vedado, is a small mall with stores selling wines, liquors, handmade chocolates, and good bread.

Miramar

Behind the Russian Embassy, rows of advertising billboards herald the former **Diplotienda** on Avenida 3ra at Calle 70. The store is now open to anyone who has CUCs and can afford to shop there; in fact, most buyers are Cubans, not foreigners. The range of food is not as good as it was, but it is still remarkably expensive.

Havana's haute couture **Maison** at Calle 16 and Avenida 7 has a series of smart boutiques selling Cuban fashions and antiques. There are also regular fashion shows, which are very entertaining.

Le Select, Avenida 5ta and 30, is an upscale department store, with an amazing lobby with marble statues and chandeliers, and there's even a swimming pool. Closed Sunday.

SPECTATOR SPORTS

Anyone interested in attending sports events should contact their nearest Cuban tourist office or check the websites of the Buró de Convenciones, www.cuba.cu/eventos, which lists all forthcoming events with contact details of organizers, or Cubadeportes, www.cubadeportes.cu.

Estadio Latinamericano
Calle Pedro Pérez 302, Cerro
Tel: 7-870 6576
Baseball, Cuba's favorite game, is played here five days a week. Your hotel should be able to give exact details. The stadium accommodates 55,000 spectators, and is about a 10-minute taxi ride from Old Havana.

Estadio Panamericano
Vía Monumental, Km 4.5, Habana del Este
Tel: 7-766 6030
Built for the 1991 Pan-American Games, the stadium was upgraded in 2008 with a new synthetic surface with eight lanes for athletics. Soccer games are also held here. It has a capacity for 34,000 spectators.

Estadio Ramón Fonst
Avenida Independencia and Bruzón, Plaza de la Revolución
Tel: 7-881 4196
Basketball games are held here.

Sala Polivalente Kid Chocolate
Paseo de Martí and Brasil (Teniente Rey), Old Havana
Tel: 7-861 1547
The main centre for boxing, this sports center also stages competitions for judo, weightlifting, handball, tennis, and badminton.

Ciudad Deportiva
Avenida Boyeros and Vía Blanca
Tel: 7-881 6979
This was a state-of-the-art indoor facility when it opened in 1958, but it is showing its age. It seats 18,000 under a domed roof and hosts local and international volleyball, basketball, table tennis games, and martial arts contests.

Velódromo Nacional Reinaldo Paseiro
Vía Monumental, Km 4.5, Habana del Este
Tel: 7-766 3776
Across from the Estadio Panamericano, but part of the same complex. Cycling is highly competitive in Cuba and world-class cyclists train and compete here.

ACTIVE SPORTS

Beach resorts usually have amenities and qualified instructors for a wide range of land and water sports. Some hotels also rent out bicycles and mopeds, but supplies vary.

There are many specialty sports tours available – cycling, fishing, birding, etc. – that can be arranged via an agency in your home country, or online. Cuba is especially well organized for scuba, snorkeling, and sailing, and these are best arranged through a dedicated travel agency.

Baseball is Cuba's favorite game.

Cubanacán's UK subsidiary has a series of package tours that include scuba diving, deep-sea fishing, birding, hiking, horseback riding, kayaking, cycling, and mountain biking. Cubanacán UK Ltd, Unit 49, Skylines Village, Limeharbour, Docklands, London E14 9TS, tel: 020-7536 8175, www.cubanacan.cu.

In Canada, Cubanacán can be contacted at 372 Bay Street, Toronto, Ontario, M5H 2W9, tel: 416-601 0343; and 1255 Rue University, Suite 211, Montreal, Quebec H3B 3B2, tel: 514-861 4444.

Birding

Birding is good all over the island but tours tend to concentrate on the Zapata peninsula, where thousands of migratory birds nest each winter (see page 222). There are also 170 species of Cuban birds here, including most of the endemics, and the best place for seeing rare species is around Santo Tomás. Other good spots are the Sierra Maestra range, the Península de Guanahacabibes in the far west, Cayo Coco, the mountains around Baracoa in the east of the island, and the Sierra Najasa region of Camagüey. Ecotur (www.ecoturcuba.tur.cu) is the travel agency in Cuba that handles all aspects of nature tourism, including birding.

Cycling

There are numerous opportunities for a Cycle Cuba vacation, often organized as a means of fundraising for various charities. Just type 'Cycle Cuba' into your search engine and you will be spoiled for choice.

Fishing

Deep-sea fishing can be arranged with **Marlin Náutica y Marinas** around the island at Marina Hemingway, Marina Tarará, Base Náutica Chapelín, Cayo Guillermo, Cayo Coco, Cayo Paredón Grande, Santa Lucía, Guardalavaca, Marina Santiago de Cuba, Marina Trinidad, Marina Cienfuegos, Jardines de la Reina, Isla de la Juventud, and Cayo Largo del Sur. Good, safe fishing boats can be rented for half a day from CUC$250–300. Fish include shark, 225kg (500lb) marlin, swordfish, tarpon as large as 70kg (150lb), sawfish, yellowfin tuna, dorado, and wahoo.

International sport fishing competitions are held mostly at the Marina Hemingway in Havana. The main tournaments include the International Ernest Hemingway White Marlin Fishing Tournament in June, the International Blue Marlin Fishing Tournament in September, and the International Tournament of Wahoo Fishing in November.

There are also great opportunities for fly-fishing in the Jardines de la Reina, off the south coast, off Cayo Largo del Sur, and in the Zapata peninsula. The salt flats at Las Salinas have recently been opened to fly-fishermen, but numbers are limited and access is controlled by the National Park Headquarters at Playa Larga, tel: 45-987 249.

Good freshwater fishing can also be found in the lakes and reservoirs, mainly for large-mouth bass (*trucha*). Good places include Maspotón in Pinar del Río, Laguna del Tesoro in the Zapata peninsula, the Zaza reservoir in Sancti Spíritus, and Redonda Lake in Ciego de Avila province.

Environmental Issues

Cuba has a good record for environmental awareness and has done much to protect and preserve the island's natural attributes. But there is, inevitably, a conflict between conservation and providing the amenities needed for the tourist industry – which is the country's main source of income. For example, hotels in certain areas must be allowed to spray against mosquitoes, even though this kills many insects that feed the indigenous and migratory birds.

'Ecotourism' is an expression bandied about a great deal, and one that is difficult to define, as it is used to cover a wide range of activities and intentions, from wilderness adventures to volunteering for activities that promote economic opportunities for local communities. And it is sometimes misused simply to promote vacations in places of natural beauty.

The infrastructure put in place to cater to our needs can have an adverse affect on a country's ecosystem, and anyone engaged in any kind of outdoor pursuit should behave responsibly, and be aware that their activities could potentially cause damage. Care should be taken at all levels, from avoiding touching coral when diving to staying on designated paths when hiking, or simply taking all your garbage home with you.

Golf

Cuba has two professional golf courses open to foreign visitors.

The **Havana Golf Club** (tel: 7-649 8918), also known as the 'DiploClub,' in Boyeros, is 30 minutes from the city center. The course is currently 9 holes but it's hoped to increase to the full 18 holes. The clubhouse has a pool, bowling alley, two bars, and a restaurant. Hire of personal caddies and trainers, and rental of clubs and balls are available at day rates. Closed Monday.

The **Varadero Golf Club** (tel: 45-668 482, www.varaderogolfclub.com), an 18-hole course covering a narrow 3.5km (2-mile) strip of land, is the venue for international events. The course, by Varadero beach, was designed in 1927 for millionaire Irénée Dupont, and the clubhouse is located next to the former Dupont mansion (Mansión Xanadú). Club and ball rental is available, and there are caddies and trainersfor hire.

Horseback Riding

Viñales and Trinidad are the main sites for horseback riding. In the former, treks can be arranged through hotels Los Jazmines and La Ermita (see page 326). In Trinidad, you can tour the Valle de los Ingenios (see page 250) on horseback. All state tour operators offer the same deals. Private guides may be cheaper, but their horses and saddles may not necessarily be in good condition. Check that your horse appears fit and healthy.

Hotels in Varadero and other resorts will also be able to arrange treks. Or, if you want a full horseback holiday, check www.captivatingcuba.com.

Rock Climbing

This is mainly done on the limestone crags called *mogotes* in the Viñales Valley; they offer fantastic climbing and the sport is becoming increasingly popular. Best months are October through April, when it is not too hot or too wet. The Hotel Jazmines (see page 326) is the central venue. Check the informative website www.cubaclimbing.com, which offers a quote from Castro: 'The Revolution was the work of climbers and cavers.'

Scuba Diving

Diving is extremely popular along Cuba's stunning coastline and all the major resorts offer diving courses and excursions. You can do it as part of an all-inclusive package or pay-as-you-go, with individual dives costing around CUC$35–40. The three marine platforms around the island – the Archipiélago del Rey to the north, the Archipiélago de la Reina to the south, and the Archipiélago de los Canarreos around Isla de la Juventud and Cayo Largo del Sur – offer a wealth of coral reefs and marine life, making diving a rewarding experience. Some of the main sites include Varadero, Santa Lucía, Cayo Largo, Isla de la Juventud, Faro de Luna, María La Gorda, and Cayo Levisa. Marlin Náutica y Marinas operates 18 dive centers and there are four hyperbaric chambers. There is also a live-aboard vessel in the Jardines de la Reina in the southeast.

Trekking

There are great opportunities for trekking in Cuba. It is possible to arrange local guides, but probably best to go on an organized trip that offers the kind of experience you want. Remember: guides are compulsory in all national parks, which is probably where you will want to walk. Pico Turquino in the Sierra Maestra is a favorite trekking destination. At 1,975 meters (6,749ft), it is the highest peak in Cuba. The landscape is stunning and there is good birdlife. Try a dedicated agency such as Andean Trails, www.andeantrails.co.uk. The Ramblers Association also take guided groups to Cuba, www.ramblersholidays.co.uk.

A – Z

A HANDY SUMMARY OF PRACTICAL INFORMATION

A

Admission Charge

There is an admission charge for most museums, galleries, and other places of touristic interest. It is generally CUC$1–5. In many places, you pay extra if you are going to use a camera, and quite a lot extra to use a video camera.

Age Restrictions

The age of consent is 18 in Cuba. Sex tourism is rife and foreign men are often seen in the company of young girls, but this is illegal and can be a blackmail trap. The minimum age for renting a car is 21, although for some types of car the limit rises to 25.

B

Budgeting for Your Trip

A good hotel in Havana will cost around CUC$160 for a double room in high season (see page 323), but there are cheaper options, and almost anywhere outside Havana is cheaper. You can choose to stay in *casas particulares*, where you will, on average, be charged CUC$25 (less outside Havana), with breakfast costing around CUC$3–5 and dinner around CUC$7–10, depending on your menu choice. Eating out is rarely very expensive. About CUC$25 per person in a smartish restaurant, but there are many restaurants and *paladares* where you can eat well for around CUC$15 or less. If you are going to drink wine, this puts the price up quite a lot. In a bar, beer costs around CUC$1.50, *mojitos* CUC$3–6, depending on location. If you go to a town such as Bayamo, where you can pay in pesos Cubanos, food and drink will be much cheaper. Car rental is expensive, around CUC$50 a day (see page 321). Taxi fares are reasonable: you can get to most places in Havana for CUC$5. Long-distance bus fares are reasonable; the longest journey you could make would be Havana to Santiago, currently CUC$51. As there are not many consumer goods for sale you are unlikely to spend much on shopping.

C

Children

Cubans love their own kids and take them everywhere with them, so they are fascinated by foreigners who do the same. Your children will be pampered guests at any hotel and the employees will quickly learn their names and interests. The beach resorts all have supervised activities for them, and family rates are offered during the low season.

Climate

Cuba has a subtropical climate, with an average annual temperature of 25°C (77°F). The mean relative humidity is 77 percent during the dry season (Nov–Apr) and 82 percent during the wet season (May–Oct).

The sun seems to shine all the time in Cuba, but temperatures are most definitely higher during the rainy 'summer' season than in the drier 'winter' months. Those who are not accustomed to melting temperatures would do well to avoid visiting the island in July and August – when most Cubans spend every spare moment either on the beach or in the shower.

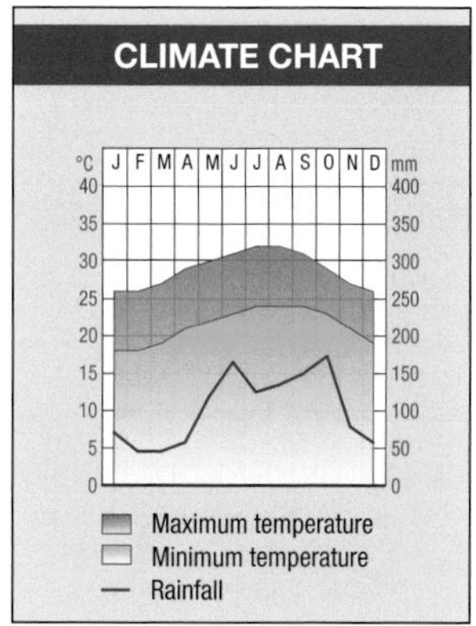

While the rain of the wet season is not often more than an inconvenience – torrential showers can be replaced by sun within the space of half an hour – the late summer is also hurricane season. Therefore, the best time to visit Cuba is from December to April, after the hurricane season is over and before the hot, muggy summer months arrive. To avoid high-season prices and crowds, visit in November or from March–April.

Crime and Safety

Crime is undoubtedly on the increase in Cuba, but it is still low by Latin American standards. Indeed, in comparison with most of the countries from which they come, visitors will find Cuba reassuringly safe. However, bag snatching and pickpocketing are not uncommon, particularly in the poorer sections of Havana and Santiago.

The streets feel safe, but visitors should still take sensible precautions. Leave travel documents, large amounts of cash, and ostentatious jewelry in your hotel, and keep a firm grip on your camera and on any bag you decide to carry – bags are best worn crossed over your shoulder.

Violent crime is rare, but there have been some incidents that have landed tourists in hospital. Most of these occurred when people tried to fight off muggers – DON'T.

Although Havana is still considered to be safer than most cities, there are some areas – such as the darker streets of Old and Central Havana – that should be avoided after dark. Be sensible and take the same precautions you would in any large, unfamiliar city, and at night keep to busy and well-lit streets (or walk in the middle of the road if there is no street lighting).

There is much less crime outside the capital, but in Santiago you must take the same precautions as you would in Old or Central Havana.

Loss of belongings

In case of theft, you should immediately report the crime to the nearest police station. Make sure you ask for the case report *(denuncia)* to back up any insurance claim on your return home. This may take time, but is essential if you intend to make a claim. The Cuban firm **Asistur** (tel: 7-866 8339 24 hours, www.asistur.cu) can help with cash advances and replacement of documents.

Emergencies

The general numbers to dial for emergencies are **106**, for police, **105** for fire, or **104** for ambulance. However, this is a relatively new system that does not function in all parts of the country, and where it does, you may not get through to an English-speaking person. There is an extensive list of alternative numbers at the beginning of the telephone directory. **Asistur** is often a visitor's best bet. The Havana office is at Prado 208, tel: 7-866 8339, and there are branches in tourist centers all over the island. Hotels are also able to help with medical emergencies.

You should report lost or stolen passports to your embassy or consulate, which can issue emergency papers to get you home.

Customs Regulations

Tourists may bring in, duty-free, personal effects – including medications for their own use or as gifts – cameras, audio recorders, MP3 players, personal computers, cellular phones (mobiles), and sports and camping equipment. All of these items should in theory be listed on a customs declaration form on arrival. Customs inspections are random.

Visitors importing electrical items as gifts – TVs, kitchen equipment, etc. – should note that 100 percent duty is payable. Certain items, mainly video recorders, modems, and photocopying equipment and supplies, are restricted: you may bring them in only for accredited people such as journalists and approved organizations. Such items will be confiscated by customs until the necessary paperwork from the Ministries of Foreign Relations and Communications is presented.

D

Disabled Travelers

Travelers with disabilities may find getting around Cuba quite difficult. Most modern hotels and many refurbished hotels have facilities, but older hotels and other buildings do not. Streets and sidewalks are narrow, with storm drains, and wheelchair ramps do not exist. Public toilets (and those in restaurants and bars) are not adapted for people with disabilities. On the positive side, Cubans are extremely helpful and will come to the assistance of anyone who appears to need it.

E

Electricity

Both 220 and 110 volts are used, but 220 is more common. Electric outlets usually take plugs with two flat prongs, but you may find some that take round prongs. It's best to come prepared with adaptors and transformers so as not to be caught out – they are inexpensive and can be bought at the airport before you travel. Power cuts are less frequent than they were, but not uncommon.

Embassies and Consulates

Havana

Canada: Calle 30 518, corner of 7ma, Miramar, tel: 7-204 2516.
Germany: Calle 13 652, corner of B, Vedado, tel: 7-833 2539, 833 2569.
UK: Calle 34 702, corner of 7, Miramar, Havana, tel: 7-204 1771.
Italy: Avenida 5 402, corner of 4, Miramar, tel: 7-204 5616.
Spain: Cárcel 51, corner Zulueta, Habana Vieja, tel: 7-868 6868.
United States: (Interests Section of the Swiss Embassy): Calzada, between L and M, Vedado, tel: 7-833 3551/9, also toll-free: 1-866-374 1769.

Etiquette

Cuba is hot and many women wear skimpy tops, but bathing suits are for the beach and should not be worn around town. Dress decently to go into a church or temple. At the Basilica El Cobre outside Santiago you will even be asked to cover your shoulders if they are bare. There are often dress codes at nightclubs: Cubans dress smartly to go out at night and men are expected to wear long pants and shirts.

G

Gay and Lesbian Travelers

The hardline Cuban policy on homosexuals has lessened in recent years (sex between consenting adults was legalized in 1979) and there is generally a more tolerant attitude (see page 21). However, it is still not the most gay-friendly place to visit, although there is a growing number of openly gay people – mostly in the capital and in some small, laid-back places such as Viñales and Baracoa.

H

Health and Medical Care

No health certificate is required of visitors unless they are arriving from areas where cholera, smallpox, or yellow fever exist, in which case they must show a certificate of vaccination against those diseases. However, it's a good idea to be up to date with tetanus, typhoid, and hepatitis A vaccinations. There are no malarial areas in

Cuba, but dengue fever, although it has been virtually eradicted through determined fumigation measures, may still occur. There is no vaccination, so do all you can to prevent mosquito bites – use a DEET-based repellent, and cover up in areas where mosquitoes are prevalent. The fever is spread by the *Aedes aegypti* mosquito which, unusually, tends to bite during the day rather than at night. The illness presents with flu-like symptoms and, while usually mild, can be serious.

On the whole, biting and stinging insects, and bugs in general, are not a great problem in Cuba.

Common medicines – such as aspirin and basic stomach remedies – can be bought in hotels, but it's sensible to bring a small supply with you. More specialized items can usually be bought over the counter without prescription from CUC pharmacies, but you should bring all your own prescription drugs with you. In Havana, the **Farmacia Internacional** is at Avenida 41, corner 20, Playa, tel: 7-204 2051, and at the **Hotel Habana Libre**, corner L and 23, Vedado, tel: 7-838 4593. There are other good pharmacies at the **Camilo Cienfuegos Hospital** on Línea and Calle 13, Vedado, tel: 7-833 3599, and at the **Clínica Central Cira García**, Avenida 20, 4101, corner Calle 41, Playa, tel: 7-204 2880, open 24 hours. Outside Havana, try the international clinics in resort areas or any high-street pharmacy in urban areas.

To avoid upset stomachs and diarrhea – the two main complaints suffered by tourists – drink bottled water, and plenty of it, and eat lightly. Be sensible about over exposure to the sun.

Medical services

All hotels have a first-aid post of sorts, and the larger hotels will have a resident doctor or nurse, plus transportation to take a patient to the nearest clinic or hospital. Unless you fall ill in a remote rural area, as a foreign visitor you will be treated in a CUC-only hospital or a special tourist clinic (run by Servimed, www.servimedcuba.com).

Most doctors and some nurses speak at least a little English, but hardly anybody is multilingual. The Cuban health-care system is free and readily available to all Cubans, but medicines are in short supply except in facilities that cater to CUC-paying foreigners.

I

Internet

Many of the large tourist hotels have Internet access and in some (the Inglaterra and the Nacional in Havana, for example) it is available to non-guests on presentation of a passport. This can be expensive, with the business centers in the top hotels charging up to CUC$15 per hour. Wi-fi is rarely available except in some of the business hotels, such as the executive floor of the Hotel Nacional or the lobby of the Hotel Parque Central. Most towns have a branch of ETECSA (the telephone and communications company), which offers Internet facilities. In 2013, 133 Internet access offices, called Nauta, opened, costing CUC$5 per hour. Be aware that telephone lines can be slow and unreliable, so it's always worth writing long emails on Word and saving them to a pen drive/memory stick in case the connection breaks. Lines may also be down completely and access unavailable.

L

Language Courses

The University of Havana, the University of Santiago de Cuba, and the Central University in Santa Clara offer intensive Spanish-language programs for foreigners and a range of specialized courses and seminars for Spanish-speaking foreigners. Low-cost lodgings and meals as well as field trips are usually part of a student package. Language courses are also offered by some tour operators, together with music and dance classes, eg Càlédöñiâ, based in Scotland, tel: +44-131-621 7721, www.caledonialanguages.com.

M

Maps

The best road map of Cuba is Guía de Carreteras by the Directorio Turístico de Cuba (on sale in Cuba for CUC$6). Freytag and Berndt's Kuba/Cuba (1:250,000) is less up to date but has useful city plans. Individual city-centre maps of larger cities cost around CUC$1–2. Hotels and bookstores in Havana and Santiago sell reasonable maps; however, they may not always be in stock when you want them.

Insurance

From May 1, 2010, health insurance has been mandatory for all visitors to Cuba. Tourists and all non-resident Cubans must hold a medical insurance policy that has been issued by one of the specific companies approved by the Cuban government. This is in fact a list of umbrella companies that provide medical and specialized assistance (repatriation) on behalf of individual insurance companies. Check with your insurance company whether they are on the approved list (they may not know and will have to find out for you). If you do not have the correct papers, you will be forced to buy an approved insurance policy on arrival at the airport in Cuba.

Media

Newspapers and magazines

The printed media of Cuba is extremely limited due to paper shortages and governmental control. Newspapers are posted on kiosks for the general population to read, and you sometimes see vendors wandering the street with copies to sell. The only daily paper is the Communist Party organ, *Granma*, which mainly offers an update on solidarity, trade and agriculture, and provides interesting rather than scintillating reading. It is published weekly in Spanish, English, French, German, and Portuguese. Tourists are more likely to find the international edition in hotel stores, but street sellers often have English-language versions.

The long-established magazine *Bohemia* offers general features, and there are other Cuban publications on sale at CUC newsstands in hotels and airports. Four- and five-star hotels (particularly in Havana) often carry foreign publications from *Time* to *Cosmopolitan*.

Television

Cuban national television is broadcast on five state-owned national channels (Cubavisión, Tele Rebelde, Multivisión, Canal Educativo, and Canal Educativo 2). National and international **news** is reported on two half-hour programs.

Sports events – especially baseball, boxing, and soccer – are often covered live. Other shows include officials and specialists **speaking** at **length** and **music** of all kinds in concerts or videos. Foreign **movies** (usually American), seven a week, are shown on Thursday, Friday, Saturday, and Sunday. Action movies are most popular, but a recent crackdown on violence and sex has resulted in an increase of 'family' movies. **Soaps**, usually Brazilian, Mexican, or Cuban, are extremely popular. North American soaps and series are also screened.

Tourist hotels all have satellite TV with more than 20 channels.

Radio

Just about everybody in Cuba has a radio, and loud music is a constant background sound wherever you go. Apart from local stations, radios pick up waves from Miami, Jamaica, and the American Forces Network at Guantánamo Base. There are six state-owned national radio stations and each province has its own station as well. Reception varies and you can't pick up the signal for all of them everywhere.

Radio Reloj (Clock Radio) gives round-the-clock news on AM, to the infuriating background noise of a ticking clock; **Radio Havana Cuba** broadcasts news and features on short wave, where the BBC also comes through, though the reception is poor (early morning on 6195, 8–10am on 15220, 10am–1pm on 17840, and mid-afternoon till late in the evening on 5975).

Voice of America broadcasts from 6pm on 7070, short wave. **Radio Martí**, Voice of America's Spanish-language propaganda service, broadcasts from Miami, and often changes its frequencies to avoid jamming, but without much success.

Money Matters

Although President Raúl Castro has announced his intention to unify the currency, at the moment Cuba still has two currencies: the *peso Cubano* (CUP or *moneda nacional*) divided into 100 centavos, and the *peso convertible* (CUC). Foreigners are expected to use CUC most of the time and will be charged in CUC for all accommodations, most food, and transportation. Euros can be used in the large resorts: Varadero, Cayo Largo, Cayo Coco, and Santa Lucía.

Some people find it useful to change a small amount of foreign currency into Cuban pesos (the exchange rate is CUC$1 = CUP24) for use on local buses (fares on most urban routes cost between 40 centavos and one peso), in movie theaters, when shopping for fresh fruit at farmers' markets, when buying food and drink from street vendors, and in some off-the-beaten-track restaurants. You can make domestic phone calls using the peso phones, saving yourself a lot of money, so you may also want to have a few 20-centavo coins for phone booths. However, most old peso phones have been replaced with the new type, which take only cards.

Changing money

You can change foreign currency into pesos convertibles at government-licensed CADECA booths and some large banks, and it is wise not to attempt to do so elsewhere. There is no black market. Branches of CADECA are fairly widely scattered. In Old Havana, they can be found on Calle Obispo and Calle Oficios and elsewhere, and in Vedado there is one on La Rampa (Calle 23) and one on the corner of the Malecón and Calle D. Every sizable town has at least one – ask at your hotel. CADECAs change travelers' checks but you must produce the original purchase receipt as well as your passport. American Express travelers' checks or any others issued by a US bank are not accepted. British banks will not even sell you travelers' checks for use in Cuba for that reason.

Change foreign currency into convertible pesos at the CADECA booth at the airport when you arrive. Bring sterling or euros if possible, as a 10 percent tax is charged on US dollars. Make sure your notes are clean, with no writing on them, as any blemished foreign currency will be rejected. Remember to keep enough convertible pesos to pay the CUC$25 departure tax, but don't take them home with you except as souvenirs, since they are not, in fact, convertible currency, despite the name. You can exchange them back into another currency at the airport in Havana, but it is unwise to count on this, as there may be delays and the exchange desk, although theoretically open 24 hours, may not be.

The exchange rate fluctuates slightly, but is approximately CUC$1 = US$1.08 (before tax), CAN$1.10, €0.80, £0.72.

Credit cards

Access/MasterCard, Visa, and other credit cards are welcome at most hotels, and some restaurants and stores, provided they have been issued outside the US by non-US banks, so American Express is no use. Check your card, as some store cards are issued by MBNA or other US bank and will be rejected.

Credit-card operations in Cuba do not always run smoothly. The centralized computer system often fails, going down for hours at a time; this affects every credit-card machine in the land, and you will not be able to use your card at all while the system failure lasts.

A credit card can also be a useful backup if you need cash in an emergency: cash can be withdrawn against a credit card at branches of the Banco Financiero Internacional, and at CADECA, but an 11 percent commission rate is currently being charged, which makes it an expensive transaction. Added to this, all purchases of cash or goods on a credit card will be converted from CUCs to US dollars, incurring the 10 percent exchange tax, before conversion to your own currency by your credit card company, which may charge you further fees and commissions. There is also an increasing number of ATMs in Havana

Banks

Banco Financiero Internacional

Open Mon–Fri 8.30am–3pm. You can get cash on a credit card here, if it's not from a US bank. In **Havana**, there are branches inside the Hotel Habana Libre; at the corner of Línea and O, Vedado (near Hotel Nacional), also open on Sat 8.30am–noon; at the Plaza de la Revolución; in Old Havana at Oficios, corner Brasil (near Plaza de San Francisco); and at Calle 18 111. In **Santiago de Cuba**, there is a branch on Avenida Las Américas, corner J Sueño. There are other branches in all major towns and holiday resorts.

Banco Metropolitano SA

Head office is at O'Reilly 402, in Old Havana, but there are many branches throughout the capital. They deal in foreign currencies (cash on credit cards, traveler's checks, etc.), and have shorter lines than the Banco Financiero).

– for example, at the CADECA office in Calle Obispo, available when the office itself is closed – each site should give the location of others in the area. Be warned that there are almost no opportunities to withdraw cash against Cirrus or Switch cards, and that these transactions are best done in Havana and Santiago.

Cash

While travelers' checks are a safe way to carry money, you should always try to have a good supply of cash with you, particularly if you head out of the city. Not all provincial hotels will be able to cash travelers' checks for you.

Getting change from big bills is often difficult, so it is worthwhile keeping a stock of 10s, 5s, and single bills in your wallet. Try to get as many small-denomination bills as possible when you change foreign currency, and always try to break big bills when you are staying at city hotels, where they are more likely to have a better supply in their tills. If your hotel can't help, you may have to go to a bank; most banks will change big bills for you. You will normally have to show your passport if you produce a 50- or 100-CUC bill in a Cuban store.

The UK Foreign Office warns that the wider use of the convertible peso (CUC) has meant an increase in the number of forged CUC bills of all denominations but in particular 100-CUC bills.

Be careful, too, when you pay for something, that the change you are given is in CUCs not *pesos cubanos* – the bills look extremely similar.

O

Opening Hours

Most banks open Mon–Fri 8.30am–3pm. Most Cuban offices open around 8.30am–5 or 6pm, often with a break at lunchtime. But it is not rare for offices, even those serving the public, to close early because of blackouts, shortages, and transportation problems.

Farmers' markets open early, from around 7am or even earlier, and close when traders decide to leave – usually between 4 and 6pm.

CUC retail stores (often referred to as dollar stores) are all over Cuba; most open Mon–Sat 10am–5pm but may stay open later.

CUC supermarkets usually open Mon–Sat 9am–6pm and Sun 9am–1pm. Tourists may be asked to show their passport at the *diplomercado*, near the Russian Embassy in Havana's Miramar suburb (see page 344). One of the city's original dollar supermarkets (before the embargo on the US$), popular with expats, the 'diplo"' sells fresh meat and vegetables, and household supplies. It is open Mon–Sat 9am–7pm. Many of the bigger stores open 9am–9pm.

P

Postal Services

Every rural town has a post office, and major cities have a central post office with municipal branches. You can buy stamps *(sellos)* here for pesos. In hotels, you will be charged the same price, but in CUCs. Some stamps are not glued, so you have to ask for a dab of glue at a post office.

Postcards and letters to Europe cost 75 cents. Domestic delivery is slow, but usually faster from city to city than within the same city. Postcards and letters to Europe and the Americas sometimes only take a fortnight but may take a month or more, even via airmail.

Mother's Day (second Sunday in May) is the one day of the year when cards and telegrams are delivered on time all over Cuba. For a week or so ahead of the mailing deadline, cardboard boxes labeled by province are stacked in the lobby of the larger post offices so senders can drop in their addressed and stamped cards. The boxes are flown to the provincial capital to be sorted and then dispatched – and they are sure to reach mother on her day.

Public Holidays

January 1 Liberation Day, commemorating the guerrillas' triumph over Batista.
Good Friday (date varies).
May 1 Labor Day, celebrated with workers' parades.
July 25–27 A three-day holiday celebrating July 26, 1953, the date of the attack on the Moncada Garrison in Santiago, recognized as the start of the revolution.
October 10 Celebrating the start of the War of Independence against Spain in 1868.
December 25 Christmas Day.
In addition to these official public holidays, there are innumerable other important dates that are commemorated, including:
January 28 The birth of José Martí (1853).
April 19 The victory at the Bay of Pigs (1962).
Second Sunday in May Mother's Day.
October 8 Death of Che Guevara.

R

Religious Services

The government blunted the influence of the Catholic Church in the early 1960s, but never cracked down on it completely. Since the Pope's visit to Cuba in 1998 there has been a resurgence of Catholic practice – and a seeming relaxation of hostility from the government. Mass is still said in churches throughout the island. Your hotel tourism bureau can direct you to the church of your choice, but service times vary.

In Havana, times of Mass in the **cathedral** in Old Havana are posted at the entrance. The **Jewish synagogue** at Línea and Calle M holds services and has a library. The **Methodist church**, a block away from the Habana Libre Hotel at calles 25 and K, lays on social activities as well as services, and has a small guesthouse. **Catholic churches** are open all over the island and anyone can walk in at any time to have a look or attend Mass.

S

Student Travelers

There are no official discounts or special deals for student travelers in Cuba, but discounts on accommodations, museum entrance fees, etc. are offered in some places to holders of ISIC cards (International Student Identity Cards). Check the website: www.isic.org.

T

Telecommunications

The Cuban local telephone service has undergone a complete overhaul and it is now possible to make crackle-free calls right across the island (sometimes). The state telecommunications company is ETECSA, also known as Telepunto in some places. ETECSA offers a full range of services, including phone rental, Internet, and international calls. There are usually lines, so allow plenty of time.

Local and international phone calls can be made through the operator from your hotel room (or sometimes hotel reception), but calls can be made far more cheaply from public phones. There are still some public phones that take coins, either 20-centavo or 1-peso cubano coins. Most have now been converted to pre-paid phonecards *(tarjetas)*. There are two types of card on offer: 'chip' and 'propia,' which cost the same but the latter has lower rates at night and can be used to make calls from a private phone as well as a public call box. The best and cheapest cards to get are the **Propia** cards priced in *pesos cubanos*, but these are supposed to be reserved for Cubans and are difficult for tourists to obtain. Foreigners are supposed to buy those priced in CUCs, which are extremely expensive. Propia cards give you a personal code that you input before using a phone. They can be bought at branches of ETECSA and cost 5 or 10 *pesos cubanos*.

Peso convertible cards, for local or international calls, can also be bought at ETECSA offices and at hotel reception desks, and come in denominations of 5, 10, 15, or 25 CUCs. Local calls cost about 5 *centavos* a minute, calls to other provinces cost about 35 *centavos* a minute. International calls with a Propia card are expensive: CUC$1.95 a minute to the US and Canada; CUC$3.65 a minute to Europe and the rest of the world (and even more if you call from a hotel), but there are reductions for calls between 6pm and 6am.

Collect calls (reverse charge/ *cobro revertido*) can be made from a regular Cuban line (as found in most homes) to the US, Canada, the UK, Mexico, Puerto Rico, Portugal, Spain, and Italy, but they are prohibitively expensive. You cannot make a collect call from a hotel or a public phone.

It is possible to rent cell phones (mobiles) at Cubacel. There is an office of Cubacel at Telepunto, Calle Habana, 406, between Obispo and Obrapía, in Old Havana, or they can be found in ETECSA offices around the country. The head office is at Centro de Negocios Miramar, Edificio Santa Clara, corner calles 3 and 78, tel: 7-5264 2266; www.etecsa.cu; and there is an office at Havana airport. Phones cost around CUC$5 a day to rent. Call charges are high, about 70 cents a minute for local calls, rising steeply for calls outside Cuba. As with your own cell phone if used abroad, you pay for incoming as well as outgoing calls, although an incoming call from abroad is free. The bill must be paid by cash or credit card. A deposit is refunded when the phone is returned and the bill has been paid. You can use your own cell phone in Cuba (where there is a signal) and sending a short text message home can be quicker and easier than struggling with the internet at ETECSA. Tariffs depend on your own service provider.

Telephone codes

Telephone services have been extensively modernized and many numbers have changed, but the system has now settled down. Telephone numbers are usually six digits, except in Havana, where they are seven digits, and cell phones, which have eight digits (beginning with a 5).

If you're phoning from outside Cuba, dial the country code (53), then the area code, and then the number. Area codes are: Havana city 7, Havana province 47, Cienfuegos 43, Las Tunas 31, Pinar del Río 48, Villa Clara 42, Holguín 24, Sancti Spíritus 41 (except Condado, El Pedrero, Topes de Collantes 42), Granma 23, Isla de la Juventud 46, Cayo Largo del Sur 45, Ciego de Avila 33, Santiago de Cuba 22, Matanzas 45, Camagüey 32, and Guantánamo 21. No area code is needed if you are dialling a cell/mobile phone.

Inside Cuba, to call another city from Havana you must dial 0 before the area code (eg Santa Clara from Havana 042-); to call Havana from another city you must dial 0 before the area code (07-); to call any city from another (eg Santa Clara from Cienfuegos) you must dial 01 before the area code (0142-). The 0 and 01 still apply if you are calling a cell/mobile phone; the initial 5 acts as an area code.

In general, don't use the area code when phoning within a province.

In listings in this guide we have not included the international code (53), and we have kept to the general rules outlined above, but be aware that there may be differences and changes. If you're stuck, ask for help in a hotel or in an office of ETECSA, the Cuban state telephone company, although in the latter you will need to speak Spanish.

To make an international call, first dial the access code 119, then the country code, area code, and phone number. International operators speak English.

Time Zone

Cuba is on Eastern Standard Time (Daylight Saving applies during summer), which is GMT -5. When it's noon in Havana, it's 5pm in London, 6pm in Madrid and Rome, and 2pm in Buenos Aires.

Tipping

Taxi drivers, waiters, and hotel staff should be tipped in CUCs – this is the only access to convertible currency that they get. Ten percent is usual for taxi drivers and restaurant staff. You should leave CUC$1 a day for a hotel chambermaid.

Toilets

The first thing to remember about toilets is that Cuban plumbing is unreliable, so you must always throw paper in the bin provided, not into the bowl – even in hotels with smart new amenities. The second thing is to take your own toilet paper with you (this doesn't apply to hotels). There are very few public restrooms and those that do exist (at bus stations, for example) are best avoided, if possible. Restrooms in bars and restaurants are usually fairly decent, and in most places they don't question whether or not you are a customer, especially as you are expected to tip the attendant who sits outside and (sometimes) proffers toilet paper.

Tourist Information

All hotels have a tourism bureau, where restaurant reservations can be made, sightseeing tours booked, etc. More complicated queries should be addressed to your guide (if you have one) or to your hotel public-relations manager (if they have one).

General tourist information offices do not really exist in Cuba. Infotur is the only tourist-information service, with kiosks at José Martí Airport, Terminal 3 (tel: 7-642 6101; in Old Havana at Calle Obispo 521, between Bernaza and Villegas (tel: 7-866 3333), and out in Playas del Este at Avenida Las Terrazas between calles 11 and 12, Santa María del Mar (tel: 7-797 1261).

Tour Agencies & Operators

There is a whole range of state tourism enterprises whose services sometimes overlap and which concentrate on offering packages or other specific services, but they can give assistance

in all areas, and most of them have improved greatly in recent years in both helpfulness and efficiency.
Amistur Cuba specializes in political tours for people wishing to see the revolutionary side of Cuba. They can be found on Paseo 406, between 17 and 19, Vedado, tel: 7-830 1220, 7-833 4544; www.amistur.cu.
Cubanacán administrates numerous hotels, promotes and arranges conventions, and organizes tours of all kinds, including health tourism, nature tourism, and water sports activities. Its main office is in Havana, at Calle 23 (La Rampa) 156, between O and P, Vedado, tel: 7-204 1658; www.cubanacan.cu. In the UK, tel: 020-7537 7909.
Cubamar specializes in ecotourism, youth activities, bicycle tours, and other general sports. It also rents self-drive RVs and motorhomes. The main office is at Calle 3, between 12 and Malecón, Vedado, Havana, tel: 7-833 2523/4; www.cubamarviajes.cu.
Cubatur was for many years the only commercial subsidiary of the Ministry of Tourism (MINTUR), the state umbrella organization for tourism. Now, Cubatur sells excursions through the tourism bureaux in most of Cuba's hotels and in their own offices, which can be found in most towns and resorts. Cubatur's headquarters and its tourism office in Havana are at Calle F 157, between calles 9 and Calzada, Vedado, tel: 7-833 3569; www.cubatur.cu.
Ecotur is the agency that deals with nature tourism, http://cubanature travel.com/ or www.ecoturcuba.tur.cu, including birding and hiking.
Gaviota books hotel accommodations, organizes excursions, car rental, dive packages, and more. The main office is at Edificio La Marina, 3rd floor, Avenida del Puerto 102, Old Havana, tel: 7-204 7683; www.gaviota-grupo.com.

Many workers rely on tips.

Gran Caribe runs most of the island's luxury hotels, including the Hotel Nacional in Havana, tel: 7-204 9202; www.gran-caribe.com.
Habaguanex is part of the Havana City Historian's office. The company runs and promotes enterprises in Old Havana, and has a number of experienced multilingual guides attached to its own travel agency, called San Cristóbal, at Calle Oficios 110 bajos, between Lamparilla and Amargura, Old Havana, tel: 7-861 9171; www.habaguanex.com.
Havanatur arranges hotel accommodations, as well as excursions of all kinds. It has its own fleet of buses and a car rental agency, Havanautos. Its headquarters is in the Edificio Sierra Maestra, Calle 1a, between 2 and 0, Miramar, tel: 7-830 8227; www.havanatur.cu.

Tour Agencies in the UK

A growing number of UK operators offer Cuba in their brochures:
Càlédöñiâ,
33 Sandport Street, Edinburgh EH6 6EP, tel: 0131-621 7721
www.caledonialanguages.com
Language courses and activity holidays, including salsa and music, trekking, diving, and cultural tours.
Cox and Kings Travel, 6th floor, 30 Millbank, London SW1P 4EE, tel: 020-7873 5000
www.coxandkings.co.uk
Cultural tours to Havana and tailor-made vacations.
Interchange
Interchange House, 27 Stafford Road, Croydon, Surrey, CR0 9NG, tel: 020-8681 3612
www.interchangeworldwide.com
Group tours to Havana, Varadero, and western Cuba plus tailor-made itineraries.
Journey Latin America,
12–13 Heathfield Terrace, Chiswick, London W4 4JE, tel: 020-8747 8315
www.journeylatinamerica.co.uk
Cultural tours, tailor-made tours, and twin-center vacations with other Latin American countries.
Kuoni Travel, Kuoni House, Deepdene Avenue, Dorking, Surrey RH5 4AZ, tel: 01306-747 002
www.kuoni.co.uk
Offices throughout the UK.
Tours include Havana, Santiago, and Camagüey. Packages to Varadero, Guardalavaca, Cayo Ensenachos, and Cayo Coco.
Saga Holidays
The Saga Building, Enbrook Park, Folkestone, Kent CT20 3SE, tel: 0800-096 0078
www.saga.co.uk Organizes cultural and general-interest tours.
Western & Oriental,
W&O Travel, Laydon House, 76-86 Turnmill Street, London EC1M 5QU, tel: 202-7666 1260
www.wandotravel.com
Cultural tours and itineraries tailor-made to meet individual requirements.

V

Visas and Passports

All visitors entering Cuba must show a passport valid for at least six months beyond the date of arrival in Cuba. In addition, visitors must have a **tourist card** *(tarjeta de turista)*, issued by the Cuban Consulate directly or, more commonly, through a travel agent. This will be valid for the length of your planned visit, but can be extended (once) up to the date shown on your return airplane ticket – as long as the total time you are in the country does not exceed 60 days. Immigration officials stamp your tourist card, not your passport. Do not lose it – you must show it when you leave the country.

Those planning to stay with a Cuban family (other than a licensed *casa particular*) must apply some time in advance for a **tourist visa**, while any commercial travelers must obtain a **business visa**. Regulations stipulate that travelers to Cuba must spend a minimum of three nights in a pre-booked hotel, but a *casa particular* is sufficient. Ask at the local Cuban Consulate (or check with your travel agent) for more information.

Visas for US citizens

These are handled by the Cuban Interests Section in Washington, DC. United States Treasury Department regulations prohibit US citizens from spending money in Cuba unless they qualify as journalists, researchers, businesspeople in specifically licensed sectors, or relatives of Cubans living on the island.

Americans who oppose their government's trade and travel blockade against Cuba regularly evade or purposely violate these restrictions, and some do so just out of curiosity: many fly in via Canada, Mexico, or Jamaica. Although they could theoretically be prosecuted, they generally aren't.

W

Websites

www.cubagov.cu – official government site, general information in Spanish and English.
www.cubasi.cu – news, culture, and general information about Cuba in Spanish and English.
www.infotur.cu – tourist information website, with information on accommodations, events, activities, etc. in Spanish and English.
www.casaparticularcuba.org – useful site for booking *casas particulares*, in English.

What to Bring

Clothes

Casual, comfortable clothes are appropriate anywhere on the island, especially light cotton garments that can be put on and taken off in layers as the temperature changes. As far as many Cubans are concerned, the less you wear the better.

Shorts and bathing suits are accepted at all seaside resorts, though more coverage is expected for dining out or visiting museums and galleries. Unless you're coming here for business you won't have much use for a suit and tie or a formal dress. You also don't want to stand out by looking too smart and 'dressed up.'

A waterproof jacket is optional – you can usually wait out a tropical shower, and if there is a real downpour, a waterproof jacket will be of minimal use – although an umbrella might be. Cubans often carry umbrellas for protection from the sun, and also whip them open at the first drop of rain.

Take comfortable walking shoes, and dark glasses for protection against harsh tropical sunlight. Straw and cloth sunhats can be bought in any tourist store if you forget to bring one. If you are going to be traveling on long-distance buses bring a fleece or warm jersey. The air conditioning usually has only one setting in Cuba – high.

Transformers and adaptors

As already mentioned (see Electricity) you cannot be sure of the voltage or the socket type you will encounter, so it is as well to come prepared.

Medical supplies and toiletries

Travelers to Cuba should bring their own medications, diarrhea remedies, vitamins, adhesive bandages, contraceptives, toothpaste, insect repellent, and sunscreen. It's not a bad idea to bring a supply of toilet paper and tissues as well, if you are going to be traveling around.

Most of the larger hotels sell basic medications at European prices. A wider range of drugs can be obtained from pharmacies (see page 348).

Emergency treatment is free, while follow-up treatment and medications are payable in CUCs. Foreigners will be treated in a CUC-only hospital, and health costs at these hospitals are as high as in the US. You are strongly advised to take out **health insurance** before leaving home. Cuba is now making insurance compulsory and you are likely to be sold a policy at the airport if you don't already have one (see page 348).

A dilemma

In many Cuban towns you will be approached by people asking you for soap, moisturising cream, or pens. These are articles that are in short supply and/or can only be bought with *pesos convertibles*.
It is difficult to know what the response should be. On one hand, it is cheap and easy to bring a small supply of these things with you and dole them out to people who have very little. On the other, it does encourage a culture in which Cubans look on tourists simply as suppliers of unobtainable goodies and pester them accordingly.
Perhaps the best way to deal with this situation, if you would like to give things that could be useful but don't want to add to the problem, is to deliver things like pens and notebooks and soap directly to schools, where teachers can distribute them – or refuse them, if they choose.

Weights and Measures

Officially, Cuba uses the metric system, but you will find that goods at places that deal mostly with Cuban shoppers, such as farmers' markets, use imperial pounds *(libras)* – a hangover from the days when the USA provided almost all of Cuba's imports.

Women Travelers

Foreign women traveling alone may opt to visit Cuba on a package beach vacation, or a cultural tour, with Cuban specialists guiding and initiating most of the action. However, Cuba is not a difficult or dangerous place in which to travel as a single woman. Cubans out in the hinterland may regard a foreign woman traveling alone as unusual, but they will normally be friendly and helpful. Women are generally safer in Cuba than in most places in the world. Although rape is uncommon in Cuba, foreign women should be aware that the Cuban definition of 'rape' is not the same as in many other places; a woman who takes a man up to her hotel room or indulges in public heavy petting will not be taken seriously if she later claims rape.

Women can expect a lot of male attention: this may be in the form of whistling, hissing (this is not perceived as rude in Cuba), or comments whispered or shouted in the street. This can be annoying but it is rarely aggressive, and is just something a woman is expected to get used to in such a macho country – Cuban women receive similar attention. Ignore the perpetrators and they will normally leave you alone. Any kind of acknowledgment is likely to be taken as a come-on.

Conversion chart

Metric to Imperial

1cm = 0.39 inch
1 meter = 3ft 28ins
1km = 0.62 miles
1 gram = 0.035oz
1kg = 2lbs 21oz
1 liter = 0.22 Imp. gallons
1 liter = 0.26 US gallons

Imperial to Metric

1 inch = 2.54cm
1ft = 0.30 meters
1 mile = 1.61km
1oz = 28.35 grams
1lb = 0.45kg
1 Imp. gallon = 4.55 liters
1 US gallon = 3.79 liters

LANGUAGE

UNDERSTANDING THE LANGUAGE

BASIC RULES

Spanish is the language of Cuba. It is a phonetic language: words are pronounced exactly as they are spelled. Spanish distinguishes between the two genders, masculine and feminine, and the subjunctive verb form is an endless source of headaches for students. As a general rule, the accent falls on the second-to-last syllable, unless it is otherwise marked with an accent (´) or the word ends in D, L, R, or Z.

Vowels in Spanish are always pronounced the same way. The double L (LL) is pronounced like the y in 'yes,' the double R is rolled. The H is silent in Spanish, whereas J (and G when it precedes an E or I) is pronounced like a guttural H (similar to the end sound of Scottish loch).

When addressing someone you are not familiar with, use the formal 'usted.' The informal 'tú' is reserved for relatives and friends. It is worth trying to master a few words and phrases. It will be much appreciated, and will also make your stay more enjoyable, as the majority of Cubans do not speak English – except for staff in the smarter hotels, who are sometimes fluent; and waiters, who know enough English to understand what you want and tell you how much it will cost. The younger generation now learns English in school, but the older generation had Russian as their second language – and they are not finding this very useful now.

The following brief lexicon is Spanish as spoken in Spain, with a few Cuban amendments. A list of 'Cubanisms' follows.

WORDS AND PHRASES

Hello *Hola*
How are you? *¿Cómo está usted?*
What is your name? *¿Cómo se llama usted?*
My name is... *Yo me llamo...*
Do you speak English? *¿Habla inglés?*
I am British/American *Yo soy británico(a)/norteamericano(a)*
I don't understand *No comprendo*
Can you help me? *¿Me puede ayudar?*
I am looking for... *Estoy buscando*
Where is...? *¿Dónde está...?*
I'm sorry *Lo siento/Perdone*
I don't know *No lo sé*
No problem *No hay problema*
There isn't any *No hay*
Have a good day *Que tenga un buen día*
Let's go *Vámonos*
See you tomorrow *Hasta mañana*
See you soon *Hasta pronto*
At what time? *¿A qué hora?*
When? *¿Cuándo?*
What time is it? *¿Qué hora es?*
yes/no *sí/no*
please *por favor*
thank you (very much) *(muchas) gracias*
you're welcome *de nada*
goodbye *adiós*
good evening/night *buenas tardes/noches*
today *hoy*
yesterday *ayer*
tomorrow *mañana (note: mañana also means 'morning')*
tomorrow morning *mañana por la mañana*
the day after tomorrow *pasado mañana*
now *ahora*
later *después*
this afternoon/evening *esta tarde*
tonight *esta noche*
next week *la semana que viene*

Getting around

I want to get off at... *Quiero bajarme en...*
Is there a bus to ...? *¿Hay un omnibús a ....?*
I'd like a taxi *Quisiera un taxi.*
Please take me to... *Por favor, lléveme a...*
How much will it cost? *¿Cuánto va a costar el viaje?*
Keep the change *Guarde el cambio.*
What street is this? *¿Qué calle es ésta?*
How far is...? *¿A qué distancia está...?*
airport *aeropuerto*
customs *aduana*
train station *estación de tren*
bus station *estación deomnibuses/terminal de guaguas*
bus stop *parada de omnibús*
platform *andén*
ticket *tickete/boleto*
round-trip ticket *boleto de ida y vuelta*
hitchhiking *autostop/la botella*
restrooms/toilets *baños*
This is the hotel address *Ésta es la dirección del hotel*

At the hotel

I'd like a (single/double) room *Quiero una habitación (sencilla/doble)*
... with bathroom *con baño*
... with a view *con vista*
Does that include breakfast? *¿Incluye desayuno?*
May I see the room? *¿Puedo ver la habitación?*

washbasin *lavabo*
bed *cama*
key *llave*
elevator/lift *ascensor*
air conditioning *aire acondicionado*
swimming pool *piscina*
to book *reservar*

Emergencies

Help! *¡Socorro!*
Stop! *¡Pare!/¡Alto!*
Go away! *¡Vayase!*
Call a doctor *Llame a un médico*
Where is the nearest hospital? *¿Dónde está el hospital más cercana?*
I am sick *Estoy enfermo*
I have lost my passport/purse (bag) *He perdido mi pasaporte/ bolsa*
I want to report... *Quiero denunciar…*

On the road

Where is the nearest garage? *¿Dónde está el taller más próximo?*
Our car has broken down *Nuestro coche se ha averiado*
I want to have my car repaired *Quiero que reparen mi coche*
It's not your right of way *Usted no tiene prioridad*
the road to... *la carretera a...*
left *izquierda*
right *derecha*
straight on *derecho/todo recto*

Dates and seasons

Days of the Week
Monday *lunes*
Tuesday *martes*
Wednesday *miércoles*
Thursday *jueves*
Friday *viernes*
Saturday *sábado*
Sunday *domingo*
Months
January *enero*
February *febrero*
March *marzo*
April *abril*
May *mayo*
June *junio*
July *julio*
August *agosto*
September *septiembre*
October *octubre*
November *noviembre*
December *diciembre*
Seasons
Spring *primavera*
Summer *verano*
Autumn *otoño*
Winter *invierno*

Numbers

1 *uno*
2 *dos*
3 *tres*
4 *cuatro*
5 *cinco*
6 *seis*
7 *siete*
8 *ocho*
9 *nueve*
10 *diez*
11 *once*
12 *doce*
13 *trece*
14 *catorce*
15 *quince*
16 *dieciseis*
17 *diecisiete*
18 *dieciocho*
19 *diecinueve*
20 *veinte*
21 *veintiuno*
30 *treinta*
40 *cuarenta*
50 *cincuenta*
60 *sesenta*
70 *setenta*
80 *ochenta*
90 *noventa*
100 *cien*
200 *doscientos*
500 *quinientos*
1,000 *mil*
10,000 *diez mil*
1,000,000 *un millón*

near *cerca*
far *lejos*
opposite *frente a*
beside *al lado de*
parking lot *aparcamiento/parqueo*
at the end *al final*
on foot *a pie*
by car *en carro/auto*
street *calle*
square *plaza*
give way *ceda el paso*
exit *salida*
dead end *calle sin salida*
wrong way *dirección prohibida*
no parking *prohibido aparcar*
highway *autopista*
toll *peaje*
one-way street *una sola vía*
road closed *camino cerrado*
diversion *desvío*
speed limit *límite de velocidad*
gas *gasolina*/**gas station** *gasolinera*
unleaded *sin plomo*/**diesel** *gasoil*
water *agua*
oil *aceite*/**air** *aire*
puncture *pinchazo*
bulb *bombilla*

On the telephone

I would like a phonecard *Quisiera una tarjeta de teléfono*
I want to make an international (local) call *Quiero hacer una llamada internacional (local).*
What is the code for...? *¿Cuál es el código para...?*
Hello? *¿Dígame?*
Who's calling? *¿Quién llama?*
Hold on, please *Un momento, por favor*
I can't hear you *No le oigo*
Can you hear me? *¿Me oye?*
I would like to speak to... *Quisiera hablar con...*
He/she is not here *No está aquí.*
Speak more slowly, please *¿Podría hablar más despacio?*
Could you repeat that, please? *¿Me lo repite, por favor?*

Banking

Where is the nearest bank? *¿Dónde está el banco más cercano?*
Can I withdraw money on my credit card here? *¿Puedo retirar dinero con mi tarjeta de crédito aqui?*
Where are the ATMs? *¿Dónde están los cajeros automáticos?*

Shopping

I'd like to buy... *Quiero comprar...*
How much is it? *¿Cuánto es?*
Do you accept credit cards? *¿Aceptan tarjetas?*
I'm just looking *Sólo estoy mirando*
Have you got...? *¿Tiene...?*
I'll take this one/that one *Me llevo éste/ese*
What size is it? *¿Qué talla es?*
small *pequeño*
large *grande*
cheap *barato*
expensive *caro*
enough *suficiente/bastante*
too much *demasiado*
a piece *un trozo*
each *cada una/la pieza/ la unidad*
check/bill *la factura (store), la cuenta (restaurant)*
bookstore *librería*
pharmacy *farmacia*
post office *correos*
bakery *panadería*
butcher's *carnicería*
cake store *pastelería*
grocery *ultramarinos/bodega*

Sightseeing

mountain *montaña/sierra*
hill *colina/loma*

valley *valle*
river *río*
lake *lago*
lookout *mirador*
old town/quarter *casco antiguo*
cathedral *catedral*
church *iglesia*
town hall *ayuntamiento*
staircase *escalera*
tower *torre*
castle *castillo*
fortress *fortaleza*
museum *museo*
art gallery *galería de arte*
tourist information office *oficina de turismo*
free *gratis*
open/closed *abierto/cerrado*
every day *diario/todos los días*
all day *todo el día*

Eating out

menu *la carta*
breakfast *desayuno*
lunch/meal *comida*
dinner/supper *cena*
first course *primer plato*
main course *plato principal*
dessert *postre*
drink included *bebida incluida*
the check/bill *la cuenta*
fork *tenedor*
knife *cuchillo*
spoon *cuchara*
plate *plato*
glass *vaso*
wine glass *copa*
napkin *servilleta*
ashtray *cenicero*

Drinks

coffee *café*
  black *sólo*
  with milk *con leche/cortado*
  decaffeinated *descafeinado*
sugar *azúcar*
tea *té*/**herbal tea** *infusión*
milk *leche*
mineral water *agua mineral*
  fizzy *con gas*/**still** *sin gas*
juice (fresh) *zumo/jugo (natural)*
cold *frío*/**hot** *caliente*
beer *cerveza*
  bottled *en botella*
  on tap *de barril*
rum *ron*
soft drink *refresco*
with ice *con hielo*
wine *vino*
  red *tinto*
  white *blanco*
  rosé *rosado*
  dry *seco*
  sweet *dulce*
house wine *vino de la casa*
half liter *medio litro*
quarter liter *cuarto de litro*
cheers! *¡salud!*

Menu decoder

Breakfast/*Desayuno*

huevos **eggs**
  cocidos **boiled, cooked**
  fritos **fried**
  revueltos **scrambled**
  tortilla **omelet**
mantequilla **butter**
mermelada/confitura **jam**
pan **bread**
queso **cheese**
sal **salt**/*pimienta* **pepper**
tostada **toast**

Meat *Carne/lomo*

cabrito **kid/goat**
carne picada **minced meat**
cerdo **pork**
chuleta **chop**
conejo **rabbit**
cordero **lamb/mutton**
costilla **rib**
jamón **ham**
res **beef**
salchichón **sausage**
solomillo **sirloin steak**
ternera **veal/young beef**
a la brasa **charcoal grilled**
al horno **roast**
a la plancha **grilled**
asado **roast**
bien hecho **well done**
en salsa **in sauce**
en su punto **medium**
estofado **stew**
frito **fried**
pinchito **skewered meat**
poco hecho **rare**
relleno **stuffed**
pollo **chicken**

Fish/*Pescado*

anchoas **salted anchovies**
atún **tuna**
bacalao **salt cod**
calamar **squid**
cangrejo **crab**
gambas **shrimps/prawns**
langosta **lobster**
langostino **large prawn**
róbalo **sea bass**
mariscos **shellfish**
merluza **hake**
pez espada **swordfish**
pulpo **octopus**
trucha **trout**

Vegetables/*Verduras*

aguacate **avocado**
ajo **garlic**
arroz **rice**
berenjena **eggplant/aubergine**
calabaza **squash**
cebolla **onion**
champiñón/hongo **mushroom**
col **cabbage**
ensalada **salad**
espárrago **asparagus**
espinaca **spinach**
frijoles **beans**
haba **broad bean**
judía **green bean**
lechuga **lettuce**
lenteja **lentil**
maíz **corn/maize**
patata **potato**
pepino **cucumber**
pimiento **pepper**
tomate **tomato**
trigo **wheat**

Fruit and desserts/*Fruta y postre*

ciruela **plum**
guayaba **guava**
limón **lemon/lime**
manzana **apple**
melocotón **peach**
melón **melon**
naranja **orange**
papaya **paw paw**
piña **pineapple**
plátano **banana (plantain)**
sandía **watermelon**
uva **grape**
pastel **cake**
helado **ice cream**

Cuban expressions

Asere/chama **friend**
Consorte/yunta **close friend**
Jevo/a **boyfriend/girlfriend/young woman**
Mango **young, sexy man**
Chama/ambia **partner/friend**
Cundango/loca/pájaro **gay**
mamey **mummy (used casually to women of any age)**
Qué bola, asere! **What's up, man?**
Qué onda/hubo **Hi there!**
Cuál es la vuelta? **How's it going?**
Bárbaro/enpingao/encojonao/escapao **cool/great!**
Di tú! **Tell me about it!**
Aquí, en la lucha **You know how it is**
No es fácil **Things aren't easy**
Chao pesca'o **Bye, bye!**
Bueno, voy en pira **Right, I'm going now**
Eres un mangón **You're looking really good**
Fula/verde **Hard currency**
Gao **house/home**
Pincha **work**
Ser un luchador **to try any means to make money**

FURTHER READING

GENERAL

Before Night Falls: A Memoir by Reinaldo Arenas. A powerful memoir tracing the struggle of a young gay writer in Cuba at a time when there was no sexual or artistic freedom, his flight to New York, and his final battle with AIDS. Later made into a movie, starring Johnny Depp and Javier Bardem, this is one of the iconic books of the late 20th century.

Cuba: A Journey by Jacobo Timerman. Conversations with Cubans from all walks of life shatter Timerman's idealized view of socialism in Cuba, encompassing the lack of political freedom, the inability of the state to feed the population and provide basic necessities, hypocrisy, and corruption at the time of the decline of the USSR.

The Cubans: Voices of Change by Lynn Geldof. Interviews with Cubans in Cuba, those who have left for the US and those who were born in the US, with their views on issues relating to the Revolution and the next 40 years.

Havana, A Cultural and Literary History by Claudia Lightfoot. Havana's history is explored through its architecture, music, dance, and literature, its treasures hidden among decay, its exuberant street life surviving amid shortages and political repression.

Walker Evans: Havana – 1933. A beautiful photographic record of Havana and its residents in 1933.

Into Cuba by Barry Lewis and Peter Marshall. First published in 1985 and, although this travelogue is affected by the passage of time, the beautiful photographs illustrate the timelessness of much of Cuba and its inhabitants.

Mea Cuba by Guillermo Cabrera Infante. Cabrera Infante chose exile after the Revolution and was a persistent critic of Fidel Castro. This collection of essays introduces the reader to Cuban writers, artists, and other intellectuals who were ground down by the brutal regime if they dared to think independently.

Memories of a Cuban Kitchen by Mary Urrutia Randleman and Joan Schwartz. Traditional Cuban recipes fusing Spanish, Portuguese, Chinese, African, and Indian influences, illustrated with pictures from the author's childhood in pre-Revolutionary Cuba.

A Taste of Cuba: Recipes from the Cuban-American Community by Linette Creen. While including very traditional recipes such as ropa vieja, there are also dishes developed by Miami-Cubans with ingredients newly available to them, such as conch fritters.

To Cuba and Back by Richard Henry Dana. Dana (1815–1882), an American lawyer, politician, and supporter of the oppressed, traveled to Cuba in 1859 when the island was ruled by Spain and this is an account of his voyage, his experiences, and opinions on colonialism and slavery.

Send Us Your Thoughts

We do our best to ensure the information in our books is as accurate and up-to-date as possible. The books are updated on a regular basis using local contacts, who painstakingly add, amend and correct as required. However, some details (such as telephone numbers and opening times) are liable to change, and we are ultimately reliant on our readers to put us in the picture.

We welcome your feedback, especially your experience of using the book "on the road". Maybe we recommended a hotel that you liked (or another that you didn't), or you came across a great bar or new attraction we missed.

We will acknowledge all contributions, and we'll offer an Insight Guide to the best letters received.

Please write to us at:
Insight Guides
PO Box 7910
London SE1 1WE
Or email us at:
insight@apaguide.co.uk

Trading with the Enemy: A Yankee Travels Through Castro's Cuba by Tom Miller. Miller spent many months traveling in Cuba, mixing with people from all walks of life and listening to their stories and jokes about Castro and their lives during the hardship times of 1990, including: 'the three great triumphs of the Cuban revolution are education, health, and athletics; the three great failures are breakfast, lunch, and dinner.'

When It's Cocktail Time in Cuba by Basil Woon. Published in 1928, this book is part recipe book, part guide, noting where the tourist of the day could find the best bars and which bartender made the best cocktails. It includes a recipe for daiquirí, as given to Woon by Facundo Bacardí himself.

With Hemingway: A Year in Key West and Cuba by Arnold Samuelson. In 1934, as an aspiring writer, 22-year old Samuelson hitched to Key West to interview Ernest Hemingway and ended up spending a year with the novelist, fishing off Cuba, sailing on The Pilar, and being mentored by him.

FICTION

Cecilia Valdés or Angel Hill by Cirilo Villaverde, translated by Helen Lane. 19th-century novel about the children of white colonizers and their black slaves, the best known of several abolitionist novels written in the 1880s.

Dirty Havana Trilogy by Pedro Juan Gutiérrez, translated by Natasha Wimmer. The protagonist, Pedro Juan, explores himself and Havana through sex, drugs, rum, music, and other self-indulgences.

Tropical Animal by Pedro Juan Gutiérrez. Pedro Juan is invited to Sweden and leaves Havana for the north where, ultimately, he misses the heat of his city and his woman and has to decide whether to adapt to the cold in spirit as well as in his sex life.

Our GG in Havana by Pedro Juan Gutiérrez. His reworking of Graham

Greene's *Our Man in Havana*. GG, who may or may not be Graham Greene, is suspected of the murder of a dancer with whom he spent the night, and the cast of characters is liberally spiced with vacuum salesmen, spies, and dead bodies.

Dreaming in Cuban by Cristina García. With the grandmother remaining in Cuba, her daughter in the US, and the granddaughter on a mission to visit the matriarch, the three generations' relationships are complex and disturbed, intertwined with politics and the Cuban condition.

Havana Bay by Martin Cruz Smith. The fourth in the Arkady Renko series of thrillers by the author best known for *Gorky Park*. This crime novel set in Cuba won the 1999 Hammett Prize.

Havana Quartet: Havana Red, Havana Black, Havana Blue, Havana Gold by Leonardo Padura Fuentes, translated by Peter Bush. Prize-winning detective novels featuring the life, work, and friends of a Havana policeman. *Havana Fever* is a follow-up after his retirement.

The Man Who Loved Dogs by Leonardo Padura Fuentes, translated by Anna Kushner. The man who killed Trotsky in Mexico turns up secretly in Havana after being released from jail and meets a Cuban writer. A detective story with a difference, an indictment of Stalinism, and a tale of politics, intrigue, and lost illusions.

The Old Man and the Sea by Ernest Hemingway. Hemingway's last novel published in his lifetime, it won the Pulitzer Prize for Fiction in 1953 and contributed to the author winning the Nobel Prize for Literature in 1954. The storyline is about old Santiago and his fight with a marlin after going 84 days without catching a fish.

Our Man in Havana by Graham Greene. A black comedy set in Havana in the time of the dictator Batista. The central character, Wormold, a vacuum cleaner salesman accepts the offer of work with the British Secret Services to earn extra money for his daughter's extravagances. His drawings of vacuum cleaner parts are accepted as evidence of military installations and his web of deceit becomes ever more convoluted as fiction and reality collide.

The Mambo Kings Play Songs of Love by Oscar Hijuelos. Two musician brothers migrate to the US in the 1950s and the story is told as reminiscences by one of them at the end of his life. In 1990, the author was the first US-born Hispanic to win the Pulitzer Prize for Fiction. The novel was later made into a movie and a musical.

Patria o Muerte! The Great Zoo and Other Poems by Nicolás Guillén. Guillén (1902–1989) was one of the foremost Afro-Caribbean poets, using sound and musical influences – primarily African rhythms – in his poetry. From the 1930s he was known as a socially committed writer and he supported the Revolution.

Tres Tristes Tigres by Guillermo Cabrera Infante translated as *Three Trapped Tigers*. A portrait of Havana's nightlife under Batista, written with humor and insight after the author left Cuba.

The Voice of the Turtle edited by Peter Bush. An entertaining collection of Cuban short stories translated into English.

Versos Sencillos by José Martí. Poems written by the national hero while in exile in New York.

CULTURE

Afrocuba, an Anthology of Cuban Writing on Race, Politics and Culture edited by Pedro Pérez Sarduy and Jean Stubbs. The relationship between Africa and Cuba is examined in essays on fiction, drama, poetry, history, and politics.

Cuban Music by Maya Roy. A comprehensive study of the roots of Cuban musical styles and the musicians involved, from rumba and son to the Buena Vista Social Club revival.

Newspaper seller, Havana.

Machos, Maricones and Gays, Cuba and Homosexuality by Ian Lumsden. An account of prejudices since the days of slavery, not only toward homosexuals but also to blacks and women. Although nearly 20 years have passed since the book was written and attitudes have evolved further, this remains an interesting study of tolerance and intolerance.
***Rumba, Dance and Social Change in Contemporary Cuba* by Yvonne Daniel**. Daniel explores the relationship between dance and political and social change in Cuba, how rumba has been used to reinforce solidarity, national identity, and cultural values since the Revolution.
Salsa: Havana Heat, Bronx Beat by Hernando Calvo Ospina. The history of salsa is examined, tracing it from the slave ships to New York clubs, taking in son, jazz, and cha cha chá along the way, and also taking into account Colombian cumbia and the Dominican Republic's merengue.
Santería from Africa to the New World: The Dead Sell Memories by George Brandon. In following the historical and anthropological evolution of the Yoruba religion, Brandon discusses broader questions of power, multiculturalism, and cultural change, not only in Cuban santería, but also Puerto Rican espiritismo and Black Nationalism in New York.

FIDEL CASTRO

In Defense of Socialism: Four Speeches on the 30th Anniversary of the Cuban Revolution by Fidel Castro. Castro defends the Cuban model of socialism even as the USSR was collapsing and the Berlin Wall was crumbling, analysing conflicts at that time in the world, such as in Angola.
Executive Action: 638 ways to kill Fidel Castro (Secret War) by Fabian Escalante. Written by Cuba's former counter-intelligence chief, Escalante reviews the hundreds of CIA plots to assassinate Castro, from the farcical to the deadly serious.
Fidel Castro Handbook by George Galloway. An account of Castro's life and achievements by an avid admirer and supporter.
Fidel Castro y la Revolución Cubana by Carlos Alberto Montaner. An account of the Castro phenomenon by a critic and victim; imprisoned after the Revolution on unproven charges of terrorism and working with the CIA, Montaner escaped.
Fidel Castro: Rebel Liberator or Dictator? by Jules Dubois.
History Will Absolve Me by Fidel Castro. Castro's defence speech in court after the 1953 uprising.
My Life by Fidel Castro (author), Ignacio Ramonet (editor) and Andrew Hurley (translator). Based on conversations in 2003–5, this is a fascinating and erudite account of Castro's life, thoughts, and principles, his vision and achievements.
***The Autobiography of Fidel Castro* by** Norberto Fuentes, translated by Anna Kushner. A 'faux autobiography' by a one-time friend of Castro's, who fell out of favour in the 1990s and escaped a death sentence. The voice of Castro reflects on his life, at times megalomaniacal, at times charming, and the people with whom he came into contact – it could be true.

POLITICS AND HISTORY

Cuba Confidential: The Extraordinary History of Cuba, Its History and Its Exiles, by Ann Louise Bardach. A controversial book, its author criticised by both Miami exiles and Havana; Bardach is a PEN-award winning journalist with close contacts on both sides of the divide.
Cuba from Columbus to Castro and Beyond by Jaime Suchlicki. An overview of the history of the island and an analysis of the problems that beset the island in the 21st century.
Cuba: Or the Pursuit of Freedom by Hugh Thomas. A comprehensive and extensive history of Cuba; one of the most authoritative and informative.
Diary of the Cuban Revolution by Carlos Franqui. Franqui (1921–2010) was a Cuban journalist who was close to Castro in the Sierra Maestra during the Revolution, when he worked as his press chief. He subsequently went into exile after disapproving of the invasion of Czechoslovakia by the USSR.
The Historical Dictionary of Cuba by Jaime Suchlicki. This is an academic tome with more than 2000 alphabetically arranged entries.

FOREIGN RELATIONS

Thirteen Days: A Memoir of the Cuban Missile Crisis by Robert F. Kennedy, Norton, New York (1969). Kennedy was US Attorney General at the time of the Cuban Missile Crisis, when his brother John was President. This is his account of the events at that tense period and the reasons for the actions of the President. The book was published after Robert Kennedy's assassination.

OTHER INSIGHT GUIDES

Other Insight Guides covering the region include: *Insight Guide Caribbean, Insight Guide Guatemala, Belize and the Yucatán, Compact Guide St Lucia,* and *Compact Guide Antigua and Barbuda.*

CREDITS

Photo Credits

123RF 19, 23L, 26TC, 65L, 70, 91, 103, 142T, 143, 144, 151, 161, 162BR, 166B, 181T, 182, 187, 193, 200T, 209, 210B, 212, 213B, 217, 227, 229B, 231T, 232, 260T, 277, 295
akg-images 25T, 111L
Alamy 29, 48L, 55, 185B, 263BR, 263BL, 266, 271, 310, 311, 313
AWL Images 5TR, 74/75
Bigstock 139, 222BL, 250, 274
Corbis 37, 38, 44, 58, 63, 64, 66, 67, 77, 78, 84, 92, 95, 100, 107, 179, 203BR, 302
Corrie Wingate 86BL, 157T
Dreamstime 2/3, 6T, 24TL, 33, 42, 83, 87ML, 149B, 168, 176, 189, 198, 200B, 223BR, 223BL, 224, 226, 229T, 230, 233, 248, 255, 269B, 272, 278, 293, 308, 314
Fabrizio Zampa 185T
FLPA 216, 222/223T, 263ML
Fotolia 24BL, 30L, 149T, 207, 218, 234B, 270B, 276, 315B
Gerardo Churches/Contemporary Dance of Cuba 109
Getty Images 48R, 49, 50, 51, 52, 54, 56, 57, 59, 60, 61, 71, 72, 73, 82, 85, 96, 99, 101, 102, 108, 110, 114, 118, 121, 123, 128/129, 203BL, 214, 262/263T
Glyn Genin/Apa Publications 28, 191, 194T, 270T, 315T
hellosputnik 181B
iStock 5MR, 5BR, 7R, 15T, 15B, 21R, 76, 80, 86BR, 88, 93, 138, 141, 153, 167, 169, 173, 195, 201, 220T, 225, 231B, 262BL, 281, 283B, 294, 309, 312
iStockphoto 357L
Las Américas 215
Library of Congress 26BL, 36, 39, 40, 43, 45, 163BL
Library of Congress/Carol M. Highsmith 186
Mary Evans Picture Library 32
Mockford & Bonetti/Apa Publications 26MR, 105L, 105R, 119, 131T, 131B, 145, 146T, 156, 257T, 268T, 269T
Photoshot 41, 184, 222BR, 223ML, 223TR, 262BR, 263TR
Pictures Colour Library 137, 253
Public domain 24TR, 25B, 27T, 35
Rex Features 53
Richter Library, University of Miami 46, 47
Robert Harding 7L, 130, 164, 220B, 296
Scala Archives 104
SuperStock 68, 79, 94, 292
Sylvaine Poitau/Apa Publications 1, 4ML, 4MR, 4MR, 4B, 5ML, 5BL, 5TL, 6B, 8/9, 10/11, 12/13, 16, 17, 18, 20, 21L, 22, 23R, 62, 65R, 69, 81, 86/87T, 87BR, 87BL, 87TR, 89, 90, 97, 98, 106, 112, 113, 115, 116, 117, 122, 124/125, 126/127, 136, 142B, 146B, 147B, 147T, 148, 150, 152, 154, 155, 157B, 158, 160, 162BL, 162/163T, 163ML, 163TR, 163BR, 165, 166T, 170, 171B, 171T, 172, 174, 175B, 175T, 177, 178, 183T, 183B, 188, 190, 194B, 196, 197, 199T, 199B, 202BL, 202/203T, 202BR, 203ML, 203TR, 206, 208, 210T, 211, 213T, 234T, 235, 236, 237, 239, 240, 241B, 241T, 242T, 242B, 243, 244, 245, 246, 247, 249, 251, 252, 254, 256, 257B, 258, 260B, 267, 268B, 273, 275, 280, 283T, 284, 285, 286, 287T, 287B, 288, 289T, 289B, 290T, 290B, 291, 298, 299, 300, 301T, 301B, 303T, 303B, 304, 305T, 305B, 306, 316, 318, 320, 321, 322T, 322B, 324, 327, 331, 338, 341, 344, 346, 352, 354, 358
The Art Archive 30R, 34
Tips Images 120
TopFoto 31
Warner Br/Everett/Rex Features 111R

Cover Credits

Front cover: Havana *4Corners Images*
Back cover: (top) Cayo Levisa beach *Dreamstime*; (middle) Musicians, Santiago *Sylvaine Poitau/Apa Publications*
Front flap: (from top) Cathedral, Havana *iStock*; Gran Parque Natural Topes De Collantes near Trinidad *Dreamstime*; Havana *iStock*; Cayo Jutias *Dreamstime*
Back flap: description *credit*
Spine: Che Guevara *iStock*

Insight Guide Credits

Distribution
UK
Dorling Kindersley Ltd
A Penguin Group company
80 Strand, London, WC2R 0RL
sales@uk.dk.com

United States
Ingram Publisher Services
1 Ingram Boulevard, PO Box 3006,
La Vergne, TN 37086-1986
ips@ingramcontent.com

Australia and New Zealand
Woodslane
10 Apollo St, Warriewood,
NSW 2102, Australia
info@woodslane.com.au

Worldwide
Apa Publications GmbH & Co. Verlag KG (Singapore branch)
7030 Ang Mo Kio Avenue 5
08-65 Northstar @ AMK
Singapore 569880
apasin@singnet.com.sg

Printing
CTPS-China

First Edition 1995
Sixth Edition 2014

www.insightguides.com

Project Editor
Rachel Lawrence
Series Manager
Rachel Lawrence
Author
Sarah Cameron
Picture Editor/Art Editor
Tom Smyth/Shahid Mahmood
Map Production
Original cartography Mapping Ideas Ltd, updated by Apa Cartography Department
Head of Production
Rebeka Davies

Contributors

This new edition of Insight Guide Cuba was commissioned by **Rachel Lawrence**, Insight's Latin America specialist, and copy-edited by **Penny Phenix**. The book was updated by **Sarah Cameron** who has spent a lifetime traveling in Latin America and the Caribbean, working first as an economist and then as an author of travel guides. The Caribbean Islands, and Cuba in particular, have become her specialty and she has contributed to many of APA Publications' guides to the region. This version builds on the work of contributors to previous editions, including **Danny Aeberhard**, **Joann Biondi**, **Jane McManus**, **Tony Perrottet**, **Sue Steward**, and **Marjory Zimmerman**. The quote from Colombian author Gabriel García Marquez from an article on his friendship with Fidel Castro is the copyright of Gianni Mina and Ocean Press, and has been reprinted by kind permission of the Talman Company.

About Insight Guides

Insight Guides have more than 40 years' experience of publishing high-quality, visual travel guides. We produce 400 full-color titles, in both print and digital form, covering more than 200 destinations across the globe, in a variety of formats to meet your different needs.

Insight Guides are written by local authors who use their on-the-ground experience to provide the very latest information; their local expertise is evident in the extensive historical and cultural background features. All the reviews in **Insight Guides** are independent; we strive to maintain an impartial view. Our reviews are carefully selected to guide to you the best places to stay and eat, so you can be confident that when we say a restaurant or hotel is special, we really mean it.

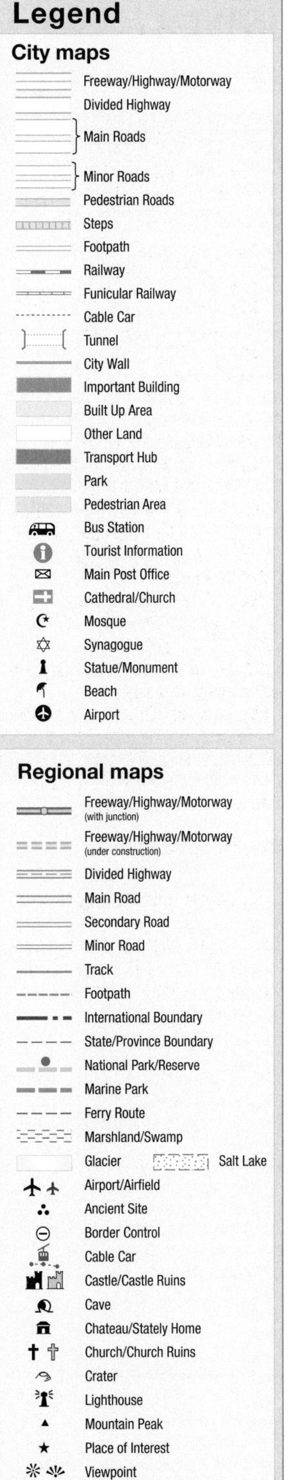

INDEX

Main references are in bold type

D

E

F

Miramar, Playa, Siboney
Monumento a Calixto García
Malecón
PARQUE JOSE MARTI (SPORTS GROUND)
Swiss Embassy US Interests' Section
Hotel Riviera
Calle 3
Casa de las Américas
Calle 7
Calle 5
Hotel Presidente
Calle 9
Calle 11
Calle 13
Avenida Washington
Calle 7 (Calzada)
Edificio Focsa
Monumento al Maine
Linea
Avenida O
Avenida N
Museo de la Danza
Calle 15
Hotel Nacional
Iglesia del Sagrado Corazón de Jesús
Calle 11
Avenida M
Hotel Capri
Hotel Victoria
Malecón
Calle 17
Avenida L
Calle 23
Calle 13
Avenida de Los Presidentes (G)
Avenida K
Avenida J
Humboldt
Avenida I
Hotel St John
Museo Casa de Abel Santamaría
COPPELIA Ice Cream Park
Hornos
Avenida H
Calle 21
Avenida F
Museo de Artes Decorativas
Parque John Lennon
Calle 15
Príncipe
Torreón de San Lázaro
Hotel Habana Libre
Hotel Vedado
Vapor
Calle 25
Calle 19
Avenida E
Calle 17
Jovellar
Calle 27
Calzada de Infanta
San Lázaro
Calle 21
(Rampa)
Avenida D
Avenida C
Universidad de La Habana
Hamel
Julio Antonio Mella
Concordia
Oquendo
Casa de la Amistad
VEDADO
Neptuno
Museo Antropológico Montané
Calle 23
Museo Napoleónico
San Francisco
San Miguel
Mariana Grajales
Espada
Aramburu
San Rafael
Hospital
Estadio Juan Abrahantes
Avenida B
Calle 25
San Martín (San José)
Valle
CENTRO (CENTRAL
Calle 27
La Tropicana
Zanja
Castillo del Príncipe
Salud
Allende
Calle 29
Avenida A
Quinta de los Molinos
Jesús Peregrino
Castillejo
Soledad
Pocito
Calzada de Zapata
Avenida Salvador Allende (Carlos III)
Paseo
Casa de Cultura de Centro Habana
Lugareño
ESTADIO RAMON FONST
Enrique Barnet (Estrella)
Calle 31
Xifré
Bruzón
Calle 32
Almendares
Plasencia
Retiro
Árbol Seco
Subirana
Franco
Oquendo
Marqués González
Calle 35
Terminal de Omnibuses Astro
Calle 4
Calle 2
Ministerio del Interior
Desagüe
Calzada de Infanta
Teatro Nacional
Peñalver
Benjumeda
19 de Mayo
Desagüe
Calle 37
Aranguren
Plaza de la Revolución
Calle 39
Benjumeda
Calle 6
Paseo
Santo Tomás
Calle 41
Panorama
Monumento José Martí
Legado Cultural Hispánico
Clavel
Avenida Carlos M. de Céspedes
Territorial
Santa Marta
Ave. 20 de Mayo
P. Vidal
Avenida de Colón
(Zaldo)
Calzada de Ayestaran
Arroyo (Avenida Manglar)
Avenida Rancho Boyeros
Palacio de la Revolución
San Martín
Panchito Gómez
San Pedro
M. Abreu
Masón
General E. Nuñez
Estancia
Marino
Ermita
Pedroso
Amenidad
L. Ferrocarril
Avenida de la Independencia
San Pedro
Auditor
Estévez
Santa Rosa
San Pablo
CERRO
Pedroso
Universidad
Campos
Fernandina
3ra
Lombillo
Pje. Vista Hermosa
Pedro Perez
Patria
Estadio Latinoamericano
Estévez
Romay
Máximo
2da
La Rosa
Clavel
1ra
Ermita
San Pedro
Mariano
Cádiz
Zequeira
San Joaquín
Ayuntamiento
Tulipán
Borrego
Unión y Ahorro
José Martí Airport